ALSO BY RICHARD FIRSTMAN

The Death of Innocents
WITH JAMIE TALAN

Men of Steel
WITH KARL KOCH III

A CRIMINAL INJUSTICE

Richard Firstman
& Jay Salpeter

BALLANTINE BOOKS NEW YORK

A CRIMINAL

INJUSTICE

A TRUE CRIME, A FALSE CONFESSION,
AND THE FIGHT TO FREE MARTY TANKLEFF

Published in the United States by Ballantine Books,
an imprint of The Random House Publishing Group,
a division of Random House, Inc., New York.

BALLANTINE and colophon are registered trademarks of
Random House, Inc.

Frontispiece photograph by Michael E. Ach/*Newsday*, July 22, 2004
Newsday photographs © 1988–1990, 2004–2008
Photographs from *48 Hours Mystery*, originally broadcast April 7, 2004, on
the CBS Television Network, © 2004 and 2006 CBS Broadcasting, Inc.
Personal photographs courtesy of Martin Tankleff and family

Library of Congress Cataloging-in-Publication Data
Firstman, Richard.
A criminal injustice: a true crime, a false confession, and the fight to
free Marty Tankleff / Richard Firstman and Jay Salpeter.
p.   cm.
ISBN 978-0-345-49121-3
1. Murder—New York (State)—Investigation—Case studies.
2. Tankleff, Marty. I. Salpeter, Jay. II. Title.
HV6533.N5F56 2008
364.152'3092—dc22   2008038287
[B]

Printed in the United States of America on acid-free paper

www.ballantinebooks.com

2   4   6   8   9   7   5   3   1

First Edition

Book design by Liz Cosgrove

For Jamie and Cheryl,
who were always on the case with us

CONTENTS

PART THREE

The Best Years of His Life

The principal characters in the Tankleff case:

THE TANKLEFFS
Marty Tankleff, Class of '89, Vandermeulen High School
Seymour Tankleff, Marty's father
Arlene Tankleff, Marty's mother

THE FAMILY
Ron Falbee, Marty's older cousin and (with his wife, Carol) Marty's legal
    guardian after his parents' murders
Marcella (Mickey) Alt Falbee, Ron's mother and Arlene's older sister
Marianne McClure, Arlene's younger sister
Mike McClure, Marianne's husband
Shari Rother (later Mistretta), Seymour's daughter from his first marriage
Ron Rother, Shari's husband at the time of the murders
Norman Tankleff, Seymour's older brother
Ruth Tankleff, Norman's wife

THE FAMILY LAWYER
Myron (Mike) Fox

THE STEUERMANS
Jerry Steuerman, "the Bagel King of Long Island"
Todd Steuerman, Jerry's son, a convicted drug dealer

THE POKER PLAYERS
Vinnie Bove, Frank Oliveto, Joe Cecere, Bob Montefusco, Peter Capobianco, and Al Raskin

SUFFOLK COUNTY POLICE HOMICIDE SQUAD
Detective K. James McCready, lead detective on the Tankleff case
Detective Norman Rein, McCready's partner
Detective Sergeant Robert Doyle, supervisor of the Tankleff investigation

SUFFOLK COUNTY DISTRICT ATTORNEY'S OFFICE, 1988–90
John Collins, Tankleff trial prosecutor
Edward Jablonski, chief of the homicide bureau
Patrick Henry, district attorney, 1978–89
James Catterson, district attorney, 1990–2001

THE TANKLEFF DEFENSE, 1988–94
Robert Gottlieb, trial attorney
Ronald Sussman, Gottlieb's law partner
Mark Pomerantz and Warren Feldman, appeals attorneys, 1991–94
John Murtagh, private investigator, 1988–90
William Navarra, private investigator, 1990–94

TRIALS OF THE JURY
Joseph Fisher, the juror who talked too much
Frank Spindel, the juror who led the charge
Peter Baczynski, the juror who blew the whistle
Theresa Quigley, the juror in the middle

MARTY'S PRINCIPAL LAWYERS, 1995–2008
Stephen Braga, lead attorney in federal appeals, 1995–98, and in the drive to reverse the convictions based on new evidence, 1999–2008
Barry Pollack, co-counsel in federal appeals, 1995–98, and litigator of the motion to reverse the convictions, 2002–2008
Bruce Barket, litigator of motion to reverse the convictions, 2002–2008
Jennifer O'Connor, principal author of Marty's final appeal brief, 2006–2007

SUFFOLK COUNTY DISTRICT ATTORNEY'S OFFICE, 2002–2008
Thomas Spota, district attorney
Leonard Lato, assistant district attorney assigned to oppose a new trial
Walter Warkenthien, investigator assigned to the Tankleff case

THE JUDGES

Alfred Tisch, Suffolk County Court, trial judge, 1990

Stephen Braslow, Suffolk County Court, 440 hearing judge, 2004–2006

Stuart Namm, Suffolk County Court, 1982–92, critic of Suffolk homicide prosecutions

Lawrence Bracken, Cornelius O'Brien, Geraldine Eiber, Vincent Pizzuto, and Thomas R. Sullivan, Appellate Division of New York State Supreme Court, Second Department, 1994

Thomas Platt, United States District Court, Eastern District of New York, 1997

Guido Calabresi, Jose Cabranes, and Fred Parker, United States Second Circuit Court of Appeals, 1998

Reinaldo Rivera, Gabriel Krausman, Anita Florio, and Mark Dillon, Appellate Division, 2007

THE REINVESTIGATOR

Jay Salpeter, private investigator, retired detective, New York City Police Department

THE SELDEN CROWD

Joseph (Joey Guns) Creedon, Peter Kent, Glenn Harris, Billy Ram, Brian Scott Glass, and Joe Graydon

THOSE WHO CAME FORWARD

Karlene Kovacs, who first came forward in 1994

Joe Guarascio, Joe Creedon's son

Terry (Guarascio) Covais, Creedon's ex-girlfriend and Joe Guarascio's mother

John Guarascio, Terry's brother

Lenny Lubrano, the first to link Steuerman and McCready

William Sullivan, who reported seeing Steuerman and McCready together

Neil Fischer, who heard Steuerman incriminate himself in 1989

Mark Callahan, friend of Scott Glass

MARTY'S ADVOCATES

Lonnie Soury, Soury Communications

Eric Friedman, webmaster of martytankleff.org

PART ONE

Unfortunate Son

CHAPTER 1

Belle Terre, Long Island: September 6, 1988

ALL ALONG THE COASTLINE, a succession of jagged peninsulas gives the northern shore of Long Island its idiosyncratic contours and most desirable real estate. Great Neck . . . Manhasset Neck . . . Lloyd Neck . . . Eatons Neck . . . eight haphazard glacial formations in all, each in its way heaven or hell to centuries of seamen. Fifty miles out from the New York City line, the last of them pushes into Long Island Sound. And then the coastline abruptly straightens, becoming as regular as a riverbank from there to Orient Point.

It is a hilly cape, this last one, smaller than the others, shaped something like a crabeater seal. The peninsula's tree-lined western edge shelters Port Jefferson Harbor, whose wharf docks the ferries that rumble by on their way to Connecticut and back. On the sound side of the neck, a line of low cliffs overlooks a stretch of rocky shoreline. There was a time, before the first land speculators came along in the early 1900s and gave it a more agreeable name, that the peninsula was known for the misfortune it brought ship captains who didn't see it in the night. Mount Misery Neck was what they called it, before they called it Belle Terre.

Now, late in the century, the cape remains serene and secluded, home to a small community of suburbanites who live in upscale homes on significant properties. Apart from a lavish estate at the end of Cliff Road, where a manor known as the Pink Mansion is inhabited by a woman known as the Contessa, the most enviable addresses are on a sleepy, L-shaped lane that runs toward the sound for a few hundred feet before turning sharply to the right to hug the coastline. It's precisely at this bend, hard by what locals know as the Cliffs, that the first waterfront home comes into view. A roadside mailbox displays the address: 33 Seaside Drive.

The residence is a sprawling, ranch-style house nestled beneath a canopy of leafy trees—if five thousand square feet of living space can be said to nestle—and shrouded in a small forest of shrubbery. In the ground out back is a gunite swimming pool surrounded by a deck of mountain laurel stone. And then, over the cliffs, an endless midnight-blue panorama. On sun-splashed afternoons, Long Island Sound sparkles, sailboats bob in the breeze, and the occasional powerboat leaves a V-shaped wake of foam. Distant on the horizon is the Connecticut shoreline—New Haven straight ahead, Bridgeport slightly to the left. Late in the day, the sun casts an orange glow across the western sky, and at nightfall the blue sea dissolves into a vista of blackness, the southern New England coast twinkling faintly in the distance.

Such is the view on this nearly moonless night in the late summer of 1988. It is the day after Labor Day, and the venerable After Dinner Club is gathered for its floating Tuesday night poker game at the house that Seymour Tankleff built sixteen years ago as his personal affirmation of the American Dream. It's the old story, give or take: Son of immigrants grows up in Depression-era New York, thinks big, makes some good moves, has a little luck and a ton of chutzpah—next thing you know he's living on a cliff on Long Island. At sixty-two, Seymour has the world whipped. At least that's what Seymour wants the world to think.

The After Dinner Club goes back thirty years, and the stakes have risen as the players have grown older and more prosperous. It's not for amateurs or the budget-conscious. The opening ante is a hundred dollars a player, and thousands can change hands by the last one. But the game is friendly and oddly wholesome: Drinking and smoking are prohibited (though swearing is permitted) and 20 percent of the weekly buy-in goes into a kitty for charities, or to send flowers when someone of local prominence dies.

Peter Capobianco—"Cappy" to all—is one of the originals and the current member of longest standing, but at seventy-seven he's not even close to being the oldest. That would be Al Raskin, who's ninety-five, which makes him a full sixty years older than Joe Cecere, who picks him up each week from his room at the Elks Hotel. Except for Frank Oliveto, who's an orthopedic surgeon, and John Ceparano, a lawyer, the players are local businessmen of one sort or another. Cappy owns Cappy's Carpets. Joe has a Goodyear Tire franchise and builds high-end homes on speculation. Leo Sternlicht is a Ford dealer, Bob Montefusco's a contractor, and Al Raskin used to have his own shoe company. There's Vinnie Bove, who owns one of the biggest wholesale nurseries in Suffolk County, and there's Jerry Steuerman, who has half a dozen bagel stores. By his own proclamation, he's the Bagel King of Long Island.

And then there's Seymour. Describing Seymour Tankleff as a business-man is a little like calling a shark a tropical fish. He made his first million in insurance, then sold the business and fashioned his voracious appetite for wheeling and dealing into a second career as everybody's partner. Friend, relative, neighbor, perfect stranger—Seymour wants to be in busi-ness with you. *Don't have the cash? You can pay me back! The terms? Never mind about the terms.* Seymour the deal maker. Seymour the conquerer. Seymour the big *macher* with the snow-white hair and the shit-eating grin. He's in deals with just about everybody in the card game, if only because he can be a son of a bitch to say no to. Ask Joe Cecere. He said yes just to get Seymour off his back; then he read the contract he came up with. *The balls on this guy,* Joe thought. Of course, this stuff with the poker pals is nothing compared with what Seymour's got going with Jerry the Bagel King.

Leo Sternlicht was due to host the game this week, but Leo and his wife went upstate for a long Labor Day weekend. The game rotates al-phabetically, so Seymour's up next. The men start arriving at 33 Seaside around seven, packing the red gravel driveway with late-model Cadillacs and Lincolns and one Mercedes that's brand-new. They troop in, pockets full of twenties and fifties. Frank Oliveto, the orthopedic surgeon, comes straight from the operating room, his shoes caked in blood. He stops to say hello to Seymour's wife, Arlene, who's in a recliner in the den, read-ing the paper and half watching the TV. Frank gives her a kiss and asks what's new—how's Marty doing? The swelling's down, Arlene says. And he got his license last week, so he's all excited about that. Jenny too, Frank says.

The card table is set up as usual in a spacious room, at the far right corner of the house, that serves as Seymour's office and doubles as a home gym. The décor is mostly sports kitsch and exercise equipment. The rear wall has sliding glass doors opening onto a deck that looks out onto the pool and the sea beyond. The early arrivals play a couple of warm-up hands. By eight there's a full house. The night officially starts in the kitchen, around the center island where the men help themselves to the turkey Arlene cooked the way her husband likes it, in champagne. There are bagels—of course there are bagels. And water-melon. Seymour brought home a good one—nice and red, the new seed-less kind.

The game's in full swing when Vinnie Bove pulls into the driveway in his nurseryman's Ford station wagon. He's a beefy man with thick white hair combed straight back. Besides selling shrubs and evergreens by the truckload, Bove—it's pronounced Bo-*vay*—serves as the mayor of Belle Terre, population 829. He's also the vice chairman of the board of

John T. Mather Memorial Hospital and president of the Port Jefferson Volunteer Ambulance Corps. So he's always got some meeting to go to and rarely gets to the card game in time for dinner, even when he's the host.

"Vinnie!" Seymour says when Bove appears in the card room. "Go get something to eat. We've got the champagne turkey." Vinnie says no—he's on one of his periodic diets—and takes his seat at the card table. "I got something for you," Seymour tells him. He sits out a hand and brings Vinnie a bag of microwave popcorn, along with a generous slice of watermelon. Hey, no seeds, says the nurseryman—what'll they come up with next?

The bets are flying, and so is Bob Montefusco. Monte looks to be headed for a very good night. The game's not going quite so well for Seymour. Maybe he'll have better luck with the horses this weekend. Between hands he goes off to make a phone call. "He's in the race," he tells Jerry the Bagel King upon his return. "We need a check." They're just about the only words between them all night. Whatever's going on between them, Seymour's not doing much better with Arlene these days. "We're at each other's throats," he tells Vinnie. "I'm getting in her hair." Vinnie has an idea: "Why don't you do some vacuuming or something for her? Make yourself useful around the house instead of bothering her." Seymour has a better idea: "Why don't you and me go down to A.C.? Get outta here for a few days." If they do, maybe Seymour will tell Vinnie what he and Arlene have really been fighting about.

Marty gets home a little past nine and stops in on the card game, carrying a bag from Pants Plus and another from Radio Shack. He's a wisp of a kid, his thick brown hair freshly cut and styled for the first day of school.

"Marty, let me see you," Vinnie says.

"Oh, he told you," Marty says with a sheepish smile, nodding toward his father. He's still wearing the tinted glasses he's been using to hide the aftereffects of the nose job his parents gave him for his seventeenth birthday. "They break your nose," he says, then lifts the glasses just enough. Oooh, says one of the guys, looks like you lost a fight. Marty says it's nothing compared to right after the operation.

"Yeah," says Vinnie, appraising the new nose. "It looks good." The others nod. Marty says thanks, then asks Cappy for the keys to his Seville. He needs to move it so he can get his car in the garage. It's a ten-year-old version of something from the card players' fleet: a dark blue '78 Lincoln Town Car. Seymour got it for Marty because Arlene wanted him driving something big and safe after two of his classmates died in a sports car in

June. Marty's made no secret of his desire for something not quite so old-mannish, but for now even a big blue Lincoln beats a big yellow school bus. He's been fixing it up with the money he makes at the bagel stores. He and Zach Suominen spent the afternoon putting in a new stereo, with dual-control speakers.

Marty returns Cappy's keys but doesn't stick around to watch a few hands, which he usually does when his father's hosting the card game. He wants to get up early to finish working on the car stereo before he has to leave to pick up Mark Perrone, his best friend, for the first day of school. He's thinking 5:30, no big deal after two years working weekends at the bagel stores. He kisses his father and says good night to the group before heading into the kitchen to see what's to eat. He helps himself to some champagne turkey, some watermelon, and brings it into the den, where his mother's still reading in the recliner. They talk for a few minutes, about the trip to the mall, about school, about Marty having forgotten to set up the card table for his father before going out. Marty apologizes and promises to take it down tomorrow. He brings his dish into the kitchen and goes off to take a shower. His mother calls it a night herself. She's in bed, watching TV, when Marty comes in a little while later and gives her a kiss good night. See you in the morning, Mom, he says.

On the other side of the house, the poker game continues into the night. Cappy quits around midnight, his usual departure time whether he's ahead or behind. The game typically breaks up around one, sometimes two, but it's been a lively night and nobody objects when Monte, who's still on a roll, suggests a few more hands. It's around three when they finally call last hand, play it out, throw in their cards, count their winnings, lick their wounds. Vinnie's the first to go. Wasn't his night. He pauses in the kitchen to cut himself one last piece of seedless watermelon. Monte, meanwhile, is all smiles—he's pocketed a tidy two grand. He's in the solarium, which connects Seymour's office to the kitchen, when he decides to go back in, maybe gloat a little and wind down the night with Seymour, who's always good for a few laughs. Monte comes to an abrupt halt, though, when he sees Seymour and Jerry alone in the room, having a conversation that's obviously private. He turns right around and heads for the front door.

One by one the card players pull out of the driveway, in reverse order of their arrivals seven, eight hours earlier, until just two remain: Cecere in his new Mercedes with Al Raskin beside him, and Jerry Steuerman at the wheel of his Lincoln. Joe was the first to arrive and should be the last to leave. But Jerry signals for him to go around him. It's an awkward maneuver and Joe's a little worried for his new car. But he has just enough room and heads out in the darkness. Half a minute later, he's sailing down Cliff Road, the only driver on the road in these peaceful moments, three hours before day breaks over the cliffs of the little cape they used to call Mount Misery Neck.

CHAPTER 2

A Darkness Before Dawn

AT 6:11 ON THE MORNING of Wednesday, September 7, a shrill tone pierces the quiet of the communications center at the Suffolk County Police Department headquarters, a sprawling two-story building in a desolate part of the county called Yaphank. An operator on the back end of the overnight shift presses the blinking button on the 911 line. "Police emergency," she says. A frantic response comes crashing through her headset:

"This is Marty Tankleff, 33 Seaside Drive in Belle Terre—I need an ambulance! Emergency!"

"All right, hold on and I'll connect you."

"Emergency!" Marty repeats.

It is just before sunrise, three hours after the members of the After Dinner Club played their last hands in Seymour Tankleff's home office. Now Seymour's seventeen-year-old son is in the office, shouting into the phone on his father's desk. The 911 system records the words of a teenager who seems overwrought but under control, a voice that could be described as the slightly groggy panic of someone who's just woken from a nightmare. Or into one.

I had set my alarm for 5:35 so I could finish working on my car. But I was too tired to get up. So I turned the alarm off and went back to bed for another half an hour. I got up around 6:05. It was still dark outside. I put on a pair of shorts. I opened the door and the hallway lights were on. The bathroom light was on. I looked into my parents' room. The TV was on but no one was there. The burglar alarm on their wall wasn't set. So I thought maybe they had gotten up already. I continued down the hallway and noticed that all the lights were on. I had this foreboding feeling that something was wrong. Every step of the way, things are not right. I went through the den, to the foyer. The front door was open. I continued toward the kitchen. The kitchen lights were on. From the kitchen I noticed that the office lights were on. And so I went into the office. . . .

"Fire Rescue Center."

"I'm at 33 Seaside Drive in Belle Terre!" Marty tells the second operator, breathing heavily.

"Thirty-three Seaside?" the operator asks.

"Seaside Drive in Belle Terre, it's off Crooked Oak Road. *Please!* My father—"

"Whoa, whoa, hold on. I can't write that fast."

"Thirty—"

"What corner?"

"—three. It's off Crooked Oak Road."

"Crooked Oak?"

"Yes, yes, hurry up!"

"No no no!" the operator shoots back. "Answer my questions! What's your name?"

"Marty Tankleff. I'm his son." Marty trembles. "He's gushing blood from the back of his neck. He's got a cut—"

"What's the phone number you're calling me from?"

"928-2242."

"How old is he?"

"He's sixty-two."

"What happened to him?"

"I don't know. I just woke up and he's in the office. He's gushing blood. *Please!*" Marty's crying now—he says the last word as if it has two syllables.

"All right, listen to me! Is this a private house?"

"Yes it is."

"All right, now listen."

"It's a red driveway."

"Listen to me. I'm sending you an ambulance. I want you to take a clean towel—"

"Yes."

"Wrap wherever he's gushing blood from."

"Okay."

"Lay him down if possible."

"Okay."

"Hold pressure on it."

"Okay."

"Get his feet elevated and we'll have someone down there for you."

Marty hangs up the phone. His father is unconscious, barely alive, laboring for breath. His neck is slashed, cut deeply and nearly all the way around. Marty's first impulse is to do the last thing the 911 operator instructed: get his father's feet elevated. He races back through the house, all the way back to his bedroom.

How can you describe what you feel in your head or how your brain works at a time like this? It's like you just operate without thinking. You're like a robot. You just automatically do what you've been taught to do from early childhood. Something's wrong, just call 911 and do what they say. The last thing they said was to elevate my father's feet. I thought: Get the big pillow, it's sturdy. I ran to my room to get the pillow. I went to the linen closet to get a towel. I ran back to the office to help my father. They said to lay him down, get him level. He's in a reclining chair with one of those leg lifts that pull out. When I tried to lift the legs up the whole chair tipped forward, and he sort of slid out of the chair a little bit. I pulled him off the chair. I put the pillow under his feet and the towel over the wound. I pushed down once and then I ran away. I wanted to go find my mother. Maybe she went out to get some milk.

Marty runs to the door to the garage. He looks in and sees his mother's car. He backtracks again toward the bedrooms. He goes to his parents' room again. This time he goes in, just a few steps. It's dark but for the flickering blue light of the television. He looks across and down and he sees her. She's behind the far side of the bed, and all he can see is her head. She's faceup, utterly still. He can't make himself go any closer.

I ran out of there screaming. I went into the kitchen and I called Shari. I got her machine. I said, "Shari, get over here. I think Mom and Dad have been murdered." I couldn't believe I was saying these words. In my head, this can't be happening. But it is happening. I went back in to check my father. He was still gagging. I went back into the kitchen and the phone rang. It was Shari. She says, "Marty, is this a joke?" I tell her this is not a joke—just get over here. Then I called Mark, my best friend. His mother answered and I told her the same thing—"I think my mother and father have been murdered." I ran next door to my neighbor's house. I didn't know what else to do. I just wanted someone to help me.

Morty Hova is in his bathroom when he hears someone yelling for help outside. He opens the front door and sees Marty Tankleff running toward him, barefoot and screaming in the darkness. Hova comes out, hears the word *murder*, and thinks at first that Marty's saying his *dog* has been murdered—but the Tankleffs have no dog. Marty's just about at Hova's front door when two county police cars barrel past. He stops and turns, then runs back. Hova goes after Marty and reaches him just as the police cars screech to a halt in the Tankleffs' driveway. A cop named Dan Gallagher emerges from one of the cars, Jim Crayne from the other. "Somebody murdered my parents!" Marty blurts, leading them into the house in full stride. He directs Gallagher toward the master bedroom. "My mother's that way," he says, pointing, then tells Crayne, "Follow me," and leads him in the opposite direction. He brings Crayne to the office, where his father is "breathing but unresponsive," as the officer will later write in his report. Crayne calls the Port Jefferson ambulance squad to make sure they're on their way, then turns to Marty. "What happened?" he asks.

"I just woke up and found him in the chair," Marty says.

"Where'd the towel come from?" Crayne asks.

"I just moved him from the chair and put the towel on his neck to stop the bleeding."

Then Marty says, "I know who did this. It was Jerry Steuerman."

"Who's that?" Crayne asks.

"My father's business partner," Marty tells him.

Crayne turns his attention back to Seymour. Marty heads back outside to wait for the rescue squad. The night is just giving way to daybreak now, and Marty sees the ambulance careening onto Seaside, another police car right behind. He waves his arms to flag them down. Three emergency medical technicians jump from the ambulance. A cop emerges from the patrol car. Seconds later a sergeant and another patrolman pull up in two more cars.

"Hurry up! Come this way!" Marty yells to the rescuers. Two of the EMTs head for the office with a gurney; the other one, a thirty-year-old registered nurse named Ethel Curley, goes toward the master bedroom. Marty follows her in and sees that his mother's been badly beaten, her throat's been slashed. He retreats to the hallway. "Is she dead?" he calls in to Curley. The EMT sees that besides her other wounds Arlene's sternum is protruding an inch out of her chest. "Is she dead?" Marty asks again and again. Curley checks for a pulse. Then she pulls Arlene's eyelids down over her eyes. "I'm sorry," she tells Marty, barely pausing before darting to the other side of the house to help her partners with his father.

The phone rings and Marty answers it in the kitchen. It's Mark Perrone. Marty tells him what's going on, tells him to go to school and let the principal know what happened. Don't tell anyone else, he says—just Mr. Neuner. Hanging up, Marty goes back outside and sees Ronnie Rother, his sister's husband, hurrying up the street. They meet in a bear hug at the foot of the driveway, and Ronnie asks Marty what happened. "I don't know, Ronnie," Marty says, "I just woke up and found my father." He's glad Ronnie's here, but wonders why Shari isn't with him. Before he can ask Ronnie where Shari is, one of the uniformed officers tells them he has to separate them—standard procedure, the cop says, so they don't "contaminate" each other's accounts. The cop asks Marty to sit in the back of his patrol car to wait for the detectives, then gets behind the wheel of the ambulance so all three squad members can work on Seymour as they race to Mather Memorial.

For the first time since he left his bedroom, Marty is still. He's not calling anyone or running into the street or screaming at people to hurry up. He's just sitting there, alone in the back of a police car. And then he looks at the blood on his hands and begins to gag and spit up. Among his family and friends Marty is notoriously squeamish. When his father was in the hospital for an angioplasty, Marty saw an open incision on his leg and was so repulsed he had to look away. He asks one of the officers if he can go back into the house and wash the blood off his hands. The patrolman has just finished sealing off the property with yellow crime scene tape and tells Marty he can't go back inside. Marty sees a puddle in front of the car and asks if he can wash his hands in it. The officer says it's okay.

Just as Marty is dipping his hands in the puddle, Don Hines drives up. He's Belle Terre's chief constable, a retired New York City cop who's the only full-time member of the constabulary, a kind of light-duty security force. Hines knows the house well: He's delivered the weekly time sheets here ever since Vinnie Bove appointed Seymour to the position of commissioner of constables.

Neighbors are converging on the scene now, but Marty barely registers their presence. Passing by on her way to school, Dara Schaeffer sees Marty standing in the street and pulls over in her yellow Mustang to ask what the commotion is all about. She will remember him babbling almost incoherently, managing just enough intelligible words to make her scream "Oh my God!" and burst into tears herself. They've known each other since nursery school, but Marty seems to barely recognize Dara, and their passing encounter will be little more than a dreamlike image in his memory. He will remember sitting with Don Hines in his patrol car, but not a thing said between them. Through the fog, though, one thought remains coherent. When Vinnie Bove drives up, Marty tells him, almost matter-of-factly, that Jerry Steuerman murdered his parents.

Marty, Bove asks, what makes you say that? Did you see him do this?

No, Marty says, but it has to be him. They've been having a lot of problems, his father and Jerry. A lot of problems. But Marty, Bove says, we played cards last night and nothing happened, nothing at all. Did you see *anything*? All Marty can tell him is what he saw when he woke up: the lit-up house, his father barely alive at one end of the house, his mother life-less in the dark at the other.

THE FIRST homicide detective arrives on Seaside Drive at 7:40. He parks a hundred feet up the road and approaches the crime scene with the casu-alness of a man who has made this walk countless times before. He's around forty, dressed in the standard dark blue sport coat, gray slacks, a pale blue tie. His hair is dark, just starting to turn gray, carefully combed; his glasses are aviator-style and tinted. Cup of coffee in hand, he strolls up to the uniformed cops and gets the essentials: two victims, Seymour and Arlene Tankleff, wife DOA, husband in bad shape. Rescue took him to Mather at 0643 hours. Son Martin, seventeen, says he woke up, found his father in the office area, called 911, went looking for his mother, found her unresponsive in the bedroom. Gallagher says son came up to him yelling, "Somebody murdered my parents." Anyone else in the house at the time? No, just the kid. That's him over there, on the railroad ties by the drive-way.

The detective glances at Marty, then turns and walks toward the house. He finds his way to the kitchen, then steps through the solarium, which leads to the office. He sees Seymour Tankleff's bloody chair and notes the spatterings on the desk and the phone that's on the desk. He pans the room: poker table, eight chairs around it. Bag of microwave popcorn on the floor, unopened. He backtracks into the kitchen. Bowl of pasta, some dishes. Half a watermelon on the counter, a knife next to it. He works his way down to the other end of the house and goes into the master bed-room. The drapes in front of the sliding glass doors are parted about three feet, splashing the room with a shard of daylight that reveals the body of Arlene Tankleff on the floor next to the bed.

The detective notes the position of the body and of the blood spatter on the bed linens. He retreats from the bedroom and sees a linen closet in the hallway. The door is open; the light is on. He moves on to the other bedroom, the son's. Built-in bunk beds, shelves on either side. A red towel on the bed. A set of dumbbells on the floor. Scanning the room, he notices some small, dark red smudges around the light switch. He looks closer. Blood.

The detective ends his initial tour of the crime scenes after ten min-utes or so and finds his way to the only witness, still leaning against the railroad ties alongside the red gravel driveway. "Martin, my name is De-tective McCready," he says. "I'm from the homicide squad, and I'll be one of the detectives working the case." Marty nods and says hello. "Why don't we go over to my car to talk?" McCready asks.

Before they reach McCready's car, Don Hines, the constable chief, pulls McCready aside for a private word. Go ahead, McCready tells Marty, have a seat in my car. I'll be right with you. He turns back to Hines, who fills him in, at one point motioning toward the puddle in the street. McCready takes some notes, then asks Hines to go down to the beach behind the house to see if he can find anything.

Sliding into his seat next to Marty, McCready starts with what the cops call the pedigree—name, address, date of birth—as if he were filling out an insurance form. Then he asks Marty to tell him what happened.

"I know who did this," Marty says abruptly.

"Really?" McCready says. "Who?"

"Jerry Steuerman."

"Who's he?"

"He's my father's business partner. He was at the poker game last night."

"And why do you think he did this?"

"They've been fighting all summer. You can ask Julie at the bagel store. Julie Mutschler—she's seen them arguing."

McCready asks the spelling of Julie's name, the name and location of the bagel store, then gets back to what happened. *So what time did you say you came home last night? What'd you do after you moved this fella's car? What'd you eat? What time was that? What'd you do after that? How long were you in the shower? What time did you go to bed? What time did you get up? What were you wearing? Where'd you go first? Then where? What did you see? What'd you do when you saw him? Which phone did you use? Where'd you get the pillow? Then what'd you do? How'd you get into the garage? Where'd you go after you saw her car? Did you touch her?*

As they're talking, McCready notices a spot of blood on Marty's right calf, another on his instep. Is that from helping your father? he asks. Yeah, Marty says. What about your hands? McCready asks. Marty says his hands were full of blood. He washed them in the puddle over there.

Okay, McCready says, stay put. I'll see you in a few minutes. He goes back up to the house. When he returns ten minutes later, he's got someone with him. Marty's out of the car now, sitting on the hood. Marty, McCready tells him, this is my boss, Sergeant Doyle. I'd like you to tell the sergeant what you told me.

Marty recounts the incongruous sequence, last night's mundane events somehow a prelude to the inconceivable ones he woke to this morning. McCready listens in, smoking a cigarette, as Marty declares once more his belief that his father's business partner is responsible for what's happened to his parents. Doyle asks what sort of business they're in. Bagel stores, Marty tells him. And horses. Trotters, he says when Doyle asks what kind.

And what's been their problem? "Steuerman owes my father a lot of money," Marty says. "My Uncle Mike can tell you a lot more about it. He's my father's attorney. Mike Fox. He knows all about his business dealings with Jerry Steuerman."

And then, a moment of uncanny timing. Marty glances down the street, back toward his driveway. "There's my Uncle Mike now," he says, pointing toward a man walking toward them. At this, McCready abruptly leaves Marty with Doyle and walks double-time toward the approaching figure, engaging him a distance away. Barely a minute later, he's back and the man is getting in his car.

"Where's my Uncle Mike going?" Marty asks.

"He's going back to his office," McCready says, a business card in his hand. "If we need to contact him we know where to reach him."

By now the first member of the news media has arrived on the scene: the photo editor of the weekly *Port Jefferson Record*, Tony Jerome. Through the windshield of his car, he captures Marty Tankleff, sitting on the hood of McCready's car now, as the two detectives stand above him scribbling in their notepads. The images will be of surveillance quality, but they will also be indelible. There will be demand for them from bigger if less nimble media organizations, as well as from the police and prosecutors of Suffolk County. While Jerome is shooting, a third detective enters his viewfinder, a tall and slender man who towers over Marty.

"Marty, this is my partner, Detective Rein," McCready says. Rein flips open his notepad and starts the process over again. While Marty talks, McCready and Doyle amble toward the Tankleffs' mailbox for a conversation.

When Ed Jablonski arrives on Seaside Drive a little while later, he knows this has the makings of his biggest case since his promotion to chief of the homicide bureau of the Suffolk County district attorney's office. Jablonski checks in with Doyle and his boss, Lieutenant John McElhone, the commanding officer of the homicide squad. The three of them enter the house together and make their way to the master bedroom. They see Arlene Tankleff splayed faceup on the floor beside the bed, her blood-soaked camisole covering only the top half of her body. Jablonski scans the room and notices several pieces of jewelry on the dresser. Among them is a gold necklace featuring a crucifix intertwined with a Star of David.

"It's not a burglary," Jablonski says, something the homicide detectives have already concluded.

CHAPTER 3

The Usual Suspect

THE LARGEST ISLAND in the continental United States runs 118 miles end to end, more than enough to uphold its name. From space, Long Island looks like an appendage to the eastern seaboard; vaguely fish-shaped, the land seems tethered so tenuously that it might float off into the North Atlantic with a stiff wind.

The eastern two-thirds of Long Island is governed by Suffolk County, a cul-de-sac of grand proportions. Separated from New York City by Nassau County, Suffolk covers nearly a thousand square miles and forks in two just past the county seat of Riverhead. Thirty and forty miles beyond—at Orient Point on the north fork, Montauk Point on the south—the roads come to the biggest dead ends in America. The county is rich with the lore of the Native American tribes who predated its establishment as a colonial entity in 1683, and its years under British occupation during the Revolutionary War.

Two centuries later, in the decades after another war, Suffolk County was under suburban occupation. Now those thousand square miles were inhabited by a million and a quarter people who transformed the state's most productive agricultural county into one of its most populous. By the 1980s, it was a place with all the social ills of any modern city, if not in such great abundance. Murder, for instance, wasn't an everyday occurrence. On average, it was a three-times-a-month occurrence. The county police department's homicide squad was always busy but rarely overburdened. It was big enough to be a world unto itself, small enough for a detective to make a name for himself.

Detective Kevin James McCready already had a name when he made the squad in 1980. His family had roots in Suffolk County dating to 1754, and a dozen generations later the McCreadys were a well-known family of cops. McCready and all three of his brothers were members of the department, following the path of their father. Eugene McCready had been one of the original ten members of the homicide unit after the county department was formed in 1960, and two of his sons later made the squad, Gene Jr. and then Jim. The McCready boys had one sister, and she, too, joined the department: She married a detective whose father was the police commissioner.

Along with a familiar name, Jim McCready arrived in Homicide with a reputation established in a singular moment of glory. One day in 1975, he was on uniformed patrol when a bulletin came over his police radio: A man had robbed a drugstore and killed a retired police captain in the process—now he was fleeing in a stolen utility truck. McCready and his partner joined the chase, and when the gunman slammed on his brakes McCready jumped out of his own car, ran alongside the stolen vehicle, and shot the suspect to death right through the window. The shooting was ruled a justifiable homicide, and McCready spent the rest of the year collecting accolades: the police department's Combat Award, the Silver Shield Award from the Police Benevolent Association, Cop of the Year from the Police Conference, Outstanding Police Officer of the Year from the American Legion. A few months later he was assigned to the district attorney's office, where he spent a year in the rackets bureau and two in anticorruption before making detective in 1979. Just six months later, he was promoted to Homicide. It was the quickest leap to the department's most elite unit anyone could remember.

Within the ranks of any police department, a man so inclined will find it much easier to get himself noticed once he has a detective's shield. McCready had a way of drawing attention to himself more than most. It wasn't long before he was one of those guys with a reputation for having a reputation, for better or worse. Crafty, tough, hard-driving—all that was true. Arrogant, reckless, hard-drinking—also true. He could turn on the easygoing charm with witnesses and suspects, reporters and fellow cops, and anyone he happened to be drinking near. Or he could sit at the bar and become a son of a bitch before their eyes. So, no, McCready wasn't everyone's cup of coffee. He had a series of partners and bosses over the years, and they all had to get used to working with an impulsive man who might do something exceptional to break a case or something inconvenient to make them cringe. There was, for instance, the Diaz case—not the department's finest hour, to say the least. The trial was a first-class fiasco and nobody could be surprised that McCready was in the middle of it. He wasn't the worst offender, but he might have done the most stammering. It didn't hurt his career, though. What saved him, it seemed, were equal measures of his own special skill and the county's lenient law enforcement culture. No one could deny McCready's work in the interview room. And no one could deny the police department's long reputation for broad-mindedness when it came to the way its homicide detectives conducted business.

The homicide squad was divided into three teams, each with six detectives and headed by a sergeant who reported to the lieutenant who was the squad's commander. In 1988, Homicide's newest sergeant was Robert Doyle, recently transferred after a tour heading up a special bicounty robbery task force. Doyle drew McCready and paired him with Norman Rein, a veteran detective with a manner as composed as McCready's was untamed. Taking stock of the old days years later, Doyle described McCready as the "epitome" of his breed. "You need three things to be a homicide detective," he explained. "You need to be a skilled investigator. You need to testify well. And you need a giant ego. You have to believe in yourself." That, McCready certainly did. More than anything, he believed in his instinct for knowing when someone was lying to him. Years after his retirement, but still speaking in the present tense, he would go on national television and matter-of-factly tell an interviewer, "Oh, I'm better than a polygraph."

McCready had worked scores of murders by the time Doyle joined the squad, some of them well publicized. So the sergeant knew him well by reputation, again for better or worse. The case that raised McCready's profile most was a made-for-TV soap opera that the press glibly dubbed the case of the "Homeroom Hit Man." The synopsis: On February 5, 1986, in the working-class community of Selden, a burly electrician and widowed father of three is found dead in his driveway, shot in the back of the head. McCready pokes around the family, checking out his lieutenant's suspicions, based on instinct and a consultation with the sex crimes unit, that the victim had been sexually abusing his sixteen-year-old daughter. The girl, a bright-eyed cheerleader named Cheryl Pierson, had found the body. McCready works on her for nearly two weeks, and eventually she confesses. Her father had been forcing her to have sex with him since she was eleven, she says, and she decided to have him killed after finding him "wrestling around the floor" with her eight-year-old sister. Cheryl and her boyfriend persuaded the boy who sat next to her in homeroom to kill her father for a thousand dollars.

A reporter named Dena Kleiman wrote about the case for *The New York Times Magazine* and later turned the story into a book in which she described McCready as "a wry investigator with Nick Nolte good looks and an uncanny sense about people." The depiction might have struck knowing readers as a bit fawning—close enough on the looks, maybe, bu exaggeration of the man's talents. In the TV movie, McCready was played by Bruce Weitz, best known as the surly undercover street cop given to referring to people as "hairballs" in the 1980s cop drama *Hill Street Blues.*

A year after the Pierson case, McCready was on Sergeant Kevin Cronin's team when their squad was on call for a double homicide in Ronkonkoma, a nearby community sliced in two by the Long Island Expressway. Daniel Kasten, a sophomore at the state university in Stony Brook, told the detectives he'd found his mother's body when he woke up in the morning. The team's rotation put two of McCready's colleagues into the interview room as the lead detectives, and before the day was out they would have a confession from the victims' son. Kasten told them, and repeated to a video camera, that he'd plotted for months to kill both his parents because they threatened to force him to quit school and get a job if his grades didn't improve. He said he shot them with a .22-caliber rifle he outfitted with a homemade silencer—a pipe surrounded by socks—and test-fired into a dictionary. After giving his statement, Kasten led the detectives to several spots off the service road of the expressway where he'd hidden the rifle, the silencer, and the dictionary.

Daniel Kasten was a young man with no history of actual violence, though he seemed to have a strong attraction to the imaginary kind. He was a devoted player of the fantasy role-playing game Dungeons & Dragons. Friends and neighbors described him to reporters as smart, kind, a little shy. His attorney said that Kasten, who was adopted, "loved and still loves his parents very much." The lawyer went for the insanity defense at Kasten's trial—Dungeons & Dragons made him do it—but on June 29, 1988, a jury took just four hours to convict him on two counts of murder. It was with that background that Jim McCready, ten weeks later, showed up at a waterfront home where a seventeen-year-old boy had reported finding his mother dead and his father barely alive.

ON CALL for the homicide squad in the overnight hours of September 7, Detective Mike Carmody reached his boss at home to let him know their team was catching a homicide, maybe two, in Belle Terre. Thirty-three Seaside Drive—up by the cliffs. Not a homicide kind of neighborhood, Sergeant Bob Doyle thought. The press will be all over it. He dispatched Carmody and his partner, John Pfalzgraf, to Mather Hospital in case Seymour Tankleff regained consciousness. He wanted the rest of his team at the scene. He paged Bob Anderson and Norm Rein to get them on their way. They both lived on the South Shore, half an hour away at least. Then he called Jim McCready. He lived closest to the scene, in Stony Brook.

McCready wasn't home, so Doyle paged him. McCready had a busy construction business on the side, and when he was on a day tour he usually went to his shop before work to get his crew squared away. McCready responded to Doyle's page from the shop and made it to Belle Terre in nineteen minutes. Doyle arrived another twenty minutes later. By the time Norman Rein showed up, his partner had already decided where this case was going.

McCready told Doyle he didn't like the kid's demeanor—too matter-of-fact, no tears. And a few things didn't look right. The police constable said he saw him washing his hands in a puddle in the street. There was a smear of blood around the light switch in his room. And there was this: The kid said that after he helped his father, he checked the garage for his mother's car. If he's telling the truth, there should be some blood on the handle of the door to the garage. I checked, McCready said. There was none. But as much as anything, to both McCready and Doyle there was the simple fact that they had three people in the house, and one of them was unharmed—why? What about the business partner? They thought the kid was bringing him up a little too much. Trying a little too hard to point the finger elsewhere. Doyle told McCready to go ahead—ask the kid to come to Yaphank.

If Doyle had any qualms about McCready and his unpredictable ways, he felt he could count on Rein. A twenty-nine-year veteran of the department, the previous five as a homicide detective, Rein's experience included assignments to assorted detective squads and a stint working directly for the chief of detectives. He'd spent time in internal affairs and was a long-time member of the department's hostage-negotiating team. Ramrod straight, Rein had an understated and methodical manner of speech that made him exceptionally effective when it came time for him to testify in court. This was in stark contrast with McCready, with his smoky voice and volatile disposition. In fact, it would be hard to find two men in Homicide who seemed less alike, and maybe that's what made their pairing effective. In the interview room, they were a classic good cop/bad cop combination.

After getting Marty's third recounting of the morning's events, Rein joined McCready and Doyle around the Tankleffs' mailbox. Doyle filled him in, and then McCready strolled back over to Marty and asked if he'd mind coming down to headquarters. I'd like to hear more about this Steuerman, McCready told him. Marty asked if they could stop at the hospital first. McCready said he'd take him there afterward.

Just as they were passing the old gatehouse at the entrance to Belle Terre, a message came over McCready's police radio: *Detective McCready, respond to Detective Pfalzgraf at Mather Hospital.* The quickest route to Yaphank would take McCready right past Mather in a minute or two. But he went the longer way through Port Jefferson, avoiding the hospital and stopping at a pay phone outside a restaurant on Main Street called the Village Way. He punched in his calling card number, had a brief conversation, then returned to the car. "They're moving your father to Stony Brook," he said. That's good, Marty replied. It's a much bigger hospital than Mather.

"Did your father have any head injuries?" McCready asked. Yes, Marty said, a bad one. It looked as if someone had hit him over the head really hard.

McCready continued down Route 112, then headed east on the Long Island Expressway, pulling off at the sixty-seventh of its seventy-two exits. The police headquarters building was in Yaphank, a locale so barren it barely qualified for a zip code and was best known for something that no longer existed. Yaphank was once the site of Camp Upton, a massive army training base during both world wars and the inspiration for *Yip, Yip, Yaphank*, a musical revue produced in 1918 by a young sergeant named Irving Berlin. One popular song came out of it: "Oh! How I Hate to Get Up in the Morning."

McCready swung around to the rear of police headquarters and led Marty across the parking lot and through the back door. They took an elevator up one flight. Homicide was just down the hall from the communications center, where the emergency operator had picked up Marty's 911 call a few hours earlier. McCready brought Marty through the squad room and into a small, square anteroom. It had a steel desk, three metal-framed chairs, and four walls. The interview room was where many of the homicide detectives thought they did their best work.

Detective Rein will be joining us in a few minutes, McCready said, and asked Marty if he could get him a cup of coffee. Yes, Marty said. Light and sweet, please.

It was 9:30. Back in Port Jefferson, third period was just starting at Vandermeulen High. Marty was as far from there as he could possibly be. He looked down and noticed that his feet were filthy. Three and a half hours after getting out of bed for the first day of school, he was still barefoot.

CHAPTER 4

Where's Marty?

A CHAIN OF TELEPHONES RANG early that morning. In Fort Salonga, a waterfront community eighteen miles west of Port Jefferson, Myron Fox, Mike to his friends, had just sat down for breakfast when his wife, Gail, picked up the phone and heard a jarring voice.

Hello, this is Shari Rother, Seymour's daughter, I have to talk to Mike!

Gail quickly handed the phone to her husband. "Shari, what's wrong?" he asked.

"Arlene's dead and my father's in the hospital! They tried to kill him, too!"

"Oh my God," Fox said. "What happened?"

Shari told him all she knew and said she was at the emergency room of Mather Hospital with her father. "It's bad, Mike," she said.

Fox grabbed his tie and jacket, jumped in his car, and headed east on Route 25A. There was hardly a prettier drive anywhere on Long Island on a sunny morning just after Labor Day, but all Fox could think about was getting there and hoping Seymour wasn't as bad as Shari said and wondering if, after thirty years of friendship and so much business advice that Seymour had mostly ignored, it had really come to this.

As Fox raced to Port Jefferson, the news was spreading. Shari had set the sequence in motion, calling her father's brother, Norman, and his wife, Ruth. Norman called their daughter, Autumn Asness. Autumn alerted Arlene's side of the family, calling Joy Piccirillo, Arlene's niece, who called her brother, Ron Falbee, and his wife, Carol. The conversations were all the same: the inconceivable news, the gasps of horror and disbelief, the scantiness of the information—Arlene's dead and Seymour's really bad—making it seem all the more unreal. Then the recipient of the call repeating the dreadful process, bringing the news to another relative.

Ron Falbee wanted more before he took that step. He needed to be sure of the most essential fact before telling his mother that her younger sister had been murdered. Ron called the Suffolk County police, reached the Sixth Precinct, and told a desk officer he was trying to get any information available about an incident at the Tankleff house at 33 Seaside Drive in Belle Terre. The officer said he couldn't tell him anything—it had to come from the public information office at headquarters. "Look," Ron said firmly, "I'm their nephew. My mother is Arlene Tankleff's sister. I just want to know—can you confirm that somebody died?"

The desk officer transferred the call to a sergeant, who told Ron he had little but the most basic information. "There is one person deceased," he said. "Another person was removed to Mather Hospital, breathing but unresponsive."

"Can you tell me who is dead?"

"The deceased is a female."

Ron was a man of solid bearing, steady even as he took in words that shook him to his core. "Do you know anything about their son?" he asked. "His name is Martin."

"I believe he was the one who called 911 for assistance," the sergeant told him. "My information is that he's fine."

Ron got in his car, his mind racing. He struggled with the image of his aunt dying violently in the night and contemplated how he was going to break the news to his mother. He tried to imagine what it meant that Seymour was "breathing but unresponsive," and the possibilities led him to think about Marty. Somewhere among the jumble of thoughts ricocheting in Ron's mind was a flashback to the day four years ago when Seymour took him out to lunch to tell him about some decisions he and Arlene had made, and to ask his blessing for the most important one. To Ron, it was a flattering gesture and a solemn obligation for Carol and him, but a contingency that he presumed, until this moment, would never come to pass.

Marcella Falbee, a self-possessed woman in her early sixties, absorbed the news of her sister's murder with the same quiet anguish with which her son delivered it. Then she turned to her own unbearable task. It was still before daybreak in Northern California. Marcella decided to wait until the hour there reached seven before calling Marianne, the younger of her two much younger sisters. Marcella was ten when Arlene was born, eighteen by the time Marianne came along. To her kid sisters, she was not Marcella but rather "Mickey," a nickname that suited her warmth if not quite her dignified manner. When she made the call and heard Marianne's voice, Marcella couldn't bring herself to utter the blunt words in her head.

"I have some very bad news, Marianne," Marcella said softly. "Arlene's gone."

"What do you mean, 'gone'?" Marianne asked.

"Hon, she's gone," Marcella repeated.

"Mickey, I don't understand what you mean."

"Marianne, she's been killed."

Marianne dropped the phone and ran to her husband, screaming. Mike McClure got on with Ron, who told him what he knew and said he and Carol were on the way to the hospital with his mother. They'd call again from there. Mike hung up, called his law office to clear the rest of his week, and booked three seats on the next flight out of San Francisco. Their seventeen-year-old, Jenny, insisted on coming. She felt so terribly for her cousin Marty. They'd spent two weeks together when her family visited his over the summer. Marty gave Jenny and her younger sister Christy his room—it had bunk beds—and slept in the guest room. He took them out on the sound in their Boston Whaler and squired them around Port Jefferson. Jenny couldn't imagine what Marty was going through now, but she wanted to be there for him.

MIKE FOX pulled into the parking lot at Mather Hospital a few minutes before eight. He was barely out of his car when he saw Shari running out to meet him, trailed by her husband. "Oh my God, Mike, I'm so scared," Shari said, sobbing. Her father was still alive, she told him, but she didn't know what was going to happen. "I want you to go get Marty," she said. "He needs to be here."

"Where is he?" Fox asked.

"He's still at the house," Shari said.

"I was over there," Ronnie said, "but the police wouldn't let me stay with him." He was the only relative who had seen Marty since all this began. That was an hour and a half ago and nobody had talked to Marty since.

"I'll go get him," Fox said, and got back into his car.

Just as he was leaving the parking lot, a pair of homicide detectives were arriving. Mike Carmody and John Pfalzgraf went to the emergency room and asked the doctors how likely it was that Seymour Tankleff would regain consciousness. Not very likely, they were told.

The ER doctors were local physicians who were unaccustomed to treating injuries such as those they saw before them. Alfred Ekstrom was an internist, Robert Roth a neurologist. Roth had been home on Cliffside Drive in Belle Terre, one street up from Seaside Drive, when he got word that a sixty-two-year-old man was coming to the hospital with traumatic injuries from an assault. He rushed to the hospital, and it was only then that he realized that his gravely wounded patient was his neighbor Seymour Tankleff. When he heard that Arlene was dead, Roth thought of his own wife, Patricia, a good friend of Arlene's. In fact she had been with her just yesterday, playing bridge on the Tankleffs' backyard deck.

Roth was stunned to find someone he knew laid out before him with some of the most vicious injuries he'd ever seen. Seymour had a deep laceration that went nearly all the way around his neck—a slashing so deep that the general impression among the ER staff was that it appeared as though someone had tried to decapitate him. It was the thickness of Seymour's neck that saved him, at least for now. As deep as the cuts went, they failed to sever any major blood vessels. Unfortunately, they weren't the worst of Seymour's injuries. He suffered several blows to the back of his head, including at least one of such force that his skull was crushed and pieces of detached bone were driven into his brain. That Roth saw exposed brain tissue oozing from the site was a very bad sign. It was miraculous that Seymour was still breathing, he thought.

Carmody and Pfalzgraf had hoped to get a look at Seymour's injuries for some indication of what kind of weapons the assailant might have used. But his head and neck were already completely bandaged. When the detectives asked Roth to describe the head wounds, he told them that the worst one was roughly round, about an inch in diameter, with several slash marks around it. It seemed to him that Seymour had been attacked with a hammer.

Roth told the detectives he didn't think Seymour would survive the day, but if he had any chance at all he needed the immediate attention of a top-flight neurosurgical team. There was one just ten minutes away, at Stony Brook University Hospital. Its chief, a renowned expert on traumatic head injuries, was on his way over.

Mike Fox was pulling into the Tankleffs' driveway in Belle Terre. He'd been here so many times over the years—he handled the purchase of the land even before there was a house on it—but now he was barred from the driveway by a Suffolk County police officer and a ribbon of yellow crime scene tape strung from tree to tree across the width of the property.

Fox parked on the street and scanned the scene for Marty. He didn't see him so he asked the cop out front who was in charge. You want the gentlemen up there, the officer told him, pointing up the road at a group of three or four men gathered at the front end of a plain black car. Fox started walking toward them, then saw one approaching at a good pace. The man pulled up with an air of casual purposefulness, cup of coffee in hand. "I'm Detective McCready," he said. "Can I help you?"

Thus began a brief but crucial encounter, one that would become the subject of fierce contention in the months ahead. Precisely what was said and done during these few minutes defies objective certainty. But some things are undisputed: That Mike Fox pulled up to the Tankleffs' house while Marty was up the road, sitting on the hood of McCready's car, answering questions for the detective and his sergeant. That Marty spotted Fox just as he was telling McCready and Doyle that "my Uncle Mike" could tell them about his father's problems with Jerry Steuerman. And that Marty pointed out Fox's arrival, saying, "There's Uncle Mike now"— at which point McCready abruptly left Marty with Doyle to encounter Fox in the street.

By Fox's account, McCready headed him off before he could get close enough to see Marty talking to the detectives, and distracted him with a deft maneuver: "He meets me in the street," Fox recalled, "and positions himself so that I have to turn to face him. He turns me around. So now he's facing the people at the car and my back is to them. I never even knew it was Marty they were talking to."

McCready turned Fox around in a bigger way. According to Fox, when he told McCready that he was the Tankleffs' attorney and that he was there to bring their son to the hospital, McCready told him that Marty was already on the way over there. "He said, 'He told us everything he knows,' and they were taking him to the hospital in a cruiser. 'They left about five minutes ago.'"

Fox handed McCready his business card, said he'd be in his office later, then headed back to the hospital, where he found a small crowd gathering. Seymour's brother, Norman, and his wife, Ruth, were there. So were Linda and Frank Perrone, Marty's best friend's parents. And Vinnie Bove. Having played in the poker game the night before, he was the last of them to see Seymour conscious. And he was the only one who had seen him this morning, comatose and wrapped in bandages behind the doors of the emergency room. As vice chairman of the community hospital, Vinnie had free rein. The group waited for word of Seymour's condition and talked about who might have done this. Ron Rother felt he knew. "This was a hit," said Seymour's son-in-law. "A hundred thousand was owed this week," he added cryptically.

When Shari saw Mike Fox, but not Marty, a look of dismay crossed her face. "Where's my brother?" she wanted to know.

"Hasn't he gotten here yet?" Fox replied.

"What? No, he's not here. What are you talking about? Where is he?"

"One of the cops said they were bringing him here. He should be here by now."

Fox and the Rothers went out to the ER reception area—maybe Marty was there. But he wasn't. Shari went looking for the detectives, Carmody and Pfalzgraf. Maybe they knew where he was. But she couldn't even find *them*. They were behind the doors of the emergency room, watching Dr. George Tyson, the neurosurgeon from Stony Brook, carefully remove the bandages from Seymour's head. When he saw the injuries, Tyson doubted the patient would survive. He would do what he could, of course. But of course not here. Detective Pfalzgraf turned to Roth. Before you move him, he said, we need some of the blood. Roth scraped the dried blood from Seymour's forearms and poured the flakes into a plastic evidence bag. Then he removed a blood-specked gold bracelet from Seymour's wrist and handed it to Pfalzgraf.

Pushing through the double doors of the emergency room moments later, Roth was surrounded by Seymour's family and friends. He was candid about the magnitude of the injuries and told Shari he needed her consent to move her father to Stony Brook. In the disarray of the moment, Shari was distracted from her brother's absence, but with still no sign of him, Mike Fox decided to take another trip up to the house. Maybe McCready was mistaken. Maybe Marty was still there.

As Fox would later recount, he arrived back on Seaside Drive just as an unmarked police car was departing. "Was that Detective McCready?" he asked a uniformed sergeant. The sergeant said it was and told him, "He's finished here. He's going to Yaphank." Can you get him on your radio? Fox said he asked. The sergeant went across the road to his patrol car but returned a minute later saying he couldn't raise McCready. So Fox headed back to Mather. Maybe McCready realized that Marty hadn't been taken to the hospital after all and was dropping him off on his way to Yaphank.

"Have you seen Marty?" Fox asked Vinnie Bove when he got back to the hospital.

"No," Bove said. "I haven't seen him since I was at the house early this morning." He told Fox he'd ask the detectives, who were out of the emergency room now and starting to interview Seymour's relatives. Bove found Pfalzgraf interviewing Ronnie Rother and asked the detective if he could find out where Seymour Tankleff's son was. "There's a lot of concern about him," he said. "His family's been told he's being brought over here but nobody's seen him."

Pfalzgraf took out a handheld radio and asked a police communications operator to have McCready call him at Mather Hospital. Then he turned back to Rother, who told him about his father-in-law. He's retired from the insurance business, Rother said, and the last few years he's been putting money in various businesses. His main partner is Jerry Steuerman, the bagel guy. Things weren't good between them. Steuerman owed Seymour a lot of money and he wasn't coming up with it. Rother told Pfalzgraf, "I think Steuerman may have done this."

"I can give you a lot of information about Steuerman," Fox interjected. He told Pfalzgraf that Steuerman was due to make a "substantial" payment that very week, that Seymour was putting a lot of pressure on him. "I have all the paperwork in my office."

"Detective," a nurse called over. "There's a Detective McCready on the phone for you."

Pfalzgraf took the call and returned to Fox and the others a few minutes later. "Martin is en route to Yaphank with Detective McCready," he told them.

"Why's he going to Yaphank?" Fox asked. "I was told he was being brought to the hospital."

Pfalzgraf told Fox that Marty was going to headquarters to tell McCready and his partner what he knew about his father's business dealings, particularly those with Jerry Steuerman, and about the events surrounding the poker game the night before. Marty would be "debriefed," Pfalzgraf told Fox, and then he would be brought to the hospital in Stony Brook to join his family.

Fox didn't think Marty should be alone at police headquarters. He wanted Rother to go to Yaphank and bring Marty back to the hospital when he was finished telling the detectives what he knew. Rother said okay. But just as Pfalzgraf was giving him directions to police headquarters, there was a commotion outside the emergency room doors. All eyes turned to see Seymour being wheeled down the hall, wrapped like a mummy from the neck up. Attendants held IV bags and Shari walked alongside, grim-faced, as the gurney was rolled out to the ambulance.

"No, I want to go with Shari and Seymour to Stony Brook," Rother told Fox.

And after talking to Shari, Fox decided that he should go there, too. She might need him should she have to make any legal decisions. And he could serve as a family spokesman, shielding her and the other relatives from reporters. So nobody went to Yaphank.

I NOTICE some hemorrhages in your eyes, Marty.

Detective Norman Rein was sitting across from Marty in the homicide squad's interview room at police headquarters. Marty explained that it was from the surgery he'd had on his nose a couple of weeks earlier. It was for a deviated septum, he said. Well, actually, it was a nose job.

Rein asked Marty if he had a girlfriend. No, Marty said, freely engaging in the small talk, incongruous as it was under the circumstances. He said he didn't have much luck with girls. Well, the nose job should help with that, Rein said, and asked if there was a girl he liked at the moment, anyone in particular. Marty said he liked this one girl he worked with at the bagel store, Christine Engels. Over the summer, he threw a birthday party for her on the Belle Terre beach. It didn't end too well—a bunch of crashers showed up and broke some of the cabanas. Marty said he got blamed and had to pay for the damage, which was embarrassing for his father, the commissioner of constables.

Any other girls? McCready asked. Marty said he always liked Dara Schaeffer, but they were just friends. They'd known each other since nursery school. And there were the Goldschmidt sisters, Audra and Stacy. He just met them over the summer. He liked them both.

And so it went. Marty thought he was there to give the detectives information about his father's business partner, but that hadn't come up so far. *What kind of interests do you have, Marty? Sure, most kids like cars. What do you drive? That's the car you took to the mall? And you like cooking with your mom? What's your specialty? Do you play any sports?*

So tell us one more time about last night, McCready said eventually. Marty started going through it again, but rather than having him give them an uninterrupted narrative as they had back in Belle Terre, McCready and Rein broke in with questions: Did he usually take a shower at night, or in the morning, or both? Did he use the same towels all the time, and if so what color were they? In my family we have our own towels, McCready said. Is that how it is in your house? Marty said his towels were red. So after showering and drying off, what did you do with your red towel?

Marty said he wrapped the towel around his waist, and then he got another towel from the bathroom and put it on his pillow because his hair was wet. And then he abruptly stopped talking about the towels and his showering habits and anything else that had to do with last night or this morning.

I was adopted when I was two days old. My mother and father had an affair a long time ago. My father owned a big insurance company and my mother was his secretary. My father got divorced and he and my mother got married, and then they adopted me when I was born. They're the only parents I've ever known. . . . We're very close. We do everything together. Everywhere they go, they take me. We went to Europe last year. They let me bring my friend. . . . I don't know what's going to happen to me. I'm an orphan now. . . .

"I want to remind you, Marty, that you're not an orphan," Rein said. "Your father is still alive."

"Well, if he dies," Marty said. "Then I'll be an orphan."

*   *   *

THE AMBULANCE pulled up at the Stony Brook medical center, a complex of modern cubic buildings across from the state university's main campus. Seymour was brought directly to an operating room, where Dr. Tyson was waiting. Shaving a patient's head before surgery was usually a task performed by a member of the surgical team. But with Seymour's injuries, even this wasn't a routine procedure. Tyson did it himself. Then he took four Polaroid photos of Seymour's head from different angles and sketched a scale drawing showing the size and location of the injuries. He gave the photos and the diagram to a police detective.

Over the next several hours, Tyson did what he could to keep Seymour alive. He removed the broken pieces of his skull and repaired a tear in one of the protective layers around the brain. But part of the brain itself was damaged beyond repair. Tyson used an aspiration machine to suck it out. He drained blood from a part of the brain that was only bruised. Then he closed the scalp.

The two sides of the family gathered in an office that housed the hospital's AIDS program. It was run by Mike Fox's wife, Gail, a nurse practitioner. Her department's suite of offices became an encampment, a place for family and friends to await word on Seymour, to grieve for Arlene, to make calls, to try to get their bearings. With each arrival there were tearful hugs and so many questions. Yet it seemed that the biggest questions— Who did this and why?—were the source of the least bewilderment. There was little doubt among them about whom the police should be talking to. "We were asking the cops, 'Has anybody gone after Seymour's partner, Jerry Steuerman? He's been having big problems with him,'" Ron Falbee recalled. "I told them that. Mike told them that. Norman told them that. Ron Rother. Everybody told them."

And nobody worried too much about Marty's continued absence. When later events forced them to think about why, the reason was as plain to them as Steuerman's involvement. The family saw no mystery here, and the police played that card exquisitely, encouraging them to believe that Marty was in safe hands, doing what he could to help solve the case, telling them everything he knew about his father's war with Jerry Steuerman. The detectives needed as much information as they could get, and Marty was privy to a lot, much more than would be expected of a seventeen-year-old. Everyone knew that Seymour was grooming his son.

At 10:15, an hour and a half after Pfalzgraf said that Marty was on his way to Yaphank to be "debriefed," Ron Rother called the homicide squad to check on his teenage brother-in-law. A sergeant named Horvath told him that Marty was in with the detectives. Rother called again an hour later. He's still in there, Horvath said. You're welcome to come out here and wait for him, or we can run him over to Stony Brook when he's done. Rother thought he should stay at the hospital with his wife.

But others in the family were starting to worry. How long should it take for Marty to give the police enough to go on? The problems weren't really all that complicated. And, really, how much could Marty tell them—more than Mike Fox, Seymour's close friend and attorney? Sure, Marty needed to help the police, but right now he needed to be with his family more. Ron Falbee asked the detective stationed at the hospital if he had any word on Marty. As far as I know, the detective told him, he's still being interviewed.

HOW'S YOUR father's health been, Marty? Not great, Marty said. He had a heart condition that put him in the hospital. They had to open up a blocked artery. And he has diabetes. *When was the last time you saw your mother alive?* When I came in to say good night after I took my shower. *What side of the bed did she sleep on?* The side closest to the sliding glass doors. *What did she wear to bed?* A nightgown. *What did the poker players eat last night?* Pasta and champagne turkey. *Did you spend any time in the card room?* A few minutes. *How rich is the game— what kind of stakes are we talking about?* You can win or lose thousands. My father usually brings a thousand dollars into the game. He takes the money from a hidden drawer in his dresser.

Eventually, McCready turned the conversation to the problems between Marty's father and Jerry Steuerman. *Was it just the usual horseshit that goes on between business partners? Was it so bad that the other card players knew about it?* My father and Steuerman put on a big act, Marty said. They pretended to be good friends like they used to be. But they really hated each other. *You seem to know a lot about your father's business dealings.* He involves me in everything. He's been grooming me.

Does your father have business relationships with other people besides Steuerman? A lot of them. He's partners in an alarm company with Mike Fox and another guy. Joe something. There's also a real estate deal with some of the other card players, and he's got some other businesses. He put money into a gym near the bagel store—Fundamental Fitness, it's called. He's also partners with my brother-in-law in a tanning business. And he's been planning to set up a cousin of mine in a marina business. If I don't go to college I might work in that business.

Any problems with those business relationships? No. The only problems are with Steuerman. *Are they involved in anything else, your father and Steuerman—anything besides the bagel business?* Racehorses. My mother's part of that, too. Jerry has fifty percent and my parents have twenty-five percent each.

Tell me, Marty, what kind of money do your parents have? Are they rich or poor? Well, they're not poor. I guess they're wealthy. *Do they have a lot of life insurance?* My father was retired from the insurance business, so he has insurance. I don't know how much.

Are there any safes in the house? There's one in the linen closet. My parents are very careful about security, especially my father. *I'd be paranoid, living in a neighborhood where everyone was so concerned about security.* My parents always lock the sliding doors and set the alarm. That's one thing I noticed when I first got up this morning, how I knew something was wrong. When I looked in my parents' room, the alarm wasn't set.

Marty, what happens to the money? Say your father doesn't make it. Who would inherit the estate? I would. I'm the main beneficiary. *What about your sister?* She doesn't get that much. *Why's that?* My mother wanted it that way. *And what would happen if your parents were dead and Jerry Steuerman was out of the picture—what would happen then?* I don't know. *Well, what do you think would happen?* I guess then I would get everything.

You know, Marty, you don't seem very upset about all this. Your mother's dead, your father's in bad shape. And we haven't seen you cry all day. Not a tear. I guess I was all cried out before you came.

Marty, how come you don't have any blood on you from helping your father? Well, I had blood on my hands. I washed them off in a puddle. *Why'd you do that?* I can't stand the sight of blood. One time, when my father was in the hospital after his heart surgery, I saw an incision in his leg. I couldn't take it. To this day, I get sick at the sight of blood.

It seems kind of strange, Marty, how you have almost no blood on you after helping your father. I mean, there was blood all over the place in there. Why don't you show us how you helped him? Let's say Detective Rein here is your father. Show us exactly what you did, how you moved him.

Marty was almost finished with the demonstration, reenacting how he got in front of his father and pulled him off the chair. As he leaned over Rein, his zippered sweatshirt, loosely fitting and halfway open, fell away from his chest, revealing several large red splotches on the front of his right shoulder and his upper chest. Seeing this, McCready caught his partner's eye, pointed to his own shoulder, and silently mouthed, *Blood.*

Did you shower this morning? No, last night. *But you said earlier that you usually shower at night and again when you wake up in the morning.* Usually. But today I found my father when I woke up. *You said you went into your mother's bedroom first when you got up, but you didn't see her. Why didn't you see her?* It was dark. And I didn't go all the way in. When I didn't see my parents in bed I went back into the hallway. *Marty, I was up at ten to six this morning and I looked out the window and it was light out. How come you didn't see her?* It was dark. And the drapes were closed. *No they weren't. The drapes were parted. And the TV was on. There was plenty of light.* No, it was dark, and my mother was on the floor, behind the bed. *But you saw her there when you went back in after you helped your father.* Yes. *But you just said it was dark.* It was getting lighter. I saw her on the floor when I looked around. Before, I only looked in the bed. *So when you see your mother, did you help her?* No. *Why not?* I thought she was dead. Her throat was cut. *Did you get right up to her?* No. *Where were you standing?* Just inside the room, by the wall. *How did you see that her throat was cut from there? I had to go right up to her and stand over her to see that.* I don't know, I could see.

What phone did you use to call 911? The one on my father's desk. *Did you go back to your room after you called?* Yes, to get the pillow. *Why would you go all the way back to the other end of the house for a pillow?* I don't know, they said to get his legs elevated and I just thought of this big heavy pillow I have in my room. *Did you go back to your room at any other point?* No. *Then how do you explain the blood around the light switch in your room?*

Marty, did you have blood on your hands when you checked the garage to see if your mother's car was there? Yes. *How about when you used the phone in the kitchen to call your sister and your friend?* Yes. *Well, after I spoke to you in my car, I went back inside and looked at the phones in the kitchen. And there was no blood on them. How do you explain that, Marty? A situation like this, you get blood in your fingernails, you get it in the crevices of your fingers. You told us you cried your heart out before the cops arrived. When you cry, you wipe your eyes, you dab your nose. I don't see any blood on your face. I don't see your eyes all red from crying. You said you never went all the way into your mother's room. You never touched her.* That's right. *Marty, I can't believe that. Do you know why I can't believe that? Because your hair was in your mother's hand. How did it get there, Marty? You don't know? You keep saying you didn't take a shower this morning. We did a humidity test, Marty. We know you took a shower this morning.*

I didn't—I swear.

Marty, how come you're the only one in that house who was left unharmed? Why were you spared?

FIFTEEN MINUTES before noon, McCready walked out of the interview room, leaving the door open. As Rein continued with Marty, a phone rang in the squad room.

Homicide. McCready. Yeah, John, it's Jimmy. Yeah? No kidding, he came out of it? Okay, great. Thanks a million.

McCready returned to the interview room and stood over Marty. *That was the detective I talked to earlier at the hospital. They pumped your father full of adrenaline, he's out of his coma and he's conscious. And he said that* you *did this.*

Marty was stunned.

He said you *beat him and stabbed him.*

I can't believe that.

They taped the whole thing. We'll play it for you later if you want.

But it's not true.

Why would he say that if it's not true?

I don't know, maybe because I'm the last person he saw.

Was your father conscious when you were giving him first aid? Rein asked, his tone much more aggressive than before. *Or are you talking about before that—when you went in the room and you beat and stabbed him?*

No, no. I didn't do that.

Your father wouldn't lie about that.

I'll take a lie detector test!

We're not giving you a lie detector test. Marty, let me ask you something. What do you think we should do to the person who did this to your parents?

Whoever did this needs psychological help.

Marty fell silent. Then he asked: "Could I have blacked out and done it?"

AT ABOUT 12:30, Mike Fox left the hospital in Stony Brook for his office in Garden City, an hour's drive away. He wanted to start collecting the paperwork he had on Seymour's association with Jerry Steuerman. And Mike wanted to retrieve Arlene and Seymour's wills. Shari was asking about them.

Shortly before he reached his office, Fox was listening to WCBS, one of New York's all-news stations, when a report came on the radio: *A fifty-two-year-old woman was found murdered this morning in her home in well-to-do Belle Terre, Long Island. The woman's sixty-two-year-old husband has been taken to Stony Brook University Hospital in critical condition after being beaten and stabbed. The couple is identified as Arlene and Seymour Tankleff. Suffolk County police are reportedly questioning the couple's teenaged son.*

Questioning? Fox didn't like the sound of that word. He got Ron Falbee on the phone and told him what he'd heard, asked if it was all right with him if he called out to Yaphank and put on record that Marty was not to be questioned. "Absolutely," Ron said. "Do whatever you think is right."

Fox arrived at his office and called the Suffolk County homicide squad. Sergeant George Horvath took his call. "Sergeant, my name is Myron Fox and I'm the attorney for the Tankleff family," Fox told him. "Do you have Martin Tankleff?"

"Yes, we do," Horvath said. "He's being interviewed at the present time."

"Well, you've had him long enough," Fox said. "I don't want him spoken to anymore. I want him released immediately."

"All right," Horvath said. "I'll inform the detectives. Where would you like him to be transported?"

"I want him taken to University Hospital in Stony Brook, where his father is."

Horvath said he would make the arrangements, then confirmed with Fox that the time of his call was 1:22 P.M.

Fox called Ron back at the hospital and told him Marty would be on his way. Meanwhile, a uniformed sergeant had told Gail Fox that Marty would be brought in a side entrance to avoid any reporters who might be outside the hospital. Another hour passed. Shari asked a detective, "Where's my brother?" The detective told her, "He should be on his way here."

Ron Falbee was getting a bad feeling that something was just not right. "They've told us fourteen times that he's on his way, they're bringing him over, they're bringing him in the back way," he remembers. "Part of me is thinking, 'I want to go out and get the kid.' But you write it off to, okay, one guy doesn't know what the other guy's doing."

After speaking with Fox at 1:22, Sergeant Horvath had walked over to the room in which McCready and Rein had been questioning Marty since 9:30. Horvath knocked on the door. McCready emerged, closing the door behind him.

You're done, Horvath told McCready. The kid's lawyer called and put us on notice.

McCready asked who the lawyer was.

"Myron Fox," Horvath said. "He wants the kid released and taken to Stony Brook."

"He's the father's business attorney," McCready said. He thought it was a distinction that might mean Fox couldn't assert Marty's right to counsel. Maybe they could keep going. Horvath thought it was a stretch. McCready said he wanted to check with Bobby Doyle. "Go ahead, let me know," Horvath said as he grabbed another phone call.

McCready's sergeant was still in Belle Terre, supervising the early work of the crime scene personnel. McCready got hold of him and explained the lawyer situation. The kid went for it, McCready told Doyle, but we don't have it in writing yet—can we keep going? Doyle said he'd check it out with the DA, and found Tim Mazzei, the deputy chief of the prosecutor's homicide bureau. Mazzei had just arrived at the scene, taking over for his boss, Ed Jablonski, who'd left to take his wife to see a doctor.

Doyle asked Mazzei whether Seymour Tankleff's business lawyer could assert Martin Tankleff's right to counsel and cut off questioning. Mazzei knew what the answer was but said he'd check with Mark Cohen, the head of the DA's appeals bureau. If the detectives kept talking to Marty, it would be Cohen who would wind up in the unenviable position of defending McCready's contorted legal logic to a panel of appellate judges. Cohen needed no time to research the question. He told Mazzei to tell Doyle to tell his men to stop questioning Martin Tankleff. They had to go with what they had. With that, Mazzei headed for Yaphank himself.

At three o'clock, Mike Fox made another call to the homicide squad and asked to speak with Sergeant Horvath. "Please hold," a secretary said. She came back on a few seconds later and said, "ADA Mazzei will talk to you."

If this concerned him, Fox didn't show it. When Tim Mazzei got on the phone, Fox made small talk. He told Mazzei his name was Myron Fox but to call him Mike, that he was from Nassau County but he knew Mazzei's father. Mazzei was used to this. You're thinking of Judge *Mazzee*, he said. I'm *May-zee*. Same spelling, different pronunciation. No relation.

Oh, Fox said, so anyway, about Marty Tankleff. He was supposed to be released an hour and a half ago and brought to the hospital to be with his family.

Well, Mazzei said, Marty Tankleff isn't going to be seeing his family today. He's under arrest for murder.

It took Fox a moment to register the words. Then a wave of fury and disbelief, and a few flurries of panic, rose from the pit of his stomach. "I don't believe it," he said. "What the hell's going on here? You held this kid despite my instruction that he wasn't to be questioned."

Mazzei told Fox that the detectives had complied with his notice, cutting off questioning when he called, just as the law required. Sergeant Horvath wrote it down—1:22 P.M. The problem, he said, was that by then Marty Tankleff had already confessed.

"*Confessed?* You're saying he admits to this?" Fox asked. "This sounds like one of those cases where the cop beat it out of him."

"Not at all," Mazzei said. "The police wouldn't do anything like that. Now, what exactly is your connection?"

"I'm the family's lawyer, and I'm a friend of Seymour Tankleff's for thirty years."

"Well, if you've been friends with these people who've been brutally assaulted, murdered, don't you want to see justice done?"

"McCready lied to me," Fox said.

"Are you absolutely certain you represent *Martin* Tankleff?" Mazzei asked.

"*Yes*, I'm certain," Fox said. "I told the cops and now I'm telling you. I want to speak to him."

Mazzei told Fox he could do that after his client was brought to the Sixth Precinct for the night. When will that be? Fox asked. Hard to say, said Mazzei. Could be nine o'clock, maybe as late as ten. Or Fox could wait till morning and see his client before the arraignment. That would be in First District Court in Hauppauge, Judge Green's courtroom, ten o'clock. The charges, for now: one count of murder, one for attempted. It might be different tomorrow.

CHAPTER 5

Life and Casualty

FOR SEYMOUR TANKLEFF, the chicken came first.

His parents, Abe and Mera, landed on Ellis Island from Russia in 1915, settling in a section of Brooklyn called Crow Hill two years before it was renamed Crown Heights. The Tankleffs quickly had two sons in succession, Martin and Norman. By the time Seymour came along in 1926, his brothers were ten and eight and their father was on his way to becoming, in his way, a pioneer of a great American industry.

Abe Tankleff and his three brothers were classic immigrant go-getters, men with heads for business who were determined to find their niche. And then along came Mrs. Wilmer Steele of Sussex County, Delaware. She looked around her chicken coops one day in 1923 and thought, All these eggs—but what about dinner? American dining would never be the same, and neither would the Tankleff brothers of Brooklyn. They jumped into the new industry, buying boxloads of "broilers" from the market on Fourteenth Street in Manhattan, distributing them by truck to butchers in Brooklyn and Queens. Chicken was a good and growing business, and it got the Tankleffs through the Depression better than most. The family's fortunes rose another step when Abe and his brothers came up with an even better idea: Instead of wholesaling the broilers to butchers, they opened their own store, and instead of selling the chickens whole, they cut them up and sold them by the part. It was visionary. "You go in and buy two pounds of legs, a pound of necks for soup—it was a huge success," recalled Seymour's older brother, Norman. And then, yet another move based on a new concept: franchising. The Tankleffs opened stores throughout Brooklyn and Queens, each with an independent owner with whom the Tankleffs split the profits.

Martin and Norman Tankleff joined the family business, and when their younger brother came of age he figured that his future, too, would be in chickens. By twenty-two, Seymour was married, a father, and a home-owner. He and his wife, Vega, and their baby daughter, Shari, moved into a house out in Levittown, Long Island, joining the massive migration of war vets and their young families from the outer boroughs of the city. But he went back to Queens each day to work in one of the Tankleff brothers' chicken stores. It was a decent living, it was the family business, but Sey-mour found himself yearning for something else. "I took to cutting up chickens like it was second nature," Norman Tankleff remembered, "but Seymour said it wasn't for him."

At his regular card game one night, Seymour asked Jimmy Wynn about the insurance game. Jimmy was an agent for the Travelers Insurance Company, and he told Seymour he'd be a natural. With your personality, he said, you can sell anything. Insurance? Practically sells itself. All these veterans getting married, having kids, buying houses—every one of them needs life and casualty. Seymour thought it sounded pretty good. He swapped his cutting table and butcher's knife for a desk and a phone in Jimmy Wynn's insurance agency. And Jimmy was right: Seymour was a natural-born salesman. "Who you got your insurance with?" he would ask pretty much everyone he knew or came in contact with, starting with his own family. "I'll getcha a better deal."

"Oh, Seymour was a dynamo," Ruth Tankleff, Norman's wife, remi-nisced one day half a century later. "He was tall and gorgeous and every-body loved him. Seymour could sell you the moon." Norman was so impressed by his younger brother's sudden upward mobility that he gave up chickens for insurance himself. Norman did fine but he couldn't keep up with Seymour. "Always going to conventions for the top sellers," Nor-man said. "Beautiful conventions."

Seymour eventually wanted more than commissions and conventions. He wanted to go out on his own. He thought of his father and uncles and their independent spirit. He admired how they looked for opportunities and took chances. The problem for Seymour in starting his own insurance agency was that he actually wasn't very interested in insurance. It was the selling he loved—hunting clients, talking them into deals, getting their money. But he hated the paperwork. So he needed a partner who could figure out premiums and deal with the home office and all that nonsense. He found a perfect complement in Al Alexander, an unassuming and dili-gent man who knew the insurance business inside out and could see the advantage of joining forces with a rainmaker like Seymour Tankleff. The Tankleff & Alexander insurance agency flourished, and eventually Alexan-der retired to California and Seymour bought him out. Over the next few years, he took over several more brokerages and made partnerships with others, absorbing them into his business and splitting the profits from the annual commissions.

Seymour enjoyed the spoils of his success, but the one thing his money couldn't buy was a happy home life. He and Vega had married young and spent much of their life together fighting. Seymour had an almost equally tough time with his daughter when she reached her teens. He complained to his friends that Shari was a wild kid who ran with a fast crowd. And so demanding. When Shari dropped out of college, she told her father that she was entitled to the cash equivalent of the money he would be paying had she stayed in school. When Seymour begged to differ, Shari sued him—actually took him to court. A judge threw out the case, and Seymour held no grudge. As a father, he believed in unconditional love. As a husband, though, he was open to alternatives. Unhappy at home, Seymour found something more appealing at the office.

EVERYTHING ABOUT Arlene Alt Dougherty said she was a city girl, so it was easy to believe her when she said her teenage years were the worst of her life. Arlene was born and raised in Queens until she was thirteen. That's when her father, a mechanical engineer, got a job with the American Locomotive Company and moved the family four hundred miles to Fredonia, a small town near the shore of Lake Erie and forty miles south of Buffalo.

Arlene was the middle of three girls born so far apart that she was the only one affected by the move. Her older half sister, Marcella—"Mickey" to her family—was already twenty-one, so she stayed behind on her own. Her younger sister, Marianne, was three when the family resettled upstate, so Fredonia became her hometown. But it never was for Arlene. She spent her teens marking time and moved back to Bayside, Queens, the instant she graduated from high school in 1952. She moved in with Mickey and enrolled in the Katharine Gibbs secretarial school. When she finished, Mickey got her a job in a friend's office. "She was so young, she didn't even know how to dress," Mickey recalled. "Oh, God—her first day she had on black stockings."

Arlene met a man named Ed Dougherty and brought him up to Fredonia to meet her parents. They wound up getting married right then and there, in the living room on Valentine's Day. They bought a small house on Long Island, and over the next decade or so, Arlene led the nine-to-five life while trying to have a child. Neither that endeavor nor the marriage itself was a success.

Arlene was looking for a new job in the classifieds one day in the mid-

1960s when she saw an ad for a secretary that looked as good as any of the others. The boss turned out to be an insurance agent with the personality of a press agent. He was big and boisterous, a man with money who wasn't a bit bashful about flashing it around. Suddenly, Seymour. He was a decade older than her, and a world apart from her husband. Arlene got the job, and then she got the boss. "Oh, she was attracted to his lifestyle—she thought it was very grand," Mickey recalled. Seymour might have thought he was having a fling with his secretary, but soon enough Arlene demanded a promotion. She was willing to leave her husband. If Seymour wanted the relationship to continue, he would have to leave his wife. Seymour conceded to her demand, a sign of things to come. The affair ended each of their unhappy marriages—Seymour's after twenty-two years, Arlene's after fourteen. They were married a few months after Seymour's divorce, the more complicated of the two.

In Arlene's family, Seymour Tankleff took a little getting used to. "I really wasn't pleased with her marrying him," Mickey readily acknowledged. "It was his ostentation, his braggadocio. I would've liked to see Sy a little . . . quieter." But that was a wish without hope. "Seymour was very, very loud, no doubt about it," said Mickey's son, Ron Falbee. "Even the way he dressed. He was just a loud guy."

Arlene didn't mind—she was no church mouse herself. And marrying Seymour, it seemed to her sisters, gave her a boost of self-worth. "She went from Ed Dougherty, the beer drinker, the Friday night bowler," Marianne said, "to the rich boss." One day she showed up at Mickey's house wearing an expensive new fur coat. "Wow—where'd you get that?" Mickey asked. "Oh, my honey got it for me," Arlene told her. And he took her on lavish vacations—or was it the other way around? When Arlene and Seymour were sailing off on a cruise to Alaska, Marianne boarded the ship before it sailed and was astonished by the accommodations. Their cabin was as big as a hotel suite. It wasn't Seymour. "He wouldn't have gone that high," Marianne said. "But Arlene wanted the best."

What Arlene did in return, though Seymour didn't ask it of her, was to undergo something of a cultural conversion. She took lessons in Judaism from a rabbi, though she stopped short of officially converting, and Seymour's friends and relatives became her new social group. Even her intonation changed, consciously or not. "She would say, 'When people hear me talk, they always think I'm Jewish,'" Mickey said, "and she was very proud of it." As a symbol of her mixed identity, Arlene wore a necklace of a crucifix intertwined with a Star of David.

In the summer of 1970, Marianne announced she was pregnant. Arlene found her baby sister's news unsettling. Though childless in her thirties, unable to conceive, she'd not been ready to give up on the idea of being a mother when she married Seymour. Now she told him she wanted to adopt a child. Seymour had a grown daughter but he was perfectly agreeable to a second round of fatherhood and to raising a child that wasn't biologically his. And so he called Mike Fox.

Seymour and Mike had met at Jimmy Wynn's card game a decade and a half earlier, right about the time Seymour was going from chickens to insurance and Mike was starting out as a lawyer. They hit it off instantly, figuring it must be kismet when they discovered they were born on the same date a year apart. They were a couple of garrulous guys from the boroughs who got along as though they were the oldest of friends from the neighborhood—laughing uproariously at a dirty joke one minute, bickering about who heard it first the next.

Myron C. Fox, attorney-at-law, did commercial work primarily, but took pretty much whatever came his way, especially where it concerned his dear friend Seymour. When Seymour needed a divorce, Mike handled it. When Seymour's daughter sued him for a bigger allowance, Mike got rid of it. Now Seymour and Arlene wanted a child. Mike made some inquiries.

If they got a boy, Seymour wanted to name him Martin Harold Tankleff, in honor of his older brother, who had died a couple of years earlier. But Mike came up with a girl, a three-year-old whose mother was planning to give her up for adoption. It would be a foster situation to start, but Arlene presumed it would be permanent soon enough and dove right into her long-delayed life as a mother. She fell in love with the little girl, lavishing her with attention and toys and a whole new wardrobe. And then the mother changed her mind. Arlene was devastated. Seymour was furious. He believed the mother had used them. Fox's memory of the episode was succinct: "It was a disaster."

It took Arlene a while to put the experience behind her. When she was ready to try again, Seymour was determined to leave nothing to chance. This would be strictly his deal. He kept Fox out of it and orchestrated an adoption that struck their families as a little bit mysterious. "Sy always had connections," is how Mickey put it. "Diamond rings—he had a connection. Horses, cars, whatever." And so it was with a child. Seymour had a connection, or made one, with a law secretary to a Surrogate's Court judge in Brooklyn. Fox's memory was succinct once again: "It was very secretive. And then suddenly they had a baby."

It was a boy. Though some of the details were elusive, it seemed that the baby was born to a woman in Brooklyn whose personal profile suggested one who might be adopting a child rather than giving hers up. She was a schoolteacher, she was married with one other child, and she was Jewish. From what Arlene and Seymour's relatives gathered, the woman's marriage unraveled after she conceived the baby and she decided well before he was born that she couldn't raise two children on her own. The adoption was arranged and this time everything proceeded without a hitch. The mother delivered a healthy baby boy in Brooklyn's Maimonides Medical Center on August 29, 1971. She signed the papers, and three days later a judge set the life of Martin Harold Tankleff on its course.

Arlene and Seymour brought their baby son home to Long Island, where Arlene, finally a mother at thirty-seven, sat in her robe, feeding him from a bottle, rocking him to sleep. And Seymour was a father for the second time, at age forty-five. His only other child, Shari, was twenty-three and now married. On the Sunday of Labor Day weekend, Seymour and Arlene's relatives and friends gathered at their house for Marty's bris. The Hebrew word for covenant, a bris represents the most important one in Judaism: the commandment that every Jewish father fulfill a biblical instruction to circumcise his son on the eighth day of life. Thus, on September 5, 1971, Seymour began his son's life with a ritual symbolic of a contract with God. It may have been the only time Seymour Tankleff ever made a deal that wasn't on his own terms.

MIKE FOX called Seymour one day and said he'd found a country club that didn't cost an arm and a leg to join—and they took Jews. It was out in Suffolk County, but worth the hike: eighteen pretty holes and a beautiful clubhouse right on Long Island Sound for the relatively modest price of $700 a year. It even had a pretty name: Harbor Hills.

One Saturday Mike invited Seymour out for a round of golf with the two guys he'd been playing with. There's Eddie Selkow, Mike said. He has a messenger service in the city. And Paul Lerner, who's in corrugated boxes. Seymour drove out with Mike and spent the eighteen holes happily hitting lousy shots, telling jokes, peppering Paul and Eddie with questions about their businesses—and by the way, who handles your insurance? They thought Seymour was one hell of an entertaining guy, and by the time they repaired to the clubhouse for lunch it was as if they were a long-standing foursome.

Harbor Hills was on the outskirts of Port Jefferson, a bustling harbor town that had been the capital of Long Island's flourishing shipbuilding industry a century earlier. The golf course was on a quiet peninsula north of town, roughly half of which was incorporated as the Village of Belle Terre. Seymour thought he was in paradise. He was taken by the magnificent views, by the tranquility of the place, and by the fact that its location, sixty miles from Manhattan, meant you could probably make yourself a pretty good deal on a piece of property. "I gotta bring Arlene out here," he told Mike, as they drove around before heading home. "We gotta look at a place. Maybe buy some land, build a house."

Seymour's instant infatuation with Belle Terre must have pleased the ghost of Dean Alvord. A far-seeing real estate developer at the turn of the century, Alvord acquired 1,300 acres on a virtually uninhabited peninsula north of Port Jefferson from a bankrupt company whose development plans had gone only so far as renaming the area Belle Terre. The French translation of "beautiful earth" was certainly apt and unquestionably an improvement over Mount Misery Neck. Alvord began building a playground for the famously wealthy to rival Newport. First came the Belle Terre Clubhouse, a three-story lodge designed in the manner of an English country inn, set on a bluff on the eastern face of the peninsula, two hundred feet above Port Jefferson Harbor. A pergola with a pair of Grecian columns overlooked the sound. Then Alvord hired Frederick Sterner, a major British architect of the time, to design a collection of luxurious "country mansions" that would be available for sale only to members of the Clubhouse. "There is nothing quite like Belle Terre in the world," Alvord declared in a brochure, promising a place "where every landholder is a king." To protect Belle Terre from "inharmonious elements," Alvord built a turreted gatehouse at its entrance.

Belle Terre quickly became a fashionable retreat for many of the pillars of Long Island's Gold Coast forty miles to the west—Astors, Vanderbilts, Whitneys, Goulds. But its glory was short-lived; for Alvord, Belle Terre turned out to be Mount Misery. The turbulent economy preceding World War I forced him to scale back his vision and eventually to abandon it altogether. He went bankrupt, leaving behind his unfinished Eden. Belle Terre eventually fell into the hands of sand-mining operators who turned the peninsula into a trough, merrily gouging out huge chunks of earth until the remaining residents finally put a stop to it by incorporating as a village in 1931 and adopting as their first ordinance a ban on all commercial activity.

Over the next few decades, a small community grew amid the vestiges of Belle Terre's moment of grandeur. The original Tudor homes of Frederick Sterner remained on Upper Devon Road and Lower Devon Road—"the English section," as it was called. The golf course survived, and the turreted gatehouse became the village hall. But the elegant Belle Terre Clubhouse burned to the ground in 1934 and the Grecian columns blew out to sea in the hurricane of 1938. In the years after World War II, ranches and split-levels went up on new streets with names like Alta Vista Road and Lost Meadow Lane. But even at that, Belle Terre was still a world apart from the archetypal American suburbs that were sprouting across the rest of Long Island. It was to the cliffs of Belle Terre, after all, that Sid Farber, Long Island's second-most-prodigious postwar builder after William Levitt, moved with his wife, Nadia.

The Farbers had second, third, and fourth homes in Manhattan, Saint Croix, and Monte Carlo. But their primary residence was a spectacular pink mansion on a twelve-acre estate at the top of the Belle Terre cape. The lady of the manor, Nadia Farber, was a bawdy, Bulgarian-born star of 1920s musical comedies whose prior marriage had been to a Spanish count. She still used the title, though she was now married to a Long Island land developer named Sid. The locals were happy to go along. They came to refer to her with deference and affection as "the Contessa." It couldn't hurt property values. And it was not unbefitting a woman who wore a flowing caftan and dazzling blue eye makeup with color-coordinated turban, and who carried a white lace parasol, spoke ten languages, and called everyone "my dahling."

Aside from the Farbers, Belle Terre was populated with doctors and lawyers and successful people of various kinds who might not be up to twelve acres on the water but could swing one or two inland without a problem. Theirs was a sleepy hamlet with a population of just under eight hundred, occupying a land area of nine-tenths of a square mile. There was not a single traffic light in Belle Terre and, since the ordinance barring businesses was still on the books, not one commercial establishment. You couldn't even count the country club since most of it was outside the village boundary. Belle Terre's main thoroughfare, Cliff Road, could be as lightly traveled as one of the bridle paths that once crisscrossed the neck, and with a crime rate near zero the village's part-time police constables had little to do but keep an eye out for the occasional violator of the second most prominent village ordinance: no parking on any street, at any time.

In the late winter of 1971, the Tankleffs bought a vacant parcel on Seaside Drive, a wooded acre at the cliffs that would provide the house to be built on it one of the most spectacular views on all of Long Island. Seymour hired an architect who designed a rambling ranch-style house, laid out on the property to maximize the views, leaving room for a swimming pool in back. For Arlene and Seymour, 33 Seaside Drive would be an emblem of a kind of prosperity neither could have imagined when they were young. But the house, though high in square footage, couldn't be called ostentatious. The front was nearly windowless, clad in vertical driftwood-colored wooden boards that gave it a look that was half rustic lodge, half beach house. The rear of the house, where the sound beckoned, was nearly all windows and sliding glass doors.

The Tankleffs moved into their dream house in 1972, when Marty was a year old, and they embraced the Belle Terre life with abandon. Seymour bought a large cabin cruiser and became a member of the Port Jefferson Yacht Club. And of course he joined Harbor Hills, where he played golf every weekend with Mike Fox, Paul Lerner, and Eddie Selkow. On Saturday nights they would go out together with their wives, turning the foursome into an eightsome. Seymour always the life of the party. Arlene loved her new life and the status she felt it bestowed. "She was a girl who came from nothing, had nothing," observed Mike Fox. "Now she was a society lady." Harbor Hills had ladies' golf days, but Arlene favored tennis, a sport that was a better outlet for her competitive nature. Her opponents thought she hit the ball as hard as a man. Losing put her in a bad mood.

Much as he enjoyed golf, Seymour's favorite sport was poker, which was, to him, pretty much the perfect activity. It involved sitting, socializing, and trying to beat your friends out of money. One of Seymour's first friends in Belle Terre was Pete Capobianco, the owner of Cappy's Carpets and one of the original members of the After Dinner Club, the oldest established permanent floating card game in Belle Terre. Openings generally occurred only when someone dropped out or dropped dead, and a prospective replacement had to be brought in by a member and approved by the others. Cappy invited Seymour into the game and he passed muster. Seymour fancied himself a man's man. He was drawn to guys who thought big, guys who looked for angles and had the stuff some called chutzpah and others called balls—guys, in his view, like himself. There was no telling when and where he might find them. It was typical for him to strike up friendships in the course of doing business, and to do business in the course of his friendships.

Soon after moving his family to Suffolk County, Seymour transplanted his insurance business there. He bought a small house on a side street off Nesconset Highway and opened an office that was easy to find because there was a beat-up old fishing boat in the driveway with a sign that said INSURANCE. Calling attention to your business is fine, except if you're running a business on a suburban street that's zoned residential. Thus came the inevitable letter from town hall, followed by Seymour's usual call to Mike Fox, who thought it said so much about who Seymour Tankleff was. "My dear old friend Seymour always had problems. And I was always on the phone trying to solve them. Somebody gave him a bargain on a boat. It was falling apart, wasn't worth fixing. But it was a bargain! So now I'm on the phone with town hall. I told Seymour, Here's what you do: Have one of your office girls move into the house as a tenant." He took down the insurance sign but kept the boat in the driveway.

Seymour wasn't looking for walk-in business anyway. In fact, he wasn't particularly looking for much new business at all. Having built his agency by buying out others, Seymour had himself a lucrative business that required little work. He had the same clients year after year and the commissions he earned on their policies were automatic. So if he didn't want to do much more than sit at his desk and schmooze on the phone, and play golf and make the rounds of his friends, he could. So he did. But sometimes it caught up with him. The time, for instance, one of those perpetual clients discovered Seymour's inattention was costing him a lot of money. "So I called Seymour—'Hi, how ya doin' and by the way you're fired.' He couldn't believe it. 'But we're family!' he says."

It was Seymour's nephew, Ron Falbee. Just out of college with a business degree, Ron was taking over his mother's failing Hallmark store in the Roosevelt Field Mall. "I figured out he was overcharging us—way overcharging us. He was selling my mother like fourteen different policies. There was a new type of policy for business owners that did the same thing but he didn't even know about it. 'Where'd you get that policy?' he says. 'Give me a day, I'll match it.'" Ron said okay. Because they were family. But he was amazed that Seymour had done so well with his business and yet seemed to know so little about it. "He was out playing golf. That was Seymour—he made the deal, signed the deal, got you in, got your money, onto the next one. He was an old-style wheeler-dealer, quick-money guy."

It was a quirk of Seymour's that while he was not much interested in the nuts and bolts of his own business, he was all over everyone else's. He had ideas about how Eddie Selkow could do better with his messenger service and how Paul Lerner could make more in corrugated boxes. "What's your percentage?" he asked Paul, a sales rep whose customers were the big cosmetics companies. "Five percent? I'll go in there and get you six." Paul told him no thanks. Let's stick to golf. "Seymour was always the instant expert," said Ron Falbee. "He could talk to a cabdriver: 'So what do you make on this cab? What do you get a month, what's your overhead, who do you pay?' And by the end of a twenty-minute cab ride he'd be saying, 'Do you need a partner? I'll tell you what—I'll buy the cabs and you get the guys to drive them. And I could run it through my insurance company.' He'd have the whole thing worked out."

Nobody was safe from Seymour's advances. When Ron's mother was still running the card store, Seymour wanted to be her partner. He promised he'd make her a lot of money. One day he came into the store and told her, "Gimme a thousand dollars, I'll give you back three thousand." Seymour laid out his scheme—"some shenanigans with taxes," Mickey recalled. When Ron took over the store, Seymour went after him even more relentlessly. He'd buy into the business with $150,000—one thing about Seymour, he always came with hard figures, even when they were off the top of his head—and together they'd become the greeting card kings of Long Island. Ron was young and inexperienced but savvy enough to deflect his Uncle Seymour's overtures, usually with a laugh. "If I did want a partner," he told Seymour, "it wouldn't be you." What's the matter? Seymour asked, genuinely baffled and a little hurt. "Because within five minutes you would be the expert in the card business and I would know shit," Ron told him. "And that would be the end of my business. Seymour, I love you as an uncle, but I don't want you as a partner."

Ron really did love Seymour, so long as they didn't talk business. There was just something about his raucous uncle-by-marriage that Ron found hard to resist. "He'd give you a big bear hug and a *'Howyadoin'?'*" Ron said, breaking into an impression of Seymour's booming Brooklyn bellow, which people tended to do when they were telling Seymour stories. It was a voice that called to mind a slightly higher-pitched Jackie Gleason. Ron once invited Seymour to a golf outing that a friend and business associate of his was hosting at an exclusive country club in New Jersey. The man was one of the largest real estate developers in the country, president of the company that owned the malls in which Ron had his stores. "We play golf, we go to the clubhouse to shower, then we come up for lunch," Ron recalled. "It's all bankers and corporate types, and everyone's in blue blazers. And here's Seymour in his chartreuse jacket and plaid pants, and he comes out of the locker room shouting, 'Where's my nephew?!' It was like showing up with Rodney Dangerfield. And of course we're seated with all the top guys and Seymour is asking a million questions about real estate and shopping malls. He wanted information, all the nuts and bolts—to Seymour there was no question you couldn't ask. By dessert he's ready to go into the shopping center business."

Seymour developed a close friendship with another of his relatives from his wife's side of the family. Arlene's sister Marianne moved to Northern California with her first husband in the early 1970s. They later divorced but Marianne liked it out there. She got a secretarial job with a law firm in Monterey, where she met Mike McClure, a lawyer with two children from his first marriage. Mike was smart and affable, and when Marianne came east with him for the first time, he and Seymour hit it off. They might have seemed like an odd pairing, the noisy New Yorker and the low-key Californian, but Seymour could have that effect on people who were nothing like him. He was full of beans and Mike found him hugely entertaining. You could say Seymour had boorish charm. After meeting Mike just once, Seymour added him to his list of guys he would call to shoot the breeze and talk about his latest business ideas. "How ya doin', is my brother-in-law in?" he would say to Mike's secretary. They weren't actually brothers-in-law, not yet, but perhaps Seymour's jovial presumptuousness helped move things along. In the spring of 1984, the two families made plans to spend a week together in Las Vegas, and when they got there, Marianne and Mike were struck spontaneously by the idea that they *should* get married, and do it that very week. And so they did.

Vegas was one of Seymour's favorite places, which he made abundantly clear when he walked over to the craps table and told the dealer, "Gimme ten thousand." Mike was duly impressed. His divorce had left him with so little money that when he and Marianne went home as newlyweds they couldn't afford even the down payment for a house. Marianne suggested they ask Seymour for some help. Seymour was happy to help. He loaned them $15,000—three years, no interest, terms he wouldn't have dreamed of giving anyone but the closest of family. As Mike reflected after consequences made it unavoidable, "Seymour divided the world into two groups, and how he treated you depended entirely on which one you were in. He kept his family and friends very, very close. If you were a relative or a friend—and I mean a real friend—there wasn't anything he wouldn't do for you. And everybody else was on a different track. If you were in business with him, he was just not the same person. Seymour didn't have a lot of close male friends. He had a lot of acquaintances. He had a lot of people like the guys he played cards with. But I don't think they got into the sort of inner sanctum of Seymour."

IN LAS VEGAS, while Seymour was betting thousands at the craps table and Arlene was cooking in cocoa butter by the pool, their twelve-year-old son was doing business. Hanging around the hotel with Mike McClure's son Doug, Marty had an idea. "Hey, let's charge people to go on the elevator." The boys did perform a service, pushing buttons and announcing floors, and with a hotel full of free-spending gamblers, they returned to the family a few dollars richer.

"I want to be like my dad," Marty explained to his Aunt Marianne.

If a father's dream is to have a son who wants his life to be a version of his, then Seymour Tankleff must have been a fulfilled man. Seymour's life was "business," shorthand for just about anything that involved money changing hands. Marty considered his father a master of his universe, and he was his eager apprentice. He grew up watching and listening, absorbing his father's ways, assuming they were the ways of the world. Other kids might have a paper route, but that was a little small-time for Marty. In elementary school he would buy candy from liquidation stores, then sell it from a briefcase at school at a nice markup. He did so well that the principal told him he had to stop because he was putting the school store out of business.

Marty's quest to make a buck always had his father's encouragement and sometimes his capital. When Seymour thought his landscaper was overcharging him, he fired him and hired Marty, who could use the mower Seymour bought to make extra money around the neighborhood. In a place like Belle Terre, where extravagant allowances tended to put kids in the upper-income bracket among their classmates from the more modest areas of the school district, you didn't find many going around with lawn mowers in summer or shovels on snowy days in winter. But Marty appreciated the value of a dollar and he didn't mind clearing a driveway to clear a profit.

Industrious though he was, Marty was certainly given plenty by a mother and father who were older, wealthier, and more doting than most of the parents of his classmates and friends. From the moment Arlene and Seymour signed the adoption papers in Brooklyn and brought Marty home to Long Island, they showered him with attention, affection—and things. They spent a good sum building a house that a kid could get lost in, on a property that promised a life of idyllic days, in a neighborhood that exuded status. Arlene and Seymour were raising their son in a cocoon of privilege and indulgence. They gave him the childhood of their dreams.

Marty got all the toys he could play with when he was young, and as he got older the toys got bigger. As soon as the Commodore 64 computer came out, when he was eleven, Marty got one. He found that the Commodore did nothing to hurt his popularity. He and his friends played Space Invaders and Pong, and Marty became a first-generation computer geek. His father had a mammoth computer for his insurance business, and Marty would go to the office and back up files and make printouts. When he got into photography in high school, his father bought him a Nikon camera with extra lenses and built a darkroom in the basement, where Marty would print the pictures he shot for the school yearbook. He had an all-terrain vehicle and went fishing and water-skiing on a Boston Whaler his father named *Mr. T's Toy*. There were family jaunts to Las Vegas and Atlantic City, winter vacations in the Caribbean, trips to Europe. And when Marty turned thirteen, Arlene and Seymour threw the requisite wedding-quality bar mitzvah, an extravagant affair at Harbor Hills featuring a Michael Jackson impersonator, clowns and game booths for the kids, and endless tables of food and drink for the two hundred adults.

It was an environment that led Marty to believe he was living in a world without limits. On the rare occasions when he was denied something he wanted, he would simply pester his father until he got it—an approach he might well have picked up from Seymour himself, a man who wasn't inclined to take no for an answer when he had his sights on a business opportunity. But there was no denying that Seymour derived pleasure from indulging his son. "My father grew up poor," Marty would say as an adult, a slight mischaracterization of Seymour's childhood, though certainly true relative to Marty's. "That's why, when I was a teenager, he kind of lived vicariously through me."

Like any other suburban boy, when Marty reached his teens he lusted alternately after girls and cars. One day when he was sixteen, he and his father dropped in on Frank Norberto. Frank had built the Tankleffs' pool, and as was often the case with Seymour, they became good friends in the process. Parked outside Norberto's office was a souped-up Toyota truck, jacked high off the ground on oversized tires and painted a luminescent pink. "Pink Panther" was branded across the hood in script lettering—and a For Sale sign was in the window. Ohhh, cool, Marty said, and pleaded with his father to buy it for him. "It's my son's," Norberto said. "He did all that crazy work on it." Seymour told Marty to forget it—no way are you getting that thing. But when Marty went to the bathroom, Seymour muttered to Frank, "Listen, don't sell it. I'll come back tomorrow and we'll make a deal." Seymour surprised Marty with the Pink Panther, but he didn't have it for long. After he ran it into a tree on a snowy day, Arlene deemed the truck as unsafe as it was hideous and ordered it gone. Seymour got a For Sale sign and parked the Panther at Pete & Al's service station. He eventually handed Marty the keys to something safer, if decidedly less cool: a midnight blue '78 Lincoln Town Car.

Perhaps inevitably, his parents' indulgence gave Marty a sense of entitlement that had predictable effects. When he began ninth grade at Earl L. Vandermeulen High School, he met kids from some of the Port Jefferson area's more middle-class neighborhoods, and over the next few years some of them would find him a little pretentious about his privilege. His older cousin Ron noticed it, too. "You know," he told Marty, "you're kind of a show-off."

As an adult, when the trappings of his youth would seem perversely ironic on many levels, Marty would readily acknowledge the skewed values of his younger self: "It's true. I was a spoiled kid. It was a fault I had."

But there was also a generosity about him, an attentiveness to the people in his life and an innate gentle nature that could be overshadowed by the veneer of conceit that came with being his parents' son. "Marty was a nice kid, a good kid," Mike Fox observed. "But they instilled in him that he was something special."

In fact, Marty was largely unremarkable. Like any other teenager, he had his group, kids he hung out with. He had a best friend—Mark Perrone, one of the kids he met at the beginning of high school, who was from middle-class Mount Sinai and saw past Marty's materialism. But most of all, Marty had his parents. If anything set him apart, this was it. They were a threesome. If Arlene and Seymour were going out to dinner with friends on a Saturday night, they routinely brought Marty with them, which some of their friends found annoying. When Marty was thirteen and Seymour was getting ready to go with Mike Fox and his law partners on their annual fishing trip to Canada, Arlene told him he should bring Marty along. Mike was none too pleased when Seymour brought it up. "Seymour, this isn't for kids," he said. "It's grown men cursing, drinking, playing cards. We don't want any kids around."

"Well, I've gotta bring Marty," Seymour said. Mike gave in when he realized that Seymour was under orders.

Marty was happy to go. He never developed the usual adolescent aversion to spending a minute more than necessary with his parents. He looked forward to the nights every couple of months when it was his father's turn to host the weekly poker game. He liked to help his mother prepare the food they would serve, and he was in no hurry to go off and watch TV once the game got going. "Oooh, look at all that money," he would say when he was younger, eyeing the pile of hundreds on the table after the opening buy-in. "Can I have some?" As Marty got older, Seymour taught him the game, patiently explaining how to fill an inside straight, the way another parent might help with math homework. Marty looked forward to joining the game someday. And at family gatherings he would gravitate to the adults. "You wanted him to sometimes be a kid more," Mike McClure remembered. "'Marty, the kids are over there—go over there with the kids.' As an outsider you might say this is a little weird. But that's the way they lived. Marty participated in everything." Seymour once told his sister-in-law, Ruth, "I love Shari—she's my daughter and I really love her. But I'm mad about Marty."

Arlene and Seymour were open with Marty about his adoption, the approach recommended by all the experts. But Marty preferred not to think of himself that way. When he was eleven, Arlene took him to see an orthodontist, who commented that the growth pattern of Marty's teeth could be hereditary. Arlene told him that Marty had been adopted. When they got outside, Marty was annoyed. "I don't want to hear I'm adopted," he told his mother. "I'm your son."

Indeed, Marty was unquestionably as much his mother's son as his father's. Arlene could be abrasive to adults, her husband certainly included, but she was devoted to Marty, maybe to a fault. In Mike Fox's blunt view, "Arlene babied the shit out of him. Seymour was trying to make a man out of him, but Arlene was always, 'He's only a child.'"

Marty was equally devoted to his mother. He would cook alongside her, accompany her on walks around the neighborhood. While Marty would grow up to see his father's failings clearly in hindsight, he would remember his mother only as "a wonderful, caring person." He realized that not everyone was a fan, but in his view, "If she was tough it was because she wanted the best that life could give, to her, to her son, and her husband." And anyone who thought she pampered him misinterpreted her purpose: "She was bringing me up to have good morals and good manners. How to treat a lady the right way, how to cook, how to clean. As early as I can remember, I could cook for myself, clean for myself, do my own laundry. I could do ironing. I think it was that they were older. If you're going to a nice restaurant, you don't want to have a bratty little kid. You want someone who has manners, who understands the difference between a shrimp fork, a salad fork, and a dinner fork."

While Marty was exceedingly close to both his parents, Arlene and Seymour themselves could be a combustible mix. In 1984 things came to a head when she threw him out. Seymour moved in with his daughter, Shari, and her family. At first he didn't mind the freedom. He bought himself a new toy—one of John Z. DeLorean's dazzling stainless-steel sports cars, with its gull-wing doors and momentary cachet—and found a regular nightspot to drive it to, a place called Strawberries. But it wasn't long before Seymour realized he'd rather be married after all. He and Arlene went into counseling, where she aired her complaints and laid out some conditions for his return. The central issue was, in a word, money.

When they were first married, Arlene was in awe of her husband's success and wealth. She fully enjoyed the benefits. But over the years Arlene had become increasingly bothered that Seymour gave her no say over business decisions involving significant sums of money. She was also concerned about Seymour's gambling. But what Arlene was most unhappy about was Seymour's will. The problem was that Shari was in it—at her expense, she felt. Arlene's relationship with her stepdaughter, who was only a decade younger than her, had never been easy. It had only grown worse over time.

One of the stipulations Arlene made for Seymour's return home was that he would include her in all his business dealings and put her name with his on documents. Seymour would also have to cut down on his gambling. And the last condition, the most important to her, would be put in writing. The last time Seymour changed his will had been in 1973. In a dramatic flourish, he'd decided to leave half his estate to Hofstra University, Long Island's largest private college. There was a catch: The money would have to be used in part to pay the way for anyone in the next two generations of his and Arlene's families who attended the school. Seymour had no connection to the university, but it was the kind of gesture that made him feel important.

Eleven years later, at Arlene's insistence, the agreement with Hofstra would be modified. The university would receive half a million dollars in trust, still a generous gift but nowhere near half the value of Seymour's assets by this point. Arlene would receive the rest. If she died before Seymour, all except the Hofstra gift would go to Marty, though not until he reached twenty-four. The big loser in all this, of course, was Shari. Under the new wills, her inheritance would be limited to the interest income on a small percentage of the Hofstra trust. In an estate that would be valued at several million dollars, it meant that Shari was all but cut out of her father's will.

There was one more order of business. Arlene and Seymour both wanted Ron Falbee to be the executor of their estates—and they wanted Ron and his wife, Carol, to be Marty's guardians in the event they both died before he reached eighteen. They asked Marty what he thought, and he said he would be fine with that, though he made it clear he was uncomfortable talking about any such eventuality.

Seymour took Ron out to lunch to tell him what he and Arlene had decided. "We trust you," he said. "We trust that you'll do what we would want done. We know you would make the right decisions with Marty."

Ron was taken aback. But it made sense. If not them, who? Shari? Arlene would never allow it. Marianne and Mike? They were in California. Ron and Carol were young parents with identical twin four-year-olds, Susanne and Carolyn, whom Marty loved as if they were his baby sisters. Ron had home videos of Marty with the girls, giving them toys and playing with them, taking care of them. That's one thing about Marty, Ron always thought—as much as he has, he's always generous.

Now Seymour dropped the bombshell. He told Ron that he and Arlene had made some big changes in their wills, and that Marty would eventually be inheriting nearly their entire estate—the house, the business interests, everything but the half million dollars they would leave to Hofstra.

Ron asked the obvious question. "What about Shari?"

"Well, she's out," Seymour said. "Except for some income on the Hofstra trust."

"Does she know about this?"

"No."

"That's not going to go down well."

"I know."

"So what's the story?"

"Well, I just don't trust Shari with money. She'd blow it all."

Seymour conceded, though, that cutting Shari out wasn't his idea. "Shari and your aunt, it's not a good situation," he said.

He was now fifty-eight, but not a young fifty-eight. He had a heart condition and diabetes, peptic ulcers and high blood pressure. He was the kind of man who needed a woman to take care of him, even in the best of health. So whatever Arlene wanted, Arlene would get. Ron and Carol agreed to be Marty's guardians, and on January 31, 1985, Seymour and Arlene went to Mike Fox's office and signed their new wills. Some time later, Seymour told Marty about his eventual inheritance. But he didn't tell Shari about hers.

CHAPTER 6

A Baby in a
Paper Jumpsuit

RON FALBEE COULD NOT BELIEVE what Mike Fox was telling him. Not eight hours ago, he and the rest of the family learned that Arlene was dead and Seymour was on the brink, both of them slashed and bludgeoned. Now Ron was in Gail Fox's office at University Hospital, waiting with the other relatives for word on Seymour—and for the police to finally deliver Marty. And Gail's husband was on the phone telling him something so incomprehensible that Ron had to repeat the words to make sure he was hearing them correctly.

They're saying that *Marty* did this? They're saying he *confessed*? Impossible. Couldn't be.

Sitting at his desk in Garden City, Fox was confronting his own nightmare. He ran the events of the day through his mind, trying to separate McCready's deception on Seaside Drive from his own lack of presence in the hours that followed. So many hours. He felt the deadweight of his failure to protect his best friend's son. The best he could do now was to get Marty a serious criminal defense attorney. His office colleagues threw out names. The quick consensus was Steve Scaring, the one with the biggest reputation. But Scaring was on a case out of town. One of the lawyers, Harold Sussman, suggested Bob Gottlieb. Sussman's nephew was Gottlieb's law partner. Is he good? Fox asked. He knew his way around the old guard of the Nassau County bar, but Gottlieb was a younger guy in Suffolk. Fox knew the name—Gottlieb had run for district attorney out there a few years earlier—but not much more. Sussman assured him Gottlieb was very good—smart, full of piss and vinegar, high-profile. The guy fights like hell for his clients.

Fox called Ron Falbee back. As Fox knew—and he was one of the few who did—Ron was now Marty's surrogate father. By the doctors' reckoning, it could become permanent at any moment. Fox told him about Bob Gottlieb. Call him, Ron said. Call him right now and get him down there. Ron got off the phone and updated the gathering of relatives. They listened blankly, too stunned to react. Then Mike McClure called. He and Marianne and Jennifer were midway through their cross-country flight from San Francisco. Mike had been using an onboard phone to check in hourly. In the last call, Ron told him Seymour was still in surgery, while Marty was on his way from police headquarters. They're bringing him over, should have him here any minute. And now Mike was checking in again. *"What?"* was the only response he could manage. He told Marianne and Jen. They sat through the rest of the flight mute, frozen, thinking this was impossible, it just couldn't be: Nine hours ago Marty lost his mother and likely his father in the worst way imaginable. What he needed now was a lawyer to fight like hell for him.

THREE DECADES on, a film was made about Shirley Chisholm's brief but exuberant campaign for the 1972 Democratic presidential nomination, a mostly symbolic quest by the first black woman elected to Congress. "Shunned by the political establishment, she's supported by a motley crew of blacks, feminists, and young voters," said the promotional material for *Chisholm '72: Unbought & Unbossed*, a PBS documentary. "Their campaign-trail adventures are frenzied, fierce, and fundamentally right on!" In the footage of Chisholm's campaign stops are glimpses of a shaggy-haired young aide who appears to be having the time of his life. That would be Bob Gottlieb, taking off his last semester from Cornell to serve as the campaign's national youth coordinator.

Gottlieb, a man of Quixotic impulses, became an underdog candidate himself thirteen years later, running intensely but unsuccessfully for district attorney of Suffolk County in 1985. Though he'd started his career in the Manhattan district attorney's office, which he pointed out at every opportunity, he found Suffolk County unreceptive to a defense attorney running as a reformer against the establishment. His major campaign issue was the conduct of homicide prosecutions in Suffolk County: If elected, he promised, he would institute a policy requiring the police to videotape all interrogations of suspects.

In the late summer of 1988, Gottlieb was mulling another run in the following year's election, but still making his living as he had for more than a decade. On the afternoon of September 7, he was in his office when Mike Fox called him, anxiously explained the situation, and asked him if he could take the case. Hearing the distress in Fox's voice, Gottlieb tried to reassure him. "I'm going to hang up the phone," he said, "and I'm going to call the homicide squad right now."

In Yaphank, Assistant District Attorney Tim Mazzei was sitting at a borrowed desk, working on a search warrant. What the police wanted to search was Marty Tankleff's body. They needed a judge to agree that they had reasonable cause to take blood and hair samples, along with scrapings of the dried blood on the front of his shoulder. A secretary announced that Gottlieb was on the line. Mazzei picked up. He listened for a few seconds, then said, "Nobody's talking to him. Unfortunately for you, he's already given an oral admission. But unfortunately for *us*, Mr. Fox put us on notice before we could take the full written confession."

"Was he videotaped?" Gottlieb asked.

"No," Mazzei said. "We were about to go in and videotape him when we were put on notice. But I can go in and videotape him right now. He can say whatever he wants."

"Absolutely not," Gottlieb said. "I'll tell you again: All questioning stops."

"Well, that's pretty strange," said Mazzei. "When you ran for DA, didn't you say that all defendants in murder cases should be videotaped? Wasn't that a big part of your campaign?"

"That's very cute," Gottlieb said. "You should have been videotaping from the very beginning. It's a little too late now."

Gottlieb said he wanted to see Marty. Mazzei told him he could do that at the Sixth Precinct, where he'd be lodged overnight, but not for a few hours. In that case, Gottlieb said, he wanted to speak to Marty on the phone right now. Mazzei told him the police were processing him—mug shot, fingerprinting. Give me twenty minutes or so. When Gottlieb called back, Mazzei got Marty on the phone. It was a short conversation, one-sided and with a single purpose. "Your family's retained me to represent you," Gottlieb told Marty. "I will see you later and we'll talk then. In the meantime, I don't want you to talk to anyone."

Marty said he'd asked to talk to his sister. "Not even your sister," Gottlieb said. "Not until I see you. Do you understand?"

An hour later, at 6:30, Norman Rein told Marty he'd located his sister at the hospital in Stony Brook. Did he still want to talk to her? Marty said he did. Rein looked at him squarely, Marty later recalled, and told him, like an angry parent, "You're going to tell your sister what you did. And you're going to tell her that you are really, really sorry."

At the hospital, Shari sat behind Gail Fox's desk with her relatives gathered around her. She was connected first with Jim McCready. He asked her if he could record the call. Shari cupped the phone. "They want to record it," she told the others. "Do I have a choice?" Of course you do, she was told; tell him no. "No, I don't want you to record it," Shari told McCready. Then she asked, "Are you going to tape it anyway?"

"No," McCready said. "You've asked me not to."

McCready was true to his word, leaving the account of the conversation—Marty's first words to anyone outside the police department—to the recollections of Marty and Shari, and of the detectives who sat with him as he spoke to his sister.

"I'm sorry, I'm so sorry, I'm so sorry," Marty said, by both his and Shari's account. "I'm in big trouble. I need psychiatric help. I need you to be with me wherever they take me."

"Marty, I will be with you. Wherever they take you, I will be with you. Marty, did you tell them you did this?"

"Yes," Marty said. "Because they made me."

The detectives sitting with Marty would later testify that Marty told his sister that he "acknowledged" to the police that he attacked his parents. That he didn't say anything about the police making him confess.

"Shari, I need to see you tonight," Marty said. Then he hung up the phone. Rein brought him back into the interview room, for lack of a better place to keep him until they were ready to bring him to the Sixth Precinct holding cell. Rein asked him if he wanted something to eat. By this point, Marty hadn't eaten anything since the plate of champagne turkey some twenty hours earlier. He'd declined the previous offers from Rein. This time, he accepted. He looked down and found a copy of *Playboy* on the table in front of him. Rein came back a minute later and gave Marty a bagel.

IT WAS AFTER ten o'clock when the homicide detectives finally brought Marty to the Sixth Precinct. Bob Gottlieb and Mike Fox were waiting for him in a small cinder-block room. The door opened and Marty walked in wearing a white paper jumpsuit and something on his feet for the first time in sixteen hours. Paper slippers.

Gottlieb was instantly struck by how slight, how meek, Marty seemed. "He looked like a baby in that paper jumpsuit," he recalled. Whatever this teenager's temperament or personality—whatever demons would have to be inside him to commit such horrendous acts—Gottlieb found it hard to square Marty's physical appearance with the kinds of injuries inflicted on his parents. But for the moment he was less interested in what actually happened in Marty's house than in what Marty had told the police about it.

"They tell me you confessed," Gottlieb said. "Did you?"

"I think I said I did it at some point," Marty said. "But I didn't do it."

"That's a bit of a contradiction. Why don't you tell us what happened?"

Marty said the detectives kept asking him why he was the only one in the house left unharmed. They kept insisting he did it, they *knew* he did it, they had proof. They did a test in the bathroom that proved he took a shower this morning and washed off all the blood. They found his hair in his mother's hand—how did it get there? And no matter how many times he denied it, they just kept telling him they knew he did it. Finally, they told him his father said he did it. He came out of his coma and said he did this to him. So just make it easy and tell them what happened. Finally, he began to think—and said it the moment he thought it—that maybe he actually *did* do this. Maybe he blacked out. And then he told them, yeah, I did it. Because, at that moment, he really believed he did. Even if he couldn't remember anything about it.

"Do you think that's what happened?" Fox asked. "Do you think you did this?"

"No," Marty said. "I didn't do it."

He remembered McCready asking a lot of questions about *how* he did it. And he tried to pull the answers out of his brain, as if he were interrogating his own psyche and his psyche were fighting back. *What knife did you use?* I don't know, I didn't do this. *There were some knives in the kitchen— did you use one of those?* I don't know. *We don't want to hear "I don't know." We know which one it is, but we need you to say it. Was it the knife next to the watermelon?* I guess so, maybe. *What did you hit your mother and father with?* I don't know. *Well, was it the barbells in your room?* I don't know, I don't remember anything. *Just say yes, Marty. C'mon, make it easy. You used the barbells, right?* I don't know. Maybe. *The knife and the barbells looked awfully clean. Did you wash them off?* I don't know. *Well, you know you took a shower. They're nice and clean. So you must have washed them off in the shower.*

If these things weren't true, Gottlieb asked Marty, why did you say they were, or even that they might be? It was a question that Marty would be asked countless times over the next two decades—a question that would come to define his life. The answer would be unfathomable to many people, but it came down to this: "They had me believing that's what happened." It was only after his release from the crushing pressure of the interrogation room—a force he was to compare to having an eighteen-wheeler bearing down on his chest—that he began to recover his bearings enough to reclaim his own reality. No, he wasn't a murderer. No, he wasn't insane. And yes, he had a pretty good idea, as he had from the beginning and as he had tried to tell the detectives, who really did this to his parents.

Gottlieb knew that night, even before putting his own investigators on the case, that Jerry Steuerman could be the foundation of his case for reasonable doubt. But would that, and Marty's version of the interrogation, be a match for what he also knew would be the two detectives' lockstep accounts of Marty's own words? The cops always got their stories straight before putting anything in writing. This was something that Gottlieb had been thinking about since he learned that Marty's alleged confession had been extracted by Jim McCready and Norman Rein. This was the same pair of detectives who, only a couple of months earlier, had been part of a team that had gone into that same room with a twenty-three-year-old man named Patrick Schoendorf. After eight hours of interrogation and McCready's false assertion that "scientific tests" proved that Schoendorf fired the gun that killed his wife, they emerged with a confession, written by McCready, which Schoendorf quickly disavowed. Ten weeks later, the case file was front and center on Gottlieb's desk when he got Mike Fox's call about Marty Tankleff.

Gottlieb asked Marty if the detectives had given him a statement to sign.

No, Marty said.

Very good, said Gottlieb.

He took it all in but reserved judgment. Though his adversaries might think otherwise, Gottlieb was neither so cynical nor naïve to go into a case thinking his client was a victim of the police, or even that he was innocent. No defense lawyer could survive with that mind-set. To Gottlieb, snap judgments of any kind were pointless. He strived to be as objective as possible, even skeptical, weighing his client's story as a jury would. The case would develop organically, layers would be peeled away, and a defense would reveal itself. Maybe even the truth. In this regard, the Tankleff case was no different than any other. That's why, in the coming days, Gottlieb would comply with Section 250.10 of New York Criminal Procedure Law: "Notice of intent to proffer psychiatric evidence." An attorney who wanted to bring a defense of extreme emotional disturbance or insanity had to file notice within thirty days of his client's arraignment. Gottlieb didn't expect to actually put up a psychiatric defense, and he could withdraw the notice at any time. But it was always best to play it safe.

No snap judgments—and yet, there *was* something different here. "What was striking and what remained striking to me," Gottlieb recalled, "was that he didn't seem to be somebody who was manipulative, cunning, callous, or anything other than a very typical teenager. He struck me, in fact, as someone who was very gentle, and very candid." That was not something that he, or any criminal defense lawyer, could say about the typical client. How this might figure in a defense, if at all, was something he wouldn't know until much further down the line. But Gottlieb found his gut impression too compelling to put out of his mind.

If Marty Tankleff really was as he seemed, Gottlieb thought, his defense could have the makings of a classic Suffolk County homicide case. That is, a case in which the defendant wouldn't be the only one on trial. "I left that night thinking, This could be very interesting."

CHAPTER 7

Princes of Suffolk County

FROM ITS ESTABLISHMENT IN 1960, it was commonly observed that the Suffolk County Police Department operated with a certain frontier mentality. This was perhaps a legacy of the days when the county was a vast, semirural outpost served by thirty-three separate police forces. The consolidation of departments into a county force was authorized by public vote but carried out against the wishes of the majority of those most directly affected.

Like everything else in Suffolk County, the police department grew explosively over the next three decades, and by the late 1980s it was the thirteenth-largest municipal police department in the nation. It had twenty-two hundred uniformed officers, four hundred detectives, and some eight hundred civilian employees. But even as it grew, the department remained at the heart of a local law enforcement culture that never seemed to gain a reputation for evenhanded justice. Indeed, it became almost a cliché to say that Suffolk County was like the Wild West in this regard. Arguably, no single entity was more responsible than the one unit of the police department that held itself above the rest: the homicide squad.

Homicide had been a world unto itself since the police department's inception. When the department moved into its modern headquarters in Yaphank in 1972, the squad was the only unit permitted to remain behind in Hauppauge, eighteen miles away. It was both an actual and a symbolic separation. But even after the squad finally moved to Yaphank in the early 1980s, its detectives continued to operate with little oversight. The squad became notorious for the outrageous interrogation tactics that sometimes surfaced in court proceedings. Told by his boss to get a confession, a detective in one case was said to have tied a rope around the suspect's legs, thrown the rope over a tree limb, and swung the man headfirst into the tree trunk until he confessed. In a variation on that theme, another suspect told his lawyer that detectives had dragged him feetfirst by boat across Great South Bay from Sayville to the Captree Bridge.

Among the homicide brotherhood, the squad's methods seemed to be quietly accepted as part of the job, and anyone who felt differently was unlikely to last. So pervasive was the squad's cowboy attitude that Joe Demma, a longtime crime reporter and editor for *Newsday*, a man renowned for his own ballsiness, recalls once being threatened at gunpoint by a group of detectives who didn't like a story he'd written. "I found out how they cracked the case, and they were pissed off because it looked like they had just gotten lucky, which they had," Demma recalled. The next day, he said, he was surrounded by a group of detectives who demanded to know his source—at gunpoint. As Demma tells it, one of the men aimed a rifle at him and said, "Either you've got somebody in the medical examiner's office or you've got our office bugged." Demma was unimpressed: "'Yeah, that's it,' I said. 'I'm bugging your office. What're you gonna do, shoot me? Now I'm walking the fuck out of here.' And I got up and walked out." The detective with the rifle later became a commander of the homicide squad.

That homicide detectives routinely used physical force and intimidation to extract confessions from suspects was an open secret in local legal circles well into the 1980s. Dozens of defendants brought such claims to court, but the county's judges—who tended to align themselves with the police and prosecutors, not a phenomenon unique to Suffolk County—almost never gave them credence. Not infrequently, the tactics involved a man's most sensitive area. A suspect named William Maerling claimed that detectives tied a piece of paper to his penis and held him over an electric paper shredder until he confessed. He did, and the judge at his trial ruled the confession admissible. A man named Christopher Gibbons alleged that a detective put on a pair of surgical gloves and squeezed his testicles. He confessed, too.

One day in the early 1980s, Michael Cahill, a Suffolk County Legal Aid Society lawyer, showed up in court to represent a young defendant who was being arraigned on a murder charge. At the county jail after the arraignment, the defendant, Timothy O'Toole, told Cahill that he had confessed only after being beaten by a detective. "He kicked me in the balls," he said. Legal aid attorneys did not try murder cases, so Cahill knew he would be turning the case over to a court-appointed lawyer for trial. But he wanted to document any evidence of police brutality before it disappeared, especially if it played a role in O'Toole's confession. So Cahill asked O'Toole to drop his pants. Sure enough, O'Toole's testicles and groin area were covered with bruises. As the case proceeded, O'Toole's court-appointed lawyer moved to have the confession ruled invalid and called Cahill as his main witness at the suppression hearing. Cahill testified to what O'Toole told him and to what he himself observed. Then the prosecutor called the detective, who denied he had hurt O'Toole. The defendant was unfortunately injured, said the detective, when he tried to escape after his arrest. The judge ruled the confession admissible, commenting in his written decision that one would have to be naïve to believe the defendant over the detective. The detective's name was James McCready.

Henry O'Brien was elected district attorney of Suffolk County in 1973 and noticed that his predecessors had historically allowed the police department to handle brutality complaints internally. When he tried to change that, the police commissioner dug in, resisting any effort to diminish the department's autonomy. Finally, O'Brien went to Governor Nelson Rockefeller, who appointed a special prosecutor to investigate the issue. The result was a scathing report by a special grand jury that condemned the "tradition" of Suffolk County district attorneys ceding authority to the police department, which had a habit of burying allegations of serious wrongdoing by its officers. It was a reflection of the balance of power in the county's criminal justice system.

At the core of the DAs' subservience to the police was the unusual political power of the county's police unions. Not only did they negotiate contracts that made them among the most highly paid cops in America, but they were not the least bit reluctant to get involved in local political campaigns—those for district attorney in particular. So it was no surprise that Henry O'Brien was out in the next election, replaced by the more police-friendly Patrick Henry, a prosecutor whose politics were not to be confused with the libertarianism of his namesake. But the changing of the guard couldn't keep the trouble in Suffolk County buried beneath the surface. By the end of the decade, prosecutors, defense lawyers, and judges could not help but notice that state appeals courts were reversing Suffolk homicide convictions with alarming frequency.

From 1975 to 1985, the appellate courts threw out ten murder convictions—one a year on average. In all these cases, the higher courts found that homicide detectives had used a range of improper methods to obtain confessions: illegally isolating suspects, denying them access to attorneys, and so blatantly crossing the line between aggressive interrogation and coercion that even the most law-and-order-minded appellate judges found it impossible to give them grace. As an appeals court wryly put it in one case, "It is obvious that the defendant's request to remain silent was not scrupulously honored."

Taken together, the cases suggested a homicide squad that followed its own rules, skirting suspects' rights so consistently that it could only be considered systematic. Implicit in the rulings was the higher courts' displeasure with the Suffolk County district attorney's office for tacitly supporting the police methods, and with the county trial judges who endorsed the illegal practices by admitting the resulting confessions into evidence. Even those who perceived an epidemic of constitutional rights that allowed criminals to get off on the proverbial technicalities had to take notice when *The National Law Journal* published a front-page article in January 1979 alleging that the Suffolk County Police Department was an institution in which homicide detectives had free rein to beat confessions out of suspects. Largely as a result of physical coercion and other improper practices, the article said, Suffolk County's homicide detectives had obtained confessions in all but one of their twenty-eight cases in the previous year—an astounding 97 percent, a rate that dwarfed the percentages that homicide squads across the country produced in their best years. The homicide squad's response did nothing to counter the image of an arrogant bunch with unchecked powers: At that year's Suffolk County Detectives Association picnic, members of the squad showed up wearing T-shirts with "97%" proudly displayed across their chests.

And for the most part, they kept doing what they were doing. "Every time one of those decisions came along, we faced a choice," a retired homicide detective named Richard Zito once told a reporter for *Newsday*. "We could knuckle under . . . or we could fight and come up with a way to get around it." No wonder the state Court of Appeals kept making the same kinds of rulings in the same kinds of cases from Suffolk County. "It was as though we were writing in the sand," recalled a judge who sat on the Court of Appeals in those years.

For his part, District Attorney Patrick Henry stuck by the cops, insisting there was nothing wrong with the way homicides were investigated and prosecuted in Suffolk County. But many defense lawyers knew otherwise—and so did some of Henry's subordinates. They wouldn't say so in public, at least not while they were still on the county payroll, but homicide prosecutors routinely went into court with cases that began and ended with a detective's word that the defendant confessed to the crime. Few knew this better than Charles Newell, the man who had to argue Suffolk's cases as chief of the district attorney's appeals bureau in the late 1970s. Years after he left the office, Newell admitted to a reporter that time and again he found himself before appeals courts defending murder convictions that were based on testimony from detectives that he strongly suspected was perjured. As he put it, "The facts in some of the cases didn't comport to what I knew to be human experience." Newell recalled once sitting anxiously in the chambers of the state's chief judge, Charles Breitel, as the chain-smoking jurist perused the record of a Suffolk murder conviction that was being appealed. "Tell me, Mr. Newell," the judge said finally. "Who runs Suffolk County? A vigilante committee?"

Patrick Henry's predecessor, Henry O'Brien, who had spent a good deal of his single term in office battling the police department, once said of the homicide squad: "All they need is a dead body and a confession. They don't want to do the work on the harder cases."

THEN CAME a judge who saw the worst and couldn't let it go.

Stuart Namm was always an outsider. He had moved his family out to Stony Brook in the mid-1960s, an abrupt transition for a man who had grown up in a neighborhood of Brooklyn that featured Yiddish theaters and socialist politicians and produced some of the most comical people of the century as well as some of the most cold-blooded. Jerry Lewis, Danny Kaye, and Mel Brooks came from Brownsville, as did the Hebrew hitmen of Murder Incorporated, who planned their contract rubouts over chocolate egg creams at Midnight Rose's twenty-four-hour candy store.

Stuart Namm, a plumbing supply man's son, dreamed of becoming a lawyer. On Saturday nights while at City College, he and his fiancée would ride the El to Manhattan to watch defendants being arraigned in Magistrate's Court. He sat in the spectators' section taking copious notes of the proceedings and knew the names of the judges as well as he knew the Dodgers' starting lineup. So taken was Namm that he decided that someday he would like to be not just a lawyer but a judge. He worked as an insurance underwriter to put himself through Brooklyn Law School at night. He spent five years enforcing truth-in-advertising laws for the Federal Trade Commission in New York. In 1966, he moved out to Suffolk County to join two friends in a law practice. One of them was Fred Block, a future state bar association president and federal judge; the other was Dominic Baranello, the chairman of Suffolk County's (and later New York State's) Democratic Party. Democrats in those days were perennial underdogs on Long Island, but Namm's moment came in 1975. Baranello nominated him for a District Court judgeship in the town of Brookhaven, and Watergate and a local Republican land-development scandal were just enough to give him the election. Out of sixty-eight thousand votes cast, Namm won by fifty-eight.

District Court was an entry-level job—the most serious cases were misdemeanors, the rest were "violations" and "infractions"—but Namm came to be known as a rigorous judge. He took that reputation with him when he advanced to the County Court in 1982. Impressed with Namm, the court's administrative judge soon assigned him to be one of the three judges presiding over all the county's homicide cases.

Namm quickly established himself as the last judge a convicted murderer wanted to see on sentencing day. It was nearly always twenty-five-to-life—and, as he was apt to tell the worst offenders, you should thank God that New York no longer has the death penalty. Defense lawyers considered Namm a prosecutor's judge, and prosecutors happily agreed. But while he might have been a favorite of Suffolk County's law enforcement community, Namm didn't fit in very comfortably with his brethren of judges, most of whom were Republicans who owed their jobs to a political system that had long been infected with corruption. Bob Greene, a legendary investigative reporter and editor for *Newsday* who played no small role in exposing the graft, later tallied that six of the eleven Suffolk County Republican chairmen in his memory had departed their posts under clouds of scandal, "three of them virtually in handcuffs." The three party leaders, who held tremendous power over which members of the Suffolk County bar got to be judges, were indicted for various acts of extortion, bribery, and tax evasion.

One day soon after his election to the County Court, Namm attended one of the regular lunch meetings of the county judges. He was deeply offended when a judge stood up and laughingly remarked, "Let's face it—we're just a bunch of political hacks." Namm skipped the lunches after that. It turned out to be a hint of just how independent he was.

At the outset of one of his trials, a defendant's lawyer complained that the prosecutor was unfairly keeping his client's peers—young black men—off the jury. When the lawyer claimed that this was standard practice by the district attorney's office, it occurred to Namm that the attorney might have a point: In his nearly two years on the bench, he couldn't remember a single young black man being seated on a jury. Namm took a bold step for a trial judge: He ordered a hearing on the question. Several prosecutors testified that they regularly impaneled young black jurors. Namm knew it wasn't true and publicly excoriated the DA's office for a practice he declared "shocked the conscience of the court." It was an extraordinary move, especially for a supposed "prosecutor's judge." But it was just the beginning of what he would come to regard as a moral awakening.

In May 1985, a sixty-three-year-old career criminal named Peter Corso went on trial in Namm's courtroom for the execution-style murder of a prominent lawyer named Archimedes Cervera six years earlier. Corso was a convicted drug trafficker with organized crime connections. But as the trial unfolded, it was the performance of the police, more than the guilt or innocence of the defendant, that seized the attention of the courtroom. The prosecutor, Edward Jablonski, had only one real witness, an informant who claimed Corso had told him he murdered the lawyer for $10,000. But the witness was a hit man himself. He admitted having committed crimes "too numerous to specify." The homicide detectives, meanwhile, made their own admissions under cross-examination: They didn't follow up basic leads to corroborate the informant's story, nor did they investigate other possible suspects before discounting them. Perhaps most remarkable was the detectives' testimony that Corso made incriminating statements to them—yet they had no written record of any such statements. And then prosecutor Jablonski discovered how hard it can be to win a murder conviction when the police auction off evidence.

On the day of his murder, Archimedes Cervera was found holding an erasing device for an IBM dictation machine, which was nearby with recordings still on its belts. But as the jury was incredulous to hear, the detectives never listened to them; instead, they had Cervera's secretary do it and asked her to let them know if there was anything important on them. (She said there wasn't.) Also in Cervera's office was an answering machine with several messages on it from men known to be associated with organized crime. But the homicide detectives never made any transcripts of the calls. And by the time of Corso's arrest five years later, the dictation and answering machines were nowhere to be found. The police property section had sold them off. In an act of desperation during the trial, the prosecution team tracked down the equipment, but the tapes had long since been erased and reused.

Peter Corso had committed a lot of crimes in his day, and he may have committed this one. But the case brought against him was so full of holes that the jurors took just four hours to acquit him. In interviews with reporters, several of them spoke angrily about the quality of the police work and the district attorney's acceptance of such a weak case. "I'm not a bleeding heart, I'm a straight citizen," said one. "This guy may have been this or that, but to hang this charge on him, it stinks." Another suggested that the Suffolk police should teach its homicide detectives how to take notes, while a third said of the evidence, "It wasn't much for a murder case." The quote of the day, though, came from Ed Jablonski. "The police work might have been less than expected," said Suffolk County's top felony prosecutor. "That can happen in a very, very complex investigation with many possible suspects."

Judge Stuart Namm had never subscribed to the notion that there might be something wrong at the core of homicide prosecution in Suffolk County. He had been just like every other judge who followed the unwritten rule that the DA's office was always to be given the benefit of the doubt. It was Namm, in fact, who rejected Timothy O'Toole's claims that Detective McCready kicked him in the groin to get him to confess, preferring McCready's story that O'Toole hurt himself while trying to escape.

But the Corso case changed him. In a highly unusual statement after the jury announced its verdict, Namm said, "I have heard things that, as a judge, I am not going to walk away from." A few weeks later, he dismissed a related drug charge against Corso, citing the "gross negligence" of the homicide detectives. "There is an aura which permeates the facts of this case which makes it difficult—indeed impossible—to give credence to the testimony of the police officers involved," Namm said in a written opinion.

But it was nothing compared with what he was to hear in his very next case.

ON JUNE 8, 1984, a six-year-old boy came home from school and found his mother's body at the foot of the stairs in the basement of their home on Market Street in Port Jefferson Station. Maureen Negus, a thirty-five-year-old nurse, had been raped and then stabbed to death. Two weeks later, the police arrested James Diaz, a twenty-two-year-old man whose most recent address was the Suffolk County Jail, where he'd served time for burglary and parole violations. In September 1985, two months after Peter Corso left Judge Namm's courtroom a free man, James Diaz sat at the same defense table with his court-appointed lawyer.

The primary evidence against Diaz was a three-page confession written by Detective Dennis Rafferty, a senior member of the homicide squad. Diaz had signed the first page, which contained only identifying information and a list of his Miranda rights, but had refused to sign the other two. Diaz later told his lawyer, Paul Gianelli, that after reading the confession he had thrown the papers and the pen on the floor. He also said that the detectives assaulted him—literally twisting his arm and shoving his head into a trash can—and blared a radio to drown out his screams.

The confession had Diaz describing how he killed Negus and then "ran out the back door into the woods. I threw my gloves in the woods. I also threw the knife in the woods." It seemed consistent with a knife the police said they found in the woods. The police couldn't prove it was the murder weapon—it had no blood on it, and Rafferty never asked Diaz to identify the knife he used—but it seemed the prosecutors planned to put it in evidence anyway. Until, that is, the day ten months after the murder when Maureen Negus's husband was retrieving an errant Ping-Pong ball in the basement and something caught his eye. In a corner of the room, behind some boards, he discovered a knife. This one had blood on it and the county's crime lab confirmed it was the victim's.

Now the police had some explaining to do. How they had managed to overlook a murder weapon just fifteen feet from the body was just the beginning. The really serious problem was what to do about Diaz's confession—the part where he said he ran out the back door and threw the knife in the woods. While the prosecutors were trying to figure out how to handle this turn of events, Rafferty, the lead detective, suddenly remembered—on the witness stand at a pretrial hearing—that at the time of the confession Diaz told him that he "never wiped the blood off the knife." This caused quite a stir in the courtroom. Such a statement had never come up before. It wasn't in the confession. It wasn't in any of Rafferty's reports or notes. It was even news to the prosecutor.

Faced with the obvious implication that he was making up a story on the fly in a desperate attempt to tie Diaz to the new knife, Rafferty then claimed that though he hadn't told the trial prosecutor about Diaz's statement about the blood, he *had* told two *other* assistant district attorneys. And not just any two. Steven Wilutis was the office's chief trial prosecutor and William Keahon was chief of the Major Offense Bureau.

Rafferty, a seventeen-year veteran of the homicide squad, liked to tell people that he and his brother homicide detectives were "doing God's work." It was men like Rafferty whom a high-ranking prosecutor named John Buonora was talking about when he once recalled, "When you're a young assistant DA, you're taught that those are the big, macho guys you should be seen with." They were men, another lawyer said, who were "almost like princes of the county, who go anywhere, do anything." Another veteran Suffolk County lawyer put it this way: "You're twenty-five years old, you're barely out of law school, and suddenly you find yourself in an interview room with a forty-five-year-old detective questioning an actual, real-life criminal. You're not going to say, 'Gee, I really think you're not going about this the right way. What about the suspect's rights?' The cops know that ADAs come and go, so they have no reason to give them a second thought. And the guys who stay and move up don't do that by being a pain in the ass to the cops."

Wilutis and Keahon, two of the highest-ranking assistant district attorneys, took the witness stand at James Diaz's pretrial hearing and later at the trial itself, and testified that yes, Detective Rafferty told them about Diaz's statement about leaving the blood on the knife. It was way back, they said. Must have been a year ago.

Taking it all in, Judge Stuart Namm was incredulous. He believed that Rafferty, Wilutis, and Keahon were all lying—committing perjury right in front of him. But there was more to come. With the discovery of the actual murder weapon undermining the credibility of the confession, the prosecutor, Barry Feldman, tried to shore up his case by calling to the stand a young man named Joseph Pistone. He was what cops and lawyers called a jailhouse snitch: someone who traded testimony against another inmate for a break in his own case. Pistone, a motorcycle thief whose father was a New York City detective, testified that Diaz told him how he'd murdered Maureen Negus. But Pistone was so eager to help himself that he claimed a defendant in another murder case also confessed to him. Namm was so dubious of Pistone's testimony that he had the jury leave the courtroom so he could question the witness himself. When he finished, he called Pistone a "pathological liar" and all but accused the prosecutor of suborning perjury. "If this defendant is guilty, I want him convicted," Namm said. "But by God, if he is not guilty of this charge, he should not be convicted, and it's not important enough to have perjurers come in this court to ensure that somebody is convicted of murder." When the jurors returned, Namm instructed them to disregard Pistone's testimony.

The prosecution had yet another problem, with another detective: Jim McCready. While canvassing the neighborhood in the days following Maureen Negus's murder, McCready had interviewed three workers at a Long Island Rail Road yard near the victim's house. According to McCready, the first railyard worker he talked to, a fellow named Butch Shumel, identified Diaz as a man who sometimes slept in train cars at the yard, and placed him in the neighborhood days before the murder. Shumel said he recognized Diaz from a picture of him he'd seen in a newspaper. And the two other railyard workers told him the same thing, McCready testified. But defense attorney Gianelli knew this couldn't be true, and confronted McCready on cross-examination: Are you aware, Detective McCready, that no picture of James Diaz appeared in any newspaper until after his arrest—two weeks after you say you interviewed these men?

McCready asked to return to the stand the next day, saying he wished to clarify his testimony. But he proceeded to do the opposite. Listening as Feldman tried to assist McCready in modifying his testimony, Judge Namm found the detective's story incomprehensible. "Wait a minute," he cut in finally. Once again, he sent the jury out and took over the questioning himself.

"Yesterday," he said to McCready, "you said that Butch Shumel told you that he saw a picture of the defendant in the newspaper on June 26, 1984. Is that correct?"

"That's correct, Your Honor," said McCready. "At that time, that was my belief."

"Are you saying now that that testimony is not correct?"

"I'm saying that that testimony was partially correct and partially incorrect."

"What was partially correct and what was partially incorrect?"

"He told me he saw Diaz in the paper and there was an assumption on my part that it was a picture of Diaz."

"An assumption?" Namm asked.

"Yes, it was," McCready confirmed.

"He saw Diaz in the paper?"

"Yes."

"What do you mean he saw him in the paper and you simply assumed it was a photo?" Namm asked impatiently. "I don't understand what you mean by that. What does that mean?"

"Last night, I was going over this thing in my mind quite a bit," McCready told the judge, "and I was trying to figure out exactly why there's a problem here, and I think the problem arose as a mistake on my part by an assumption that I had made based on the conversation that I had with Shumel and the other two men."

"Detective McCready," Namm responded, picking up a document, "on June 26 and 27, 1984, you wrote a report, a Supplementary Report. . . . You wrote in your report, 'He stated that he saw the newspaper containing a photograph of James Diaz and recognized him as being a person who slept in the railroad cars.' Is that what you wrote on that date?"

"Yes, correct," said McCready.

"Are you telling me now today that after thinking about it last night, about what the problem was, that it's now your belief that he never told you that he saw a photograph of the defendant in the newspaper but that you simply assumed he saw a photograph of the defendant in the newspaper?"

"Your Honor, last night when I went over this and over this in my mind I tried to recall as best I could the exact conversation with Mr. Shumel. In doing so, I realized that this was an assumption on my part."

Sitting in his retirement home in North Carolina twenty years later, Namm would recall the exchange vividly. "He comes back and says, 'I spent all night thinking about it and now I know what happened. I just *assumed* they saw a photograph in the newspaper.' Now, this was interesting to me because when we were discussing this when the issue arose on the previous day—myself, Mr. Gianelli, and Mr. Feldman, out of the presence of Detective McCready—Feldman said, 'You know, I'll bet what happened here was that McCready just assumed there was a photograph in the newspaper.' And sure enough . . ."

McCready never explained what Shumel might have seen in the newspaper if not a photograph, or how it was that he asked the other two railroad workers if they saw the same nonexistent photo and both said they did. But McCready didn't stop there. In reconstituting his testimony from the day before, he added something brand-new. When Namm asked if there was anything more to his interview with Shumel that day, McCready said the railroad worker identified Diaz from a mug shot. "I show him the picture of Diaz. He said, 'That is the guy.'"

This was news again to Feldman. McCready had never told him about such an identification, nor made any record of it. The prosecutor had earlier told Namm and Gianelli that no hearing on identification evidence would be necessary because he had none to offer: Diaz had not been identified through either police photos or a lineup.

After the lawyers delivered their summations and the jury departed to deliberate its verdict, Namm launched a tirade that stunned everyone in the courtroom. He called the police investigation of the case "a disgrace" and blasted the DA's office for its use of the jailhouse informant Joseph Pistone. "A perjurer was brought before this court with an open eye by the prosecutor," Namm said, adding that "there have been other perjurers"—an apparent reference to the various detectives and assistant district attorneys whose testimony he also considered patently false. "The greatest tragedy," Namm said, "is that a person who may be guilty may walk free because of prosecutorial misconduct." And finally, perhaps most startling, he accused the police and prosecutors of trying to intimidate *him*. Leaving the courthouse a few days earlier, Namm heard howls and taunts coming from a fifth-floor window in the DA's office. "You lose, Stu!" someone yelled. On another day, the judge found his car damaged by a long scratch, the kind made with a key.

But it wasn't Namm who lost when the jury returned. As with Peter Corso, there were reasons to believe that James Diaz may have committed the crime of which he was accused. But as in that case, the jurors found that the police had botched the case so badly, and given so much testimony that couldn't be trusted, that they had no choice but to find him not guilty. Namm told the jury after the verdict: "You spoke only two words. But you spoke volumes with those two words."

They spoke many more words with reporters afterward. "What it came down to is twelve people got together and decided that the police were lying to us," said one juror. Another said it was plain that the police believed Diaz did it and fabricated the evidence to prove it. "If someone close to me was murdered," another juror remarked, "I'd rather have a small-town police department investigate it than the Suffolk homicide squad with all its resources."

Two days after the Diaz verdict, Namm wrote to Governor Mario

Cuomo and asked him to appoint a special prosecutor to investigate the conduct of the Suffolk County police and prosecutors. "In two consecutive highly publicized murder trials," he wrote, "I have witnessed, among other things, such apparent prosecutorial misconduct as perjury, subornation of perjury, intimidation of witnesses, spoilation [*sic*] of evidence, abuse of subpoena power and the aforesaid attempts to intimidate a sitting judge."

Cuomo referred Namm's allegations to New York State's Commission of Investigation, a bipartisan six-member panel appointed by the governor and leaders of the state legislature. The commission, commonly known as the SIC, had no prosecutorial powers, but its staff of lawyers could subpoena witnesses to testify at both private sessions and public hearings. The commission concluded each of its formal investigations with a report of its findings and recommendations that could carry political weight.

To the SIC's commissioners—who included Bernard C. Smith, a former Suffolk County district attorney and Republican candidate for state attorney general—Namm's allegations had a familiar ring. In recent years, the commission had received and investigated twice as many complaints about the Suffolk police and district attorney's office as it had about law enforcement agencies in any other county in the state. A prior SIC investigation had found that District Attorney Patrick Henry had mishandled allegations of misconduct within his office. In January 1986, the commission announced it would conduct its first full-scale investigation of the law enforcement institutions of Suffolk County.

Namm's courageous public battle with two immensely powerful institutions triggered one other investigation, and it would reverberate for years. Going back to 1954, when it won its first Pulitzer Prize for public service, *Newsday* had been known for its fearless investigations of Long Island's most powerful political and government institutions. Starting in late 1985, two of the paper's top young reporters—Thomas Maier, a Suffolk County native who had covered both of Namm's recent murder trials, and Rex Smith, a minister's son who grew up in the Black Hills of South Dakota—spent a year examining the way Suffolk County investigated and prosecuted homicides. The result, published a year later, was a devastating five-part, 25,000-word series titled "The Confession Takers."

Maier and Smith examined 361 Suffolk murder cases going back a decade and found that the police had claimed that suspects made incriminating oral statements in 94 percent of them, nearly the same percentage *The National Law Journal* reported when it looked at just one year's worth of cases eight years earlier. It was a staggering statistic, one that experts from across the country told the reporters was without parallel. Assisted by computers, Maier and Smith analyzed seven hundred cases from six other large suburban counties in five states. Confession rates in those jurisdictions ranged from 54 to 73 percent. Homicide detectives in Suffolk's Long Island sibling, Nassau County, obtained confessions in just 55 percent of their cases.

The confession takers themselves, present and past, reacted predictably to the suggestion that too many people seemed to be confessing to murder in Suffolk County. They scoffed, then circled the wagons. The high confession rate, said a recently retired homicide commander, meant that "we're the best." Because, said another, "We try harder." But others drew a somewhat less laudable inference—none more bluntly than Charles Peterson, a lawyer who had once been a deputy police commissioner in Suffolk County as well as a high-ranking official of the New York City Police Department. "When it's this high here and much lower elsewhere," Peterson said flatly, "you have perjury somewhere."

Newsday found that the Suffolk homicide detectives relied so much on confessions that they seemed to consider corroborating evidence an annoyance. This was at a time when better police training and more sophisticated criminalistics techniques were moving the national trend toward forensic evidence and away from confessions. But Suffolk County's crime lab had been notoriously understaffed and poorly equipped for years, another indication of where the priority was.

These were all symptoms of a broken system. Here was a jurisdiction in which it seemed the innocent might be prosecuted and the guilty might go unpunished and in which twelve evenhanded people might consider the evidence presented and be unable to say with any confidence, let alone certainty, what they were looking at. Reasonable doubt is a cornerstone of the justice system, but too many cases with too much reasonable doubt was a sign that something was wrong. While prosecutors in Suffolk County were twice as apt to come to court with confessions as their counterparts in Nassau County, they were half as likely to come away with full convictions. In 1985 and 1986, *Newsday* found, only 23 percent of Suffolk's murder defendants were convicted as charged.

There were many potential victims of such erratic justice—an innocent defendant, of course, and the families of the murdered whose killers go free—but among them, too, were all those in the district attorney's office and the police department who did their work honorably. An isolated instance of injustice might be forgiven, but what was going on in Suffolk County suggested something wider and deeper, something at once obvious and obscure: If misconduct on the scale being exposed was deemed acceptable, what subtler transgressions were being tolerated? It tainted the entire institution.

For their part, the two men who ran the agencies in question offered only pious dismissals of *Newsday*'s findings. "We're not doing anything wrong," District Attorney Patrick Henry told the newspaper. "We're not laughing up our sleeves, abusing somebody's rights or abusing the system. We take our responsibilities very seriously." Both he and the police commissioner, DeWitt Treder, insisted the Corso and Diaz cases were unfortunate but isolated. According to Treder (whose son was married to Jim McCready's sister), the people of Suffolk County could rest assured that they had a "professional, working criminal justice system that works."

DECEMBER 1986 was not a good month for the Suffolk County homicide squad. Just as the "Confession Takers" series was dominating the pages of *Newsday*, the State Investigation Commission was issuing subpoenas to the key detectives involved in the Corso and Diaz cases. By this point, three of the six men called to testify had retired from the department, and only one of the other three was still in homicide. That was James McCready.

When his day came, McCready, like all the other detectives subpoenaed to testify behind closed doors, was accompanied by Thomas Spota, a former chief trial prosecutor whose most important client, now that he was in private practice, was the Suffolk County Detectives Association. It did not go unnoticed by the commissioners that Spota had a vested interest in their investigation. Among the controversial homicide cases they were reviewing was one that Spota himself had prosecuted: the conviction of four teenagers in the 1979 murder of Johnny Pius, a thirteen-year-old boy who was found in a school yard, beaten and suffocated, with half a dozen rocks stuffed down his throat.

The Pius case was one of Suffolk County's most notorious murders, both for the hideousness of the crime itself and for the way it was handled. The journalist Jesse Kornbluth had been the first to seriously question the case against the four teenagers who were accused of murdering Pius to keep him from reporting their theft of his motorless minibike. Kornbluth spent a year examining the case and *New York* magazine published his findings in a two-part series in September 1982. Two of the defendants, brothers Peter and Michael Quartararo, who were fifteen and fourteen at the time of the murder, had been found guilty by a jury that rejected their lawyer's claims that the confessions used to convict them had been coerced and invented by the police. The other two defendants, Robert Brensic and Thomas Ryan, were about to go on trial. They would be convicted.

After conducting some 150 interviews and poring over a thousand pages of documents, Kornbluth thought that all four boys might be innocent. The stories they told did, "in the main, check out," he wrote. "The story the Pius family, the homicide squad, and the district attorney all tell does not." The police had made a mistake, Kornbluth believed; prosecutor Thomas Spota and his boss, District Attorney Patrick Henry, had compounded it by pressing the case with willful blindness to its many holes. And the judge who declined to suppress the problematical confessions sealed the defendants' fate. That judge, ironically, was Stuart Namm. Eight years after the murder—just as the SIC was examining the case as part of its wide-ranging investigation—the New York Court of Appeals overturned three of the four convictions. As the state's highest court wrote in one of the cases, "The confession was the product of the custodial questioning of a 15-year-old boy for six and a half hours, without his parents' knowledge, by two police detectives . . . under circumstances which suggest that it was induced by the hope of leniency." With his altered perspective, Namm now agreed that he should have suppressed the confession.

With the case of his career still being disparaged a decade after its prosecution, Tom Spota found himself at the center of a storm that threatened even greater damage to Suffolk County's law enforcement establishment. Spota's first move was to go to court to fight the commission's subpoenas. It was the first of numerous attempts by Spota and his counterpart with the Police Benevolent Association to sidetrack the investigation with court orders. They lost every time.

In January 1987, a year into its investigation, the SIC held its first public hearings, two days of harsh questions and tense exchanges in the auditorium of the Suffolk County Legislature building. Chairman David Trager, the dean of Brooklyn Law School, opened with a strikingly blunt statement about the commission's findings thus far. "There is a startling lack of professionalism in the Suffolk County Police Department," he said, "shamefully tolerated by the district attorney's office."

Testifying that day, District Attorney Henry, a hefty man with a patrician air, declared that he was "shocked" by such characterizations. "It suggests that I should be ashamed of myself for not doing something about it. I resent that." Henry also took the opportunity to scold *Newsday* for its own investigation. "*Newsday* would have you believe that all confessions are contrived. I think that is a disservice to the reading public."

In the course of eight hours that stretched into the night, the commission took testimony about the Corso and Diaz cases and a number of others that made Henry's protests look feeble. Contrived confessions did not seem a rarity. And in a more insidious way, what the commission heard suggested a squad of detectives who operated in a culture that allowed for the occasional, if not routine, manipulation of evidence. *Newsday*'s Maier and Smith had conveyed that impression vividly through the words of the homicide men themselves. "In my mind, the end justifies the means," the retired detective Richard Zito told them. "Now, as far as anybody else knowing what I did? Not really. Because I kept most of my stuff to my-self." Others tried to explain the mental toll on homicide detectives and how it could intrude on their work. "There's a certain anger and frustra-tion in dealing with a murdered person that colors your behavior," said Bob Dunn, a former homicide squad commander. "The young detectives come in and say they'll be objective, unbiased in their approach to the job. But there's that certain case that pushes you over the edge—the young child who is missing for so long, and then you find her brutally murdered. You become personally involved." As yet another veteran put it, most suc-cinctly: "Homicide, it's different."

Set against the SIC's investigation, the candid reflections carried frightening implications. If evidence was considered flexible, where was the line? *Was* there a line? In that sort of environment, did some detectives find it too difficult to resist the temptation, or the pressure, to take some liberties here and there? In light of the Diaz case, it was not unreasonable for the SIC to wonder how many corners a detective like Dennis Rafferty might have cut in his seventeen years in the squad. Rafferty was a classic of the mold, a homicide man who liked to say he was "doing God's work." But the SIC turned up yet another instance in which Rafferty showed a "convenient talent for producing crucial testimony and evidence at the eleventh hour." After a rare instance in which a Suffolk County judge ruled a defendant's confession inadmissible, Rafferty suddenly produced a .22-caliber bullet that turned out to have the same ejection marks as those made by the murder weapon. He said he had found it in the defendant's pocket when he arrested him but had forgotten all about it. Questioned by the SIC five years later, Rafferty denied any inference that something was amiss. Where he erred, he said, was in not initially realizing the signifi-cance of the bullet. This was because "every black guy in Amityville has a twenty-two." Also, "I'm not really on top of guns and that's probably what got me messed up on that."

Feeling ambushed by the SIC on the first day of the public hearing, members of the police department showed up the next day ready for bat-tle. Some 250 off-duty police picketed outside the legislative building while others went inside to heckle the proceedings from the audience. The commissioners continued their probe of the Diaz case, questioning prosecutor Barry Feldman as Tom Spota sat beside him. Feldman was an-swering a question when he was interrupted by a skeptical commission member. "Give him the opportunity to answer fully," Spota cut in, inter-rupting the interruption.

"And honestly?" asked the commissioner, an assistant United States at-torney.

"Mr. Chairman, that is absolutely uncalled for!" Spota yelled, jabbing a finger as the police in the audience burst into applause and catcalls.

When another commissioner, an attorney from Buffalo, asked Spota if he was representing Feldman as counsel to the detectives association or as his private attorney, Spota wouldn't say. Trager directed him to reply, but Spota refused, which sent the audience of police into another round of cheering. "This isn't *The Price Is Right*," the commissioner from Buffalo informed the audience. At this point, Spota asked to speak privately with Trager, and when he returned to the witness table he asked his clients and their supporters for a little decorum. "Emotions have been running high on both sides," Spota said, a remark to which the commission's chief counsel took exception. "We are really making an effort to be objective," she said.

"Bullshit!" came a voice from the crowd.

Afterward, the president of the Superior Officers Association announced that he'd sent a letter to the United States attorney general, Edwin Meese, asking for a federal investigation of the state investigation. In a statement that struck the police department's critics as almost too clueless to be believed, the police union chief complained that his members' "civil rights" were being violated by the New York State Commission of Investigation.

No one who'd spent much time around the Suffolk County Courthouse could be surprised by the defiance of the police and prosecutors. Nor did they expect the investigations triggered by Stuart Namm's allegations to lead to serious changes anytime soon. The county's law enforcement establishment was too entrenched to be uprooted by a single whistle-blowing judge, or a newspaper series, or even by a state investigation. Its attitude was perhaps expressed most keenly in a casual remark by a homicide detective during a recent murder trial. Cross-examining him about his methods, the defense attorney asked the detective whether he followed the department's rules when he investigated homicide cases. The detective shrugged. "The police department has many, many rules," he said.

CHAPTER 8

He Was Angry at His Parents

The son of Belle Terre's commissioner of constables was charged with stabbing his mother to death and slashing his father's throat during an early-morning attack yesterday in the family's rustic waterfront home, Suffolk police said. Seventeen-year-old Martin Tankleff—described by neighbors as a polite boy whose parents doted on him—was arrested less than 12 hours after he called 911. . . .

Authorities last night said they had not recovered any weapons and declined to discuss a motive for the attack. Sources close to the investigation, however, said that it was not prompted by an argument, but apparently by anger and hostility that had been building over a period of time. . . .

—*Newsday*, Thursday, September 8, 1988

IN PORT JEFFERSON, the school year at Earl L. Vandermeulen High opened with a disturbingly familiar jolt. During the previous year, six Vandermeulen students had died—one of heart failure, another shot to death by her boyfriend, four in a car accident a week after school let out for summer. And now this. Port Jefferson's weary schools superintendent, Philip Magnarella, remarked to a reporter that he felt as if he'd "like to have the district exorcised."

Instead the news brought the customary exercise in group trauma— hallways abuzz with rumor, the deployment of the grief counselors, the reporters descending on students and teachers who reflexively began referring to the boy in question in the past tense. It was shocking, everyone said—Marty was a nice kid, a quiet and unremarkable student, not the kind you'd ever expect to do anything like this. But wasn't that what people always said? Most of his classmates knew Marty, some since they were in kindergarten—but did they *really* know him? Marty's close friends did, and to them it was impossible. Mark Perrone and Zach Suominen had been with Marty the day and night before. They rewound their memories eighteen hours but couldn't detect even a moment when Marty wasn't himself—easygoing, mild-mannered, preoccupied by how he looked to girls. But then you had the police saying he did it, saying Marty *said* he did it. They don't just make up this kind of thing, do they?

Marty's business teacher, Randy Stander, knew that Marty idolized his father, but was there more to their relationship, some kind of father-son psychodrama nobody knew about that finally erupted? Estelle Block, the head of the guidance department, heard the news from Dara Schaeffer, who had heard it from Marty herself when she came upon the scene while on her way to school. Neither of them could imagine Marty doing this— but could they just dismiss it outright? After all, Marty confessed, didn't he?

The next morning, Marty emerged through a side door of a small courtroom at the county center in Hauppauge. Handcuffed, dressed in a white jumpsuit, he was led to a bench in front of District Court judge Edward Green, where he was joined by his lawyer, his sister, and his brother-in-law. Marty stared blankly, head bowed, as prosecutor Ed Jablonski read the charges against him: one count of murder, another of attempted murder that could be upgraded as necessary.

"He committed the crimes," Jablonski told the arraignment judge, "because he was angry at his parents."

From the front row of the spectators' section, Marty's aunts and uncles and cousins looked on, grim-faced. Mickey Falbee shook her head as Jablonski continued: "The defendant planned these attacks so carefully that he purposely was naked so he wouldn't get any blood on his clothing. Then he washed the murder weapons and put them in plain sight to throw the police off. He left the knife he used on the kitchen table next to a watermelon. The other weapon was a barbell. It was found in the defendant's bedroom."

The judge decreed that the defendant would be held without bail. More upsetting to Marty, in the short term, was the judge's denial of Gottlieb's request that he be allowed to attend his mother's funeral. Gottlieb assured him he would take the matter to a higher court. As he told the family outside the courtroom, keeping Marty from the funeral was a violation of his fundamental right to the presumption of innocence.

As Gottlieb talked to the family, Jablonski expounded on Marty's motives for murder, offering a list of grievances: "His parents spoiled his summer. They restricted the use of a Boston Whaler. They made him drive a '78 Lincoln to school as opposed to another car, a newer Lincoln."

Also, he was unhappy that his parents were planning to have someone stay with him when they went on a cruise in the fall. He felt they were fighting a lot and putting him in the middle. And finally, he was upset because his father had gotten angry with him for not setting up the poker table before going out to the mall on Tuesday night. "It was a temper tantrum that turned into violence," Jablonski said. "He's a boy that had everything in life and thought he deserved more."

The quote provided the next day's headline in *Newsday:*

DEADLY TEMPER TANTRUM? PROSECUTORS: ANGER LED TO SON'S ATTACK.

Thus did Marty Tankleff join the annals of Long Island crime, an archive of strange and notorious deeds that was coming to represent the darker heart of the endless American suburb as it grew into maturity a generation after the glorious innocence of Levittown. Starting that night in 1974 when Ronnie DeFeo slaughtered his family in Amityville, Long Island became a reliable setting for crimes of passion, greed, madness, and Buttafuoco. There was a kidnapper who kept a little girl named Katie in a dungeon, a doctor who gave his wife a shot of Demerol and declared her dead from a stroke, a berserk gunman on the Long Island Rail Road at rush hour, a serial killer in a pickup truck who hauled his dead prostitutes, seventeen of them all told, alongside his landscaping equipment. The excess of exceptional true crime did not go unnoticed, and the reasons were often pondered. "What the hell happened?" the writer Ron Rosenbaum wondered in the opening paragraph of a cover article in *The New York Times Magazine*. "What happened to the incredibly boring place I grew up in, where I swear nothing ever happened?"

Marty Tankleff—accused but not convicted—instantly took his place in this pantheon of atrocious behavior. He was the quintessential spoiled, Jewish, North Shore kid—a stereotype taken to psychotic extreme. In the months to come, prosecutors, ably assisted by the media, would burnish the image, turning the story of Marty's murderous fit into a kind of perverse suburban folktale. As the case proceeded, they would famously allege that Marty, in his confession, described the car that was said to be at the root of his discontent as a "crummy old Lincoln," and the words would attach to his name and his face like a tattoo.

But was any of it true? Among Marty's circle of family and friends, it was as if the police and prosecutors were conjuring an alternate universe to fit a concocted confession. To them it made no sense, this idea that Marty would kill his mother and father over the kinds of things teenagers and parents quarreled about all the time. Marty decided to hack his parents to death because he didn't like his car? Even beyond the absurdity of it, as far as anyone knew Marty seemed to like the Lincoln just fine. Over the summer, the McClures had spent ten days visiting the Tankleffs and

Marty had driven them to the airport the day they flew home. "The whole time we're riding in that car, all we're hearing is how excited he is about all the things he's going to do with it," Mike recalled. "'Uncle Mike, I'm gonna put in these speakers that you can switch from front to back.' And he was going to have it reupholstered. He and Seymour had gone to a place. He says, 'It's really cool, all black.'"

And even if Marty had become disenchanted with his car since then, even if he were really annoyed by everything else on the prosecutor's list, nobody who knew him could reconcile the brutality of the attacks with their image of Marty. This wasn't a single moment of rage but two distinct acts of determined, sustained, savage violence. It was murder with a purpose. Could a brain just short out like that, without any warning in the hours and days and weeks preceding it—to say nothing of the seventeen years before? And there was the question of Marty's *physical* ability to carry out these slaughters. Arlene and Seymour were both much bigger and stronger than Marty. Seymour had a hundred pounds on his son. Arlene had fifty, and she could be every bit as fierce as Marty was mild. "Arlene would have picked him up and thrown him through the window," her sister Mickey said. At the very least, she would have defended herself mightily—and she did. This became evident to Ron Falbee and Mike McClure when they went to the morgue to formally identify her body. "We saw enough to know that she put up a hell of a battle," Mike said. "Nobody was going to kill Arlene easily." Said Ron: "Everything about Arlene was tough—her personality, her size, her strength. It was who she was. Whoever did this would have looked like he went through a war."

And yet. In these first hours, even Marty's closest relatives could not say with certainty what had happened here. Their minds were awash in speculation and vacillation, grasping for some plausible reality—even one that said that Marty did it, if that was to be the truth. "In a way, that would have been easier to deal with," Mike would later reflect. "If Marty did it, then fine—we can bury Arlene and they can put Marty away and we will never see him again the rest of our lives." But if Marty didn't do it, then the entire family had an enormous fight on its hands. Their need for a glimpse of clarity was so overpowering that Mike found himself praying for a real-life version of McCready's fantasy. If only Seymour could come back, just long enough to whisper the truth into someone's ear.

Short of such a miracle, the family was left to its own powers of reason. Arlene's side sat together late into the night at Mickey's house and tried to mesh what they knew with what they were being told—a kind of family jury struggling to come to some objective judgment. "And the more you thought about it," Mike said, "the more it didn't ring true. All these things we know about Marty and we know about Seymour and we know about

Arlene—it's not adding up to Marty, in a fit of rage, getting up that morning and saying, 'Okay, I'm going to kill them before school.' Nothing I can put in my mind is making that round peg fit in that square hole. And then you add the select facts of the confession, the motives according to the prosecutor. We're all sitting there saying, 'Well, that's bullshit, and that's bullshit, and that's bullshit.'" And then they put Jerry Steuerman into the mix. If they couldn't get their heads around Marty's pet peeves as a motive, how about Steuerman and all that money? "Finally," Mike said, "we're all looking at each other saying, 'No. It's not Marty.'"

Ron and his mother wanted to hear it for themselves. Later on the day of the arraignment, they drove out to Riverhead to see Marty at the Suffolk County Jail. They entered the crowded visiting room and saw Marty on the far end of a row of tables with plastic partitions.

Ron, straightforward as ever, came right to the point. "Did you do it?" he asked.

"No," Marty said. "I didn't."

"I don't think you did it, either," Ron said.

Mickey asked Marty to open his shirt. All the way, she said. She silently surveyed his upper body—chest, shoulders, neck, stomach, arms—searching for any evidence of a fight. There was not a scratch on him. From that moment on, Mickey was resolute in her belief that her nephew did not kill her sister. And so was her son. "I knew the heart of him," Ron said. "This kid was no murderer. I knew it that day."

The next day, the Falbees and the McClures drove to Belle Terre to pick out clothing from Arlene's closet for her funeral. They were met at the door by Jim McCready, who told them that the house was under the control of the crime scene team. There were detectives and technicians all over the place. Virtually every surface was covered with black fingerprinting powder.

McCready introduced the group to his partner and their sergeant, then herded them into the dining room and asked them to sit. "I just want to tell you that we do have the person who murdered your sister, and it's Marty," McCready said. "It may be hard for you to accept, but that's the way it is." Now, he said, is there anything you folks would like to say that might be helpful to the case?

"I would like to say one thing," Mickey said.

Two of the other detectives opened their notebooks.

"I want you to go out and find out who really killed my sister. Because Marty didn't do it."

The detectives closed their notebooks. The family gathered an outfit for Arlene. Then they drove to the courthouse in Hauppauge to watch Bob Gottlieb ask a judge to allow Marty out of jail for a few hours so he could attend his mother's funeral. At noon the next day, a pair of sheriff's cars pulled up at the O. B. Davis Funeral Home. Marty emerged from one of them, unshaven, his ankles shackled, his hands cuffed in front of him. Escorted by three sheriff's deputies, he shuffled into the chapel and offered a slight, pained smile toward the small group of relatives and family friends in attendance. He's incarcerated, the sheriff's department had told them. You can't touch him. You can't talk to him. They managed some brief words of comfort but were otherwise left to express their support in a less traditional way. WE LOVE YOU MARTY signs were taped to the windows of their cars outside.

The service was brief: a few generic religious verses, a eulogy for Arlene by her older sister, Mickey. There were no allusions to the manner of her death. Marty sat alone, under guard, sobbing. Then the group moved to Pinelawn Cemetery, the cars lining up behind the hearse in a procession reminiscent of the entourage that had followed the ambulance transporting Seymour from one hospital to the other five days earlier. This time, nobody was asking, "Where's Marty?" He was in the sheriff's car at the end of the line. At the cemetery, he sat on a folding chair a few feet from his mother's coffin as a final prayer was recited. The casket was lowered into the ground, and then one by one those who loved Arlene Tankleff tossed flowers into her grave. All but Marty, who remained in his seat, still shackled, as his aunts and uncles and cousins squeezed his shoulder and patted his knee as they passed. And then he was taken back to jail.

CHAPTER 9

The Loan Shark
of Seaside Drive

TO JIM MCCREADY, the Tankleff case was simple. So simple that it hardly took any work at all. "Everything we needed to know about this case," he was to say years later, "we pretty much knew on the first day."

It may have been McCready's most revealing comment about the Tankleff case. Having announced the confession of their suspect as they had most others, the police considered this case closed, and closed tight. There would be no further investigation. No need, for instance, to interview Seymour and Arlene Tankleff's closest relatives and friends. "What were they gonna add to my case?" McCready asked.

They could have told him quite a lot about Seymour and Arlene and Marty Tankleff. Not just about what a nice kid Marty was, and how he loved his parents, but about how Seymour and Arlene lived their lives, and what it might have had to do with how they died. They might have started the story nearly four years earlier, late in 1984, when Seymour, with Arlene's agreement, decided the time was right to sell his insurance business.

Seymour began negotiating, naturally, with a friend of his. He'd known Tom Ness since he'd moved his business to Port Jefferson in the early 1970s. Though competitors, they'd become close enough to go on vacation together with their wives. Ness was very interested when Seymour asked if he wanted to buy his business, but he didn't have the kind of money Seymour wanted. So he acquired a partner who did: a Lufthansa cargo pilot who had made so much money flying freight back and forth across the Atlantic that he was willing to unload some of his cash in a Long Island insurance agency. They agreed to buy Tankleff Associates for $1 million.

The deal called for Seymour to get $250,000 up front, with the rest to be paid, with interest, over five years. The papers were signed, the check cut. Seymour was officially retired from the insurance racket. He bought a Harley-Davidson but got rid of it after driving by an accident in which another motorcyclist had been killed. He replaced it with a gentler Vespa motor scooter, the Italian-made moped ridden by Cary Grant in *Roman Holiday*. Seymour and Arlene also used some of the cash from the sale of the insurance business to add a large room to the east end of their house, which was connected to the kitchen by a solarium in which Seymour raised orchids. The new room became Seymour's home office and the family's home gym, and the place where the After Dinner Club convened on the Tuesday nights every ten weeks or so when it was Seymour's turn to host. On those occasions, Marty would unfold the felt-topped poker table, which featured chip wells and cup holders, and squeeze nine or ten upholstered chairs around it.

For Seymour, getting out of the insurance business didn't mean retirement; in some ways it meant the opposite. Having time and money on his hands truly unleashed his inner wheeler-dealer. His desire to make deals became a kind of compulsion, an impulse as strong as a gambler's craving for a bet. He wasn't particularly discriminating, nor was he much concerned about complications. In his quest for places to put his money and for partners with whom to share the risk, he had to look no further than the men seated around the poker table. He was in deals with most of them.

Like any kind of social club, the After Dinner Club was a source of connections. Leo Sternlicht owned Riverhead Motors, which was why the Lincoln Town Car was a favorite among the poker players. If you needed carpeting, you didn't go to one of those huge carpet showrooms, you went to Cappy. The group had two professionals, a lawyer and a doctor, which was handy whenever someone needed some free legal advice or a quick diagnosis of his latest joint pain. The doctor, Frank Oliveto, was a happy-go-lucky orthopedic surgeon who sometimes came to the game straight from the operating room at Mather, still in his scrubs. And of course there was Vinnie Bove, who had to be the busiest guy in town. There was hardly an organization whose board didn't include Vinnie—the local Rotary, the local amateur theater, the local advocacy agency for group homes for the mentally disabled—and he was vice chairman of the hospital board and president of the volunteer rescue squad that brought patients to the emergency room. He had a slew of political appointments: to the county board of health, the Pine Barrens Commission, the draft board, and the ferry board—the list went on and on. And for twenty-eight years, starting in 1977, Vinnie Bove was the mayor of Belle Terre. In that capacity, he appointed Seymour chief of constables for Belle Terre. There were few duties and no pay—the main job was signing off on the weekly time reports—but Seymour considered it a feather in his cap.

The men of the After Dinner Club had varying tastes in investments, but the one thing they agreed on was real estate. (Conveniently, the lawyer in the group, John Ceparano, specialized in real estate and zoning matters.) In eastern Suffolk County in these years, farmland was being sold for development at a rapid clip. Seymour put together a deal with Frank, Cappy, Vinnie, and Leo—Seaside Associates, as he dubbed the group in its partnership papers. For a million dollars they bought seven acres of farmland in Riverhead from the Long Island Cauliflower Association, pooling $200,000 in cash for the down payment. It was a smart deal: The property was right on Route 58, a prime location for a pair of office buildings. But Seymour was just as apt to get involved in all sorts of risky businesses, from wine speculation to tanning machines to the chestnut of all dubious deals—Texas oil wells. On this one, his partners were Vinnie Bove and Bob Roth, the neurologist who worked at Mather Memorial. Though his wife was a good friend of Arlene's, Roth didn't like Seymour very much; he thought his life was all about money. But if that's what it was all about, he figured, he must be pretty good at it. Roth wrote a check.

When Seymour told Mike Fox he was putting money into Texas oil wells, Fox just shook his head. "Do you know these people?" he asked. Not the Texas people, Seymour conceded, but the guy who was bringing them into the deal was from Belle Terre. Frank Giuffrida—lives on Fairway Drive and he's loaded. "Don't worry," Seymour said. "We're going down to see the oil wells." He flew to Texas with Bove and Roth, and when they came back Seymour told Fox that they'd signed the deal in a trailer next to the oil rig.

"Was anybody working on the rig?" Fox asked.

"No," Seymour said, "it was at night."

"Oh, okay. Let me know when you get a check."

A month later, Seymour got a check. "*Now* what do you think?" he asked Fox.

"What I think is they're going to ask you for more money on another oil well," Fox told him. "The first check is always a come-on."

A few months later, Seymour sheepishly told Fox that he was right. He, Bove, and Roth lost their money. And Frank Giuffrida? The feds eventually nailed him for fleecing four thousand people out of $30 million in a nationwide tax-shelter scheme. Off he went to federal prison for fifteen years.

*   *   *

AS SEYMOUR CONTINUED on his perpetual quest to build a personal fortune, he took his teenage son along for the ride. Seymour's redrawn will would leave Marty nearly everything he had. In the meantime, Seymour would teach him everything he knew.

Other fathers and sons might go to a ballgame together. Seymour and Marty took an accounting course together. Not that they didn't bond over baseball; they did that by going into the baseball card business. Marty devoured magazines, trying to figure out what the next hot card might be, like a stock or a piece of real estate, and Seymour bankrolled his moves. "You could buy a card for half a penny apiece, buy a thousand of them, and then six weeks later all of a sudden the player's a star and they're up to sixty cents," Marty recalled. He put a lot of money into Don Mattingly rookie cards. He had stacks of them in plastic cases. On weekends, he and Seymour would drive around to card stores and collectors' shows, buying and selling cards. Backed by his father, Marty amassed a formidable collection and had a profitable little business. Seymour was proud of Marty, bragging to his friends about what a natural his son was. Eventually they expanded into baseball kitsch—statuettes, plates, posters, and such. Seymour's office was filled with the stuff.

On the card circuit one weekend, Seymour found his latest business opportunity. As usual, his consigliere was skeptical. "He says this guy needs money to buy a complete line of baseball cards for his store," Mike Fox recalled. "He'll lend it to him and he'll own the baseball cards until they're sold. And of course this guy never paid him back a nickel and Seymour winds up with cartons of unsold baseball cards in his garage."

Reflecting years later on his father's seemingly ravenous appetite for new business connections, Marty would see roughly equal parts avarice, vanity, and attention deficit disorder: "I think he liked the fast pace of it. He was easily bored and he liked the excitement of something different. But I also say he was a greedy businessman. He was never satisfied with what he was making. And I think he also got enjoyment out of the power he felt at having control over businesses. There was a level of arrogance that came with that." Of course, in his youth Marty had seen things through a much less jaundiced lens. With everything his father's success had wrought—the house on the water, the cars and boats, the wherewithal to lose thousands at poker without blinking—Marty, at sixteen, was not inclined to judge him.

In his postinsurance life, Seymour spent a lot of time making the rounds, dropping in on Vinnie at his nursery, Cappy at his carpet store, Frank Norberto at his masonry yard. One of his favorite stops was Pete & Al's, a Getty gas station and garage at the corner of Bicycle Path and Route 112. Seymour would bring Marty along, hoping he'd soak up a few things.

He would explain why he'd negotiated a deal the way he had and expound on the right way to do business: There was his way and there was the sucker's way. But sometimes, if Marty paid close attention, he could see hints that his father's bluster was only skin-deep. Seymour loved to regale Marty with tales of his life as a businessman, and one story went back to his days in the family chicken business in Queens. Seymour once met a restaurant owner in Manhattan and persuaded him to stop buying his chickens from his regular supplier and start buying them from Seymour. And then one day Seymour got a visit from a couple of serious characters who came out to Queens to ask him what the fuck he was doing selling chickens in Manhattan. "*We* sell chickens in Manhattan," he was told. "We'll tell you where you can sell chickens, and it ain't Manhattan. Got it?" Marty asked his father what he did. "I stopped selling chickens in Manhattan," Seymour said.

It's a tough world out there, Seymour wanted Marty to know. He had great pride in his son's ambition and the business sense he had shown from a young age, but he worried that Marty was too soft. He thought Frank Norberto might be of some help here. Besides considering him one of the savviest men he knew, Seymour thought Frank was one of the toughest—a real no-bullshit guy, a burly man with the gravelly voice of the Italian neighborhood in the Bronx where he grew up. The pool builder once owned a nightclub. Seymour was always trying to get Norberto to move up to Belle Terre but Frank said he wasn't a North Shore guy. He wouldn't even go up there to play cards. "There's a lot of people up there pretending," he said. "I play cards with working people." Seymour and Frank were talking about buying some land out east and building a shopping plaza. Seymour wanted to bring Marty along when they went out to look at properties. "I want him to hang around you," he told Norberto. "Maybe you'll rub off on him a little bit."

Norberto understood what Seymour meant. He thought Marty was a nice kid, but weak—physically slight and noticeably passive around his father. The kid seemed a little short on cojones, in Frank's opinion. But he also thought Seymour was at least partly responsible for raising Marty to think life was easy. He remembered the day they came over and Marty wanted the souped-up Pink Panther the minute he saw it parked outside with a For Sale sign in the windshield. Seymour said no, just to tease him, and bought it the next day. Giving your kid everything you never had might make you feel good, Frank thought, but it probably wasn't the best way to toughen him up.

*   *   *

"IT'S NOT THE MONEY—it's the chase," Seymour once told his sister-in-law, Ruth. Of course, as she herself said, Seymour could sell you the moon.

Whatever it was that drove him, there came a point when Seymour crossed a line he couldn't see. His father and uncles had been entrepreneurs who found ways to maximize their profits with ideas as old as capitalism. Sixty years later, Seymour used a tried-and-untrue method of enlarging the pot of money he was receiving from the sale of his insurance business. He took up the ancient practice of usury.

"What you have to understand about Seymour was that he lived for cash," Mike Fox explained. "He hated paying taxes. So he got the brilliant idea that he could deal in cash by lending out some of his money at exorbitant rates of interest. I'm talking about thirty or forty percent. But who's going to pay these rates except desperate people? People who need money to keep their businesses going but can't get it from the bank. So first of all Seymour becomes a part owner. 'Now we're partners,' he would say. 'I own fifty percent. And you're going to pay me x dollars on my investment every week, in cash. And at the end of the year if there's any profit I get fifty percent.'"

Seymour wouldn't argue if you called him a loan shark. When you're charging 30 or 40 percent interest and calling it *vig*, calling it *juice*, you're not pretending to be anything else. Apart from any ethical or even legal considerations, Seymour's plan struck Fox as unwise from a strictly business point of view. "I used to say to him, 'Seymour, how do you know you're going to get your money back?' 'I'm on it,' he would say. He would go around collecting, and if anyone gave him trouble, he had the Hammer Clause."

In Seymour's philosophy of negotiation, a compromise was when the terms were less one-sided than he'd like. When he called something fifty-fifty, there was likely to be a catch, some proviso that weighed the deal in his favor. And when Seymour was owed money, he expected to be paid—not a minute late, not a penny short. And if he wasn't? The Hammer Clause: It stipulated that he could call in a loan anytime he wanted. So if someone wasn't holding up his end, Seymour could simply demand his money back, immediately and in full. But to Fox it was an illusion: If someone was in such dire straits that he would agree to such onerous terms in the first place, and then couldn't make his regular payments, how on earth was he going to come up with the whole thing all at once? Seymour wasn't the type to do what real loan sharks did in such situations. So he would have to sue people to get his money back, Fox thought, and probably wind up losing his shirt. "But you couldn't tell Seymour that," he said. "He thought he was the best businessman in the world, that when it came to negotiating a deal, there was nobody better than Seymour Tank-leff." In case there was any doubt, anyone who entered his office—say, to play poker—was reminded of Seymour's self-appraisal by a framed sign hanging on the wall behind his desk: NOBODY DOES IT BETTER.

Seymour was so brazen that he thought nothing of playing hardball with people who weren't desperate or naïve—in one case with someone who didn't even want to be in business with him in the first place. Between hands of poker one night, Joe Cecere mentioned that he was about to make a $1.2 million deal for a parcel of land in an area that was heating up. Seymour pounced. He'd love to get in on that, he said. Joe politely side-stepped him but Seymour persisted. "He kept on asking me to get him in-volved in the project," Cecere later said, and he finally relented, just to get Seymour off his back. They shook hands on the particulars, but a few days later Cecere was stunned to receive a contract in the mail that was, as he put it, "a whole different story." The deal was no longer a partnership or even an investment. It was a high-interest loan—with Seymour's famous Hammer Clause.

"He comes to me and wants me to draw up the contract," Mike Fox re-membered. "But the terms were unbelievable. I told him, 'Seymour, you can't get this.' He says, 'Yes I can.' I said, 'If you can get these terms, then there's something wrong.' 'Oh, I hate dealing with you,' he says."

Cecere called Seymour and told him the deal was off—no discussion. Ah, c'mon, Joe, Seymour said, let's have dinner and talk about it. Cecere agreed to dinner, but only in the interest of maintaining the cordiality of the After Dinner Club. "All right if I bring Marty?" Seymour asked. No, it's not all right, Cecere said. They had their dinner and Cecere told Sey-mour, in no uncertain terms: I'll play cards with you, but I won't ever do business with you.

By this time, though, Joe Cecere was the least of Seymour's problems. It was the summer of 1988 and Seymour was becoming consumed by his deteriorating relationship with another of the poker players. Unlike Ce-cere, who had no problem telling Seymour what he could do with his one-sided terms, this man had eagerly taken Seymour's money, and taken some more. He was just the kind of guy Mike Fox worried about.

CHAPTER 10

The Bagel King

IN 1907, THREE HUNDRED Jewish bakers formed a labor union that was to become one of the strongest and most clannish in New York. They were Eastern European immigrants who had arrived on Ellis Island with a product said to have originated two centuries earlier. As legend had it, their specialty was conceived in 1683 by an Austrian baker who fashioned a hard roll in the shape of a stirrup for the king of Poland, a gesture of appreciation for leading his cavalry into Vienna and saving the city from Turkish invaders. Whatever the mythology of its origins, the round roll, hard on the outside and doughy on the inside, was standard fare in the bakeries of Eastern Europe. It was called a *beygl* by the Yiddish-speaking men who made them, a word derived from *beugel,* the German for "ring." The Americanized spelling was *bagel.*

The International Bagel Bakers Union, Local 338, was an insular group that kept its recipe secret and its membership restricted: Only the sons and sons-in-law of members could join the bagel-making fraternity of Local 338. It was so tight that even bialy bakers couldn't get in—they had to form their own local. The union controlled all the bagel bakeries in New York and its members enjoyed benefits other workers could only dream of—pensions and life insurance to go with enviable wages: nineteen cents for every box of bagels they made.

Jakob Fruchtman was eleven when he arrived on the Lower East Side from Austria and began baking bagels in the basement of his family's tenement. It was 1905. Two years later he became one of the founding members of Local 338, and eventually he was elected its president. Bagels became a family tradition. Fruchtman's daughter married Max Steuerman, a Teamster bakery driver from Brooklyn, and the couple had a son named

Jerry, who joined his father when he was a teenager, helping him load and unload bagels from his truck. Jerry got married at nineteen and became a union baker himself, learning the trade the old-fashioned way, as an apprentice. He put in long days in cellars that were so hot that he worked in his underwear. "After work you collapsed dead," he once recalled. "But you were paid well." It was the late 1950s, and the bagel bakers' union was at the height of its powers. A skilled man could earn $500 a week.

Jerry Steuerman was ambitious and headstrong though held back somewhat by a pronounced stutter. In 1963, when he was twenty-four and the father of two, Jerry and his wife, Elaine, moved from Brooklyn to Long Island. They bought a house in the South Shore community of Seaford, and Jerry made plans to open a bagel shop nearby, in Merrick, with his brother-in-law and another partner. It was a bold move. As *The New York Times* noted in a 1960 article, some people regarded the bagel as "an unsweetened doughnut with rigor mortis." So opening a place called Bagel City was something less than a sure thing.

Steuerman wanted to blaze a new trail in another way. Though his family had been intimately involved with the bakers' union since its inception more than fifty years earlier, and though he himself had benefited greatly from its strength, Jerry was determined to open the first nonunion bagel shop in New York. Not only did it mean betraying a deeply rooted family ethic, but it would require him to take on one of New York's most entrenched union locals. The response was swift: Union picketers showed up in Merrick and began handing out free bagels to Jerry's customers. Among those walking, Steuerman later recounted, was his own father. "I understood his position," Steuerman said, recalling his beginnings for a business reporter for *Newsday* in 1986. "He was told he'd lose his pension if he didn't."

The union protesters came every day, and eventually Jerry and his partners gave in and signed a contract with Local 338. But it wasn't the end of their union problems. The bagel bakers were so strong that their contract prohibited owners of bagel stores from using their own ovens. Only a union member could bake a bagel. One day Jerry decided to bake some bagels. One of his union bakers threatened to report him to the union office. Jerry evicted him from Bagel City. This was a mistake. The next day the picketers were back, along with union officials who promised they would be there every day until Jerry Steuerman wasn't. Steuerman's partners told him they were sorry, but he had to go. They offered him a buyout and Jerry reluctantly took it. It was a tough business, bagels.

Jerry had a relative named Marty Schwartzberg, who had a bagel store in a strip mall a few miles away, in North Massapequa. It was called S&S Bagels, for Schwartzberg and his partner, Steve Saperstein. They hired

Jerry to work in their store and eventually allowed him to buy into the business as a partner. In Steve Saperstein's view, Steuerman was a conniver, always looking for ways to pull a fast one. According to Saperstein, Jerry once discovered how easy it was to get stuff for free by applying for credit cards under phony names and simply ignoring the bills. When an investigator from one of the credit card companies showed up at the store, Jerry tried to talk his way out of it. The investigator pointed out that he'd put his actual Social Security number on the application. Jerry agreed to pay the money back rather than face criminal charges.

Saperstein lived out in Setauket, thirty miles to the east in Suffolk County, and in 1973 he heard that a bagel store on Nesconset Highway was for sale. Seeing his chance to work close to home and be on his own, Saperstein sold his share of S&S to his partners and opened for business out east. He renamed his new store Strathmore Bagels, after a trio of upmarket housing developments built in the area by William Levitt's company. Back in North Massapequa, meanwhile, Steuerman and Schwartzberg's partnership quickly deteriorated. "I was getting phone calls from both of them, accusing each other of stealing," Saperstein recalled. "They were at each other's throats." At the same time, he was without a partner for the first time and working ungodly hours. Desperate, he asked Steuerman to join him. In 1974, Jerry became a partner in Strathmore Bagels. The timing was perfect. Setauket was growing and the bagel was booming. Steuerman and Saperstein prospered, though their partnership wasn't easy. Steuerman was impulsive and hot-tempered, especially when he felt wronged, which was often. But his stuttering put him at a distinct disadvantage. "I won every argument because he couldn't get the words out," Saperstein said.

Saperstein got to know Steuerman as only a business partner could, and he was astounded by Jerry's craving of extravagances that were way beyond his means. For a while, Jerry leased a Maserati sports car for $1,700 a month. He bought a hundred-thousand-dollar boat with a loan from a bank, which repossessed it after Jerry failed to make a single payment. "That's how Jerry does things," Saperstein said with a shrug in his voice.

Jerry eventually conquered his stutter, which made him more assertive, though for someone with his scheming inclinations that wasn't such a good thing. Saperstein would invariably hear about his latest scam because nothing pleased Jerry more than bragging about beating some big company or government bureaucracy out of money. When his father-in-law died, Steuerman saw no reason why his Social Security checks had to stop. He told Saperstein that he paid the funeral director $500 to neglect his legal obligation to send the death notification to the Social Security Administration. So the checks kept coming every month, and every month Jerry forged his father-in-law's signature. It went on for a couple of years until the government caught on, at which point, apparently, Jerry managed to avoid prosecution by paying the money back. "Jerry never thought things through," Saperstein said. "So he always wound up getting caught. But somehow, every time he managed to land on his feet."

Steuerman's proudest moment came when he claimed his few minutes of fame as the Bagel Guy Who Fought Wall Street. It was the summer of 1978, and Jerry, a betting man, was all excited about the coming of gambling to Atlantic City. Jerry had never invested in the stock market, but he was bullish on A.C. He went to the Long Island office of Merrill Lynch, Pierce, Fenner & Smith and told a broker he wanted to buy stock in Bally's and some other casino-related companies. The broker told Jerry that the Bally's stock was "pink-sheeted"—it wasn't being traded yet on one of the major exchanges, so investors who wanted the stock had to make bids and wait to see if their offers were accepted. Pink-sheet stocks weren't for novices. They were volatile, and their "bid-and-ask" procedure could be tricky. The broker asked Jerry how high he wanted to go in his bid. Jerry decided $24 a share was his limit and opened an account with $800.

The next day, Jerry was thrilled to hear that Bally's stock had already made a big jump and the price was going up virtually by the hour. But then came the bad news: The broker hadn't bought the stock. He'd bid up to Steuerman's limit but the offer hadn't been accepted. Jerry was furious. He denied he'd put a limit on his order and demanded his day's profit. The broker told him it wasn't possible. Jerry called the Securities and Exchange Commission. Someone there told him his problem sounded like an unfortunate failure of communication between him and his broker. Jerry's temper was rising like the Bally's stock.

On Monday morning, Steuerman called *Newsday*. He was just a humble bagel baker, he said, a small investor getting screwed by Wall Street. And he wasn't going to take it. Come to the Merrill Lynch office in Melville at three o'clock and you'll get a good story. At the promised time, Jerry walked inside the Merrill Lynch office with a brown paper bag and announced a sort of reverse holdup. He dumped $13,000 in hundreds and fifties on the floor and demanded it be invested in Bally's stock at Thursday's price. The manager told Jerry it couldn't be done. So Jerry took a pair of handcuffs from the paper bag and shackled himself to the front door.

For the next hour and a half, Jerry politely opened and closed the door for customers and employees as a photographer took pictures. "At about 4:30 P.M.," recounted the story in the next day's paper, "Police Officer James Galasso used his own key to open the $17 manacles that Steuerman had bought at a police supply store, then replaced them with official police handcuffs. 'There was no problem. He was real nice because he didn't want any trouble,' Galasso said after arresting Steuerman on a charge of criminal trespassing." Steuerman put his thirteen grand back in the paper bag, used twenty-five bucks of it for bail, and emerged from the Second Precinct vowing to shackle himself—hands *and* feet this time—to Merrill Lynch's corporate headquarters in Manhattan. The next day he drove into the city and managed to get a meeting with Merrill Lynch's vice president for litigation, though only after promising no more publicity stunts. They haggled awhile, and when the Merrill Lynch man raised his offer to $2,400—contingent on Steuerman promising to take his future business elsewhere—Jerry accepted. He took the check directly to E. F. Hutton and invested it in casino stocks.

IN 1978 the Steuermans moved to Suffolk County. Jerry and Elaine had four kids, so they needed a decent-sized house. Jerry went to a real estate office in Port Jefferson and said he was interested in the community of Belle Terre. An agent named Lee Ekstrom, a doctor's wife who had just gotten her real estate license, took him on a tour. Jerry regaled her with stories along the way. "When my grandmother died, my grandfather disappeared for three days," he said, apropos of nothing. "We thought maybe he killed himself out of grief. But then we found him holed up in his mistress's house!" Ekstrom hurried the tour along. "I really thought at one point, 'Should I just jump out of the car?'" she said later. "I just wanted to get rid of this guy."

The Steuermans couldn't afford Belle Terre and so they wound up renting a house just to the east, on the only road on a narrow spit of land called Cedar Beach, in the hamlet of Mount Sinai. Their home was a driftwood-clad house, the kind usually associated with weekends and vacations. Their backyard was Long Island Sound and a stretch of rock-strewn beachfront, with the cliffs of Belle Terre sitting enticingly off to the left.

In 1980, Steve Saperstein decided he'd had enough of bagels and sold his share of the business to Steuerman. It proved a major turning point for the Steuerman family. Running the business without a partner for the first time, Jerry was joined by his wife, who rose at four in the morning seven days a week, and their children, who joined them on weekends. "We're all born bakers," Jerry said. He opened new stores and expanded into a wholesale trade. By the middle 1980s the Steuermans owned two busy retail shops in adjacent, upscale communities, Stony Brook and East Setauket. They had interests in three other stores and supplied bagels to two major supermarket chains and to wholesalers that sold baked goods to diners, delicatessens, and institutions. Every week, the Louis Hackmeyer Flour Company of Queens delivered twenty-five tons of high-gluten flour to Jerry Steuerman's bagel bakeries. Jerry bought a $14,000 mixer to stir the flour with water, salt, yeast, and malt to make the dough. To roll it into bagels, he went for the Excalibur, a $26,000 apparatus that churned out 3,360 bagels an hour. His five large-capacity ovens—$20,000 apiece—each baked fifty dozen bagels at a time, and Jerry ran them twenty-four hours a day. By 1985, he was turning out 300,000 bagels a week and bringing in $3 million a year. Jerry anointed himself the Bagel King of Long Island.

Jerry may have been born to bake, but long gone were the days of laboring in his underwear in front of searing ovens on the Lower East Side. He made the rounds of his bagel kingdom "watching, yelling, and screaming," as he once put it, and presided over the flagship—a 3,500-square-foot emporium of bagels and deli specialties. He drove expensive cars—a Cadillac one year, a Ferrari the next—and dressed in a manner that he apparently considered befitting a bagel *macher:* open-collared shirts with gold chains strung around his neck and, in winter, a long fur coat. He wore a large gold ring with a floating diamond and covered his bald pate with a curly brown hair weave that required regular "servicing" by Hair Club for Men. When he wasn't making bagels, he could often be found making bets. He loved it all—high-stakes poker, trips to Vegas and A.C., and especially the ponies. He didn't just bet on them—he owned a few, trotters he raced under the name Strathmore Stables.

PEOPLE CAN GET attached to their bagel stores, and such was the case with Seymour Tankleff and Strathmore Bagels. Seymour being Seymour, he would kibitz with the owner of the place whenever he came in. Steuerman had pictures of his racehorses on the walls, and this got them talking about the track, gambling, money, business. Seymour, naturally, was curious about Jerry's operation. How much did that dough-rolling machine set you back, he'd want to know, and what about those ovens? What's your profit margin on, say, a poppy seed with scallion cream cheese? Jerry was only too happy to share the particulars. Not every bagel man could afford an Excalibur rolling machine. The Bagel King could, and he was proud of it. Seymour was fascinated by the numbers—five ovens, five racks apiece, ten dozen bagels a rack. That's two hundred and fifty dozen bagels an hour. A lot of bagels, and a lot of cash. Before long, Seymour had a new friend and a yen for the bagel business.

Seymour and Jerry seemed cut from the same cloth. They were hard-nosed, self-made men whose elders came from another continent and another century and established themselves in the commerce of hard-scrabble, immigrant New York—Jerry's people with their bagels, Seymour's with their chickens. Like Seymour, Jerry was noisy, brazen, impetuous, overconfident. Like Jerry, Seymour was hyperconscious of money and covetous of status. They both badly wanted people to see them as they saw themselves: as big shots. But Seymour was the much bigger shot. Jerry realized this the first time Seymour invited him to the palatial home he'd built at the cliffs of Belle Terre. It wasn't long before Jerry decided it was time to move. He wanted to live in Belle Terre. He wanted to buy a property there and build a dream house.

Taking another crack at the exclusive community that beckoned across the way, Jerry went to Janette Drexler, one of Port Jefferson's leading real estate brokers. He left a distinctive impression on her, as he had on Lee Ekstrom when she showed him around. "He was very excitable, very edgy—if he was a kid, you would say he had attention deficit disorder," Drexler later said. "He wanted to get into Belle Terre. It was a prestige thing for him. He came in, very bombastic, very full of himself. 'I'm gonna do this, I'm gonna do it *now*.' I showed him a property on Cliff Road and that was it." The lot was an acre and a half bordering the golf course, and Jerry snapped it up for $150,000. He caused a small uproar by showing up at the closing with the whole thing in cash—in a brown grocery bag. "The attorneys just stared at him, they were in shock," Drexler said. "His attorney said, 'I *told* you to bring a certified check.' Steuerman said, 'I didn't have time, what's wrong with cash?' The attorneys didn't even want to look at the money. They were going to adjourn the closing. But I wanted to get it done so I took the cash into the ladies' room and counted it, then I walked over to the bank and got a cashier's check. Oh, Steuerman was a nut job."

Though Seymour and Jerry were alike in ways, there was a fundamental difference in their temperaments. Seymour could be demanding and difficult in his business life, but on the whole he was smiling Seymour, the good humor man. Jerry was quick-tempered and petulant. He had a broad face and droopy eyes that suggested a man who'd never lived a day without discontent. The impressions of the two men were common around town. While Jan Drexler considered Jerry "a nut job," she thought Seymour was "very warm and open, like a big teddy bear."

Much as he tried, Jerry had neither Seymour's unlikely charisma nor his gift for schmooze. These were two of the things most responsible for Seymour's possession of a considerably larger heap of money, and money being the measure they both revered, Jerry was all too aware of the disparity. By his own succinct account, he didn't see himself as Seymour's equal: "He was a multimillionaire. I wasn't." So when Jerry found himself a little behind, it was Seymour he turned to for help.

After buying the land in Belle Terre, Steuerman hired a builder to construct an ultramodern six-thousand-square-foot manse that would stand out to anyone driving on either Cliff Road or the seventh tee of Harbor Hills. But in the spring of 1985, with the cost of construction soaring past three-quarters of a million dollars, Jerry found he couldn't pay the builder. So the builder packed up. It was the latest in a series of problems, financial and otherwise, that had been accumulating in Jerry's life. There was his wife's illness, a chronic pulmonary condition so serious that it put her in the hospital. There was a downturn in the bagel business, a result of poorly managed expansion. There was the effect of Jerry's unrestrained gambling. And there was the trouble with Todd.

The Steuermans' younger son had been a problem nearly all his life, and by seventeen he was using and selling cocaine and marijuana. In the winter of 1983, a customer came into the small office in the back of the bagel store in Stony Brook. "How much blow you lookin' for?" Todd asked. "One g," the guy said, just like the other times. Todd fished a plastic bag of cocaine from his jacket pocket, took a small scale out of a desk drawer, and measured out a gram. "That's one hundred dollars," he said, as casually as if he were selling a baker's dozen and a pound of whitefish salad. "Just call here anytime you want more blow," Todd told his customer before he left. "My father owns this place so it's cool." It wasn't until he received a letter from the Suffolk County district attorney's office informing him that evidence of six felony drug charges was to be presented against him to a grand jury that Todd realized his customer was an undercover cop.

To defend his son, Jerry Steuerman hired one of the most prominent lawyers in Suffolk County. Gerard Sullivan was a former assistant district attorney of local acclaim. In 1974, he prosecuted the most notorious murder case in Long Island history: when Ronnie DeFeo took a shotgun and killed his mother, father, two sisters, and two brothers. The case went on to inspire "The Amityville Horror"—the books, the movies, the myth—and made Gerry Sullivan's career. Sullivan had since left the DA's office and opened a law practice with another former prosecutor—Tom Spota. As defense attorneys in private practice, Sullivan and Spota were now handling more prosaic criminal matters than those of their glory days as young homicide prosecutors. Cases such as Todd Steuerman's arrest for selling cocaine to an undercover cop. Sullivan thought he could keep Todd out of jail by making the case that the boy had long-standing psychological problems. He sent him to see Dr. Harold Zolan, the forensic psychiatrist he'd used as his expert witness when Ronnie DeFeo's lawyer tried to go for the insanity defense.

"He is not a very prepossessing looking youngster," Zolan wrote of Todd Steuerman in his report to Sullivan, noting that after ten sessions with the young man he'd never seen him without a baseball cap. Todd explained that his brain would become "fuzzy" if he didn't wear a cap and he would make "all kinds of mistakes." Todd's records showed he was once classified as having "borderline intelligence" and was virtually illiterate. At restaurants, he told Zolan, he always ordered steak because he couldn't read the menu.

"He works at one of his father's bagel stores and allegedly is the 'manager,'" Zolan wrote. "However, during my most recent contact with him, on October 26, 1983, he indicated that during the preceding week he and his father had barely talked to each other because he had painted the store while it was open and the Board of Health apparently cited them for the odor. This naturally resulted in the father being angry." As "hostile and negativistic" as Todd was toward his family, he worked hard for the acceptance of outsiders. "His over-weaning motivation is to get people to like him and approve of him," Zolan observed, noting that Todd twice showed up for his appointments "with large quantities of bagels and on one occasion accompanied the bagels with approximately 10 different flavors of cream cheese." It seemed to Zolan that Todd tried to buy friends, "whether it is with cocaine or bagels."

After three months of sessions, Zolan found Todd to be chronically depressed and withdrawn. Clearly sympathetic to Todd as well as his family, Zolan concluded six pages of reports by saying that jail would be counterproductive. Sullivan sent them to the assistant district attorney, who agreed to a deal: five years' probation and both psychiatric and substance-abuse counseling. Lucky as he was to avoid jail, though, Todd considered living with his family only a slightly better alternative. He spent several nights a week in a motel so he could be away from them, and asked his father to build *two* houses on the property in Belle Terre, the second one a small residence for him.

Steuerman was in such dire financial straits that he was having trouble building even one house. In the spring of 1985, he needed a quick transfusion of cash to get his contractor back to building his dream house. He and his wife added $249,000 to a bank loan they'd taken the previous summer, consolidating the two into a single debt of $325,000. But it wasn't enough. Overextended and mortgaged out, Jerry asked his friend Seymour Tankleff for a loan. Turning friends into business associates was practically Seymour's policy, and a pairing with someone like Jerry Steuerman was all but preordained to involve money changing hands. How much do you need? Seymour asked. Two hundred thousand, Jerry said.

Seymour laid out his usual terms, and then some. There was the absurdly inflated interest rate. There was the obvious requirement that the loan was to be repaid in cash—fifteen hundred a week, every week, which would be barely enough to cover the interest. And there was, of course, the Hammer Clause allowing him to call the loan any time he liked. But that wasn't all. Seymour wanted a half interest in one of Jerry's stores, the Bagel Factory in Stony Brook. And if the bagel store grossed at least $20,000 a week, Seymour would get half the profits. Jerry accepted all of Seymour's terms.

Mike Fox didn't like the deal when Seymour told him about it: A guy so desperate to borrow money under such oppressive conditions was a guy who couldn't be trusted to pay it back. "And where's the bank in this?" Fox wanted to know. "He's got to pay them first or they'll foreclose. And then where will you be?" When Fox did a record search, he found virtually nothing in Steuerman's name. The deed and mortgages on the Belle Terre property listed only his wife.

Fox also reminded Seymour—in case he didn't realize it—that the money he was lending out, to Steuerman and others, was from the principal payments Tom Ness and his partner were making for their purchase of the insurance agency. In effect, Seymour was taking the business equity he'd built for thirty years and tossing it into the wind, hoping more money would fall from the sky. That Seymour would hold half a bagel store as collateral didn't persuade Fox that this was a good way for him to invest his money. But Seymour's money it was, and Fox had long since given up trying to tell him what to do with it. It was a kind of dance they did: Mike would point out the problems and Seymour would tell Mike he had everything covered. Mike would say he shouldn't do it and Seymour would tell him he worried too much. Just draw up the contract. And Mike would finally say, Okay, Seymour, but don't say I didn't warn you. On May 2, 1985, Seymour wrote his new partner a check for $200,000.

Over the next few months, Fox was pleased to hear that Steuerman was making his payments, in cash and on time. Seymour, meanwhile, made himself at home at Jerry's bagel store. He'd stop in just about every day and go behind the counter for a nosh, and he relished telling people about his latest business adventure. "Hey, brother-in-law, I'm in the bagel business," he said over the phone to Mike McClure. "Just don't eat all the profits," Mike told him. It was also an opportunity for Marty: At fourteen, he had his first real job, working in the bagel stores on weekends. But mostly, of course, Seymour was happy about the money. "Happy as a pig in shit," Ron Falbee said, "because he's got all this cash coming in."

Jerry was happy, too, all things considered. Work resumed on the house on Cliff Road, and he was solvent, more or less, for the moment. And though the provisions of their business deal were hardly terms of endearment, Seymour and Jerry had the look of two men forming a close friendship. It was as if money were the lifeblood of their relationship, and the more it flowed between them the closer they became. Eventually Jerry brought Seymour into his hobby business, owning harness racehorses. "What the hell are you doing in quarter-horse racing?" Mike McClure asked Seymour, who blithely conceded he didn't even know what a quarter horse was. Seymour never ceased to amuse his brother-in-law.

Steuerman made Seymour and Arlene the proud half owners of a pair of standardbred three-year-olds named Ali Khan and Precious Cammy, which together cost about $35,000. They stabled them near the harness track at the New Jersey Meadowlands and Jerry registered the horses under his corporate name, Strathmore Stables. For Arlene, owning racehorses became an outlet for her intensely competitive nature. Harness racing had a deserved reputation as a sport of cheats, so Arlene had plenty to feed her suspicion that when her horse lost it was because the race was fixed. Seymour, meanwhile, didn't much care whether his horses won or lost, or even whether he made money on them. "He just liked to be able to go to the track with Arlene and sit in the owners' section like a big shot," said Mike Fox. Seymour tried to get him to go to the track with him, but Mike wasn't interested—he didn't like horse racing and he didn't like Jerry Steuerman. But another member of their original golf foursome, Paul Lerner, came several times with his wife, Myra. It was at the Meadowlands, one night in the spring of 1987, that the Lerners had a memorable first encounter with Steuerman. By this point, his wife's illness was so serious that she was too weak to go to the track. When Jerry showed up with another woman, not for the first time, no one was more offended than Arlene, a woman easily irritated by the shortcomings of men. "You fucking bastard," she told him, and left the table.

Jerry made no secret of his image of himself as a ladies' man. He seemed sincerely proud to say he had been married to the same woman for twenty-nine years and yet never considered himself out of circulation. Steve Saperstein remembers that Steuerman habitually even went after teenage girls who worked at the bagel stores: "I had a sixteen-year-old come to me crying. He tried to deny it but I said, 'Jerry, I don't want to hear any excuses. I know you. You just can't do that.' I used to say to him, 'One of these days you're gonna get yourself shot—not by a jealous husband but by an irate father.'" In fact, in 1976 a bullet came through the store's front window and lodged in Jerry's chest. The police never solved the case: Jerry Steuerman was the kind of guy who always seemed to have somebody mad at him. And he always seemed to land on his feet: He left the hospital with a scar across his chest that he found useful.

Early in 1986, Seymour asked his fellow After Dinner Club members if he could bring his friend Jerry into their Tuesday night poker game as an alternate. Jerry was honored to play in such esteemed company. "It was all multimillionaires, let me tell you," he once said. "It was a choice game." Jerry played when there was an open chair, and eventually, to his delight, he was accepted as a full-fledged member. One night he opened his shirt at the table, proudly revealing his scar, leaving the story somewhat mysterious. Once Jerry joined the poker game, it was a rare Tuesday when Seymour left with empty pockets, regardless of how he did at the card table. He told Jerry to bring his weekly cash payments to the game and pay him at the end of the night.

Seymour's loan kept Jerry afloat, but only for so long. In the early spring of 1986, eleven months after he borrowed $200,000, Jerry asked Seymour for another $150,000. Mike Fox, once again, advised against it. "This guy kept borrowing money at these exorbitant rates of interest," Fox recalled. "To my mind, this is a house of cards. It's got to come tumbling down somewhere." Seymour, of course, ignored Fox. He told Steuerman he'd lend him the $150,000, but he wanted a larger stake in the bagel business: a half ownership of Jerry's other store—his flagship Strathmore Bagels in East Setauket. The deal also increased Jerry's weekly payment obligation to $2,500. Fox prepared the papers for the second loan as he had the first. And two months after that, there was yet another deal. Feeling his oats as a bagel partner, Seymour went in with Jerry on a new store, in Nassau County. Seymour supplied the entire $179,000 start-up cost. Jerry's contribution was his know-how, along with a $50,000 note. They named the store T&S Bagels, and Jerry's twenty-five-year-old son, Glenn, got it up and running, coming to work each day on his Harley-Davidson. Nine months later, they sold the store for a little more than $200,000. All of it went to Seymour, who got his money back, with a modest profit. But under the terms of the deal, Jerry found himself still owing Seymour $50,000.

As the deals piled up, Steuerman seemed oblivious to his own recklessness. If he felt in any way abused by Seymour, he didn't show it. Seymour's loans were allowing him to finish building his millionaire's house. But he couldn't ignore the pressure that was building. In addition to all his other obligations, Steuerman had to come up with nearly $11,000 a month just to cover the interest on the money he owed Seymour.

Steve Saperstein was six years removed from his partnership with Steuerman by this point, but one day he ran into a mutual friend who told him how weighed down Jerry was by his obligations to Seymour, and how upset his wife was about it. "Jerry was paying Seymour twenty-five hundred a week in juice," Saperstein said. "Elaine told Jerry, 'This guy is killing us.' She wanted him to get this burden off their backs." Jerry himself later told Saperstein that he wouldn't have been able to make his payments if not for the money he won at the weekly poker games. Was Jerry that good a poker player? "No," said Saperstein. "The other guys were that bad."

Steuerman was so cash poor that even after he and his family finally moved into the house on Cliff Road in early 1987, his contractor had to win a court judgment to get his final payment of $62,861. The Steuermans needed yet another loan, but they were already in so much debt that the only institution that would extend them credit was a commercial lender that charged them an interest rate of 16.5 percent. It was way above the national average of about 9.5 at the time, but a bargain compared to the rates Jerry was paying the Bank of Seymour. On April 13, 1987, State-Wide Capital issued a check for $110,000. Once again the loan was put in Elaine Steuerman's name only.

Two months later, Elaine died. And a few months after that, in the fall of 1987, Jerry moved out of the house on Cliff Road. After going into tremendous debt to build it, he lived in the house for barely a year before selling it at a loss of more than $300,000. When Leo Sternlicht, the Ford dealer, heard Jerry had it on the market for only $600,000, he offered to buy it on the spot. But Jerry told him he was too late; he'd already sold it—to a Pontiac dealer. It was indeed a house of cards. Steuerman, his divorced daughter, Bari, and her five-year-old son moved in together in Old Field, on another neck of land about fifteen minutes west of Belle Terre.

And still, Jerry owed money everywhere. In the early part of 1988, creditors of every variety were closing in with lawsuits and court judgments. Jerry hadn't paid for his wife's anesthesia—or her funeral. He owed three different casinos in Atlantic City more than $9,000 each. Even one of the other poker players, Cappy Capobianco, had to go to court to get Jerry to pay him for the $4,100 worth of carpeting he'd put into the house on Cliff Road. And the Suffolk County Department of Finance and Taxation was after him for $141,863.

Inevitably, early in 1988, Jerry Steuerman began having problems paying his largest creditor of all.

CHAPTER 11

Squeezing Jerry

FOR A FELLOW who was supposed to be famously unaccommodating with people who owed him money, Seymour Tankleff didn't seem overly concerned when Jerry Steuerman first told him he needed a little breathing room on his weekly payments. Maybe it was that Jerry had kept up for more than two years. Maybe it was a real affection for Jerry. Or maybe it was that Seymour was not so ruthless after all. Whatever it was, when Jerry asked if he could lower his weekly payments for a while, Seymour let it slide.

Not for long, though. When Seymour settled for only two of Jerry's four payments for the month of May 1988, Arlene stepped in. She told him he had to put a stop to it. He had to come down hard on Jerry before things got out of hand.

On the golf course with Mike Fox and Ron Falbee one day, Seymour confided that he was having some problems with Jerry Steuerman. Hearing this, Mike pounced. "I told you not to trust that son of a bitch!" Ron recalled, "Mike was really riding Seymour. He didn't like Steuerman, didn't trust him at all." But it was one thing for Seymour to say he was having a problem with Steuerman. It would be quite another for him to admit he couldn't handle it. On the way to the Meadowlands one night, Seymour mentioned the situation to Paul Lerner. Seymour didn't appear too concerned, though, and when they met Jerry at the track and sat down for dinner, Seymour seemed to be taking matters in stride. "What have we got in the horse account—fifteen thousand?" he asked Jerry. "I'll take the money from there and then you can pay it back into the account when you can." Jerry liked that idea.

The next time he went to the track, a couple of months later, Paul found Seymour alone. "Where's Jerry?" he asked.

Seymour said Jerry wasn't coming. They were barely talking. Jerry was still behind in his payments, Seymour told Paul, and then he had pulled a maneuver that Seymour couldn't believe. A horse trainer had come to him and asked him to invest $30,000 in a yearling he wanted to buy. "So I told the guy I don't do anything without discussing it with Jerry," Seymour told Paul. "And he tells me Jerry already put up his thirty thousand!"

"When he heard that," Lerner recalled, "Seymour went kind of bananas. Here Jerry owes him so much money and he's putting up thirty thousand dollars for a yearling."

And then came the day Seymour went to the bagel store, asked where Jerry was, and was told, "He's at the new store."

New store? What new store?

As Seymour learned, Jerry was in the process of opening a bagel store in Lake Ronkonkoma for his son Todd to run. Apart from Jerry's recent delinquency on his loan payments, Seymour regarded the move as a cardinal violation of his personal code of business practice. "Seymour had a philosophy," Mike Fox explained. "If you were his friend and you were doing business with him, anything you did he was your partner, automatically. You couldn't go without him anymore, or at least without giving him an option. He even tried to do it with me. But I could control him. If I didn't like the deal, I could tell him to shove his terms up his ass."

Seymour confronted Jerry, igniting a furious argument that employees and customers overheard. "For the first time," Fox said, "Seymour was worried for his money." But not nearly as much as his one true business partner. Arlene was worried, and angry—not just at Steuerman but at Seymour.

Arlene and Seymour found it especially infuriating that Todd was involved. It had been nearly five years since Todd's drug conviction, and his probationary period was winding down. But in certain circles, it was common knowledge that he had become a far more serious drug dealer in the years since Gerry Sullivan had spared him a jail sentence. Young people would frequently leave his father's bagel store in Stony Brook with small plastic containers holding little heaps of a white substance that wasn't cream cheese. Was Jerry involved in his son's side business? Was this why he wanted to set up an outpost of the family business for Todd, of all his children? Seymour shared his discovery with Mike Fox, who could do little but shake his head. "You're dealing with shit," Fox told Seymour. "And when you deal with shit, you end up with shit."

Fox wasn't the only one of Seymour's friends trying to help him deal with his problems with Steuerman. Frank Norberto knew Steuerman only by reputation—"He was a chiseler, that was the word on him"—and when Seymour told him what was going on, Norberto had a simple solution. "Just foreclose. Get away from him, end it. You don't need this bullshit. Get it over with." Seymour would have liked nothing more. But as Fox had pointed out on any number of occasions, collecting on debts from someone like Jerry Steuerman wouldn't be easy. Seymour decided to take it a step at a time. The first step: calling the $50,000 note he held from the Nassau County store, the smallest of Jerry's three debts. On June 29, 1988, Seymour sent Jerry a succinct letter by certified mail.

> Dear Mr. Steuerman:
> Demand is herewith made for payment of your note dated June 2, 1986 in the sum of $50,000 payable to the undersigned. Unless payment is made immediately, I will take all legal steps necessary to collect the same.
>
> Very truly yours,
Seymour M. Tankleff

The demand was delivered to the Strathmore bagel store in East Setauket. Julie Mutschler signed for it. Jerry Steuerman ignored it.

THOUGH HE TRIED to expose Marty to his rough-and-tumble world, Seymour was guarded with him about the most difficult business issue he'd ever faced. Marty knew the essentials of his father's deals with Steuerman—how much he had out to Jerry, how much cash he was getting back each week—but there were things Marty didn't know. He didn't know that Jerry's weekly payments were for interest so usurious that they qualified for gangland parlance—the vig. And he didn't know how worried his father was for his money. "My father was a guy who felt nothing would stop him," Marty reflected years later. "He could just look at everybody and say with a straight face, 'Oh, nothing's wrong.'"

So by most outward appearances it was business as usual for Seymour. Even as he fretted over Steuerman, he trawled for new deals. Don Hines, Belle Terre's chief constable, introduced him to a friend of his son's, a personal trainer named Dan Hayes who wanted to take over a closed-down fitness center on Nesconset Highway. Seymour wrote him a check for $50,000 and added another half a business to his grab bag of investments. In late June, in the same week that Seymour sent his certified demand letter to Steuerman, the Fundamental Fitness Center opened in the strip mall adjacent to the one containing Strathmore Bagels. Marty would go there sometimes to work out, but Hayes could see that he was just a dabbler. He set the weights higher when Marty's mother came down.

Early in the summer, Marty started hearing rumblings about his father's trouble with Steuerman. Julie Mutschler told him about the argument she'd overheard between them over Jerry's plan to open a new store. Julie had always found it unusual how much Marty seemed to know about his father's business dealings, so she was surprised he didn't know about this. Marty told Seymour what he'd heard from Julie, and his father told him what was going on. But he assured him he had the upper hand. Jerry Steuerman, after all, was no match for Seymour Tankleff. Marty one day was talking with Frank Perrone, his best friend's father. Perrone was always impressed with Marty's interest in business, and how his father was already taking him under his wing. He liked hearing about Seymour's ventures and asked Marty what his father had going lately—anything new? Among other things, Marty mentioned that things weren't great between his father and Jerry Steuerman. In fact, his father was calling a $50,000 note. Geez, Perrone said, that's a lot of money—how's Steuerman gonna come up with that kind of cash all at once? Marty shrugged. His father wasn't losing any sleep over it.

Marty had more important things to think about himself. Girls and cars and how best to enjoy his summer vacation. There would be driver's ed, days out on the sound in the Boston Whaler, nights hanging out with his friends, and who knew what else. When you're sixteen going on seventeen, anything's possible. There'd be work, too, and Marty was figuring on making enough at the bagel store to pay for all the things he wanted to do on the Lincoln Town Car he'd be driving to school in the fall, after he got his senior license on his birthday, which was August 29. He'd put in new upholstery—black, definitely—maybe give it a paint job. And a new stereo system with dual-control speakers. Not that this would be permanent. Marty was working on his father for something a little flashier—a secondhand Porsche, maybe? Seymour let it be known that he might be open to an upgrade if Marty worked a little harder in school this year, at least until he got accepted to college. In the meantime, for his birthday, Arlene and Seymour were giving Marty something he really wanted: a nose job. Or, as Marty took to telling people, surgery to correct a deviated septum. Seymour had found a plastic surgeon near his old insurance office and negotiated a reasonable fee. Marty would go back to school with a big car and a smaller nose.

Marty was looking forward to his senior year—more precisely, he was looking forward to finishing his senior year. He had never been academically inclined. His teachers and guidance counselors considered him a classic underachiever whose performance in school didn't match his IQ scores. You're such a bright boy, they would tell him—*if only you'd apply yourself.* But Marty was the kind of kid who applied himself selectively, doing well in whatever interested him and letting everything else slide. So he excelled in his business classes, and he wasn't bad in math. But the rest of his grades were mediocre. It didn't bother him, though. With his future set, he thought, why worry about high school—or college, for that matter? Why not go straight into business with Dad after graduation? Out of the question, Seymour would tell him. It was really the only thing they fought about on a regular basis. Sometimes Seymour would use boat privileges as leverage: bad grades, no Boston Whaler. True, Seymour himself had dropped out of college and gone to work in the family chicken business, but that was the point: He wanted better for his son. But Marty didn't see it, and in this, unbeknownst to him, he had an unlikely ally. Before their friendship began to fracture, Seymour would complain to Jerry about his struggle to get Marty to try harder in school. "Seymour, leave the kid alone," Steuerman would tell him. "Why does he need to bother with school? He's got you, he's got millions. Why bother?"

By the end of Marty's junior year, Seymour and Arlene had come up with an idea to get Marty a little more enthusiastic about college. A good friend of Marty's had moved down to Florida after tenth grade and was about to start at Miami-Dade Community College. You can go to school there, Seymour told him. As an inducement, they bought a condo in Royal Palm Beach. Marty liked the idea but still wouldn't commit to it. He really wanted to go right into business with his father. He could see it: Tankleff & Son Enterprises.

One day that summer, Marty and his father went to the high school to make a change in his schedule for senior year. They saw the head of guidance, Estelle Block, a gregarious woman known around town as Cookie and married to a well-known lawyer. After they chatted awhile and took care of Marty's schedule, Mrs. Block asked about Marty's plans for the future. Seymour jumped in, telling her that Marty was very interested in business and would someday take over his various interests.

"And how do you feel about that?" she asked Marty.

"Oh, definitely, that's what I'm going to do," Marty said. "My father's a great businessman." He pointed out that Mr. Stander, the business teacher, frequently had his father in as a guest speaker.

What about college? asked Mrs. Block. Marty said he didn't know yet, but Seymour brought up the Florida plan. "You can go there for two years and prove yourself," he told Marty. "Then you can go to the Wharton School of Business."

Marty said he'd rather just go right into business. His father told him to slow down. "No one becomes a millionaire overnight," Seymour said.

"There's a lot of hard work. You'd have to start at the bottom and work your way up."

"I know that," Marty said. "You know I have no problem doing that."

"It takes a long time. Unless I drop dead." Seymour laughed at his own morbid joke, but Marty didn't think it was funny. "Why are you saying that?" he asked.

"You know I'm not that well," Seymour told him. He turned to the guidance counselor. "I'm taking twenty pills a day," he said.

"Tell Mrs. Block how you eat hot dogs when you're told not to," Marty said.

"I've given up smoking, I won't even tell you what else I've given up," Seymour said. "My one vice is that I eat a hot dog. My son is begrudging me a hot dog. At least it's Hebrew National."

"You're in much better shape now," Marty told him encouragingly. "Just lose some weight and don't eat hot dogs."

Before they left, Seymour reached into his pocket and handed Cookie a pair of passes to his latest enterprise, the Fundamental Fitness Center. "Use 'em anytime you want," he told her.

IN JULY, Marianne and Mike McClure and their daughters, Jenny and Christy, flew in from Northern California for a reunion of Arlene's family. From various points on Long Island came Arlene's sister, her nieces and nephews, and their own children. Ron and Carol Falbee brought their eight-year-old twin girls, Susanne and Carolyn. Ron's sister Joy and her husband, Tom, came with their baby son. Up from Gainesville, Florida, came Arlene's father, Harold Alt. It would be two weeks of sunny days around the pool, jaunts on the Tankleffs' boat, chauffeured rides to the racetrack, the good times recorded for posterity on Joy's video camera: Here's Arlene splashing in the pool with Joy's baby. There's Seymour at the deluxe gas grill—"filet mignon!" he announces, turning to the camera. There's Marty on a chaise longue, squinting in the sun, smiling and waving at the camera, 1950s-home-movie-style. The video betrayed no hint of the tensions radiating from Seymour and Arlene that were to become the enduring memory of a last family gathering.

Ron and Carol felt it the moment they walked into the house the morning after the McClures got in from California. Arriving for a day-long barbecue, the Falbees heard Seymour screaming from somewhere in the back of the house. In the kitchen they found Arlene looking angry and agitated as Seymour continued to yell on the phone in his office, his barks wafting through the solarium connecting the two rooms.

"What's going on?" Ron asked Arlene.

"That son of a bitch Steuerman," Arlene said.

As Ron recalled, "Seymour could be vociferous and loud, but you never saw him get really angry. This was a very loud, very angry, aggressive conversation. And we kind of looked at Arlene, and she started ranting and raving about the problems they were having with Steuerman—all the things he'd done, that he had threatened them, that she was getting very scared about what he was going to do."

Seymour ended his conversation and came into the kitchen. He told Ron that the problems with Jerry had reached the point of no return. "We're getting out of the deal," he said. "We've put up with enough."

Seymour and Arlene tried not to let their problems with Jerry wreck the family gathering, but the subject had a way of coming up—literally, in one instance. One day, Seymour and Arlene and Mike and Marianne went out together to the P. C. Richard store on Nesconset Highway to pick out appliances for the condo in Florida. They were inspecting washing machines when Arlene nudged Marianne and nodded toward a man walking toward them. "That's *him*," Arlene whispered. "That's Steuerman." Marianne registered the image: "Gold chains, shirt buttoned down to here, a little Afro, thick, thick glasses." Mike said later that he thought Jerry looked like a pimp.

"This is my partner Jerry," Seymour said, making the introductions. "And these are my relatives from California, Marianne and Mike." There were awkward hellos all around, then Arlene said it was time to look at the refrigerators. Afterward, the couples went out to lunch. The subject was nothing but Steuerman. Seymour assured everyone that he was in control of the situation. "I got him right by the balls," he said. "That guy opens a store, I'm part of it."

"We're part of anything he does," Arlene added.

Sitting at breakfast with Mike a couple of mornings later, Seymour was fuming about a conversation he'd had with Jerry the day before. "He wants me to sign over the ovens and the dough machines so he can use them in the store he wants to open for his kid," Seymour said. "Can you believe the balls on this guy? I told him I'm not releasing anything. I told him, '*I'm* your partner. If you're opening another store, you're opening it with *me*.'" At another point that week, Seymour told Mike that Jerry had asked—not for the first time—if he could skip that week's payment. "I told him, 'Don't fuck with me, Jerry. I want my money and I want it on time. I want it in cash at the poker game.'"

Seymour told Mike that he insisted Steuerman bring the money to the poker game. He knew it irritated Steuerman to be paying him in front of the others. Mike didn't understand why Seymour seemed so intent on exacerbating the tensions. Once during the visit, Seymour got off the phone

Father and son, 1971:
Martin Harold Tankleff
was adopted at birth and
named for Seymour's late
brother.

Adopting Marty made Arlene a mother at last.

To Marty, his childhood
was nearly perfect.

Clockwise from above: Arlene and Seymour
not long before their murders; Marty in his
senior high school portrait, taken that summer,
and with his mother the previous winter.

With his half sister, Shari,
at his bar mitzvah at Harbor
Hills in 1984.

The rear of 33 Seaside Drive, shot from a police helicopter over Long Island Sound the winter after the murders.

The two crime scenes (above and right): After hosting the poker game in his office, Seymour was attacked while sitting behind his desk. Arlene was murdered in the bedroom at the other end of the house. (Suffolk County Police Department photos)

0739 AT SCENE

Son Says Jerry Steuerman
Bagel Guy /Mitchen-Prt-In.
Bagel Business
Mother said Jerry
Would Do - 2 wks ago

Left: Detective Jim McCready (right) briefs his sergeant, Robert Doyle. Above: McCready wrote in his notebook that Marty thought Jerry Steuerman was responsible, saying that his mother had expressed fear of Steuerman two weeks earlier.

After sending Mike Fox away, McCready listens in as Doyle interviews Marty.

At police headquarters, McCready and Norman Rein asked Marty to draw a diagram showing the position of his mother's body. After his arrest, Marty was photographed as he was that day: zippered sweatshirt, shorts, bare feet. The bloodstains on his front shoulder and upper chest—tagged in the photo above left—played a critical role in the interrogation.

Marty is transported to jail
after his arrest for the murder
of his mother and the attempted
murder of his father.

Deadly Temper Tantrum?

Prosecutors: anger led to son's attack; he pleads not guilty

By Shirley E. Perlman

A Belle Terre youth cut his parents' throats and bludgeoned them with a barbell because they had spoiled his summer and would not let him stay home alone when they took a planned cruise and vacation in Florida, prosecutors said yesterday.

"It was a temper tantrum that turned into violence," said Assistant District Attorney Edward Jablonski, chief of the Suffolk County homicide bureau. "He's a boy that had everything in life and thought he deserved more," he said.

Martin Tankleff, 17, pleaded not guilty to charges of second-degree murder and second-degree attempted murder before District Court Judge Edward Green in First District Court, Hauppauge, in the death of his mother, Arlene, 54, and the wounding of his father, Seymour, 62. Officials said Tankleff was being held in Suffolk County Jail last night under a suicide watch.

Defense attorney Robert Gottlieb said prosecutors do not have a strong case. "There is a great deal more to this case before this issue is finally resolved," he said.

Police responded to a 911 call from Martin Tankleff at 6:14 Wednesday morning. His mother was discovered on the floor of her bedroom at 33 Seaside Dr., a sprawling waterfront ranch home with sweeping views of Long Island Sound. She was pronounced dead at the scene. Police said that her throat had been slit and that she had been bludgeoned with a blunt instrument — later identified as a barbell — and stabbed.

The father was found in the den on the opposite side of the house suffering from blows to the head and a cut throat. He remained in critical condition last night at University Hospital at Stony Brook. The bodies were discovered three hours after family friends had left the house following a weekly poker game.

During the tense arraignment yesterday, Jablonski said Tankleff planned the attacks to the point that he "purposely was naked when he committed the crime so he wouldn't get any blood on his clothing."

The youth washed the knife and the barbell, Jablonski said, adding, "He left the knife on the kitchen table next to a watermelon" so that police wouldn't suspect that it was the murder weapon.

Jablonski said Tankleff "was an intelligent person . . . and he committed the crimes for a number of reasons . . . He was angry at his parents." He did not elaborate in court.

But in a later interview he said Tankleff was angry because "they spoiled his summer, restricted the use of a Boston Whaler in the driveway . . . and made him drive a '78 Lincoln to school as opposed to another car, a newer Lincoln" or the family Cadillac. Tankleff also was angry about his parents' plans to go

away and leave someone to stay with him, Jablonski said. "He thought he could stay by himself." The youth also told police that his parents were having marital problems and that he felt they were asserting themselves through him.

He also said the father had been angry at Tankleff Tuesday night because the youth had not set up the card table for the poker game before going to the mall.

Yesterday, clad in a white prison jumpsuit, Tankleff stood with head bowed as Green rejected arguments for reasonable bail.

"There is an allegation that he committed these crimes," Gottlieb said before a hushed courtroom packed with spectators. "There is no written state-

Newsday / Cliff De Bear

Martin Tankleff, right, is arraigned on murder and attempted murder charges yesterday. With him, from left, are his half-sister, Shari Rother, her husband Ronald, and defense attorney Robert Gottlieb.

ment, no signed confession, no videotaped confession."

But the judge, noting the "serious nature of the crimes," ordered that Tankleff be held without bail and denied a request by Gottlieb that the boy be allowed to attend his mother's funeral. Last night, Gottlieb said he would ask a County Court judge to allow the boy to attend the services. The defense lawyer, who also was critical of the police investigation, asked Green to instruct Jablonski to preserve all original police notes and tapes on the case.

Among those in cou. were Tankleff's two uncles, a half-sister, Shari Rother, 40, and her husband, Ron-

Please see TANKLEFF on Page 33

The Tankleff case instantly took its place in the annals of famous Long Island murders. As *Newsday* reported, prosecutor Edward Jablonski declared at Marty's arraignment, "He's a boy that had everything in life and thought he deserved more." Defense attorney Robert Gottlieb contended that the police had it all wrong and pleaded with the judge to allow Marty to attend his mother's funeral.

June 4, 1988: Though they were all smiles after their horse's first-place finish, the gulf between the Tankleffs and Steuerman (at left with his future wife, Sharon) was evident. Three weeks later, Seymour took a pivotal step, sending Jerry a certified letter demanding immediate payment of a $50,000 note.

September 8: The day after Arlene and Seymour were fatally assaulted, Steuerman nearly cleaned out the joint bank account he shared with the Tankleffs. He disappeared six days later, but the homicide squad managed to keep the news under wraps for another week.

Newsday
THE LONG ISLAND NEWSPAPER

TUESDAY, SEPT. 20, 1988 • NASSAU   35¢

Jerry Steuerman

MISSING

Partner of Seymour Tankleff, Belle Terre Stabbing Victim, Had Told of Death Threats

Last Seen Wednesday; Car Found, Engine Running, Outside Hauppauge Disco

Page 3

September 30: Tracked down in California, Steuerman was escorted home by (left to right) Jablonski, Doyle, and McCready, arriving at Kennedy Airport to a throng of media.

October 11: Three days after his father died of his injuries, Marty was released from jail on a $1 million bond put up by his family. Left: Flanked by Shari and Bob Gottlieb, Marty read a short statement to the media. Below: The next day, he attended his father's funeral.

RSA 101-103 **POLICE DEPARTMENT**
COUNTY OF SUFFOLK, N.Y.

9/7/88

MARTIN TANKLEFF being duly Sworn deposes AND Says that I AM 17 years Old having been born on August 29th, 1971 in Brooklyn N.Y. I Live AT #33 SeASide Drive Belle Terre. I'm a Senior in Port Jeff High School.

I have been Advised of my Rights As Follows.

I Know that I have the right to Remain Silent.

I Know that Anything I Say Can and Will be used against me in a Court of Law. I Know that I have the Right to have AN Attorney Present Before or during any Questioning. I Know that if I Cannot afford to hire AN Attorney one will be Furnished For me Free of CHARGE.

I UNDERSTAND each of the Rights Detective McCready has explained to me. I do Not WANT to Contact AN Attorney. Having my Rights in mind I WANT to Tell Detectives McCready AND Rein what happened to my PARENTS this morning.

Yesterday I WENT to the mall shopping. I was supposed to be

RSA 102
POLICE DEPARTMENT
COUNTY OF SUFFOLK, N.

2.

home eArly enough to Set up the CArd Table For my Father AND his Friends. When I got home about 9:10 pm my mother was MAD AT me because I didn't do it. My Father Punished me mostly But my mother had been Siding with my father Lately. I was Hngry Because my Father's PARTNER Don Hays was going to stay with me when they WENT to Florida in October. they Ruined my Summer by Not Letting me use the Boat as much as I wanted. they WANTED me to drive the Crummy old Lincoln. they were Fighting Alot AND Taking it out on me. when my mother Sided with my Father About the CARD Table I was ReALLY MAD. I decided I WANTED to Kill them Both. I Set my AlARm For 5:35 to MAKe Sure I Would be up before them. I decided to use the BARBell when I WENT to Bed. When I got up I was Surprised to See the lights still on. When I looked in my PARENTS Room my mother was there. she was sleeping. I WENT down to the office AND Saw my FATHer sleeping in the Chair. I decided to Kill my mother First. I Ran Across the Bed. I got to her Quick.

RSA 103
POLICE DEPARTMENT
COUNTY OF SUFFOLK, N.Y.

3.

I hit her 4 or 5 Times on the head. she Fought me. I WENT to the Kitchen AND got a Knife. I RAN BAck with the Knife. I Cut her throat. I don't Know how many Times But I STABBed AT her Also. Mostly I Cut AT her throat AND Neck. I Left to

1322 D/sgt Horvath States
Atty myron Fox CAlled - Nothing Further

with Steuerman, furious. Mike had never seen him so exercised. "Seymour, what are you getting so upset about?" he asked. "Are you tired? Just calm down." Seymour told him that he couldn't. Jerry had screwed him in the horse business and now he was trying to screw him again. To Mike, the lawyer in the family, it seemed that these were two hotheads with opposing perceptions of reality. "According to Seymour, if it wasn't for him, Jerry would be nothing. 'Bagel King, my ass,' he said one time. '*I'm* the Bagel King.' And Jerry didn't think he owed Seymour anything. It was two guys with flamethrowers trying to talk."

At lunch one day, Arlene added a peculiar aside to the saga. She told her sisters that Jerry had gone out with several women while his wife was dying—and that he had made several passes at *her* over the previous months. "I told him, 'Why would I go out with Avis when I'm married to Hertz?'" Arlene said, proud of her tacky but effective line. "It really pissed him off. He said, '*I'm* Hertz, and you'll never do better.'" When they talked about it later, Mickey and Marianne agreed that Steuerman had probably come on to Arlene simply to get at Seymour. It seemed to them that Seymour and Jerry's relationship had been reduced to a contest of "who was going to get whom first," as Mickey put it.

And Arlene put herself right in the middle of it. One day she was seething about the poor performance of one of the horses Steuerman had signed over to the Tankleffs in lieu of a loan payment. The night before, the horse had gotten off fast but broke stride, a disqualification in harness racing. Arlene thought the jockey had thrown the race. Her sisters watched in dismay as she and Seymour handed the phone back and forth, yelling first at Steuerman and then at the horse's trainer. "That goddamn jockey pulled on purpose!" Arlene said. Marianne asked Mike if he thought her sister was edgier than usual. Much edgier, Mike thought. They were well aware of Arlene's anxiety about the Steuerman situation, but only later would they come to believe that beneath her tough exterior was real fear. After they returned to California, Arlene persuaded her father to stay the entire month. And Mickey, who lived only an hour away, wound up spending much of the summer. "She was very clingy," Mickey remembered. But the strange thing about it was that it was Arlene more than Seymour who was forcing the issue with Steuerman. She wanted that money back, she told Seymour, and he'd better get it. *She* was bringing down the Hammer Clause this time. On *him*.

DESPITE THEIR festering tensions, Seymour and Jerry continued to play together in the Tuesday night poker games. But as the summer wore on it became apparent to the other players that this was a pair of friends having a serious falling-out. Seymour and Jerry barely spoke to each other at the games, and one day Jerry volunteered to Bob Montefusco that the problem was that he and Seymour had different views of friendship. "Seymour's just out for himself," he complained one morning when Monte came by the bagel store for breakfast. And there was the night, at the poker table, when Steuerman tried to get Frank Oliveto to bail him out.

The orthopedic surgeon had been aware that Jerry owed Seymour a lot of money and that he'd been paying him back at the games each week for nearly two years. "He passed envelopes every Tuesday, full of money," Oliveto remembered. "But now Seymour wanted his money out. One night, we're sitting at the card table. Seymour gets up and Jerry turns to me and says he wants me to go into a deal with him, a cash deal. Whatever he owed Seymour, he wanted me to put up the money. I said, 'Jerry, I'm not into those kinds of deals. I don't invest that way. So no, absolutely not.'"

While Steuerman made no secret of his financial pressures—besides his debt to Seymour, he moaned about the bath he'd taken on his house and talked about being audited by the IRS—Seymour was more circumspect. So nobody knew that Jerry wasn't the only debtor Seymour was worried about. Even as his conflict with Steuerman was coming to a head, he saw another disaster looming—with Tom Ness, the insurance broker who had bought the insurance business four years earlier. Ness and the Lufthansa cargo pilot still owed a sizable chunk of their $750,000 note, and according to Mike Fox, they, too, were starting to show signs of falling behind, maybe even defaulting. Between the hundreds of thousands of dollars he had out to Steuerman and Ness, along with some other failed investments, "Seymour was going downhill rapidly," Fox said, "and he was starting to realize it." Seymour and Jerry, it seemed, were hurtling toward each other from opposite ends of the track.

It's not clear exactly when it occurred, but there did come a point that summer when Seymour seemed to confront his life, when he realized that tossing buckets of cash into a sinkhole of dubious ventures, making dangerous liaisons, and playing loan shark to a gallery of rogues had not been a successful business model. Jerry Steuerman bought into Seymour's image of himself as the quintessential "shrewd businessman," and Seymour's son thought that all he had to do to be wealthy and successful was to be just like his father. But Seymour seemed to finally grasp that it was a charade. He was not a shrewd businessman, and he had nobody by the balls but himself. "Everything I've ever invested in has turned to shit," he told Mike Fox. "I can't even get my business back. I'm sorry I ever sold it." He had a look in his eyes that his old friend had never seen. "Mike," he said, "I don't know what I'm going to do."

Mike didn't know what to tell Seymour. "Even if he could have gotten back in the insurance business," he later observed, "Seymour was not the type who was going to hitch up his britches and go back in there and start working again."

So Seymour reverted to form. Even as he sat amid the ruins of his misjudgments, he looked for new deals, new ways to apply his principle that one man's problem was another man's opportunity. When he dropped by Pete & Al's service station one day and Pete mentioned that they were having trouble negotiating a new lease with the Getty people, Seymour pounced: I'll buy the land and we can be partners. But Getty wasn't selling. No matter. Seymour always had irons in the fire. He and Frank Norberto were checking into the zoning situation on a piece of commercial property in Manorville they liked. And Seymour had hired a land surveyor to move ahead with the office park he and his poker partners had in mind for the cauliflower farm in Riverhead. He and Frank Oliveto had an appointment to meet the surveyor on September 7, the morning after that week's Tuesday night poker game.

MARTY GOT his birthday present a week before he turned seventeen and came home black-and-blue and swollen, nose packed in bandages and ice, eyes red from broken blood vessels. Ruth Tankleff called to see how her nephew was doing, and Marty told her he felt as though he'd been beaten up. "Aunt Ruth, you wouldn't believe what I look like," he said. "Mom didn't sleep at all last night. She was putting ice on my nose all night."

Even through his codeine-induced postoperative haze, Marty couldn't help but be conscious of the agitation that was in the air as the summer drew to a close. But it wasn't until he overheard his father and Jerry arguing one day at the bagel store that he realized how much their hostilities had escalated. It was followed by his mother's expressed fear—after Seymour told her that Jerry had reached across the counter at the bagel store and threatened him—that Steuerman was capable of doing "something terrible." But Marty thought his mother was exaggerating. His father had things under control. A few days before his nose job, Marty went on an overnight fishing excursion with Mark Perrone and his father. Frank Perrone asked Marty if his father had gotten his fifty thousand from Steuerman. No, Marty told him, but he's supposed to get it at the card game next week.

In the waning days of August and into the first week of September, Seymour Tankleff had a number of conversations with people who would remember them vividly—encounters that, considered together, revealed him to be consumed by his distress over Jerry Steuerman, his frame of mind swinging almost on a daily basis, from his usual bravado to moments of genuine fear.

Seymour went to see Frank Norberto one day and told him that he had informed Jerry that he intended to go to the Lake Ronkonkoma store with a Suffolk County sheriff's deputy and take the equipment that belonged to him. Frank thought it was a good idea, but then Seymour said something that he'd not said to anyone else. "Frank," he said, "I'm scared of this guy."

Frank knew that Steuerman had a lousy reputation, but he scoffed at the idea that some bagel guy was making Seymour cower. "What's he gonna do—beat you up?" he asked.

Seymour wasn't comforted. "All right," Frank said, "here's what you do. You call the district attorney and make a report—and you let Jerry know you did that." Frank had friends who were cops, and he knew his way around. The DA's office won't do anything, he told Seymour, but you'll be on record about what's going on. And if Jerry knows that, he won't try anything. Why not the police? Frank thought the district attorney's office had a more serious ring of authority. But Seymour apparently didn't take his advice.

On Friday, August 26, Seymour had a golf date with Mike Fox, and from the first tee, Mike saw that Seymour wasn't his usual garrulous self. They finished the second hole and were waiting at the third when Mike turned to his old friend and said, "Seymour, what's up?"

"Why?" Seymour asked.

"Something's bugging you, what's up?" Fox asked again.

"It's that goddamn Jerry," Seymour said. "I've had it with that son of a bitch. I'm calling in *all* the notes."

Fox wanted nothing more than for Seymour to get his money and run from Steuerman as fast as possible. But he pointed out the obvious problem, the one he'd always worried about. "Seymour," he said, "what makes you think he can come up with three or four hundred thousand dollars just like that?"

"He better," Seymour said.

"Why?"

"Because I know where the bones are buried. And I'm gonna let him know I know unless I get my money back."

Fox didn't have to ask Seymour what he was talking about. It was obvious to him that it was the dope dealing by Steuerman's son, whose prior record would mean a prison sentence if he were to be arrested again. Fox didn't like it. "Now, listen to me, Seymour," he said. "You're playing with dynamite. You understand? Guys like this don't hold still for threats."

"Enough's enough," Seymour said, displaying none of the fear he'd expressed to Frank Norberto. He said he would see Steuerman at the next poker game, at Frank Oliveto's house, and give him a week to come up with the money. That would make the deadline the Tuesday after Labor Day. With Leo Sternlicht going out of town for the long holiday weekend, it would be Seymour's turn to host the game.

"Seymour, I don't know about this," Fox said.

"Don't worry," Seymour said, words Mike had heard so many times before. "I'll handle it."

One afternoon a few days later, around the first of September, the real estate agent Jan Drexler was arriving at Harbor Hills when Seymour rolled up to her on his Vespa motor scooter as he was leaving. She asked how he was doing, and Seymour told her. "Arlene and I are fighting a lot," he said with an openness Jan was accustomed to but a glumness she wasn't. Seymour went on to explain that what he and Arlene were fighting about was Jerry Steuerman. "He owes us money and she's on my case to get it back."

"Steuerman, the guy with the bagel stores?" Drexler asked.

"They're not his bagel stores—they're *mine*," Seymour corrected her.

Drexler had learned long ago that indiscretion was bad for business, so she didn't pry into Seymour's situation, nor did she mention her own peculiar experience with Steuerman a few years earlier, when he'd shown up with a paper bag filled with cash to close on his property on Cliff Road. So neither of them realized the link between them: Seymour was trying to get back the money he lent Jerry to finish building the house on the property whose sale Jan had brokered.

"Well, I hope everything works out," she said, then continued into the club for a meeting on another deal as Seymour scootered down Fairway Drive on his Vespa.

Every Tuesday and Friday, Marie Vieira came to the Tankleffs' house to clean. On September 6, the day after Labor Day, she showed up at the usual time and went through her usual routine, which put her in Seymour's office in the early afternoon, a little after one. Seymour was at his desk, as he often was when Marie came in to clean. The phone rang as she was dusting, she would recall, and Seymour answered it. He was barely past "Hello" when his face became contorted with anger. "I don't give a shit!" he screamed into the phone. "I'm coming tomorrow morning to get my money. So you better have it!"

Marie pretended not to pay attention and continued cleaning. A few hours later, the card table would be unfolded and the men of the After Dinner Club would stream into the room and take their seats for a friendly night of poker that would last into the wee hours of the morning.

CHAPTER 12

A Suffolk County Homicide Investigation

ON THE MORNING of September 7, Detective Charles Kosciuk, the head of the Suffolk County crime scene team, began his initial tour of 33 Seaside Drive at around 9:30, just as Jim McCready and Norman Rein were starting their interview with Marty Tankleff in Yaphank.

Kosciuk had been a member of the Suffolk County Police Department for twenty-three years, nineteen of them assigned to the crime laboratory. The lab was run by the county medical examiner's office, not the police department, but it didn't make Kosciuk any less a cop. He and his fellow crime scene detectives were here to comb every square inch of the Tankleffs' rambling house and the grounds outside, looking for blood, fibers, footprints, anything that might help make a murder case. The buried treasure was a weapon or two—a knife, obviously, but also whatever instrument might have been used to cause the victims' blunt-force injuries.

The doctors who worked on Seymour Tankleff that morning thought he had been hit over the head with a hammer, but by early afternoon Kosciuk and his team were told to retrieve something else: The news from Yaphank was that Marty Tankleff had confessed to attacking his parents with a dumbbell from his room, along with the knife they found on the kitchen counter, next to the watermelon left from the poker game the night before.

The various sections of the crime scene team spent the better part of four days exploring the house. One detective from the identification section shot rolls of film, photographing everything of possible relevance, first in wide views, then close in with identifying tags and a two-inch ruler placed inside the frame. Another man surveyed the house with a video camera. The house was dusted for fingerprints, and the two crime scenes were searched for hair and fiber evidence. In the master bedroom, Kosciuk focused on the bed. Blood was splattered in wild patterns across the sheets and pillows and the comforter, evidence not only of a vicious attack but of a mighty struggle.

With word coming that the victims' son had confessed to washing himself and his weapons in the shower, the crime scene team paid special attention to his bathroom. There were two slightly damp red towels, a loofah sponge, and two shampoo bottles in the bathtub shower. All of it was placed in plastic bags and brought out to the van that would transport it to the crime lab. There was a small amount of water around the drain of the tub, and it was collected for analysis. After everything else in the bathroom was photographed and processed, the crime scene men removed the entire drain assembly from the tub so the lab could take it apart and test it for the presence of blood or human tissue. In Marty's bedroom, they cut out the bloodstained section of wallboard around the light switch.

The second crime scene, the office on the other side of the house, was in a different state of disarray than the master bedroom. There was as much evidence of the rescue squad's frantic work to save Seymour Tankleff's life as there was of the brutal assault that had brought them there. Seymour's large wooden desk was at an angle, moved aside by the first cops on the scene so the squad could do its work. First-aid equipment was strewn about, left behind in the rush to get him onto the ambulance. But the scene appeared somewhat less gruesome than Seymour's wounds might suggest. Most of the blood was pooled on the seat of the swiveling leather chair; it blended with the dark brown leather. Still bright red was the pile of blood-soaked clothes on the floor at the foot of the chair— the underwear and khaki pants that had been cut off Seymour by the EMTs. There were blotches of blood on the carpeting and a few spots on some of the papers spread across Seymour's cluttered desk. Red dots flecked the Supplemental Income page of the Tankleffs' 1988 tax return. Nearby, the poker table remained open, surrounded by eight chairs. On the floor next to one of the chairs was the bag of Pillsbury microwave popcorn Seymour had made for Vinnie Bove. It was fully popped but unopened.

As he took everything in on that first day, one thing was conspicuous to Kosciuk almost from the moment he entered the premises. The two crime scenes were as far apart as two locations could be in this rambling house. And yet there seemed to be no blood anywhere in the hallways or rooms in between. Indeed, with the exception of the smudge of blood around the light switch in Marty's room, the crime scene detectives saw no blood anywhere inside the house other than in the two rooms in which the victims had been found.

*   *   *

ON SATURDAY, after five days of work, the crime scene units packed up and released 33 Seaside Drive to the victims' family. Ron Falbee and Mike McClure went into Seymour's office first. Ron was looking at the papers arrayed on Seymour's desk. "Look at this," he told Mike. In plain sight, right on top, was a copy of the letter he had sent to Jerry Steuerman by certified mail on June 29, demanding immediate payment of a $50,000 note. The letter was flecked with blood.

To Mike and Ron, the letter was significant in two ways. Obviously, it could be used in Marty's defense—a vivid piece of evidence of the pressure Seymour was exerting on Steuerman. But equally revealing was that the police left it behind. Could they have been so careless that they'd over-looked it? Or were they so sure of their case that they considered it irrelevant? Ron and Mike took the letter and gave it to Bob Gottlieb.

Marty's relatives weren't the only people who thought the cops had it wrong. Frank Oliveto didn't get to bed after the poker game until nearly 4 A.M. He didn't operate on Wednesdays, and the only thing he had scheduled for the day was the trip to Riverhead with Seymour to meet the land surveyor at the cauliflower farm. But Margaret Oliveto woke her husband up early after she heard from their daughter Jenny what happened at the Tankleff house. "My first thought was, Oh, my God, somebody tried to hold up the game," Oliveto recalled. "My second thought was that Jerry did it."

Since Steuerman had joined the After Dinner Club a couple of years before, it was the consensus of the other players that he was not like anyone else they knew. Jerry proudly told of escapades like beating Merrill Lynch out of $2,800 and loved making himself out to be a tough guy, showing off his gunshot scar and once claiming to be "an enforcer for the mob." Nobody believed him. But it was the kind of thing they came to expect. Oliveto remembered going with Vinnie Bove to see Steuerman's new house on Cliff Road. "He took out this sawed-off shotgun and he went outside and shot it off. Crazy."

When Oliveto heard about what happened at the Tankleffs' that morning, it seemed to him that Steuerman had to be involved. But then came the news, just hours later, that Marty had reportedly confessed and was under arrest. Oliveto didn't believe it. With everything he knew about Marty, it just didn't make sense. Steuerman—*that* made sense. And he wasn't alone. Later that week, the poker players met at John Ceparano's law office. Ceparano hadn't been at the game that week, nor had Leo Sternlicht. They wanted to talk to those who were there—and those who were there wanted to get together and compare their thoughts about what might have happened after they left. Oliveto and Bove came, along with Cappy Capobianco, Bob Montefusco, and Joe Cecere. The only one not invited was Jerry Steuerman.

There were some things that everyone knew. That Jerry and Seymour's friendship had deteriorated precipitously the last few months. That the bad blood was all about those envelopes of cash Jerry had once passed to Seymour with such regularity. That Seymour wanted his money back and that Jerry had serious cash flow problems. Oliveto recalled the night Jerry tried to get $100,000 out of him. It wouldn't be until much later that Oliveto would learn that even if he'd lent Jerry the money, all it would have bought him was time. Jerry owed Seymour a lot more than a hundred grand.

Maybe they hadn't thought too much about it at the time because Jerry and Seymour had done a decent job of checking their hostilities at the door. And the idea that someone wasn't getting along with Seymour Tankleff wasn't exactly news. Even Oliveto, the most good-natured of the group, found that half the time you loved Seymour, half the time not so much. But now he and the others had to consider their shared impressions in light of the mental image of Seymour lying there in his leather chair with his head nearly sliced off and their last hands still on the poker table a few feet away. Here they had Seymour and Jerry—two volatile guys, one of them known for putting the squeeze on people, the other for trying to wiggle out of his debts. The shylock and the chiseler—not a good combination. To the poker players, everything pointed to Jerry. "We all knew he was capable of doing it," Oliveto said.

So what about Marty? None of the card players could say they knew him really well, but what they did know absolutely didn't jibe with the specter of him viciously beating and stabbing his parents. Not this mild-mannered wisp of a kid. And why would he do it? The stuff the cops were saying made no sense. The players recalled Marty's cameo at the card game, seven hours before he was supposed to have exploded in rage. They saw nothing off. Oliveto was in the kitchen when Marty came in and asked Frank to check out the bruising around his eyes. Oliveto looked him over and said he looked good. Marty smiled and said thanks.

So it seemed that Jerry, more than Marty, had the motive. What about the opportunity? They went around the room, trying to piece together how the game broke up. Cappy quit early, as usual, going home around midnight. Vinnie was the first of the remaining group to leave, three hours later. He remembered stopping in the kitchen and cutting himself a last piece of watermelon on his way out. Then there was Montefusco, the big winner with two grand in his pocket. He remembered that he was making his way from the sunroom to the kitchen when he decided he wasn't ready to call it a night. He went back into Seymour's office to wind down with him, but when he got there he found Seymour and Jerry talking. They weren't arguing or anything, but it was obviously a private conversation, so Monte turned right around and left. But Seymour and Jerry's conversation couldn't have lasted long. Because by the time Joe Cecere came out with Al Raskin, Jerry was sitting in his car. Waiting. Jerry was nearly boxing him in and should have pulled out first. But Jerry waved him around. Why'd he do that? And funny thing: He didn't see Jerry follow him out. Never saw his headlights behind him.

The poker players' postmortem was the first of two gatherings they had in the days after the attacks on the Tankleffs. The second one was organized by Detective Jim McCready, and it turned their perceptions on their head. McCready asked all the players who had been at the game on the night of September 6 to meet him at Vinnie Bove's house. He wanted to fingerprint everyone so their prints could be ruled out when the crime lab compared them with those found on various items in the Tankleff house. But when they met, McCready didn't simply fingerprint them. He hung out, and when Vinnie offered him a beer, he said sure. He drank several, and he drank alone. Between swigs, McCready told the poker players that whatever they thought of Jerry Steuerman, whatever they thought of Marty Tankleff, none of it was evidence. We *do* have the evidence, McCready said, and it comes straight from Marty himself. He told us he did it. He told us how he did it and he told us why he did it, and we've got the physical evidence to *prove* he did it. We've got him six ways to Sunday, so don't waste your time thinking we have the wrong guy. We even know why he picked that night to do it. It was so he could blame Jerry Steuerman.

McCready could be awfully persuasive, especially with people who were not disposed to believing that someone would confess to a horrible crime he didn't commit. Or that a pair of veteran police detectives might fabricate a confession. Or that one of the largest district attorney's offices in the state would throw itself behind the prosecution of an innocent boy. With a personal pitch from Jim McCready, even Frank Oliveto and Vinnie Bove, who had as much firsthand knowledge as anyone, began to think that, yes, Marty must have done it.

This was one case in which the police chose not to interview the victims' relatives, judging them to be adversarial and of no benefit to their case. But McCready and his partner, Rein, did make the rounds of Marty's friends, hoping to pick up some corroboration of Marty's motive for murder. When they paid a visit to the Perrones, the detectives made it clear from the start that they weren't interested in hearing anything about Marty being innocent. He's guilty, and he's going to be convicted. Just ask yourselves this, McCready told them: Why is Marty still alive? Why was he the only one who wasn't touched?

Rein asked Mark if he was aware that Marty and his parents had been fighting a lot about the car and the boat. Mark said no, not that he knew of. In fact, in the two years he and Marty had been close friends, he'd never known Marty to fly off the handle at anyone, including his parents. That just wasn't Marty. Rein showed Mark a photo of the weights taken from Marty's room. Do you recognize them? he asked. Yeah, said Mark, I've seen them in his room. So what? he thought.

McCready and Rein interviewed Zach Suominen, who spent a good part of the day and night before the attacks with Marty, helping him put the new car stereo in the Lincoln and going with him to the mall that night after they kept blowing fuses. Zach told the detectives that Marty was perfectly normal the whole time, but he found them intimidating. "They came out with things before I answered them," he said later. "They were trying to make me see things the way they wanted me to."

Sometimes McCready would go out alone to talk to potential prosecution witnesses, taking along a visual aid to help them see his point of view. Many years later, new investigators would interview old witnesses and discover that McCready showed several of them photographs of the crime scene. It was serious misconduct in any police manual, which McCready well knew and may even have used to his advantage: I shouldn't be doing this, he would confide conspiratorially, so let's just keep this between us. Apparently, they did. It wouldn't come out for twenty years.

At the same time, McCready enjoyed making his case to strangers, as a social activity. On several occasions, Jan Drexler, the Port Jefferson real estate agent, was in a restaurant called George's Handlebar at lunchtime and saw McCready holding forth at the bar. "He was very loud—'I've got that little shit,'" she recalled. "He'd tell anybody at the bar, especially any female who would listen. He was in his glory."

McCready's partner was more circumspect, but he wasn't reluctant to defend his work if pressed. Frank Norberto lived near Norman Rein in Patchogue, and their sons went to school together. So when Norberto saw Rein one day, he wasn't bashful about telling him what he thought: Norm, I know this kid. And I know what his father was going through with Steuerman. And I'm telling you the kid didn't do it. He wouldn't have it in him. But to Rein, Norberto was like the Tankleffs' family. You don't know, he said, you weren't there. We've got the evidence. Hard, physical evidence. It'll all come out eventually. So forget about Steuerman. The kid did it.

Norberto liked Rein, thought he was a good cop and a decent man. But he felt in his bones that Rein was wrong. He was always organizing community fund-raising events and so he decided to get something going for Marty's defense. But almost immediately after he began talking it up around town, he got a visit from a uniformed Suffolk County cop. As Norberto recalled it, the cop, whom he knew, told him, "You got two teenage sons in this county. I wouldn't get involved in Tankleff if I was you." Norberto was hardly a man easily intimidated, but neither was he reckless when it came to protecting his family. His wife insisted he drop the idea for a Marty Tankleff defense fund, and he did. Later, when Norberto finally got a look at the "hard evidence" against Marty, he realized Rein had sold him a bill of goods. After that, Rein refused to talk to him about it.

AT MID-MORNING on the day the Tankleffs were attacked, homicide detectives Robert Anderson and Anthony Laghezza were interviewing Vinnie Bove at his nursery business when Bove got a call from Jerry Steuerman. He'd just heard about what happened, Jerry told Vinnie, and asked what he knew. Bove knew a lot, having arrived at the scene that morning even before the detectives. He started with the most compelling piece of information he had. "I spoke to Marty at the house," he told Steuerman, "and he says you had something to do with this."

"What the hell are you talking about?" Steuerman asked.

"I can't talk to you right now because I've got two detectives here," Bove said. He told Steuerman to hold on a second, and asked the detectives if they wanted to speak to him. One of them got on the phone and arranged to meet Steuerman at his bagel store in East Setauket later in the day. But the detectives didn't make Steuerman a priority: Under instructions from their sergeant, they went to see three other poker players first. Thus began what the police and prosecutors were to describe as their "thorough investigation" of Jerry Steuerman as a possible suspect in the Tankleff murder case.

According to Detective Anderson's report, neither Bob Montefusco, nor Peter Capobianco, nor Al Raskin was aware of any problems between Seymour Tankleff and Jerry Steuerman. "There was no tension between any of the card players to the best of Mr. Capobianco's knowledge," Anderson wrote, "and he didn't notice anything out of the ordinary that night." As far as Bove knew, "there were no known problems between Seymour and Jerry."

The comments attributed to the men, however, did not quite reflect reality. A week later, for instance, Capobianco told Robert Gottlieb's private investigator, Jack Murtagh, that Jerry and Seymour, once the best of friends, had hardly spoken over the last few months. And Bob Montefusco had told others of Jerry's complaint that "Seymour's just out for himself."

But to Anderson and Laghezza, it was a moot point. By the time they called on Steuerman, Marty Tankleff was under arrest and it was the consensus of the homicide squad that the bagel king was a red herring: Marty's accusations were nothing more than desperate attempts to deflect suspicion. Thus Anderson and Laghezza's report of their interview with Steuerman had an air of the pro forma. Sitting at a table in the bagel shop, Jerry described himself as just one of Seymour Tankleff's many business associates. He told the detectives about his partnerships with Seymour in bagels and racehorses—nothing, though, about usurious loans or Hammer Clauses, and no mention of how he'd gotten himself in a bind and swapped half the interest in his bagel business for a fancy house in Belle Terre. Summing up Steuerman's thoughts about Tankleff, Anderson wrote: "He considers Seymour a very shrewd and excellent businessman and was fortunate to be in business with him."

As for the events of the night before, Steuerman confirmed that he'd been the last to pull out of the Tankleffs' driveway after the poker game broke up. He said he drove straight home to Old Field, about fifteen minutes away, and he had a witness. "Jerry said he arrived home at about 0315 hours, and his daughter had to let him in because he forgot his keys," Anderson, apparently on a first-name basis, wrote. "He said he first heard about the homicide when his son called him at about 0900 hours. His son was told about it by Jerry's accountant, one Lenny Lesk, who heard it on the radio. . . ."

The detectives wrapped up the twenty-minute interview by asking Jerry for his thoughts about the Tankleffs. Marty was "a nice kid with no school smarts." Arlene "did not appear to be a very friendly person and the impression she left on [Steuerman] was that of a woman who didn't like men." Overall, though, Steuerman "said he did not pay any attention to the personal lives of the Tankleff family. His relationship with Seymour was strictly business aside from the poker group." Anderson concluded: "Having knowledge of Martin Tankleff's accusations of Jerry Steuerman that he made at the scene . . . it is this officer's opinion and also the opinion of Det. Laghezza, after interviewing Mr. Steuerman, that he should not be considered a suspect in this homicide."

The detectives that first day also interviewed one of Seymour Tankleff's other business partners: Danny Hayes, who was using Seymour's money to operate the Fundamental Fitness Center. He was also the man who was to stay with Marty when his parents went on their cruise in October. Early that morning, Hayes was about to leave for Seymour's house to pick up a $5,000 check when one of his employees came in and told him what she'd just heard on the radio. Unlike the card players, Hayes knew firsthand that Seymour's relationship with Jerry Steuerman was anything but harmonious. Seymour talked to him about it on a regular basis. So when the detectives came to talk to him, Hayes told them about all the money Steuerman owed, about the pressure Seymour was putting on him to pay it back, and about the furious argument the two men had in the bagel store over the summer. He told them that Seymour was upset that Todd Steuerman was selling drugs from the back of the store. And one more thing: "Seymour told me this was going to happen."

As Hayes recalled years later, Seymour was driving him back to the fitness center after they signed their business contract. Marty had come with them and was in the backseat when Seymour started talking about Steuerman with more urgency than before. "He said, 'I want you to realize that a lot of things are going on. It's a bad situation, and if anything should happen, everything goes to Marty. That's why I want him to learn the business, and I want your help with that. And should anything occur, I need you to promise me you'll go right to the police with this and tell them what's going on.' Which I did, and everyone ignored me entirely." Hayes's information was never mentioned in any reports by the homicide squad.

Soon after the detectives left the gym, Hayes had another visitor: Jerry Steuerman. It seemed to Hayes that Steuerman was trying to find out, rather unsmoothly, whether the police had talked to him and, if so, what he had told them. Hayes found the conversation odd—they barely knew each other—and he played it close to the vest. He told Steuerman that he'd talked to the detectives mostly about his own business with Seymour. Then the conversation shifted to the attacks themselves. Hayes said he'd heard from Ron Rother that the doctors at the hospital thought Seymour had been hit in the head with a hammer. No, Jerry told him, not a hammer—"a weight." And his throat was cut. Hayes was struck by how much Steuerman seemed to know. True, the news media were already reporting that the Tankleffs' throats had been slashed and that they had been "bludgeoned." But it wouldn't be until the next day, after Marty Tankleff's arraignment, that prosecutors would disclose the allegation that Marty had attacked his parents with a barbell.

Two days later, Steuerman had a second visit from the homicide squad—this time by Jim McCready and Norman Rein. It was a virtual replay of his conversation with Anderson and Laghezza. Steuerman sat at a table with the detectives, answering routine questions. McCready and Rein apparently didn't ask Steuerman a single question about the half-million dollars they knew he owed Seymour. Instead, it seemed from Rein's page-and-a-half report of the interview that they considered him no more or less important than any of the other card players who'd been in the Tankleff house in the hours before the assaults. Like the others,

Steuerman was asked about when he arrived, who else was there, what they ate, what time the game began, what time it ended. Though suspicions about Steuerman had been coming at the police from all directions since the first hours, the subject warranted only one sparse sentence in Rein's report: "Steuerman said that he is a business associate and friend of both Seymour and Arlene Tankleff."

There was, however, one notable difference between Steuerman's two interviews with the homicide squad. With McCready and Rein, he was considerably more expansive on the subject of the Tankleffs. Indeed, it seems from Rein's account that Jerry was eager to assist the detectives with information that might be helpful to their prosecution of Marty Tankleff, starting with his implication (unsupported by anyone else at the card game) that there had been a coolness between father and son when Marty came home that night. "According to Steuerman, Marty said hello to his father, but it was not like normal when he would stay in the room for about half an hour. There was not the usual exchange of hugs and kisses between Martin Tankleff and his father, Seymour Tankleff." And while he told Anderson and Laghezza that his relationship with Seymour was "strictly business" and that he "didn't pay attention to their personal lives," Steuerman now had plenty to say about the Tankleffs: He talked about Seymour and Arlene's marital difficulties and suggested that their relationships with Marty were thorny. "According to Steuerman, Marty was grounded daily for academic and other reasons," Rein wrote. It was Seymour who did the grounding, while Arlene mostly coddled: She kept Marty from playing sports and said "my baby's staying home with me" when the subject of college came up.

McCready and Rein heard a variation on that theme when they spoke to Julie Mutschler, Steuerman's longtime employee. "She said that he needed a lot of love, hugs, attention, and praise. She stated that Marty was spoiled. He bragged about all the material things he had, but she said they never seemed to be enough, that they were insufficient to give him security. Julie said that Marty did a lot of things with his father. She said that Seymour Tankleff praised Marty to no end, but that she didn't sense that a true warmth existed between the father and son. Mutschler said that the parents did not let Marty do 'boy things' with other kids. Mutschler said that she thought that Marty was trapped by his parents. . . ."

Like many things that could be said about Marty and his relationship with his parents, Mutschler's armchair psychology would have been innocuous under usual circumstances. But they took on dark insinuations with his arrest. More important, arguably, was what Mutschler knew about another relationship—the one between Seymour and Jerry. It was Julie, after all, whom Marty brought up almost immediately at the house that morning, telling McCready he should talk to her because she had seen a heated argument between his father and Steuerman. McCready would later acknowledge that he and Rein did indeed learn about the argument from Mutschler. But Rein's report left out any mention of what she knew about how her boss and Marty's father had been getting along.

Thus did the Suffolk County homicide squad begin and end its consideration of Jerry Steuerman as a possible suspect in the Tankleff case.

ON THURSDAY, September 8, a little more than twenty-four hours after the Tankleffs were attacked and the day between his two half-hour meetings with the homicide detectives, Steuerman went to the Port Jefferson branch of KeyBank. He and Seymour and Arlene had a checking account there for their racehorse partnership. It was a joint account, but Seymour insisted on keeping the checkbook.

Steuerman told a bank teller he wanted to draw cash out of his account but didn't have a check with him. The teller looked up the account. There was a balance of a little more than $20,000. She gave Steuerman a generic check, which he made out for $15,000, payable to himself. He endorsed it and left the bank with an envelope stuffed with hundreds and fifties.

A few days later, Jerry called Frank Oliveto at Mather Hospital and asked a question that stopped Oliveto cold. "Is he dead yet?"

What? No, Oliveto stammered. He reminded Jerry that Seymour was at Stony Brook, not Mather. Well, Jerry said, you must know people over there. Have you heard anything? No, Oliveto told him, he hadn't talked to anyone at Stony Brook. As far as he knew, Seymour was still hanging on. Then he got off the phone as quickly as possible. "I hung up," Oliveto recalled, "and thought, 'Oh boy.'"

Seymour was indeed hanging on, defying the odds with every breath. It seemed that Seymour was exhibiting the kind of stubbornness that marked his conscious life. To the public, the gravity of his condition was assumed but unspecified. Reporters who called the hospital's public relations office for updates were told only that Seymour Tankleff's condition was "critical," and that at the request of his family no other information was being released. But some might have gathered from that week's *Port Jefferson Record* that he had been at least semiconscious that morning and might not be in such grave condition. A police officer who had been one of the first at the scene was quoted saying, "He didn't know what was going on. He was breathing but out of it."

So for all anyone knew, each day that passed without the announcement of Seymour Tankleff's death kept alive the possibility that he might survive another, and then another, until the moment when he might open his eyes and speak. Faint though it might be, the possibility even came up at Marty's first bail hearing, when Ed Jablonski and Bob Gottlieb offered equally compelling versions of the case. Apparently mystified, the judge expressed hope that the police would eventually be able to talk to Seymour Tankleff and clear this whole thing up.

CHAPTER 13

Pistachio

AT 6:15 ON THE MORNING of Wednesday, September 14, seven days virtually to the minute after the attacks in Belle Terre were reported to the authorities, Jerry Steuerman arrived at his bagel store in East Setauket in a sullen mood. He stayed just a couple of hours before driving twenty minutes to Smithtown, showing up unannounced at the office of his lawyer, Michael Grundfast. After a brief conversation that Grundfast found baffling, Steuerman left.

Three hours later, the Suffolk County Police Department's Fourth Precinct received a report from a restaurant called Ribsters. It was next to the Ramada Inn at the intersection of Veterans Memorial Highway and the Long Island Expressway in Hauppauge. Behind the restaurant some-one had noticed a car with its engine running, the driver's-side door open, and no one in sight. The police impounded the vehicle, a 1987 Lincoln Town Car. The plates came up stolen from New York City. The car was registered to Jerry Steuerman. The following morning, Bari Steuerman filed a report with the police. She had not seen her father in twenty-four hours.

Jerry Steuerman was a missing person.

The news triggered a wave of acute discomfort among the detectives and prosecutors who had spent a good part of the previous week promot-ing Marty Tankleff's confession and suppressing any alternative theory of the crimes. They had done a good job: To date, Jerry Steuerman's name had not appeared in the media. Whatever Marty's relatives and the poker players thought, to the general public Steuerman didn't exist. And the au-thorities wanted to keep it that way.

At police headquarters in Yaphank, the homicide squad declared jurisdiction of the missing-person case and scrambled to find Steuerman before the press heard he was gone. "Homicide has no reason to believe that Steuerman's absence is connected with the murder," the missing-persons section noted in the first entry of its running report, adding that according to Sergeant Robert Doyle, "Steuerman has been thoroughly questioned and Homicide does not believe he was involved."

Jim McCready didn't quite agree that Steuerman's "absence" was unrelated to the murder. When word first reached Homicide that Steuerman's car had been found with its motor running in a restaurant parking lot, McCready dashed to the scene. Peering inside the car, he saw a gold bracelet on the driver's seat and a single sneaker on the floor. It seemed just a little too staged. But why would Steuerman flee? McCready thought he knew: Mike Fox paid him to get lost and take the heat off Marty. McCready later said he thought it could be nothing else.

Fully aware of the damage it could do to the prosecution of Martin Tankleff, to say nothing of the embarrassment to the homicide squad, Doyle took the lead role in investigating Steuerman's disappearance. Homicide's commanding officer, Lieutenant John McElhone, and chief homicide prosecutor Ed Jablonski also got directly involved. They put a description of Steuerman on the national missing-persons wire: forty-eight-year-old white male, six feet two, 190 pounds, brown eyes, curly brown hair with beard and mustache, last seen wearing blue jeans, a beige sweater, white Addidas sneakers, with a gold Longines watch and "a gold neck chain with gold bagel."

Doyle, McElhone, and Norman Rein started with Mike Grundfast, who told them that Steuerman had shown up at his office on Wednesday very upset, wanting him to "put his affairs in order." According to Rein's summary of the interview with Grundfast, "Steuerman did not sit down. He appeared to be highly agitated and he stated that he was very upset. Steuerman stated that he received two life threatening phone calls. He told Mr. Grundfast that he had not lived an exemplary life, and he had done things of which he was not very proud. Steuerman stated that the calls were received subsequent to Seymour Tankleff's murder [*sic*]. Steuerman told his attorney that some people in his poker card game believed what Martin Tankleff had said about Jerry Steuerman's involvement in the murder. Steuerman told Grundfast that he was close to breaking down, that he was terrified, and he had many problems which were too much for him to handle."

Before leaving, Steuerman had given Grundfast a sealed envelope, telling him to open it "only if something happens to me." Now a group was gathered in Grundfast's office: Doyle, McElhone, Rein, and Steuerman's three oldest children, Glenn, Todd, and Bari. "The mysterious manner surrounding Steuerman's disappearance was sufficient cause for the envelope to be opened," Rein wrote. "In the presence of all the people at the meeting, Michael Grundfast opened the envelope."

Inside was a note addressed to Steuerman's oldest child, twenty-eight-year-old Glenn. Jerry started with a list of money he owed—to his girlfriend, to casinos in Atlantic City, to Grundfast, and to Seymour Tankleff. There was a copy of one of Jerry and Seymour's loan agreements, along with an amortization schedule. A note was attached instructing Grundfast "not to pay Myron Fox." Glenn explained what this meant. He said that over the weekend his father told him that Fox had written him a letter demanding he continue sending his payments to Seymour, in care of him at his law office. Jerry's reaction, though, didn't interest the detectives in the loan agreement any more than the blood-splattered demand letter they'd left on Seymour's desk. Doyle looked at it but didn't ask Grundfast for a copy or take any notes. Testifying later, he would recall it only as "some sort of a business document between Mr. Steuerman and Mr. Tankleff."

Steuerman's letter continued with a list of instructions to Glenn about the bagel stores, the racehorses, and various insurance policies. After all the financial business, he closed: "Now going to see your mother." But Jerry's none-too-subtle suggestion of suicide was less than convincing. After all, he'd handed the note to Grundfast right after claiming that *other* people were threatening to kill him. Glenn, meanwhile, told the police that on Sunday, four days after the murder, his father told him that he'd gotten a phone call from someone who said, "Got enough of your shit, you'll be sleeping with the fishes." Bari said her father told her he would no longer have anything to do with anyone in the card game.

After interviewing Steuerman's children, the homicide detectives fanned out to interview his friends. One of his former bagel partners from the old days, Danny Fleischman, told them that Jerry had called him the previous Thursday, very upset about what had happened to the Tankleffs the day before. According to Fleischman, Jerry was also sad about his wife's death a year earlier. "They were very close, best friends, did everything together," the police quoted Fleischman saying. "He's more upset about her death than people realize."

Jerry's girlfriend, Sharon Freifeld, told the detectives that he had been "very quiet" over the weekend. "He had a lot on his mind, and he was very tired." Jerry told Sharon that he wanted his lawyer to draw up a will "because Seymour Tankleff's death was a sudden reminder of how important it was to tie everything together." He also told her "he was no longer going to carry a wallet. He said it took up too much space."

Neither Steuerman's girlfriend nor his children had heard from him or had any clues where he might be. But Jim McCready learned a few things when he went to the Ramada Inn next to the parking lot where Steuerman's car had been found. McCready showed a picture of Steuerman to the front desk manager, who told him that Steuerman had taken a room before his disappearance. She also said he was a regular. He checked in "three or four times a week," usually in the company of a woman in her early thirties with medium-length dark brown hair. He registered under an assortment of aliases—"Jerry Josephs," "Jerry Stevens," "Jerry Steveman"—which the manager found odd, considering he came in so often and usually bantered with the desk clerks. But this last time was different. First of all, there was no woman. Then he registered under a new name: "Joseph Qualigreen." And he stayed overnight, registering late on Tuesday and checking out in the early afternoon on Wednesday. And when he left, he looked completely different. He shaved off his beard and cut his hair weave, and he was without his usual array of flashy jewelry. Instead of his gold bagel chain, he had an ascot around his neck. He wore dark glasses.

The police managed to keep the news of Steuerman's disappearance out of the press for the better part of a week. But there were rumors around Port Jefferson, and by Friday it was all over town. Jack Murtagh, Gottlieb's investigator, was interviewing the card players that morning. When he got to Vinnie Bove and started questioning him about Steuerman, Bove looked at him and asked, "Are you not aware that Jerry Steuerman is missing?" He said he'd heard it from his wife, who heard it from a friend at Dreamland Realty. The rumors came complete with details, most of them true or close enough. "From what I understand," Bove said, "they found his car running in a parking lot at a disco. He wrote two letters, one to his lawyer and one to his son, saying that people were after him and his family was being taken care of."

Murtagh could not have given Gottlieb better news. It was all so bizarre and beyond obvious, he thought—like something out of a cheap novel. *The DA will* have *to look at Steuerman now. They'll have to reconsider the whole case!*

Gottlieb called Ed Jablonski. "I assume you've heard about Steuerman," he said, containing his enthusiasm.

Yes, the prosecutor said, betraying no hint that he'd thought about little else for days. What about it?

What about it? You've got to take another look at this whole case now.

Why would we want to do that?

Why? Tankleff lingers, Steuerman vanishes—what does that tell you? You know this guy owed Tankleff all this money. This changes everything.

Actually, Jablonski said, it changes nothing. Marty Tankleff still did it. He told us he did it—remember? Steuerman going missing doesn't change that. There's no indication this is even related to the homicide.

Not related to the homicide? How can you say that before you even talk to the guy? You don't even know where he is.

But Jablonski wasn't interested. Gottlieb got off the phone, flabbergasted. He figured the cops to take the absurd position that Steuerman's disappearance wasn't the least bit suspicious, but Jablonski? Even after a decade as a defense attorney in the perilous precincts of Suffolk County, Gottlieb still wasn't so cynical to think that one of the highest-ranking law enforcement officials in the county—an officer of the court, as lawyers liked to say when they felt the need to remind one another of the sanctity of their profession—would put winning a case above discovering the truth. Did backing the cops, saving face, really trump a basic devotion to justice? Gottlieb would forever remember the conversation with Jablonski as a revelatory moment.

"It was bizarre to me," Gottlieb recalled. "He's actually telling me, 'Oh, come on, you don't really believe this has anything to do with the case.' I was disgusted. It was clear to me that they were just locked in. They had already told the world that they had gotten a confession from this young kid and held press conferences announcing they had solved this case in a matter of hours with these crack homicide detectives. So now I know there's no interest in getting to the truth. I can very well be representing somebody who did not commit these crimes and I now know that the Suffolk DA and the homicide squad will do everything possible to destroy Marty and any attorney who tries to vigorously represent him. I knew at that moment that we were involved in a war."

Though Steuerman's disappearance was the buzz of Port Jefferson, it was five days before the police confirmed it to the media. On Tuesday, September 20, *Newsday* finally broke the story that Seymour Tankleff's business partner was missing. The development "may be a bizarre twist" in the homicide case, the newspaper said, the cautious language indicating that this was the first time Steuerman's name had appeared in the paper's coverage of the case. In the same instant, Jerry Steuerman vanished from sight and surfaced as a central character in this suddenly much more intriguing murder case.

The police and prosecutors, of course, discouraged any such thoughts. All the media reports came equipped with the authorities' assurance that Jerry Steuerman was nothing more than a missing person. There was "no indication of a connection" between Steuerman's disappearance and the Tankleff case, homicide commander John McElhone told *Newsday*. Yes, the homicide squad was handling the missing-person case, but it was "separate and distinct" from the homicide case. If that weren't ambiguous enough, Jablonski told the paper, "The man had been receiving death threats since the homicide." Aside from the fact that there was no reason to believe that was true, was the disappearance related to the homicide or not? Jablonski said it didn't really matter because it wouldn't change the only thing that did matter: Martin Tankleff confessed to killing his mother and trying to kill his father.

Whatever spin the prosecution put on it, one thing was clear: Steuerman had presented Marty's defense with an extravagant gift. But that was down the road. For now, Gottlieb would use the disappearance to make a renewed pitch for Marty's release. Two judges had already rejected his applications for bail—first at the arraignment and then at a bail hearing eight days later, when the judge was unswayed by thirty letters of support from Marty's relatives, friends, classmates, and teachers. It didn't matter to him that Marty Tankleff was "a loving, kind, gentle, responsible and hard-working sweet soul" to his Aunt Marcella. Or that, according to his business teacher, "Marty was in the Future Business Leaders of America Club . . . one of our finest fundraisers." Or that Estelle Block, the head of the guidance department at Earl L. Vandermeulen High School, found Marty to be "polite, respectful, friendly, and personable" and recalled that he sat with his parents at Junior Night "and appeared to be proud of them." Or that one of his classmates considered him "a good reliable friend since fourth grade" and another found that "he has a way of making even the dullest classes fun."

The day the story of Steuerman's disappearance broke in the media, Gottlieb went back to State Supreme Court justice James A. Gowan, the same judge who had allowed Marty to attend his mother's funeral, to ask for another bail hearing. Gowan granted the request, and the next morning Gottlieb and Jablonski met in court to debate once more the strength of the case and whether it warranted the defendant's indefinite incarceration. Knowing that Gottlieb was primed to make Steuerman's disappearance Exhibit A in his latest argument for bail, Jablonski came in with something new of his own. He revealed that Marty had emerged from his house that morning with a splotch of blood on his shoulder—proof, he said, that, as "Martin said in his confession, he was not wearing any clothes when the crime was committed."

First of all, Gottlieb told the judge in response, the blood on Marty's shoulder isn't proof of anything—except, perhaps, that he was telling the truth when he told the police how he had tried to help his father. And now we have the disappearance of Jerry Steuerman. "The flags and sirens should be blaring here," he said. Then, in a moment of between-us-lawyers candor, Gottlieb told the judge that this was not the usual bail application "where, I have to say, you have to stretch a little bit" to make a bad guy look not so bad. "This is not a case where we're playing games." This time, he was convinced he had a truly innocent client—a teenage boy sitting in jail, ensnared in a mistake of tragic proportions.

Having heard the arguments for and against, the judge decided that Marty could be released on bail—a million dollars' bond or half a million in cash. He also agreed to a stipulation requested by Jablonski: that Marty not be allowed to enter his father's hospital room unless he was accompanied by a member of the hospital staff.

THE STORY OF Jerry Steuerman's disappearance encouraged exactly what the police and prosecutors wanted to suppress: speculation about Steuerman's possible involvement in the Tankleff homicide—and, necessarily, the first serious questions about the veracity of Marty Tankleff's purported confession. Some who had presumed his guilt on the basis of simple faith in the police now weren't so sure. Among those suddenly a little shaky was Vinnie Bove. He had heard all the speculation about Steuerman—from Marty himself on the morning of the crimes and from some of the other poker players. But the cops told him not to believe it: Marty confessed. "The professional people tell me they have the right person," Bove told a reporter. But now? "I'm so confused."

Around Port Jefferson, attention focused on Steuerman's checkered reputation. The day the story broke, an officer in the police department's missing-persons section wrote in the case log: "Anonymous male caller advises Steuerman finances his son Todd, aka Toad, in major cocaine dealings. Caller states he saw Steuerman and Todd in a room together with several kilos of cocaine. Also states last business venture he heard them working on was a whorehouse on the East End. D/Sgt. Pepper of Homicide notified of conversation." (Todd himself seemed to think the whole disappearance thing was kind of funny. "He's probably down in Atlantic City with some blond's legs wrapped around him," he told a TV reporter, off camera.)

Inevitably, Steuerman's disappearance opened for public discussion the possibility that the Suffolk County homicide squad was at it again. In *Newsday*, under the headline "One Side Isn't the Truth," Paul Vitello, the paper's incisive news-side columnist, pointed out incongruities in the Tankleff case that were reminiscent of some of the notorious homicide prosecutions now being examined by the State Commission of Investigation. For instance: that Martin Tankleff, a defendant described by prosecutors as "highly intelligent," carefully plotted his parents' murders and their cover-up but "somehow missed a spot of blood the size of a fist around his armpit when he took an alleged shower after the alleged rampage." Whatever the police and prosecution's version of events, Vitello wrote after attending the bail hearing, "The territories at stake in this case are vast, and, apparently, mostly unexplored. Either Martin Tankleff has lied, and lied his whole life to create an impression of himself that is sweeter than his true nature, or the Suffolk County police have lied about his admission, or they have extracted incriminating statements from a terrified boy after a long interrogation on the day of his mother's death."

ON SEPTEMBER 23, nine days after Steuerman's idling Lincoln was found behind Ribsters restaurant, his girlfriend, Sharon Freifeld, came home to a one-word message on her answering machine. The word was "pistachio," and it was spoken by a male voice that sounded a lot like Jerry Steuerman's. Freifeld notified the police. Pistachio was their favorite ice cream, she explained. Another call came later in the day. The caller hung up. The device placed on her phone by the police identified the source: the Galleria Park Hotel in San Francisco.

Doyle called the hotel and asked an assistant manager to check his registration records for Jerry Steuerman and the four aliases Steuerman had used at the Ramada Inn. The manager had no record of a guest by any of those names. Then Doyle faxed a picture of Steuerman. The manager called back and said that another hotel employee recognized the man in the photo as a guest who'd registered under the name Jay Winston. He'd checked out the day before. Detective Mike Carmody called American Airlines in San Francisco and learned that a Jay Winston had been aboard the previous day's flight 898. It left San Francisco at noon and arrived in Los Angeles an hour and twenty minutes later. Phone records at the hotel, meanwhile, indicated "Jay Winston" had made several calls from his room to two phone numbers in the L.A. area. One belonged to a woman named Carolyn Beaver, the other to a Trudy Polsky.

On Monday, September 26, Doyle, McCready, and Jablonski flew to Los Angeles, rented a car, and took three rooms at the Sheraton Hotel in Redondo Beach, a surf town south of the airport. The next day they drove to Hollywood to see Carolyn Beaver. Shown a photograph of Jerry Steuerman, Beaver said that it was Jay Winston, though he no longer had a beard and his hair was shorter. She'd met him the previous weekend at a place called Esalen, a retreat about a hundred miles south of San Francisco. He called her a few times after she got home. Was he in some kind of trouble? No, no, the detectives told her, but he's a material witness in a homicide case. They asked her if she was planning to see "Jay." No, she said, she thought he was strange.

The next day, McCready, Doyle, and Jablonski went to talk to Trudy Polsky. They tracked her down in the Long Beach court building. She also identified the man in the photo as Jay Winston, said she'd met him at Esalen, and gotten calls from him since the weekend. In the last one, he said he was staying at the Holiday Inn outside the Long Beach airport. Polsky was a lawyer. She told the men from Suffolk County that she would represent "Jay" if he were a suspect in any crime. They assured her he wasn't. They just wanted to talk to him.

Jay Winston had a room on the second floor of the Holiday Inn. Doyle booked the room across the hall, then the group went upstairs and knocked on Steuerman's door. No answer. McCready went back downstairs to the lobby to call his wife. He was in mid-sentence when he stopped and told her he'd talk to her later. He approached a man who'd just come through the hotel's front doors.

"What are you doing, Jerry?" McCready asked.

Jerry Steuerman began to cry.

McCready brought him upstairs, where Doyle and Jablonski finally laid eyes on the peculiar bagel man who had given them twelve days of agita and may have wrecked their case against Marty Tankleff. McCready looked squarely at Steuerman and said: All right, Jerry, just what the hell is going on here? Did Myron Fox pay you to get out of town?

No, Steuerman said, looking down, shaking his head, crying. That's not what happened.

He didn't make a deal with you? asked Doyle, who found McCready's theory plausible enough. He didn't bribe you to stage your disappearance and take the heat off Marty Tankleff?

No, Jerry said. Mike Fox had nothing do with it.

Then why did you leave? McCready asked. You're not a suspect. You've never *been* a suspect. Marty Tankleff confessed. So why *the fuck* did you disappear?

Steuerman said he staged the whole thing to look as if he'd been abducted. He'd disappear, people would think he was dead, and his family would get $2 million in insurance. "I'm a coward," Jerry said. "I can't even face my own problems." McCready later wrote in his case report, "It was apparent that Steuerman was emotionally upset over the deaths of Arlene and Seymour Tankleff," notwithstanding that Seymour was still alive. "In addition, he was upset over the fact that Tankleff's family and friends would think that he could be involved in something of this nature. Furthermore, Steuerman was extremely upset with himself as a person in general. He talked about family problems and where he felt he was going with his own life. He thought the life insurance he had would help make up for the mistakes he had made during his life." According to McCready, Steuerman cried as he unburdened himself, sometimes uncontrollably.

So where had Jerry spent these last two weeks? He left his car in the parking lot near the Ramada Inn off the Long Island Expressway because a bus to Atlantic City stopped there. After changing his appearance and setting the scene of his faked abduction, he took the bus to Atlantic City. But he didn't stay there. He took a limousine service to Newark Airport, deciding somewhere on the New Jersey Turnpike that he should buy his ticket to Los Angeles under an alias. The limousine company was called Winston.

During the cross-country flight, Steuerman struck up a conversation with the woman sitting next to him. She was a psychologist, and he took the opportunity to tell her his troubles: He was in debt. His wife died a year ago and she was the backbone of the family business, which was bagels, which wasn't what it used to be, what with all the competition. Now he had a girlfriend he was supposed to marry, but he wasn't sure about it. And on top of all that, last week his partner and his partner's wife got murdered. Well, his partner was still alive, but he was in a coma. The psychologist told Jerry she had the perfect place for him: Esalen. If she had a brochure with her, Jerry could have read that Esalen was founded in the early 1960s as an "alternative educational center devoted to the exploration of the world of unrealized human potential that lies beyond the imagination." A place where he could immerse himself in "East/West philosophies, Gestalt therapy, and experiential/didactic workshops on 27 acres of spectacular Big Sur coastline blessed with natural hot springs and the Santa Lucia Mountains rising sharply behind." Where "philosophers, psychologists, artists, religious thinkers, and historical luminaries like Aldous Huxley, Joseph Campbell, Jack Kerouac, Allen Ginsberg, and Joan Baez have gathered to develop revolutionary ideas, transformative practices, and innovative art forms."

Not exactly Jerry Steuerman's kind of place. But he figured, why not? The plane landed in Los Angeles and Jerry checked into a hotel at the airport. The next day, he got on another plane and flew three hundred miles north and checked into Esalen for a weekend retreat. He participated in group sessions, sharing his woes with people such as Trudy Polsky and Carolyn Beaver. (Years later, Scott Christianson, a former New York State criminal justice official, talked to both women while working on a documentary about the Tankleff case. Beaver told Christianson that Steuerman was "a strange man who stuck out like a sore thumb" at Esalen and who told a lot of stories that she found hard to believe—his business partner's murder, in particular. Polsky, meanwhile, recalled that Steuerman said he hated his partner but did not kill him, as some people back home thought.

His partner's "crazy son" did it because he didn't like his car. Both women told Christianson that the Suffolk County authorities didn't ask them whether Steuerman talked about the murders. All they wanted to know was whether they knew where Steuerman was.)

Whatever personal growth Jerry may have achieved in his three days at Esalen, he did experience one important revelation. Confiding his staged disappearance to another retreat member who was in the insurance business, he learned that his scheme to fake his death had a fatal flaw: Life insurance policies on people listed as missing didn't pay off until they were declared dead—and that didn't happen until they were gone for seven years. "*Seven years?*" Jerry said. "My kids couldn't even pay the premiums for seven years."

Jerry left Esalen on Sunday and headed north to San Francisco, where he made his pistachio call to Sharon Freifeld from the Galleria Park Hotel. He also went across the bay to Oakland to have his hair weave "serviced." Then he flew down to Los Angeles. It was there, in the room at the Holiday Inn, that the Suffolk County police finally asked Steuerman about his business dealings with Seymour Tankleff—not because they now considered him a possible suspect but because his bizarre odyssey was certain to be the centerpiece of Bob Gottlieb's defense of Marty Tankleff. Steuerman's affairs with Tankleff, hardly a concern to the police and prosecutors two weeks ago, was now an issue they couldn't ignore.

Steuerman conceded that he and Tankleff hadn't been getting along. He said he was paying Seymour the money he owed at a clip of $2,500 a week in cash, taking it off the top of the bagel business. But that wasn't a problem, according to Jerry. The problem was that Seymour thought he was entitled to half of everything Jerry owned. So when Jerry opened a store for his son to run, Seymour insisted it was half his. They had an argument about it. But it wasn't as if he and Seymour were mortal enemies. Just not as friendly as they'd been. They were still playing cards together.

McCready offered Steuerman some friendly advice. "After talking to Steuerman," he wrote in his case report, "we explained to him that he did not have to return to New York with us if he did not wish to. In view of what Steuerman had told us, [I] explained to him that he might be better off returning with us, taking care of his personal problems, and then returning to California at a later date if he wished to do so. Steuerman then decided to return to New York with us."

That afternoon, Jablonski called Shirley Perlman, a crime reporter for *Newsday*, and told her that Jerry Steuerman had been found in Southern California. He described Steuerman's flight as nothing more than a stressed-out man's misguided escape from personal problems. "I can't stress enough that we didn't come out here looking for a killer."

And then Jerry himself got on the phone with Perlman. "A lot of people were looking at me," he told her. "Not that they accused me, but I felt it would be easier if I would just go. I figured my kids would not have to worry and the woman that I loved would have enough and they would not need me in their life anymore. Well, the plans of mice and men went astray. They don't pay off life insurance policies on people that are missing." Jerry said he was relieved to be found: "I couldn't stay away any longer. . . . It's been a trying experience for me."

Wearing his Esalen T-shirt, Jerry posed with McCready for a photographer hired by *Newsday*. Then he packed his things and moved over to the hotel in Redondo Beach where McCready, Doyle, and Jablonski were staying. The group—detectives, prosecutor, and former missing person—were there another two days, though it was never explained what they did over that time.

Jerry's reappearance was nearly as strange as his disappearance. Arriving with his police escort at Kennedy Airport, he was met by his daughter Bari and a cluster of reporters, photographers, and TV crews. *Why'd you disappear?* they wanted to know. Clutching his daughter, whimpering as he walked, Jerry repeated his explanation with a hint of his old stutter. "A lot of people thought that I did it," he said. "I couldn't take it anymore. I had too many, uh, prob-problems, and it's twenty years of building up, that's all. So I staged my death."

Exercising its prosecutorial discretion, the district attorney's office lodged no charges against Steuerman related to his self-professed attempted fraud. The prosecutors didn't even charge him with possession of stolen license plates.

Discussing Steuerman's vanishing act years later, Erin Moriarty, of the CBS program *48 Hours*, asked Jim McCready if he'd been angry at Steuerman when he found him in California. "I mean, didn't you say to Jerry, 'You're messing up my case'?"

McCready chuckled weakly. "Something to that effect," he said.

"Steuerman's disappearance must have made your case harder," Moriarty suggested.

"Not that it made it harder," McCready said, then spent several seconds searching for the rest of his thought. "It just . . . it just added . . ." Another long pause. ". . . more questions."

More questions, indeed. But questions that McCready and everyone else connected with the prosecution of Marty Tankleff were determined never to ask.

CHAPTER 14

Long Island Railroad

ON THE AFTERNOON of September 14, Jim McCready had gone to Bob Gottlieb's office to make a personal delivery from the district attorney's office. It was seven days after the assaults on the Tankleffs. And though neither McCready nor Gottlieb knew it at the time, it was also the day Jerry Steuerman was making himself disappear. Gottlieb's office was five minutes from the Ramada Inn.

McCready handed Gottlieb an envelope containing a thin stack of stapled pages. Gottlieb read the line at the top of the first page:

ORAL STATEMENTS—MARTIN TANKLEFF

It was the heart of the prosecution's case: McCready and his partner's account of what Marty said to them on the day his parents were brutally attacked. It began the moment McCready introduced himself on the driveway at 8:10 that morning:

> His date of birth is 8/29/71. He resides at 33 Seaside Drive, Belle Terre. His phone number is 928-2242. He believes Jerry Steuerman, his father's partner in bagel stores, murdered his mother and father.

It ended five hours and thirteen pages later, with Mike Fox's phone call to the homicide squad, demanding that all questioning stop, at 1:22 in the afternoon.

The three-thousand-word narrative was a reconstruction that McCready and Rein produced at some point after the interview and was based on their memories and Rein's notes. It recounted Marty's statements to the detectives and their sergeant at the scene, what he said to McCready during the drive to police headquarters, then moved on to the opening moments in the interview room, when McCready and Rein asked him a series of questions that roamed from the personal to the material, sometimes in ways that revealed the detectives' notion that the subjects were inseparable. They brought the conversation to Marty's relationship with his parents, and from there to questions of aspiration, wealth, and inheritance. The account, at this stage, seemed less significant for what Marty was telling the detectives than for what they were asking him: "Marty knew his father and mother were extremely wealthy. . . . He was aware of the contents of the will and knew that he would be the primary beneficiary when they both died. . . . If Jerry Steuerman was out of the picture, and his parents [were] both dead, he would own it all."

The detectives didn't write that Marty wouldn't inherit anything for another seven years. Perhaps this was because he didn't mention it, his mind on other things. Or perhaps he did tell them. It was one of countless questions, though hardly the most critical one, that only a recording could have answered. But what did seem clear by this point in the account was that Marty and the homicide detectives were not on the same page. When Marty tried to get back to the man he thought they should be talking to, they asked him to take them through the morning's events one more time.

The report confirmed Marty's own recollection that at a certain point McCready and Rein became more aggressive, challenging him on details and taking an increasingly accusatory tone. On the tenth of the thirteen pages, the account arrived at McCready's faked phone call to the hospital, and Marty's reaction to the fictional good news–bad news. His father had been revived with a shot of adrenaline. But he had identified Marty as his attacker. If his father said that, Marty responded, it was probably because he was the last person his father saw. When McCready refused to accept that explanation, Marty asked to take a lie detector test. The account didn't include the detectives' response. It went directly to the game-changing question they said he asked:

> Could he have blacked out and done it? Maybe that wasn't him, but another Marty Tankleff that killed them. Could he have been possessed? It was starting to come to him. That he understood his rights. He did not want to contact a lawyer. Having his rights in mind he would tell us what happened. He needed psychiatric help. He knew what happened, but it felt like it was another person who was inside of him who did it. His mother, father, and he once had a loving relationship, but he got caught up in their fighting. It

changed everything in his life. He hasn't been able to be himself. He said he would tell what happened and asked what the Dets. wanted to know. He said, yeah, he did it.

According to McCready and Rein, Marty told them why he did it before he told them how. He began recounting his many dissatisfactions and resentments, a list that included specific complaints as well as the general one that his parents were "looking to him for more attention and they were smothering him." By their account, "This relationship was a nightmare to him. He resented that he had to ride around in the crummy old Lincoln and he wanted something more sporty. His parents felt the Lincoln was safer. He also resented that Dan Hayes, his father's partner in a health and fitness center, was going to move into their house to babysit when his parents were away on vacation. He was never allowed to play any contact sports. He was restricted this summer in his use of the family boat, and the ATVs."

What Gottlieb couldn't know until much later, when he received the reports the detectives wrote of their other investigative work, was that several of the grievances they attributed to Marty bore a striking resemblance to the opinions expressed to them by Jerry Steuerman and Julie Mutschler. In Mutschler's estimation for instance, Marty was never satisfied with what he had and was "trapped" by his parents. McCready and Rein conducted those interviews two days after Marty's arrest, and before they wrote up their account of his statements.

The narrative arrived at the crimes themselves. According to the detectives, Marty told them he went to bed planning to murder his parents and that he got up at 5:35 to do it. He decided to attack them naked so he wouldn't have any clothes with blood on them. He killed his mother first. He "got to her quickly," hitting her with a dumbbell, then going to the kitchen and returning with a knife he found next to the watermelon on the counter. "He didn't know how many times he stabbed her. . . . He hit her at least four to five times on the head. He kept on trying to hit her, she fought with him. She was in pain calling for help, saying why? and help me." Then he went to the office, where he found his father sitting at his desk, awake from the commotion at the other end of the house. "He got behind his father and hit him with the barbell first. His father asked him why he was doing this. He knocked him silly. . . . He slashed his father's neck. He didn't know how many times he hit or cut him. He couldn't believe all the blood."

Then, according to the detectives, Marty told them how he went about trying to cover his tracks. He washed the knife and barbell in the shower, then went back to his bedroom, laid down, and "thought about what to do next." At 6:10 he decided to call 911. He went down to the office and found that his father was still alive. But he figured he would die before the ambulance arrived. He went back into his mother's bedroom and saw that she was dead. He made the call from there. Then he got a towel and pillow to make it look as if he had followed the 911 operator's instructions. "He made sure that he got his father's blood on his hands to show that he tried to help his father. He missed the blood on his shoulder when he showered. He screwed up."

Gottlieb went to the jail to show Marty his interrogators' account of his "oral statements." Marty was incredulous. He told Gottlieb it was a nearly complete fiction. All the details came from *them*. They pressured him to acknowledge each point. He kept telling them he didn't know. They kept telling them he *did* know. They wrote it up as if they were simply taking dictation. In some instances, it seemed that the cops took things Marty told them earlier and put them into his confession. The part about being naked: At one point they had asked him what he wore to bed and he told them he slept nude. This became a convenient explanation for why he had no blood on his clothes.

Marty's close relatives, meanwhile, saw dead giveaways in some of the language. For instance, how Marty was said to have described the attack on his father: He hit him with a barbell and "knocked him silly." It wasn't how Marty spoke. And if he were really confessing after realizing he'd done something horrible and then "blacked out," would he really have used such a glib phrase?

The account attributed one more thing to Marty that he didn't recognize: "He agreed to give a written and videotaped statement." He didn't remember agreeing to either, or even being asked. Of course, there was a lot he didn't remember about those hours. But while there was no videotape, the prosecutors did have a three-page document purported to be a written confession. It was a statement written in Marty's first-person voice, but not by his hand. It seemed that when Mike Fox called and put them on notice, the police were in the process of preparing the confession of Martin Tankleff—as told to K. James McCready.

The ghostwritten confession was executed in black felt-tip pen on lined white paper with the words POLICE DEPARTMENT COUNTY OF SUFFOLK, NY, in the upper right corner of each page. McCready opened with a recitation of the Miranda warnings—Marty's right to remain silent and his acknowledgment that anything he said could be used against him; his right to an attorney and his agreement to speak without one. After each one, McCready drew a line for Marty to initial. But Marty never did; the spaces remained blank. "Having my rights in mind," he wrote next, "I want to tell Detectives McCready and Rein what happened to my parents this morning." He began with a summary of the motives.

> . . . They ruined my summer by not letting me use the boat as much as I wanted. They wanted me to drive the crummy old Lincoln. They were fighting a lot and taking it out on me. When my mother sided with my father about the card table I was really MAD. I decided I wanted to kill them both. I set my alarm for 5:35 to make sure I would be up before them. I decided to use the barbell when I went to bed. When I got up I was surprised to see the lights still on. When I looked in my parents room my mother was there. She was sleeping. I went down to the office and saw my father sleeping in the chair. I decided to kill my mother first. I ran across the bed. I got to her quick. I hit her 4 or 5 times in the head. She fought me. I went to the kitchen and got a knife. I ran back with the knife. I cut her throat. I don't know how many times but I stabbed at her also. Mostly I cut at her throat and neck. I left to

And there it ended. Underneath was McCready's final entry:

> 1322 D/Sgt Horvath states atty Myron Fox called—nothing further.

Fox's call apparently came while McCready was midway through writing the confession—before he had a chance to write that Marty had slashed his father with the watermelon knife and "knocked him silly" with the dumbbell (or "barbell"—the detectives used the two words interchangeably in the two documents, a point that would become significant); before he could write that Marty washed himself and his weapons in the shower but "screwed up" by missing several large bloodstains on his shoulder and upper chest. Fox's call bringing everything to a halt explained why Marty never initialed his Miranda rights or signed the unfinished confession—why he never even knew of its existence before his lawyer showed it to him. If nothing else had gone right for Marty that day, Gottlieb was pleased that at least Fox called before McCready finished writing the statement and handed Marty the felt-tip pen. Given his state of mind in those moments, it wasn't hard to envision him signing it. *That* would have been a problem. Much more than this—a statement written by the arresting detective, that stopped in mid-sentence, that was unsigned and unsworn.

The specter of McCready and Rein's testimony, though, was another matter. Gottlieb's first plan of attack would be to seek to have Marty's alleged statements suppressed. He believed he could make a strong case that the police had violated Marty's rights against self-incrimination by isolating him, denying his right to counsel, and giving the Miranda warnings much too late in the process. That, and manipulating him into a false confession.

But Gottlieb also knew that getting a confession tossed was always a long shot, especially in the political halls of justice of Suffolk County. And if he couldn't make it fly—if the detectives were permitted to tell a jury that Marty Tankleff told them he killed his parents, quoting him in the manner of their report of his oral statements—the consequences could be devastating to his defense. At that point, Marty's life might well depend on whether the twelve people chosen to judge him were skeptical enough to come to the same conclusion that two other juries in murder cases of recent vintage had reached: that the Suffolk County homicide squad sometimes behaved less like an elite unit than a rogue one.

For that reason, Gottlieb was very eager to receive another package from the district attorney's office: the results of the forensic investigation. If the detectives fed Marty the means and methods of the attacks, how would those details match up with the findings of the crime lab? So far, it seemed to Gottlieb, the reports were slow in coming.

ON OCTOBER 6, seven days after Jerry Steuerman returned to New York, Seymour Tankleff died. He had been in a coma for twenty-nine days.

Marty was still in jail, waiting for his relatives to put up bail, when the news came that he was now both an orphan and an accused double murderer. The district attorney's office prepared the new papers for the grand jury while Marty's family scrambled to get him out for his father's funeral. Bob Gottlieb would go to court for a second temporary release if he had to. But the family was so desperate to avoid another funeral with Marty sitting alone in shackles that they delayed the burial for six days. Finally they put together enough cash and pledged the value of their homes to make the $1 million bond.

Marty emerged from the county jail wearing his own clothes for the first time in five weeks: khaki pants, a sweater pulled over a polo shirt, Top-Sider shoes instead of paper ones. His hair, which had grown thick since the haircut he'd gotten the day before school opened, was meticulously combed. His black-rimmed glasses sat on the bridge of his reshaped nose. Marty was met in the jail's waiting room by Gottlieb, his sister and brother-in-law, and his Aunt Marcella. Gottlieb briefly conferred alone with Marty, and then Marty asked, "Can I hug my sister now?" Gottlieb smiled and stepped aside, and Marty kissed and hugged Shari and then each of his relatives. Ron Rother took his young brother-in-law's face in his hands and kissed him on the cheek.

Flanked by the group, Marty walked outside into a phalanx of reporters and cameramen. He pulled a half sheet of yellow paper from his pocket and nervously read a brief statement as he held hands with Shari. "This has been the roughest time in my life," he said, his first public words something that went without saying. A soundman from one of the TV crews asked him to speak up. "I have not only lost my parents, but I've lost my best friends," Marty continued. "I would like to thank all the people who are behind me. If it wasn't for these people, I wouldn't be as strong. My life will never be the same. Someone has taken my parents away from me in a brutal manner. I can't wait until all the truth comes out."

Seymour's funeral the next morning was attended by a large gathering that included his first wife, Vega. Their daughter delivered a brief but emotional eulogy, talking about the way things used to be, how her father meant so much to everyone in his family, and oddly making a point of Marty's adoption. "The thought I want to leave you with is this," Shari concluded. "If you look up on a starlit night, you will see my father watching over you." The assemblage moved on to Pinelawn Cemetery for Seymour's burial next to Arlene. It was a rainy day, and the mourners huddled under a canopy at the grave site, all but Seymour's four most immediate relatives standing. Up front on folding chairs sat his son and daughter, flanked by his brother and their nonagenarian mother. Marty and Shari sat close, leaning into each other, their heads touching, their hands clasped.

After the funeral, Marty went home with Shari. Though Ron and Carol Falbee were to be his legal guardians until he turned eighteen in ten months, Marty told them he preferred to stay with Shari and her family in Port Jefferson Station so he could return to school with his friends and to a semblance of his life as he prepared for his trial. He imagined he'd be welcomed back to Vandermeulen High with open arms. He presumed that everyone had to know he was innocent.

For the most part, Marty's perception was correct, if the year's first issue of the school newspaper was any indication. "The initial reports of the press painted a picture of Marty as being a spoiled young man who was angry at his parents for having ruined his summer by restricting certain privileges. But now it seems that the assessments were a bit premature," read the front-page article in *The Purple Parrot*. "Regardless of the real answer, this has proved to be a trying time for many students at ELVHS, especially friends of Marty. Many have maintained his innocence from the beginning, even when everything seemed to be stacked against him. Now that the recent information has come up, more and more people are believing in his innocence." An editorial chastised *Newsday* and other professional media for covering the case too unskeptically, accepting statements by the prosecutor as facts. "We the editors of 'The Purple Parrot' believe in 'innocent until proven guilty.' We are far from convinced of Marty's guilt, and therefore presume him innocent. We welcome him back to school, and wish him luck."

But on the day of his father's funeral, it was announced that Marty would *not* be welcomed back at school. The news came not from the school administration but from the district attorney's office. Ed Jablonski told reporters that school authorities had decided to bar Marty because of an incident the previous spring that, under the current circumstances, made them uncomfortable about having Marty back in school. It was a "knifing incident," Jablonski said.

At the high school two weeks earlier, Marty's friend Chris Pellegrino had been called to the office by the principal, Albert Neuner, who was with the superintendent of schools. They wanted to know about "the incident with Marty Tankleff and the knife." Chris had no idea what they were talking about. Last spring, the principal reminded him. When Marty pulled a switchblade. Remember? "Oh, that?" Chris said. "It was nothing. We were just fooling around."

The whole thing started with the junior prom, Chris explained. He had taken Jonna Cerbone and Marty had gone with Jennifer Oliveto. But Chris and Jennifer had a better time with each other than with their official dates, and after the prom they started talking on the phone a lot. In the hallway before third period one morning, Marty kidded Chris about "stealing my girlfriend." He took out an ornate switchblade and said with mock menace, "I oughta kill you." Then he broke into a smile, and they both laughed. Just then, Chris noticed a teacher spying on them and told Marty to put the knife away. The next period Marty found himself in Mr. Neuner's office. The principal confiscated the knife and called Marty's father, who apologized for his son's poor judgment and assured the principal that Marty was no danger. The knife was a souvenir from a family trip to Italy. Marty liked to show off new things, Seymour told the principal, but he'd see to it that the knife stays home from now on. Mr. Neuner was satisfied. He returned the knife to Marty and told him he didn't expect to see it again. Then Marty and Chris went out to get some pizza for lunch.

Now, four months later, the principal had Chris in his office. He and the superintendent wanted to know if, in retrospect, he felt threatened by Marty Tankleff. Not at all, Chris told them. They were horsing around. Would he be afraid if Marty returned to school? Of course not, Chris said. What about kids in general—how did they feel about Marty? Chris thought most agreed with *The Purple Parrot*. Neuner thanked Chris and sent him back to class. But the next day he came to the Pellegrinos' house and told Chris and his parents that the school district's lawyer had decided to report the knife incident to the Suffolk County police.

The case got a full investigation from the Suffolk County homicide team. Jablonski, McCready, and Rein visited the principal, spending two hours talking about Marty and the knife. Over the next few days McCready also made several trips and phone calls to interview Chris Pellegrino, pursuing him so aggressively that Pellegrino's father hired a lawyer, and a major one: Paul Gianelli, whose clients had included Long Island's most notorious teenager—and McCready's most famous conquest—prior to Marty Tankleff: Cheryl Pierson of "Homeroom Hit Man" fame.

With Gianelli beside him, Chris Pellegrino told McCready that the incident with Marty Tankleff was nothing, just two friends fooling around. "I don't want to know if you thought it was a joke or fooling around," McCready replied, "and I don't care whether you and Martin Tankleff are friends or not. I just want the facts." McCready also called Frank Oliveto and told him he wanted to talk to Jennifer, who knew nothing about the episode other than that she had gone to the prom with Marty and liked Chris more. All told, the homicide team did considerably more investigation of Marty Tankleff and the case of the souvenir knife than they did of Jerry Steuerman and whether he had something to do with the deaths of Marty's parents.

It would have been reasonable for the Port Jefferson school administrators to observe that the law enforcement authorities seemed to be ginning up an innocuous incident for their own purposes. After all, the principal had been so unconcerned at the time that he'd not only found it unnecessary to punish Marty but had given the knife back to him to take home. But that was then and this was now. The school officials decided to play it safe. They barred Marty from school for his senior year, sending tutors to his home instead. And since it was "district policy not to discuss student matters with the press," as the school board's lawyer explained, the district attorney's office took the initiative of alerting the media. To the portrait of Marty Tankleff's life he was carefully drawing for public consumption, Ed Jablonski now added the first suggestion that this was a teenager with a history of dark impulses: He announced that Marty had been involved in a "knifing episode," and that the school officials considered it so serious that they were afraid to let him back in school. The story he provided the media didn't let the facts get in the way. "Tankleff allegedly pulled a switchblade knife on a friend of his and said, 'I ought to kill you,'" *Newsday* reported. "Tankleff allegedly was angry because his friend had started to go out with Tankleff's date from the junior prom."

Gottlieb and Gianelli told reporters that Jablonski's maneuver was a shameless distortion. "Let them deal with this case and not throw up a lot of phony smoke screens," Gottlieb said, fuming, but the smoke didn't quite clear. One reporter asked Jablonski whether the knife in question had been among those recovered from the Tankleff home after the murders and, if so, whether it was a possible murder weapon. Jablonski said the police took a lot of knives out of the house; he wasn't sure if the Italian switchblade was one of them. "We have a knife that he says is the one," he said, "but who knows. . . ."

And myths sometimes have a hard time dying—especially when they fall into dangerous hands. Twenty years later, a psychologist named David Kirschner, a self-professed expert in "adoption forensics," would include Marty in his pet theory of "Adopted Child Syndrome." His belief was that adopted children were at a heightened risk for growing up to become pathologically violent, up to and including killing their adoptive parents. Long after he should have known better, Kirschner would write on a website devoted to true crime that Martin Tankleff, whom he never met but read "volumes" about, exhibited a "classic Adopted Child Syndrome (ACS) pattern of behavior." Among the "symptoms," according to Kirschner: "Marty was suspended from high school for threatening a student with a switchblade knife, when the other student began dating a girl Marty had taken to the junior prom. One key sympton of ACS is a pathological reaction to rejection, real or perceived."*

AS THE SCHOOL PAPER of Vandermeulen High had noticed, the daily news media were covering the Tankleff murder case as they did most other crime news: based on the information they were getting from the police and prosecutors, and operating under the time-honored principle that only a person officially charged with a crime could be accused in print. That system worked well enough when the case was typical and the information from the authorities was accurate. But this was not such a case.

The editor in chief of the school paper was Marc Howard, a senior who had been a classmate of Marty's since elementary school. By high school, they were traveling in different circles and had distinct personal ambitions: While Marty was single-minded about business and struggling with the idea of going to college at all, Marc was captivated by government and was soon to be accepted by Yale. But he knew Marty well enough that he had no reservations about speaking up for his right to the

* See Notes and Sources, pp. 584–93.

presumption of innocence. Though some adults might have thought Marc's editorial predictably naïve about the ways of the real world, the fact was that his media criticism was on the mark. It could even be argued that he and his fellow newspaper novices were among the *least* naïve journalists covering the Tankleff story. For it took a publication named *The Purple Parrot* to point out the early inconsistencies in the case against Marty: "For example," said the school paper's front-page story, "the prosecutor stated that Marty had premeditated the crime; his 'proof' was that Marty was naked, so that he wouldn't stain his clothes with blood. Well, now the defense has revealed that Marty usually slept nude anyway."

Oddly, it was *Newsday*, the locally dominant and nationally regarded paper whose series about the homicide squad had been published less than two years earlier, that was as guilty as any media outlet in reflexively propagating the story being fed to it by the police and prosecutors. What made it all the more surprising was what was going on behind the scenes at the newspaper.

In the months after the murders, the paper's reporting was overseen by Joe Demma, the veteran investigative reporter and editor who had played key roles in several of *Newsday*'s Pulitzer Prizes. While his colleagues were covering the day-to-day developments of the case, Demma was quietly pursuing alternatives. Twenty years of crime reporting in Suffolk County told him there might be something more to the story. At first he'd been intrigued by the juxtaposition of the murders to a high-stakes poker game. Then Jerry Steuerman disappeared. Demma spent a couple of months pulling together interviews by several reporters and accumulating a thick file of public documents on the Tankleffs, Steuerman, and some of the other card players. There were real estate transactions, business records, horse racing license applications, court judgments, probate filings.

Finally, Demma dropped in on Steuerman at his bagel store and found him happy to talk. They sat down at a table as Demma turned on his tape recorder. "No strawberry!" Jerry called over to a deliveryman who was wheeling in cases of Yoo-Hoo. "I got more here than you got on the truck!" He turned to Demma. "So what can I tell you?"

Like a detective, Demma started with small talk and background before getting down to business. "I've heard you and Tankleff were having some bitter fights," he said.

"The last couple of months, not bitter fights, but we weren't as close as we were," Steuerman replied. "Seymour was a businessman first. I appreciate that."

"Was he squeezing you?"

"There was no squeeze put on. It was just that his idea of business and friendship were not my idea. I trusted him like my own brother, my own flesh and blood. Not that he's ever done anything to hurt me. Everything I signed with Seymour, I signed. I knew what I did. There was nothing where he came after me afterwards, that I didn't do of my own accord."

Demma asked Steuerman if it was true that he was the last to leave the card game that night. Sure, said Steuerman. He was the first one to arrive so the last to leave—nothing unusual about that. Did the police ever consider him a suspect? No, never. Never took blood or hair samples? Nope.

Why'd you disappear? Demma asked.

"I left because I couldn't take the pressure. Police, TV cameras, my wife just died," Steuerman said, notwithstanding that the police were decidedly not pressuring him, that there were no TV cameras until he returned, and that his wife had died more than a year earlier. "Then the woman I'm going with, there's all kinds of bullshit. So I couldn't take it anymore, I had to get my head together. You know, sometimes you get in your car and you just drive and say, 'Hey, let me just go out somewhere with myself and sit down with myself in thought.' But when they found me I was ready to go home anyway."

As for Marty: "He had an attitude because of his father. 'I'm Marty Tankleff, my father owns the place.' I said, 'Marty, I'm the boss here. Your father's a silent partner. *I'm* the boss.' Marty was Marty. It's a rough thing. If he wouldn't have confessed to the police and you asked me, 'Did he do it?' I probably would say no."

Demma asked what other possibilities there might be.

"I heard rumors that you wouldn't even know about, okay?" Steuerman said. "It didn't come from me, all right? There are rumors from neighbors. I told you Seymour and the kid were close. Seymour was impotent. He couldn't—he was finished, okay? And in Belle Terre, the talk is that the kid and Arlene were having a thing, okay? Maybe Seymour found out and killed her and he killed him. Who knows what's true? I don't know. Who knows? Only the killer."

Demma had his interview with Steuerman transcribed and kept it for future use. (Except for a few brief quotes, it was to remain unpublished.) In early November, he wrote a memo to his superiors. "We've developed a lot of information, still have a lot of leads to check out and have more than our share of wild and crazy rumors. There are still, however, a lot, a lot, of questions. Many questions center on the cops and Suffolk DA targeting Martin Tankleff from the start and refusing to let go of him."

But Demma's instincts ran counter to the attitude that prevailed among reporters on the daily crime beat, whether at his own paper or other news organizations. Their view of the case was shaped largely by what they were told by their sources in the police department and the DA's office. From the beginning, those sources had been promoting their case by creating and marketing a narrative of Marty Tankleff's life that bore little resemblance to the inconveniently ordinary one he had actually been living. And in the wake of Steuerman's two-week disappearance, they were working overtime to get the focus back on Marty. "Sources say Martin talked 15 pages worth about how and why he committed the crime," a *Newsday* police reporter wrote in a memo to Demma, adding that "a very savvy guy with heavy homicide experience—I can't ID him in any way—told me 'the crime points to the kid.' He says the modus operandi was not one of the stranger-intruder because both Arlene and Seymour were 'overkilled in a very brutal way.' He also questioned why Martin would be spared. 'Who else could have killed them? All of Tankleff's associates were wealthy. If they wanted to hire someone to kill him, they'd get a pro. This was clearly the work of an amateur.'"

The detectives and prosecutors, meanwhile, continued their work as amateur psychologists. Marty did it because "his parents were smothering him," McCready told the reporter, while his sergeant, Bob Doyle, said that Jerry Steuerman had been ruled out as a suspect because "the motivation isn't there." According to Doyle, if Steuerman had decided to kill the Tankleffs to get out of a financial obligation, he would have had to kill the primary heir to their estate as well. This presumed that Steuerman knew the terms of their wills and that he was a levelheaded person. Upon his return from California with Steuerman, meanwhile, Jablonski was quoted in *The Port Jefferson Record* as saying that Steuerman had been repaying Tankleff over time and that by the time of the assaults he owed him what the weekly newspaper termed an "insignificant" amount of money—just $2,500, according to Jablonski.

As was usually the case, the defense had no interest in trying the case in the media, a necessary approach even if it made it easier for the prosecution to shape the story with "background" information that reporters could use but attribute only to "sources." Gottlieb told Marty's family not to talk and he was careful himself about what he said. But he did tell a *Newsday* reporter, off the record, that what Steuerman owed Tankleff could not be called insignificant: It was in the area of several hundred thousand dollars. Doyle's theory notwithstanding, Demma and some others wondered if this was like a lot of murder stories—entangled in unknown complications and not entirely rational. Maybe it came down to who these guys were. A former business associate of Seymour's named Robert Horowitz told another reporter, "Anybody who is Seymour's partner starts out happy at the beginning, but isn't so happy at the end. Jerry was just one of the little toys that Seymour had, and people don't like being played with. When you play with fire you get burned." And Steuerman? As he'd amply demonstrated, Horowitz remarked, "Jerry is not the most sane person in the world." So maybe Jerry just wanted to get out from under the Tankleffs and deal with whoever wound up controlling the estate. Between the son and the business partner, which of them was really being smothered?

But almost none of this ever made it into *Newsday*. In late November, Demma wrote a memo to his colleagues outlining leads to be followed and developments to be watched; he turned over the notes and transcripts of all the newspaper's interviews. Then he left on a long-planned six-week vacation. A few weeks later, on December 13, *Newsday* published its first major piece on the case. It was a three-thousand-word Sunday cover story that firmly established public perceptions of Marty Tankleff and the case against him. The headline read: A CHILD OF SUBURBAN WEALTH: MARTIN TANKLEFF'S HOUSE WAS A PLACE OF LUXURY—AND TENSION.

The story catalogued Marty's privileged upbringing, made much of his penchant for showing off, and implied that his home life was, in retrospect, a ticking time bomb: "When it came to happiness, his home in Belle Terre was somewhere east of Eden. According to friends and relatives, tensions swirled about the family." The parents bickered "as they had through twenty years of marriage" and argued with their son about college. "Martin was in conflict with his parents more and more. His father teased him about not having girlfriends and criticized his grades."

Though the ominous reports were attributed to "relatives and friends," none were named. That was because the claims didn't actually come from them, but from the police and prosecutors. And most of what they were saying was untrue. "Martin told police that there were daily arguments in the house and that the family had been getting psychiatric counseling," a reporter wrote in a memo that was a basis of the story. "He reportedly told police that 'it was someone inside of him who did this.'"

As for the relatives and friends who supposedly described "deep tensions" and "more and more" conflict between Marty and his parents, the author of the story wrote in one memo: "Family members are absolutely unanimous in their defense of Martin and their criticism of police. All describe him as an average teenager whose family situation was typical of that socio-economic group." Yet in the story that was published, the newspaper seemed at pains to cast Marty's relationship with his parents in dark tones that supported the claim that he felt "smothered" by them: "Several people who knew the Tankleffs felt parents and son were almost too close." The observation was attributed to "several people," but only one was cited: Jerry Steuerman. He was also quoted disparaging Marty's character, describing him as conceited and saying, "I fired him once."

While Steuerman was quoted as if he were a disinterested observer, his own role in the case was virtually an afterthought. His disappearance wasn't mentioned until near the end of the long story, and it came with barely a passing reference to his business relationship with Seymour Tankleff. There was no information at all about what the police had done to so quickly dismiss Steuerman as a suspect. Instead, the paper reported damning, but nonexistent, evidence against Marty. According to the police, said the story, Marty gave them this account of his actions after he called 911 that morning: ". . . He pulled his father from the chair, propped up his legs and put a towel around his head. Then he showered, put on a shirt and shorts, ran next door to a neighbor and hysterically told him what happened."

Had Marty actually told the homicide detectives he'd taken a shower in the four or five minutes between the time he gave first aid to his father and when the police and rescue squad arrived, they would have had every reason to consider him a prime suspect. And anyone reading this account in his Sunday newspaper would have had every right to think that Marty must be guilty as charged. But as McCready and Rein themselves would later testify, Marty kept denying their insistence that he'd taken a shower in the morning. Even their confession had him showering before the 911 call, not after it.

IF, AS MARTY and everyone around him thought, the prosecutors seemed all too eager to use the media to demonize Marty while portraying Jerry Steuerman in the most innocent light possible, one plausible reason emerged the day after his father's funeral.

For weeks Gottlieb had been waiting for the results of the county criminalistics lab's analysis of the forensic evidence taken from the scene. When he called the DA's office to see what was taking so long, Jablonski told him there was a backlog at the lab. Gottlieb wasn't buying it. He wrote to Jablonski's boss, District Attorney Patrick Henry. This was a double homicide, he said, one of the most high-profile cases in years. A month was more than enough time to do basic tests on blood and hair. When the first set of lab reports finally came, Gottlieb was delighted by what he read. No wonder they were sitting on this, he thought.

The crime lab had analyzed all the strands and fragments of hair recovered from Arlene Tankleff's body—in her hands, and on her arms, knees, and stomach—as well as from the bed and floor around her. None of the hairs matched Marty's. All were determined to be "similar to" Arlene's, which meant they could be hers—or some unknown person's. Of particular interest to the defense was that the hairs were rootless. Jerry Steuerman wore a hair weave, a form of hair extension that was made of rootless human hair.

Gottlieb considered the initial forensic findings so compelling—and he was so infuriated by Jablonski's attempts to manipulate perceptions through the media—that he went public with the crime lab's report himself. Proclaiming that the prosecution's own forensic evidence provided "additional positive proof that they have arrested the wrong man," Gottlieb called on the district attorney's office to admit its mistake and start from scratch. "Please," he said, "it's time to dismiss it and find out who the real murderer is."

"Ridiculous," replied Jablonski. He recited the prosecution's mantra: "I can't make clear enough that Marty Tankleff told us he killed them, he told us how he did it and he even indicated the weapons that he used. There will be no investigation of whether someone else did it."

Jablonski had a point when he said that the hair evidence hardly proved Marty's innocence. But what he didn't say—what he had yet to release to the defense—was that the forensic investigation was yielding strong indications that the key details attributed to Marty's confession were not true. That the Tankleffs were *not* killed with the weapons that McCready and Rein claimed Marty told them he used. The crime lab had failed to find any trace of blood on either the dumbbells or the knife, both of which, according to the detectives, Marty said he returned to their original places after washing them in the shower.

Like any experienced forensic investigator, the chief of the lab's serology section, Robert Baumann, knew that blood had a way of getting into the slightest gaps and crevices of an instrument used in a violent attack. It would seem to be the case here, given the injuries described by the various doctors who worked on the victims. These, for instance, were the observations of Dr. George Tyson, the neurosurgeon who operated on Seymour Tankleff at the Stony Brook medical center: "It appeared Mr. Tankleff was first hit with a blunt instrument four to six times on the back of the head. There were several deep scalp lacerations and a depressed skull fracture. . . . The knife wounds were as deep in front of his head as they were in the back. It appeared to me that the knife wounds were administered in an angry or vindictive state, as if the individual was attempting to do more than just injure him. In my opinion, the individual or individuals who administered the blows and the knife wounds attempted to decapitate Mr. Tankleff."

As an expert in blood evidence, Baumann wasn't concerned with how "angry or vindictive" a seventeen-year-old would have to be to commit these acts on his own parents. All he was interested in was whether that young man had left even the slightest trace of blood evidence for him to find on the murder weapons. Given the carnage inflicted on both victims, Baumann had good reason to believe he would find what he was looking for, regardless of how thoroughly the defendant might have thought he cleaned his weapons. There were just too many places for blood and tissue to hide.

Baumann started his hunt for trace evidence in the most obvious place. The knife was recovered by the crime scene team with a sliver of pinkish substance along the edge of the blade. To the casual eye, it could resemble a trace of bloody body tissue. But that wasn't what Baumann found when he put the knife under his microscope. It wasn't blood, and it wasn't tissue. He brought the specimen to the histology unit, the section of the medical examiner's office where body tissue was dehydrated and mounted on slides for high-powered microscopic analysis. He later received a call from histology: The material dissolved during the processing. But of course its identity was not much of a mystery. The knife was found next to the remnants of a watermelon. The poker players said they used the knife to cut the watermelon. The substance looked like watermelon. It dissolved like watermelon. Chances were it was watermelon.

Continuing his search, Baumann disassembled the knife and inspected it microscopically. He looked in the tiny gaps where the wooden handle met the blade, and in the spaces between the handle and the round metal rivets that held the blade in place. He found nothing. The knife was clean. How was it that a knife that had supposedly been used to nearly decapitate two people, and was then supposedly washed clean of any trace of blood or tissue, came to be found with a piece of watermelon residue on it? If the police account were true, the only possibility would seem to be that Marty Tankleff took the knife from beside the watermelon, murdered his parents with it, cleaned the knife in the shower, went back into the kitchen, used the knife to cut a piece of watermelon or deliberately placed a tiny bit of residue on it, and returned the knife to its original location. But if he actually did carry out such a careful cover-up, wouldn't there be some mention of it in a confession that included such details as "He made sure that he got his father's blood on his hands to show that he tried to help his father"?

The results were the same when Baumann examined the dumbbells taken from Marty's room. He inspected the fine crosshatch pattern engraved on the bar section and all the grooves and channels of the threaded clips and collars that secured each of the two weights to the bar. He examined everything microscopically and then tested it chemically. There was not a trace of blood or tissue. He also inspected every other knife taken from the house (including the Italian souvenir switchblade that got Marty in trouble), along with two hammers found in the garage. In each case, Baumann found nothing. This raised the question: If Marty's confession was true, how could that be? It was only logical that he would have had to do as meticulous a job of cleaning the implements as the crime lab did in examining them. He would have had to take them apart. But in their account of Marty's oral statements—which included so many far less significant details of the murders and their attempted cover-up—McCready and Rein reported no such explanation. All they said was that "he washed off the knife and barbell in the shower. He put the barbell back in his bedroom."

It wasn't often that a government forensic lab provided exculpatory evidence for a homicide defendant rather than the corroborating proof expected by their fellow county employees over at the district attorney's office. But in this case the Suffolk County crime lab couldn't seem to stop coming up with findings that challenged the veracity of the confession produced by McCready and Rein.

Seeking to substantiate that the defendant had tried to wash away the evidence of his crimes, the forensics team had removed the drain assembly in the tub in his bathroom, and, to cover all the bases, the drain of every other shower and sink in the house. They delivered the plumbing to the lab, where Baumann examined the components for trace evidence. On the underside of the drain stopper in the tub in which Marty allegedly told McCready and Rein he'd washed himself and the murder weapons, Baumann found a clump of soap residue, hair, and bits of red fiber consistent with a washcloth. But no blood or body tissue.

In the drain trap itself, Baumann found more hair and soap scum, and 5.2 ounces of water. He put a few drops of the water in a test tube and added a chemical called phenolphthalein reagent, the most common test for revealing the presence of blood. If the mixture turned blue after thirty seconds, it was presumed to have blood in it. Then further tests would be performed to identify it more precisely. But Baumann got no reaction from the trap water taken from the drain in Marty's bathroom, or from the water taken from any of the other traps in the house. In each case, he also performed a second test with hydrogen peroxide. All the results were still negative. Finally, he put the water in a beaker and evaporated it, then tested the "residual debris." This, too, was negative for blood.

If the police account was true, how could the accumulation of hair, cloth fibers, and soap scum in and around the tub drain include not a molecule of blood? And how could Marty have cleaned up so fastidiously that he left not one drop of blood anywhere else in the bathroom—yet miss a splotch of blood on his own front shoulder? As the detectives told it, Marty said it was simple: "I screwed up."

There was yet one more glaring inconsistency between the confession attributed to Marty—the sole basis for his arrest and indictment—and the physical evidence found at the scene. This one was evident from the very day of the murders, and required no microscopes or chemical agents.

The police claimed that Marty described the sequence of his actions this way: He went naked into his parents' bedroom and hit his mother four or five times on the head with the dumbbell, fighting with her until she dropped. Then he went to the kitchen, which was at the opposite side of the house, and grabbed the knife next to the watermelon. He backtracked to the bedroom and sliced his mother's throat, then ran back again to the other side of the house to kill his father with the dumbbell and the knife. In the office he hit his father four or five times on the back of the head, hard enough to crush his skull and expose brain matter; then he cut his neck, deep enough and nearly all the way around to nearly take his head off. ("He couldn't believe all the blood," McCready and Rein wrote in their report of Marty's oral statements.) Then it was back to the other side of the house to wash off in the shower. In all, according to this account, Marty made four trips from one end of the house to the other, blood on his naked body, weapons in hand. So how was it that the crime scene team failed to find so much as a drop anywhere between the two ends of the house?

While it was largely the absence of blood in important places that cast doubt on the confession, there was one instance in which the forensic investigators provided some help to the defense with blood that it *did* find. Analyzing the blood found on the sheets, pillowcases, and blankets taken from the bedroom where Arlene Tankleff was killed, the crime lab's serology section identified some that matched Seymour. This was logically inconsistent with the confession: According to the police, Marty said he killed his mother first, then his father. He then showered, according to the statement, and never went back into his mother's room. How, then, did his father's blood become mixed with his mother's?

And what of the blood found on the wall around Marty's light switch? The section was cut out and sent to the lab, where the bloody impressions were examined under a microscope. They were found to have a "consistent honeycomb pattern," revealing that the impressions had been made by someone wearing rubber gloves. No gloves turned up during the crime scene team's three-day search of the house and property. Nor did they turn up in Marty's purported confession.

As they absorbed the crime lab's findings, Marty's relatives found themselves returning to the Question: Why did Marty say he did it? It was such a mind-bender that some found it hard to resist the impulse to be angry with him. Mike Fox recalled Ron Falbee's reaction when he briefed him after seeing Marty that first night: "I had asked Marty, 'Marty, do you think you did it?' And he said, 'No, I don't think so.' Ron went ballistic when he heard this. He said, 'That stupid fucking kid.'" But over the next few days and weeks, Ron turned his ire on the detectives. When he finally had a chance to talk to Marty at length after his release from jail, it all began to come together. "I actually thought I did it—they had me convinced," Marty told Ron. "I don't even remember half of what I said. It was like a nightmare, and I just wanted to wake up."

As hard as it was for them to imagine, Ron and the rest of the family—respectful citizens who never had cause to mistrust the authorities—came to believe that the police had essentially brainwashed an innocent teenager. They had used emotional coercion to elicit a false confession—or as Gottlieb's partner Ron Sussman called it, a *concession*. Here was a seventeen-year-old kid in shock over what he'd woken to. Isolated from his family. Questioned for hours. Lied to. Manipulated so expertly that he became convinced that what the police were saying was true. It was, it seemed to Marty's relatives, something approximating a psychological rape. And now the accumulating forensic evidence was supporting Marty's memory, spotty as it was, of where the details came from in that nearly seamless narrative of the crimes McCready and Rein claimed he gave them.

According to the reports the prosecution turned over to the defense as part of the discovery process, McCready made two brief inspections of the crime scenes that morning: once when he first arrived, before he talked to Marty, and again after getting Marty's initial statement. It was obvious to Gottlieb that McCready fed Marty his theory of the crimes based on what he had seen during those two walk-throughs, and then put his presumptions in Marty's mouth. "Either Marty's just volunteering all this patently false information, which just doesn't happen in the real world, or the confession was a fabrication by the police," Gottlieb said. "To me, it was clear. It was what they thought happened."

Gottlieb had seen and heard a lot over the years. But he found it hard to imagine homicide detectives so arrogant—so cavalier about a teenage boy's life—that they would fill in the blanks of a double murder and simply assume the crime lab would prove them right. This was beyond the pale, Gottlieb thought, even for Suffolk County.

AFTER SEYMOUR TANKLEFF'S DEATH, his family sat shivah at his daughter's house in Port Jefferson Station. Judaism's ritual mourning period lasts seven days from the funeral and comes with a long list of restrictions. So Marty and his father's side of the family found themselves incongruously buoyant when Gottlieb delivered the good news from the crime lab the day after Seymour's burial. The initial forensic reports were so encouraging that both sides of the family agreed that the time was right to go on the offensive. Though the Tankleffs couldn't be there, the next day Arlene's sisters, nieces, and nephews held a press conference at Gottlieb's office and announced a $25,000 reward for information leading to the arrest and conviction of "the real killer or killers of Seymour and Arlene Tankleff." "We know Marty is innocent," Ron Falbee told the assembled reporters. "The wrong person has been arrested and charged with this brutal crime." Then, in a veiled reference to Jerry Steuerman, he added: "We're very unhappy with the investigation to date and the refusal by law enforcement to follow up on all leads that have been brought to their attention."

When the reporters made their obligatory calls for comment to the DA's office, Jablonski scoffed at the news that Marty Tankleff's family was offering a reward. "I hope the Suffolk County Police Department enjoys it in their coffers," he said, before turning serious. "I guess it's nice that the family is supporting him. But the family wasn't there when he was admitting the crime to the police."

Like many attorneys who tried high-profile cases and knew how to use the media, Jablonski was always good for a pithy quote. But two weeks later, the chief homicide prosecutor of Suffolk County was off the Tankleff case, and so was his deputy, Tim Mazzei. They were barred by the presiding judge because both would be called as witnesses at the pretrial hearing on the defense's motion to suppress Marty's self-incriminating statements. Jablonski was among those present at Marty's side of the phone conversation he had with Shari on the evening of his arrest. He was prepared to testify that the defendant told his sister that he "acknowledged" to the police that he had murdered his parents. Mazzei, meanwhile, would be a *defense* witness, called to testify about another phone conversation—the one in which Gottlieb instructed him *not* to arrange the call between Marty and his sister. Gottlieb would argue (successfully, it would turn out) that the police and prosecutors arranged the phone call as a way of getting additional statements from him after he was represented by counsel—an attempt to skirt the law and a clear violation of his rights.

With both Jablonski and Mazzei disqualified, the prosecution of Marty Tankleff fell to the next in line, a rising star in the DA's office named John Collins. Most of the twenty or thirty homicides committed in Suffolk County each year were of the unsensational variety, the kind in which drugs turned up somewhere and justice was achieved without too much complication. These were generally the sorts of cases John Collins had handled since his promotion to the homicide bureau a couple of years earlier. Then he'd been given a plum assignment: the case of the Angel of Death.

Richard Angelo was a pudgy, bearded, bespectacled nurse at Good Samaritan Hospital in West Islip. He was a volunteer firefighter in his working-class town and a former Eagle Scout. At twenty-six, though he looked a decade older, he seemed a thoroughly unremarkable fellow. Until the day in 1987 when he was hauled away in handcuffs, arrested for injecting an undetermined number of patients with lethal doses of a muscle-relaxing drug called Pavulon. From the confession that he gave up with little fuss, it seemed Angelo was a stealth killer in white uniform with a brain full of crossed wires and a locker full of poison. He explained that he was simply someone who "felt very inadequate" and meant only to cause his patients respiratory distress sufficient for him to perform heroic acts to save their lives and inject his own with a dose of self-esteem. He failed on all counts. He may have killed more than two dozen people, though he was charged with only ten and eventually convicted of four. The "Angel of Death," he was inevitably dubbed by the media.

The Angelo case was a complex affair that was to consume John Collins for more than two years and assure him a footnote in the annals of American serial murder. But to nearly all but his victims' loved ones, Richard Angelo would eventually fade into history—tried, convicted, shipped off to oblivion.

And then came Marty Tankleff, a name that was not to fade away. A case that an assistant district attorney might look back on, for better or worse, as the one that defined his career. The kind of case that people might talk about for twenty years.

CHAPTER 15

Shari's Choice

WHEN SHARI ROTHER was growing up, her father wasn't nearly so prosperous as he would become a generation later. Shari followed him out to Port Jefferson from Nassau County after starting her own family in the mid-1970s, but proximity didn't bring parity with her adoptive half brother. "Marty was the prince and Shari wanted to be the princess," Ron Falbee observed. "But she wasn't. It was too late."

As Marty grew up, it became increasingly evident to him that Shari begrudged his pampered life. It was a resentment that often took the form of a kind of sibling rivalry by proxy. Her two children were just a few years younger than Marty, and by Shari's lights they were entitled to live in comparable style. "I guess she felt that since she didn't have what I had during her childhood, she wanted her kids to have it," Marty said.

As it was, Seymour and Arlene were exceedingly generous with Shari and her family. Over the years, Seymour tried to boost Shari and Ron's fortunes by giving them money to start a variety of businesses, all of which failed. There was a tanning business, a clothing store, vending machines. "Sy was always putting them in a position where they could make money," Arlene's sister Mickey said. For years he did it with Arlene's support, but there came a time when it began to wear on her. "Arlene tried really hard to keep Shari happy, but it was never enough. Shari was just extremely jealous of Arlene."

And Arlene began to return the hostility. Shari's ability to get money out of Seymour infuriated her. The relationship between wife and daughter deteriorated to such an extent that it would not be an exaggeration to say that they despised each other. Whether because Arlene barred Shari from her home or Shari refused to set foot in it, Seymour had to go to

Shari's house to see his daughter. The antagonism was an overriding factor in Seymour and Arlene's brief separation and their ensuing execution
of new wills, which would virtually cut Shari out of her father's estate. But
Seymour was determined to maintain the relationship. For Shari's fortieth
birthday, just months before he was murdered, he took her to Atlantic
City, picking her up in a limousine and sharing a two-bedroom suite,
treating her to everything from gambling to shopping. But he never told
Shari about the will.

The day after Seymour died, Mike Fox asked Ron and Carol Falbee,
Norman and Ruth Tankleff, and a man from the legal department of Hofstra University to come to his office for the reading of the will. Absent
would be Seymour's two children: Marty had not yet been bailed out of jail
and Shari wasn't invited. It was Fox's decision. He knew he would have to
deal with her sooner or later, but right now he just wanted to get the will
filed in Surrogate's Court so some of the assets could be freed up to pay for
Marty's defense.

Fox and Ron Falbee's preliminary calculations put the worth of the estate at roughly $3.2 million, not including a $500,000 insurance policy
that was to be used to establish a scholarship at Hofstra University. Nearly
a third of the estate's value was in the house on Seaside Drive, which
would eventually be appraised at slightly more than a million dollars.
There was another million or so in stocks, bonds, and liquid assets. And
there were Seymour's business holdings. They were the hardest to reckon.

Since the week of the murders, Fox and Falbee had spent hours together trying to make sense of the business affairs Seymour left behind. "It
was all just a mess," Ron recalled. "Everything was handshakes with him.
He was in a deal with this one, a deal with that one, making deals over the
card table. There was minimal documentation. He carried a lot of it
around in his head. And some of these people disappeared when Seymour
died. He was right when he told Mike that his empire was crumbling. Because everything he had was just crap. I went to the gym he opened. It was
a hole in the wall. You could see studs hanging and it's musty and there's
leaks all over. And I'm thinking, 'Oh, my God, Seymour, what were you
thinking?'"

In the basement of the house, Ron and Mike found the remains of
some of Seymour's failed schemes: cartons of unsold baseball cards, cases
of wine that Seymour bought as an investment. "I remember Seymour always talking about this wine that supposedly went for four hundred dollars a bottle," Ron said. "But he didn't keep it in a wine cellar. Just the
cellar. I pulled one out and poured some." He and Mike took a sip. "It was
like vinegar," Fox said. "Shari wanted it anyway, thinking she could sell it.
I said, 'You want it, take it.'" And Shari wanted some other things from the

house—Arlene's things. "Her jewelry, her furs, her car—a Cadillac Eldorado that was falling apart," Ron said. "Shari Rother wanted everything that Arlene Tankleff had."

The group was seated around a table in a conference room, with Fox about to begin reading the will, when the door opened. The group looked up to see Shari and Ron Rother. "Mike said, 'Shari, what are you doing here?'" Ron Falbee recalled. "She said, 'I'm here for the will, of course.' Mike said, 'Shari, you're not involved in this.' And she pointed to me and said, 'What's *he* doing here?' And that's when Shari found out that I was the executor and the trustee and that Carol and I were Marty's legal guardians. In other words, we were controlling the whole ball of wax. It was obvious she had no idea." Of course, that was the least of what Shari didn't know as she and her husband took their seats at the table.

"To my beloved wife, Arlene Tankleff," Fox began, "I devise and bequeath . . ." Arlene would have received everything had she survived her husband. With her death, the Hofstra trust would now receive the Tankleffs' liquid assets, roughly a million dollars, about a third of the estate. Shari listened carefully to see how she and Marty would be dividing the rest.

"As to my business interests and my interest in my home in Belle Terre, New York," Fox read, "and in the event that my wife, Arlene Tankleff, predeceases me, I give, devise and bequeath to my son, Martin Tankleff, to have and to hold for any purposes he deems advisable."

A baffled look crossed Shari's face as Fox continued with a long paragraph stipulating that Marty's inheritance would be held in trust until he reached age twenty-four. Several more paragraphs spelled out how he was to be taken care of in the seven years until then.

Shari was visibly in shock at the realization that her father had left her almost nothing. "She was white as a ghost," Fox recalled. And she reacted as he and most in the family expected: She hired a lawyer within the week. But she didn't take any immediate action to challenge the will. Instead she tried to persuade Marty to make some adjustments on his own. As Marty recalls, "She was trying to recruit me to her position and it started with wanting me to change the guardianship." Then it moved on to suggestions about changing some of the financial terms of the will. During these months, Marty was living with Shari and her family to be near his friends, but he spent most of his weekends with the Falbees in Nassau County. "The whole time he's out there, she's working on him," Ron recalled. "'You can change the will. We can split it down the middle. We can do this, we can do that.' I said, 'Marty, if she wants to question the will, you just tell her you have nothing to do with it. She should come to Mike Fox or me.'"

A few days before Christmas, Shari called Ron and said she needed to talk about Marty. They met at a diner in Port Jefferson, where Shari told him that things with Marty weren't going well. She had a list of complaints. "They were so petty and nonsensical that I knew something else was going on," Ron said. "Putting it together from what Marty was telling me, I think she was getting angrier and angrier that he wasn't agreeing to change the will. Shari said to me, 'Look, this just isn't working.' And I said, 'Fine, I'm happy to have him, let's get his stuff together.' She had it with her. So we went outside and just took it out of her trunk and threw it in my trunk."

It was that same week that Shari took the first step toward formally challenging her father's will. At a hearing in Surrogate's Court, her lawyer spent three hours questioning Mike Fox about the circumstances under which the will had been changed in 1985. During a break, the attorney told reporters that Shari would decide in the next few weeks whether to proceed with a lawsuit. But whatever she decided, it had nothing to do with her feelings toward Marty: "My client is very supportive of her brother and believes strongly in his innocence."

Ron told Marty not to believe it. "I've known your sister a long time," he said. "And I'm going to tell you a hard fact of life. Marty, she is going to turn on you. She is going to turn on you, and it's going to be about the money."

Even Jerry Steuerman thought the same thing. During their conversation at the bagel shop, Steuerman told Joe Demma that Shari only *seemed* like Marty's biggest supporter. "You're gonna see," he said. "Next year at this time Shari's gonna go the other way. Right now, there's nothing she can do to get that money. If she sticks with Marty, God forbid they find somebody else that did it, she and Marty maybe will share in this thing. Maybe, if Marty allows it. But if Marty gets sent away, she gets everything."

How much was everything? To a significant degree, it depended on Jerry himself. Of all the things Mike Fox and Ron Falbee were trying to figure out, what confounded them most was what Steuerman owed Seymour before he was murdered. In an encounter of the strangest kind, Fox and Falbee met with Steuerman and his lawyer, Michael Grundfast, to talk about settling the debt without a protracted legal battle. Ron had never met Steuerman, and he was surprised by his first impression: "I knew he killed my aunt and uncle—there was no question in my mind that he was involved. But he came across as very unassuming, not threatening at all. Almost kind of swishy."

Less surprising was that Steuerman was even more disinclined to pay what he owed Seymour after his death than before it. He threatened to dissolve his corporation and declare personal bankruptcy if the estate didn't accept considerably less than the total debt. The estate called his bluff. He held. They sued. Less than two months after Seymour's death, Jerry was served with papers from his estate seeking $900,000.

In January, Shari filed a suit of her own, formally contesting her father's will. She claimed it was a fake. She also claimed that Mike Fox, in preparing the will, misunderstood her father's wishes, and that the terms were the result of undue influence by Arlene. Even people who were no fans of Shari had to concede she had a point about Arlene, but a bossy wife wasn't likely to win the day for a contentious daughter. And if her challenge failed, Shari would not get what she considered her rightful share of her father's estate unless Marty gave it to her—or he was convicted of murdering his parents. As the newspapers noted each time they covered a development in this battle of wills, in New York State a convicted murderer couldn't inherit money from his victims.

THE FIRST TIME Marty spent a weekend with the Falbees, a couple of months before he moved in with them, Ron talked to him late into the night about the events of September 7. They talked and watched TV until Marty fell asleep on the couch around midnight. Ron woke him up at two and talked to him some more. He wanted to make sure his answers didn't change. There was the tiniest part of Ron that was still testing Marty, still making sure his own belief in him was based on truth, not just family loyalty. "I knew he didn't do it, but I've got two little kids and my wife upstairs. If you had to measure it, it would be .00000001 percent. By the end of that weekend, it was zero percent. I knew this kid didn't do this."

After he moved in, Marty would help his young cousins with their homework and drive them to school in the car that replaced the notorious Lincoln. And he would go back to Port Jefferson for his own lessons, meeting his tutors at Mark Perrone's house. Ron, meanwhile, put Marty to work in one of his Hallmark stores and tried to instill in him values that were different from what he was used to—a deprogramming of sorts. "Marty," he said, "I loved your dad, but he was a shitty businessman. What he did is not the way you do business. A good deal is when each side is satisfied. Your dad made one-sided deals, and one-sided deals are not good deals. They don't last, they don't build relationships. They just suck someone dry."

And that, Ron told Marty, is why your father is dead.

Marty listened, but Ron wasn't sure he was really getting it. Someday he will, Ron thought.

There was something else Marty didn't really get, Ron thought, something much more important right now, and that was how much trouble he was really in. The adults around Marty thought he would be acquitted, but they were cautious about their confidence. They knew there was plenty to worry about, and Gottlieb let them know from experience that anything could happen in a trial. But Marty seemed nearly oblivious. In jail, he'd met Suffolk County's other notorious murder defendants of the moment—Richard Angelo, the Angel of Death of Good Samaritan Hospital, and Matthew Solomon, a twenty-three-year-old accused of killing his wife of two months on Christmas Eve in 1987, then stuffing her body in a plastic garbage bag and joining the search party. Marty said they both seemed nice. He seemed not to grasp that he was now even more infamous than they were. Because *he* was innocent. Nice as they seemed, they probably weren't. When he thought about the period between his arrest and trial years later, Marty heard his own voice saying the same thing over and over: "Innocent people don't get convicted."

His first consciousness of reality might have come one night after work, when he went out to a diner with one of Ron's warehouse employees and stayed out till 10:30 without calling. Ron was furious when he finally showed up. "I picked him up and threw him against the wall," Ron remembered, "and I said, 'You don't seem to understand something. You're facing jail on *murder* charges. You better realize this is not a game, and you are in big, serious trouble. You are not like everyone else. Not anymore. Another kid gets a speeding ticket, he gets some points on his license. You get a speeding ticket, you have a chance of going back to jail.' Marty was never late again after that. I think it was a little wake-up call. It got him a little closer to the reality of how much trouble he was in. But not all the way there. He still thought there was not a chance in the world he would be convicted."

PART TWO

Trial and Error

CHAPTER 16

Shenanigans

OUT OF NOWHERE, Jim McCready had thought of his periodontist. A strange thing to occur to a homicide detective in the middle of an interrogation of a suspect in a double murder. But that was McCready. At any given moment, it was anybody's guess what thought might pop into his head.

McCready and his partner didn't have all the time in the world. Their suspect was only seventeen, and he had to have family looking for him—to say nothing of the family lawyer. The guy could call at any second and say the magic words that would bring everything to a screeching halt. McCready felt he had the kid on the edge. He knew it. That's when his mind flashed to the last time he was in the chair, and the dentist telling him how the adrenaline in the anesthetic he was about to give him could cause a sudden increase in heart rate and bring on palpitations. This, McCready was to say, was his inspiration for the ruse that pushed Marty Tankleff over the edge. *They pumped your father full of adrenaline. . . .*

Minutes later, Marty was falling into the abyss, wondering aloud if it could be possible that he blacked out and massacred his parents without remembering it. Years later, someone asked McCready what he remembered thinking at that moment. McCready's face instantly brightened with self-satisfaction. "I *gotcha*," he said. "I *gotcha*. I *gotcha*." By the third *gotcha*, his face was atwitter with glee. "That's a good feeling, when you get somebody to roll over. It's an art."

It wasn't the artistry of McCready's performance that was at issue six months later, but the legality of it. In early March 1989, Bob Gottlieb began trying to make the case to Suffolk County Court judge Alfred C. Tisch that Marty's alleged statements to the police should never reach the ears of a jury. Newly assigned as the trial judge, Tisch would make that crucial decision after conducting a pretrial hearing to determine whether the confession was voluntary, reliable, and legally taken, or whether it failed to meet one or more of these standards and should be suppressed.

For more than two decades, such a proceeding had been a New York defendant's best chance to challenge the validity of self-incriminating statements. Coerced confessions, even those that might be true, had been barred as evidence by the U.S. Supreme Court since the 1920s. So by law, judges throughout the country were obliged to suppress confessions they found to be involuntary. But what if the circumstances were in dispute? In New York, the question was for the jury to consider as part of its ultimate decision. Jurors were instructed to disregard the confession if they deemed it involuntary or unreliable. In 1960, a lawyer for a convicted defendant centered his appeal on a flaw in the system: What if the jury decided the confession was coerced but *didn't* disregard it? More to the point, how could anyone know, since the verdict didn't say? Four years later, the appeal reached the U.S. Supreme Court, which declared that New York's long-standing method of determining the admissibility of a confession—which was used in fifteen other states and six of the ten federal districts—violated the defendant's constitutional right to due process.

In the wake of the Supreme Court decision, the New York Court of Appeals devised a new system to give defendants who had confessed a way to challenge the admissibility of their statements. A judge would hold a hearing in advance of the trial, at which he would review the defendant's statements and hear testimony about how they had been obtained. If the judge found the confession valid, the defendant's lawyer could still, as under the old system, contest it before the jury. To illustrate how the new procedure would work, the Court of Appeals chose the case of a man from the West Side of Manhattan who was appealing his conviction for a robbery that was based largely on a confession he claimed the police beat out of him. The man's name was Charles Huntley, and from then on the new pretrial proceeding was known as a Huntley hearing. A few months later, Huntley lost his own Huntley hearing.

A quarter century and thousands of Huntley hearings later, Robert Gottlieb hoped to demonstrate that any testimony about what Marty Tankleff said to Detectives James McCready and Norman Rein on the morning of his parents' murders—or, more precisely, what they said he said—should be suppressed because it was the result of an illegal interrogation that led to an involuntary and unreliable confession. The issues would involve legal distinctions of the most subtle kind, and the magnitude of Judge Tisch's decision could not be overstated. Marty's statements were not just the heart of the prosecution's case—they were its *entire* case. With the crime lab's failure to find any physical evidence tying Marty to the murders, the case would live or die by Tisch's decision. In a paradoxical way, this made suppression an even tougher sell for the defense than it usually was.

In the courtrooms of Suffolk County, perhaps more than in other places, justice was not necessarily administered without consideration of political obligations. And politics were certainly in the air as the case of *People v. Tankleff* moved toward trial. For months it had been an open secret that District Attorney Patrick Henry was probably not going to run for a fourth term in the fall. It was also evident that Judge Al Tisch was interested in succeeding him. And if Tisch were to win the Republican nomination, his opponent in the fall was almost certain to be the same combative Democrat who had made a run at the office four years earlier. Robert Gottlieb had decided he had one more campaign in him.

At fifty, Judge Tisch was a slender, bespectacled man with thin, straight black hair that reached from one side of his head to the other—a comb-over, but a commendable one—matched by a dark mustache. He had a low-key manner and a reputation as an able and fair-minded judge and a likable fellow out of his robes. Gottlieb wasn't displeased when he learned that Tisch would be presiding over the Tankleff case. He wasn't one of those judges defense lawyers hated to draw, the kind who was always putting roadblocks in front of them with his rulings on evidence. "I went in thinking he'll let me try my case," Gottlieb said, "and that's all I ever want."

But just as the Huntley hearing was starting, Patrick Henry made it official that he would not be running for reelection in the fall, and for the first time Al Tisch's name appeared in print as a leading contender to succeed him. But Tisch insisted he wasn't an active candidate. If he were, under the state's canons of judicial ethics he would have to give up his seat on the bench. When *Newsday*'s Joshua Quittner asked him about his intentions, Tisch candidly said he'd run only if his party handed him the nomination. To resign his judgeship to run in a contested primary, Tisch said, "I'd have to be an idiot."

Tisch said much the same thing when Gottlieb broached the subject in the judge's chambers on the morning the suppression hearing was to begin. "Considering the circumstances, Judge, I've got to ask you: Do you feel comfortable sitting on this case?" Gottlieb asked. *Entirely* comfortable, Tisch replied. He pointed out that he was not yet an actual candidate; he didn't even think he was the front-runner for the nomination.

Then he turned the question around: Do *you* feel uncomfortable with me? No, Judge, said Gottlieb. And you, Mr. Collins? Not at all, Judge.

"All right, then," said Tisch.

WHETHER OR NOT political developments would actually lead to the untenable conflict Gottlieb envisioned—the judge against the defense lawyer, the winner becoming the prosecutor's boss—it was lost on no one that the case would play out against a backdrop of the issues that had ignited the previous campaign for DA and might well come up in this one: the conduct of the county's homicide prosecutions and the question, pressed by Gottlieb four years earlier, of why police interrogations in Suffolk County were not videotaped. No case brought up that issue more vividly than the one Gottlieb was defending now.

Videotaping of suspects by police and prosecutors had come into wide use over the previous decade, as prosecutors throughout the United States realized that putting a camera into the picture was a simple means of removing doubt from cases built around contested oral confessions. The district attorney of the Bronx, Mario Merola, had instituted a videotaping policy as far back as 1974, leading Manhattan DA Robert Morgenthau, among others, to follow suit. Where videotaping was adopted, recording a suspect's ultimate confession was most common, but the more progressive jurisdictions began at the beginning and captured every moment of the interrogation. By the mid-1980s, the police in Southern California's Orange County, the nation's largest suburban county, would not talk to a suspect without at least an audiotape running. In 1985, the Alaska Supreme Court made its state the first to require police to tape all questioning of suspects. The failure to do so, said the court, denied a defendant "an objective means for him to corroborate his testimony concerning the circumstances of the confession." In Alaska, a criminal defendant could no longer be tried, much less convicted, solely on the basis of an unrecorded confession.

That same year, a continent away, Suffolk County was exploding with questions about the integrity of its homicide prosecutions. Gottlieb pledged that he would institute a videotaping policy if he were elected DA. A week after the election, the incumbent victor, Patrick Henry, announced that henceforth, homicide suspects who made oral admissions would be asked to repeat their confessions on camera, and in the presence of an assistant district attorney. The new policy came a decade after nearby jurisdictions began videotaping suspects, and it fell far short of recording not just confessions but the interrogations that preceded them.

Nevertheless, Henry made the announcement with fanfare. The equipment had already been installed, he told reporters at a press conference, and "we're doing training now, waiting for our first customer." He declined to attribute the decision to the botched cases over the previous months that led Judge Stuart Namm to complain to the governor about homicide prosecutions in Suffolk County. Nor did it have anything to do with his election opponent's repeated criticism of the office for failing to institute a videotaping policy.

With Henry leaving office four years later, his chief homicide prosecutor told *Newsday* that he loved going to the videotape. "It's great having these things," Ed Jablonski said. "When you only have a written confession, it's always the cop's word against the defendant's. Now, with videotaping, it's not a question." According to Jablonski, eighteen murder defendants had given oral or written confessions in the past year, and fifteen of them "went on videotape." That the suspects "went" on videotape meant that the camera was turned on only after the suspect had been questioned for any number of hours, by any number of detectives, with any number of interrogative techniques, and was then, as Henry put it, "willing to make a statement." So juries would not see unabridged reality, with all its context and nuance, but a kind of rehearsed soundbite. It could be a credible summary of a truthful, legally obtained confession. Or it could be something else.

The confessions-only policy adopted by Suffolk County in 1985 wasn't unusual—other police departments around the country also chose not to videotape interviews and interrogations. The rationale typically offered was that videotaping made suspects nervous, kept them from telling the truth. But that was less a reason than an excuse. Many departments installed cameras and microphones behind walls and ceilings, which was legal and effective. Whatever their official reasons, the fact was that jurisdictions that didn't put cameras in the interview room were guided mostly by a single concern: You never know what might show up on that tape. Such was the reasoning in Suffolk County, as it was explained years later by a former homicide sergeant. "Sometimes you have to get in people's faces," said the detective, "and with a camera in the room, it can inhibit a detective. You have to be careful. You don't want people to see what goes on in there."

The homicide detectives who claimed Marty Tankleff confessed to them said that Marty agreed to go on videotape, but that his lawyer interceded before he could perform his final act of procedural contrition, confessing to the camera. But who would have been seen on that tape—the Marty of the police account who lucidly and matter-of-factly confessed to slaughtering his parents that morning because he didn't like his car? The Marty who was said to have given a nearly perfect narrative of the crimes but for the fact that it described exactly how the murders had *not* been committed? Or would the tape have revealed him to be what he claimed from that day forward: a teenager dazed by the horrors he'd woken to, reeling from five hours of questioning and one mind-bending lie. All of this raised one more hypothetical question: What if Mike Fox had called later than he did? What would the detectives and prosecutors have done if they'd had the chance? Would they have turned the camera on?

As with so many homicide trials before, neither judge nor jury, prosecutor nor defense attorney, would ever know precisely what went on in that little room in Yaphank. In the pursuit of absolute justice, secondhand truth was all there was. Starting with the Huntley hearing's jury of one, it would have to do.

ON THE MORNING of March 6, 1989, a day short of six months after the murders of Arlene and Seymour Tankleff, Judge Alfred Tisch began the prelude to the trial of their son.

To reach his decision, Tisch would have to consider the testimony of more than a dozen people about several pivotal moments on that chaotic day in September. To establish the confession's validity, Assistant District Attorney John Collins planned to call six detectives, two assistant district attorneys, two uniformed officers, the mayor and the chief constable of Belle Terre, and the photographer from *The Port Jefferson Record*. Bob Gottlieb, on the other hand, would rely on his cross-examination of the police and the testimony of but a single witness of his own: Mike Fox. Gottlieb could only hope that Fox, an attorney for thirty-six years, would make a believable witness.

On the afternoon of Marty's arrest, Gottlieb had asked Fox to write an account of everything that happened that day. Fox's memo focused on his initial encounter with McCready on Seaside Drive at around eight o'clock. He described how McCready intercepted him in the street, distracted him from seeing Marty, then sent him on his way by telling him that Marty had just left for the hospital in a patrol car. But whatever McCready did or did not do, it was what Fox said or didn't say in those moments that mattered most. He claimed that before leaving, he identified himself as Marty's lawyer and told McCready that the detectives were not to question him outside his presence. But Gottlieb had been worrying about Fox's story for months, ever since the day back in September when McCready came to his office to deliver the police account of Marty's confession. McCready had read about Fox's claim in *Newsday* and couldn't wait to tell Gottlieb what a problem he had.

"You know, I saw Fox at the scene that morning," McCready said. "I spoke to him."

"I know you did," Gottlieb replied.

"The problem was he didn't say the magic words," McCready said. "He didn't tell me he was a criminal attorney representing the kid. He didn't put us on notice. And now he's kicking himself in the ass because he fucked up."

"That's not my understanding," Gottlieb said cautiously.

"Well, if you want to let him perjure himself in a court of law, that's your business," McCready said. "Because my guess is no judge in the world is going to believe that man put me on notice at eight o'clock in the morning and turned around and put me on notice again at 1:22 in the afternoon."

Six months later, McCready took the witness stand and delivered a tidy account that began with his initial conversations with Marty outside his house and ended in the interview room at homicide headquarters, where McCready—as he now revealed publicly for the first time—tricked Marty into confessing to his parents' murders by staging a phone call from the hospital. The ploy was the big news in the day's media coverage, but it was another part of McCready's testimony that was of more crucial interest to the defense lawyer: the detective's version of his encounter with Mike Fox.

McCready testified that he and his sergeant, Robert Doyle, were interviewing Marty in front of McCready's car when Marty noticed Fox's arrival and pointed him out. At that point, McCready left Marty with Doyle and met Fox in the street. They introduced themselves, Fox telling McCready he was Seymour Tankleff's business attorney for thirty years, McCready responding, Yes, Marty told us that. "And he asked me how it was going. I said, 'Fine, the kid is telling us everything that he knows about what happened.' At one point in time I heard [Marty] say to him, 'Hi, Uncle Mike.' Mike Fox waved back to him. Mr. Fox asked me what I was going to do with the kid when I was finished. I said, 'What would you like me to do with him?' . . . And he asked me if I would bring him to the hospital when I was finished. I said, 'Sure, when I'm finished.'"

Aside from the absence of any legal warnings by Fox, the news here was McCready's claim that Marty and Fox acknowledged each other. If true, it would support the prosecution's assertion that Fox saw Marty talking to the police and did nothing to intercede. But McCready seemed a little unsteady when Collins asked him if Fox said anything to Marty when he waved to him.

"No, sir," McCready said. But then he changed his mind. "I believe he may have asked him, 'How is it going, Marty?' Or something to that effect. Can I check my notes to be sure?"

McCready opened a folder and flipped through a few pages. They weren't the original notes he wrote in his pad the morning of the murders—those contained no mention of any exchanges between Fox and Marty, verbal or otherwise—but a typed report of the day's events he and Rein composed a week later. After checking this report, McCready testified that Fox asked, "Are you okay, Marty?" and that Marty replied, "Yeah, I'm okay."

Fox had always insisted that he never even saw Marty. It was the cornerstone of his version of events, and he would have his chance later in the hearing. For his part, Marty told Gottlieb that the moment was one of the few things he remembered vividly: He recalled how strange and upsetting it was that his father's best friend, his "Uncle Mike," drove off without coming over to see him. Marty wouldn't be testifying at the hearing, but Fox's version would be supported by Shari's testimony that she was upset when Fox returned to the hospital without Marty. She asked him where he was, and Fox said he thought Marty was already at the hospital. The police told him they'd brought him over in a police car.

McCready's direct testimony took four hours. His cross-examination lasted four days. Gottlieb grilled McCready, and later Norman Rein, about their words and actions throughout that day, focusing on the key moments. "Let's go through this again," Gottlieb said, like a detective himself, after McCready repeated his version of Fox's appearance at the scene. "How far is Marty from Mike Fox when you say he had this conversation?"

"About thirty-five feet," McCready said.

"You recall that clearly?"

"I do so, sir."

Gottlieb sidled over to the defense table and picked up a court transcript. He returned to the lectern and read the relevant section of McCready's grand jury testimony. Then he returned his eyes to McCready. "There is no mention here about this conversation between Mike Fox and Marty Tankleff, is there?"

"No, sir," McCready said.

With that concession, Gottlieb began drawing attention to a curious sequence of events. According to McCready, it was from an article in *Newsday*, on September 9, two days after the murders, that he learned that Fox was claiming he had put the police on notice at eight o'clock that morning. And it wasn't until five days later, after he and Assistant District Attorney Ed Jablonski discussed this "legal problem involving Mr. Fox," as he put it, that he made any record of the purported exchange of greetings between Fox and Marty.

"As a matter of fact," said Gottlieb, "in your original notes that you were making contemporaneously on September 7, there is *no* mention of Mike Fox, is that correct?"

McCready said that was true.

When Sergeant Robert Doyle followed McCready to the witness stand, he, too, testified that Marty and Fox acknowledged each other. And he, too, conceded that he had made no record of it.

Gottlieb's obvious insinuation was that McCready added a fictional exchange of greetings and hand waves to undercut Fox's coming claim that he didn't see the police talking to Marty at the scene—an assertion that was the linchpin of his much bigger claim that he told McCready that Marty was not to be questioned outside his presence. But Gottlieb's endeavor had a significant obstacle. For the judge to believe it, he would have to believe that Doyle was backing up McCready's lie with one of his own. Despite the homicide squad's sullied reputation of late, it was a lot to expect from Tisch. Another Judge Namm he was not.

But the real rub for the defense had less to do with McCready and Doyle's credibility than with Fox's. Even if it was true that McCready had isolated his suspect from the family attorney and was lying about it now, it only sharpened the logical question that went to the heart of one of the defense's two grounds for suppression: If Fox never saw Marty speaking with the police, and he returned to the hospital believing Marty was already there or on his way, why would he have told McCready that Marty was not to be questioned? Especially since he would have had no reason to think Marty was a suspect.

Gottlieb weighed the options, and the balance tipped ever so slightly in favor of taking a shot. He decided to put Fox on the stand and pray that the judge believed him.

After three weeks of testimony by police witnesses, Fox climbed up to the witness box. Gottlieb asked him about his professional background, seeking to convey that here was a lawyer of long experience and sound credibility. Fox said he graduated from law school in 1952, spent a few years as the house counsel for a holding company on Wall Street—"I traveled all over the world for them"—then started his own practice in Nassau County. He'd represented clients of just about every kind over the years, both civil and criminal. "I have handled federal acts in drugs, possession and sale. I have handled kidnapping, I have handled attempted murder, I have handled fraud, grand larceny, burglaries, and then a whole series of misdemeanors as well."

Gottlieb asked about his friendship with Seymour Tankleff. "It was a very close relationship," Fox said. "I would say as close as men can get." Gottlieb asked him to elaborate. "Well, I was involved with his family, he was involved with my family," Fox said, his voice starting to crack. He stopped to fight back tears. "Excuse me," he said to Tisch.

"Sure," said the judge.

"How would you describe it?" Gottlieb asked, impatient with Fox's display of emotion, which he considered unhelpful.

"Well, we cared for each other very deeply," Fox said.

Gottlieb turned to September 7, and Fox recounted the steps that led him to pull up to the Tankleffs' house, where an officer directed him toward a group of men standing in front of an unmarked police car parked up the road. "I must have taken between five and ten paces, when this gentleman who was coming from that far car arrived, stands on the lawn, not in the street, stands on the lawn, holding a white plastic coffee container with the lid on but a piece torn out to drink from with both hands, and he stood there and said, 'I'm Detective McCready. Can I help you?' At that point, I reached into my wallet and I pulled out a business card for purposes of identification. I handed it to him and I said, 'I'm Myron C. Fox. I'm the Tankleff family attorney. I'm here to represent Marty Tankleff. I don't want him questioned except in my presence and I'd like to see him.'"

How did McCready respond?

"He said, 'That's fine, but we don't have Marty here. He told us everything he knew, including his father's business associates and his problems and we sent him over to the hospital to be with his father.' I said to him, 'How and when?' and he said, 'Well, within the last five minutes. . . .' I said to him, 'Well, if there's anything you're going to want to know about Seymour's business, I have been his attorney for thirty years and I'll probably be in my office this afternoon.'"

Fox said he drove back to the hospital, but Marty wasn't there. A while later, he asked a detective, John Pfalzgraf, if he could find out where Marty was. Pfalzgraf said he'd try and came back fifteen minutes later. "And he said, 'Marty is in Yaphank with Detective McCready.'" (Pfalzgraf would later testify that he told Fox that Marty was "en route" to Yaphank, a version supported by McCready's phone records.) "I got very upset," Fox continued. "I said to him, 'What the hell is he doing in Yaphank, when I was told he was on the way to the hospital and I gave instructions for him not to be questioned?' He shrugged his shoulders. He said, 'Well, he's not being questioned, he's volunteering information concerning his father and his father's business partners, and as soon as he's through'—I think he used the words *being debriefed*—'we're going to bring him right over.' And I said, 'You're going to bring him right over now,' and Detective Pfalzgraf said to me he would take care of it." Then, "I said to Ron Rother, 'Ron, maybe you ought to go over to Yaphank and get the kid.' . . . Ron said, well, he'd rather stay with Shari and Seymour."

Fox joined the family at the hospital in Stony Brook. Why go there and not to police headquarters? Gottlieb asked him. "To be with Shari," Fox said, "in case there might be any consents, requirements or things like that, to make sure that the family was out of the eye of the press, and to see if Marty was there." He stayed at Stony Brook for nearly three hours, then drove to his office, forty-five minutes in the opposite direction of Yaphank. He had the radio tuned to a news station. "And on it I heard that Marty was being held for questioning by the Suffolk County police."

By this point—even before he was cross-examined—Fox was shaping up as a disaster for the defense. He revealed himself to be a man who had operated that day less as a savvy criminal attorney than as a close family friend. Like everyone else, he was shocked, grief-stricken, and sure he knew who was responsible. Told that Marty was being "debriefed" about his father's business with Steuerman, Mike Fox—who knew more about the situation than anyone else—believed the police were correctly focusing on Steuerman. One of the first things he planned to do when he arrived at his office was to gather documents for the detectives. It didn't even occur to Fox that it was actually Marty they considered their prime suspect all along.

The problem, as it was becoming obvious to people on both sides of the case, was that Fox could not live with that truth. McCready was probably right when he said that Fox was kicking himself because he had failed to see what was going on—failed to protect his best friend's son. Desperate to undo the damage, it seemed, Fox rewound the clock to that critical moment on Seaside Drive and inserted the magic words, trying to create a new reality, praying it would save Marty, and himself. If this seemed evident enough from Fox's direct testimony, Collins peeled away whatever doubt remained. Just as Gottlieb had raised the possibility that McCready fabricated a moment to back up his testimony, Collins suggested that Fox whipped up some fictional dialogue to support his own.

Collins showed Fox two documents. The first was the typed account Fox wrote for Gottlieb on the day of the murders. It described his conversation with McCready this way: "Informed Mr. McCready that I was the family attorney and, in fact, gave him one of my business cards and asked to see Marty. He informed me that they had already sent Marty over to Mather Hospital to be with his step-sister and the family."

The memo supported half of Fox's account. But it was the other half that interested Collins. He asked Fox if he wrote that he informed McCready that he represented Marty, and that the police were not to question him.

"No, I didn't in so many words, I didn't," Fox conceded.

Then Collins called Fox's attention to a second document, this one handwritten on yellow legal paper. Fox described it as an "in-depth" account that he wrote later the same day. It said he told McCready, "I am here to represent Marty Tankleff and he is not to be questioned without my presence and I want to see him."

When did you first give this report to Mr. Gottlieb? Collins asked. Fox said it was "somewhere near the inception of this hearing or a little after that." He conceded, when pressed, that it was "about a week ago." Where was it all that time? "It was in my desk drawer. I informed my secretary that in the event anything happened to me it was there and it was for my purposes of enlightenment only, because I was getting funny phone calls."

Fox's last comment, weirdly reminiscent of Jerry Steuerman's disappearance six months earlier, seemed to befit testimony peppered with cringeworthy moments for the defense. Earlier, there had been winces all around when Fox, in the middle of his testimony, winked at someone in the press section. It might have gone unnoticed but for Collins, who leaped to his feet to ask the judge to take note that "in the course of the answer to this question the witness was winking to the reporters." Fox later explained that he was just acknowledging a photographer he recognized from the hearing on Seymour's will a few months earlier.

When Fox stepped down, Gottlieb knew he'd just witnessed the collapse of one of his two main grounds for suppression. "I was not happy," he recalled. "Fox did not come across in a way that I would expect of an attorney, which is absolutely straight, no shenanigans. You never want to give a judge a reason to go against you, especially when you know going in that you have to bowl him over."

But Gottlieb had one other basis for his move to suppress the confession. He was thankful it had nothing to do with Mike Fox.

THE CONCEPT OF police custody is not as simple as a pair of handcuffs or a jail cell. In New York State, the legal standard is this: If a reasonable person, innocent of any crime, had been in the defendant's position, would he have believed he was free to leave? If the answer was no, the law deemed the defendant to have been in custody.

By this definition, and factoring in Marty's age, Gottlieb believed he had a strong case that Marty was in custody and should have been advised of his rights even before he got in McCready's car. At the very least, the "interview" had to be considered a custodial interrogation the moment it became accusatory. By McCready and Rein's account, that was at about 11:15. Since McCready didn't advise Marty of his rights until much later—at 11:54, after the fake phone call and ensuing accusation, and after Marty made his first incriminating statements—his confession should be suppressed. As Gottlieb put it, "You can't just say custody suddenly happens when he starts doing what you want him to do, which is confess."

Knowing that the custody issue would be his best chance for suppression, Gottlieb dissected the seven hours from Marty's 911 call to the point when Fox stopped the questioning in Yaphank at 1:22 in the afternoon. One of Gottlieb's primary objectives was to demonstrate that McCready, as the lead investigator, immediately settled on Marty not only as the prime suspect, but as the only suspect. This wasn't difficult to do. When Gottlieb questioned him about Marty's repeated assertions that Jerry Steuerman was responsible for the attacks on his parents, McCready had to concede that he dismissed this possibility without any investigation whatsoever. Gottlieb found his disregard of Steuerman so inexplicable that he asked him if he knew or "ever heard the name Jerry Steuerman" before that day.

"Oh, God, no," McCready replied. "I never heard of him."

Gottlieb's cross-examination became a duel that brought out McCready's volatility. When Gottlieb asked him to repeat what he'd told him about Mike Fox that day at Gottlieb's office, McCready replied: "I said, 'He's kicking himself in the ass right now because he fucked up,' is what I said."

"And you said it just like that," Gottlieb said.

"You're damned right I did," McCready snapped.

At another point, Gottlieb and McCready skirmished about the point in the interrogation when Marty was asked to demonstrate how he had moved his father from his chair. "What I'm telling you," McCready said finally, exasperated, "is I cannot recall the specific, absolute movements of this moving of the chair. . . . The chair was moved, okay?"

"But you don't know who moved it?" Gottlieb asked.

"I do know who moved it," McCready replied. "We moved it."

"Detective, please, I don't mean to trick you. I want to go step-by-step."

"You're not tricking me," McCready fired back. "You couldn't trick me if your life depended on it."

Gottlieb paused, as if taken aback. "The way you just talked to me now," he asked, "would you describe that as a way that you were talking to Marty Tankleff on this day?"

"No, sir," McCready said.

"You just saved that for me?"

"Yes, sir."

"Thank you. . . . Detective, are you angry at me?"

"Am I angry at you?"

"Yes. Are you angry at me?"

"Yes, sir."

"Well, you're an experienced homicide detective, you've been questioned many times on the witness stand. Do you get angry with all the defense attorneys, or just me?"

"I don't have a problem with defense attorneys. I understand very, very much that a defense attorney comes into this courtroom and he has a job to do, and I have a job to do also. But I am very, very upset at the defense attorneys when they come in and they lie and they make up things, they say I said things that I never said. That upsets me, yes."

McCready was still ranting about liars when he encountered the *Newsday* columnist Paul Vitello in the hallway after his testimony. Vitello was struck by McCready's hot temper on the witness stand. The detective seemed more emotionally involved than the usual homicide cop.

McCready scoffed. "Martin Tankleff means nothing to me," he said. "He's just like all the others. They all lie."

A FEW DAYS after the hearing ended, Gottlieb opened his Sunday newspaper and saw a headline that ruined his weekend: GOP LEADERS BACK JUDGE FOR DA. Meeting privately the day before, the Suffolk Republican Party's executive committee—the county chairman and the party chiefs from each of the county's ten townships—had voted unanimously to support Judge Alfred C. Tisch for district attorney.

Gottlieb put down the paper and called his partner, Ron Sussman. "How can he sit on this case?" he asked.

"He can't," Sussman said. "He has to recuse himself. He's got to know that."

Sussman was confident of this not only because he knew the law, but because he knew Tisch. They were friendly outside the courthouse, even played together in a regular poker game. Sussman told Gottlieb their first move had to be to find out from Tisch himself whether he was going to accept the nomination, and if so, whether he planned to step down from the bench, as judicial rules required, or at the very least recuse himself from the Tankleff case. Sussman also thought Gottlieb shouldn't be the one to ask Tisch these questions. It might come off as a political play. Sussman, on the other hand, had both a personal relationship with Tisch and built-in credibility: He had long been active on the county bar association's ethics and grievance committees. "Coming from me, he won't see it as political," he told Gottlieb.

First thing Monday morning, Sussman called Tisch's chambers in Riverhead, and asked for an immediate conference. John Collins was sum-

moned to the courtroom, and within the hour Sussman was standing before his poker chum. Even before a word was said between them, Sussman
knew he had miscalculated. Tisch was glowering at him.

"Your Honor, I have an application," Sussman said. "I am here, Judge,
to emphasize that the application I am about to make is not a matter of
politics." He wasn't questioning the judge's personal integrity, Sussman
assured Tisch, but the weekend's political developments left his firm with
no choice. They were duty-bound to their client, "whose fate, in large
part, is in your hands." Sussman began reading aloud from the New York
State Canons of Judicial Ethics: "'A judge should not engage in other political activities. A judge should resign his office when he becomes a candidate. A judge should conduct himself in a manner that promotes public
confidence in the integrity and impartiality of the judicial arena.'"

Sussman felt Tisch's silent gaze as he spoke, but pressed on. He closed
the book on judicial ethics and began quoting from two other volumes,
reciting the definition of "candidate" from *Black's Law Dictionary*, and then
from *Webster's*. Then he looked back up at Tisch. As he remembered years
later, "He didn't say a word during my whole pitch. He's just glaring at me,
looking at me like I'm stabbing him in the back."

And then Sussman came to the point. The Republican leaders were on
record; the question now was whether he planned to accept their nomination. "If the answer is yes, I have no choice but to move for recusal. If the
answer is no, I need it on the record and we can move forward again."

Finally Tisch responded. He said he had no answer to give because he
didn't think there was even a question at this point. All he knew, the judge
professed, was that his party's leaders were "prepared" to "indicate" that
"they believe" the nomination should "be tendered" to him. Until then,
"I'm not in a position to either agree to accept it or to decline it."

Sussman thought Tisch was being disingenuous. "The issue as to
whether or not you're a candidate exists right now," he insisted, adding
that the official nomination would be a formality by the time it occurred.
That wouldn't be for another month—a month too late to comply with
the judicial canons. "The time would be now," Sussman said.

Now—as in *before* Tisch ruled on the motion to suppress Marty Tankleff's confession. However they felt about Tisch before the hearing,
Marty's lawyers now had serious reservations about his ability to be impartial. As Gottlieb recalled, "I knew that our best shot of winning the case
was right now, in our motion to suppress, and we needed a judge strong
enough to say that this confession as a matter of law was not admissible. I
couldn't allow it to be used by some guy who wanted to show how he's
tough on crime to pander to the electorate."

Tisch's adamant refusal to relinquish the Tankleff case did nothing to discourage courthouse scuttlebutt that he had sought and been assigned the case as a way to raise his profile in advance of his run for district attorney. The year before, Tisch had been among several criminal court judges temporarily transferred to the county's civil courts to relieve a backlog of cases there. Back in the criminal court later in the year, Tisch was given both of the county's two biggest homicide cases—two of the biggest in decades. One was a case Tisch had been assigned before his temporary transfer: the prosecution of Richard Angelo, the nurse charged with giving fatal drug injections to patients at Good Samaritan Hospital. Then, with the Angelo case still working its way toward trial, Tisch was given the Tankleff case as well. Another judge had handled the case's initial proceedings, but in January 1989, four months after Marty Tankleff's arrest, the administrative judge transferred the case to Tisch.

After Sussman put forth his motion, Tisch asked Collins what the People's position was. The prosecutor said his office opposed the motion— that he agreed with everything Tisch said and had full confidence in the judge's ability to preside impartially. Tisch turned back to Sussman and told him to put his arguments in writing. He'd make a ruling within the week.

Sussman and Gottlieb filed their brief two days later, and included a photocopy of a news article published the day after Sussman's appearance in court. It reported that Tisch's nomination—despite his insistence to the contrary—was virtually a done deal. Party leaders were on record saying they had already arranged a temporary job for Tisch, as a law secretary to a fellow Republican judge once his candidacy became official and he would be forced to leave the bench. But Tisch was no more persuaded by the defense's written motion than by its oral one. A week later, he wrote that he found himself to be in no violation of judicial ethics and therefore declined to either step down from the bench or to recuse himself from this or any other case.

Was Tisch trying to hang on long enough to make a ruling that would be good for his image as he embarked on the first major political campaign of his life? Or was he simply hedging his bets? In either case, it was hard to avoid seeing him as a man whose primary concern was his own career. Thus some people saw a bit of poetic justice in how Tisch's bid for DA fizzled in the days ahead. Indeed, his stubbornness turned out to be an exceptionally bad career move.

The turning point was a story by *Newsday*'s Joshua Quittner revealing that the judge had apparently not been quite the noncandidate he claimed over the previous month. He had in fact been actively campaigning for the nomination behind the scenes at the very time he was presiding over the Tankleff hearing. Halfway through the monthlong proceeding, Quittner reported, Tisch had his secretary arrange a meeting with a number of county Republican leaders, including four of the party's ten town chairmen, "to discuss what we're going to do this year for the district attorney's replacement," according to one of the participants. A few days later, on March 22, Tisch adjourned the hearing's morning session early, at 11:45, for a reason that was now apparent: The judge—and his law secretary—had to get to the political meeting scheduled for noon at an office near the courthouse. The meeting went well. It led to the party leaders' vote two weeks later to recommend Tisch for the nomination.

But if the party's support was unanimous, so was the criticism Tisch got from legal experts. There was no question, they told reporters, that Tisch had violated state judicial rules barring sitting judges from "participation, either directly or indirectly," in any activity "of a partisan political nature." So focused was Tisch on parsing the language of the judicial canons that he seemed to miss the overriding one: It wasn't enough for a judge to avoid actual impropriety; he had to avoid the appearance of it. "He should not be sitting on *any* criminal cases," Hofstra law professor Monroe Freedman, one of the nation's foremost legal ethicists, told *Newsday*. "He shouldn't wait for an objection."

But Tisch *still* refused to recuse himself, or even to say whether or not he planned to accept the nomination. This annoyed even the party leaders, who began to see Tisch's clumsy maneuvering as evidence that his political instincts were perhaps not of the highest caliber. By early May, Tisch's repeated insistence that nobody had offered him anything became a self-fulfilling prophecy: The party voted to nominate Tisch's chief rival, a failed congressional candidate named James Catterson.

The turn of events didn't ease Gottlieb and Sussman's discomfort. "After the firestorm in the press and the nomination was withdrawn," Sussman recalled, "it came back to me from multiple sources, though he never said it to me directly, that Tisch was telling people, 'Sussman stabbed me in the back' and that I ruined his political career. Great way to start the case. We eventually talked about it, years later, and he told me that he did take it personally. He felt what I did was for Bob as a political candidate. He couldn't believe I would question his integrity, and I told him, 'Al, that's not what I was doing at all. It just wasn't right.'"

Sussman and Gottlieb had to believe that Tisch would not allow his personal feelings to influence his decisions. But could they ever know for sure? It was even more to ask of those with the most at stake—Marty Tankleff and his family and friends—who knew nothing about Tisch and had no reason to give him the benefit of the doubt, beyond the presumption that no judge would put his bruised ego above someone's life.

* * *

ON MAY 8, Tisch issued a thirty-five-page ruling on Marty Tankleff's statements to the police: They were voluntary, legal, and proper for the jury to consider. "The testimony of the police witnesses," he wrote, "was generally frank, candid and apparently trustworthy, marked by no substantial or serious inconsistencies or contradictions and possessing the flavor of credibility. . . . The testimony of the defense witness, Myron Fox, however, impressed this Court as wholly without candor, incredible to a large degree in the face of overwhelming evidence to the contrary, and generally unworthy of belief."

In Tisch's judgment, Fox didn't behave as a lawyer that day and this was clear from the moment he first arrived at Mather Hospital and Shari Rother asked him to fetch her brother. Fox's claim that he put McCready on notice was patently unbelievable. He would have had no reason to think his friend's son was a suspect, so he would have had no reason to warn the police not to question him. Moreover, his claim was belied by what he did once he learned that Marty was en route to Yaphank or already there. "We suspect any lawyer, experienced or not, would have been on the phone immediately or in his car, going as fast as the speed limits permitted to intercept his client at Yaphank. Yet we know he did none of the above. . . . We do know he did accompany his mortally wounded friend to Stony Brook Hospital. This is the conduct one would expect of a longtime friend of the family as opposed to an attorney representing a defendant." And when Fox heard on his car radio that Marty was being held for questioning, "Did he make a U-turn and head back to Yaphank to extract his 'client' from the clutches of the police? No! Did he immediately call police headquarters on his car phone to insist that they honor his earlier advice that he was representing defendant? No! He tells us that he called the defendant's cousin, Ron Falbee, from his car phone and asked Falbee if it was all right for him to call the police."

Gottlieb was chagrined to see his main witness ridiculed so mercilessly, but he was more disappointed by the judge's rulings on the claims he considered his stronger arguments for suppression: that the police failed to advise Marty of his rights until long after they began a custodial interrogation, and that they used psychological coercion to extract an unreliable confession from a teenager in shock. Tisch didn't buy any of it. He ruled that Marty was not in custody at any time earlier than the point when he was given his rights. Based on their accounts, which he found highly credible, Tisch judged McCready and Rein's questioning of the defendant to be straightforward, devoid of any coercive tactics. The detectives were simply trying to find out the truth, Tisch wrote, and McCready's ultimate ploy was within the bounds of acceptable police conduct according to federal case law. It was not so great a deception that it would "truly compel" a confession, least of all a false one.

IT WAS DOUBTFUL that anyone savored Judge Tisch's rulings more than Jim McCready. The judge validated both his methods and his results, and McCready surely didn't mind the attention he got for his inspired deception in the cause of justice, which he described on the witness stand with a dose of his characteristic swagger. Coupled with the case of the "Homeroom Hit Man," Marty Tankleff's arrest made McCready arguably the most prominent of the Confession Takers.

McCready was riding the wave of his triumph in the Tankleff case when he got another splash of positive press from *New York Times* reporter Dena Kleiman's book about the Cheryl Pierson case. *A Deadly Silence*, published just a month after Marty Tankleff's arrest, was a police procedural that didn't look too closely at the procedures of its hero. McCready was commonly viewed by people on the job and off as arrogant, alcoholic, and largely unmanageable—but nobody said he couldn't play people. Kleiman described him as a highly intelligent detective who was "at his best when faced with an unsolved murder"—a model of open-mindedness, scrupulousness, and patience: "The way McCready looked at it, time was always on his side in a murder case: Let those who are guilty think they have gotten away with it. Let them get sloppy. No matter how many years he had been a detective, it never ceased to amaze him how often criminals sabotaged themselves if only given time. Patience was one of his great virtues as a detective. Careful methodology was another. A compulsive researcher, he was the kind of stickler for detail who always said he would rather be late and right than first and made a fool. 'If I have six nails in a coffin it might stay closed,' McCready liked to say. 'But if I have forty . . .'"

If this portrayal of McCready bore little resemblance to the detective who showed up on Seaside Drive on September 7, 1988, a decidedly less flattering depiction appeared in another publication a few months later: *An Investigation of the Suffolk County District Attorney's Office and Police Department*. Its author was the New York State Commission of Investigation. Three years after Judge Stuart Namm's official complaint to Governor Mario Cuomo, the investigation he triggered was now complete. The findings more than vindicated him.

The SIC had launched its investigation on the basis of Namm's allegations of perjury and incompetence by the police and prosecutors in two consecutive murder trials over which he presided. But the commission went on to conduct a much wider investigation of law enforcement in Suffolk County, and its final report, 199 pages long, included revelations of many varieties of misconduct and mismanagement, in assorted units and at all levels. But it was still the investigation and prosecution of murder cases that accounted for the commission's most disturbing findings.

In the late fall of 1986, toward the end of the first year of the investigation, the commission had subpoenaed six detectives and two prosecutors to testify behind closed doors about their actions in the cases of murder defendants Peter Corso and James Diaz. James McCready was the only one of the six detectives still working in the homicide squad by then. The commission had a few questions about his convoluted and dubious testimony about the railroad workers and the phantom photographs in the Diaz case. McCready chalked it up to an honest mistake, but the SIC commissioners found him culpable of much worse. In their final report, they said that McCready "knowingly gave false testimony" in the trial of James Diaz.

To be sure, McCready's evident perjury was only one of numerous instances of corruption in the pursuit of justice, by any number of detectives and prosecutors, alleged by the SIC after its examination of numerous homicide cases. In the Diaz case alone, the commission found that no fewer than six prosecution witnesses had given perjured or otherwise untrustworthy testimony—and five of the six were members of the prosecution team itself: two detectives, two senior assistant district attorneys, and the deputy director of the county crime lab, who had since pleaded guilty to criminal charges of lying about his credentials in this and more than twenty other major felony cases. (No less troubling than his perjurious résumé-padding, said the SIC, was how two senior assistant district attorneys buried the allegations for three years.) The one perjurer who was not a member of law enforcement was Joseph Pistone, the motorcycle thief who claimed that Diaz, as well as another accused murderer, confessed their crimes to him in jail. Pistone admitted to the commission that he lied in the Diaz trial and that his perjured testimony was facilitated by two detectives who showed him Diaz's alleged confession and told him, "This is how it happened."

The Diaz case was a debacle by anyone's measure. Yet, as the SIC said it was "shocked" to discover, the police department never conducted an internal investigation, much less disciplined any of the detectives involved. It was only after the SIC itself exposed a pattern of serious misconduct by the case's lead detective that he was transferred to the robbery squad after seventeen years in homicide. But McCready was neither transferred nor disciplined. He had since gone on to lead investigations of several high-profile homicides, culminating in the Tankleff case.

In examining Diaz and several other cases in the context of the homicide squad's long-standing reputation for having a confession rate that was too high for comfort, the commission came to the same conclusions as *The National Law Journal* and later *Newsday:* that Suffolk County homicide detectives relied far too much on confessions, had far too little concern for physical evidence and fundamental investigation, and could count on prosecutors going to court with whatever they gave them, no questions asked.

The SIC report cited one remarkable exchange it had during a closed-door session, when members of the commission were quizzing a detective sergeant about the county crime lab's work with blood evidence. Asked what the lab's technicians could tell from a stain recovered from a murder scene, the sergeant said, "I guess they can tell you if it's blood." If it was blood, he was asked, what else could they tell you? The sergeant said he had no idea. He had been a homicide squad *supervisor* for eleven years but didn't know that the crime lab could determine blood type.

But nobody drew more criticism from the investigations commission than District Attorney Patrick Henry. The SIC excoriated Henry's office for its tolerance of shoddy and even fraudulent police work, and the DA himself for his blasé attitude about the quality of the prosecutions yielded by those investigations. The report cited one of the more stunning moments at the hearings, when Henry testified that his entire review of the Diaz fiasco consisted of talking to trial prosecutor Barry Feldman and "possibly" reading "part" of the trial transcript, after which he decided that Feldman had done nothing wrong. Questioned by an incredulous commission member, Henry said, "I think that if he had done something wrong, and coupled with my questioning him on the subject, it would have been obvious that he did something wrong."

In its report, the SIC revealed that a few weeks after the public hearing, Governor Cuomo's criminal justice director arranged a private meeting between Henry and commission chairman David Trager "in an effort to resolve questions raised at the public hearing and to bring about needed reforms." According to Trager, the DA opened the meeting by saying, "I probably can't run again." Still, he was trying to make some changes. Among other things, he had already relieved Barry Feldman of his duties as chief of the felony trial bureau. Trager wasn't impressed. The man should be fired, he told Henry.

The district attorney's softened attitude, such as it was, didn't last. After the SIC's investigation expanded to include allegations about illegal wiretapping and other wrongdoing in narcotics cases, Henry went to court to try to quash the commission's subpoena of his chief narcotics prosecutor, and later to block the public release of the SIC's final report. Both efforts were rejected by the state Supreme Court, as were more than a dozen lawsuits aimed at hindering the commission's investigation that were filed by the three unions representing members of the police department. When the report was finally released, two weeks after he announced he would not run for a fourth term, Henry blasted it as "the bastard child born out of the political rape of Suffolk County law enforcement." It was unclear what the motive might be for a "political rape" by a bipartisan commission that was chaired by a law school dean from Brooklyn and included a career federal prosecutor and a former Suffolk County district attorney who was, like Henry and most other elected officials in the county, a Republican.

The SIC report was released on April 24, 1989—right in the middle of the five weeks Judge Alfred Tisch spent deliberating whether the homicide squad had extracted a proper and voluntary confession from Martin Tankleff. But neither the report's accusation of perjury against the case's lead investigator, nor its finding that the homicide squad was an institution with a deeply embedded history of misconduct, had any effect on Tisch. The testimony he heard from McCready and the other detectives was, in his view, "frank, candid, and apparently trustworthy."

Stuart Namm, the judge who found McCready, among others, to be none of the above, paid for his whistle-blowing with his career. In March 1988, he testified before another watchdog agency, the state Commission on Government Integrity. He said that no other judge in the county would join him in reporting police and prosecutorial misconduct to the SIC because they feared offending political leaders whose support they needed for reelection. Within a few weeks of that appearance, the county's administrative judge, Arthur M. Cromarty, transferred Namm from the criminal to the civil part of the court system, where he remained for two years, even as the backlog of criminal cases exceeded a thousand. Cromarty, for whom the County Court complex was later named, told the press he wouldn't dignify the suggestion that the extended transfer was punishment.

That Namm's courage was political suicide became official when his seven-year term drew to a close in 1992 and the two major political parties, which had cross-endorsed him in the previous election, declined to renominate him. The Republicans were so intent on purging Namm that they gave the Democrats three new judgeships in return. With that, Stuart Namm, who dreamed of a life as a judge, was out. Abandoned by his own party, Namm was hardly consoled by the chairman, Dominic Baranello, his former law partner. "Stuart," Baranello told him, "this just wasn't your year."

CHAPTER 17

Burdens of Proof

IN JUNE 1989, a month after his statements to the police were ruled admissible, Marty graduated from Earl L. Vandermeulen High School. He received his diploma after a school year of home tutoring, but he wasn't allowed to attend the graduation ceremony, just as he wasn't allowed to go on the senior class trip to Florida, or to stand with his classmates for the senior picture on the school's front lawn. And that fall, when most of his friends and classmates were going off to college, Marty stayed behind, living with his cousins and working in their greeting card stores. His life was in a state of suspension.

The American justice system promises a defendant a speedy trial, but some are less speedy than others. In Marty's case, justice was delayed: The judge and the prosecutor had a prior engagement with a serial killer and the defense attorney was running for district attorney. Bob Gottlieb spent that fall doing battle with James Catterson, who owed his Republican nomination to Al Tisch's blunders. While Gottlieb promised new vision and higher purpose, Catterson determined that after twelve years under Patrick Henry, all the DA's office needed was a little "fine-tuning." He said of Henry, "History will judge him a great district attorney."

Catterson was an insider, a man who practiced law in the civil courts and politics in the back rooms. At fifty-nine, he was looking for his first election to public office. But he proved a ferocious campaigner, essentially running on the proposition that a defense attorney couldn't be district attorney. "Who will Bob Gottlieb fight for—the victim or his murderer?" Catterson asked in television commercials. In response, Gottlieb spewed righteous indignation. "He is a *dangerous* man," he said, noting that "Abraham Lincoln also represented criminal clients." He pointed out, as he often did, that he started his career in the Manhattan district attorney's office and within two years was assisting the office's top homicide prosecutor in convicting a gang of Croatian terrorists who planted a bomb in Grand Central Terminal that killed a member of the NYPD bomb squad.

But Catterson's ad campaign was music to the ears of the county's law enforcement community. In announcing his organization's endorsement a month earlier than usual—"because the right choice is so clear and so important"—the head of the Police Benevolent Association declared that the PBA's candidate screening committee was aghast at the Democratic candidate's representation of "the most heinous criminal element." Asked to clarify his reference, the PBA president said he was talking about Martin Tankleff, of course. The man responsible for Marty's arrest, meanwhile, was happy to share his thoughts on the campaign. "He doesn't have the experience to be the DA of this county," opined Detective James McCready, adding that Gottlieb's failure to win their most recent courtroom battle—the murder trial of Patrick Schoendorf—demonstrated that he was a weak trial attorney. It was typical of McCready's penchant for unwitting remarks: His implication seemed to be that Gottlieb should have gotten an acquittal because the case he and Norman Rein made against Schoendorf was weak.

"It is *inappropriate* and *unprofessional* for Detective McCready to be getting involved in this campaign," Gottlieb fumed when he was informed of McCready's comments. Easily goaded, he took the bait of McCready's barbs about his competence. He ticked off cases he'd won for his criminal clients: Antoinette Corona, the woman who drowned her baby? Got that one reduced from murder to criminally negligent homicide. David Rubinstein, the big-deal land speculator they made a big deal of arresting for grand larceny and forgery? Got him acquitted. In view of Catterson's campaign theme, Gottlieb's self-defense was probably not the best strategy.

A few days before the election, Catterson announced that Gottlieb's election would cost the taxpayers of Suffolk County more than a million dollars. This was his calculation of the legal fees the county would have to pay outside attorneys to prosecute Gottlieb's pending cases. Catterson's cost estimates might have been a little on the high side, but he was right that Gottlieb's election would throw his cases into disarray—the Tankleff case, in particular. Not only would he be unable to stay on as Marty's defense attorney, but as the new district attorney he would have to recuse his entire office from the prosecution and hand the case to a special prosecutor appointed by the governor. So John Collins would have to be replaced as well, even if he didn't find the prospect of working for Gottlieb so odious that he quit.

However Gottlieb's election might have changed the trial and its outcome, the questions became moot when Catterson won by a comfortable margin. It presented an unlikely juxtaposition of odds. Of the hundreds of homicides that had been committed in Suffolk County over the previous decades, the murders of the Tankleffs were the first ever recorded in the village of Belle Terre. And while the village's 839 citizens accounted for less than one-sixtieth of one percent of the county's population of 1.32 million, the man now responsible for prosecuting the case was one of their neighbors. The new district attorney lived on Druid Hill Road, a short walk from the scene of the crimes.

JOHN COLLINS spent the 1989 election season waging a successful campaign of his own. In the courtroom of Judge Tisch, he won multiple convictions of Richard Angelo, and Tisch sentenced the sociopathic nurse to the maximum, a total of sixty-one years. In the weeks between verdict and sentencing, the judge conferred with Collins and Bob Gottlieb, and together they made a date. The trial of Martin Tankleff would commence with jury selection four months hence, on April 2, 1990, nineteen months after the arrest of the defendant.

It would be hard to imagine two lawyers whose worldviews and personal styles were more different than Bob Gottlieb and John Collins. Gottlieb was Jewish, liberal, a man of his generation who was still rebellious at forty. He had grown up in the suburban heartland of Hicksville, the same middle-class, middle-island town that produced Billy Joel. He was the middle of Doris and Harold Gottlieb's three sons. Doris was a school secretary, Harold a furrier. When Gottlieb began working on the Tankleff case, he took note of the name of the bagel business his client's father was involved in. While he was growing up, Gottlieb's father and a partner owned a shop called Strathmore Furs. But unlike some other sons—those of Seymour Tankleff and Jerry Steuerman, for instance—Gottlieb never thought of joining his father's business. He was destined for a career in law and politics. Like his campaign style, Gottlieb's courtroom manner was passionate and tenacious, sometimes to a fault. He didn't care if he irritated his adversaries, or the judges, and he certainly wasn't the kind of lawyer about whom a prosecutor could say, "He works well with us."

John Collins was Irish Catholic and Bronx-born, a graduate of Fordham Law School who was right at home among the police, prosecutors, and judges who made up Suffolk County's insular criminal justice establishment. Collins was a battler, but not in the observably zealous manner of some others in his line of work. At trial he was methodical, efficient, controlled. If a case called for outrage, he would summon it sparingly and coolly. He seemed more comfortable expressing his emotions through sarcasm. But beneath Collins's almost drab exterior lurked a street fighter. No doubt it contributed to his rise in the DA's office. At thirty-four, Collins was the deputy chief of the homicide bureau, about to begin his second straight very high-profile multiple murder case.

The prosecution's pretrial propaganda campaign simmered down somewhat after Ed Jablonski departed the case, but Collins was not above making his own out-of-court contribution to the legend of Marty Tankleff, psychopathic spoiled brat. He told Carolyn Gusoff, the reporter covering the case for Long Island's all-news cable TV station, that it had occurred to someone in the homicide squad at one point that the Tankleff case bore a striking resemblance to an old Charles Bronson movie, *10 to Midnight*. Maybe the kid saw it and got inspired, Collins said, so the police went around to video stores to see if Marty ever rented it. He hadn't, but Collins still liked the theory, enough to mention it to Gusoff, who thought it was interesting enough to include in an article she later wrote for the Long Island section of the Sunday *New York Times*. "There are an awful lot of parallels," Collins told her, and Gusoff's story left it at that. So what were all those parallels? In this "scummy little sewer of a movie," Roger Ebert wrote when *10 to Midnight* was released in 1983, Bronson starred "as a Los Angeles police captain on the trail of a mad slasher. . . . The creep is a psychopath who gets his kicks out of anonymous phone calls to women. After he warms up over the phone, he likes to crawl into their apartments, take off his clothes, and run around stark naked carving them up with butcher knives. There are, of course, the usual shots in which horrified naked women cower in the corners of shower stalls, etc."

So it was that Judge Tisch's first order of business in the matter of *People v. Tankleff* was to call Collins and Gottlieb to his chambers to discuss the procedures they would use for jury selection—specifically, how they would minimize the influence of pretrial publicity. They agreed to an unusual process. First, the prospective jurors were to be brought into the courtroom in groups and asked whether they had already formed any opinions about the case based on media coverage, or wished to be excused because the trial would probably last two or three months. Those remaining would be questioned individually in the judge's chambers, asked by Tisch and the lawyers what they knew of the case, how they heard about it, and to what extent their impressions would influence their ability to judge the evidence impartially.

The prescreening process lasted a week, and at that point the eighty-nine people who remained were seated in groups of sixteen in the jury box and subjected to the usual voir dire by the attorneys. Beyond further questioning about pretrial publicity, Collins and Gottlieb tried to tease out any hidden biases that might hurt their respective cases. Collins rejected any-one who indicated sympathy for Marty because he was young. He was wary of parents with teenage children. And more than in most cases, he wanted no jurors whose attitudes suggested skepticism of the police. Gott-lieb, on the other hand, asked the prospective jurors whether they would be *less* skeptical of police witnesses. And while Collins was on the lookout for anyone who thought a seventeen-year-old could not possibly kill his own parents, Gottlieb had the opposite concern. In California the previ-ous summer, Jose Menendez, a wealthy entertainment executive, and his wife, Kitty, had been found riddled with bullets from a 12-gauge shotgun in the library of their Beverly Hills mansion. Their sons, Lyle and Erik, were arrested just two weeks before the opening of jury selection in the trial of Marty Tankleff.

Gottlieb was also concerned about a spate of sensational cases involv-ing killers who happened to have been adopted (though none killed their adoptive parents). One of them was a local boy: Joel Rifkin, who had the distinction of being Long Island's first serial killer and the first in the New York area since David Berkowitz, the notorious Son of Sam, who was also adopted. Gottlieb asked the prospective jurors whether they believed that someone who was adopted would be more likely to commit a violent crime than someone who was not. And he wanted to know whether they thought that different people reacted in different ways to traumatic expe-riences.

ON THE MORNING of April 23, Judge Tisch swore in the jury of twelve and their four alternates. The panel was comprised of eight men and four women whose occupations ranged from psychiatric nurse to postal carrier. The first juror chosen, Ronald Clipperton, would serve as the foreman. He was a technical supervisor at Brookhaven National Laboratory, an in-stitute of the U.S. Department of Energy whose slogan was "A Passion for Discovery." Tisch congratulated the jurors on their selection, then took note of another group in the courtroom. "Today we have a class visiting us from Smithtown East High School. It's a criminal justice class, and we welcome them."

From a corner of the courtroom, a television cameraman and a print photographer trained their cameras on Tisch as he spoke. It was an un-usual sight in New York. The state legislature had recently lifted a ban on cameras in the courtroom dating to 1952, and the Tankleff trial would be the first to be covered in its entirety on live television in state history. The local all-news channel, News 12 Long Island, planned to air the trial from opening statements to verdict, providing feeds to the New York City stations and Court TV. During breaks there would be commentary by Eric Naiburg, a prominent local defense attorney watching from the studio after spending two years defending the Angel of Death. Naiburg's partner for the trial would be Ken Rosenblum, a lawyer by training who had been working for Channel 12 as a producer and host. During lunch and other extended breaks, the station would return to its regular format of local news, weather, and soft features such as "The Garden Spot with Stan Dworkin." When testimony was about to resume, the station would cut in with a graphic featuring a photo of Marty as an announcer with a Movietone style intoned: *This is a News 12 Special Report: The Murder Trial of Martin Tankleff.*

In the opening scene, John Collins stood behind a lectern and addressed the twelve chosen ones and their four backups: "Ladies and gentlemen of the jury. On September 7, 1988, between the hours of three o'clock and six o'clock A.M., the lives of Arlene and, for all intents and purposes, Seymour Tankleff came to a brutal, bloody, and violent end. More horribly, it came at the hands of the son that they lovingly brought into their home some seventeen years earlier. Sitting there"—Collins motioned toward Marty, dressed in a dark suit, his hair carefully styled—"it may yet be difficult to picture the defendant as the attacker who beat his mother and father about the head and sliced their throats and necks as if they were pieces of meat. However, as the evidence develops throughout this case, your doubts, your concerns about his capability of committing these most heinous crimes, will fade, as well as the much-talked-about presumption of innocence with which he is now cloaked."

Collins skimmed his circumstantial evidence—no forced entry or burglary, only the defendant left unharmed, blood found around the light switch in his room. He offered a preview of the heart of his case, the testimony of the police detectives who would tell the jury that Marty Tankleff confessed to them before noon on the morning of the crimes. But a good deal of Collins's opening statement seemed designed to discourage the jurors from worrying too much about what they might come to regard as weaknesses in his case. How a teenager with no history of violence or mental illness, for instance, could wake up one day and butcher his parents over the most trivial of teenage gripes. "You must understand," Collins said, "that motive is a function of the inner workings of the killer's own mind, and no one else owns a passkey to that protected territory but the killer himself. . . . Whether these deaths are the result on the one hand of an adolescent tantrum gone haywire or on the other hand the result of perhaps an even more distasteful, yet ancient motive for murder—greed— do not expect that motivation to acquit for you in your minds a reasonable, acceptable justification for these crimes. There is no rational justification for crimes like these."

Collins readily conceded there were some holes in the physical evidence. It was a strategy meant to beat Gottlieb to the punch, diminish his impact, and telegraph to the jury that forensic testimony wasn't all that important when you had the defendant confessing to the crimes. Thus he admitted that while bloodstains revealed that the killer wore gloves, "We don't have the gloves." Likewise, he was eager to lower the jury's expectations of the county medical examiner's testimony about the murder weapons. It's not TV, he told them. "He cannot come in here and say for sure this is the knife that did it, for sure this barbell did it. But what he *will* tell you is that the injuries are not inconsistent with having been caused by those items." What Collins left unsaid was that the forensic scientists at the county crime lab could not even say *that* much.

Finally, Collins wanted the jurors to hear about Jerry Steuerman from him before Gottlieb, and with a spin that would turn the defense's prime argument for reasonable doubt on its head. "You will learn that from moment one the defendant claimed his father's business partner was the person who had done this." In Steuerman, Collins suggested, Martin Tankleff saw a convenient scapegoat: He knew that Steuerman was "indebted to his father" and that their relationship "was not what it once was." Then Collins attacked head-on the Achilles heel of his prosecution: Steuerman's disappearance. "Was this a smart, honest undertaking on Mr. Steuerman's part?" he asked. "Of course not. But does it cast reasonable doubt on this defendant's guilt? I submit to you that at the end of the case you will find it does not."

ROBERT GOTTLIEB began his opening statement by underscoring the principle that every defense attorney emphasizes in every case, but one that he argued was especially salient in this one: He didn't have to prove anything to them. The burden was completely on the prosecution to establish, *to prove beyond a reasonable doubt*, that Marty Tankleff murdered his parents. It was a burden, he insisted, that the prosecution could not bear. "Marty Tankleff was not the person who brutally beat and stabbed his mother and his father. Marty Tankleff is an innocent boy."

So why was Marty Tankleff here, in this courtroom, accused of the worst crimes imaginable? "Ladies and gentlemen," Gottlieb said, "you are about to see and you are about to bear witness to a police investigation that was so sloppy, so inept, so unbelievable and so objectionable that it will shock your conscience and it will send tingling and shivers down your spine." The police decided Marty did it, relied on interrogation instead of investigation, "and when they couldn't get what they wanted, they turned to lies, to deceit, to tricks. . . . Yes, you will certainly hear what Marty Tankleff ultimately uttered to the detectives. What you didn't hear during the opening statement a few moments ago was what the detectives were saying to *him*." By the end of the trial, he promised, "You will then realize the absolute meaninglessness of their supposed confession, statements that only show the length of desperation the detectives went on September seventh to get Marty to confess, even if it meant getting a *false* confession."

What of the motives attributed to Marty? "They are absurd, they are ridiculous, and they simply are not true," said Gottlieb. "You will hear from family and friends who love him and will tell you about Marty's loving relationship, up to that moment of their horrible deaths, that Marty had with his mother and father."

Now it was Gottlieb's turn to talk about Jerry Steuerman. Indeed, he left no doubt of his intention to make a shadow prosecution of Steuerman a primary element of the defense. What the prosecutor didn't tell you, he said, is that Marty's entire family was telling the police to look at Steuerman. But the detectives made the classic mistake of jumping to a conclusion without following other leads and gathering all the facts. By the afternoon, they were announcing that Marty Tankleff confessed, another case quickly solved. So when Steuerman disappeared a week later, the police and the prosecution were already locked into their story. They proclaimed that Jerry Steuerman was not involved, then set off on a manhunt. "And two weeks later Detective McCready and an assistant district attorney traveled to California, where Steuerman is found alive and well, after fleeing Suffolk County, having faked his own disappearance, having changed his appearance, having used aliases to avoid apprehension."

Gottlieb let the words hang in the air for a moment before closing with a plea. "Ladies and gentlemen," he said, "there's much more to this case than just set forth by the prosecutor. And I ask you, please recall your sworn oath to abide by the laws of this country. This trial will be a search for the truth. . . . Please do not assume that Marty is guilty as others did on September seventh. Don't do that. Because Marty Tankleff is innocent."

FROM LATE APRIL to the first day of summer eight weeks later, the jury heard the evidence: thirty-five witnesses for the prosecution, seventeen for the defense, their testimony illustrated by 277 exhibits ranging from the dumbbell and knife said to be the murder weapons, to the bloodstained bedding taken from one murder scene and khaki slacks from the other, to the gruesome photographs of the victims. Throughout the trial, an eight-foot-long scale model of the Tankleffs' labyrinthine house was displayed on an easel. People in the courtroom were struck by how newspaper photos and TV footage failed to do the house justice. "It is the model of an almost limitless home," Paul Vitello wrote. ". . . It is a complicated house, all angles and doorways and new discoveries at every turn. It is a house big enough to get lost in, and whatever happened there on September 7, 1988, Martin Tankleff got lost in it."

Prosecutors in murder cases like to begin at the beginning, unfolding their stories piece by piece and laying the groundwork for their best evidence. And so one of the first voices the jury heard was that of Marty Tankleff himself. As his opening witness, Collins called Patricia Flanagan, the emergency services dispatcher at the receiving end of Marty's 911 call, and during her testimony he placed a large portable tape deck on the ledge in front of her. He hit the play button. The jurors followed along with a transcript.

*This is Marty Tankleff, 33 Seaside Drive in Belle Terre—I need an ambulance! Emergency!**

The 911 call was standard prosecution evidence, but in Gottlieb's view it was much more helpful to the defense—so helpful, in fact, that he would have introduced it had Collins not. One of the principal themes of the prosecution was that the police had first become suspicious of Marty in good part because he seemed too calm, too unemotional, in the aftermath of the horrific assaults on his parents. But with the tape of the 911 call, the jurors could judge for themselves. It would be the only such chance the jury would have. Everything else they would learn about Marty and the events of that day—his demeanor, his actions, his words—would come from testimony by others.

In the first half minute of the tape, Marty's sobbing pleas for help certainly seemed the sound of a panicked teenager who'd just woken to a nightmare. He gained control of himself as the call progressed, but Gottlieb suggested through his own questioning of Flanagan that this was largely because she was a well-trained emergency operator who did her job well. She screamed at him to slow down, get hold of himself, and he did. But whatever the jurors made of Marty's demeanor on the tape, Gottlieb hoped they picked up on something much less subjective: Marty told Flanagan only that he'd found his father. His mother didn't come up at all. It was consistent with what he told the detectives—that he didn't find

---

* For the full transcript of the 911 call, refer to pages 10–11.

her until after he hung up the phone, tended to his father, and then went looking for her. And there was this: If Marty had actually carried out an elaborate plan to slaughter his parents and cover up his guilt, would he have called for help while his father was obviously still alive?

Collins continued his story line with testimony from the various people who converged on 33 Seaside Drive in the hour that followed the 911 call—the uniformed police officers, the rescue workers, the neighbors, each of them contributing a brushstroke to the picture Collins was painting of Marty as the immediate and obvious prime suspect.

Morty Hova, the dictating equipment distributor who lived next door, honored his pledge to tell the whole truth by recalling that he was sitting on the toilet at 6:15 that morning when he heard someone screaming outside. Opening the front door, he saw Marty running toward him, yelling something about murder. As soon as Marty reached Hova's front door, two police cars whizzed by. Marty turned on his heels and Hova followed him. "All this time, Marty was screaming 'Murder, murder.' I thought the dog was murdered"—even though the Tankleffs had no dog—"because I just couldn't imagine. He said, 'No, they murdered my parents!' and I asked, '*Both* of them?' And he said, 'Yes, both of them.'"

Police officers Daniel Gallagher and James Crayne testified that Marty rushed up to them in the driveway, barefoot and frantic, holding up his bloody palms and yelling, "Somebody murdered my parents!" He led them inside the house, directing Gallagher in one direction and Crayne in the other. Under Gottlieb's cross-examination, the officers described Marty variously as "agitated," "excited," "hyper," "jumpy," and "whimpering." According to Gallagher, "He said that the only person who had motive to do this was Jerry Steuerman."

DON HINES, the chief and only full-time employee of the Belle Terre constabulary, recalled that he was working his summer hours that morning—4 A.M. to noon—but stopped by his house a couple of hours into the shift. "I had responded there to change a short-sleeve shirt that I had put on at four A.M., because it was cold," he said. "And while I was there, I heard a call, 33 Seaside Drive, 10-8, which is injury."

Hines knew the address well. He and Seymour Tankleff were friends. And ever since Vinnie Bove appointed Seymour commissioner of constables, the chief would often go over to his house to review time sheets and equipment and such. Seymour made his home the constabulary's "relief point," where the constables passed the village's patrol car from one shift to the next, parking their personal cars in the Tankleffs' lower driveway.

Hines's explanation of such details might have seemed extraneous but Gottlieb liked the testimony. That Marty was trustful of the police, knew them as good guys always there to help, was a joist in the framework of his defense. "Sometimes, my patrol car blocked Arlene from the garage," Hines said. "And I asked Marty to move it, and he did it, and he was extremely cooperative."

Hearing the radio call that morning, "I immediately finished changing my shirt and responded to that location. I got there as quickly as I possibly could." He saw several Suffolk County police vehicles and an officer stringing yellow crime-scene tape around a tree. He saw Marty in the street, bending over a puddle. "I said to him, 'What happened, Marty?' Or 'Buddy, what happened?' I have a habit of calling people 'Buddy.' And he said to me, 'Jerry Steuerman murdered my mother and my father.'" He brought Marty to his car, where he heard a litany about Steuerman: "That there was bad blood between the families, that there was some involvement with money, and that his mother two weeks prior to this situation had advised both he and his father that she thought that Jerry Steuerman was going to do something terrible. 'And he did. He killed my mother and my father. He was at the card game last night and he was the last one to leave.'"

"Did you say anything to the defendant?" Collins asked.

"Yes, I did," Hines said. "I advised him that his father was still alive and that there was a police officer with him and that should he regain consciousness the police officer would find out and be able to verify that Jerry Steuerman was indeed the perpetrator of this act."

"And how would you describe his demeanor when you had this conversation?"

"Well, up until that time, the defendant, Marty, was looking at the ground, at his feet, at the floor of the car, at something other than me. He had his head down. When I made that statement, he picked his head up and he looked directly at me. His eyes widened, he stopped talking, and didn't say another word."

Hines's testimony was chilling in its implication, and for those in the defense camp, hard to fathom. Marty himself was of little help. He hardly remembered talking to Hines, much less what his facial expressions might have been. Gottlieb considered how he might counter the damaging image of Marty sitting in the constable's car looking startled and guilty.

Hines had been a New York City police detective but was twenty years removed from that life. Recalling his arrival at the scene earlier in his testimony, Hines said he'd approached a uniformed Suffolk police officer. "He advised me that there was a crime scene and I couldn't go in there."

A while later, when he asked if he could be of some help, McCready told him to go down to the beach and see if he could find anything. "Well, I went down to the beach and I found that the scene had already been secured by the Suffolk County Police Department, and they were conducting a search of the area."

Gottlieb stood at the lectern and asked Hines what his duties were as chief constable. "Littering, trespass on village property, vehicle and traffic law," Hines said. "Noise ordinances, dogs, and to assist Suffolk County in any endeavor that they are engaged in within the village."

"Now, Chief Constable, what happened on September seventh was a very emotional experience for you, wasn't it?"

"Oh, it certainly was."

"In fact, because of your relationship with Seymour Tankleff, when you first arrived, you became very upset, didn't you."

"Yes. I was upset, yes I was."

". . . Is it fair to say that the professionalism sort of went out the window?"

"Yes, I think that's fair to say."

Gottlieb elicited from Hines that Marty was "excited" and "talking rapidly" when they were in the patrol car, but he steered clear of Hines's remark about Marty's "widened" eyes. When Hines started to refer to it, Gottlieb cut him off and changed the subject to his next encounter with Marty. That was ten minutes later, when Hines returned to the scene after driving over to Vinnie Bove's house to tell him what was going on. "I saw that Marty was wandering around, more or less, by himself," Hines said. A teenage girl in a yellow Mustang stopped to talk to Marty. Then she drove off. "He appeared to me to be lost, I guess the word would be. I said, 'Buddy, why don't we go to the car and sit down and relax.'" Marty started talking about Steuerman again. "He was very repetitious about it."

On his redirect examination, Collins asked Hines whether either of the Tankleffs had ever shared any concerns about Jerry Steuerman. "Never," Hines said.

"Other than the time his eyes widened when you told him that a police officer would remain with his father at the hospital, did the defendant ever register any other emotions that you could see?"

"Some excitement."

"Did you ever see him cry?"

"No, he didn't cry."

"Did you ever see him sad about what happened?"

"*Oh—*" Gottlieb moaned.

"Sustained," said the judge.

*   *   *

THE GIRL IN THE yellow Mustang was Dara Schaeffer, a classmate and neighbor of Marty's since they were in nursery school. She was heading for school when she saw the police cars parked in front of his house and Marty milling around the foot of the driveway. "I said, 'Hey, Marty, how's it going?' And he said, 'Last night someone killed my mother, tried to kill my father, and molested me.'"

There was a murmur in the courtroom. Pens hit pads in the press section.

"And I couldn't believe it," Dara continued. "I was—just started to cry. And he said something about his father being stabbed, he was in the hospital, and I was just—I couldn't believe anything. I was crying. I said, 'I'm really sorry. Is there anything I can do for you? Whatever you want, I'll do it.' And he said, 'Well, can you just go into school and tell Mr. Neuner I'm not in school and tell him what happened?'"

Marty's brief encounter with Dara was one more blur in his mind. But one thing he was sure about was that he didn't tell her he had been molested. Why would he say such a thing, and only to her? She obviously misheard him. Even in normal conversation, Marty had a tendency to speak rapidly and swallow his words, and his agitation that morning was well established by now. As Dara herself had told Gottlieb's investigator, Jack Murtagh, Marty was "babbling," "in shock," and "out of it."

Murtagh had interviewed Dara a few weeks before the trial, soon after Gottlieb learned, through discovery, that Dara had told Detectives Doyle and Rein about the "molested" statement when they interviewed her at the University of Connecticut. Murtagh caught Dara on the ferry as she was heading back to college after a weekend home and called her later at her dorm room. He taped the phone call (recording phone calls in New York doesn't require both parties' consent), and after a discussion with the lawyers in his chambers, Judge Tisch told Gottlieb he could play it during his cross-examination.

"Dara, you're not really sure about this statement that you just told us concerning molesting, are you?" Gottlieb asked.

"I'm sure that's what I heard," Dara replied. "When I first heard it, I was positive and I told everybody. And then I didn't hear about it again, and I started doubting it. But then I've been thinking about it a lot and I don't know what he could have said if he didn't say it."

Gottlieb played the tape of Murtagh's phone interview. Dara listened uncomfortably as her recorded voice echoed in the courtroom. She sounded very unsure of what she heard that morning, and she told Murtagh that she had expressed her uncertainty "over and over" to Doyle and Rein when they came to talk to her. "I told them, 'You know how your ears play tricks with you?'"

Questioned by Gottlieb after the tape was played, Dara said she had thought hard about whether Marty might have said something other than "molested me." But she had come up with no other possibilities. "It's what I believe I heard. And I can't tell you anything that I don't think I heard. I'm just, I'm just trying to tell the truth."

"I see," said Gottlieb.

"That's what I think," Dara added.

"Dara, you were very upset that morning . . . you were crying a great deal, correct?"

"After he told me what happened, yeah."

"And when Marty was speaking to you, you described him as 'babbling,' correct?"

"After I greeted him and he told me about the initial statement, yeah, then he started going off."

Dara Schaeffer's testimony made for baffling news. A NEW TWIST IN TANKLEFF TRIAL was the headline over the next day's story in *Newsday*. The story struggled for evenhandedness but left the impression that Marty actually did say he was molested. The testimony was part of the prosecution's effort "to show the inconsistencies in Tankleff's statements about what happened the morning of the attack," said the newspaper. On the other hand, it could signal a new avenue for the defense: "Schaeffer's testimony is the first time in the case that anyone has said that Tankleff claimed to have been molested by his parents' killer, a claim that carries with it the implication that he may have seen the killer."

But it was to be the first and last time anyone would hear about it. Only later would Marty realize what he probably said: "They killed my mother and tried to kill my father and *must have missed me*." But whether people thought Dara heard Marty correctly or not, her testimony that Friday afternoon closed the first week of the trial with a clear impression of Marty as confused and frantic. The question was whether it was because he was an innocent teenager in shock or because he was a guilty one desperate to deflect suspicion. On Monday, Collins brought to the stand a man who made a case for the harshest view.

JOHN MCNAMARA was the quintessential big man in town. Along with owning a large General Motors dealership, McNamara Buick-Pontiac, and the weekly *Port Jefferson Record*, he was a real estate developer who was credited with doing more than anyone else to revitalize Port Jefferson's downtown in the 1980s. By the end of the decade, he was one of Long Island's largest developers and a man whose far-flung business interests—an oil company, real estate in Germany, exports of GM cars and trucks to Kuwait and Saudi Arabia, an actual gold mine in Nevada—were said to put his net worth in the hundreds of millions of dollars. For years he lived in a house overlooking the sound in Poquott, just west of Port Jefferson, but he'd recently moved into an expansive house on Seaside Drive in Belle Terre.

McNamara had just begun his regular early morning walk that September day when he saw Morty Hova coming out of the Tankleffs' house looking very upset. There were just two police cars in the driveway and the ambulance had yet to arrive. McNamara stopped to see what was going on. Since he was new to the neighborhood, he knew Seymour and Arlene only casually and Marty not at all. Yet McNamara testified that soon after he happened onto the scene, Marty came up to him and told him that his parents had been murdered and that Jerry Steuerman had done it, and then Marty went into a moment-by-moment account of what happened in those ten minutes after he woke up.

Then, McNamara said, "I asked him: If he lifted his father onto the floor, why didn't he have any blood on him?"

"And did he answer that question?" Collins asked.

"No. He didn't reply. He looked at me and did not reply." And then, McNamara said, Marty walked away. But he came back a short time later and began telling him again what happened. This time he added some details—that he had been sleeping in the nude, for instance, and put on shorts and a sweatshirt; and that he'd found his mother when he checked her bedroom a second time, after doing what he'd been instructed by the 911 operator to aid his father. Once again, McNamara said, he asked Marty a question: Why didn't you help your mother? Once again Marty didn't answer and walked away. And a short time later, Marty came back to him yet again.

"He started again with the same scenario, that he woke up, looked into the hall, saw that the lights were on in the house, thought it was unusual. . . ." And as before, Marty gave him more information, adding a fuller account of finding his mother. "[He said] he realized his mother was dead and he was too scared to go in, into the bedroom, and ran out of the house screaming that a murder had taken place."

"Would it be fair to say," Collins asked, "that each of those questions to which you got no response was the end of that particular conversation?"

"Yes, that's correct," McNamara said.

"And on each occasion when he returned did he seem to have an answer for the question that he had left unanswered?"

"Well, each time he told me the story there was a little more to it."

McNamara's testimony did no harm to Collins's goal of portraying Marty's behavior as strange and suspicious. But on cross-examination, Gottlieb suggested it was McNamara whose behavior that morning, and whose veracity now, were questionable. Gottlieb wanted the jury to consider whether it rang true that Marty would come back again and again, explaining himself in ever greater detail, to a man he'd never met. Wasn't it odd for a man, chancing upon this horrible and chaotic scene while on his morning walk, to hang around asking accusatory questions of the victims' shocked and distraught teenage son? And wasn't it curious that McNamara, without the benefit of any notes, was able to quote Marty at length and virtually verbatim, a year and a half later; that he recalled each of the three conversations so distinctly that he had no trouble keeping track of which details Marty related in which rendition?

But Gottlieb's most important message was the same one he applied to the prosecution's other early witnesses: Even if everything McNamara said were true, so what? Under the circumstances, who was to say that anything Marty said or did was outside the bounds of "normal" behavior? There was some circular logic to this: To give his behavior wide latitude because of what he had found that morning, one had to first believe his story—believe he was innocent.

Whatever the impact of McNamara's testimony, the jury couldn't know the extent to which it might have been shaded by his belief from the beginning that Marty was *not* innocent. There were some hints. McNamara delivered much of his testimony with a kind of sneer, his deep-set eyes accentuated by perpetually arched eyebrows. And as Eric Naiburg pointed out in his television commentary, McNamara did little to hide his hostility to the defense, particularly when Gottlieb asked him if it was true that while he had met with members of the prosecution team several times, he had refused to even talk to the defense's investigator. "That is absolutely right," McNamara snarled. But what the jury didn't hear was what he told Jim McCready during an interview at his car dealership a month after the murders. He said that Marty that morning "had a guilty look on his face" and "kept changing his story." That while the emergency squad was working on his father, Marty "was walking up and down the street talking to everyone who came by." That he had challenged Marty more than once about "why he didn't have blood all over him" and that he had told Morty Hova, "The kid did it."

Allowing these statements into evidence would obviously be prejudicial to the defense, so in chambers prior to McNamara's testimony, Gottlieb had asked the judge to require that the witness "be instructed not to volunteer his expert opinion" that "the kid did it." Replied Tisch: "Well,

Mr. Collins has already told the jury that the kid did it. But I think we'll refrain from having McNamara emphasize that."

There was one more thing the jury didn't know, something *nobody* would know until long after the trial. John McNamara was not the man he presented himself to be. He was a con man—not simply a shady operator but a swindler of epic proportions. In April 1992, nearly two years to the day after he testified for the prosecution against Martin Tankleff, McNamara would be accused by a federal grand jury of carrying out the largest corporate fraud in American history. In a scheme the United States attorney called "the mother of all kiting schemes," McNamara bilked no less a rock of American business than General Motors of $436 million over an eleven-year period.

As Port Jefferson and the rest of Long Island was stunned to learn, since 1981 McNamara had borrowed $6 *billion* from GM's financial arm, General Motors Acceptance Corporation, for nonexistent cars and trucks that he claimed to be exporting to the Middle East. He used the proceeds to assemble his $400 million business empire, which itself was built partly on bribery and fraud. As he later told the authorities, for years he had paid off local officials to approve his development projects, bribing them with everything from bags of cash to free brake jobs. A flight risk if ever there was one, McNamara was held on a staggering $300 million bail. A few months later, facing twenty years in prison, he agreed to a plea bargain, trading the names of those he claimed to have bribed for a lighter sentence and a ticket into the witness protection program. (He eventually served five years in federal prison.)

John McNamara, the big man in town, turned out to be a man of big lies and deep secrets, of frauds small, medium, large, and extra-large. Was his provocative testimony at Marty Tankleff's trial, a brick in the foundation of the prosecution's case, one of those frauds?

CHAPTER 18

Witnesses to Circumstance

ON TUESDAY, APRIL 24, a procession of teenage girls walked down the center aisle of the courtroom and past the wooden gate separating the business half of the room from the spectator section. One by one, they stepped gingerly up to the witness chair. Marty knew who they were and why they were here. And he knew it would not be good for him.

Over the summer of 1988, in the month or so before his parents' murders, Marty had been friendly with Stacy Goldschmidt and her younger sister Audra. He'd met Stacy through their mutual friend, Christine Engels, with whom Marty worked at the bagel store in Stony Brook. On a Saturday night in late August, the Goldschmidt girls were home, and Audra's friend Danielle Makrides was over, when Marty stopped by. As the three girls recalled, they were sitting around the kitchen table with Marty, just hanging out. Stacy was waiting for her boyfriend to pick her up to go out to the movies. She and Marty were flipping through a book of expensive imported sports cars. A Ferrari caught Stacy's eye.

"And did Marty make a comment?" Collins asked her.

"He said that if he could get a hit on his parents he could have that car," she said.

"And can you relate to us please the tone of voice in which he said that?"

"He said it kind of nonchalantly, an everyday conversation."

"And did you say anything to him in response to that?"

"No. I was just kind of flabbergasted."

Audra Goldschmidt repeated the statement when she followed her sister to the stand. She said her own reaction was to nudge Danielle under the table. Danielle testified that she thought Marty's comment was weird.

Collins asked her if she'd ever heard any of her other friends say such a thing about their parents. "Jeez, Your Honor, objection," Gottlieb cut in—but it was one of those questions-in-no-need-of-an-answer that lawyers like to sneak in.

The testimony by the three girls caused a stir in the courtroom. The prosecution team couldn't have scripted better support for its most astonishing allegation, that Marty Tankleff was a spoiled rich kid who slaughtered his parents in part because he wanted a car sportier than his "crummy old Lincoln." To his lawyer's dismay, it was Marty himself who inadvertently led the police to this small but potent piece of testimony. Marty had mentioned Stacy and Audra when the detectives asked him, in the casual opening moments of their questioning in Yaphank, which girls he liked.

Marty told Gottlieb that the girls were exaggerating what he actually said that night. As he remembered it, Stacy was leafing through the car book and stopped to linger over the Ferrari. Then she snapped back to reality and the Nissan Maxima she'd be getting when her sister left for college in a few days. It was at that point, Marty said, that he offhandedly remarked, "I could have any car I wanted if my parents weren't around." A less chilling sentiment than the one attributed to him, but still an unfortunate remark whose poor timing was impeccable.

The dilemma for the defense was how to respond. It was Gottlieb's burden to cope with the special challenges of defending a client who was young, impulsive, often oblivious—a typical teenager in most respects—but also one whose personality quirks could be magnified and fashioned into circumstantial evidence against him. No lawyer wants a jury to see his client in an unfavorable light, but Gottlieb realized he had no choice but to try to soften the impact. If the prosecution painted Marty as a spoiled brat of the most pathological kind, Gottlieb painted him as, at worst, a spoiled brat of the most common kind: an insecure boy with a penchant for trying to impress girls in the clumsiest ways imaginable. A boy who had grown up in a community in which it wasn't uncommon for teenagers to talk about their parents' wealth and where hanging out might revolve around a book of Ferraris and Lamborghinis.

"During the short period of time that you actually knew Marty, he bragged quite a bit about money, didn't he?" Gottlieb asked Stacy.

"Pretty good amount of time," she replied.

And when Marty made this comment about a "having a hit" on his parents, "he only said it in a very nonchalant, regular manner, correct?"

"Right."

So said Audra and Danielle.

"Typical Marty, wasn't it?" Gottlieb asked Audra.

"I guess so," said Audra.

Despite Gottlieb's best efforts, the girls' testimony was a damaging blow. The only good thing was that it came so early in the trial. He hoped that by the end, the jurors would hear enough evidence of reasonable doubt that they would see Marty as nothing worse than an immature and overindulged teenager.

THE FIRST HINTS of reasonable doubt came from the prosecution's own witnesses. Having presented those who converged on 33 Seaside Drive just after dawn on that Wednesday morning after Labor Day, Collins backtracked to the group that had departed only three hours earlier: the men of the After Dinner Club, now the most famous poker game on Long Island. It was mostly scene-setting testimony, but in calling up three of the eight poker players Collins would provide testimony that was, on the whole, more useful to the defense. And then he would call one more poker player and hold his breath.

It was an August day in April when Bob Montefusco took the witness stand, and because the county didn't normally turn on the building's air-conditioning until June, the courtroom was so unbearably hot that spectators were fanning themselves with newspapers, *To Kill a Mockingbird*–style. Montefusco, who had a heart condition and was visibly nervous to begin with, constantly mopped his brow with a handkerchief. Collins was scarcely into his questioning when he asked the judge if it would be all right if he took his jacket off. One of the court officers thought it might be a hundred degrees in the courtroom and brought in an oxygen tank as a precaution. Gottlieb pleaded with Tisch to adjourn the proceedings until the county turned on the air-conditioning or the heat wave broke. "It does seem to get a lot warmer in here when Bob speaks," Collins remarked. Tisch gave Gottlieb's appeal due consideration but ruled against him, not for the last time. The jurors seemed alert and willing to keep going, Tisch said. And Montefusco told the judge he'd rather just get this over with.

"How did the game go that particular evening?" Collins asked him.

Montefusco said it was just like any other game, though he did better than usual, going home the big winner, $2,000 richer. Was that a lot to change hands? Collins asked. "It's a little on the high side," Montefusco said. "That's considered a lucky streak."

Now Collins employed a tactic he would use at various times during the trial, eliciting a piece of testimony that was arguably unfavorable to his case. The reason was twofold: to signal to the jurors that he was being upfront with them, and to introduce the evidence on his own terms, rather than letting Gottlieb present it later as a dramatic revelation.

"Could you tell us, please, what occurred at around the time the game was breaking up?" Collins asked Montefusco.

"Well, everybody left, and I was getting ready to leave myself," Montefusco replied. "The only people there were myself, Steuerman, and Tankleff. So I left the card room and I was in the sunroom ready to walk through the kitchen and out the front door, and I decided to go back in and talk to Seymour, just, you know, about how the game was or whatever."

"Tell him how much you won?"

"Right, something like that. So I walked back in, and I saw Steuerman and Tankleff having a conversation." It seemed private to him so he turned around and left.

Gottlieb tried to get a little more out of Montefusco in his cross, asking whether the conversation appeared to be "serious." But Montefusco wouldn't bite. "It appeared to be private" was all he would say.

"And you left and went home with Jerry Steuerman and Seymour Tankleff in their private conversation," Gottlieb said.

"Right," said Montefusco.

It proved nothing, of course. They were business partners, and Jerry typically paid Seymour the money he owed him after the game broke up. And while Montefusco recalled that Steuerman had complained to him "once or twice" over the previous months that "Seymour's out for himself," he could report no tension between them that night. Still, the testimony provided Gottlieb his first opportunity to suggest that Steuerman had both motive and opportunity. He was able to suggest this much more strongly through Collins's next witness.

"Tell us what happened when you left," Collins said to Joe Cecere, once again taking ownership of unhelpful testimony to blunt its impact.

"Since I was the first one there, everyone was parked behind me," Cecere said. "So I waited until all the cars left and I was ready to leave, and I looked to my left. [Steuerman] should have exited first, and he just waved to go ahead. And I left."

Eager to make much more of Cecere's exit, Gottlieb asked him to step down from the witness chair and use the scale model of the property to explain why it would have made sense for Steuerman to go first. Cecere used a pointer to show where each of them was parked and why he was worried about Steuerman hitting his new Mercedes.

"But Mr. Steuerman doesn't pull out first does he?" Gottlieb asked.

"No, he doesn't," Cecere said. "He just waved, said, 'Go.'"

"And that seemed odd to you?"

"For a second." But he was able to make the awkward maneuver and head out of the driveway.

"And do you see Mr. Steuerman's car follow right behind you?"

"No, I didn't."

"And when you leave and you go down Seaside Drive, do you see the headlights of a car behind you?"

"No. No one was behind me."

Cecere made one other contribution to the defense, testifying about the time Seymour pushed his way into one of Cecere's real estate investments, only to send him a contract that was "a whole different story" from the deal they shook hands on. Gottlieb asked Cecere if Seymour's business practices offended him. They certainly did, said Cecere. He told Seymour he'd play cards with him, but he'd never do business with him.

"DO YOU RECALL Mr. Tankleff in the course of the evening making or receiving any phone calls?" Collins asked Vinnie Bove.

The silver-haired nurseryman was the third of the poker players called as a witness for the prosecution, and it became clear very quickly that he, Montefusco, and Cecere were not three of a kind. Among the men with whom Seymour Tankleff spent the last hours of his conscious life, Bove was probably the closest to him, and as the events unfolded that day he seemed to be everywhere. By virtue of his positions as mayor of Belle Terre and vice chairman of Mather Memorial, Bove arguably saw more that morning than any single person, homicide detectives included. He talked to Marty at the scene, saw Seymour in the emergency room, and was back in his office being interviewed by two homicide detectives when Jerry Steuerman called and asked him what he knew. It was from Bove that Steuerman learned that Marty was accusing him. On top of all that, Bove found himself playing a role in the physical evidence of the prosecution's case, such as it was. According to their theory of the crime, Bove was the last person to touch the watermelon knife before Marty Tankleff took it from the kitchen counter and used it to slash his parents' necks.

So Vinnie Bove had a lot to tell.

"He made a phone call. I don't know to whom," Bove replied when Collins asked him whether Seymour Tankleff used the phone during the poker game. "He talked to someone, hung the phone up, and said to Mr. Steuerman, 'Jerry, he's in. We need a check.' And I assume he's talking about their racehorses."

How bad could things have been between Seymour and Jerry, Collins wanted the jury to think, if they were not only still playing cards but racing their horses? And what did Bove think when Marty rushed up to him that morning and declared, before Bove even got out of his car, that Jerry Steuerman murdered his parents? "I said, 'Marty, what makes you say that? We played cards last night and nothing happened, nothing at all. Did you *see* him do it?'"

Like John McNamara, Bove had made it no secret around Port Jefferson that he thought Marty was guilty. Unlike McNamara, though, he'd not been sure about it from the start. It took some persuading by McCready. The jury knew none of this, but Bove didn't make it hard for them to figure out where he stood. He seemed at pains, for instance, to describe Marty that morning as being suspiciously composed. "He looked pretty calm and he knew what he was saying," he said at one point during cross-examination. When Gottlieb challenged him, asking whether Marty seemed "'agitated,'" Bove said, "I don't know what you mean by "'agitated.'" When Gottlieb asked if Marty appeared "very excited," Bove replied, "Well, I really can't answer that." Asked again, he said, "I don't know what you call excited." When Gottlieb asked if he'd used those very words with a reporter from *The Port Jefferson Record* the week of the murders, Bove said he couldn't remember.

In contrast with his spotty recall of Marty's demeanor that day, Bove had no trouble remembering precisely what he did when the poker game broke up. On direct examination, Bove testified: "I left first. I lost. I had no chips to cash in. And I was going through the kitchen and Seymour left the watermelon out on the counter. And the watermelon was good. So I took a knife out of the block, and I took the Saran Wrap that he had the melon covered with and sliced a piece and laid the knife directly in front of the melon. And I ate the melon on the way out and left."

Collins handed Bove a photograph taken by the crime scene team showing the watermelon and the knife on the counter. "But I didn't lay the knife there," Bove said. "I laid it perpendicular to the watermelon, right on the edge of the counter."

The implication was clear, and Collins presented it with an air of momentousness. But Gottlieb had little trouble demonstrating it was a red herring: There was no reason to believe Bove was the last person to touch the knife. In fact, he was the *first* of the poker players to leave, departing before the others passed through the kitchen. So any one or more of them might have stopped to cut himself a last piece of that seedless watermelon. And anyone who was in the house early the next morning could have brushed against the knife before the picture was taken several hours later. Maybe that's why the knife wasn't in exactly the same position as Bove remembered. But apart from all that, the entire question was arguably irrelevant. For as Collins himself had admitted during his opening statement, he couldn't prove the knife had anything to do with the murder.

All told, the poker players did little to advance the prosecution's case. Given that the burden of proof was on Collins, there seemed to be a net gain for the defense in the testimony by all three men that Marty's demeanor that night was entirely normal; that there was no hint of hostility between him and either of his parents. But on the stage of this trial, Vinnie and Joe and Monte were mere supporting players. It was the next and final poker player whose appearance everyone in the courtroom and everyone watching from home was anticipating most. "We go now to one of the crucial moments of the Martin Tankleff murder trial," commentator Ken Rosenblum was saying the next morning on News 12. "Perhaps *the* most crucial moment."

CHAPTER 19

And It's Not Fair!

AFTER JERRY STEUERMAN fled like a fugitive a week after the Tankleff murders, it was the highest hope of the Suffolk County lawmen who brought him back from California that he would refrain from any further acts of screwy behavior before the trial. Their hopes lasted about six months.

First came the case of Sol Klein, Tropicana salesman. He told Jerry he owed him for four cases of orange juice. Jerry told Klein he shorted him on the juice. They argued back and forth, Jerry threw Klein out of his store, Klein sued Jerry in small-claims court. Jerry had quite a bit of experience as a small-claims defendant, and his record was unblemished. He'd lost every time. In his case with Sol Klein, Jerry decided to try a new approach. He wrote a letter to the court saying that he wished to drop his case against Jerry Steuerman. *Sincerely, Sol Klein.* All this succeeded in doing was to move the quarrel from small claims to criminal court, where Jerry was ordered to pay a $2,000 fine, plus the money he owed Sol Klein for the four cases of orange juice.

But the Tropicana escapade was just a case of first-degree chutzpah compared with what came a month later. On April 23, 1989, a thirty-year-old man arrived by ambulance at Community Hospital of Western Suffolk, bleeding from a gunshot wound to his right arm. He told a detective who showed from the Sixth Squad that he had been shot by Todd Steuerman.

In the course of building his drug business, Todd had come to rely on the services of enforcers—bill collectors, as it were. The man he was alleged to have shot was one such enforcer. His name was Joe Creedon. On the streets of central Suffolk County, he was known, ironically enough, as

Joey Guns. The problems started two weeks ago, Creedon told the detective, when Todd asked him to come to his bagel store in Stony Brook. "Todd is a drug dealer and sells cocaine, pot, and valium," Creedon said in his police statement, which was written by the detective, standard procedure even if Creedon's arm weren't in a sling. "He said that a number of people owed him money for drugs that he sold them. He told me he wanted me to collect sixty thousand dollars for drugs that he sold." (Creedon wanted to make one thing clear: "Todd came to me because he heard that I was a collector for other drug dealers. I told Todd that I didn't want to get involved in collecting drug money.")

Todd had some other work for him, said Creedon. "Todd also told me that I should talk to his father about cutting Marty Tankleff's tongue out of his mouth. He also told me that he wanted somebody wacked for ten grand but wouldn't tell me who."

That was two weeks ago, Creedon told the detective. Then, today, Todd called him and said he wanted to talk—about what, Creedon didn't say. They arranged to meet in a parking lot early that evening. Todd showed up in a pickup truck with someone Creedon didn't know at the wheel. Todd got out, and after they talked for a few minutes Todd's friend "started to get stupid. I said to him, 'What do you think, you're a gangster?' He then pulled out a small chrome automatic handgun and pointed it at my head. I said, 'You're no gangster. You won't pull the trigger.' Todd then said 'give me the gun.' Todd took the gun and shot me in the right forearm near the elbow." Todd and his friend took off; Creedon ran to his car and chased them. But he could only drive with one hand and lost them. He went to a friend's house and told him to call an ambulance. "I am now in severe pain from the bullet, which went through my right arm," Creedon's statement concluded. He signed it with a left-handed scrawl.

Todd was charged with assault with a deadly weapon. His lawyer, Gerry Sullivan, who had spared him a jail sentence once before, got the DA's office to knock the charge down to third-degree assault. But the lesser charge was subsumed by much bigger trouble. Six years after his first arrest, he was collared again on felony cocaine-dealing charges. Gerry Sullivan once again pleaded the case down to possession, but no psychiatric report was going to keep Todd out of prison this time. It was curious how Todd, not the sharpest or most cautious of young men, had managed to go six years freely dealing significant quantities of drugs from a bagel store, only to be arrested now. With the Tankleff case moving toward trial and Todd showing signs of the kind of erratic behavior for which his father was known, he was shipped off to Dannemora, the northernmost prison in the state.

Nobody was happier about Todd's arrest than Bob Gottlieb. It was the consensus among Marty, his lawyers, and his family that Jerry Steuerman was the sort of man who didn't have it in him to kill Seymour and Arlene with his own hands, but that he was certainly capable of arranging for someone else to do it. Where would he find such a killer for hire? Gottlieb believed that was where Todd came in, and he was hoping Judge Tisch would allow him some leeway when he cross-examined Jerry Steuerman. He wanted to bring up Todd's "history" to suggest that it gave his father "access" to the sorts of characters who might do other people's dirty work.

What Gottlieb didn't know as the trial got under way was anything about Todd's *other* situation. The DA's office had apparently decided that the arrest of Jerry Steuerman's son for shooting a drug enforcer had nothing to do with the Tankleff homicide case. So it had no obligation to inform the defense. But Gottlieb did find out about it—a year later, and in a very unusual way. One afternoon during the first week of the trial, Gottlieb was in his office after court when he got a phone call from a lawyer named Harold Shapiro, who said he had a client who wanted to give him some information he might find useful. Gottlieb listened to the synopsis. He told Shapiro he needed to talk to his client right away.

After court the next afternoon, Gottlieb's secretary told him that a Joe Creedon was on the line. Gottlieb picked up and Creedon told him that not only had Todd shot him but Todd's father offered him $10,000 to drop the charges. And that when he refused, Jerry told him, "What are you, crazy? You're fucking with the wrong people. I can have you dead."

Gottlieb wanted details. Where did Steuerman make this threat? Over the phone, Creedon said. Are you positive it was *Jerry* Steuerman you were talking to? It was Jerry, Creedon assured him. How do you know? I know his voice, Creedon said. I've talked to him on the phone before.

Gottlieb saw a provocative new line of inquiry and implication, but he also saw a major hurdle: The judge might not allow him to use any of it.

ON MAY 1, 1990, the day before Todd Steuerman was scheduled to begin his seven-year prison sentence, his father came to court as a witness for the prosecution in the trial of Marty Tankleff.

As those who proceeded him had done, Steuerman waited in the district attorney's office until his time came. But he waited longer than most. The lawyers were holed up in the judge's chambers, arguing about how far Gottlieb should be allowed to go in cross-examining Steuerman with allegations involving his son. Collins contended that Gottlieb shouldn't be allowed to go there at all, and he had a good argument. To use Todd Steuerman to connect his father to the murders, Gottlieb first had to show a basis for saying that Todd himself might have been involved. To do that,

he would need to bring up Todd's criminal record. To do that, he would
have to demonstrate its relevance to the cross-examination. And to do
that, he had to persuade the judge that Todd's record challenged the view
of his father as a morally upright person with no involvement in the murders. It all came to this: In order to propose a father-and-son murder plot
as an alternative to the son-murders-father-and-mother plot being prosecuted, Gottlieb had to overcome a catch-22 so that he could then bring in
a piece of oblique evidence through the back door.

"Judge, if I may . . ." Gottlieb said, beginning his difficult pitch. "Todd
Steuerman, in addition to having pled guilty to an A-1 drug felony, was
also charged with assault on a Joseph Creedon. Joseph Creedon has filed
a sworn statement with the police department concerning many matters,
including that Todd Steuerman, at the behest of his father, wanted to
know whether or not Creedon was willing to rip out Marty Tankleff's
tongue. We also have, based on conversations with Creedon, that Jerry
Steuerman threatened Creedon as a result of Creedon having been shot
by Todd. So it is connected to Todd Steuerman. . . ."

"Okay, okay," said Tisch. "Look, there's no question . . . that on cross-
examination of Jerry Steuerman you can inquire as to whether or not he
ever threatened Joseph Creedon." But if Steuerman denied the accusation, that would be the end of it. Under the rules of evidence, Gottlieb
could not then put Creedon on the stand to say that Steuerman *had* threatened him. That would constitute "collateral impeachment"—bringing in
someone to attack a witness's credibility on an issue not directly related to
the case. And, said Tisch, Gottlieb couldn't get into any of the criminal
charges against Todd. "The only rationale for bringing that in," he said,
"would be to suggest that birds of a feather flock together and if his son
was in trouble with the law, therefore this is not a worthy witness."

Of course, Jerry Steuerman's worthiness as a witness was not quite the
point. Gottlieb realized he had to show his hand. "It could very well be
that somebody at the *behest* of Jerry Steuerman committed the murders,"
he told Tisch. This area of questioning, he implored the judge, was vital
to his goal of demonstrating that Steuerman, who clearly had a motive for
arranging the Tankleffs' murders, also had the opportunity: The poker
game put him in the house—ultimately alone with Seymour—and his son
gave him access to people who might kill for money.

Tisch said no: Three appellate court decisions told him that Todd
Steuerman's criminal record could not be introduced to attack his father.
But to Gottlieb, no argument was over until the judge said no at least
three times. This case isn't like those, he insisted. This is a witness who
might have *committed the murders*, or been behind them. Gottlieb pleaded
for leeway, declaring that virtually his entire defense depended on casting

Steuerman as a more likely perpetrator than Marty. "It would almost be as if we are prosecuting the case, Your Honor. . . ."

But Tisch wouldn't budge and Gottlieb finally let it go.

For now. He had an idea about coming back one more time for permission to use the shooting incident and its aftermath in his cross-examination—of Jim McCready. To Gottlieb, the whole episode raised too many questions that suggested a connection to the case and should have been explored. That they weren't spoke to the defense's fundamental argument that the police seized on Marty Tankleff and never actually investigated the case.

IT IS SAFE TO SAY that of all the witnesses John Collins brought to the witness stand in his prosecution of Marty Tankleff, none made him more nervous than Jerry Steuerman. The police detectives who would follow Steuerman to the stand were clearly more crucial, but Collins didn't have to worry about them. They knew how to testify. Jerry Steuerman, on the other hand, was the very definition of a loose cannon.

Collins planned a relatively brief direct examination of Steuerman, little more than the same thirty minutes or so he'd spent with the other poker players. But he prepared Steuerman—and himself—for a cross-examination by Gottlieb that was sure to be relentless. Here was one of Long Island's most dogged criminal defense attorneys, fighting for that rarest of clients—one whose innocence he truly believed in—and finally getting his shot at something rarer still: confronting a man he could legitimately and in good conscience offer up as the actual murderer. And if one thing seemed clear about Jerry Steuerman, it was that he didn't respond very well to pressure.

Though he had yet to face a single question from Gottlieb, Steuerman had already given him plenty to work with—both bizarre actions and tantalizing words, frequently spoken to people with notepads and cameras. Jerry just wasn't a "No comment" sort of guy. And if Collins didn't have enough to worry about, on the eve of the trial he found himself staring at a truly astonishing remark. What made it so astonishing was that it was uttered not by Steuerman, but by Collins's former boss, the prosecutor from whom he inherited the case. In late March, *Newsday*'s court reporter, Carolyn Colwell, was putting together a story to run on the trial's opening day—a "curtain raiser," in newspaper parlance. She found Collins unwilling to talk about the case so she called Ed Jablonski, the homicide bureau chief at the time of the murders. He had since left the DA's office for private practice and was happy to share his thoughts.

During the interview, Colwell asked Jablonski about his trip to California with McCready and Doyle to find Steuerman. Did he come back feeling differently about Steuerman as a possible suspect? Not at all, said Jablonski. "Nobody could convince me he did it." What made him so sure? "It's just a feeling you get." Having dismissed the possibility of Steuerman's involvement based on "a feeling," Jablonski was moved to elaborate. He recalled a conversation in California when Steuerman was talking about Seymour Tankleff. "He wanted the guy dead," Jablonski said, "but he felt bad when he was dead, and then he felt bad wanting him dead. He cried."

Thank you, Ed, Gottlieb thought when he read the quote. Early on, he had complained bitterly about Jablonski's use of the press to hype his case, sometimes with information that was patently untrue. Now Gottlieb relished the opportunity to finally use Jablonski's words to his own advantage.

COLLINS SET UP Steuerman's testimony with a prelude: a witness who gave him an alibi.

"Please state your name and address for the record," said the court clerk.

"Bari Steuerman," said the witness.

Followers of the case might have recognized Jerry Steuerman's curly-haired daughter from the television news coverage of his disappearance following the murders. She had met him at the airport upon his return from California, and the wild scene of the two of them locked in a walking embrace, Jerry tearfully explaining himself to the trailing media horde, became one of the most memorable images of the case. Now, a year and a half later, another camera was trained on Bari Steuerman as she sat in the witness box, dressed smartly in a gray business suit with bulky shoulder pads.

Collins asked Bari where she was living, and with whom, in September 1988. She said she was living in Old Field with her son and her father. "All right," said Collins. "What I'd like to do is direct your attention to the very early morning hours of September the seventh, 1988. Do you recall that day?"

"Yes I do."

"And how is it that you recall that day?"

"Because it was the first day of first grade for my son. It was a big day for him."

"And did anything unusual, or anything happen during the early morning hours prior to that?"

"I was awoken by a doorbell at 3:17—between 3:17 and 3:18 A.M.,"

Bari testified, adding that she looked over at her digital alarm clock. "I went downstairs, opened the door, saw it was my father. I let him in."

According to Bari, it wasn't unusual for her father to wake her up like that: "He forgot his keys, which he normally does." Collins asked her to elaborate. "My father leaves one ignition key in his car at all times in the ignition," Bari explained. "He has a combination lock on his car so he leaves the bulk of his keys in the house. He's supposed to carry it with him. But he leaves it in the house. And I said to him, 'Dad, again you woke me up.'" Then the two of them went upstairs to their respective bedrooms.

After your father disappeared, Gottlieb asked on cross-examination, did you tell the police that his behavior in the week following the attacks on the Tankleffs had been "strange"? The characterization appeared in a detective's report of the interview, but Bari said she had no recollection of it. She also had little recollection of talking to her father about the events of that September. Just one "five or ten minute" discussion in the nearly two years since then. After her father returned to New York following his faked abduction and disappearance, she didn't ask him why he did that. "I don't discuss everything with my father," she explained. "We are very close and he does not like to get me upset. . . . So we do not discuss this elaborately."

Gottlieb didn't directly challenge the veracity of Bari's testimony. He didn't accuse her of fabricating an alibi for her father, or comment on how convenient it seemed that he'd forgotten his key that night and had to wake her up to let him in the house, or delve into her claim that there was nothing so unusual about this, that he did it all the time. Sometimes, Gottlieb thought, it was better to leave the questions hanging in the air, unanswered, and let the jurors wonder about them on their own. So Gottlieb didn't ask Bari Steuerman if she would lie for her father. He simply asked her again if she loved him very much. And Bari said yes, she did.

DRESSED AS FEW had seen him—in a muted glen plaid sport coat, black slacks, a white button-down shirt, a maroon tie, and not a piece of gold jewelry in sight—Jerry Steuerman took the stand and described himself as a fifty-year-old bagel maker, a father of four grown children, married for a year to his second wife.

John Collins asked him if he had known Seymour Tankleff.

"Yes, I did," Steuerman said. "Seymour was a customer and we became very good friends from that time on."

"And would you describe, please, the relationship that you had with him up until the time of his death?"

"We were very close. Seymour was like a father to me."

Steuerman recounted his business partnerships with Seymour—the bagels and the horses and the two loans, totaling $350,000, that Seymour made to him two years before his death. Collins asked him what he needed that sort of money for. "I was building my home in Belle Terre," Jerry said, "and I ran a little short."

Since Gottlieb was defending Marty Tankleff in large part by mounting a virtual prosecution of Jerry Steuerman, Collins found himself playing the role of Steuerman's virtual defense attorney. When he moved on to the events at hand, he questioned Steuerman as if he were no different from the three card players who preceded him. That is, until he arrived at the end of the poker game, when he had Steuerman address two pieces of their testimony.

"What did you do upon the card game breaking up?" Collins asked.

"I spoke to Seymour for a minute or so, like we always do after a card game," Steuerman replied. "'How much did you win, how much did you lose?'"

"After you had the conversation with Mr. Tankleff, where did you go?"

"Filed out of the house and everybody was getting into their cars and leaving. I got into my car, which was alongside Joe Cecere's. Joe started his car. I started my car. I waved Joe to, to go ahead."

"Why did you do that?"

"Well, Joe had Al Raskin in the car with him. Al's ninety-five years old. And I just thought it was, you know, he, just tell somebody like that to go before you."

"Did you return back into the Tankleff house at any time?"

"Oh, never."

"Where did you go?"

"Straight home." That turned out to be a problem. "I'm very bad with keys," he confessed.

"Why was it, Mr. Steuerman, that you left New York and took the trip that you did?" Collins asked.

"At that time of my life, my wife was just recently passed away a year before. I was married for twenty-nine years. I had four children and four grandchildren. And one of my children was in bad legal trouble, and that—and my cash flow and my business was not what it used to be and then the murder of Arlene and Seymour after that, and the accusations by the son just—it got to me. I thought everybody would be better off just without me, that's all."

"Mr. Steuerman, did you have anything to do with the deaths of Seymour and Arlene Tankleff?" John Collins asked, closing his direct examination.

"No," Steuerman replied emphatically. "I would never do anything like that."

ARMED WITH page after page of serious questions, Bob Gottlieb decided to open his crucial cross-examination of Jerry Steuerman by mocking him. "Mr. Steuerman," he asked, "your name isn't Sol Klein, right?"

Gottlieb hammered Steuerman about his two arrests, the recent one for forging a letter to small-claims court from the Tropicana man, followed by his stunt twelve years earlier to get his money back from Merrill Lynch. Of that, Steuerman said, "I did what I had to do."

But it was the question of what he had to do to finish his house in Belle Terre that signaled the true beginning of what was to be an epic of public interrogation.

"It was a big house, wasn't it?" asked Gottlieb.

"Big house," Steuerman confirmed.

"And you found that you were in a little over your head. So you needed money to finish this very big house. And you go to Seymour, who you had met through your bagel business. And you ask him whether or not he can loan you some money."

And borrowed $350,000, on top of the $600,000 he'd already spent on it, and which he wound up selling for $550,000. "You took quite a beating, didn't you," Gottlieb said.

"Yup," said Steuerman.

For the rest of the day and into the next one and through the day after that, Gottlieb interrogated Steuerman about his web of debts to Seymour Tankleff. He presented Steuerman with one document after another: the agreement on the first loan giving Seymour half the ownership of Jerry's Stony Brook shop, and the second one giving him an equal partnership in his main store; documents stipulating their arrangement in the store they opened together in Nassau County, and the baking equipment Jerry signed over to Seymour after they sold that place a year later; copies of licenses and financial documents concerning the horses they raced in New Jersey. Gottlieb was relentless in his cross-examination, often asking Steuerman the same questions in different ways at different times. Questions about how much he owed Seymour, and how much he paid back each week, each month, each year; questions about when he paid him and in what form; questions about the various terms of the various contracts that, however they started out, came to define their relationship.

". . . By the way, how much money did Mr. Tankleff give you at the time he entered into this agreement?"

"It was a hundred and fifty thousand."

"He paid a hundred and fifty thousand dollars for the shares in Strathmore Bagels, correct?"

"It was a loan. He would not give me the hundred and fifty thousand dollars if I did not give him—I had to give him fifty percent as collateral."

". . . And it bugged you, didn't it. It bothered you?"

"At that time, no."

"Doesn't it bother you that you sold fifty percent of Strathmore Bagels to Seymour Tankleff?"

"It bothered me that Seymour was a very close friend and—and that friendship was beautiful, and it just disintegrated."

Why was that? Gottlieb wondered. Was it because Seymour wasn't just a tough businessman, but because he was an underhanded one? A man who charged even a supposed friend outrageous interest rates that became an unbearable burden?

Steuerman wouldn't go for it—wouldn't even say that the loan rates were usurious. Not even when Gottlieb pointed out that he was contending in his still-unresolved legal battle with the Tankleff estate that he owed nothing—in fact, the estate owed *him*—"due to the fact that said moneys actually represented, as set forth in my counterclaim, interest that was usurious and which should be returned." Not even when Gottlieb did the math for him, calculating the interest rate to be 39 percent and reminding him of his earlier testimony that in 1987 he paid Seymour $52,000, which was $6,000 more than he reported as his personal income that year.

Gottlieb tried another approach: Steuerman's statement to McCready, Doyle, and Jablonski in California that "Seymour thought he should own one-half of all of my property." Was that one of the reasons their beautiful friendship deteriorated?

"It began to deteriorate," Steuerman replied, "because Seymour got very sick, he got diabetes along with the bad heart and the bad blood, and I think it just got to him, and he put friendship aside, which we were—he was a father to me, and he started to be—he started to be one hundred percent businessman, which I understand because that's what he did. But we were friends, too, very close friends."

"Didn't you believe at that point," Gottlieb pressed, "that one of the problems was that Seymour Tankleff now believed he owned one-half of all of your businesses?"

"I'll answer it by, Seymour believed he owned one-half of *me*, not one-half of my businesses."

"Your Honor," said Gottlieb, "I have nothing further this afternoon."

*   *   *

GOTTLIEB CONTINUED grilling Steuerman the next day, questioning him so relentlessly on the minutiae of financial transactions that someone wandering into the courtroom might have presumed the case to be a civil suit between warring business partners, or perhaps a prosecution of some sort of white-collar crime. "When are we going to start litigating the murder case?" Collins grumbled as he rose to join Gottlieb behind the bench for one of their many sidebars, "We *have* been litigating the murder case," Gottlieb fired back. "Your Honor, I object to that!"

"Enough," Tisch said, like a weary parent. "Behave yourselves, both of you."

But Gottlieb couldn't let this pass. Arriving behind the bench, he was as livid as one could be without talking above a whisper. "It's absolutely unprofessional for him to make gratuitous comments like that when I'm cross-examining a witness. I object to it. It's inappropriate. And I'm going to right now ask for a mistrial."

"Denied," said Tisch.

But Gottlieb wasn't finished. "The problem right now is Mr. Collins stands up in front of this jury, says something about, 'Let's start litigating the murder case.' That is so highly objectionable. Why is there any sort of tension with me?"

"You already made your motion for a mistrial and I denied the same," replied Tisch, who then got to the point of the sidebar—Gottlieb's habit of questioning Steuerman about a document before it was formally in evidence. "I've told you time and again that in this courtroom we abide by the rules of evidence." Gottlieb straightened, and Tisch told him, "I don't think it's necessary that you walk away. I'm still speaking."

"Your Honor," said Gottlieb, "I've never walked away from you. I just stood up. I was leaning over the sidebar here."

After the conference broke up, Tisch instructed the jury to disregard the tensions. "Obviously, from time to time the passions of counsel become somewhat inflamed," he said.

Undaunted, Gottlieb continued building the alternative narrative that was the centerpiece of his defense: that Jerry Steuerman found himself in an ever-deepening financial hole in the months before the murders and finally did something desperate. Gottlieb gathered his next set of documents—court judgments against Steuerman by an assortment of creditors—and started with the $2,364 he owed the I. J. Morris Funeral Home.

"Oh, goodness," Collins groaned. Tisch agreed that asking Steuerman about his failure to pay for his wife's funeral was "degrading to the witness," as he put it in yet another sidebar. But his other debts were fair game.

"During the time that you say that whatever Seymour Tankleff put in front of you, you signed, your debts began to mount, correct?" Gottlieb asked.

"I don't remember at that time what my financial status was in the way of debts and not debts," said Steuerman.

Gottlieb refreshed his memory. There were court judgments in that period for casinos in Atlantic City—Trump Plaza, Harrah's, and Caesars, totaling about $29,000—along with a $7,743 debt to a condominium association. Gottlieb asked Steuerman about each of them and then about his county tax delinquency of $141,863.

"Do I remember that?" Steuerman asked.

"Do you remember that?" Gottlieb confirmed.

"Against me?"

"Against you."

"That's what that says, personally? I'm asking you, this is against me, $141,000?"

"Do you recall that, Mr. Steuerman?"

Steuerman bit his lip. "Yes," he said.

"Money was getting very short during this period of time that you were dealing with Seymour Tankleff, correct?"

"No."

"There comes a time, Mr. Steuerman, that by the summer of 1988 Mr. Tankleff is beginning to call in his notes, correct?"

"Not that I remember."

"You don't recall Mr. Tankleff demanding immediate payment of a $50,000 note by way of certified letter dated June 29, 1988?"

"I don't remember the letter."

Gottlieb wanted to get the letter into evidence—it was actually the blood-specked copy found on Seymour's desk—but Tisch wouldn't allow it. "The purported author is dead, and he did not sign it," he said. Instead Gottlieb handed Steuerman the certified mail receipt Julie Mutschler signed the next day at Strathmore Bagels. Steuerman looked at the receipt. "This wasn't signed by me," he said. "It was signed by 'J. Mutschler.'"

"As you sit there now, is this coming as a shock to you that he was demanding payment on this fifty-thousand-dollar note?"

"Yes," Steuerman said, and he insisted under further questioning that he never talked to Seymour about it and had no knowledge of any letter.

Gottlieb wanted to challenge Steuerman on this by showing him another certified letter, this one sent by Mike Fox a week after the murders. It was delivered to Steuerman's home, where his daughter signed for it. The letter referred to earlier demands for payment of the $50,000 note, and Gottlieb argued that it should be admitted because it revealed Steuerman's claim that he was unaware of the June letter to be "a bald-faced lie."

Tisch again ruled against him, at one point mocking his "very nice, tortured logic" to try to get around hearsay rules. But Gottlieb kept trying. He began reading from Fox's letter. "It indicates, 'It has come to our attention that Mr. Tankleff made demand on June 29 for payment and'—Your Honor, please, there's no reason to laugh."

"Mr. Steuerman," Gottlieb said, back before the jury, "you indicated to us yesterday that by the summer of 1988 your relationship with Seymour Tankleff began to deteriorate, correct?"

"Towards the end of that summer," Steuerman clarified, conceding for the first time that he and Seymour were at odds in the period just before the murders. Gottlieb seized the opportunity. He asked Steuerman what was causing this tension.

"I was opening up a new business and Seymour wanted fifty percent," Steuerman said. "He thought we were partners."

"Seymour Tankleff told you that he was entitled to fifty percent?"

"Entitled, yes . . . in *his* mind."

Gottlieb served up a sampling of comments—things Steuerman was quoted saying about Seymour to friends, poker players, reporters. "Do not recall it," Steuerman said in each instance. Then Gottlieb brought up Joe Cecere. "Did you ever tell Mr. Cecere you were having problems with Seymour?" he asked.

"I would say no more problems than Mr. Cecere had with Mr. Tankleff," Steuerman said.

"Mr. Cecere did not enter into any agreement with Mr. Tankleff, correct?"

"He's lucky."

". . . Isn't it true that by the summer of 1988 you were really feeling the pinch, you were really feeling strangled by the agreement that you had signed with Seymour Tankleff?"

"I have always needed money," Steuerman replied. "That's me. I begged and borrowed all my life."

"And once Seymour Tankleff was killed and Arlene Tankleff was killed, you haven't paid . . . any of the moneys that you had been paying Seymour Tankleff each week, correct?"

"It's in litigation."

"And while it's been in litigation, you haven't paid one dime, correct, Mr. Steuerman?"

"Correct."

"The pressure is really off, isn't it, Mr. Steuerman?"

"No."

"You still have pressure, Mr. Steuerman?"

"Worse than before."

* * *

STEUERMAN SAID he didn't remember going to KeyBank the day after Seymour and Arlene were attacked and nearly cleaning out their joint account. Gottlieb refreshed his memory with the $15,000 check he wrote to himself. Now Steuerman remembered.

"Did you get the money in cash?" Gottlieb asked.

"I don't remember," Steuerman said.

Lapses of memory were by now the leitmotif of Steuerman's testimony. He neglected few opportunities to claim not to recall the obvious or to deny the seemingly undeniable. Sometimes he denied statements he'd made earlier in his testimony. He was especially at a loss when it came to his disappearance. Gottlieb pounded him about whether the homicide group questioned him about his business with Tankleff when they found him in California. "I cannot recall every single question they asked me two years ago," Steuerman finally snapped. "I cannot do it and I won't do it. It's impossible." The problem was he hadn't recalled *any* questions they asked him. So Gottlieb tried this: Did any of these three men, at any time during those two days, ask you any questions about your financial dealings with Seymour Tankleff?

"Could be," Steuerman said. "If you keep on asking me the same question, I'll get you off my back by saying 'Could be.'"

Eventually, Gottlieb brought up Ed Jablonski's stunning quote in *Newsday*. "Did you tell Assistant District Attorney Jablonski that you wanted Seymour dead but were sad when you heard it happened?"

This, Steuerman remembered very well. But he remembered it very differently. "Exact conversation was I thought I wish *I* was dead, not Seymour was dead. When they found me, I told them I wish I was dead. That's why I went to California."

Steuerman professed no memory of telling Shirley Perlman of *Newsday*, on the phone from California the night he was found, that his plan to fake his death went awry when he found out his family wouldn't get any insurance money for seven years. This began an exchange that slowly escalated to a moment that seemed to flip a switch, detonating what was to be one of the defining moments of the entire trial.

Gottlieb held a photocopy of a newspaper clip with a few lines highlighted in yellow. "Do you recall telling reporters after you were located in California, Mr. Steuerman, that, 'Well, the plans of mice and men went astray because they don't pay life insurance policies on people that are missing'?"

"If you're asking me if I recall," said Steuerman, "I say no."

"In fact, the plans of mice and men did go astray, Mr. Steuerman, correct?"

"Is that a question?"

"That is a question."

"Are you asking me—what are you asking me? Ask me the question."

"I will."

"I'm waiting."

"Your plan to have life insurance paid to Sharon and to your children upon your disappearance didn't work out, did it?"

"I still do not know what you're talking about. I answered no to all those questions about life insurance and about plans. I think it's enough already."

"Mr. Steuerman, your plan was that if you staged your own disappearance people would think you were dead, correct?"

"*Yes,*" Steuerman said finally.

"And your plan was that if they thought you were dead Sharon and the children could receive the moneys from your insurance?"

"*Yes.*"

"And in fact it didn't work out that way . . . because you learned when you were out in California that insurance companies don't pay out for seven years."

"I didn't know that."

"You never learned that?"

"Never learned that."

"Did you learn that your plan would not work? Did you learn that after you fled Suffolk County?"

"I took a five-hundred-thousand-dollar life insurance policy," said Steuerman, getting more and more agitated, starting to stammer, "and made my wife the beneficiary before, a long time before, and my wife, my wife, my girlfriend at the time and my kids were beneficiary of that policy. I don't think there's anything wrong in that."

"And the plan was—" Gottlieb began to ask.

"If I died."

"—that if you—"

"If I died, my kids and my girlfriend get the money. That's what life insurance is for."

"And you staged a whole scenario to make it appear as if you had died, correct?"

"I staged the scenario because I did not want to be going through what I'm going through here!" Now he was churning. His droopy eyes widened, his voice filled the room. "*Three days* on the witness stand and I didn't do a thing! And it's *not fair*. It's not fair that I'm put through this. And *Marty Tankleff* sitting over there is accused of this, and *I am not*! And I'm sitting here for *three days* baring my soul to the world and it's *not fair*! And nobody—nobody cares, okay? And I'm here and things out there—everybody knows everything about my life!"

"Mr. Steuerman—" Gottlieb tried to cut in as the court stenographer's fingers danced double time and the reporters scribbled furiously.

"The *only* mistake that I made in my life, my lifetime—"

"Mr. Steuerman—"

"The *only* mistake is—"

"Your Honor," Gottlieb said, "can we have a direction to allow this—"

"—I live on—I was a poor man living like a millionaire—"

"No question, Mr. Steuerman," Gottlieb said, an unintended double entendre.

"—all my life, and it's *not fair*."

"There's no question posed to you, Mr. Steuerman."

"No question," Steuerman muttered.

"Please," the judge said to Steuerman.

"It's three days, Your Honor," Steuerman said, "and I'm tired."

Steuerman's eruption shook the courtroom, a jarring moment after many hours of painstaking, often tedious questioning. His outburst, on live television, was better than any melodrama the other channels were offering at that moment, and made for a clip that was to become essential footage for TV newsmagazines. But the moment may not have been as spontaneous as it seemed.

Some years later, Steuerman ran into Steve Saperstein on a flight from Florida. The former bagel partners hadn't seen each other in a few years, and when the Tankleff murders inevitably came up, Steuerman told Saperstein that his famous courtroom explosion had been planned in advance with the assistant district attorney; that he had waited for the right moment. Whether John Collins was in on it or not, a performance of premeditated histrionics would not have been out of character for Jerry Steuerman. The question was whether the jury would see his rant as a self-serving, narcissistic rage—or as the genuine protest of a humiliated and wrongfully accused man. The entire cross-examination was a test of the jury's sympathies, and Marty's fate could very well turn on where they fell. So when he resumed his questioning, and Steuerman began to unburden himself again, Gottlieb tried to rein him in.

"I wanted everybody to think I was dead. I had enough. I couldn't take it anymore. My life was not what it used to be. It was in shambles. I was a man that for years and years and years was living way above my means—"

"Mr. Steuerman—"

"—and living like a millionaire, and I couldn't do it anymore. . . . I did a foolish thing. I did foolish things throughout my ten years of this thing going on. I'm not—I made a lot of mistakes in my life."

"Mr. Steuerman—"

"I am no murderer! I did not do this!"

"Your Honor, please. There was no question before the witness."

"I should not be here."

THAT AFTERNOON, Gottlieb moved into the final act of his cross-examination. He introduced a new cast of characters and hoped he could make them something more than bit players.

"Mr. Steuerman, do you know a person by the name of Joseph Creedon?"

John Collins inched his chair away from the table in front of him and leaned forward. For the better part of three days, Collins had tried to contain Gottlieb's efforts to portray Jerry Steuerman as an erratic and desperate man who could be imagined at the center of a murder plot. Now Gottlieb was signaling the beginning of his ultimate gambit, much contested in the judge's chambers, to confer credence on his theory of the crimes by bringing in the sins of his son. As of the day before, Todd Steuerman was Inmate 90A-5945 of the New York State Department of Corrections. Collins sat straight, ready to pounce the instant he heard something objectionable.

Steuerman said he didn't know a person by the name of Joseph Creedon.

"Well, do you know about any legal dispute between your son, Todd Steuerman, and another individual?"

"Objection."

Sidebar, said the judge. There followed a lengthy discussion of the proper way for Gottlieb to get to where he wanted to go. Gottlieb suggested that Collins be allowed to tell Steuerman, out of the jury's presence, that the question concerned his son's arrest for shooting Joseph Creedon and the allegation that he himself had subsequently threatened Creedon. "I thought John would have already advised him what I was going to be addressing," Gottlieb said.

"I did," Collins said. "About two days ago I asked him if he knew a Joseph Creedon and did he ever threaten a Joseph Creedon. No, he told me."

"We don't have to have a trial outside of a trial here," Tisch said. "Why don't we just ask him if he is now aware that there had been a complaint made about his son Todd?"

"I'll do it step by step," Gottlieb said agreeably. They returned to their places and Gottlieb resumed his questioning. Steuerman said he knew nothing about any incident or accusation involving his son. Nor did he call anybody who was making such an accusation and offer him $10,000 to drop the charges.

And finally: "Do you recall having a conversation with an individual who was involved in a legal dispute with your son and saying to him, 'What are you, crazy? You're dealing with the wrong person. I can have you dead'?"

"*No!*" Steuerman boomed.

And that was that. The judge's ruling allowed Gottlieb to go no further. The jury would not hear about Todd Steuerman's drug convictions or the allegation that he shot Joe Creedon in the arm. But Gottlieb had achieved at least some of what he wanted. Even if he couldn't bring Creedon in to back it up, and even though Steuerman denied it, he had gotten that quote before the jury: "*I can have you dead.*"

Gottlieb had one more thing to bring up. "Do you know a Kwame Wani?" he asked.

In the year and a half since his disengagement from Seymour Tankleff, Steuerman had begun selling franchises in Strathmore Bagels. A man by the name of Kwame Wani had been one of the first to sign up. Gottlieb knew this because Wani had called him after Steuerman began testifying earlier in the week, and told him that he and Seymour Tankleff might have something in common. According to Wani, he and Steuerman were involved in an ongoing dispute that recently escalated to the point of violence: His shop was vandalized by five men, one of whom told him they had been hired by Steuerman to force him out. Wani called the police and the men were arrested. Gottlieb found Wani's statement to the police helpful to his line of defense. It was an instance in which Steuerman seemed to have brought in muscle—the five men would later be identified as Hells Angels—to take care of his problems.

For Gottlieb, the question again was how much of the story he could get before the jury. When he started to ask Steuerman about it, Collins objected and Tisch sighed. "All right," said the judge. "Let's sidebar again." Gottlieb briefed him about what he had, and Tisch ruled as he had with the incident involving Todd Steuerman and Joseph Creedon. "The question may be posed. He can deny it. And that will put an end to it. We're not bringing in Mr. Kwame Wani, whatever his name is."

Now it was Collins who refused to go down without a fight. The allegation shouldn't come in at all—it was "prejudicial and inflammatory," he said—unfair to Steuerman. "The man's been hit over the head for three days."

Gottlieb went one last round with Steuerman, who denied everything and said it was all Kwami Wani's fault. Along with the rest of his testimony, the episode was enough to judge Steuerman an elusive and discontented man whose life seemed to be an endless series of quarrels that made him wide-eyed with indignation. But did it make him a murderer? Gottlieb hadn't come close to proving Steuerman was anything of the sort. But neither did he have to. All he needed to do was prove that it was a reasonable enough possibility to raise reasonable doubt about Marty.

Perhaps there was a hint of whether Gottlieb accomplished his objective in the reactions to Steuerman's three days on the stand by the congregation of media people who had watched it all. Yes, Steuerman was frequently evasive. Yes, it was hard not to notice how he constantly bit his lip. Yes, he seemed all too comfortable playing the victim—first of his own cravings for a life beyond his means; then of Seymour Tankleff's exploitation and betrayal of friendship; and finally, of Seymour's son's outrageous finger-pointing and his lawyer's ruthless interrogation.

But Steuerman's protests of innocence struck some as possibly authentic—if for no other reason than their anticipation of the prosecution's principal witnesses. If Marty Tankleff confessed to these murders—as Detectives McCready and Rein would swear he did—didn't that have to mean his lawyer's accusations were as unfounded as Steuerman proclaimed? Years later, one reporter remembered thinking, This guy's wacky, but somehow he's kind of convincing. He may be a murderer or he may be just a hapless bagel maker with delusions of grandeur, a poor schmuck forced to confess his failings and regrets under penalty of perjury.

The danger for the defense was in pushing the jury to decide which one he was. There was a fine line between presenting Steuerman as the embodiment of reasonable doubt and mounting a parallel prosecution that subtly shifted the burden of proof. If Steuerman said one true thing in three days under oath, it was that he wasn't the one on trial here.

CHAPTER 20

Microscopic Proof

THE SIGHT OF Jerry Steuerman finally stepping down from the witness stand might have been John Collins's best moment to this point. But his relief was short-lived. He followed Steuerman with another man whose testimony did little to dispel the defense's elemental assertion that the police had been a bit impetuous in falling in love with the first suspect they met and tying the knot before lunch.

The witness was Dan Hayes, the man Seymour Tankleff was bankrolling in the storefront gym a parking lot away from Strathmore Bagels. Collins had a single purpose in calling Hayes, and that was to confirm one of Marty's many supposed complaints about his parents that led him to murder them. But the prosecutor committed a classic blunder in putting him on the stand: He apparently had no idea what his witness was going to say. Hayes had read in the newspaper that according to the police, Marty was angry at his parents because they were having Hayes stay with him when they went on their upcoming cruise. "I said, 'You've gotta be kidding me,' when I read that," Hayes recalled years later. "It was such a lie. Everything was so twisted."

On the stand, Hayes followed his lawyer's advice not to volunteer anything—just answer the questions. So when Collins asked if Marty had been annoyed when he found out that Hayes would be staying with him, Hayes said yes. And then, with Gottlieb's first question on cross-examination, he told the rest of the story.

Did you and Marty have any further conversations on the subject? Gottlieb asked in his first question on cross-examination. Yes, said Hayes, in the gym one day around the third week of August: "Marty came over, and he said, 'When are you going to be moving in?' I said, 'Well, probably not until your parents leave.' And he said, 'Why don't you move in as soon as you can? I think we can have a good time.'" Hayes said he politely declined the invitation, telling Marty he didn't want to impose on his parents. When Marty tried to cajole him, said Hayes, "I was like, 'Well, I'll think about it. We'll talk about it.' And I think that was probably the last time I saw him. But he seemed very happy about it."

After watching his own witness refute the one thing he expected him to corroborate—and expose a piece of prosecution mythology in the process—Collins looked on as Hayes morphed into a virtual witness for the defense. He testified about Seymour and Marty's close relationship and spoke as a kind of expert witness on the matter of whether Marty had the strength to commit the murders. When Gottlieb asked for his opinion of Marty's physical abilities, the fitness trainer replied with a pertinent comparison: "I'd say I was setting a lot of the Nautilus equipment about the same weight as his mother's, if not a little bit less in certain machines." Marty was "fairly weak," he said, and quite a bit smaller than his mother.

And finally, Hayes recalled the day Seymour and Arlene were attacked. That afternoon, a pair of homicide detectives came to the gym to ask him some questions. Soon after they left, Jerry Steuerman came in. "He asked me if the detectives had mentioned anything or had questioned me about him," Hayes testified. "And I said, 'No. I didn't really speak to them at length.' . . . He said, 'What did they tell you?' I said, 'They really didn't tell me anything. I just heard that Seymour had been bludgeoned and that he was still possibly alive.' And then he said he had heard that Seymour had been bludgeoned with a ballpeen hammer. I said I didn't hear that, and it was disgusting—the whole affair was rather upsetting and that I had to get to work. And he said, 'Well, if you hear anything, let me know.'"

"How did he appear while he was speaking to you and asking you these questions?" Gottlieb asked.

"Nervous," said Hayes.

BRIEF THOUGH IT WAS, if Hayes's testimony made one thing clear it was that Collins needed to rid the courtroom of the scent of Jerry Steuerman. He needed to get to the cops. They were his whole case. But he had one last area of testimony to get through first, and it was a big one: the physical evidence. As he had reluctantly intimated in his opening statement, it was the most problematic part of his case. Collins, it seemed, would have to hope that the jurors wouldn't pay so much attention to the forensic evidence that they realized it contradicted the prosecution's theory of the crimes in just about every regard.

Collins continued his tactic of portraying himself as an objective and evenhanded seeker of truth who held nothing back, whether it helped his case or not. The county's crime scene investigators and forensic scientists spent hundreds of hours collecting and analyzing trace evidence, and Collins presented it all. This had two practical effects: It conveyed how thorough and professional the forensic investigation had been, giving the case a patina of integrity. And it inundated the jury, hour after hour, day after day, with monotonous, technical testimony that tended to obscure the true meaning of their findings. It was a kind of prosecutorial sleight of hand.

Over the course of five days, Collins brought to the stand eight people with some of the most specialized skills of any employees on the Suffolk County payroll: three crime scene detectives, four forensic scientists from the criminalistics lab, and the county's deputy chief medical examiner. The crime scene detectives recounted the four days they spent hunting and gathering evidence of the crimes. They described all they had taken from the house and how they had gone about collecting and cataloguing it. A detective named James Barnes recalled the crime scene team's exhaustive but ultimately fruitless search of the grounds: the detectives with metal detectors, the blood-sniffing dog from the canine unit, the seven men from Emergency Services who searched the bluffs, scaling them with ropes.

The forensic scientists then took the witness stand to explain the techniques of their respective specialties and report the results of their tests in this case. Years later, the field of crime scene investigation would inspire a franchise of TV dramas featuring glamorous actors and spectacular computer-generated simulations. But then as now, jurors in real-life murder trials found that genuine forensic investigators were decidedly unglamorous people whose work involved peering into microscopes for weeks on end and then coming to court to report what they saw, often in a fashion that was spectacularly tedious. The Tankleff jurors heard from Robert Baumann, the crime lab's serologist, that when it came to the genetic markers in blood, "adenosine deaminase is the most stable enzyme, with AK second, PGM and ACP tied for third, and esterase D probably last." They learned about blood spatter castoff and pooling tendencies. About "comparison values" between "question specimens" and "known sources." About the catagen and telogen stages in the life cycle of a hair.

After describing their methods, the forensic witnesses presented their analyses of the trace evidence recovered from the scene, specimens now gathered before them in stacks of heat-sealed envelopes. Led by Collins, they recited the exhibit number of each one, described what it was and where it came from, how it had been collected and by whom, the methods used to examine it, and finally what had been learned. And when all the witnesses had spoken, giving testimony that would fill 1,156 pages of transcript, there was only one conclusion to be drawn: that all this diligence had yielded nary a piece of physical evidence linking Martin Tankleff to the murders of his parents.

Collins handled this awkward situation in the manner of any number of Suffolk County homicide prosecutors before him. His job was to work with what he was given—to turn the homicide squad's work into a conviction, whether that work was good, bad, or indifferent. From the moment Collins had taken over the Tankleff case, this had meant ignoring the inconsistencies. It meant taking on faith that the police account of the confession was unassailable. McCready and Rein would testify that Marty told them he killed his mother and father with the knife found beside the watermelon on the kitchen counter and the bar of a dumbbell taken from his bedroom. So the prosecutor could take only one position: that Marty killed his mother and father with that knife and that dumbbell. Even if all Collins could say, as he had in his opening statement, was that the victims' fatal injuries were "not inconsistent with having been caused by those items." Even if painstaking analysis and common logic showed the chances of that to be microscopic.

So here was Dr. Vernard Adams, the medical examiner, showing pictures comparing a dumbbell bar to Arlene Tankleff's head wounds and saying they were consistent—but acknowledging on cross-examination that the wounds were also consistent with any number of other blunt objects. And here was Charles Kosciuk, the lead crime scene detective, holding the watermelon knife, still in pieces from the crime lab's pursuit of trace evidence tying it to the murders. And here was Baumann, the forensic serologist who performed that search, recounting all his ultimately negative microscopic and chemical tests—first on the presumed murder weapons and then on the plumbing of the shower tub in which the defendant was alleged to have washed them clean.

From the drain trap, Baumann explained, he removed clumps of hair, soap scum, fibers from a washcloth, and 5.2 ounces of trap water. Trying to detect the presence of blood, he tested the water with phenolphthalein reagent, and when that was negative he tested it with hydrogen peroxide, and when that was negative he evaporated the water and tested the residue, and when that was negative he gave up looking for blood in the shower drain. Then he gave the entangled hairs to one of his colleagues, Susan Ryan, whose specialty was hair and fiber analysis. She took the witness stand and described how she tried to identify whose hairs they were. It would be significant if the drain in Marty's bathroom contained hairs matching either of his parents. But Ryan found that the hairs had been down there too long to identify. Most of them had taken on the green tint of the copper piping, and some were further degraded by soap residue. "I believe the hairs were sitting in the drain for a period of time," Ryan said.

As they reported their findings, the forensic experts revealed the case to be a kind of hall of mirrors. The jury had learned early on that the knife had been found on the morning of the murders next to the remnants of watermelon the poker players ate the night before. Much was made of Vinnie Bove's last slice of watermelon before he departed. So when Baumann disclosed that there was a bit of "pinkish material" along the edge of the blade, that it was negative for blood and tissue, and that it dissolved in solution when a lab technician tried to mount it on a slide, he left no doubt what the substance on the watermelon knife was. It was beyond his expertise to explain how a sliver of watermelon could have possibly gotten on a knife that had supposedly been used to murder two people and was then cleaned of all traces of the crimes. But it remained the prosecution's position, if only by inference.

There were also some peculiar things about the dumbbell bar. In their initial reports, McCready and Rein referred to the implement allegedly used to bludgeon the Tankleffs as a "barbell" or a "dumbbell," using the words interchangeably, though they are different implements. (A barbell is five to seven feet long and used by weight lifters. A dumbbell is a free weight, a kind of miniature barbell. That's what Marty had in his room.) But at the trial, by which time the medical examiner's report was a factor, it became specifically "the bar part of the dumbbell"—without the weighted disks—that was being held out as the weapon used to crush the Tankleffs' skulls. But when Baumann tried to disassemble both dumbbells taken from Marty's room to examine them for trace evidence, he found the weights screwed to the bar so tightly that he had a hard time taking them off—hard enough to mention in his testimony. Again, the police attributed to Marty no mention of taking the dumbbell apart to murder his parents, then reassembling it after washing it in the shower.

The prosecution's forensic scientists made several other contributions to the defense's contention that Marty's confession was a fabrication by the police. According to Baumann's analysis, some of Seymour Tankleff's blood was mixed with his wife's on a bedsheet and on one of the walls of the master bedroom. This finding was inconsistent with the account, attributed to Marty, that he killed his mother first, then went to the office and killed his father, and never went back into the bedroom.

Even more striking was Kosciuk's testimony that the crime scene investigation yielded not a trace of blood anywhere on the path between the two rooms, much of which was covered with light-colored rugs and carpeting. This single fact discredited the police account of the murders, which described Marty going back and forth through the house, blood all over himself and his weapons.

Finally, there was Robert Genna, the crime lab's assistant chief. His specialty was pattern analysis. Using a high-powered magnifying glass, Genna testified, he examined the bloodstains on the bedding in the master bedroom and the smudges of blood left on and around the light switch plate in Marty's room. These stains, all of them Arlene's blood, made imprints that Genna described as a "chain link honeycomb pattern." He found no such patterns on anything removed from the room in which Seymour was murdered. Arlene's killer, he determined, was wearing gloves—most likely latex, though a tightly woven fabric was also possible. The reason he couldn't be definitive was that the gloves were never found. They didn't turn up during the crime scene team's intensive search of the house and its grounds in the days following the murders. And they weren't found during a specific search conducted after Genna informed the homicide squad of his discovery in the lab.

In the prosecution's view, all this meant was that Marty Tankleff did an exceptional job of getting rid of the gloves. But it wasn't just the gloves' absence from the array of exhibits offered by the prosecution that was significant. Just as conspicuous was their absence from the confession. According to McCready and Rein, Marty told them all about how he did it, why he did it, and how he tried to cover it up. They said he told them he made sure to commit the murders naked to avoid having to get rid of bloody clothes. Yet, according to their account, he didn't mention that he wore gloves (but only while killing his mother), or tell them how he managed to dispose of them so ingeniously that they would elude a search of several days by teams of detectives and a blood-sniffing dog.

Because the jurors had not yet heard the police rendition of Marty's confession, the inconsistencies with the physical evidence would not be readily apparent to them at this point. But even if Collins obscured the meaning of the forensic findings by presenting them out of context, it would all become clear eventually. Gottlieb would make sure of that in his summation. And then the prosecutor's case would rest on whether the jury came to his position that life, as he'd nimbly suggested in his opening statement, isn't perfect. That this was just one of those cases with a few loose ends that shouldn't divert them from the simple fact of the defendant's confession to the crimes. The part where he said he did it, not where he said *how* he did it or what he did or didn't do to cover it up.

In the meantime, Collins tried to make the most of a few items of evidence, and some expert testimony, that he considered persuasive evidence of guilt.

At police headquarters on September 7, the homicide detectives took three tissues that Marty had in his pocket. One of them was found to have a spot of blood that was consistent with his mother's. From that day forward, the prosecutors promoted this single tissue as primary physical evidence sufficient to tie Marty Tankleff to the murders of his parents. In the months after the murders, the police and prosecutors told reporters that Marty had been seen using this tissue to wipe blood off his ankle. The insinuation, repeated in several news stories, was that Marty lied when he said he never touched his mother's body, and that he tried to get rid of incriminating evidence. But it wasn't true. There would be no testimony by anyone claiming to have seen Marty wiping blood off his ankle with any tissue, let alone this particular one. Still, there *was* that spot of blood matching his mother's on a tissue Marty had in his pocket. So how did it get there?

Marty had no idea, but Gottlieb had a few. It could have happened at any point when he was running from room to room, in and out of the house, during the chaotic first half hour after he woke up that morning. He could have touched the area around the light switch in his bedroom, the only place outside the master bedroom that the crime scene investigators found Arlene's blood. Since Marty said he was using the tissues to dab his eyes as well as his nose, the dampness could have caused the transfer of blood even if it were dried.

In the shower, investigators found a coarse, body-scrubbing sponge called a loofah. They testified that the loofah sponge was wet when they found it, suggesting that Marty had showered that morning, as the confession said, and not at eleven o'clock the night before, as he claimed. But there were flaws in this allegation. First, the rest of the shower and tub were dry, save a small amount of water around the drain. And the investigators were unable to say with any precision *how* wet the sponge was. They offered no evidence about the absorbency of that kind of sponge, or that it was inconsistent with having been used just seven hours earlier.

But Collins suggested there was more to the loofah sponge. At the crime lab, Baumann had examined it under his microscope, looking for blood or tissue. He found none. But he did notice a slit that appeared to be cut along half the sponge's twelve-inch length. Asked by Collins what made him think the sponge had been cut, Baumann testified that the edges of the fibers were "very sharply defined, a very straight edge," and a consistent one-fifth-inch deep. Collins wanted the jury to suppose that Marty cut the sponge while using it to clean the knife. But it was speculation without support. Marty himself would later testify that the sponge came with the slit. Baumann's failure to find any blood or tissue in the slit—or anywhere else on the loofah sponge, whose distinctively webbed structure would likely have soaked up and trapped trace evidence—made that claim credible.

UNABLE TO CORROBORATE the details of the confession, Collins focused on challenging Marty's account of his actions in the ten minutes after he woke up that morning. His star witness was Charles Kosciuk, whose specialty was reconstructing the scenes of crimes and accidents. Kosciuk testified that the patterns of blood he observed in Seymour Tankleff's office betrayed two of Marty's statements as lies. He showed the jury a series of photographs of Seymour's leather chair. The blood on the seat and on the inside back of the chair wasn't smeared, he pointed out. So Marty's description of how he helped his father couldn't be true: "It's obvious that nobody was dragged from that chair."

Kosciuk also discerned evidence of guilt in the blood spatter left on the telephone on Seymour's desk—the one Marty said he used to call for help. Kosciuk displayed photos showing bloodstains on the coiled phone cord draped over the side of the desk. Based on the way the bloodstains lined up, he said, "It does not appear to have been moved since the blood was deposited on it." He showed a close-up. "You can see the cord is intertwined, indicating that it was not pulled out or stretched out." In addition, the blood on the phone itself was not smeared. The implication of all this was that Marty's 911 call was a ruse—that he actually made the call from another phone. And the absence of blood on any other phone in the house was consistent, in the prosecution's view, with Marty having cleaned himself in the shower before he made the call.

During a long and detailed cross-examination, Gottlieb challenged Kosciuk's conclusion that the blood on the phone would have been smeared if Marty had used it to call for help. That opinion assumed—incorrectly, according to other testimony—that the blood was wet. Moreover, Kosciuk's appraisal of the phone cord assumed that Marty "stretched out" the cord when he called 911, and that the cord would not recoil to its original position even if he did. His testimony on this question was vague and perfunctory, unsupported by the kind of careful examination and analysis that gave credibility to the work of his colleagues in the forensic sciences section. Without knowing how Marty handled the phone or how dry the blood was when he made the call, there seemed no real basis for Kosciuk's observation that it didn't "appear" that the cord was moved after the blood landed on it.

Kosciuk's less than rigorous analysis of the telephone suggested a forensic version of what scientists call "investigator's bias." In their coming testimony, McCready and Rein would say that Marty ultimately admitted making the 911 call from the phone in his parents' bedroom. Was the crime scene detective's job to dispassionately evaluate the evidence or to come up with support for the prosecution's case? Kosciuk seemed to have an alarmingly casual approach to work of serious consequence.

The relevant question was how the jurors would ultimately weigh the evidence the prosecution was selling against the evidence it was ignoring—how disposed they would be to interpreting it in favor of guilt because they believed the confession.

AS A PROSECUTION WITNESS, Dr. Vernard Adams's primary function was to describe the injuries of the victims and offer his opinions about the implements that might have been used to cause them. To do this he displayed a series of gruesome photographs of the victims, at the scene and on the autopsy table.

"The wounds of the scalp were lacerations—that is, tears caused by blunt impact," Adams said, showing a photo of Arlene's shaved head taken at autopsy. "There were eleven of them, including one which involved a rip through the ear. They had a variety of shapes. Some were linear, some were curved, some were formed star-like. This one is cross-shaped. The fatty tissue beneath the scalp became pulped with the blunt impact, so there is an excavated area, if you will." And the skull: "There were five circular to oval depressed fractures. Some of them were connected one to another by linear fractures and by traumatic separations of the cranial sutures, which is where the cranial plates grow together in childhood." Beneath the skull fractures were "thin bleedings" under the layer of tissue that forms a case for the brain.

When he finished describing Arlene's skull fractures, Adams compared them to the bar of the dumbbell taken from Marty's room. Collins asked him what he concluded. "In my opinion," Adams replied, "the skull fractures are consistent with having been caused by the bar in the photograph."

As the jury understood by now, *consistent with* was a phrase forensic investigators used to describe evidence that was neither conclusive nor exclusive. Collins was up-front about it, asking Adams whether he could say that Arlene's head wounds were consistent with "having been caused by that particular bar and no other instrument on the face of the earth." No, said Adams, he could not say that. Gottlieb picked it up from there. Could it have been caused by a hammer? A tire iron? Adams agreed that the head wounds were consistent with those and any number of other implements. In fact, the injuries were not inconsistent with having been caused by more than one blunt instrument. The same went for the stabs and cuts: Beyond saying they were caused by a sharp blade, Adams couldn't match any of the wounds to any particular size or type of knife, or say they weren't caused by more than one.

Though there was little doubt that the Tankleffs had been killed with similar if not identical weapons, Adams's description of their injuries revealed two very different scenes of violence. Arlene's head wounds were serious enough to have knocked her out, he said, but not to kill her. The slashing, though, was fatal. It severed two major arteries and a vein on the right side of her neck. According to the medical examiner, Arlene Tankleff bled to death. Her husband also sustained deep neck wounds, but somehow they didn't involve any major blood vessels or the airway. It was why Seymour survived the attack, if only until he succumbed to the effects of his brain injuries a month later.

The medical examiner's findings supported Detective Kosciuk's conclusion that Seymour was struck from behind while sitting in his chair and never got up. The attack was so savage that the emergency doctors found brain matter oozing from his head. This was significant for a question it raised about the confession. According to McCready and Rein, Marty said "he got behind his father and hit him with the barbell first. His father asked him why he was doing this. . . ."

Adams's description of Arlene's murder created an even more horrific image—and another reason to doubt the police account. Judging from the locations of the various bloodstains in relation to where Arlene's body came to rest, it was evident, said Adams, "that she moved between the time that the injuries started to occur and the time that she died." Just as clear was that she battled her attacker. Among her many defensive wounds were cuts on two knuckles of her left hand and one on her right hand, suggesting she had her hands up, back sides out, in an effort to shield herself. There were also two bruises and two stab wounds on the underside of her left arm, one of which went completely through the arm, and another gaping stab wound on her right forearm. Arlene Tankleff was a strong woman who weighed 191 pounds at her death; it was unlikely her killer left that room without some evidence of a fight on his own body. Between the police photographs taken that day at police headquarters and the image of the slight young man sitting at the defense table a year and a half later, Arlene's son would not seem the likeliest of suspects.

REAL MURDER TRIALS aren't like the ones on TV, Collins had declared in his opening statement. Sometimes we don't have all the answers. The medical examiner, for instance, won't be able to give a precise time of Arlene Tankleff's death. As it turned out, the medical examiner couldn't even hazard an estimate.

The question of the time of death was extraordinarily relevant. But, said Dr. Adams, "In this case, I have nothing to offer." This was because the crime scene investigators, for reasons unexplained, didn't call Adams to the scene until *nine hours* after the homicides were first reported.

Gottlieb asked Adams to speak about the processes that occur in the human body in the minutes and hours after death, and how observing those processes can narrow the time of death.

There's rigor mortis, said Adams, the stiffening that comes as oxygen is depleted from muscle. But a better indicator is livor mortis, or lividity, the gravitational settling of blood in the blood vessels. It causes gradual changes in skin color until a point comes when the process ends and the discoloration of the skin becomes fixed. Observing the body before then is an important element of estimating a time of death. It's not an exact science, but generally speaking, the sooner a medical examiner sees the body, the better his estimate will be.

"But in this case," Gottlieb asked, "because you arrived at the home some ten hours after you understood the body to have been found, you lost that opportunity to check for the livor mortis to try to narrow the time when you could conclude the death occurred, correct?"

"Yes," said Adams.

Gottlieb asked how arriving at, say, eight that morning, rather than at four in the afternoon, might have affected his ability to judge whether Arlene died closer to three o'clock, when she was last known to be alive, or six A.M., when she was first known to be dead. All things considered, said Adams, "I may have been able to give an opinion as to whether death occurred at the beginning of that three-hour bracket, or at the end. I don't know. But I may have been. I was not able to do so, having arrived at the scene at four o'clock."

Collins seemed taken aback, and more than a little annoyed, by Adams's agreement with the suggestion that the police had blown any chance to address what might well have been the case's single most relevant forensic question. On redirect, Collins tried to get Adams to back off. But the medical examiner realized how critical a question the time of death had become, and he seemed almost wistful at the lost opportunity. "It's possible that I could have given an opinion as to whether the death occurred closer to three o'clock or closer to six o'clock A.M.," he told Collins.

Though Adams couldn't say when the Tankleffs were murdered because he wasn't there soon enough, some indications could be found in the accounts of those who were. Officers James Crayne and Daniel Gallagher found that Seymour Tankleff was no longer actively bleeding when they arrived, that the blood on his body was mostly dry and some of it crusted. Gallagher testified that Arlene looked discolored when he saw her at 6:20. Ethel Curley, one of the rescue workers, also testified that Arlene's skin was pale and dry, and that much of the blood she saw on both victims was already dry. On Seymour's chair she noticed a large clump of coagulated blood.

And Curley offered a vivid recollection—one of the more unpleasant images of the trial, but perhaps one of the most revealing. "When we were getting ready to move Mr. Tankleff, I heard something drop to the ground," Curley said. "I thought it was possibly some piece of equipment. I turned to see what it was. And it was a large clot of blood, perhaps the size of a golf ball, that dropped from his upper extremities."

CHAPTER 21

Watching the Detectives

BY THE TIME OF Marty Tankleff's trial, the Confession Taker was taking it easy. Detective K. James McCready was retired from the Suffolk County Police Department at age forty-two, not entirely by choice.

A year earlier, the State Commission of Investigation had accused McCready of committing perjury in the murder trial of James Diaz and expressed its dismay that he faced no consequences. It seemed that the period for disciplinary proceedings permitted by the county's contract with the detectives' association had elapsed.

In the investigation of homicides in Suffolk County, it was sometimes hard to imagine what sort of conduct might be considered unacceptable. The basic rules seemed to be: Get a conviction. And whatever you do, don't get caught. But in the Diaz case, McCready did get caught. And there was no conviction. If his successes had allowed him to avoid the consequences of his less-than-stellar personal reputation, the SIC investigation was something else. The one thing the institution could not tolerate was embarrassment.

At the point when the SIC report was released, McCready was six months shy of twenty years on the job, the magic moment when cops can retire with full benefits, still young enough to start new careers and cash two checks. McCready was not one of those guys who longed for that day. He already had two incomes, and he loved his job. "What can you do with your life that is more interesting than investigating a murder?" he told Dena Kleiman. "It's for real. It's not read a good book. Watch a good movie. This is the real thing where you can really make a difference." Even years later, McCready would use the present tense and the pronoun *we* when he talked about the work of a homicide detective. But his time was up. Whether or not anyone in the hierarchy had any misgivings about McCready's work in the Tankleff case was a subject too dangerous to seep through the great blue wall.

"I STOOD and looked around the defendant's bedroom. And one of the things I noticed almost immediately was that there was blood on a light switch plate cover. . . ."

McCready was recounting his initial walk-through of 33 Seaside Drive on the morning of September 7, 1988. He was the picture of self-assurance in the witness chair, a man who seemed to swagger even while sitting. He rested his chin between his thumb and forefinger as he listened to John Collins's questions, and sometimes while answering them. He took frequent sips of water, and often kept the glass in his hand between swallows, swinging it nonchalantly as he spoke. One reporter recalled thinking McCready looked as if he were regaling his buddies at their favorite watering hole. The image was undiminished by his voice, which sounded like cigarettes and scotch.

"I walked out to the driveway, where I met with the defendant. I introduced myself. . . . He told me that he had gotten home at about 9:10. He said his father had a card game going on at the house. I asked him for the names of the card players. He rattled off about eight or ten names. And while he was giving me these names, he said to me, 'I know who did this.' . . ."

It wasn't the first time the jury had heard about Marty's first statements to the police that morning. Norman Rein arrived on Seaside Drive a while after McCready but preceded him to the witness stand. He and their sergeant related their own conversations with Marty at the scene and recalled conferring at the Tankleffs' mailbox as Marty sat nearby on the hood of McCready's car. On the basis of "inconsistencies that we found in the story," said Sergeant Robert Doyle, "I thought it would be a good idea for Detective McCready to invite him to go out to police headquarters and talk to him."

It was not surprising that Collins chose to lead with Rein rather than with McCready, the case's lead detective. As a police witness, Rein was a prosecutor's dream. He came across as seasoned, straightforward, by-the-book. He delivered a seamless narrative of the interview with Marty, and he was as unflappable as his former partner was volatile—something demonstrated later, during Gottlieb's cross-examination. "Detective McCready has a bit of a temper, correct?" Gottlieb asked. "He's a colorful person," Rein replied smoothly.

There was an irony in how Rein's nearly robotic dispassion made him so effective a witness. Some of his more damaging testimony, aside from his account of the interrogation itself, was his characterization of Marty's composure that day as so inappropriate that it constituted evidence of guilt. Asked by Collins to describe Marty's demeanor during the fifteen minutes he spent with him on Seaside Drive, Rein said, "Well, the defendant was sitting on the hood of the car. His arms were folded and his feet were up on the bumper and he was calm. He was businesslike. He spoke very forthrightly and was unemotional." At another point, Collins made use of Rein's background as an emergency medical technician and hostage negotiator. "Based on your experience," he asked, "did the defendant appear to be in shock at any time that you were speaking with him that day?" Replied Rein: "No, not in the least."

After an hour of preliminaries, the detectives eased toward the accusatory phase of the interview. Even by their account, Marty seemed to have no clue of their suspicions. But there was a suggestion of his state of mind—a hint of disconnection from reality—in one passing moment of Rein's narrative. McCready was questioning Marty closely about the shower he said he'd taken the night before. Marty answered the questions and then abruptly drifted into a kind of stream-of-consciousness about his parents and his life: "We asked the defendant what he did next, and at that time the defendant said to us, 'I was adopted when I was two days old.' And he continued talking. . . . He said, 'My father got divorced and he and my mother got married, and they adopted me when I was two days old.' And he said, 'They're the only parents I've ever known.'"

Whatever Marty's emotional state, there came a point when it dawned on him that it was not Jerry Steuerman who was under suspicion by the detectives. "I asked the defendant what would happen if we arrested Jerry Steuerman, and he got convicted," Rein said, "and the defendant said that if Steuerman was out of the picture the defendant would get everything." (Both Rein and McCready attributed the expression "out of the picture" to Marty—one of several instances in which they quoted him using a glib phrase that would seem less natural coming from an accused teenager than an accusing detective.)

At about 11:15, McCready told Marty he didn't seem very upset. "I said, 'Marty, I haven't seen you shed one tear. You haven't cried at all. You don't seem very upset about what happened to your parents.' And he didn't respond."

It was at about this point that McCready had an idea that was to become pivotal. Between their initial interviews in Belle Terre and now at homicide headquarters, Marty had recounted half a dozen times what he'd been told to do by the 911 operator and how he had followed her instructions. Now McCready asked him to demonstrate what he'd done, using Rein as his father. "I moved my chair away from the desk," Rein said. "The defendant came up on my left side and took his right hand and arm and placed it on my back. He took his left hand and put it on my left arm and urged me forward"—Rein was demonstrating the demonstration from the witness chair—"like I'm doing right now." After some maneuvering, "he pulled me several inches forward on my chair, and he slid his hands from my waist down to my hip. He's in front of me, leaning over me." At that point, Marty's half-zippered sweatshirt fell off his shoulder. Rein looked up at McCready. "He was pointing to his own right shoulder. And then he pointed to the defendant and he mouthed the word 'blood.'"

The blood on Marty's shoulder intensified the tone and pace of the interrogation. The detectives asked him to go through his story again, pressing him about what he did at each moment. They asked him to draw a diagram of his parents' bedroom, showing how far in he went when he first got up in the morning, where he was standing when he came back after calling 911, and where his mother's body was when he spotted it. Marty sketched a rough rectangle to represent the bed, with two ovals at the head for pillows. Next to the bed he drew a stick figure and wrote "Mom." McCready looked at the diagram and told Marty that his story didn't make sense—that he would have seen his mother from where he was standing the first time he looked into the room. When Marty said it was dark, McCready told him no, it wasn't. Then he asked him how blood got on the light switch in his bedroom. Marty had no idea.

But he did know how he got blood on himself—his hands mostly. It was while following the 911 operator's instructions. "And we asked the defendant, 'Well, then how come you don't have any blood on your clothes, at least on your sleeves?'" Rein recounted. "And he said, 'Well, before I gave first aid to my father and helped him, I rolled my sleeves up.' And he pulled the sleeves of his sweatshirt up above his elbows."

With that, McCready confronted Marty about the blood he'd seen on his shoulder and upper chest during his reenactment. "I said, 'But Marty, if that's the case, how come'—and I reached over and I opened his sweatshirt—I said, 'How come you have blood right there?' And he just looked at me. And then all of a sudden he's sitting there, and he goes, 'Well, my sweatshirt was down like this,' and he pulled his sweatshirt down off his shoulders. And I looked at him and I said, 'Marty,' I said, 'that's ridiculous.'"

"And I said to him, 'Now that's absurd, Marty,'" said Rein. "'You're telling us that in a moment of your father's most critical life-threatening situation you took the sweatshirt and you dropped it down around your elbows, making flippers out of your arms, rendering yourself totally ineffective to give first aid to your father?' I said, 'Your father could have been bleeding to death and you're concerned about getting blood on your clothes?' And the defendant said, 'No. Maybe I put on my sweatshirt after I gave first aid to my father.' And we said to him, 'You have blood on your hands, you have blood on your shoulder. When did you have time to get your sweatshirt? Where was it? Did you go back to your room? You never went back to your room. You would have gotten blood on it.' And the defendant said, 'I put the sweatshirt on after the police arrived.' And we told him he was wearing a sweatshirt when the police arrived. And then Detective McCready said to the defendant, 'You also told us earlier that when you woke up, you left your room, you were wearing a towel around your waist.' And the defendant said, 'Well, maybe that's what I did.' And we said to the defendant, 'You've told us five different stories, all in the course of this short matter of time.'"

If Rein's account suggested the detectives themselves may have caused the confusion they were describing, McCready took it another step when he reached the same point in his testimony. In his version, he played a more active role in the confrontation, pushing Marty to explain why there was blood here and not there, there and not here, suggesting possibilities. "I said, 'Well, Marty, maybe—maybe you didn't have the sweatshirt on when you administered first aid to your father,'" McCready testified. "'Maybe you were wearing the towel. Remember you told me you put a towel on?' He said, 'Yeah. I had the towel on when I helped my father.'"

Absorbing Rein's testimony and then McCready's from his seat at the defense table, Marty scribbled on a legal pad and occasionally leaned over to whisper something to Gottlieb. Rein's account was no surprise: He seemed to be reciting almost verbatim the report of the interrogation he and McCready composed seven days after the fact. But McCready's testimony was sloppy and changeable—at times it seemed almost improvised. His account of the interrogation matched Rein's in essence, but his sequence of the key moments barely resembled the order of things as his partner recounted them. He was unsure whether Marty came up with the towel scenario or *he* suggested it to him. He settled on the latter, which was not the version he'd gone with at the Huntley hearing, as Gottlieb later pointed out.

In one instance, McCready recalled challenging Marty's story that he didn't see his mother's body when he looked into the bedroom after he first got out of bed that morning. "And I said, 'Well, did you go into the room?' And he said, 'No, I was afraid to.'" McCready was jumbling two different moments. As both he and Rein had previously testified, Marty said he didn't go all the way into the room when he first woke up because he could see from the entryway that nobody was in the bed. It was *later*, when he checked the room again and spotted his mother's body on the floor, that he was afraid to go all the way in because he thought someone might be hiding in the dark.

Seeing McCready and Rein on the witness stand, hearing their voices, Marty couldn't help flashing back to that day and those moments. He knew there was a chasm between the truth and their version of it, but so much was still a blur in his mind that he couldn't tell Gottlieb where the lies were. Did he try to explain the absence of blood on his sweatshirt by saying he rolled up his sleeves? Or say there *was* blood on his shoulder because he dropped the sweatshirt down—the explanation McCready and Rein said they dismissed as "ridiculous" and "absurd"? He didn't think so—because it wasn't so: He wasn't even wearing the sweatshirt when he helped his father. He was shirtless after first waking up, and stayed that way until he got the sweatshirt from his bedroom just before going outside to wait for help to arrive. *That's* why there was blood on his shoulder, and why there was none on his sweatshirt. Was that what he told them? Marty didn't know. But by their own accounts, it was clear they were trying to trip him up, baiting him to change his story.

So here again was a battle in the war between two versions of truth: The prosecution was presenting the confrontation over the sweatshirt and the blood spot as the moment Marty Tankleff realized the jig was up—the prelude to his eventual confession. Gottlieb's task was to picture the same scene through a different lens. It wasn't a young murderer's cover coming apart. It was a false confession in the making: a dazed teenager cornered by a pair of shrewd fifty-year-old murder cops who are absolutely sure he hasn't said one truthful thing yet. Gottlieb wasn't even concerned, necessarily, about discrediting McCready and Rein's account of the run-up to the confession. Their own depictions were enough to imagine Marty in a state of such fear and confusion that he didn't know *what* happened, or what he was or wasn't wearing when it did.

The jurors' perception of that moment was critical. If they saw it as the defense did, they might see what came next through the same lens. Of course, the opposite was also true.

IT WAS NOT in dispute that McCready turned up the heat after the confrontation over the sweatshirt. He shelled Marty with one accusation after another, grilling him with questions he couldn't answer. And then, finally, came the point when McCready went for broke, and the point in his testimony, his last as a homicide detective, when he told how he got Marty Tankleff to confess.

"I walked out into the main squad room," McCready said. "I picked up an extension. I dialed another extension to another desk in our office that was close to the interview room. When that phone rang, I walked over and I picked up that phone, and I made believe I was having a telephone conversation with Detective John Pfalzgraf."

The jurors were rapt.

"I said, 'Homicide. McCready.' Answered the phone the way I usually do. And then I said, 'John, yeah, this is Jimmy,' and I proceeded to have a conversation with myself, saying, 'Really, really. You're kidding me. Okay. Thanks a lot.' And I hung up the phone."

As McCready was setting up his ruse, his partner, alone with their suspect for the first time, pulled his chair close, put his hands on Marty's knees, and looked him straight in the face. "I told him that I had been in rescue work since I was eighteen years old, and that I handled a lot of excessive-bleeding calls," Rein said. ". . . And I told the defendant I'm finding it very hard to believe or explain to myself why he didn't have any blood on his clothes after rendering assistance to his father."

When Marty didn't respond, Rein overheard his partner talking on the phone in the squad room. "It seemed to me that he was receiving a progress report from the hospital," he said. He had no idea at that point what his partner was up to. "It sounded real."

Returning to the interview room, McCready resumed his position, sitting at the corner of the desk, looking down at Marty. "I told the defendant that I had just had a conversation with Detective Pfalzgraf, and that he told me that his father was—that the hospital had pumped his father full of adrenaline, that he came out of his comatose state and that his father was now saying that it was you, Marty, you who beat and stabbed your father."

Rein said that McCready sounded convincing here again, though he was "perplexed" that adrenaline could revive someone with Seymour Tankleff's injuries. But he didn't linger on the question. His attention was drawn to Marty's response to the news.

"The defendant said, 'If my father said that, it's because I'm the last person he saw,'" Rein said. "And I asked him if his father was conscious while he was giving his father first aid." How did Marty respond to that question? The detectives had different recollections.

"He gave no response," said McCready.

"He said yes, he was," Rein said. "And I said to the defendant, 'Or are you referring to when you went in the room and you beat and stabbed him before he went unconscious?' And the defendant didn't say anything for about ten seconds and then he said, 'I'll take a lie detector test.' And I said, 'We're not going to give you a lie detector test.'"

They had a better way to get the truth.

Rein: At that point, I said, "Marty what should we do to a person that did this to your parents?" And the defendant said, "Whoever did this to them needs psychiatric help." And then he said, "Could I have blacked out and done it?" I said, "Do you think that's what happened?" And he said, "It's not likely it's me but it's like another Marty Tankleff that killed them." And I said, "Why don't you explain to us what you're talking about." And he said, "Could I be possessed?" And I said to him, "If there's a part of you that knows what happened, why don't you tell us about it." And he said, "It's coming to me, it's coming to me."

McCready: I asked the defendant—I said, "Marty," I said, "do you know that you're in police headquarters, that you are talking to two homicide detectives?" And he sat there and he nodded. . . . I then told him, I said, "Marty, I'm going to advise you of your constitutional rights." [From the witness chair, McCready recited the Miranda warnings and said Marty acknowledged his rights, verbally and then with his signature on a Miranda card, and then waived his right to have a lawyer present.]

I asked him what happened. He said—the first thing he said is, "I need psychiatric help." And I said, "Marty, do you know what happened?" He said, "I know, but it, it felt like a, some other person inside of me who did this." And I said to him, "Why did you, why did you do this, Marty?" He said that his parents and he had been fighting recently, that they once had a good relationship in their house, that since this fighting had started that everything in his life had changed. I then asked him, I said, "Marty, just tell me what happened." He said to me, "What do you want to know?" And I asked him, I said, "Did you, did you murder your mother and hurt your father?" And he said, "Yeah, I did it." I asked him why he did this.

Rein: The defendant said that he wanted to go to college. He wanted to go to a junior college in Florida for two years. . . . He said that his mother didn't want him to go away to college, she wanted to keep him home under her thumb. . . . Detective McCready said to him, "Is that why you killed your mother?" And the defendant said, "Not entirely."

McCready: . . . And he said, "No, not entirely." And I said, "Well, why, you know, why, why did you do this?" He said, well, because of the fighting that was going on in the family that he was afraid that his parents were going to separate. He said that he was adopted and that he was afraid that if his parents did separate he didn't know what would happen to him, who he would live with. He said that they were having daily arguments in the house, that these arguments—that between the combination of his parents fighting between themselves and then fighting over him he felt that he was being pulled, pulled apart and pulled and twisted by his parents.

Rein: He said it used to be that if there was an issue concerning him, his mother would side with him even if his father didn't, and the defendant said lately, with all their fighting, he couldn't depend upon that, his mother didn't always side with him. The defendant also said that because of his mother and father arguing amongst themselves, he said they would turn to him for attention. They were smothering him. It was like a nightmare. He found it very difficult to cope with that.

McCready: He said that his father had asked him to set up the card table before the card game. He said that he was supposed to be home early enough to set that up, that he did not get home early enough to do that and that when he did get home his mother was furious with him that he had not set up the card table. He said that this card table business was the last straw, and he said that he couldn't stand the whole scenario, as he put it, in the house. I asked him what else was bothering him. He said that his father was—had made him drive around in what he said was a crummy old Lincoln. He said that he wanted a smaller, sporty car. He said that additionally he wanted to use the boat more often. He said that his parents wanted him to—every time he wanted to use the boat he had to bring somebody with him on the boat. They would never let him take the boat out by himself. Again, I asked him what else was bothering him, and he said that he resented the fact that a Dan Hayes was going to come and stay with him while his parents went away on a cruise in October. He said that they treated him like a baby, that he did not need a babysitter and that he resented that Dan Hayes was coming to stay with him.

Rein: . . . And the defendant said he also resented that his parents wouldn't let him play ball. His mother wouldn't let him play any contact sports. He really wanted to play baseball or soccer.

McCready: His mother over the years would not let him play football. She was afraid he would get hurt. Additionally, he told us that he had an ATV, an all-terrain vehicle, and that his parents were afraid that he was going to get hurt on this ATV vehicle.

Rein: Detective McCready asked the defendant again, "Tell us what happened to your parents." The defendant said, "After the business with the poker table I decided that I was going to kill them both." The defendant said that he went to bed that night and he decided that he was going to kill them. The defendant said that he had set his alarm clock for 5:35 A.M. and he said he got out of bed. He said he was naked and he remained that way, didn't want to get blood on his clothes. The defendant said he took a dumbbell from his room and he went to the master bedroom. He was going to kill both his parents. But he said he was surprised that there were lights on in the house and he was surprised not to see his father in bed. The defendant said he walked down to his father's office and saw his father sleeping in the chair at his desk. And we asked him what he did, and he said he then walked down to his—to the master bedroom, and we asked him what he had with him, and he said he had a dumbbell.

McCready: I asked him if he had the dumbbell with him at that time, and he said, "Well, it was really the bar part of the dumbbell." He said that he came back to his mother's room, decided that he was going to kill his mother first, that he went into her room, that he got to her quickly, that he hit her in the head. . . .

Rein: He said she was sleeping on her back, and he leaped across the bed and he got to her quickly. The defendant said he hit her on the head with the barbell and his mother started fighting with him. He said his mother was screaming out "Why?" and "Stop," and he said his mother was in a lot of pain. She kept fighting and he said he hit her on the head about four or five times and she fell on the floor. The defendant said that he thought the noise might attract his father or wake him up. So the defendant said he started looking for a knife, he said, to cut his mother and stop the noise.

McCready: He said that he ran out of his mother's bedroom, that he ran to the kitchen, that he grabbed a knife off the counter next to the watermelon, that he ran back into her bedroom and that he cut her throat. I asked him if his mother was dead when he left the room. He said no, that she was moving a little bit. He then said he went down to the gym-office area where his father was, that he walked into the room, that he had the knife and the dumbbell behind his back, that his father was now awake and his father asked him, "Marty, what are you doing?"

Rein: And the defendant said, "I just knocked him silly." The defendant said he then took the knife and he slashed his father's throat. He said he couldn't believe all the blood. He said he cut him and stabbed him. We asked the defendant how many times he hit his father with the barbell. The defendant said he didn't know.

McCready: He said that he then went down to the bathroom, that he took a shower and that he washed the knife and the barbell off in the shower. I asked him what he did with the knife and the barbell. He said that he put the knife back on the counter next to the watermelon and he put the barbell back into his room. . . .

Rein: He laid down in bed and thought what to do next. At about 6:10 A.M. he got out of bed and he walked down to the hall and into his father's office. He said his father was still gagging. The defendant said he went to his mother's bedroom, that is the master bedroom, and his mother was dead. The defendant said he called the 911 operator from the phone in his mother's room and he was instructed by the 911 operator to render first aid.

McCready: I asked him, "Well, when you got up, why did you call 911 when you found that your father was still alive?" And he said that he thought that his father would die before the police got there. I asked him, "Well, what did you do—you know, what did you do to make it look like or how did you do this to make it look like you were going to try to help your father?" He said, "Well, I intentionally got my hands covered with blood so it looked like that I—you know, I had tried to help my father."

Rein: . . . And Detective McCready asked him, "And how about the blood on your shoulder?" And the defendant said, "Well, I showered and I must have screwed up." . . . I asked the defendant, "Do you regret what you did?" And he did not answer me. And I said to him, "Are you upset by what happened, by what you did?" And there was no answer. And I said to the defendant, "There's been a question that's been lingering in my mind, and I think I know the answer to it now." I said, "When you went with Detective McCready to headquarters, I stayed behind at the house and looked around that house and looked inside. And do you know what I saw?" And the defendant said he didn't know what I saw. I said, "I looked in your mother's room and I saw rage and I saw hate and I saw anger, and I saw your mother's desecrated body and all that blood." And I said, "And then I walked down to your father's office, I looked in there and do you know what I saw?" And he didn't answer me. And I said, "I saw all that blood and I can only imagine what you did to your father. And now I know why you're not crying. Do you know why?" He didn't answer me. I said, "That's because you're not upset. And you know why you're not upset?" And the defendant did not answer me. I said, "You're not upset because you're not angry anymore. Because you left your anger at 33 Seaside Drive."

MCCREADY AND REIN delivered their direct testimony like soliloquies, relating their accounts with little interruption from Collins save an occasional "Please go on" or "What did the defendant say at that point?" But Gottlieb's cross-examinations were marathons of scrutiny, frequently laced with scorn. He deconstructed the entire day, interrogating the detectives about virtually every moment they spent with Marty, every word uttered in that windowless room at headquarters. And about why they brought him there in the first place.

Gottlieb took several approaches to attacking the homicide squad's work in this case, but they were all threads of a single theme: that virtually from the moment McCready arrived on Seaside Drive, they were guided not by open-minded and evenhanded investigation but by one snap judgment followed by a string of hasty assumptions to back it up. Gottlieb pressed the two detectives, as well as their sergeant, about their judgment that Marty's behavior made him an instant suspect, and the only one. Were they aware that virtually everyone who encountered Marty in those very first moments, two hours before *they* did, described him in testimony as being variously agitated, talking fast, at times babbling incoherently, wandering around "out of it" and in a state of shock? Their responses when Gottlieb recounted the testimony of Dara Schaeffer, Don Hines, the uniformed police, the rescue workers: "I didn't hear that testimony." "I no longer recall his observations." "I have some recollections of that." "That sounds accurate."

Gottlieb questioned McCready about the "inconsistencies" he found in Marty's story that told him he had his killer. Chief among them, according to McCready, were Marty's statements, during their initial conversation in his car, that he got "wet blood on his hands" when he helped his father and that he then went to check the garage for his mother's car. He went back into the house and found no blood on the handle of the door leading to the garage. McCready had always said that this was evidence that Marty was lying, and the first indication to him of his guilt. Whatever had been learned since then, Collins carried it to trial as a key piece of his catalogue of roundabout circumstantial evidence: Though it didn't support the confession itself, Collins adopted McCready's position that it belied Marty's story—and *that* supported the confession. Collins had made much of the door handle during the testimony of his forensic witnesses—as did Gottlieb, who spent considerable time on cross-examination establishing that many factors determined whether blood might be transferred from a person's hand onto an object, not the least of which, obviously, was how wet the blood was.

"You are aware, based on your experience," Gottlieb said now to McCready, "that every time you touch an object, even if you have blood on you, blood will not necessarily adhere to that object, correct?"

"If that's wet blood, there's going to be a transfer," McCready said.

The question was whether the blood on Marty's hands was, in fact, wet. When Gottlieb pressed this question, McCready changed his testimony in a small but significant way. He no longer claimed, as he had in his direct testimony, that he knew the blood was wet because Marty specifically told him it was. "It was a general discussion about his hands, him telling me that his hands were covered with blood," McCready said. "Based on what he had told me, the blood would not have been dried."

With that, McCready conceded that his instant conclusion that Marty was lying, that he was guilty, was based on an assumption. Was it a valid assumption? Not when the testimony of the first responders was considered. All the rescue workers, along with the police officers who arrived at the same time, agreed that the blood on Seymour was largely dried when they saw him.

Another of McCready's assumptions was that Marty tried to get incriminating blood off himself when they arrived at police headquarters and started walking from the parking lot to a rear entrance of the building. "I turned around and looked at him, and he was dragging his right foot across the grass," McCready said. He thought it was suspicious because Marty "had a blood spot on his right leg at one point, and that blood spot was now gone."

Gottlieb pointed out that Marty had been barefoot all morning, had been walking back and forth across his stone driveway and the street in front, and now the parking lot behind the police building. Maybe his foot was dirty. But McCready was sure Marty was trying to get rid of evidence—he told that to Rein when he arrived a few minutes later. Gottlieb reminded McCready that Marty washed his hands in a puddle back at the scene—in full view and after asking an officer's permission.

"Did you go back to the spot where you say he dragged his foot?" Gottlieb asked. "Did you seize that grass?"

"A clump of grass," McCready said, "no, I didn't seize the clump of grass."

"HE TOLD ME that his mother had said some two weeks earlier that Jerry Steuerman was going to do something like this," McCready said.

"And at that point did you ask Marty, 'Well, Marty, can you give me any details about why your mother may have said that?'"

"No, sir," said McCready.

"That was an important issue to follow up, correct?"

"Yes, to a degree, yes it was."

But he and Rein didn't follow it up. And he was a bit hazy about how they responded to the information Marty gave them about his parents' various business arrangements with Steuerman. "Geez, I, I don't recall right now," McCready said. "I remember we talked to him about—in addition to talking about these businesses and the buyout agreement and everything, he told us about the, uh, his father being involved with the, with horses with Jerry and the other partnership with the horses and whatnot. That's as much as I recall right now."

"Can you give us some estimate of when you first became aware of promissory notes being signed by Jerry Steuerman?" Gottlieb asked at another point.

"I, I think it was during the course of this trial," McCready said.

Gottlieb seemed genuinely incredulous. He asked McCready to confirm that he was actually saying he knew nothing of one of the main financial agreements between Jerry Steuerman and Seymour Tankleff—the subject of the demand letter Seymour sent to Jerry by certified mail—before it came up during Steuerman's testimony two weeks ago.

"Yeah," said McCready, "I think that's—yeah, I don't remember anything about promissory notes before that."

It was also true that he and Rein didn't speak with Steuerman until three days after the crimes, when they sat at a table in Steuerman's shop, drinking coffee and munching bagels. McCready had no quarrel with Gottlieb's description of the conversation as "congenial." The next time he saw Steuerman was in California. This time he was anxious to talk to him.

"Why was that?" Gottlieb asked.

"Because I felt that Mr. Myron Fox had bribed him to take a hike."

"And you had concluded that?"

"I had concluded that because I ruled out any other possible reason for Mr. Steuerman leaving Suffolk County."

Once Steuerman disabused him of his theory, did it strike him as odd that Steuerman would stage his own disappearance? Not at all, said McCready. It wasn't as if he left the day after the murders—it was a week later. Nor were his suspicions aroused when Steuerman said in California that he felt that "Seymour Tankleff thought he owned half of me."

"Do you confront him at any time?" Gottlieb asked.

"Confront him about what?" McCready asked.

"Inconsistencies."

"Well, the only thing I found inconsistent was the fact that he left and there was no reason in the world for the man to have left, unless somebody paid him to leave. So I confronted him about that."

"But it turned out that you were wrong about that conclusion. So did you consider that you may be wrong about other things he was telling you?"

"No, because I can—see, I can show that he didn't have anything to do with this."

Gottlieb revisited the subject of Steuerman as a nonsuspect throughout his many days of cross-examination of McCready, Rein, and Doyle. One such sequence veered off in an unexpected direction and led to an extraordinarily intriguing comment that somehow went unnoticed at the time. Gottlieb was questioning McCready about what Marty told him regarding his father's business situation with Steuerman. "Did you consider the information he was giving you important?" he asked.

"That information that he told me about Jerry Steuerman did take a significant role in this case at a certain time," McCready replied. "At that point in time that this young man was telling me this stuff, though, there was other operations of my mind going on, based on what I had seen and learned at that scene that morning, and, quite frankly, what he was telling me was lies, sir."

"You hadn't tried to confirm or obtain any information to find out whether or not Marty Tankleff was lying to you, correct?" Gottlieb asked.

"Sir, the demeanor of the defendant at the time I spoke to him, from the very first moment when I spoke to him, was totally—his whole, his whole demeanor was totally inappropriate. His emotional response to what was going on, what had happened in that hour, to what had happened to his father and his mother was totally, totally inappropriate."

". . . You had never seen Marty Tankleff before that day, correct?"

"No, but—"

"You don't know how Marty Tankleff reacts to stress, do you?"

"He remembered phone numbers, addresses, names. He remembered, I'll tell you. . . . People in shock don't do that, sir."

"Detective, can you tell us your background and training in medicine?"

"I'm not a doctor, sir."

"Can you agree that different people react differently to stress?" Gottlieb asked McCready.

"Certainly they do."

"As a matter of fact, some people become very calm in dealing with stress."

"That can occur, yes, sir."

"And would you agree that it can be a very stressful situation to find one's father brutally stabbed, Detective?"

"Oh, I—God, I would never want to find my father or mother the way he found his."

The way he found his. Was this an innocent trip of the tongue by McCready? Or was it an unconscious slip—a moment of involuntary confession of his own? Whatever he meant to say, McCready was acknowledging that Marty found his parents as he said he did. But Gottlieb, perhaps expecting pro forma answers to his rhetorical questions, didn't pick up on it. "And you can then agree it is a very stressful situation, correct?" he asked, letting the moment pass, though prompting one of the memorable quotes of the trial.

"Oh, I think anybody in this room other than the defendant would probably be a box of rocks if they found their parents like that," McCready replied.

"AND THEN I said to him, 'Well, if that's the case, how did you get the blood'—and that's when I pointed to his shoulder."

Gottlieb was now at the main event of his cross-examination, grilling McCready about the first accusatory moments of his interrogation of Marty. "He kind of looked at me and he had a look of shock or surprise on his face," McCready said. That's when Marty dropped his sweatshirt off his shoulders and the detectives told him it was ridiculous and absurd. And that's when McCready suggested that maybe he was wearing a towel. "I threw him some bait, is what I did."

When Gottlieb read McCready's testimony from the Huntley hearing, in which he said that it was Marty who came up with the possibility of the towel, McCready was unfazed. "That's exactly what I said," he agreed.

"And while you're suggesting those various scenarios . . . is Marty saying anything to you as you're asking each of those questions?"

"No. He was—actually, he was nodding in agreement."

"And then you say, 'Maybe you were wearing a towel.' Does he nod in agreement at that point, also?"

"At that point in time, he said—I believe he did nod in agreement with me on that, yes."

But when McCready asked Marty how blood got on his light switch, Marty didn't answer. And he found that suspicious. "He indicated to me by his body language that he was trying to think of an answer."

"And did you find that suspicious, that the person you are interrogating wanted to think about an answer?"

"At that point in time, as this confrontation was going on, I thought it was *very* suspicious."

"Because you thought he was lying, correct?"

"That's quite correct, sir."

". . . And early on the morning of September seventh, before any forensic reports are completed, you have very quickly decided that Marty Tankleff is lying to you, correct?"

"I had arrived at a conclusion that the defendant, by his conduct, by his demeanor, by his lack of emotion, by his illogical acts, by a number of other factors, I arrived at the conclusion that I reasonably suspected the defendant at that time as possibly having committed this murder, yes, sir."

"And when you're confronting Marty . . . you start telling him your conclusions based on your observations in the house, correct?"

"No, sir. What I started telling him was what I knew to be facts."

". . . Well, how long had you been in the house earlier in the morning?"

"I was in the house approximately ten minutes."

McCready's passing glances at the crime scenes might have explained why he didn't notice the one thing a homicide detective would be expected to check right after the body. He didn't see that the sliding glass doors in both rooms were partly open. (The sliding screens behind them were closed and, according to Detective Kosciuk, locked.) But McCready did notice some things in the master bedroom that told him that Marty was lying when he said he didn't see his mother the first time he looked in, just after waking up. "I said to him that there was enough light in that room that he should have seen someone. I told him that it was not dark in that room." McCready said he told Marty that he'd looked out his own bathroom window at *5:50* and saw that it was "a bright, sunshiny day." But sunrise that day was at 6:25, fifteen minutes after Marty looked in the room. He told Marty that the drapes were "open." The drapes were mostly closed, parted about three feet. But McCready was certain even now that Marty would have *had* to see his mother's body—on the floor, almost completely obscured behind the bed, in the darkness of that hour, with just a quick look to the bed from the doorway fifteen feet away.

"And then you confront him with some more of your conclusions. . . ."

"Yes, sir." He asked Marty one more time what time he got dressed. When Marty said 6:10, "I said, 'Wait a minute. You just told me you woke up at 5:35.'"

"Is that what you found suspicious?" Gottlieb asked, confident it was abundantly clear by now from the various police witnesses that Marty told all of them, over and over, that he first awoke at 5:35 but didn't get out of bed and put his underwear and shorts on until 6:10.

"You found them to be inconsistencies, Detective?"

"What I found them to be were what I would say are futile attempts by the defendant to come up with a story. He's trying, he's being—he was being tripped up and he's continued to be tripped up and now he, at this point in time I felt that he, he's tripping himself all over the place at this point in time based on his answers, based on the way he's giving us the answers, based on what he's saying, and based on what he is not saying."

"Detective, in the questioning this morning and today, were you tripped up?"

"Was I tripped up?"

"Yes."

"I was tripped up because Mr. Gottlieb"—McCready seemed so tripped up that he was now referring to his questioner in the third person—"misstated several questions that occurred at different points in time, and I was confused."

"Did you ever consider that a seventeen-year-old boy who's being questioned nonstop by two experienced homicide detectives might at times be confused? Did that ever cross your mind? Yes or no, Detective. Did that ever cross your mind?"

"He only appeared confused to me when he attempted to come up with his story. As I pointed out, his demeanor—"

"Thank you, Detective."

"THIS IS ALL part of your game, correct?" Gottlieb asked, finally reaching the climax of the interrogation—Marty's as well as McCready's. ". . . And you looked at Marty, and you looked right in his face and you gave him this information about what his father was accusing him of doing. . . . And you did it in your most convincing tone of voice, correct? . . . In fact, Detective Rein didn't even know you were lying, correct?"

Gottlieb's questions continued: You had polygraph machinery and a polygraph expert at headquarters, correct? A lie detector is used by law enforcement as a way to cancel out suspects, correct? And what's your response when Marty says, "I'll take a lie detector"? And after you say he said, "Yeah, I did it," what did he say when you asked him why he killed his parents?

"He said he wanted to go away to college," McCready said.

"Were those his first words after you asked why?"

"That statement encompassed what he was saying, yes. That's close enough."

". . . Did either you or Detective Rein ask Marty, 'Do you have any other resentments?'"

". . . At one point I said what I saw inside him was somebody who's angry, and I asked him if, you know, what else was bothering him. . . . He mentioned Dan Hayes. He resented that Dan Hayes was going to come and stay with him while his parents were away on a cruise. That was what he was telling me. 'I resented it. That's why I killed my parents.' That's what he's telling me."

"And did you then say, 'What else is bothering you?'"

"I believe I may have said that to him several times. . . . The way he was relating this to me, this was a building up of resentment over the last four or five years. . . ."

IN PREPARING his cross-examination of McCready, Gottlieb had studied all the usual things: police reports and case files, the transcript of McCready's testimony at the Huntley hearing. But he also had to do some unusual legal research. To support his overall objective of exposing the Tankleff investigation as wrongheaded, reckless, and otherwise nonexistent, Gottlieb wanted to bring in the State Investigation Commission's withering criticisms of the way the Suffolk County police and prosecutors generally conducted business in homicide cases. It was perhaps his hardest sell of all.

In Judge Tisch's chambers on the morning of June 4, Gottlieb presented Tisch with a pile of case law to support his argument that the SIC's findings were proper for the jury to consider. His hopes were characteristically unrealistic. Ideally, he told the judge, he'd like to put the entire 199-page report into evidence. Failing that, he would be satisfied with just a few relevant pages, which he specified for the judge's convenience. Collins, of course, vehemently opposed Gottlieb's request. He dismissed the entire SIC investigation as a "witch hunt"—a protest often heard from the DA's office during the three-year inquiry—and the allegations against McCready as overblown and prejudicial. The police department's internal affairs division investigated all the allegations against McCready as well as the other detectives accused of misconduct in the James Diaz case. "They have been found to be unfounded," Collins assured the judge.

Tisch ruled against Gottlieb, though not entirely. The report was out. Gottlieb could not so much as mention the State Commission of Investigation in his cross-examination of McCready. But he could question him about his testimony in the Diaz case—without directly accusing him of perjury. He could only present the record of the case and let the jury decide.

Gottlieb laid it all out, reading McCready's testimony in the Diaz case and forcing him to publicly explain his actions for the first time. So incomprehensible was McCready's testimony in that trial—when he asked to return to the stand to "correct" his previous testimony and found himself being questioned by Judge Namm—that listening to it five years later, Judge Tisch stopped Gottlieb's reading and called a sidebar so that he, too, could try to figure it out. When Gottlieb returned to his questioning, McCready became visibly rattled and gave an even more convoluted ex-

planation than he had in the Diaz trial itself. When he was through, Gottlieb left Marty's jury with the same choice as Diaz's: Either McCready lied
about crucial evidence and then lied again to wiggle out of it when he was
trapped, or his work was so shoddy, his approach so cavalier, that he turned
a careless assumption into critical testimony in a murder trial.

USUALLY, witnesses are asked for their background and credentials at
the beginning of their testimony. With McCready, Collins waited until
the end, after Gottlieb's three days of cross-examination. On redirect, he
asked the battered retired detective to review his experience as an investigator. McCready recalled his early career, when he spent several years on
investigative assignments before being promoted to detective—a stint
on the narcotics squad, another in rackets, two years in the anticorruption
bureau of the DA's office. He became a detective in 1979 and worked in
the Sixth Squad for just nine months before being assigned to Homicide.

"In the history of the Suffolk County Police Department," Collins
asked, "has any detective ever been promoted to Homicide faster than
that?"

"No, sir," said McCready.

He spent fully half his police career investigating murders. By the time
of his retirement, he had worked on more than two hundred cases. He received seventeen department commendations over his twenty years.

A few minutes later, McCready stepped down from the stand, his last
case closed, his testimony finished, his career over. In the hallway afterward, McCready walked by Ron Falbee with a sneer, murmuring something about telling the truth but not all of it.

You son of a bitch, Ron thought.

McCready was done. But his last case was to have a long afterlife.
Whatever his retirement papers said, it would make Jimmy McCready
forever a Suffolk County homicide detective.

CHAPTER 22

Being Marty

A TRIAL, it is said, is not about the truth, but about whose version of it emerges from the admissible evidence as more persuasive. It is, least of all, about knowing the accused.

A jury will spend weeks in close proximity to the defendant, watching him, searching for clues. It will hear a procession of witnesses talk about him—what they saw, what they heard, what their expertise reveals about his guilt or innocence. If he testifies in his own defense, he will speak to those sitting in judgment of him in the most unnatural fashion. His thoughts will not be spontaneous, his words will be wrapped in fear and calculation. The jurors will take their measure of him and consider all the evidence soberly, rationally, and, it is assumed, without preconception. But whatever their ultimate judgment of the defendant, they will complete their civic duty without ever knowing who he really was.

By the time the prosecution rested its case, what the jury saw in Marty Tankleff was an eighteen-year-old defined by the acts of which he was ac-cused. His physical presence, despite his slight stature, did not necessarily detract from that portrayal. His hair was thick and top-heavy, meticu-lously coiffed in a fashion that on some days called to mind a 1950s-style pompadour. He wore his contact lenses and always a dark suit. Arriving from California as the defense was to begin its case, Mike McClure, the lawyer in the family, found his nephew's look worrisome. *He needs to look like the innocent, naïve kid that he is. Mess up his hair a little. Make him wear his glasses. Put him in a sweater.* That's what Mike did any time he had a young criminal client. *He looks too slick—he looks like one of the lawyers.*

Whatever the jurors made of Marty to this point, it had to be assumed that they were heavily influenced—if not convinced—by McCready and

Rein's accounts of what he told them in the interview room. As Gottlieb began his defense, it was clear to him that there was only one way to contest their story. But the decision was ultimately Marty's, and he made it without hesitation. "I want to testify," he told Gottlieb. "Innocent men testify, and I'm going to testify."

But it would not come without long and serious discussions among the family. There are always risks when a defendant takes the stand, but they were even greater with a young person whose temperament was something of a paradox. Marty could be impulsive even as he came off as perhaps a little too controlled.

As supremely crucial as Marty's testimony would be, there was a limit to what Gottlieb could do to prepare him. He went over the ground he intended to cover in his direct questioning, but knew that the worst thing to do was rehearse. The testimony could not seem scripted. "You've got to be real," he told Marty. "Just tell the truth and be yourself." Well, not exactly. "I wanted Marty to cry," Gottlieb recalled. "Because I know that's what jurors want to see. But I also knew Marty well enough by then that clearly he was incapable of crying. He's incapable of really showing a range of emotion. That's his personality."

Indeed, it was Marty's outward manner that the police had promoted as the reason they suspected him in the first place. Jurors so disposed could find this assessment not inconsistent with Marty's demeanor in the courtroom. Though he wrote frequent notes to Gottlieb and conferred with him at breaks in the questioning, for the most part he listened to the testimony impassively, maintaining his composure even during the most difficult moments.

All this crystallized what Gottlieb and everyone in Marty's circle considered one of the most infuriating and frightening aspects of the case: the extent to which Marty's life depended on other people's notions of an *appropriate* response to *his* trauma. First came the police with their amateur psychology and convenient disregard of Marty's observed behavior in the two hours before they saw him. And now the jury was being asked to validate this dangerous assumption that outward appearance revealed inner feeling—and guilt in a murder case. So here was Gottlieb telling Marty to be himself, while hoping he could find a way to also *not* be himself in order to satisfy the presumed expectations of the jury.

Whether Marty would testify had been a much-discussed topic in the hallways of the courthouse. He had given no interviews since his arrest, and he said little but "Good morning" to reporters as he arrived at court each day, shielded by his phalanx of aunts and uncles and cousins. At lunchtime they retired to a van they had rented to have a private place to eat. Sometimes they went to a park near the courthouse. The family had also avoided the media, convinced, not without reason in some cases, that reporters were virtual mouthpieces for the prosecution. So Marty remained an enigma to the public, silent but for the brief statement he had read upon his release from jail nearly two years earlier. So when Collins rested his case, the question of Marty taking the stand in his own defense moved front and center. Even the judge was curious. "Since we're about to go into the courtroom," Tisch said after a discussion in his chambers on the morning Gottlieb was to begin his case, "do you have any objection to telling me who the first witness is?"

"No, Judge," said Gottlieb.

"Who might that be?"

"Marty Tankleff."

"MARTY, you have been charged with killing your mother and your father. Did you kill your mother?"

"Absolutely not."

"Marty, did you kill your father?"

"Absolutely not."

"On September 7, how would you describe your feelings about your mother?"

"I loved her. I loved her very much."

"And on that same day, Marty, what were your feelings about your father?"

"I loved him very much, too."

After nearly two months of prosecution testimony about what sort of a person Marty Tankleff was, Gottlieb wanted the jury to know some other things, starting with what his life was like before everything changed. He was seventeen then, Marty said, about to start his senior year at Earl L. Vandermeulen High School. He was a member of Future Business Leaders of America and Students Against Drunk Driving. He was the class historian and one of the top photographers for the yearbook. "And we held the homecoming-float building at my house two years in a row." Did you also work part-time? Gottlieb asked. "Yes I did," Marty said. "I worked for Jerry Steuerman and Glenn Steuerman in three different bagel stores. And I worked for Tankleff Associates."

"Marty," Gottlieb said, "I now want to direct your attention to Tuesday, September 6, 1988. Do you recall that day?"

As he had so many times for the police, Marty began to recount the events surrounding the murders of his parents. On the day before, he went out for a haircut at about noon. He had spent most of the afternoon in his garage with Zach Suominen, putting a new stereo system in his car. They needed a part and decided to go to the Smith Haven Mall that night. He planned to get up early before school the next morning to finish the job. Did he have any arguments with his parents that day? "None whatsoever."

He went to the mall with Zach and Zach's girlfriend, Margaret Barry. They went to Radio Shack and Pants Plus; they ran into some friends and chatted with them a bit. They left the mall around 8:30, and Marty dropped Zach off, then Margaret, and got home himself around nine. "I went into the card game. I gave my father a hug and a kiss hello. I then asked Cappy for his keys, I went outside to move the car. The keys were in it so I knew it wasn't Cappy's. I then pulled my car into my garage. . . . I brought the keys back to Cappy and the card players commented about my nose."

He went into the kitchen, got himself a plate of turkey and pasta, brought it into the den, and ate while talking with his mother. She was sitting in a reclining chair, reading the newspaper.

"And Marty, please tell us what you recall your mother saying and what you said to her."

"Objection," Collins cut in. Gottlieb asked for a sidebar. He wanted an exception to the hearsay rules to allow Marty to fully rebut McCready and Rein's claim that Marty told them that his mother was furious with him because he hadn't set up his father's poker table—that it was the "last straw" that led him to decide to get up early the next morning and kill them both. Marty told Gottlieb that this was as ridiculous as it sounded. But Arlene's side of the conversation was hearsay—"There are only two people privy to that conversation, and one of them is dead," observed the judge—and Collins wanted him to bar Marty from testifying about it. Tisch said he would allow him to describe the "general subject matter" of the conversation and, of course, relate his end of it.

"What did you say to your mother about the card table?" Gottlieb asked.

"I said I was sorry that I forgot to set it up before I went to the mall and that I would take it down the next day." She wasn't angry, and "the whole conversation was a few seconds." Then he went to his room to put away his new clothes.

Around eleven o'clock, he took a shower in his bathroom. Then he went into his parents' bedroom to say good night to his mother. "I gave her a hug and a kiss good night and I said, 'I'll see you in the morning.'" Then he went to bed. Gottlieb asked him to describe his bed. "It's almost like a cave," Marty said. "I've got two walls on either side of me that extend out about three feet, and my head's against the wall."

His alarm rang at 5:35 the next morning. "I got out of bed, walked over to the alarm, shut the alarm off, and then got back into bed. I was too tired to get up." Half an hour later, about 6:05, he got out of bed, put on a pair of shorts, and headed into the hallway. "The bathroom light was on, the hallway lights were on. I looked into my parents' room to see if anybody was there. No one was there. So I thought they had gotten up already. I continued down the hallway and noticed that the hallway lights were on. The front door was open. I continued along, noticed that the kitchen lights were on. From the kitchen I can notice that the office lights were on and then I proceeded into the office." He saw his father, "sitting in his office chair with blood on him."

"And what did you do?" Gottlieb asked.

"Ran up to him screaming, 'Dad, Dad, Dad,' and when I got up to him I saw that his throat was cut and I called 911."

"Marty, at that time, at that moment, how do you feel?"

"Out of it."

"After calling 911, what did you do then?"

"I did what they told me to do. I ran to my room to get a pillow, I went to the linen closet to get a towel, and then I came back to try to help my father." He tried to fully extend the reclining chair. But when he lifted the footrest, "the whole chair tipped forward and he sort of slid out of the chair a little bit." He pulled his father the rest of the way onto the floor, then put the pillow under his feet and the towel around his neck. "I just put the towel over the wound, pushed down once, and then ran away."

"Why?" Gottlieb asked.

"I was scared."

He went to look for his mother. "I first went to the garage. I thought she might have gone out. Her car was still there. I started looking through the house. I don't recall if I went through the den or the living room, but I ended up in the bedroom area."

"And what happened?"

"I saw my mother from inside the bedroom."

"What do you recall about seeing your mother?"

"She wasn't moving . . . she seemed lifeless."

"And then what did you do?"

"Ran out of there screaming."

To the kitchen, where he called his sister. . . . "I said, 'Shari, get over here. I think Mom and Dad have been murdered.'" Then he called Mark Perrone's house and spoke to Mark's mother. He went to his bedroom to put on a sweatshirt. He ran outside, to the Hovas' house next door. "I just wanted somebody to help me."

Marty recounted the arrival of the ambulance and the first police cars—"I was yelling, 'Hurry up, come this way, hurry up, come this way.'" He accompanied one of the squad members, Ethel Curley, toward the master bedroom. "I walked with her right up to my mother. As soon as I saw my mother, I ran right out of there." Why? "I was scared of what I saw."

"MARTY, does there come a time that you recall seeing Detective McCready for the first time?"

To a large degree, Gottlieb's defense depended on how successful he was in portraying Marty as the third victim in this case. He had to persuade the jury that two of their county's most experienced homicide investigators took the lazy way out of a double murder, isolated an innocent and traumatized boy, and subjected him to a manipulative interrogation rather than actually investigating the case. And had lied about it ever since. To make this case, Gottlieb had to draw a convincing picture of McCready, in particular, as devious and calculating—starting with the way he kept the family lawyer away from Marty.

Gottlieb had decided he couldn't have Mike Fox testify at the trial— not after his disastrous performance at the Huntley hearing. So it would be left to Marty alone to dispute the homicide detectives' assertion that his family's lawyer said hello to him, asked if he was all right, and left with full knowledge that the police were talking to him.

When he noticed Fox approaching and pointed him out to Doyle and McCready, "Detective McCready took off." He returned a minute or two later. "I asked Detective McCready, 'Where's my Uncle Mike going?' And he says, 'Well, he's going back to his office and if we need to contact him we know where to reach him.' . . . I said, 'I can't believe that.' And he said, 'Well, he said he's busy and we know where to reach him.'"

It was at this point that Detective Rein arrived and asked him to go through his story for him. A few minutes later, "Detective McCready asked if I would mind going to homicide headquarters and speak with him about Jerry Steuerman and my father's business interests." He told McCready he'd like to go to the hospital first to check on his father. "He said, 'Well, I'll take you there later.'"

Gottlieb asked Marty to recall how the interview at headquarters began. "Detective Rein commented about my nose," Marty said. There were some personal questions and then Rein asked Marty to repeat his story. "I did that as best I could." And what happened after he repeated his story? "They asked me to go over the story again."

Marty's recollection of the various confrontations that came as the interrogation wore on were not nearly as detailed as those of the detectives. But there were a few things in his account that weren't in theirs—harsher language and more aggressive intimidation, along with at least two lies by

McCready that preceded the big one. "We were talking about myself going into my mother's room and Detective McCready turned around and said, 'Marty, I can't believe that because your hair's in your mother's hand. How did it get there?'" At another point, "When I said I didn't take a shower that morning, Detective McCready said, 'Marty, I can't believe that.' He says, 'We did a humidity test and we know you took a shower in the morning.'"

In each case, Marty recalled being more confused than skeptical—it didn't occur to him that McCready was lying to him. "I was brought up to always believe and trust cops and he was saying it as if it was a fact." So when McCready told him that a "humidity test" proved he took a shower in the morning, "I was surprised because I knew I didn't take a shower that morning. I took one the night before." But McCready wouldn't believe him. "He said, 'We know you took a shower this morning.'"

Marty testified to something else that wasn't in McCready and Rein's accounts. "I asked to speak to Uncle Mike a few times and every time that happened, Detective McCready turned around to me, he was standing, he said"—here Marty turned to the jury, giving his best imitation of a homicide detective's bullying sneer—"*If you want to speak to your Uncle Mike, you're a criminal, we're gonna lock you up!*"

Finally, McCready's charade: "He turned around to me. He was standing. He had his finger pointed towards me. He said, 'Marty,' he said, 'get off the fuckin' bullshit about Jerry Steuerman because I just got off the phone with the detective at the hospital and they shot your father full of adrenaline,' and he said, 'You beat and stabbed him, Marty.' He said, 'You did it, Marty.' And then he continued to say, 'And your father said just tell us what we want to hear and help us.'

"He said they taped the whole conversation that they said that my father said, that they would play it for me later. I said, 'I can't believe that.' And they said, 'Well, why would your father say that?' I said, 'Because I helped him this morning.' And they continually said, 'Well, you know, your father wouldn't lie about that.' And I said, 'Well, I'll take a lie detector test.' And they stated to me, 'We're not going to give you one now. We'll give you one later.' And they said, 'Well, Marty, you know your father said you did this. We've got your hair in your mother's hand. Just say you did it.'"

"And then what was your response, Marty?"

"I said, 'Could I have blacked out?'"

"Why did you say that?"

"I started believing them that I did do this."

"Why?"

"Because they were saying my father said I did this." He paused. "My father never lied to me."

Then, "I recall them saying, 'Marty, you know, there's—there's a Marty inside of you that knows what happened and have that Marty tell us what happened.' And then I recall saying, 'Yeah, I did it.'"

"Why did you say 'Yeah' at that time, Marty?"

"They had me believing that I did it and that's what they wanted to hear."

"Did you kill your mother?"

"No, I didn't."

"Did you kill your father?"

"No. I loved my parents. I had nothing to do with this."

To this point, Marty's version of his confession was not all that different from McCready and Rein's. He confirmed their testimony that he asked if he might have blacked out (though they quoted him saying "blacked out and did it"). And most damaging, notwithstanding his explanation, he admitted saying, "Yeah, I did it."

Now, though, Gottlieb moved on to the phase of the interrogation that he hoped would raise serious questions about the validity of that statement: how the detectives elicited the details of the murders they attributed to Marty. And how that explained why those details were inconsistent with the forensic evidence. And what that said about McCready and Rein's account of the interrogation—and the prosecution's entire case.

"The questioning after this point," Gottlieb asked, "can you describe the tone?"

"It was very fast," Marty said, "and it wasn't so much questioning. A lot of it was suggesting."

"What do you mean by that?"

"Statements were made to me like, 'Well, you killed your mother first, didn't you?' When I said no, they said, 'Well, Marty, we don't want to hear no. Just say yes.' . . . Detective McCready said, 'Well, what knife did you use?' I said, 'I don't know, I didn't do this.' And he said, 'Well, Marty, I saw some knives in the kitchen. Did you use one of those?' I said, 'I don't know.' He says, 'Well, we don't want to hear "I don't know." Just say yes.' He said, 'Well, was it the knife next to the watermelon? Was it the knife next to the sink? Was it one of those?' And I finally said yes."

"Why did you finally say yes?"

"Because that's what they wanted to hear. Detective McCready stated to me, 'Well, Marty, what did you hit your mother and father with?' You know, 'Was it the dumbbells in your room?' And I said, 'I don't know.' They said, 'Well, just say yes. Make it easy.' And I did say yes."

McCready then suggested that since he had no blood on his clothes, he must have been naked when he killed his parents. "He said, 'Well, when you got out of the shower, all you had on was a towel, so you must have been naked. So, you did this while you were naked, weren't you?' I believe I just said, 'Yeah.'"

"Why did you say that?"

"They had me believing that's the way it was."

"Do you recall any questions regarding the shower and what the shower was used for?"

"I can recall Detective McCready saying, 'Well, when I looked at the knife, it looked clean. Did you wash it off in the shower? I said, 'I don't know.' He said, 'Well, Marty, you know you took a shower. They're nice and clean. So you must have washed the knife off in the shower.' And I believe I said, 'Yeah, I guess I did.'"

In their testimony, McCready and Rein said that Marty volunteered these details, that he matter-of-factly delivered a complete narrative of his crimes with little prompting. In their version, he told them how he committed the murders only after he told them, also in expansive detail, *why* he did it. But by Marty's account, the detectives fabricated his motives by weaving together distorted versions of information he had given them earlier, before the interview became confrontational, and then inserting them into his purported confession.

Marty had already related how his mother's innocuous reminder about his father's poker table became, in the confession, a furious argument that triggered lethal rage. Now he described other instances of how McCready and Rein concocted his motive. Earlier in the interview, they asked him whether his father had any business partners other than Jerry Steuerman. "I can recall talking about his business dealings with Dan Hayes, and I said, you know, Dan Hayes was going to come in and move in with us, and that at first I wasn't too happy about it but after about a day thinking about it I thought it was really great."

He also remembered being asked whether he ever played any contact sports. "And I said I've played every kind of contact sport except football. And they asked why and I said, 'Because my mother didn't really want me to.'" In the scenario that emerged from the interview room, this was part of Marty's supposed resentment of his mother's desire to keep him "under her thumb."

What of the "crummy old Lincoln" that had become such an emblem of Marty Tankleff's murderous tantrum? According to McCready and Rein, the car first came up early in the interview, when they asked Marty what he drove. He told them the Lincoln was his parents' choice—"He said that although he agreed with them that it was a safer car, he wasn't quite happy with it, but he was going to fix it up." Marty had no recollection of the car coming up again, or of ever calling it "crummy." It seemed to him that his passing remarks about the car during the early stage of the interview later became fodder for the collection of exaggerated and invented resentments later attributed to him as his motive for murder.

"Marty, when you told them, 'Yeah, I did it,' did you consider what would happen to you?"

"No, because I thought this was all a nightmare and I was going to wake up and it would be all over."

Gottlieb handed Marty the Miranda card that McCready testified he used to inform him of his rights. According to McCready, this was at 11:56 A.M., the moment after Marty uttered his first incriminating words. Collins had put the card into evidence, but a careful examination raised questions about whether the detectives really did advise Marty of his rights even at the late point they claimed. And whether they had lied about it in their testimony.

The card was not a standard form meant for a suspect's signature. So McCready had Marty sign his name over the "Rules of Interrogation," which listed the four rights and three questions of the Miranda warnings. He had him write the date but not the far more important element—the time. Moreover, the card bore the initials and shield numbers of two detectives. *KJM #563* was McCready. The other—*RD D/Sgt 463*—was Robert Doyle, his sergeant. Doyle was still back at the scene during the interrogation, so couldn't have initialed the card until he arrived at police headquarters later in the afternoon. This would be consistent with Marty's recollection. "I recall signing it when the police report was filled out," he testified. He didn't know what report was being written or what time it was, only that "it was later on in the day."

"NOW, MARTY . . . can you tell us what you told the detectives while at the homicide squad regarding Jerry Steuerman?" Marty said he told them about the debts, the arguments, the fight about Jerry's new store, the $50,000 note that his father told him was due that week. "And I told him approximately three weeks before September seventh, there was some type of threat made to the family and that my father and mother were getting worried that Jerry Steuerman might break into the house, steal all the original notes and the bagel contracts, and they thought we should put everything in the safe."

"Now, Marty, how did it come about that you knew the details concerning Jerry Steuerman and your parents and the business?"

"I wanted to grow up to be just like my father so I always asked to be

involved in whatever business dealings he had, and he always liked that because he wanted to train me to be just like him."

Gottlieb approached the end of Marty's direct testimony with an intriguing moment. Earlier, Marty had described Rein as the far less harsh
and intimidating of his two interrogators. Though Rein sometimes challenged him aggressively, Marty found him to be generally unthreatening,
at times even sympathetic. It might have been the standard good cop/bad
cop act, but Marty recounted a moment later that day that suggested that
Rein might have had reservations about the words he and McCready had
extracted from their young suspect.

"It was when Detective Rein was taking me down to get fingerprinted
and photographed," Marty said. "Detective Rein asked me, 'Marty, do you
believe you did this?' And I turned around and I said, 'No, but you're
telling me I did.'" Rein was to have an opportunity to dispute the exchange a few weeks later, when Collins brought him back to the stand to
rebut a few points of testimony by defense witnesses, including Marty. But
he would leave this point unchallenged.

"Marty," Gottlieb said, bringing the testimony to a close, "did you kill
your mother?"

"I loved my parents," Marty said. "I had absolutely nothing to do with
this."

He said this with as much force and emotion as he could manage. But
he didn't raise his voice. And he didn't cry.

AS CRUCIAL AS Marty's direct testimony was, as anxious as he and everyone around him were about his ability to win over the jury, they knew it
was the easy part.

To prepare Marty for cross-examination—and really, to make sure it
was a good idea to put him on the stand at all—Gottlieb had recruited a
friend to put him through a mock cross. He and Ben Brafman had worked
together early in their careers, in the rackets bureau of the Manhattan district attorney's office, and Brafman had gone on to become one of New
York's top criminal defense lawyers (and in the years to follow, one of the
nation's, with a list of high-profile clients that would include Michael
Jackson). Brafman was a brash figure with a reputation as a superb cross-
examiner, and this wasn't the first time a colleague had asked him to put a
client through a practice run. A few years earlier, he'd done it for Barry
Slotnick, whose client was about to testify before a grand jury that was
considering indicting him on four counts of attempted murder. Brafman
spent a Sunday afternoon grilling Bernhard Goetz about why he shot four
young men on a subway train after one of them asked him for money.

Gottlieb brought Marty to the federal courthouse in lower Manhattan, where Brafman was defending a pharmaceutical company accused of price-fixing. They found an empty conference room and Brafman sized up the kid Gottlieb had been telling him about. Marty made the same impression on Brafman as he had on Gottlieb the night he was arrested: "Sweet, soft-spoken, socially immature. I couldn't put him in the role of a brutal murderer."

But it wasn't Marty's appearance or personality that convinced Brafman that Gottlieb did indeed have an innocent client—that was no more a basis, after all, than a lack of emotion was evidence of guilt. It wasn't that the motives made no sense, or that the oppressed business partner disappeared a week after the murders, which was a defense attorney's dream. To Brafman the case simply failed the plausibility test: "It would have been virtually impossible to commit crimes like that without leaving *any* forensic evidence. Maybe if you're a thirty-five-year-old professional killer, you figure out a way to do that. But the idea that this kid could so sanitize himself from physical evidence—that just doesn't make any sense. It was beyond my comprehension even as a former prosecutor that he could have committed these murders."

But Brafman knew that the jury would be focused on Marty's confession and his testimony explaining it. In the mock cross, he asked Marty all the hard questions, grilled him with the kind of sardonic tone that he would have to expect from John Collins: *Why is it you didn't seem upset that morning? How do you account for the fact that you had no blood on you, except for your hands, after helping your father? Are you asking this jury to believe that you confessed to something you didn't do? The slaughter of your own parents? Is that what you would have this jury believe? Can you explain how that could possibly be the truth?*

No, he couldn't, not really. And that was the ultimate conundrum of the case. "It's stuff that's almost impossible to explain," Brafman reflected. "That's the reason we have the presumption of innocence—because it's almost impossible to *prove* you're innocent. It's proving a negative." But the practical reality of this case in particular was that the defendant did have to prove he was innocent. Presented with a confession, the jury would demand it. As Brafman saw it, you've got the government on the other side, the guys with the badges in their wallets and the American flags on their lapels. And you're over here, trying to explain the unexplainable.

Homicide prosecutors don't usually get the chance to cross-examine the person they're trying to convict. Presumably, John Collins couldn't wait to go after Marty Tankleff. But it wasn't immediately evident. He ambled over to the lectern, glanced down at his legal pad for a few seconds, then looked across at the witness and addressed him with his usual low-key monotone. The only difference was that he didn't say good morning.

"Mr. Tankleff, you told us yesterday afternoon . . ." Collins began, signaling his desire for the jury to see the defendant as a functional adult, not the naïve child of the defense's reckoning. Not *Marty*, the victimized teenager. *Mr. Tankleff*, the calculating murderer, accountable for his actions.

"Your relationship with your mother was changing at this point in time in 1988, was it not?"

"No, it wasn't," Marty replied emphatically. "It was getting *better.*"

"You resented being babied by your mother and not being treated like a man, or not being treated like a senior in high school and being made to drive an automobile, because of some accidents that you had, that you felt was not sporty enough to you, is that correct?"

"That's *not* correct," Marty said, meaning the whole mouthful.

"And your mother wanted you driving that particular automobile because it was safer after you had an accident with her custom Cadillac convertible, is that correct?"

"That Lincoln was my third car. The car after the accident was a truck I had."

"And you had accidents with that as well?"

"I went out on a snowy road one day and I hit a tree."

The car talk continued when Collins turned to the day before the murders. "Following getting your hair cut, you and your father then went to a service station with the old Lincoln, did you not?" he asked.

"I don't recall that," Marty replied, baffled.

"Let me see if I can refresh your recollection." Do you remember having a problem with the seal on the manifold, Collins asked, and going with your father to Pete & Al's Getty station on September 6 to discuss it? And being told by Pete that it wasn't worth fixing? And having a loud argument with your father "wherein you called the car a piece of shit, you were embarrassed to take to school"?

"I don't recall that at all," Marty said.

"Do you recall your father being angry with you when you got to Shari's house and an argument ensuing in Shari's living room?"

"No, I don't," Marty said, growing perplexed.

"Let me see if I can refresh your recollection some." Do you recall arriving at your sister Shari's house after leaving the service station and your father telling you, "If you think you're going to any University of Miami playboy school and living in your father's condominium you've got another thing coming?" Do you recall that?

"No, I don't," said Marty.

For Marty, this was a devastating moment—the moment he realized his sister's betrayal was complete. Shari was giving ammunition to the prosecution, and lies, at that. More worrisome was the signal it gave the jury—that the defendant had lost the support of his own sister, the daughter of one of the victims. If she was on the prosecution's side, she must think he's guilty.

Collins left the implications hanging in the air and moved on to the morning of the murders. He had Marty recount one more time his call to 911, then asked, "Can you tell us, Mr. Tankleff, how it is that you managed in the course of that frantic telephone call not to smear any of the blood on that phone and not to disturb the cord from its original position?"

The question was an echo of the interrogation twenty-one months earlier, and so was the answer. "I don't know how," Marty said.

"Would you tell us again how you got your dad out of the chair?" Marty began explaining how he extended the chair's footrest, how the chair tipped forward. Collins stopped him. "I'm not following you so good here. Can we do this again?"

"Surely," said Marty. He went through it again, clearly enough for Collins to picture it.

"And you were able to get your two-hundred-thirty-pound father out of the chair in one movement such as that?"

"I really don't recall. I got him off the chair though."

Collins constructed the dilemma: With blood all over his father and on the chair, how did Marty get blood only on his hands, a spot on his shoulder, and some on his lower leg—but none on his chest or shorts? At the defense table, Gottlieb maintained a poker face as Marty came precariously close to giving credence to McCready and Rein's skepticism. How *did* he get his father off the chair without getting any blood on his midsection? Was the truth too improbable to be persuasive? Would the jury view the many instances when Marty said he didn't recall something as an honest reflection of his understandably spotty memory of that day—or as the predictable evasions of a guilty defendant? That was a paradox of Marty's situation: The more candidly he testified, the less candid he might seem.

"I believe you testified yesterday that after having checked the garage you went to the kitchen and called your sister," Collins said, apparently trying to lay a trap.

"No, that's not correct," Marty said.

"What did you do next?"

"I went into the bedroom area."

"Do you recall the testimony of Ethel Curley being that you never at any time entered the master bedroom while she was there?"

"No. I recall her saying that she couldn't recall how far I entered or if I did."

Collins looked high and low for discrepancies in Marty's story. Long before the trial, Gottlieb had arranged for Marty to be interviewed by a forensic psychiatrist named Dr. Daniel Schwartz. When Marty said at one point in the cross-examination that he got back into bed that morning after turning off his alarm clock, Collins confronted him: Isn't it true that you told Dr. Schwartz "that you shut the alarm off before it rang"? But Collins seemed annoyed that he couldn't use Schwartz's interviews with Marty to find more inconsistencies. In a sequence laced with perfect irony, Collins grilled Marty about whether Schwartz took notes during their two meetings, and why he didn't videotape them. "Would it not be fair to say that it is important to have as an exact a record and as accurate a record of that particular meeting as possible?" he asked.

"It wasn't my decision," Marty said with bewilderment.

"MR. TANKLEFF, did you tell Detectives Rein and McCready that you did kill your mother and hurt your father by saying, 'Yeah, I did it,' is that correct?"

"That's correct."

"You did tell Detectives Rein and McCready that you did that to your parents using the barbell and a knife from the kitchen, is that correct?"

"That's correct," Marty said.

To Marty's lawyer and his family, Marty had held up well to this point. But now they were wincing. He was giving ground, it seemed, from his explanation of how the confession came to be. It wasn't that he *told* the detectives he did it with the barbell and the knife, but that, under duress, he accepted their insistence that he did. It was almost as if Marty were back in that interrogation room, a victim again, it seemed, of his guileless compliance with authority. Gottlieb would try to repair the damage on redirect.

"Mr. Tankleff, you want this jury to believe that Detectives Rein and McCready got you to admit to brutally killing your mother and hurting your father in a mere matter of forty minutes by telling you, 'I don't believe you. Tell us what we want to hear. Your father says you did it,' and because your father never lied to you? That's what you want these folks to believe, Mr. Tankleff, that those are the reasons you said the things you did?"

"I want them to believe what really happened in that room," Marty said.

Marty was surrounded by his family and friends when he stepped down from the witness chair and walked through the wooden gate into the spectator's gallery. "He did just fine," Gottlieb told the relatives. "Collins didn't touch him—factually, he didn't touch him. He was consistent."

But there was more to it than that. The real question was whether Marty made an emotional connection with the jurors, one strong enough for them to take his word over McCready and Rein's. In this, there was no middle ground—doing just fine wasn't enough. Either they believed him or they didn't. The rub was that they were very likely starting from the premise that the confession was true, and it was up to Marty to convince them otherwise—to *prove* his innocence. It wasn't supposed to be that way. But as Marty was learning, a little bit each day, few things were as they seemed in the altered reality of a criminal courtroom. Even himself. "I was acting like I was told to act," he recalled of his testimony years later. "It wasn't like *I* was up there."

Gottlieb knew Marty's task was nearly impossible: to explain the unexplainable. He hoped his next witness could help with that.

CHAPTER 23

Hypnotist for the Defense

ONE NIGHT IN SEPTEMBER 1973, a woman named Barbara Gibbons was murdered in her bungalow in the northwestern Connecticut town of Canaan. Her body was discovered by her son, a sandy-haired teenager who had begun his senior year of high school a few weeks earlier. He told the Connecticut State Police that he had come home from a meeting at the teen center of the local Methodist church and found his mother on the floor of her bedroom, covered with blood. The investigators were immediately dubious of his story: Peter Reilly did not seem stricken with grief.

At the state police barracks, the investigators' skepticism turned to accusation. They held him overnight and resumed their questioning in the morning, tape-recording the interrogation. Eventually he signed a confession. The next day he recanted it.

No one who knew Peter Reilly could imagine him committing the horrific crime to which he had allegedly confessed, especially when an autopsy revealed that his mother, besides being slain in the most brutal manner—her head had nearly been severed and both her legs and three ribs had been broken—had also been sexually assaulted. What they *could* imagine, even at a time long before false confessions became a recognized phenomenon, was a team of experienced police detectives manipulating Peter—an insecure teenager respectful of authority and easily influenced by others—into confessing to something he didn't do. "If you insist to Peter often enough that black is white and white is black, then Peter will say, 'Yeah, I guess you're right,'" one of his neighbors told a reporter. On the night he confessed, Reilly asked the commander of the state police station if he could go home with him.

At Reilly's trial, just four months after his arrest, his attorney argued that her client was being tried solely on the basis of an involuntary and uncorroborated confession. There was no physical evidence linking him to the murder and no weapon was found. The state's attorney presented witnesses who said that Peter sometimes quarreled with his mother and that he didn't seem very upset after her murder.

But it was the taped confession, portions of which were played for them, that the jurors considered most. What the tapes revealed were long stretches of suggestive questioning and a young man who seemed increasingly confused and eager to please. "We have, right now, without any word out of your mouth, proof positive," said a police investigator. "That I did it?" Reilly asked. "That you did it." Reilly replied, "So, okay, then I may as well say I did it."

The jury found Reilly's admissions credible enough to convict him. But the verdict suggested uncertainty and compromise. He was found guilty not of murder but of manslaughter and sentenced to six to sixteen years in prison.

It was Peter Reilly's good fortune that his small working-class town happened to be in Litchfield County, a region of the lower Berkshires favored by upper-echelon New York celebrities. Arthur Miller, the eminent playwright, lived in the area and heard about Reilly from a friend. The author of such great American tragedies as *Death of a Salesman* and *The Crucible* became consumed by the young man's case. He talked to witnesses, reviewed trial records, and read the transcript of the interrogation. He became convinced that Reilly was the victim of a terrible injustice and turned the case into a cause célèbre. He got Reilly a new lawyer and raised money to hire a private investigator with the help of a couple of his Litchfield County friends, the novelist William Styron and the director Mike Nichols.

Miller went to New York to present the case to editors at *The New York Times*, and the result was a front-page, two-part series that included new evidence uncovered by the private investigator. The articles brought national attention to the case and to the larger criminal justice issues it raised. And it helped Reilly's new attorneys persuade the judge who presided at his trial to reopen the case.

In the spring of 1976, the judge conducted a hearing of new evidence to determine if Reilly's conviction should be set aside and a new trial granted. The key piece of new evidence was a latent fingerprint that turned out to belong to a young man who lived nearby and whose brother had been feuding with Reilly's mother in the months before her murder. There was also evidence of perjury on a key element of the timeline by a hospital nurse who was married to a state trooper, and new forensic testimony discrediting the county medical examiner's testimony that it was possible for Reilly to have committed the murder without being splattered with blood.

That left the confession. To attack its validity, Reilly's lawyer, T. F. Gilroy Daly, brought in Dr. Herbert Spiegel, a forensic psychiatrist who was at the time one of the few authorities on interrogations and confessions. After conducting an examination of Reilly and reading transcripts of the interrogation, Spiegel testified that the police "brainwashed" Reilly into believing, essentially, that because he had no memory of killing his mother, he must have done it. "He had no proof that he did not do it," Spiegel testified, "and in deference to police authority he accepted responsibility for the killing."

The judge ruled that Reilly's lawyers had made their case to overturn his conviction, saying, "It is readily apparent that a grave injustice has been done." Though there was evidence of prosecutorial misconduct, the judge laid a good deal of the blame on Reilly's trial attorney. Among the defects in her defense, he said, was her failure to present an expert witness such as Spiegel to support the contention that the confession was not only coerced but false. Reilly was never retried and despite strong circumstantial evidence that trickled out over the next few years, neither were the brothers who lived nearby.

A YEAR AFTER Peter Reilly's release, T. R. Gilroy Daly was appointed a federal judge in Connecticut. Daly was in his chambers in Hartford one day thirteen years later when he got a phone call from Bob Gottlieb. Gottlieb had been a rookie prosecutor in Manhattan when Daly won Reilly's release, and he remembered reading about the case. Gottlieb was astonished by the similarities to Marty Tankleff's case, and he was especially interested in Daly's use of an expert on coerced confessions.

Reilly's eventual exoneration was perhaps a hopeful sign for Marty. What was less encouraging was that Reilly had first been convicted, and by a jury that actually heard the police extracting an ambiguous confession from a traumatized teenager. It reinforced how difficult it was to convince people that there were circumstances under which a person, particularly a young and impressionable one, could be driven to confessing to something he didn't do. And it made clear to Gottlieb that he needed to bring before the jury someone who could convincingly explain how such a thing could happen.

Gottlieb reached Dr. Herbert Spiegel at his office in New York and told him about his case. Spiegel said Marty Tankleff sounded a lot like Peter Reilly, though of course he'd have to examine Marty and learn what he could about the interrogation. Was it recorded? he asked. Unfortunately no, Gottlieb told him. All he had were Marty's recollections, which were limited, and the police account, which he believed to be a sham.

Herbert Spiegel had graduated from medical school in 1939 and based much of his thinking on work he first did as an army psychiatrist during World War II. He studied how soldiers responded to the trauma of combat—why some could endure the most intense situations with apparent ease while others would fall apart under the slightest stress. He became fascinated by the most extreme response, one in which a person was overcome by a sense of powerlessness so acute that he could lose touch with reality. It was called "traumatic neurosis."

Spiegel had the curriculum vitae of a man respected by his profession—faculty appointments to major medical schools, a long list of publications, constant invitations to speak at conferences and seminars—but his interests took him to places far afield from the mainstream. He became captivated by hypnosis, and with his son, David, developed a test they called the Hypnotic Induction Profile, a ten-minute procedure that measured a person's susceptibility to hypnosis and related it to personality styles and psychological makeup. The test was widely used around the world, and their 1978 textbook, *Trance and Treatment: Clinical Uses of Hypnosis,* was considered the bible of medical hypnosis. Spiegel eventually combined his two areas of expertise, using hypnosis to treat patients who suffered traumatic experiences. While he continued to call the condition traumatic neurosis, others were starting to call it post-traumatic stress syndrome. And at some point Spiegel began to consider whether it could play a role in the criminal justice system.

A month before his trial was to start, Marty went to Spiegel's Manhattan office. The doctor gathered some information about Marty's background, then asked him about the day his parents were attacked, particularly those hours he spent with the police: what they said to him, what he told them, how he perceived the events, how he felt as they were unfolding. He compared this with McCready and Rein's account of the interrogation. Spiegel conducted two personality tests that day and more a week later. The third was the Hypnotic Induction Profile, in which Spiegel put Marty in a trance and noted his responses. At Gottlieb's request, he videotaped it.

Three months later, Marty sat in the witness chair and swore that he confessed to something he didn't do. The next day, Spiegel took the same seat and tried to explain how that could happen. It was a gamble for the defense. Spiegel's testimony would be the furthest thing from hard, tangible evidence the jury would hear, and there was a chance he could make the idea of a false confession seem even less plausible than it might already be. Not only did Spiegel offer unconventional expertise, but he tended to deliver it in a manner that came off as something less than authoritative.

He was a pleasant, polite man, unassuming to the point of sometimes seeming oblivious. He was slightly built, completely bald, and seemed hesitant even about his mustache: It was so excessively trimmed that it could go unnoticed from a distance.

Spiegel touched on the highlights of his fifty-year career, then described the tests he performed to assess Marty Tankleff. First was a "personality inventory," which gauged where he fell in the spectrum of personality styles, with organized and logical at one end and sensitive and intuitive at the other. The test found him to be right in the middle. Next Spiegel sought to determine whether Marty was, in general outlook, the kind of person who felt he was in control of his own destiny. "Which of these statements best describes how you feel," asked one question. "1. What happens to me is my own doing. 2. Sometimes I feel that I don't have enough control over the direction my life is taking." The results of this test would seem to be skewed by Marty's current situation, but Marty scored in the normal range again. Finally, the Hypnotic Induction Profile: Spiegel said he put Marty into a trance and considered "how he responded to entering, experiencing, and exiting the trance state." This measured "his ability to concentrate in a disciplined manner under instructed conditions" and helped assess whether he was more rigid or flexible in his responses to situations. Most people with serious mental disorders are unable to maintain this "ribbon of concentration," Spiegel noted. Again Marty fell into the healthy range.

If Spiegel's testimony thus far struck some people as so much mumbo-jumbo, what followed hardly brought him closer to the questions at hand. When Gottlieb asked Spiegel to discuss the state of "traumatic neurosis" he'd mentioned earlier, the learned psychiatrist went back to his experiences in World War II. "Because of the army's way of doing things, I ended up as a battalion surgeon, and that job meant that I lived with a thousand men in my battalion. I swam in North Africa with them, and I knew the men, and as a result—"

"Your Honor, if I may," Collins interjected, "with all due respect to the doctor, I believe the question was what's the first stage of traumatic neurosis."

Spiegel said he was just getting to that. "A suspension of our usual critical judgment is one of the first things that occurs," he said. ". . . There's such a need to deny the implied threat of the circumstances that many men become dumbfounded. It's like going into a zombie-like state. On the surface, they seemed to be perfectly normal, cool, collected, but underneath it all they were, in a sense, paralyzed. . . ."

Spiegel was still talking about the World War II soldiers, so Gottlieb cut him off and asked that he fast-forward five decades to his work with

Marty Tankleff. "It was clear to me," Spiegel said, "that he was confused and he had all the main features of this acute traumatic state, including the zombie-like quality, his suspension of judgment, and his need to deny the implications of what was going on."

Do people react differently to stress and trauma? Spiegel confirmed the obvious with a vivid example from his arsenal of war stories that Gottlieb thought timeless. A sergeant went out on a mission and saw his closest friend killed by a dive-bomber. "And the heat of the bomb not only blew up the body, but it just burned into like a purple ash. And now he was in a daze seeing this. He managed to find his way back to our company, and he carried an arm and a leg, and in a very cool, collected way he just put it down and he says, 'Here's Ken.'"

Gottlieb asked Spiegel to assess how each of the events of September 7, individually and then cumulatively, would have influenced Marty's reactions and behavior. The police bringing him to headquarters, isolating him from his family, betraying his trust by accusing him of the assaults on his parents, was like "one punch after another that insulted him right and left, up and down, to the point where he could be made dizzy by the process." The detectives' lies made him doubt what he knew to be true and even "who he is as a person," to the point that "he wonders does he exist at all." And finally, McCready's ploy: "It's hard to imagine a psychological, emotional blow or insult to be greater than that when you consider that he had an overall loving and good relationship with his father and his mother." But with his naïve trust of the police still unbroken, he began making desperate efforts to comprehend what he was being told—wondering whether he could have blacked out, whether he could be possessed. Grasping at such outlandish possibilities opened the door to Rein's seemingly sympathetic coaxing—*If there's another Marty inside you that knows that happened, have him tell us.* "That was the ultimate seduction. He was tricked into making use of his uncertainty. . . . He is so suggestible at that time and his critical judgment is so suspended that he would look for that to get immediate relief."

"Can a person confess to killing his parents when he did not do it?" Gottlieb asked, hoping to finish with a final compelling declaration. Spiegel, though, saved his most esoteric answer for this most fundamental question. He spoke of Marty's "establishment of disassociation" and described the cumulative impact of what happened to him that day as a "bedazzlement." But the answer, finally, was yes, false confessions certainly did happen. And he found it unsurprising that a mentally healthy person such as Marty had been coerced into giving one. "A psychopath knows all the devious ways to deal with authority," said Spiegel. "He is much less subject to the pressure that can be put upon by police authority than a healthy, normal, innocent man who's not onto the tricks of pressure inter-rogation."

IN THE COLLECTIVE judgment of the media corps, Dr. Spiegel's appraisal of Marty Tankleff's confession was largely impenetrable, his theories too abstract. Too *out there* to sway the jury. And this was his direct testimony.

Doctor, said John Collins, you don't seem to have any notes from your conversations with the defendant, other than the date and place of his birth.

"I know them up here," Spiegel said, pointing to his head. Collins asked Spiegel if he took notes in his other cases, "or do you keep them all up here, too?" He pointed to his own head. "It depends," said Spiegel. "If it's very complicated and involves some deep intra-psychic conference, then I take a lot of notes and might even record interviews."

Collins didn't bother asking what a "deep intra-psychic conference" was. He cross-examined Spiegel on his methods and conclusions for a while, then got to a moment he clearly relished. A television was brought into the courtroom on a rolling stand with a videocassette recorder on the bottom rack. Collins bent down, put a tape in, pressed the play button. Up on the screen came a grainy, overhead image of Spiegel sitting close to Marty. "Lean your head back, close your eyes very slowly, take a nice, deep breath. Now imagine you are floating, your body is floating. Concentrate on this imaginary floating. Floating . . . floating . . . Now let your left hand lift up. Just like a dancer, let it float up. . . . This might amuse you. . . . Imagine a huge floating balloon. That's right, all the way up. Now raise your *right* arm. Are you aware of a difference in sensation between your right arm and your left arm? How would you describe the difference?"

The video lasted only ten minutes, but they were unquestionably the ten strangest minutes of the trial, and for the defense among the worst. A video reminiscent of the Amazing Kreskin hypnotizing a volunteer from the audience on *The Tonight Show* made the defense's coerced-confession argument seem almost desperate.

Years later, Gottlieb recalled, "I knew I had to try to explain to a Suf-folk County jury why somebody could believe he killed his parents when in fact he didn't do it. Spiegel was considered the guy that got Peter Reilly out of jail. So he was my guy." But, he conceded, "He didn't do great." The twist, as it would turn out, was that however eccentric Spiegel and his methods seemed, his appraisal was hardly ridiculous. "What he said was right on. It was just that in 1990 it was too much in a vacuum. People weren't knowledgeable or open to the notion of coerced, false confes-sions."

*　　*　　*

GOTTLIEB HAD one more witness to address a question he presumed would be on the minds of the jurors. She, too, was not the standard expert witness.

Bonnie Schnitta-Israel held a doctoral degree that combined expertise in ocean physics, mathematics, electrical engineering, and computer science. In her professional area of "signal processing," she had worked for the Department of Defense and NATO, developing sound-measurement technology used to verify nuclear weapons treaties. And now she was testifying in a murder trial. As an expert in how sound travels, Schnitta-Israel had been hired by the defense to determine whether a loud scream from the Tankleffs' bedroom would have been heard in the cavelike corner bed unit in Marty's room.

Gottlieb had found Schnitta-Israel after thinking about something his investigator, Jack Murtagh, had told him early in the case. Frank Perrone, Marty's best friend's father, told Murtagh that people were saying Marty must have done it because he couldn't have slept through his parents' murders. "I'm in the construction business," Perrone said. "I've been over there, and I can tell you sound doesn't travel inside that house." Perrone thought Gottlieb should have a sound expert prove it.

Schnitta-Israel offered a brief seminar on sound waves and explained how she conducted her tests at 33 Seaside Drive. She used Defense Department–approved equipment and spent nearly an entire day calibrating the equipment according to "the environmental factors that were in effect on the night of the murder"—everything from room temperatures to the number of pillows and the position of the drapes in the master bedroom. She turned on the television. Some critical factors were unknown, though, and in these cases Schnitta-Israel assumed the conditions that would have produced the greatest sound in Marty's room. She called this the "worst-case scenario." For instance, she performed the test assuming that Arlene was at the foot of the bed, where her body was found, and that she was standing up and screaming directly toward the door.

Finally—"since I was doing the screaming"—Schnitta-Israel had asked the family if there were any recordings of Arlene's voice. "They gave me a home video. My assistant is a sound engineer and he confirmed that her speaking voice was very similar to mine." She displayed for the jury Defendant's Exhibit ZZ: a readout of two graphs showing frequency and decibel levels. One was labeled "Bonnie's voice," the other "Mom's voice."

When everything was set up, Schnitta-Israel went into the master bedroom and stood at the foot of the bed, facing the door. "I then screamed as loud as I could." In terms of decibel level, "It's halfway between the sound of banging cymbals together as loud as you could and an air hammer hitting a metal plate." The sound was measured by a spectrum analyzer in Marty's room, which plotted the signals on graphs. She repeated the test numerous times, changing only one variable. The results: With both bedroom doors closed, the equipment recorded almost nothing—the equivalent of white noise, "or maybe a bird chirping outside or the ocean waves." With Marty's door closed but the master bedroom door fully open, Schnitta-Israel's screams registered the equivalent of "the average whisper."

Litigators love nothing more than the chance to irritate their adversaries by ridiculing their witnesses. "Good morning, ma'am," Collins greeted Gottlieb's sound expert. "Did Mr. Israel know you could scream as loud as a jackhammer on a metal plate when you were married?"

"It's *Doctor* Israel," she replied.

"There's a worst-case scenario you left out, ma'am, is there not?" Collins asked. "If the defendant was in his mother's room and pounding and slashing the life from her body, is there any doubt that he could have heard that?"

"I don't think that's why I was hired," Schnitta-Israel answered.

THE BALANCE OF Gottlieb's defense fell primarily into two categories. One was meant to demonstrate that Marty had a close and healthy relationship with his parents and that his behavior on the day before the murders was entirely normal; the other had to do with Jerry Steuerman.

On both counts, one of the best witnesses for the defense, potentially, was Marie Vieira, for four years the Tankleffs' house cleaner. She worked from eight in the morning until two in the afternoon every Tuesday and Friday, so had been there until mid-afternoon on the day of the Tuesday night poker game. Vieira said she first saw Marty when he and his mother came in from a morning walk, something they did often. How were they acting? "Nice, like they always were, friendly. They walked in and they had breakfast together." Then Marty went outside and spent several hours doing yard work.

Around one in the afternoon, Vieira was cleaning Seymour's office when Marty came in and asked his father for money to get a haircut for the first day of school. "So his father goes in his pocket and he takes out twenty dollars. So Marty says, 'Dad, this is not enough. How about some more?' So Dad says, 'Gee, twenty dollars is enough for me, so twenty dollars should be enough for you.' They were joking around. So then Marty left with the twenty dollars. . . . They were kidding around, smiling, and, you know, they were funny."

Now Gottlieb came to a moment he thought could be pivotal. A few minutes after Marty left for his haircut, while Vieira was still cleaning the office, Seymour got a phone call that made him instantly irate. She had related the incident to Jack Murtagh early in the case, but the prosecution didn't hear about it until a month into the trial because the detectives didn't interview Marie until they saw her name on Gottlieb's witness list.

The phone call would be excellent circumstantial testimony for the defense—but for the problem that had plagued Gottlieb throughout the trial. Vieira got as far as saying that the phone rang and Seymour answered it. Then Gottlieb abruptly interrupted his own questioning to ask the judge for a sidebar. There followed another debate with Collins on hearsay and another ruling by Tisch that gave Gottlieb some leeway but not enough to serve his purpose. "It doesn't take a rocket scientist to figure out that you wish the jury to infer that the person on the other side of the phone is Jerry Steuerman," the judge said. He ruled that the maid could testify that there was a phone call, that Seymour appeared agitated, and that he slammed the phone down. But she couldn't quote anything he said.

"Would you at least—while I agree with the ruling, I will accept it," Gottlieb stammered, "will you at least, as to the subject matter—"

"No," said Tisch, cutting him off. Gottlieb tried again: Could Vieira simply say that the angry phone call was about money? No, Tisch said. Gottlieb retreated. He was halfway back when he suddenly stopped, turned, and asked for another sidebar. Back at the bench, he explained that he was now worried that with what he was being permitted to elicit, the jury might be left with the impression that it could have been Marty on the other end of the phone. Tisch said he would allow Gottlieb to lead the witness in this instance: He could have Vieira say that it wasn't Marty, since he had just left.

Returning to his witness, Gottlieb got out what he could: Seymour was "extremely upset" during the phone call, said Vieira, and then "he slammed the receiver." Fair to say the phone call wasn't between Seymour and Marty? "It wasn't," she said. But she was not permitted to say what she heard: Seymour screaming into the phone, "I don't give a shit! I'm coming tomorrow morning to get my money. So you better have it!"

Gottlieb tried again to cast suspicions upon Steuerman when he called Mark and Frank Perrone. With each witness came a request for a sidebar and an appeal to the judge for a lenient interpretation of the hearsay rules. So while Frank Perrone waited in the witness chair, Gottlieb told Tisch that his witness was prepared to testify that during the summer of 1988 he had two conversations with Marty about his father's move to call in the $50,000 note from Steuerman. The second one was during a fishing trip in late August. "This is a *week* before the card game," Gottlieb told Tisch. "How can we not be permitted to bring that in?"

Here's how, said Tisch: Your client could have testified about this himself when he was on the stand. It's not admissible in the form of hearsay testimony from someone he talked to on a fishing boat. Gottlieb was reduced to eliciting testimony from Perrone that was so cryptic that it resembled a round from *What's My Line?:* Mr. Perrone, in the summer of 1988 did you have conversations with Marty Tankleff about his father's business? *Yes.* Were any of those conversations before the fishing trip in August? *Yes.* Were there additional conversations after the fishing trip? *Yes.* Did you have any conversations with Marty regarding his father's partner in the bagel store? *Yes.* Was the conversation regarding the business partner connected with the conversations about his father's business? *Yes.*

"I have no further questions," Gottlieb said with a note of resignation.

By now, Gottlieb was convinced that Tisch had not presided over this case impartially. It wasn't just the judge's rulings but the way he sometimes conveyed his disdain for Gottlieb and his case in front of the jury—an arched eyebrow, even a roll of the eyes. Whether this was so or not, there was little question that Tisch and Gottlieb were wearing on each other. It was perhaps most evident during a sidebar when Gottlieb was trying to get in some testimony to counter one of the many claims being made by McCready and Rein.

"We have had incredible amounts of testimony that the defendant said this or that," Gottlieb told Tisch. "This comes in—"

"It comes in if I *say* it comes in," Tisch snapped.

"Your Honor, I always mean that . . ."

"I don't know that you always mean that."

"I have another offer, if Your Honor please."

"What offer now?"

"Because—first of all, Your Honor, I don't understand why you would even be reacting that way when this trial has been chock full of statements made by Marty regarding—"

"I didn't react at all," Tisch cut in.

"Just now in your comment you did react."

Gottlieb knew the risks of arguing with a judge. But by now he figured he had little to lose. And he wanted his comments on the record, for an appeals court to see, should the verdict go the wrong way.

When Mark Perrone came to the stand, Gottlieb asked him to recall the morning of the murders, when he and his parents went to Mather Hospital after getting Marty's call. Specifically, Gottlieb wanted Mark to relate seeing Ron Rother arrive at the hospital and hearing him say, in the presence of a detective, "This was a hit. A lot of money was due this week." But it was another hopeless cause: The best source of that information, the judge told Gottlieb behind the bench, was Ron Rother himself. It wasn't coming in through the hearsay testimony of the defendant's best friend. The problem for Gottlieb was that Ron Rother was not available to testify for the defense. As careful observers had deduced, Marty's half sister and brother-in-law had abandoned him.

Gottlieb was, however, finally able to get in some testimony that might refocus the jury's view on Steuerman. Mike and Marianne McClure had been getting daily reports of the trial from Ron Falbee, and in early June they flew in from California to testify about the ten days they and their daughters spent with the Tankleffs in July 1988.

As a lawyer who had tried a number of murder cases himself, Mike had plenty of thoughts about his nephew's trial, but he'd restrained his impulses to tell Gottlieb how to try his case. He limited himself to a seven-page letter recounting pertinent information to which he could personally testify. Most important to Gottlieb was his knowledge of the Steuerman situation. Mike wrote that Seymour told him he had Jerry "by the balls" and would force him to make him a partner in any new bagel stores; that Seymour had Steuerman pay him at the weekly poker game because he liked to make him "kowtow"; and that Seymour became more and more emotionally upset during those two weeks. "At one point I asked him why he was getting so worked up, why didn't he just calm down," Mike wrote. "Seymour responded that he just couldn't, Jerry had upset him because he was trying to screw him."

Gottlieb wanted Mike to relate all that and more on the witness stand, but Tisch ruled that he could testify only about instances in which Seymour told him about specific conversations he'd had with Steuerman. There were two such occasions. In one, Seymour related an angry phone conversation he'd just had with Steuerman about his plan to open a new bagel store with his son. "Seymour said that he told Jerry, '*I'm* your partner. If you're opening another bagel store, you're opening it with *me*. . . .'" The other conversation concerned a phone call a few days later. "Jerry asked him if he could avoid paying him the—either two thousand dollars or twenty-five-hundred dollars—in 'vig,' as Seymour referred to it, and whether he could skip the payments or not pay them for a while. And Seymour told me that he told Jerry, 'I want you to pay me. I want you to pay me weekly. I want it in cash. And I want it in an envelope and I want it at the poker game.' And do you want me to say exactly what he said?"

"Yes, please," said Gottlieb. "With the court's permission."

"Excuse me," Mike said. "He said, 'Jerry, don't fuck with me. I want my payment and I want my money on time.'"

McClure's testimony was the only time Gottlieb was able to convey to the jury a sense of the kind of pressure Seymour was exerting on Steuerman prior to the murders. Seymour discussed the situation with numerous other people, but none could recall him relating any specific conversations with Steuerman that would be admissible under the hearsay exception granted by Tisch. Paul Lerner could not testify about all the things Seymour told him at the golf course and the racetrack; Ron Falbee could not testify about Seymour's growing mistrust of Steuerman; Frank Norberto could not testify that Seymour told him he was "scared of this guy"; and Jan Drexler could not testify how upset Seymour was when he told her that Arlene was insisting he put more pressure on Steuerman. And Mike Fox, who knew more than anyone else, couldn't have testified to any of it.

ASIDE FROM providing a glimpse of the tensions between Seymour Tankleff and Jerry Steuerman, Mike McClure's appearance had another purpose. He was one of several people Gottlieb put on the stand to counter the image of Marty created by the prosecution, and because the McClures spent a period of concentrated time with the Tankleffs just a month and a half before the murders, Gottlieb also called Marianne and Jennifer.

"They were a great family," Mike said of Marty and Arlene and Seymour. Marianne recalled a moment during the July visit when she and her sister talked about how they felt about their children. "And without saying what Arlene said," Gottlieb asked—hearsay, again—"can you please tell us what you said?" "I said that my relationship . . ." Marianne began, then suddenly broke into tears. "Excuse me. . . . My relationship with my daughter was one of the purest and most honest I've ever had. And that's how we felt about our children."

"And that's how you felt about your children?" Gottlieb echoed, hoping the jury would properly infer that Arlene felt the same way about Marty as Marianne felt about Jennifer.

"Yeah," Marianne said, still sniffling.

The McClures testified to Marty's devotion to family. Jennifer talked about how attentive her cousin was during their visit, how nice a time he showed her and her younger stepsister, Christy. They testified to his industriousness. He was already at his job at the bagel store before they were up and they marveled at how much he did around the house—anything to help out, what with Uncle Seymour's health not being too great. They testified to Marty's contentment with his car. "We were in his car driving home," Jennifer recounted, "and I said, 'Don't you wish you had a smaller car?' Because it was so big. It was like driving a boat. And he said, 'No, because this is safer. My mom feels better with me in this car.'" Did he ever complain about his father restricting him from using the Boston Whaler?

Never, said Jennifer. In fact, "Uncle Seymour encouraged Marty to take us around on the boat."

The car and the boat were, by necessity, as much a recurring theme of the defense case as they were of the prosecution's. It was an element of the testimony by several of Marty's friends who followed the McClures to the stand. "We basically spent the whole summer together. We did everything together," said Mark Perrone, and "since I didn't have a car, we used his car all the time, wherever we went." How did Marty feel about his car? "He wanted to fix it up, mint it out, meaning making it perfect, you know, fixing it up totally, complete."

"What if any complaints did Marty ever make about his car?" Gottlieb asked.

"He never made any complaints about his car," Mark said.

Like most of Marty's peers who found themselves in the unnerving position of testifying in his murder trial, Mark was uneasy on the stand, straining to conduct himself properly. He referred to his best high school friend as "Martin," and said he and his parents had "a very loving and caring relationship." What sort of tone did Marty use when he spoke to them? "In a tone that was very loving and caring, like I said."

Gottlieb employed Mark in his effort to portray Marty as being physically incapable of inflicting the injuries that took the lives of his parents. "We used to fool around and wrestle once in a while, and he never won, put it that way," Mark said. "And one time I threw him in the pool because he was trying to Saturday-morning-karate on me and it didn't work. And then there was another time when we went out fishing in the tournament. I got a fish on and I gave the pole to him and he couldn't reel it in. So my father took the pole and reeled in the fish." Marty had so much trouble reeling in the bluefish, Mark's father added during his own testimony, "If we would have waited any longer, the fish could have grown up to be the winner of the contest, I'm telling you!" He broke into an uproarious laugh, then stopped abruptly as if suddenly realizing where he was.

Gottlieb asked Zach Suominen about Marty's strength. They lifted weights together once or twice, Zach said, and Marty was pretty weak. "I would say towards wimpy and being embarrassed, not wanting to work out."

The night before the Tankleffs were attacked, Zach went with Marty to the Smith Haven Mall to get a fuse for the car stereo Marty was putting into his Lincoln, and to pick up some last-minute clothes for school. Marty's demeanor, according to Zach: "Average, friendly, casual. Typical Marty."

On the way to the mall, Marty wanted to stop at the Perrones'; they had just come back from a canoeing trip. "He wanted me to come out and see his nose job," said Frank. "And he wanted to see my truck that I sunk." He had been pulling the canoe out of the water, he explained, but forgot to pull the emergency brake on his truck. "It went down the side of the mountain into the river. So Marty wanted to see the fish and the seaweed and all. They were kidding me, Marty and Zach and Mark."

Mark didn't want to go to the mall, so Marty and Zach went on to pick up Zach's girlfriend, Margaret Barry. She lived around the corner from Marty and had been a classmate since elementary school. "Happy, friendly, talkative," Margaret said when Gottlieb asked her to describe Marty as he drove to Smith Haven Mall on the night before the first day of their senior year at Earl L. Vandermeulen High.

Marty got what he needed at Radio Shack and picked up a pair of slacks at Pants Plus. "To me they were like preppy and funny looking," Zach said, "but, for Marty, I guess, they were regular." Marty's mood when they left the mall? Still "friendly and comical, you know," said Zach. "Same as it was throughout the evening," according to Margaret. Same as it was in all the years she'd known him.

Returning from the mall, Marty dropped Zach off first. "Could you do me a favor?" Zach recalled Marty asking him as he got out of the car. "Can you call my mom and tell her I'm on my way?" He had told her he'd be home between eight and nine. Marty headed back up to Belle Terre and dropped Margaret off. "I said thanks," Margaret said, "and he said, 'No problem. See you tomorrow.'"

CHAPTER 24

Make No Mistake

ON JUNE 20, after the last of fifty-seven witnesses had been heard and the lawyers were set to deliver their summations to the jury, Shari and Ron Rother made their first appearance at the trial. They had stood with Marty at his arraignment the day after his arrest and they had taken him home from jail a month later. But because they were potential witnesses, they had been barred from the courtroom during the trial. As it turned out, neither was called to testify.

With her pink leather skirt and black fishnet stockings, Shari was hard to miss as she and Ron strode down the center aisle of the gallery and sat in the front row of the left side—the side opposite the rest of the family. But what she wore was less remarkable than whom she was with. She and her husband walked into the courtroom with Jim McCready.

Though they hadn't testified, Shari and Ron had played a central role in the prosecution's effort, late in the trial, to bolster its case by suggesting that Marty had fought with his father the afternoon before his parents' murders. Shari had told Collins that her father came to her house with Marty and quarreled about college, and that Seymour complained that he was fed up with Marty. "Arlene's had him long enough," Shari quoted her father saying, and "now I'm taking control." Then, halfway through the trial, Pete Cherouvis, the Pete of Pete & Al's auto repair and Getty station and an old friend of Ron Rother's, told the prosecutors that on September 6, Seymour and Marty brought the Lincoln into his service station and argued about the car while they were there.

Marty was baffled when Collins used this information in his cross-examination but instead of denying the incidents outright, he simply answered the prosecutor's questions, as he'd been instructed by his attorney.

Collins asked Marty if he recalled these incidents. Marty said he didn't recall them at all. Now, with the defense having rested, Collins was permitted to bring in rebuttal witnesses. Shari and Ron would have been an obvious call—if not for the specter of Gottlieb cross-examining them about the two or three million dollars they stood to gain from Marty's conviction. That left Pete Cherouvis.

"The car had an offensive exhaust noise on it, and they dropped it off for me to look at," Cherouvis testified. He determined that the exhaust system had a broken manifold, and when Seymour and Marty came back in the afternoon he told them it would be a big job. "And Seymour turned around and said, 'Well, it's only going to be for another couple of months or so. Leave it be.'" Marty's reaction, according to Cherouvis: "He told his father that he didn't want to drive that 'piece of shit' to school." Seymour got "flustered" and "red-faced," which was "out of character for him," and finally told Marty to "go sit the fuck outside."

To the defense camp, it all had the whiff of a setup. Collins had done little to corroborate the gripes he claimed to be Marty's motives. Now, after the defense rested, along came Pete Cherouvis to say that Marty and Seymour had a big fight about his car just the day before the murders.

"And you first spoke to the detectives about this information back in 1988?" Gottlieb asked Cherouvis on cross-examination.

"No, sir," said Cherouvis.

"Then you spoke to them in 1989, correct?"

"No, sir."

When, then?

About a month ago, Cherouvis conceded.

Gottlieb asked him whether other customers of his, besides the Rothers, were involved in this trial. Jerry Steuerman? "Yeah, Jerry," Cherouvis said. And did he know the district attorney, Jim Catterson? "About fifteen years," Cherouvis figured, and he considered him a friend. Catterson gave him a personal reference when he was starting his business. And did he ever discuss the Tankleff case with Mr. Catterson? "I think I remember at one point speaking to Mr. Catterson but it was very early on in the investigation." Wasn't it odd, Gottlieb suggested through his questioning, that Cherouvis never mentioned to anyone, including Catterson, that on the day before Marty Tankleff was said to have murdered his parents for reasons that included his dissatisfaction with his car, father and son fought about that very car right in front of him?

Gottlieb exposed another hole in Cherouvis's story: He said the Lincoln had been noisy since Seymour bought the car and that by September it was so loud and "offensive" that Marty could have gotten a ticket for it. Yet in all the interviews conducted by the homicide squad, no one mentioned that the notorious Lincoln was in obvious need of an exhaust repair. Anticipating Cherouvis's testimony, Gottlieb had asked Zach Suominen and Margaret Barry, who were in the car with Marty three hours after the alleged visit to Pete's garage, whether the car had a noisy exhaust problem. None at all, they testified. And finally, there was this: Cherouvis said that the reason Seymour didn't want to repair the car was that he was planning to replace it. In fact, Cherouvis himself told Marty that the Lincoln was only temporary, that he was planning to go with his father to an auto auction to get something a little sportier.

GOTTLIEB WAS RELIEVED that Shari and Ron Rother didn't testify for the prosecution, but he knew that Collins had another way to use them against Marty—in his summation. "Judge, I just want to make sure that there would be no reference to any witness not being called by the defense," he said in Tisch's chambers before the summations. He was concerned not only about Shari and Ron, but about Mike Fox.

"Well," said Collins, "I intend to do that up, down, left, and right."

"Judge, I believe that's reversible error," Gottlieb said, asserting that the law in this circumstance barred Collins from implying in his summation that it was suspicious that the defense didn't call a particular witness. But Tisch waved him off. "He's perfectly entitled," said the judge. In that case, said Gottlieb, he intended to object to it.

By procedure, the attorneys delivered their summations in the opposite order of their opening statements. By nature, they delivered them in the diametrically opposing styles to which the jury and the gallery and those watching on television had become accustomed. Gottlieb was passionate, painstaking, and indignant. Collins was methodical, steadfast, and highly selective about the evidence.

"An incredible failure"—that was the district attorney's case, Gottlieb told the jury. Over the next two hours, he recounted and emphasized all the evidence that showed the prosecution to be misguided from the very beginning.

He played the tape of Marty's 911 call—as Collins had on the first morning of the trial—and asserted, "That conversation—the way he sounds, what he says, how he says it—that's reasonable doubt right there." But not just the panic and the fear and the sobs. "What strikes you is that he is frantic and getting help for one person. The entire call is about his father. . . . If this 911 call was all part of the cover-up, part of his grand scheme to fake out the police, he would be saying, 'My God, I just found my mother, both of them, they're bleeding, somebody give me help.' He wouldn't just happen to leave out any mention of his mother."

Gottlieb recalled McCready's memorable line, that anyone would be "a box of rocks" if they found their parents as Marty said he found his. "That was Detective McCready's attempt to serve as an amateur psychologist. He knows—he *knows*—how every single person should appear." And he made his instant and irrefutable judgment without worrying about how Marty might have appeared in the hour and a half before he got there. Or what his normal temperament might be. "You saw Marty testify," Gottlieb said, trying to bring the jury to his view of Marty's composure on the stand. "You saw a person under incredible stress, a defendant in a murder case charged with killing his parents."

It wasn't unreasonable for the police to initially suspect Marty, Gottlieb acknowledged, and he wasn't here to say that they set out to frame an innocent boy. "But there is more to any investigation, and there's more to your job," he told the jury, "than just suspecting or feeling or having a gut reaction. Because later their quick assumption, their quick conclusion, once the facts were learned, proved to be wrong. One by one, the blocks that their case was built on began to crumble. . . .

"*But Marty, you have blood on your shoulder.* Of course there would be blood on his shoulder." He helped his father—and if really did take a shower to cover up his crimes, he wouldn't have missed a splotch of blood right on the front of his shoulder. The prosecution would argue that the blood on his shoulder, hands and forearms, ankle and calf wasn't *enough* blood. But the rescue workers and uniformed police all said the blood on Seymour was mostly dry. Ethel Curley said it was coagulated—recall the image of a clump falling to the floor with such a thud that she thought it was a piece of equipment. Moreover, there was no testimony that the rescue workers themselves got blood on them. This not only explained why Marty didn't get more blood on him but indicated that his parents were attacked much earlier than the prosecution claimed—closer to the end of the poker game. "So that is also a piece of the puzzle that begins to show you: Wait a second. They're wrong. He's right. . . .

"And what happens in that interrogation room is so disgraceful and so reprehensible that yes, it should send shivers down your spine. What the prosecution calls a confession is ultimately shown to be nothing more than the detectives' own version of what they believe had happened earlier that morning in the house." And the story they fed him was a lie from beginning to end: "Consider this: At 5:35, they would have Marty waking up. He walks out of the room." Gottlieb began pacing back and forth, gesticulating. "We have Marty going in with dumbbells, Marty hitting his mother, running out to the kitchen, getting a knife, coming back in, viciously slashing, stabbing his mother, running out, going to the father, pausing at the door at the father's office, standing there nude with the dumbbells behind his back, his father saying, 'Marty, what are you doing?' Come back in, go to the father, hit the father with the dumbbells, take the knife, slash the father's throat. Time is ticking away. From there, what do you have to do? Well, now you have to clean up. Therefore, you have to ditch the murder weapons, then you have to go in the shower, you have to wash yourself off. . . . Not only that, you have to clean up the bathroom, you have to dry the bathroom. . . . You have to go through the house, clean it up, make sure there's no blood around, even between the rooms, and then you can call 911 at 6:10. Ladies and gentlemen, that's absurd. It didn't happen. Their own testimony defeats their claim of a truthful confession."

The presumed murder weapons: "McCready had been in the house and saw knives, saw dumbbells. He was trying to quickly piece together this case." But while the confession talked alternatively about dumbbells and barbells, by the time they got to trial McCready and Rein and Collins were talking specifically about the *bar* part of the dumbbells. That's because the dumbbells came up clean. "So they grab the bar and torture themselves to say it had to be *this* part of the bar. But even there you know that can't be, because the bars are also tested for any signs of blood, human tissue." The same went for the watermelon knife. "Surely some blood would have seeped underneath the wood. Nothing. Clean. That's a problem for them." And so was what the crime lab *did* find. "The detectives didn't know about the watermelon on the knife on September 7. They only learn about it later. So they blew it here again. This murder weapon they have Marty admitting to using cannot be the murder weapon. It's a lie. It's what they assumed. They were wrong."

Something else that didn't fit: "They have Marty, after committing these murders, going into that bathroom, hopping into that shower and washing everything off." But there was no blood or tissue in the drain, and the entire tub area was completely dry—as was Marty's hair. "My hair might dry faster than others because it's thin," Gottlieb said. "Look at Marty's hair. If he had just washed his hair, it would still be wet when the police officers first arrived. They all described it as dry. . . .

"Rubber gloves. You heard a confession that they want you to rely on because it's truthful. At any time, according to their testimony, did Marty say, 'By the way, I also used rubber gloves'? Nothing about rubber gloves. Why? Because they didn't know anything about rubber gloves yet." Not until the crime lab told them. So then they went back to the scene to search for gloves. They couldn't find them. Something else from the forensic scientists: They found some of Seymour's blood mixed in with Arlene's in the bedroom—after they had Marty saying he killed his mother first, then his father, never went back in the bedroom, then showered off?

"So now they are forced to settle for, 'Here, Marty confessed.' But all the details are lies. So don't believe the details. Believe, 'Yeah, I did it.' And believe the motives they attributed to him. He was angry that Dan Hayes was coming to stay with him. Except that Hayes himself blew that one out of the water. He's unhappy with his car. But how did he spend the afternoon before? Putting in a new stereo system in time for the first day of school. Greed? That's absurd. He wasn't wanting for anything. And recall, on direct examination, they said Marty started talking about the will and the inheritance. As if moments after his father is brutally assaulted and his mother's dead, he's talking about the will. But on cross-examination, they admitted they were the ones posing the questions: 'Marty, what happens if your parents died and Jerry Steuerman is out of the picture?' They're setting him up. Is the prosecution really going to argue that the rage is building all day leading to the brutal murder?" He was joking around, regular Marty. Rage? Dropping Zach Suominen off after the trip to the mall, Marty asked him to do him a favor when he got inside: Call his mom and tell her he was on his way home. When he got home, he came into the card game and gave his father a kiss hello.

Try to imagine it, Gottlieb told the jurors: "You're Marty Tankleff, you're seventeen, you've led a sheltered life, you love your mother and father, you grow up respecting the police, and you wake up for the first day of school to that horror. You believe it's a nightmare. You're alone. You're a sitting target to two very experienced, tough, calloused detectives. You think you are helping them. You're in the interrogation room and it's ten-by-ten, there are no windows, the door's closed. They're firing questions at you, they're making comments, they're telling you it's absurd, it's ridiculous. Do this do that, draw the diagram. The questioning picks up, the pace picks up, it becomes confrontational. They start asking you questions about your sweatshirt: 'When did you put the sweatshirt on, did you roll up the sleeves? How did you get the blood there?' One detective, McCready, is yelling. He's jabbing his finger. He's intimidating. He says: 'I don't believe you.' The other detective, Rein, is nicer, he's soft-spoken. He has training in hostage negotiations. . . . 'Marty, you're lying. Marty, we don't believe you. Because we found your hair in your mother's hands. Marty, we know you're lying about when you took a shower. We did a humidity test, Marty.' These are lies, but Marty doesn't know it because it's coming from the detectives, people he respects, people he trusts. And it goes on and on, and you've been at it since 6:10 A.M. And then suddenly McCready walks out and you hear him place a phone call, and while he's out, Rein, who you like and respect, he comes over to you and he sits close to you and he puts his hands on your knees. 'Marty, I don't believe you.' It's devastating. And then McCready walks back in. He comes up to Marty and points his finger and says: Marty, that was the hospital. And they pumped your father full of adrenaline, and he woke up, Marty, and he said you beat and stabbed him. That's what they say to Marty Tankleff when he's at his weakest. That's his *father*. He *loved* his father. He *respected* his father. And these detectives are looking him right in the eye and they're pointing their fingers. And Rein didn't even know it was a trick. It was that convincing. And what becomes important is that Marty doesn't then say: 'All right, you got me. I'll tell you everything.' Marty's comments and questions reflect the turmoil he was in. 'I'll take a lie detector test.' And they refused to give him a lie detector test. And then the transition. 'Could I have blacked out? Could I be possessed? Could it have been another Marty Tankleff?' And even the later comments to Shari—'I need psychological help'—underscore that turmoil and that doubt, where he's trying to reconcile what he's being told is the truth and what he knows to be true."

If you think this was an honest, professional attempt to get the truth, Gottlieb told the jury, consider one small piece of the detectives' testimony. "After the interrogation's completed, he's given *Playboy* by them. They set him up. Let's give him *Playboy*. And isn't this cute, now we can come into court before a jury and say, Look at that—a boy who lost his parents and he's reading *Playboy*. That's a setup, and it's offensive."

Finally, if they were still looking for reasonable doubt after all that, Gottlieb told the jurors: When you consider whether this case was investigated professionally—whether, in fact, it was investigated at all—think of Jerry Steuerman. Immediately, the police were told—not only by Marty, but by Mike Fox and Ron Rother, among others—that Jerry Steuerman should be their leading suspect. He owed Seymour a lot of money—a big payment was due that very week. There had been threats. How could they not check this out before rushing to judgment? How could Marty Tankleff be a more likely suspect than Jerry Steuerman at that point—let alone the *only* suspect?

Gottlieb went through all the evidence with obvious relish, as if delivering his second closing. *Reasonable doubt?* Steuerman owed Seymour Tankleff a ton of money at larcenous interest rates, and now he's being squeezed. "You hear, if I may, that Seymour Tankleff said to Jerry, 'Don't fuck with me.' It's getting hot. Was Jerry Steuerman reaching the breaking point? You bet he was. The problem, he said, was that 'Seymour thought he owned one-half of *me*.' Do you want to talk about motive? You hear that Jerry Steuerman handcuffed himself to Merrill Lynch over three thousand dollars. What would he do for *half a million* dollars?" *Reasonable doubt?* He was the last to leave the poker game—remember how he waved Joe Cecere around him, and that Cecere never saw his headlights behind him. Steuerman's alibi, his daughter Bari, "is lame, so convenient." The next day, Steuerman cleans out the bank account he shared with the Tankleffs and a week later he vanishes. Why would he flee, even if he were guilty, when he knows Marty's under arrest and they're saying he confessed, when he knows the doctors don't think Seymour's going to make it? Why does he wait a week to take off? Both questions had the same answer: Seymour's not dying so fast. The days go by: Thursday, Friday, the weekend, Monday, Tuesday. "This is going wrong. I better get out of town fast, and I better look as if I'm dead, too." When they find him in California, "they treat him like lost royalty out there." They still avoided the obvious questions. They didn't even bother looking at his business documents until the trial.

"Why?" Gottlieb asked. "Because they had gone too far. They had arrested Marty. They told the world they had a confession. They announced that Steuerman was not a suspect. They were boxed in. And that's unacceptable. They should have said: 'Maybe we made a mistake. Maybe we got the wrong guy.' But they refused to do that. They didn't have the sense, they didn't have the professionalism once they got the truth, once they got the forensic reports, to say: 'Time out. Let's take a fresh look.' They didn't have it within themselves to do that. And the consequences of that have been tragic and frightening."

There remained so many unanswered questions. Why was Arlene killed? She was closely involved with all of Seymour's business. Why was Marty *not* killed? "There was no need to kill him. But let's go further. To make sure he's sleeping, they go in and they're wearing rubber gloves and they touch the light switch and they open the light and they see that Marty is sleeping in his cubbyhole in the cave there. He's asleep, everything's okay. Or they're prepared to kill him but something happens, they hear some noise, we're here too long, they leave. Anything could have happened. You don't know. You can't speculate. But it's not our obligation to prove anything.

"The entire investigation by the homicide detectives got off on the wrong foot because of their snap, erroneous conclusions, and everything they did after that was to justify their initial mistakes, their initial decision to arrest Marty and tell the world that they had a confession. What a nightmare." The nightmare began at 6:10 that morning, and it wasn't over yet, nearly two years later.

"No one can bring back Marty's mom and dad or erase those images from his mind," Gottlieb said. "But, please, let him finally grieve in the open, out from under the cloud of being accused, of being thought of as the person who killed his parents. He's innocent. Marty is innocent. . . . I ask that you do your duty. And I ask you to see that justice for Marty, his family, and for us all, sees the light of day in this court."

*　　*　　*

GOTTLIEB HAD USED two words—"incredible failure"—to describe the prosecution's case. John Collins had two words of his own: "common sense." That is all you need, he told the jurors, to see that the credible evidence proves the defendant guilty. "Not speculation, not maybe coulda. The evidence. Your common sense will tell you that during the early morning hours of September 7, 1988, someone did not just drop out of the sky and commit the savage attacks on Seymour and Arlene Tankleff, and leave this defendant blissfully asleep in the room across the hall. Your common sense tells you that you do not admit to crimes such as these after a minimal amount of confrontational questioning unless you did it." The prosecutor had one word for the defense contention that the confession was coerced and false: "preposterous."

Collins reminded the jurors that he had spent considerable time during their selection three months earlier addressing "the very old, very basic difficulty in getting past the hurdle that a human child, adopted or not, could be capable of anything such as this." That's what the defense is relying on, he asserted. "Whatever we all wish or hope is true, make no mistake. It happens. It's happened continually through history. Unfortunately, it's going to continue to happen. For God sake, there are nursery rhymes, chants, rope jumping songs about Lizzie Borden and her ax and she gave her mother forty whacks and when she saw what she had done she gave her father forty-one. It's a fact."*

With that, Collins embarked on the substance of his summation, but not by reviewing the evidence he had presented to support his case. Brazenly, he began by virtually suggesting to the jurors that, whatever they might have heard, the burden of proof was on the defense. "The defendant and the defense in the opening statement promised to deliver you certain things," he said. "I submit that they have not done that—"

"Objection, Your Honor," Gottlieb interrupted. Tisch told Collins he could keep going, so long as he stuck to commenting about the evidence.

"You were promised by the defense in their opening statement," Collins continued, "that you would hear from family and friends as regards to the loving relationship between the defendant and his parents. Let's take a look at who did testify. With all due respect to the McClure family, their testimony can be summed up in four words: *Ten days in July. Ten days in July. Ten days in July.* They live in California. You heard from

---

* Other facts about that 1893 case: Lizzie Borden, a thirty-two-year-old woman, was acquitted after just an hour of deliberations by a jury that found overwhelming reasonable doubt—despite so much prejudicial national publicity that the case became known as America's first trial-by-media. The famous jump-rope verse was composed by a newspaper writer who greatly inflated the number of whacks to get it to rhyme.

the defendant's cousin Jennifer, who testified about some activities that occurred during the summer of 1988. But she also testified to you that even upon her questioning the defendant if he would wish for a nicer or sportier or a smaller car—I think the word might have been 'smaller'—that even upon being asked that, and she used the word 'wish,' the defendant said no. Overjoyed with this '78 Lincoln. I submit to you that that just does not have the ring of truth and you cannot credit or give such weight to that testimony." One more thing about the McClures: "The only person to have shown any emotion or any grief in this courtroom for the last twelve weeks was Mrs. McClure. Now, that says a lot, but it doesn't say it about her.

"You heard from Mr. and Mrs. Perrone, two obviously very nice people. However, they didn't know Seymour and Arlene Tankleff. . . . Their impressions all come from him"—Collins pointed to Marty—"and he's a liar." As for the Perrones' son, Mark, and Marty's other friends: "What seventeen-year-old has, in the words of his peers, a 'loving and joyful relationship' with his parents? What seventeen-year-old on this earth has no complaints about anything? That's all seventeen-year-olds do."

Exactly, thought many in the defense camp.

Collins eagerly pointed out what happened when he cross-examined Marty's friends. "Mark Perrone admitted telling the defense investigator that the defendant was a light sleeper and came in and told you folks on direct examination moderate to heavy. Why? Because it's important to the defendant. Zachary Suominen told you, I believe, that the defendant is always prompt. We heard about two times that the defendant was out with Zachary Suominen, once at the mall and once on the boat. Both times he was late." (Apart from its irrelevance, the citation of evidence was inaccurate: Zachary actually said Marty was "usually" prompt.)

Collins also found great significance in the memories of Marty and his friends about how long they spent at the mall that night twenty-two months ago. "The defendant told you in his testimony that he went between 5:30 and six o'clock with Zach to pick up Margaret Barry and that they went to the mall until 9:10. Margaret Barry says they didn't get there until 7:30 and spent approximately an hour and a half, two hours there. Zachary Suominen says that it was four hours and they left at five o'clock. When confronted with their prior statements, they didn't come around, they didn't even admit maybe having said that before, 'but I think my recollection is different now.' It's like, 'I don't recall saying that.'"

Though apparently confounded by how long Marty and his friends spent at the mall, Collins offered no relevance between their imprecise recollections and what happened the next morning, and hence why they would be motivated to lie about it. The one thing they were all consistent about, in any event, was that they left the mall around nine.

You heard from the relatives from California, Collins told the jury, but "where were the family members that saw and talked to the defendant that day? Where were Uncle Norman and Aunt Ruth?"

"Objection."

"Overruled."

"Where was the favorite Aunt Marcella from Nassau County? Where were Ron and Carol and their children, Carolyn and Susanne, with whom the defendant now lives?"

"Geez, Your Honor, *objection.*"

"Overruled."

"Where was Uncle Mike? Not Uncle Mike McClure who came from California. Where was Uncle Mike Fox from Garden City, Seymour's attorney and family friend for thirty years who's known the defendant since he's two days old? Where was the defendant's sister and brother-in-law from Port Jefferson, Shari and Ron Rother? And the nephew and the niece who was the apple of Seymour's eye? Where were these folks who had regular contact with the Tankleffs and with the defendant? Why did we have to sing three verses of 'Ten Days in July'? Maybe all was not so well—"

"*Objection.*"

"—in the paradise the defendant would have you believe was his home."

"Overruled."

"If the police are lying, as the defendant would have you believe, then where was Mike Fox, the attorney, to come in here and tell you that he and the defendant did not speak or exchange greetings in the street? Where was he to tell you that the police misled him? Where was he to tell you that he gave that business card to Detective McCready on the street that morning because he was there to represent the defendant?

"We did hear from the defendant himself. You got an interesting opportunity to not only observe his conduct and his demeanor here during the trial but you got a firsthand look at the real Martin Tankleff here in this courtroom. Ask yourselves, after you review that testimony in your own minds, was that a malleable, trusting, and powerless and truthful young man? Was that a son consumed by the loss of his quote-unquote 'best friends' that took the stand before you? Or were his demeanor and answers more consistent with an intelligent, cold, and self-centered person with a convenient and selective memory?"

Gottlieb had found layers of exculpatory evidence in the 911 tape, but

Collins encouraged the jurors to keep it simple. "The defendant appears to sound upset or frantic," he said, "but isn't it amazing how Mrs. Flanagan's able to just bring him out of it, get the instructions across? They have a calm exchange. Remarkable." He laid out a timeline that he argued didn't add up: Marty couldn't have done all the things he said between the 911 call and the arrival of the ambulance about five minutes later.

Collins tried to discredit, as well, Marty's account of the moments *before* the 911 call. Though Gottlieb had made the case—based on the testimony of Collins's own witnesses—that the blood on and around Seymour was largely dry when Marty called 911, he asked how it was that none of the blood was smeared. "How is it that the telephone cord remains intact with the blood spatter all facing forward, indicating, as Detective Kosciuk told you, that the cord had not been disturbed from the original position when the blood hits the cord? All the while doing this in the course of this frantic phone call, reaching around his father." But there had been no testimony that Marty "reached around his father." Collins then demonstrated the game that could be played with forensic testimony, quoting a defense witness, the Stony Brook neurosurgeon George Tyson, way out of context. "Dr. Tyson testified that the one fracture on the right side of Seymour's head was consistent with a fall," Collins said, trying to bolster his assertion that Marty's description of pulling his father out of his chair was not to be believed. After Tyson testified that one of Seymour's skull fractures was somewhat different from the others, Collins had asked him whether it could have been caused by a fall. Tyson replied that it was only "one of several possible explanations for it."

"I called Jerry Steuerman," Collins said, beginning his own second closing, in his role reversal as the alternate suspect's simulated defense attorney. "You had a right to see him. The defense would have you believe that Jerry Steuerman either committed or orchestrated these acts. I submit that after having watched him, I'm sure very carefully, over those three days, you each developed some very definite feelings about him. However, I submit to you that none of you believes that he had anything to do with these attacks. He may have come across as many things. But I submit to you a cold-blooded killer is not one of them. While he did go and pull one of the incredibly stupid stunts of all time and made this case a heck of a lot more complicated than it need have been, his antics do not detract from the proof of the defendant's guilt beyond a reasonable doubt. The defendant would have you believe that Jerry Steuerman or people working at his behest had Seymour and Arlene brutally beaten and their lives taken from them, yet left the defendant, the acknowledged heir, untouched in the next room. It doesn't make sense. I wouldn't lend Jerry Steuerman ten dollars. But it's become obvious that debt is a way of life and a lifestyle for him. He still owes the money. He still owes the estate. And wouldn't you think, based upon the relationship that he had, he had a better chance of working something out with Seymour than he will with Mike Fox?

"These supposed threats by Jerry Steuerman against the Tankleffs or the fears by the family that Jerry was going to do something wicked, to whom did the commissioner of constables report this? Mayor Vinnie Bove? No. Chief Constable Hines? No. The Suffolk County Police Department? No. Why, if those threats were real or there was any legitimate fear, would you have a person such as that in your home? It doesn't make sense. Why, if Jerry was going to do something dastardly that night, why in God's name does he wave Joe Cecere and Al Raskin on so he's the last one there? If he's going to do something, isn't he going to leave and maybe come back later? Why does he wave them on so they can see that he's the last person at the house? Mr. Steuerman was obviously no nuclear physicist, but he's far from that dumb."

As for Marty's accusations that morning: "The defendant knew about the debt. The defendant knew that the friendship was deteriorating. The defendant had been let go from one of his stores." Collins continued on, despite the obvious dishonesty of his logic. "And doesn't a guy who uses an alias like Jay Winston and does things like 'pistachio,' I mean, wouldn't he strike you as a perfect patsy? No, the defendant just didn't anticipate the suspicions that were aroused immediately in people like John McNamara and the detective that responded to the scene. He didn't anticipate Mr. Steuerman having an alibi.

"Trick phone call. Ask yourselves this question: Would that tactic cause a nonguilty person to admit their guilt to a crime such as this? Period. Chief Hines may have unwittingly planted that seed in the defendant's mind when he spoke to him on the street. Remember Chief Hines's testimony, where he's sitting with the defendant in his car . . . and he tells him, 'Don't worry, Marty. There's a police officer that went in the ambulance and he'll be with your father in the event he wakes up.' And at that point the defendant stopped speaking and looked up from his feet and looked Chief Hines straight in the eye with a wide-eyed expression and said nothing further.

"You're also going to be asked to consider the voluntariness of the defendant's statements. . . . He made the diagram of the card players' cars, didn't miss a card player, got them all. He made a diagram of the layout of the house. He participated in the demonstration of how he supposedly gave first aid to his father. You don't have a zombie-like, powerless person participate in a demonstration such as that. . . ."

Now, finally, Collins began dealing with what Gottlieb argued was the fatal flaw in the prosecution's case: the complete inconsistency between Marty's alleged confession and the physical evidence. "No one has come in here and told you that the defendant's statement is completely true," Collins said. "No one has come in here and told you that the defendant's statement is a complete lie. The detectives reported to you what was said to them. The detectives testified that they did not believe all of it, and they thought that there was more coming but they're required to tell you what was said to them. I submit to you that had the detectives not been stopped at 1:22, we would have had more than the portion of the story that we have at this point. . . .

"The defense would like you to believe that none of the information in the defendant's statement has been corroborated. I beg to differ. The defense would also like you to believe that men like Norman Rein, Jim McCready, and Bob Doyle are willing to throw away sixty-five years' worth of police career, all sorts of commendations, and fine, fine careers to come in here and lie to you rather than admit they had made a mistake. If they did not get this information from the defendant, then where the heck did it come from? And if they did make it up, they're two or three of the luckiest sons of guns that ever walked because they came up with head injuries to Arlene Tankleff they didn't know about, they came up with transfers of hair that they couldn't possibly have known about at that point in time."

Though he didn't elaborate about "transfers of hairs," Collins was apparently referring to a finding by the county's forensic hair and fiber analyst that was later refuted by an expert from Chicago who testified for the defense. The defense expert, Richard Bisbing, explained in detail how his prosecution counterpart did only a cursory examination of a bloody clump of hairs found near Seymour and incorrectly determined that some of Arlene's hairs were mixed with his. As for Collins's claim that the detectives didn't know about Arlene's head injuries, this was contradicted by McCready's own testimony: He said he observed Arlene's body close-up during his initial walk-through, as any homicide detective would have, and recounted how he challenged Marty at one point by telling him, "I had to stand right over her to see" that her throat had been cut.

Collins offered nothing else to explain why he "begged to differ" with the defense's assertion that the physical evidence revealed the details of the murders to be a fabrication. "I submit to you that it's the defendant who's lying," he said resolutely, coming to the defense of McCready, Rein, and Doyle once more. "And I submit to you, based on what you've seen here in this courtroom, that if you were unfortunate enough to have something like this happen in your family you'd be damned glad to see those three guys show up. . . .

"How is the defendant's confession corroborated?" Collins continued. "Discord in the house. Dissatisfaction with the car. The Goldschmidt girls, if you recall, didn't even come forward until March of '89. . . . Peter Cherouvis, who came forward only a week or so ago. How would the detectives know these people were going to come out of the woodwork? Are they clairvoyant?"

More corroboration, according to Collins: "The mother mad at the defendant that night." There was no testimony supporting this statement. Rather, Collins's basis was that Zach Suominen said Marty asked him to call his mother and tell her he was on his way home, and that Margaret Barry said Zach later told her he forgot to make the call. *Obviously*, Marty's mother would have been angry at him for being late, and *obviously* they would have fought about it. Collins's circular logic was that this corroborated the defendant's statement to the detectives that his mother was angry with him when he returned home. "How do they know about these events?" Collins said of McCready and Rein.

"What did the defendant tell the police that only the killer could have known? The defendant told Detectives Rein and McCready that even after he beat and stabbed his mother she was still moving." The pattern of blood in the room is "indicative of Arlene having been moving around in the course of this attack. You and I didn't know that until the doctor told us that." (But McCready and Rein knew it before they entered the interview room.)

The forensic evidence pointed to a single killer, Collins argued, notwithstanding the absence of any blood between the two crime scenes. He reminded the jury that Marty had a tissue with a spot of blood consistent with his mother's. "The defendant would have you believe that somehow, some way he managed to pick up the only stray spot of blood in the house on that tissue. That should offend your intelligence and your common sense. The chain link and honeycombed glove prints put the killer in the defendant's room without question. . . . I submit to you he lived in that room. There are just too many forensic coincidences. Either everybody else is lying or the defendant is lying.

"The bottom line is that the defendant was not as smart as he thought he was. He thought he was smarter than the cops and he thought he was smarter than his neighbors, and I submit to you that two weeks ago he thought he was smarter than you. The problem is, his story started to unravel as early as the conversations in the street with John McNamara, Don Hines, and Vinnie Bove, and it just unraveled further and further as the day went on.

"For God's sake, and for Seymour and Arlene's sake, use your common sense. We've had a trial here that has encompassed both Mother's Day and

Father's Day. Let's not forget whose rights were violated here. Go ahead, please, do your duty, deliberate and come back with the one reasonable verdict that's consistent with the credible evidence, and I submit to you that verdict is guilty."

THERE ARE NO rebuttals of summations, so Gottlieb could not say another word to the jury. But he had a few to say to the judge. At six o'clock that evening, he and Collins followed Tisch into his chambers, where Gottlieb promptly asked for a mistrial—over the judge's own conduct. He was livid that Tisch had permitted Collins to repeatedly suggest to the jury that the defense had somehow failed to prove *its* case.

"A defendant at no time is required to do anything, to rebut anything, to present any witnesses," Gottlieb told Tisch, fuming that he had to state something so obvious. "Your allowing the prosecutor to ask over and over and over again why the defendant didn't call this witness or that witness, allowing the prosecutor to imply that it's somehow suspicious that the defendant didn't call Shari Rother or Mike Fox, is improper. By clear implication the burden at some point shifted to the defendant. That is *grossly* improper." Gottlieb told Tisch that it was unconscionable that Collins had gotten away with insinuating that Shari wasn't called because she would contradict Marty's version of the phone conversation they had on the evening of his arrest. Collins knew that Shari would have confirmed Marty's account because that's what she did at the Huntley hearing.

"It was grossly improper," Gottlieb continued, "for you to allow the prosecution to question why Marcella Falbee was not called, Ron Falbee, Norman Tankleff, when both Your Honor and the prosecution knew darn well that every single one of those individuals was present in the courtroom from the beginning of jury selection." By that Gottlieb meant that most of the family members couldn't have testified. Before the trial, the judge had designated Ron as the only one who could be in the courtroom with Marty and still testify. The judge's ruling left a choice: Keep the rest of the family out so they could testify, or have them in court and let the jury see the support Marty had day in and day out. On balance, Gottlieb didn't think the testimony would necessarily be a net gain. But now, it seemed to him, Collins had cynically, and improperly, used it against Marty. And Tisch had let him do it.

But for all his righteous indignation, Gottlieb knew he was literally going through the motions. All he could really do at this point was create a record for an appeal should things go badly.

"The Court is confident in its rulings," Tisch said when Gottlieb was finished. "I will decline to grant a mistrial."

CHAPTER 25

Eight Days

A JUDGE'S CHARGE to the jury is an overlooked procedure in most high-profile criminal trials. But to jurors, the judge's instructions on the law at the conclusion of testimony is one of the most critical hours of their service.

The judge will explain the difference between direct and circumstantial evidence, discuss the fine points of corroboration and the perils of speculation. He will illuminate legal concepts the jurors may have heard of but never had occasion to think much about: What makes a doubt *reasonable*? How heavy is that *burden of proof* on the prosecution? And the judge will caution the jurors to take nothing from the mouth of either of the attorneys as gospel. The only thing that matters is their own appraisal of the evidence.

When it came time for Judge Tisch to charge the Tankleff jury, his most crucial instructions concerned the many questions swirling around the defendant's alleged confession. To begin with, they could only consider the statements as evidence if they determined they were given "voluntarily," an ambiguous word by legal definition. One thing that could make them involuntary, for instance, was if they were induced by deception or trickery. It was not in dispute that the police used deceit to obtain statements from Martin Tankleff, Tisch told the jurors. What they would have to decide was whether "the deception was so extreme that it offends our notions of fundamental fairness or that the deception could have induced a *false* confession, or that it resulted in the defendant's will being overborne." To make this determination, the jury was to examine all the circumstances—the duration and conditions of the questioning, the "manifest attitude" of the police, and factors such as the defendant's age, intelligence, and mental state. If the prosecution failed to prove that Martin Tankleff gave the statements attributed to him voluntarily, the judge instructed the jurors to disregard them—"strike them from your minds as though you have never heard them"—even if they believed the statements to be truthful.

Left unsaid was that the jury would have to make this judgment based on the conflicting versions of that day offered in testimony. The burden of proof was on the prosecution—but the homicide squad's policy against recording interrogations reduced proof of anything about what went on in that room to the jurors' subjective judgment of whom to believe.

Aside from the relevant legal concepts, the judge had to explain the different ways in which the charges themselves could be defined. Accused in the deaths of two people, Marty Tankleff faced four counts of murder. If the jurors found him guilty of two counts of intentional murder, their work would be done. If they found him not guilty, in either death, they would go on to consider another version of the accusation: murder committed "under circumstances evincing a depraved indifference to human life." This charge was such a complex legal concept that to convict on this count a jury had to find that it satisfied six different requirements, but lawyers commonly illustrated the idea this way: A person walks into a crowd and starts shooting people randomly. His intention might not be to kill any specific person, but by his actions he is recklessly and knowingly creating a grave risk of death to that person. By consciously disregarding that risk, he is exhibiting a depraved indifference to that person's life.

Considering the brutal manner in which the Tankleffs were slain, it would be hard to argue that their murders, regardless of who committed them, were carried out with anything but intent. But the prosecutors wanted to give the jurors an option should they have a hard time believing a seventeen-year-old boy could really mean to kill his parents. The theory Collins expressed in his summation was that Marty did it in a kind of premeditated rage. A theory so broad that it could be considered an oxymoron had to come with more than one option for conviction.

TISCH SENT the jury off to begin its deliberations. Everyone else began the ritual known as jury-sitting.

As Marty and his aunts and uncles and cousins filed out of the courtroom, they saw reporters and television cameras gathering around Jim McCready. He was holding an impromptu press conference to announce something he had clearly been waiting a long time to disclose: For a year and a half, Martin Tankleff's sister and brother-in-law have been "on our side." In fact, he had the exact date of their conversion. On January 4,

1989, he had a long talk with Shari Rother. "I told her to forget about cops and lawyers and question Marty herself. Shari told me, 'I did, and I didn't like the answers I was getting.'"

A *Newsday* reporter went to the Rothers' house in Port Jefferson. Shari wouldn't say directly whether it was true that she thought Marty was guilty, but she indicated that McCready was to believed. "I don't want to make any comments about my support or nonsupport of Marty until the verdict is in," she said. "This whole thing is in the hands of God and those twelve men and women."

The news of Shari's defection was hardly a surprise to Marty or his other relatives. He hadn't spoken to her in more than a year, and it was the opinion of the rest of the family that Shari's betrayal was about just one thing, and that was money. Shari herself made a veiled allusion to this when she told another reporter that her estrangement from Marty was the result of "outside forces that drove a wedge between us." For now, though, "The estate is such an inconsequential thing to me. I don't care about the money."

McCready's hallway news conference was just one more thing for Bob Gottlieb to be upset about. He went to the judge's chambers and told him he was worried that McCready's announcement about the Rothers—and other comments, including his declaration that "none of you standing here right now would ever admit to killing your mother and father if you didn't do it"—could reach the jury, even as it was being sequestered at a motel near the courthouse. "There might be a TV in their room," Gottlieb said. "Or they might walk by a newsstand tomorrow morning and see a front-page headline."

Dismissing the jurors for the evening a few hours later, the judge cautioned them against coming into contact with any media. "The televisions in your rooms will be disabled," he said, "and I would ask you not to undertake any endeavors to try to make them work."

The headline in the next day's *Newsday:* SISTER FEELS TANKLEFF GUILTY, EX-COP SAYS.

"THE JURY WOULD like to know if we can visit the location at 33 Seaside Drive," read the first communication to the judge. It was written by the jury's foreman, Ronald Clipperton. Tisch read the note to the attorneys in his chambers, then handwrote a response: "Regarding your request to visit 33 Seaside Drive, the answer is no. You must decide the issues based on the evidence and exhibits received during the trial." The jury responded by asking for the next-best thing. Tisch had the crime scene video sent in.

On Day 2, the jurors asked to hear the 911 tape again and requested their first readback of testimony: that of the rescue worker Ethel Curley and the parts of the testimony by the county forensic scientists Robert Baumann and Robert Genna about the bloody glove prints on the pillow-cases, pillow sham, and bed sheet in the master bedroom. Trying to read into the jury's requests was an irresistible part of jury-sitting, and some in the defense camp found it encouraging that the jury seemed to be interested in the missing gloves. But Gottlieb cautioned against trying to interpret any of it. Especially the next day, when the jury sent out another note: "Can we hear the testimony of Constable Hines regarding his conversation with Marty while they were seated in Hines' car?"

By the fourth day, tensions were beginning to show. Gottlieb asked Collins to stop saying good morning to the jurors when they passed in the halls. Well, Collins replied, they're saying good morning to me, I'm just saying good morning back. Gottlieb went to the judge. "I'm compelled to go on the record," he said, "and ask that even if the jurors say something, that John not make the type of eye contact where he winds up saying anything to them as they're deliberating."

"Judge, just to keep the record clear," Collins responded, "I did not precipitate any of that contact."

"Okay," Tisch said. "Let's try to keep the contact between counsel and the jurors to a minimum. I'm sure they're all aware that everybody wishes them the best."

The jurors were showing signs of strain, too, and Tisch tried to accommodate them. When one of them kept asking for some baseball news, the judge granted a momentary suspension of the media blackout. "I can tell you that the Mets swept the series against the Phillies," he told the jury during one of its visits to the courtroom for a readback. "We're now two games out of first place."

Back to work, the jury asked to hear Norman Rein's testimony about Marty's demonstration of how he helped his father and then a readback of Marty's testimony in its entirety. They returned to the jury room, emerging a while later to ask the judge to clarify an area of his instructions: Were they allowed to consider their "feelings"? The question seemed to annoy Tisch. "I think I made it abundantly clear the evidence in this case is the testimony and the exhibits," he told them. Later, the jury sent out a note asking, "If we use testimony and exhibits to arrive at a decision, is this speculation?" It might be, Tisch told them, or it might not be.

Late in the day, Tisch summoned the attorneys to his chambers to tell them that one of the two alternate jurors was asking to be released. Pleading, actually. "She's been crying and just really starting to come apart at the seams." He needed the consent of both sides to release her. "I consented the other day," Gottlieb said. "Let her go," said Collins. What made the alternate's departure noteworthy—and unsettling to the defense side—was that she promptly announced that she would have voted to convict had she been a regular juror. "In my own mind, he was guilty," she told a reporter on her way out. Her only elaboration was that she wasn't bothered by Jerry Steuerman.

Gottlieb and the defense camp found that hard to fathom, but they were relieved that the woman had only been an alternate and now she was gone. And they couldn't help thinking about Joseph Fisher and a bar down in Lindenhurst called Frank & Irene's. Fisher had been Juror Number 2 until the day, during the third week of the trial, when allegations surfaced that he had been talking about the case with his fellow patrons at their favorite tavern—and telling them what he thought of the prosecution's case. The source of this information was a secretary in the district attorney's office who said she had heard it from her mother, who sometimes tended bar at Frank & Irene's, and her brother, who patronized it. The secretary told her boss, who told John Collins, who told the judge, who summoned mother and son to court. They told him that Fisher had been making it known that he thought Seymour Tankleff's business partner should be the one on trial, not his son.

When Tisch asked Fisher to explain himself, the juror claimed it wasn't that he was going around talking about the case, but that certain patrons of the bar were constantly trying to bait him into it. He promised the judge he hadn't made up his mind about the case and wouldn't set foot in Frank & Irene's until it was over. But Tisch tossed Fisher and replaced him with the first alternate. It meant that perhaps the strongest pro-acquittal member was no longer on the jury.

On Day 5, the jury wanted to see photos of the bloodstained towel in Marty's bedroom, of the bathtub, of Seymour's chair. They wanted to see the loofah sponge. They asked for readbacks of specific sections of lengthy testimony—a second readback of "Marty's direct testimony regarding his trip through the kitchen, finding his father, up to the point where he says, 'Dad, Dad.'" Perhaps tellingly, they had yet to ask for anything related to Jerry Steuerman.

Marty and his family spent most of their time waiting out the verdict around the van in the parking lot, returning to the courtroom each time there was a note from the jury. The anxiety grew each day, but it was always buffered by a belief that a conviction could not be where they were headed. Ron Falbee recalled, "I watched the whole trial and I said, 'Jesus, this is going to be a slam dunk. They have no evidence.'" Before the McClures arrived from California, Ron called them at the end of each day. Marianne recalled, "It was all positive. 'Steuerman was on the stand today and Bob really got him good.' Then the stuff on the murder weapons being clean. We're all going, 'Great, great. It's looking good.'" Gottlieb encouraged the optimism, unable to remember another case when he felt so strongly about what the verdict *should* be. But he also knew that juries were unpredictable.

Marty himself often seemed to be the calmest one of the group. Of course he was nervous—you just couldn't tell from looking at him. Amazed and even a little curious about Marty's outer tranquility during the trial, Ron Falbee had put his hand on Marty's chest at one stressful point to see what might be going on *inside*. "And his heart was pumping so hard you'd think it was going to explode," Ron said.

Marty recalled, "Everyone felt great after Gottlieb's summation. He had court officers coming up to him, 'That was the best closing I ever heard. I don't see how Marty can be found guilty.' Then one day, two days, three days . . ."

Shortly before lunch hour on Day 5, the jury sent out two notes. The first read: "We need some clarification from the Judge's charge regarding the question of at what point the defendant was actually in custody as compared to the time his rights were read to him." This note buoyed the hopes among the defense. But the second note obliterated them. It asked the judge to repeat "the points that are to be considered in charge one and charge two decisions." When a jury is focused on the differences between intentional and depraved-indifference murder, it usually means it has decided that the defendant is guilty of one or the other. A blood-draining somberness washed over the family as they listened to the judge methodically spell out the elements of the two legal definitions of murder and recite the indictments: ". . . the defendant stabbed Arlene Tankleff, hit her about the head. . . ." It seemed to go on forever, and when the judge was finally done and he sent the jury back into the deliberation room, several of Marty's relatives left the courtroom in tears.

But the jury was not on the verge of a verdict. The notes kept coming for two more days. One said, "Please read back the following if it did occur: Anywhere in Detective McCready's testimony did he state to anyone that he saw barbells in Marty's room on either of his walk-throughs that ended at 8:35 A.M." After he and the lawyers reviewed McCready's testimony, Tisch said he would write "None found" and send the note back in to the jury. Nerves fraying, Gottlieb saw a lack of precision in the response. "You know," he said, "I want it worded, 'Not found one way or the other.'"

"Right," said Tisch. "'Not found.'"

"'Not found *one way or the other*,'" Gottlieb repeated.

"We can't find it," said Collins. "'None found' I think covers it. Doesn't mean it didn't happen. We just can't find it."

"You can't answer that way because it's misleading," Gottlieb insisted.

Tisch suggested: "No testimony with regard to this has been found in McCready's testimony."

"That's better," said Collins.

"That's fine," said Gottlieb.

"Okay," said Tisch.

WEDNESDAY MARKED Day 7. A full week of deliberations. The jury had heard countless readbacks of testimony and asked to see 220 of the 287 exhibits. But the day ended like all the others. Marty thought it meant the jury was doing its job, and that had to be good for him. That night, he baked chocolate chip cookies and Rice Krispies treats for his twin cousins, Carolyn and Susanne.

The next morning, just after eleven o'clock, there was yet another knock from inside the jury room. A court officer opened the door and the foreman handed him the latest note.

"We have reached a verdict," it said.

Word went around like a lit fuse. Marty and his family grouped in one of the legal conference rooms before returning to the courtroom. Carol Falbee called home. Her sister was staying with the twins. The verdict is in, Carol said, so confident that she told her sister to turn on the TV and let the girls watch. And then Carol watched as the weight of the moment finally hit Marty. His much-remarked-upon composure crumbled and he began to sob. Ron put his arm around his young cousin and held him against his chest. Marty cried for several minutes, his tears soaking Ron's shirt. And then he pulled himself together, recovering so quickly that when he arrived in the courtroom he betrayed no hint of his emotional release.

Marty took his seat at the defense table with Gottlieb and his second, Craig Parles. The television camera was in a new place—in the front of the courtroom, looking back. It provided the first head-on shot of Marty, with his family over his shoulders in the first two rows of the gallery. For the first time the defense table was empty: no legal pads, no case files. Marty stared straight ahead, leaning slightly forward, motionless. His hair was in perfect order, as always, though his burgundy tie was slightly askew. The television camera remained trained on him as he and everyone else waited for the judge to return to the bench.

Finally Tisch appeared and made his way to his high-backed leather chair. He sat, shuffled some papers, and looked up. "We've received communication from the jury that they have reached a verdict," he announced for the record. He instructed the court officers to bring the jury in. All eyes were now cast upon the door to the jury room. All but Marty's. He was still staring straight ahead, as if frozen, even when the door opened and the jurors filed in and took their seats. He was afraid to look. Behind him, his relatives sat close—Ron and Carol, Marianne and Marcella, Norman and Ruth, and half a dozen others—bracing themselves and one another, wishing they could reach across the barrier and hold Marty.

"Case on trial, *People versus Martin Tankleff*," said the court clerk, a burly man with the voice of a train station announcer. ". . . Jury, defendant, counsel all present."

"Let the record indicate," Tisch said, prolonging the tension, "we have asked Marguerite Sutton, our remaining alternate, to join in the jury box for the verdict being delivered."

"Ladies and gentlemen of the jury," the clerk said finally, "have you agreed upon a verdict?"

"Yes we have," said Clipperton, the foreman.

"Will the defendant please rise and face the jury? Will the foreman please rise?"

Marty rose slowly, along with his lawyers. He turned toward the jury almost robotically. His eyes were big and full of fear.

"How do you find as to the defendant, Martin Tankleff, as to Count 1, Murder Second Degree?" This count charged him with the intentional murder of his mother.

"Not guilty," said Clipperton, and yelps of joy rang out from the right half of the spectator section. Everyone knew the depraved-indifference count was still to come, but getting past the one charging intent *had* to mean an acquittal. Marty himself didn't react, not even a little.

"How do you find as to the defendant, Martin Tankleff, as to Count 2, Murder Second Degree?"

"Guilty."

Now it was anguished screams that filled the courtroom, and then, a split second behind, Marty's eyes flashed with shock. His face contorted and he broke into a tearless sob.

"How do you find as to the defendant, Martin Tankleff, as to Count 3, Murder Second Degree?"

"Guilty."

Another wave of shrieks from behind. Marty's eyes stayed locked shut, his body shuddering. He gasped for air.

"Number four will not be considered . . ."

Marty fell into his chair and buried his head in his hands. Gottlieb sat, too, staring blankly, his hands folded on the table in front of him. "Poll the jury please," he murmured, barely looking up at the judge.

"Ladies and gentlemen," said the clerk, "harken to your verdict as the court records it. You say that you find the defendant, Martin Tankleff, as to Count 1, Murder Second Degree, not guilty; as to Count 2, Murder Second Degree, guilty; as to Count 3, Murder Second Degree, guilty; Count 4 not considered. So say you all?"

"Yes," the jurors said in unison. "As the court recorded your verdict, Juror Number One," said the clerk, "was that your verdict?"

"Yes," said the foreman.

"Juror Number two, was that your verdict?"

"Yes."

"Juror Number three, was that your verdict?"

"Yes."

And the nine others: Yes. Yes. Yes. Yes. Yes. Yes. Yes. Yes. Yes.

"Ladies and gentlemen," Tisch told the jury, "I wish to thank you for the thirteen weeks that you spent with us. It's been a lengthy trial, lengthy deliberations. It's been a tremendous strain on you all. . . ."

Marty's face was still buried in his hands.

". . . I'm certain that you're all looking forward to going home. I wish, however, to express my appreciation to you for the service that you've` rendered. . . ."

In the first two rows of the gallery, his aunts and cousins sat in stunned disbelief, sobbing. "Impossible," Ron Falbee kept saying, shaking his head, his face ashen, the wind knocked out of him. Carol collapsed into his chest, her face resting in Marty's tears. "I can't believe it," Ron said.

". . . As long as folks such as yourselves are willing to come in here and devote your time, talents, and energies to the administration of criminal justice, I'm sure that our criminal justice system, the finest in the history of the world, will continue to endure."

A pair of sheriff's deputies approached the defense table. One of them asked Marty to stand and empty his pockets. Marty dug into his pants pocket and handed his car keys and wallet to Craig Parles. The deputy handcuffed him behind his back, then led him toward the front of the courtroom. Wails could still be heard as Marty was escorted past the model of the house he grew up in and then disappeared through a door in the corner of the courtroom.

Within minutes, Marty was back at the county jail, exchanging his clothes once again for a jailhouse jumpsuit. "Marty, what are you doing here?" an officer in the property room asked him. "There's no way they could have found you guilty."

Back in the courtroom, Gottlieb made one final motion. The split verdict was inconsistent, he told the judge. The evidence didn't support any conviction, let alone one that concluded that Marty killed his father with intent but his mother with "depraved indifference." Gottlieb asked Tisch to set aside the verdicts "or ask the jury to reconsider." The judge swiftly rejected the request. Collins told reporters afterward that there was nothing inconsistent about the verdicts. "They may well have felt that the situation with the mother occurred first and it somehow got out of hand, and then after having had the situation occur with his mother he then went to intentionally kill his father."

That would seem to be the only logical explanation, and it would later be confirmed by the jurors themselves. But it *was* inconsistent—both with the physical evidence, which showed that Seymour was killed first, and with the prosecution's account of Marty's confession. McCready and Rein said he told them that he went to sleep the night before intending to kill both his parents in the morning. But then, to convict Marty the jury would have had to discount most of what the police said he told them. As several jurors were to say, that's exactly what they did.

Gottlieb and the family went to see Marty in the jail later in the day. They were heartbroken at the sight of him back in that orange jumpsuit, sitting across from them in that miserable visiting room. We've got a strong appeal, Gottlieb assured Marty. Nobody's giving up, Ron told him. Neither can you.

Marianne and Jenny drove Marty's car back to Westbury in silence. When they arrived at Ron and Carol's house they saw the tray of chocolate chip cookies and Rice Krispies treats sitting on the kitchen counter. Nobody knew what to do with them. They couldn't eat them. They couldn't throw them away.

AFTER THE VERDICTS, reporters fanned out for reactions. Jerry Steuerman came out of his house and said, "As far as I'm concerned, it's over with. Thank God." *Are you relieved?* "It is an absolutely big relief. It has been a nightmare for this entire family." *How did it feel to be accused by Tankleff's defense?* "I know I didn't do it. Even if Marty would have been found innocent, I never had anything to hide." *Are you bitter?* "I don't think I'm bitter. I feel just sorry for my family that they had to be put through all of this. My life from this trial is an open book. It was rough. I was put through hell." *Any thoughts about Tankleff?* "Marty, he worked for me. He wasn't a stranger. I feel sorry that somebody has to spend fifty years in jail."

A few miles away, Shari Rother finally revealed her thoughts about her brother. Sitting on a sofa, smoking one cigarette after another, she told a *Newsday* reporter that watching the verdict on television, seeing Marty crying, broke her heart. Nevertheless, the jury's decision was "beyond reproach"—and she'd made up her own mind well before hearing it. "I supported my brother from the onset, I believed in his innocence. I still find it inconceivable that he could have been capable of being the instrument of this heinous crime." But she believed that he was. "I guess at some point, perhaps five or six weeks into the trial, I started questioning the evidentiary testimony as being inconsistent with what I had come to believe had happened. It seemed overwhelmingly conspicuous in pointing in one direction." Then Shari, like Steuerman, spoke of the toll all this had taken on her own family: "It will never be behind us. Our lives have changed immeasurably. We can only hope that with time, the hurt lessens."

In a more extensive interview a few months later, Shari and her husband discussed how their thinking evolved between Marty's arrest and conviction. They said they began having doubts during the two and a half months he lived with them. He seemed too unaffected by his parents' murders. And they thought about the day before the murders. "Whenever Daddy was blue or a little angry, he would come to me or Ronnie," Shari said. "This day, on Tuesday, the sixth, he walked in and he was red-faced. He and Marty. Marty was in and out of the room, and I said to Daddy, 'What's the matter?' He said, 'I need a hug.' We sat down and had a conversation. He said to me, 'I'm fed up with this kid.' I said, 'What did he do now?' He told me the kid was acting up."

Ron Rother said he began to turn against Marty after he began doing his own "detective work." According to the article, this entailed "putting together little points of information dropped by Tankleff in casual conversation, things he read in the newspaper, and items he picked up by keeping his ears and eyes wide open. Little points, like the view out of Tankleff's bedroom window and where certain lights were in the house."

Shari, meanwhile, said that the turning point didn't come until the later stages of the trial—when she watched Marty's testimony on television and heard him say something that didn't jibe with what he had told her. "In so many words, he said this: That he had gone into Arlene's bedroom and seen her and had touched her and gotten blood on his hands. 'My God'—that was my reaction. 'Oh my God.' Because he had told me that he had not gone into that room. He insisted on that. It was an article of faith. Now, here he was saying he *had* gone in." This, according to the *Newsday* story, was Shari's "epiphany, her blinding moment of truth," when she realized her brother was the killer of his mother and their father.

The only problem with Shari's epiphany was that it had no connection to reality. The reporter, who had covered the case only sporadically, apparently wasn't familiar enough with the details to know that Marty's testimony was no different from what he had always said: that he saw his mother's body twice—when he first spotted it from the doorway and then when he followed Ethel Curley into the bedroom—but that in neither instance had he touched her or gotten her blood on his hands.

Whatever Shari's "blinding moment of truth," Marty's conviction paved the way for her, instead of him, to inherit the bulk of their father's $3.5 million estate. It would be years before Shari spoke frankly about the money, acknowledging her efforts to convince Marty to change the terms of the will, her threats to take him to court, and her fierce resentment when he rebuffed her. She offered her version in 1998, and to a most unlikely interviewer: Stuart Namm. The former judge was retired in North Carolina and decided to make a television documentary about Marty Tankleff, whose case had always fascinated him.

Sitting in her living room, Shari told Namm what had happened when she brought up the will during the two and a half months Marty lived with her after his release from jail: "I said to Marty, 'Look this is not right, you know that Daddy, you know, this is not right. You and I need to talk because at the very least you know who's gonna make out on this? The lawyers. We don't want that.' And he looked at me, sitting on *my* couch with a face as straight as all get-out, and he said to me, 'Sorry, it's all mine.'"*

Namm asked Shari how she felt about that.

"I wanted to choke him," she said. "I wanted to choke him. I felt that"—she paused in thought—"he wasn't a part of this family. He was brought *into* this family. Don't throw your weight around with me. Because with everything that I have, I will fight you."

---

* Namm's film was completed with a partner but never broadcast. Marty learned of Shari's comments in 2008 and denied the remark she attributed to him. However, the thrust of the interview supported his long-held belief that Shari turned on him after he refused to discuss the will with her during those months, as he was instructed by Ron Falbee, his legal guardian.

CHAPTER 26

The Defense Does Not Rest

A GUILTY VERDICT in a murder trial is commonly followed by the sentencing of the defendant sixty days later. But there was nothing common about the case of *People v. Tankleff.* Convicted on June 28, Marty was scheduled to be sentenced on August 28, a day before his nineteenth birthday. But what happened in between was as strange and inscrutable as anything that came before.

In the two months after the verdict, Bob Gottlieb's office received more than three hundred letters about the case. Most were addressed to Marty, expressing support for him and anger at his conviction, and were from people who didn't know him, who had become absorbed by the gavel-to-gavel television coverage of his trial. Gottlieb brought the mail to the county jail, and Marty added it to the stacks of letters sent to him directly. He answered them all, albeit with a form letter. ("Thank you for taking the time to express your support . . . it's very comforting to hear from people who believe in me.") So many friends and relatives wanted to visit him—more than he could see in the one hour every other day he was allowed—that he wrote another letter of thanks to them and asked Ron and Carol to hand out copies. All of it was vital emotional sustenance for Marty, who was so stunned by the verdict that Gottlieb arranged for him to spend the first few weeks in the jail's sick bay. Marty wasn't suicidal—as crushing as the verdict was, that wasn't him—but Gottlieb wasn't taking any chances.

Marty was in shock, totally unprepared for the verdict that came. "'Marty, you're going to be found not guilty, there's no doubt in our minds'—that was ingrained in me for that year and a half," he said years later. "So you could imagine at the end . . ." He faced a maximum sentence of fifty years to life—twenty-five years for each count—but Gottlieb and the family told him, and told him every time they saw him, that however long he had to serve, he was going to get out. This conviction was wrong and it would not stand. They would appeal and they would win. Marty heard the words and nodded. He read a quote by his uncle Mike McClure in the newspaper: "We have not yet begun to fight."

The fight began with a public show of defiance. Other than Gottlieb, no one around Marty had spoken publicly since soon after his arrest. Now Ron Falbee was emerging as an effective family spokesman. Five days after the verdict, reporters and cameramen crowded into a conference room at Gottlieb's offices as Ron, surrounded by more than a dozen relatives and family friends, spoke poignantly of how devastating a blow the verdict was. "We've been through every piece of evidence for two years, we've done our own investigation," Ron said. "We don't know who killed Arlene and Seymour Tankleff, but we know one thing for damn sure, and that is Martin Tankleff didn't kill his parents. As we see it, Marty was guilty of three things: Number one, he was alive the morning of September 7, 1988. Number two, Marty doesn't show outward emotion in the accept-able fashion as everyone expects it. He has one of the best poker faces I've ever seen in my life. And three: He trusted the police."

After sitting through every day of the trial, Ron watched it again on videotape. And he still couldn't imagine how the jury convicted Marty. Where was this "overwhelming" evidence, as one juror was quoted saying on the day of the verdict? He and others wondered if it had been a mistake for Marty to testify. Or, conversely, if the fatal flaw in Gottlieb's defense was his failure to convey who Marty really was. They had winced when Collins mockingly asked in his summation why only the relatives from California had testified. Gottlieb had his own anguish. He was still in-censed by how cavalierly the judge disregarded the prejudicial effects of Collins's tactics. It would certainly be part of the appeal.

At the same time, Mike McClure was regretting his decision to lay back and let Gottlieb try the case as he saw fit. He wished he had pushed him to have Ron testify. He wished Gottlieb had kept Marianne on the stand for more than a few minutes and had asked Mike himself about more than Seymour's conversations with Steuerman and whether Marty ever complained about his car. In his eight-page letter to Gottlieb, Mike had written about more than just Steuerman. He had written about all the times he and Marianne and their kids had been with Marty and Arlene and Seymour. It wasn't just ten days in July. "We were all together in Arizona, Las Vegas, our house, their house, family things, Marty's bar mitzvah—we weren't questioned about any of it," Mike later said. He thought Gott-lieb did a fine job establishing how flimsy the prosecution's evidence was but didn't recognize how much the case was about the character of the accused. "Marty was never developed as a person. A trial is like a painting on a blank canvas. When you're finished, you want it to look like a painting. All the jurors knew about Marty was that he's the defendant—the guy sitting over there in the suit. Those people did not know Marty Tankleff at all."

Struggling to understand the verdict, Marty and his lawyers and supporters got few clues from the snippets of comment that reporters were able to draw out of a few of the jurors in the days that followed. Certainly they revealed nothing about what the jury made of the case for reasonable doubt offered by the defense.

"I checked the evidence over and over. There was no doubt the kid did it."

"A normal person doesn't crack for something he didn't do. The kid just snapped."

"His conviction was not solely based on his confession because it was just a statement that he didn't sign. Each piece of evidence played a part."

"No one came to a decision on anything other than the facts that were presented to us. For that, I will not have a hard time sleeping at night."

The only juror who gave an extended interview was Teresa Quigley, a psychiatric nurse who spoke to *Newsday*'s Carolyn Colwell the day after the verdict. But her account raised only more questions. She said that she and other jurors believed Marty's statements at police headquarters were taken illegally, that for all practical matters he was in custody and should have been advised of his rights even before he got in McCready's car for the trip to police headquarters. So they disregarded the confession, as the judge instructed. On what basis, then, did they find Marty guilty? "It was his testimony that determined his guilt." Specifically, what he said he did after waking up that morning.

As Quigley explained it: Marty said that the first time he got blood on his hands was when he pulled his father out of his chair. But, she said, a photograph of bloodstains on the chair showed that the person who got Seymour Tankleff out of the chair and onto the floor already had blood on his hands. It was a bizarre and disturbing statement by Quigley: There was no testimony supporting such a conclusion. It wasn't even among the arguments Collins made in his summation. Had Marty been convicted by jurors who assumed the role of forensic experts, creating their own evidence to justify a conviction?

Quigley recounted several other suspect conclusions. She said the jurors looked at the diagram the detectives asked Marty to make of the master bedroom, showing his mother's body and where he was standing when he spotted it. In the converse of McCready's insistence that Marty *would* have seen his mother the first time he looked in, the jury apparently didn't think he *could* have seen her the second time. But why? The diagram clearly showed—and crime scene photos confirmed—that his mother's head would have been directly in Marty's line of sight once he looked down to the floor.

Beyond her appraisal of any particular piece of evidence, it seemed from Quigley's comments that Collins succeeded in focusing the jurors on Marty's account of his actions after he woke up that morning, distracting them from the prosecution's lack of proof regarding the murders themselves. Even more fundamentally, the interview raised the question of whether the jurors—despite the seriousness of purpose they demonstrated in staying out as long as they did—truly understood the two most basic concepts of their task—burden of proof and reasonable doubt. Quigley said, astonishingly, that she voted for conviction without reaching a conclusion about the events that occurred that morning. "I don't think they gave us enough evidence to deduct what happened there," she said. "I felt there was a big piece missing." And because the jurors were instructed that they did not have to find motive to find guilt, she didn't concern herself with whether it made sense that Marty brutally murdered his parents over the trivial—and largely unproven—complaints attributed to him. "I took the evidence and made the evidence speak for what happened," she said, inscrutably. Quigley and the other jurors also forgave the quality of the police investigation. "We didn't conclude that it was excellent," she said.

WITH THE RETIREMENT of his longtime private investigator, Jack Murtagh, Gottlieb hired another agency to gather information that might be of use in the appeal. The new investigator was a retired police detective named Bill Navarra, and he began by trying to interview the jurors. Among other things, Gottlieb wanted to know whether their verdict was influenced by Collins's summation. Navarra started getting vibes of something unusual when he talked to a juror who seemed to have something on his mind.

Peter Baczynski was Juror Number 9. A mail carrier in his early thirties, he was the juror whose longing for sports news led Tisch to announce the baseball scores from the bench. Navarra called Baczynski and said he wasn't out to bother him about the verdict, that he was just trying to get some background. From the other end of the phone came the kind of silence that told an investigator he'd struck a nerve. As Baczynski later recalled, "I was thinking about all the things I knew that I wanted to come forward with but I was afraid to."

There were some things that went on, Baczynski said, things that still bothered him nearly two months later. But he didn't know what to do about it. "To be honest," he said, "I've been afraid. I didn't know who to go to—the defense, the prosecution, the judge? The media? Should I tell it to a lawyer?"

You can tell it to me, Navarra said. And Baczynski did. He told him about Frank Spindel. Sometimes on a jury, one person emerges as a driving force, more opinionated than the others and eager to spread his influence. In the Tankleff case, Frank Spindel was that juror. But he was more than that. According to Baczynski, Spindel obviously made up his mind that Marty was guilty long before all the evidence was in, and he led the charge for conviction from the moment the door to the jury room closed. But that wasn't the problem. It was the things he would say during the trial, and especially during the deliberations. Implying he had a connection to the DA's office, dropping hints that he had some kind of relationship with John Collins. There was just a lot of stuff that happened, Baczynski said, that really, really bothered him. Navarra asked if they could get together and talk about it. Baczynski said he'd think about it.

Gottlieb was tantalized when Navarra told him there might have been a rogue juror. But there was one thing that didn't surprise him, and that was the juror's name. Frank Spindel. Juror Number 11. The cabinet-maker. Gottlieb flashed back to the day early in the trial when Spindel showed up to court late, full of explanations. It seemed he had gotten stopped for speeding, and when the cop checked his license it came up as suspended for failure to pay fines for previous violations, one of which was also for driving without a license. Summoned to Tisch's chambers, Spindel chalked up the situation to a bureaucratic mix-up that went back fourteen years. Tisch said it wouldn't be the first time someone had a problem with the computers at the Department of Motor Vehicles. Anyway, he wasn't here to try a juror for speeding. All he wanted to know was whether anything that happened that morning would affect Spindel's ability to evaluate this case impartially. Spindel assured the judge it wouldn't and apologized to him and the attorneys. Gottlieb tried to lighten the moment. "You see the impact you're having already?" he joked.

Four months later, Gottlieb's quip echoed with prescience. On August 20, Navarra showed up at Peter Baczynski's house, a miniature tape recorder in his pocket. "I'm not interested in doing this," Baczynski said. "Thought about it a lot, and I don't really want to get involved in it. I don't want to second-guess myself."

Catching the implication, Navarra tried some gentle persuasion. "I don't want to question your judgment," he said. "I just wanted to get a little bit of a background, just a feel, that's all. Can you give me fifteen minutes?"

"I'm just really trying to forget about it," Baczynski said.

"I want you to," Navarra replied reassuringly. "All I need is a quick overview, and it'll only take ten minutes."

But Baczynski just wanted to let it go. It was the hardest thing he'd ever had to do, he said. Halfway through the trial, the jurors talked about getting together for a barbecue after it was all over. "And when the time came, everybody wanted to just forget about it. If it was an acquittal, maybe we'd be more friendly. But everybody was pretty upset that day."

"I can imagine."

"We were all crying. It was really, really bad."

"Well, what do you feel was the turning point on the thing?" Navarra asked, trying to keep Baczynski talking, hoping he'd let him past the doorway.

"His own testimony, everything he said. When you look at the evidence, his testimony doesn't back anything up. He said his father was all bloody and everything and he helped him out of the chair. If you look at all these pictures they introduced, there was no blood on him. . . ."

"Did you, at the beginning of the deliberations—"

"Ah, come in, the hell with it," Baczynski said finally. He led Navarra into the kitchen. "I just really don't want to get into this too heavily, you know. I feel just so bad for a long time. I came home, I was really messed up by it and I actually had nightmares for like five nights in a row. I couldn't imagine my own kids, you know, doing something like that. It shook me up. I wanted him to be innocent, I really, really did."

But Spindel didn't. "He really wanted to hang the kid from the get-go," he told Navarra. "He was a very dominating force in there. He said, 'Guilty, Guilty, Guilty. I'm not leaving this room with a not-guilty verdict.' I said I don't know how anybody can have their mind made up. I said, 'Let's look at the evidence and see where things are.' We took a count that first day. Five people said guilty, two people said not guilty, and five were undecided. I was one of the undecided."

But Spindel wasn't just too gung ho for conviction. "This is all gonna be off the record," Baczynski said.

"Yeah," said Navarra. "Go ahead."

"I don't know for sure," Baczynski said, "but I have a funny feeling that either he knew Collins from the golf course or he had a friend that knew Collins from the golf course. He definitely said he knows Collins from golf. And at the end, he actually made some slips, saying that Collins was looking at him and he told Collins that one person was holding us up and—"

Navarra stopped him. "He told Collins? How did he tell Collins? Where did he see him?"

It was on the last full day of deliberations, Baczynski said. There was only one juror still voting for acquittal, and they were in the courtroom for one more readback. "Frank's looking at Collins, he's going like this, just holding his head like this with one finger up." Baczynski rested his chin in his hand, with one finger raised, tapping it against his cheek. "And Collins was shaking his head and looking at us." At dinner that night, Baczynski mentioned what he saw—that Collins appeared to be looking the jurors over and seemed annoyed. "And Frank said, 'Yeah, I put my one finger up, to say that one person is holding us up.' It was incredible. I said, 'Geez, Frank, how the hell could—why are you even signaling to this guy one way or the other?'"

Baczynski found himself wondering whether Spindel might have had anything to do with the removal of Joe Fisher, the pro-defense juror who was reported by the mother and brother of a secretary in the DA's office. The day the judge suspended the trial to hold a hearing on the situation, Fisher told Baczynski that he was in trouble for talking about the case at a bar. "I said, 'Joe, was it really bad?'" Baczynski said. "He says, 'It really wasn't. I didn't say hardly anything about it, just that I was on a murder case.'"

"Do you think he was set up?" Navarra asked.

"I wonder about that," Baczynski said. "I think that Joe really felt that Jerry did it all along, and, you know, when Jerry was on the stand and we went back inside Joe would be laughing about some of the things Jerry would say." Could the DA's office have found out about Fisher from Spindel? "I don't know. But it was just so convenient that somebody would be in that bar and hang the poor guy."

Gottlieb had also thought it was a little too convenient. So when he heard Baczynski's story, he revisited his suspicions about how it was that the one juror who saw right through Jerry Steuerman, the one juror who might have blocked Marty's conviction, found himself sitting in a bar with relatives of an assistant district attorney's secretary.

GOTTLIEB THOUGHT Baczynski's story could be the foundation of a motion to set aside Marty's conviction on the basis of juror misconduct—if Baczynski could be persuaded to put his allegations on the record, and if they could be fleshed out and corroborated by other jurors.

But the interview with Baczynski was also revealing in what it said about how things went so terribly wrong for Marty. As he talked, Baczynski provided an extraordinary picture of the jagged route the jury took to conviction. "There was a lot of yelling and screaming the first few days," Baczynski told Navarra, and much of it was between Spindel and the two jurors whose initial vote was for acquittal. One of those votes came from

Terry Quigley, the juror who gave such flawed reasons for her eventual vote to convict when she spoke to *Newsday*. Baczynski confirmed one thing Quigley said: that the jury decided Marty should have been advised of his rights long before he was, and so they were obliged to disregard the confession. "We all agreed he was coerced, the police really hammered him," Baczynski said, "so I threw out everything from the time he left the house."

But did they really "strike it from their minds" as if they'd never heard it, as the judge instructed them? "I know he's only a kid and everything but I don't care," he said only seconds later. "If I'm a seventeen-year-old kid and I honestly didn't kill my parents, I would be outraged that they would even try to question me, try to make me say this. I would never admit to it, they would have to beat me up, like in the army or something like that. Plus, I would say, 'I'm going to that hospital, I want to see my father *now*. If I'm not under arrest, I'm gone.' We all thought that was strange why he didn't go."

There was no movement through the first four days—still five for guilty, two for acquittal, five undecided. And then, after the fifth day, two of the undecided jurors made up their minds: guilty. Baczynski was one of them, and it was Marty's testimony that turned him around. "If he didn't take the stand, I think it would have been a lot more difficult to pinpoint. A lot of us were undecided and people were saying, 'Oh, I think he said this' or 'I think he did this,' and everyone had a different version of what he said. So we said let's have the whole thing read back. So we did that and we went back in and we looked at the evidence and said how the hell could this be? This doesn't add up."

One reason some things didn't add up may have been that the jurors couldn't get basic facts straight—even after readbacks. "The blood on the light switch in his room," Baczynski said. "He said he had the door locked and the killer went in." This would indeed have been a damning inconsistency, but Marty testified only that his bedroom door was closed. He didn't say it was locked. At the same time, it seemed from Baczynski's account that the tale of the missing rubber gloves didn't hold anyone up.

Something else Baczynski pointed out to the other jurors: "The blood was only around the mother's and father's bodies." It was an odd thing for him to find suggestive of guilt. The absence of blood between the two crime scenes had been one of the *defense's* strongest circumstantial arguments, not the prosecution's. The more Baczynski talked, the more it seemed Marty's life had rested in the hands of people who meant well and were certainly in no rush but whose powers of reasoning could surely be questioned.

GEORGE ARGEROPLOS/NEWSDAY

John Collins was a rising star in the Suffolk County district attorney's office, and the Tankleff case certified his status as its top homicide prosecutor.

DICK KRAUS/NEWSDAY

Judge Alfred C. Tisch presided over the trial after stumbling in his bid for district attorney.

DICK KRAUS/NEWSDAY

JOHN H. CORNELL, JR./NEWSDAY

At the Huntley hearing (above), Bob Gottlieb tried to have Marty's alleged statements to the police suppressed. His key witness, Mike Fox, broke down when he talked about his friendship with Seymour, then offered an account of September 7 that Tisch dismissed as "unworthy of belief."

Poker player Joe Cecere uses a model of the Tankleff house to show where the cars were parked that night and why it was odd that Jerry Steuerman waved for him to leave first. Cecere testified that Steuerman didn't follow him out.

Gottlieb cross-examined Steuerman relentlessly, often with documents related to his business arrangements with Seymour Tankleff. Finally, Steuerman exploded in protest: "Three days on the witness stand and I didn't do a thing!"

NEW YORK STATE
DEPARTMENT OF CORRECTION

NAME STEUERMAN, Todd
DIN 90A5945   HT. 5'11"
NYSID 5099359R   WGT. 160
DOB 07-20-65   EYES Hazel
DATE   HAIR Brown

Todd Steuerman began a seven-year prison sentence the day before his father took the stand. Gottlieb wanted the jury to consider the possibility that Todd's drug business gave his father access to the sort of people who might kill for money.

Vinnie Bove testified that he cut a last piece of watermelon after the poker game but left the knife in a different position from the way it appeared in the photo taken by the crime scene team. Collins presented the testimony as momentous, though he failed to prove that the knife was used in the murders.

Examining the watermelon knife at the county crime lab, forensic serologist Robert Baumann noted a "small visible bit of material . . . pink in color" on the blade—but no blood (below).

CRIMINALISTICS LABORATORY
WORKSHEET

ST Plas Bag/

One Knife / "SABATIER HOFFRITZ" 14 1/8" oL·; 9 5/8" B
B.W.= 1 1/4"   Silver-colo finish w/ blk plastic hdl
STEREOSCOPICALLY: Nothing resembling blood stains, however

Small visible bit of material was present along edge.
blade approx. 5" from tip. (43A) Size of piece ~
& pink in color. (Sent to Hildbry for micro prep) - Dissolved a
preserving of stain questioned)
Km/LMG: neg on entire blade & handle.

			9/21	Catalytica	ANTI-B	ANTI-HD	Direct	Reverse	Lewis	Elution/Inhib	Lattes	EsD	PGM	Pep A	GLO I	EAP	ADA	BLOOD EXAMINA
	SPECIMEN																	
31	Pl. Cont w/ Trap Water fm Kitchen Sink (of south wall of kitchen)			-				No	Blood	Detected								
32	Pl. Cont w/ Trap Water fm Kitchen Sink (north wall of kitchen)			-				No	Blood	Detected								
36	Pl. Cont w/ Trap Water fm Bathrm (east sink) between master & Sec'd Bedrm			-				No	Blood	Detected								
37	Pl. Cont w/ Trap Water fm Bathrm (west sink) between master & Sec'd Bedrm			-				No	Blood	Detected								
40	Pl. Cont w/ Trap Water fm Tub Drain in Bathroom			-				No	Blood	Detected								

Submitted by: 9/5-8
Date: 9/11
TRAP WATER

According to the prosecution, Marty confessed to bludgeoning his parents with a dumbbell, but all four taken from his room (left) were negative for trace evidence. According to the prosecution, Marty also confessed to cleaning the dumbbell and the knife in the shower. Baumann tested the trap water in all the showers and sinks in the house. "No Blood Detected," he wrote for each one (above).

McCready: "The defendant said he hit her on the head with the barbell and his mother started fighting with him. He said his mother was screaming out 'Why?' and 'Stop.'"

Rein: "The defendant said he then took the knife and he slashed his father's throat. He said he couldn't believe all the blood."

WHERE GO AFTER P.D. ARRIVE?
HALL & KITCHEN
DIAGRAM   MOTHER
PHONY CALL   11:45

PFALZGRAPH
ADRENALINE
FATHER SAYS YOU
LAST ONE HE SAW

Rein testified that he took notes of the interrogation as it was happening, and Collins offered the notes as evidence to support the detectives' account. But in the critical sequence, Rein wrote, "Phony Call 11:45"—yet he testified that McCready's lie to Marty was so convincing that he didn't realize it was a trick until later.

A necessary gamble: Marty takes the stand in his own defense. Under cross-examination, he points out the towel he used to wipe his hands and left on the bed.

For Marty and his family, a rented van was a refuge in the parking lot as they waited for the jury's verdict. On Day 7, sitting with Ron and Carol Falbee and Marianne McClure and her daughter Jennifer, Marty was the picture of confidence.

June 28, 1990: the verdict Marty never thought possible.

Moments after the verdict, Gottlieb's associate Craig Parles eased Marty back into his chair, a hand on his shoulder small comfort.

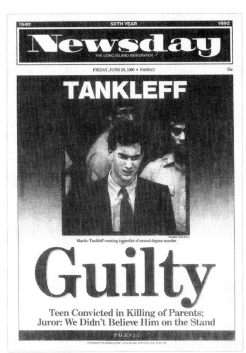

Newsday
THE LONG ISLAND NEWSPAPER

FRIDAY, JUNE 29, 1990 • NASSAU   35¢

TANKLEFF

Martin Tankleff reacting to verdict of second-degree murder

Guilty

Teen Convicted in Killing of Parents; Juror: We Didn't Believe Him on the Stand

PAGES 2-3

October 23, 1990: fifty years to life.

Frank Spindel, Juror Number 11, led the charge for conviction. Two months later, he showed up for Marty's sentencing, but was disappointed when it was post-poned.

At the juror-misconduct hearing, Peter Baczynski testified that Spindel used a discreetly up-raised finger to signal to John Collins that there was one holdout.

Marty's aunts, Marianne (left) and Marcella, and cousin Ron lash out at the jury's verdict during a press conference with Gottlieb. "We don't know who killed Arlene and Seymour Tankleff," said Ron, "but we know one thing for damn sure, and that is Martin Tankleff didn't kill his parents."

"The only other thing that really swayed me," Baczynski went on, "even though I threw it out because I thought that he was coerced in that police room . . ." So he was "really swayed" by something that he "threw out." What he found so compelling was that McCready and Rein couldn't have fed Marty details of the crimes, as the defense contended, because they didn't know about his parents' injuries yet. "How would they lead him on about the head injuries and he used the barbell. So right there that was something that really bothered me. He had to do it, because the detectives can't bring him into all these details at that time because they didn't know what was going on themselves."

But of course they did. McCready even testified that he specifically discussed Seymour's head injuries with Marty after talking to Detective Pfalzgraf while en route to police headquarters. Moreover, Baczynski's logic assumed that the barbell was in fact one of the murder weapons. The question he might have asked was the one Gottlieb posed in his summation: Why would Marty confess to killing his parents with an implement that forensic tests showed could not have been the murder weapon? But he and the other jurors apparently didn't ponder this question, or the many other forensic findings that betrayed the confession to be fiction— because they disregarded the confession.

On the sixth and seventh day of deliberations, the three remaining undecided jurors changed their votes to guilty. That left Terry Quigley and James McMillan, the two who had been for acquittal since the beginning. In each case, Baczynski told Navarra, it wasn't the evidence that was holding them back so much as their expressed feeling that a kid like Marty couldn't be capable of doing what he was accused of. "I think Jim felt very guilty, he didn't think he would be able to handle it, send the kid away. It was more of a sentiment thing." If that was all that was holding them up, it wasn't surprising that Quigley and McMillan eventually fell in line. It might also explain why Quigley's reasons for conviction were so far off track. McMillan dropped his opposition on the afternoon of the seventh day. Quigley, the last holdout, followed the next morning.

Aside from suggesting the verdict was the result of a good bit of muddled thinking and perhaps the influence wielded by a juror with an agenda, Baczynski's account supported the family's criticism of Gottlieb—and Gottlieb's anger about Collins's summation. "These three people from California were only there for a few days in July the year before," Baczynski told Navarra, parroting Collins, if inaccurately. (The McClures visited the Tankleffs that summer, less than two months before the murders, not the year before.) He wanted to know why all those people sitting in the courtroom—Marty's aunts and uncles and cousins—didn't testify for him.

"The people that really knew him and knew the family. Why weren't they up there saying, 'Hey, you know, they might have had some problems but they had a good family relationship and we know him and this is why we believe he's innocent'? When they didn't go up there, that annoyed me. Uncle Mike Fox—why wasn't he up there, too? Those were parts of the puzzle that we never really knew the answer to."

So it was that the jury's only portrait of Marty seemed to be the one drawn by the prosecution. "I think the father and the mother babied him too much and kept him under their thumb," Baczynski said. "They made him landscape around the house. They wouldn't let him go out, go to college in Florida. I think they just built up the anger and resentment that they wouldn't let him be a man, and I think that's how the kid actually snapped. My own theory, anyway. 'Cause my folks were very protective of me. I was an only child, too, and they wouldn't let me go out and do things and I kind of rebelled. I rebelled in a different way."

What about Jerry Steuerman? "The guy was a sleazy person and running away certainly complicated things, but we honestly said, and they told us at the beginning of the trial, Jerry is not on trial here. We have to evaluate everything with Marty. Not to think, 'Well, we don't think Marty did it, do we think Jerry did?' Is Marty innocent or guilty? We're really not concentrating on Jerry. We're not here to play detective."

Baczynski's verdict also paid no heed to the dim view he took of the defense's other villain: Detective McCready. "I thought he was a bum. He's not a type of cop I would trust." Do you think he did his job on this case? Navarra asked. "I honestly think he didn't," Baczynski said. "I really had no respect for him. He was on a par with Jerry Steuerman. I thought they were like birds of a feather."

The more Baczynski talked, the more he sounded like the juror with reasonable doubt that he was for most of the deliberations. "I was leaning for not guilty when I went into that deliberation room. I really was. As the trial was going on, I thought, Oh, he's not going to be guilty, it's going to be okay, 'cause it would be a lot easier to say not guilty. I said to my wife, I says, 'I really can't see how I'm gonna come back with a guilty vote.' And when I came home with a guilty vote, my wife said, 'What happened, how could you? You were so sure.' And I said, 'Yeah, I thought I was too until I saw all the evidence, those pictures and what Marty said, it just didn't add up.' I said to myself, if the evidence could have been a little bit the other way, I would have been more apt to let Marty go. I can see he's not such a bad kid. I mean, for ten, twelve weeks you're sitting in the same courtroom, and when you go out for lunch, you see Marty over there with the family, you see what a nice kid he is, he seems so well-mannered and the family looks so nice. You feel like you know him."

"I don't want to change your mind," Navarra said. "I mean, if he's guilty, he's guilty. I mean, that's it. That's your feeling, and all of us have different feelings."

"I wish the hell it could have been different, I honestly do. It does bother me."

"I can see it in your eyes."

"I feel like crying. Honest to God, I can't even look at you. The family, what does the family really feel? About the jury, I mean. Do they, I mean, I know we're not popular."

"It's just something that's done. I mean, they're not happy with it, but it's something they'll have to live with."

"If you see the family, could you tell them we all wanted him to be innocent, we honestly did. I wish I could actually tell some of those people. I feel so, so terrible."

AMONG THE HUNDREDS of letters and phone calls that flowed into Bob Gottlieb's office after the verdict were a few from people who had something more to offer than sympathy and support. Just a week before Marty's scheduled sentencing date, Gottlieb got a call from a man named Richard Monte, who said he had some information that might interest him. During the week of Jerry Steuerman's disappearance in September 1988, Monte was at a pub down on the South Shore when Norman Rein came in and started asking people if they knew anything about the whereabouts of two men—a guy named Eddie Cavallo, who owned a bagel store in East Islip, and his partner, Jerry Steuerman.

Monte knew Rein in addition to the two people he was looking for, and he knew they were both missing. Steuerman's disappearance was all over the papers. As for Eddie—well, the bagel store had been closed for days, ever since a day or two after the murders, and nobody had seen him since. Monte said he hadn't seen either Steuerman or Cavallo and had no idea where they might be, but Rein didn't believe him. He brought Monte to the Fourth Precinct, where he was joined by McCready. The detectives questioned him for half an hour and several times more over the next month. Monte told Gottlieb that he got the clear impression from the detectives that they thought Eddie Cavallo's disappearance had something to do with the Tankleff murder investigation.

When Gottlieb told Marty's family about the phone call, Mike McClure remembered Seymour telling him during the July visit that he was putting some money into a new bagel store in East Islip that was going to be run by a guy named Eddie.

On the day of his scheduled sentencing, Marty climbed out of his jailhouse jumpsuit and into his gray trial suit, which he wore with his maroon tie. Back with Gottlieb at the defense table in Judge Tisch's courtroom, he looked pale, his hair tousled. His close relatives returned to their seats in the first two rows. They were joined by another fifteen supporters— friends of Marty's, members of the extended family, even a few from the ranks of strangers who had watched the trial on TV and came to lend their moral support. Everyone entered the courtroom wearing large yellow buttons, adorned with ribbons, that declared MARTY IS INNOCENT. When Tisch saw the buttons, he instructed a court officer to have everyone take them off.

Gottlieb told Tisch that he had a motion to make. He said he was in possession of potentially significant new evidence that he hoped would allow him to file a motion to set aside the verdict. He had received it only days before and needed some time to develop it. He asked the judge for a month's postponement of the sentencing. "The information we are pursuing goes to the very heart of someone else being involved," Gottlieb said, unwilling to say anything more in open court. Tisch brought Gottlieb and John Collins into his chambers, but even there Gottlieb respectfully declined to divulge what he had. Tisch asked whether it had something to do with Steuerman. Gottlieb wouldn't confirm even that much. But in view of the magnitude of the case, Tisch told him, he would give him his thirty days.

Cries of "Yes!" and "Thank God!" rang out when Tisch made the announcement in the courtroom. "This could finally be a breakthrough," Marcella Falbee told a reporter.

Gottlieb spent the next four weeks scrambling to put together enough evidence to file a viable motion. The new evidence to which he alluded in court didn't include the possible juror misconduct, and this began to eclipse the intriguing but vague information that had come to him from a tipster. The turning point came when Gottlieb and Bill Navarra visited Peter Baczynski at his home and found he had a lot more to share than what he'd told Navarra during their first meeting. According to Baczynski, Spindel's apparent signal to Collins from the jury box was hardly the first instance of troubling conduct by Juror Number 11. Strange things had been going on almost since the beginning of the trial.

There was, for instance, the case of the mysterious cigarettes. In the crime scene video that Collins had presented early in the trial, the jurors had noticed a lingering shot of a pile of cigarette butts in a garbage pail outside the Tankleffs' house. There was testimony that none of the Tankleffs smoked and that the poker game had a no-smoking policy. "It was sort of a big mystery to everyone," Baczynski said. "No one knew how these cigarette butts got there." But Frank Spindel knew. "Frank told a few of us that he knew where they came from, and that it was a certain woman who played cards with Arlene Tankleff. She smoked like a chimney and they wouldn't let her in the house because they were very particular about smoke in the house. She would go outside in the back and smoke there, and she would take the ashtray and empty the butts into the trash can. I said, 'How do you know this, Frank?' He either said he knew the woman directly or someone in his family knew her, and he was able to speak to her and find out a lot of inside information about Marty, about how the relationship was going at home with Marty and his family. The woman told him a lot of things."

The cigarette butts were mentioned a few times as the trial continued, and according to Baczynski, "All of us had a hard time keeping a straight face in the jury box. We thought it was incredible we knew about it and nobody else in the courtroom did." At one point, Spindel told the others that the prosecution would put an end to the speculation by bringing in the smoker herself. And he was right. On the last day of the trial, after the defense rested, Collins called Dot Depping to the stand. The day before the murders, she testified, she had played in her weekly bridge game with Arlene and two other women on the deck outside the kitchen. She smoked Carlton 100s. And she dumped her ashtray in the pail near the garage before leaving, as she always did. Depping said she had first spoken to the police just a week before she was called to testify.

Baczynski said Spindel had more to share on the first night the jury was sequestered: "I got big news for everybody. The kid's sister is on the prosecution's side. She thinks he's guilty." How did he know this? Spindel said he had figured out how to make a call out—just go through the motel operator and bill it to your home phone so there's no record of it—and when he talked to his wife she told him about McCready's announcement that Shari Rother had been supporting the prosecution for a year and a half. Baczynski, for one, took the information seriously. He started out undecided and leaning toward acquittal, but the news about Marty's sister became a significant factor in his eventual decision to convict. "I thought, 'Why doesn't his own sister support him?'"

Obtaining that information and sharing it with other jurors was Spindel's most serious breach of the sequestration, according to Baczynski, but it wasn't the only one. Spindel made numerous phone calls (his home phone records would later document eight calls on the first night alone) and told Baczynski and others that he had watched videotapes of the trial and taken notes. All this was of course a clear violation of the judge's admonishments, repeated every time the jury left the courtroom every day of the trial, not to "read, listen to, or view any report or account of the case."

Baczynski agreed to go on the record with an affidavit and said he would testify in court if necessary. But Gottlieb needed to corroborate his extraordinary claims, and Navarra was having little success getting other jurors to talk to him. The one exception was Terry Quigley. She told much the same story as Baczynski and agreed to swear to it in an affidavit only days before the rescheduled sentencing.

Quigley said she did not see the signal Baczynski claimed he saw on the last day of deliberations, but that Spindel did tell her, a few days earlier, that he was trying to communicate with Collins through hand signals. She also confirmed that Spindel told his fellow jurors about McCready's announcement about Shari Rother on the first night they were sequestered, and that, during the trial, he revealed the source of the cigarette butts and correctly predicted the mysterious smoker's appearance as a witness. And Quigley had some stories of her own to tell, instances when Spindel seemed to know things no one else did and advocated positions that revealed a bias in favor of the prosecution. She recalled one point during the deliberations when she raised questions about the legality of the homicide detectives' questioning of Marty. Spindel told her that the judge had already "predetermined" the legitimacy of the detectives' techniques. It was an apparent reference to the pretrial Huntley hearing, a proceeding that the jurors should not have even been aware of.

According to Quigley, Spindel had a habit of revealing his preconceptions, and his flouting of the judge's instructions, when he got angry. She recalled his words during one heated argument: "The kid is guilty. You know it, I know it, my lawyers told me, the police said so. I am not having any mistrials. I came here to make him guilty and that's what I'm going to leave here with." She recalled arguing with Spindel about a piece of Marty's testimony. She thought he said one thing, Spindel insisted he said something else. "I know you're wrong because I saw the Channel 12 tape," she said Spindel told her. She recalled him also saying that he watched the commentary by attorneys Eric Naiburg and Ken Rosenblum that Channel 12 aired from its newsroom during pauses in the testimony. Gottlieb found this particularly troublesome because Naiburg and Rosenblum commonly mused about strategies, evidence, and other matters that the jury should not have been exposed to, and that might have influenced their deliberations.

MARTY'S SENTENCING had been rescheduled for September 27, and when that day came Gottlieb asked Judge Tisch to postpone it yet again. He preferred the judge focus his attentions on an eleven-page motion he had filed a day earlier. It asked Tisch to set aside Marty Tankleff's conviction on the basis of juror misconduct and the assorted other allegations he had accumulated in the three months since the verdict.

In addition to the sworn statements of Peter Baczynski and Teresa Quigley, Gottlieb submitted his own thirty-two-paragraph affidavit outlining the new information. He argued that Baczynski's and Quigley's statements suggested that jurors might well have believed that Frank Spindel "had some special bond to the prosecution, perhaps inside information that Martin Tankleff was indeed guilty, all creating a situation which placed Spindel in a superior position in the jury room during deliberations."

Gottlieb also disclosed that a background check of Spindel revealed that he lied on his juror questionnaire—and in a way that was relevant to the case. Spindel answered that he had never been a party to a civil case. But a computer printout that ran five pages said otherwise: Spindel and his wife were defendants in ten cases that resulted in judgments against them, including a foreclosure action against their home. This could have colored Spindel's view of Jerry Steuerman, Gottlieb said, and he never would have allowed Spindel to serve on the jury had he known about it.

The balance of the motion laid out the information about Eddie Cavallo, Jerry Steuerman's missing bagel partner, if somewhat cryptically. "Our investigation is proceeding full throttle," he explained, "and we do not want to risk the possibility that premature disclosure will terminate the investigation or dry up leads." But already the information was showing that the police investigated other avenues early in the case that were never shared with the defense. Gottlieb argued that it constituted suppression of potentially exculpatory material that would warrant a reversal of the verdict on appeal.

Gottlieb's allegations brought a swift reaction from John Collins. He told reporters he was "personally insulted" at the suggestion that he received signals from a juror during deliberations. "I had no, absolutely no, communication with Mr. Spindel or any other trial juror," he said, ". . . either by way of telephone calls, personal conversation, hand signals, mental telepathy, or otherwise." But he didn't discourage the intrigue when he acknowledged that he did meet Spindel after the trial—and played golf with him. "There's nothing really improper about it," he said. The trial was over, and besides, "I did not reach out to any of the jurors. This juror reached out to me." He didn't say, but it would come out later, that the round of golf included a third player: Jim McCready. They played at McCready's club.

For his part, Spindel denied everything. "You can put that one down as totally ludicrous," he said when a reporter asked him about his alleged hand signaling to Collins. He even denied playing golf with him, despite Collins's acknowledgment. Spindel called the whole thing a witch hunt by a defeated defense lawyer "and two jurors second-guessing what they did."

Spindel was right about one thing: Peter Baczynski was second-guessing his verdict. The process of going public with his allegations had pulled Baczynski's mind back into the case. He found himself ruminating about the evidence and whether he had analyzed it correctly. He realized that a lot of his conclusions were actually speculation and that he'd given the benefit of the doubt to the wrong side. He regretted that he'd allowed himself to be influenced by Spindel's announcement that Shari Rother supported the prosecution. He saw Marty's face in his mind, and couldn't stop thinking about what a nice kid he seemed to be. Before long, Baczynski came to the conclusion that he had made a terrible mistake. Spindel knew this, and it allowed him to dismiss Baczynski's allegations as the fabrications of a weak-willed man suffering a bout of juror's remorse. What Spindel didn't know, yet, was that Terry Quigley could not be so easily discounted.

The battle moved into the courtroom the next day, and a clot of new lawyers joined the fray. An attorney for Spindel was there to say for the record that his client denied the allegations as well as to fight Gottlieb's issuance of a subpoena for Spindel's phone records. Collins, meanwhile, was joined by two other assistant district attorneys: the head of the office's appeals bureau, along with another prosecutor to take on the juror misconduct issue in which Collins now found himself enmeshed. Once Tisch agreed to consider the allegations, which he would almost have to do, Collins would be off the case. But he wouldn't depart without a statement of personal outrage and a plea to the judge to proceed with the sentencing despite the defense's maneuvers to avoid it.

"There is nothing other than my family that I cherish above my reputation," Collins declared. "In the course of this trial, I was lied to by the defense. I was called a liar in the course of a sidebar. I am now being attacked personally at the postverdict motion. My initial Bronx-born instinct to that attack is to request to speak with the defense in the parking lot." But instead he forged ahead with the statement he'd been waiting for months to read. "I ask the court to speak now and today for Seymour and Arlene, whose voices were forever silenced by this ungrateful son. I ask that the court in imposing sentence recall their battered skulls and gaping wounds. I ask that this court show this defendant all the compassion he showed his mother as she struggled mightily and fiercely against the rain of blows brought down upon her and his father as he was, in the defendant's own words, knocked silly. . . ."

Collins's outrage notwithstanding, Tisch realized he had no choice but to put off the sentencing once more and sort out Gottlieb's array of accusations. He would start by hearing from the two jurors, and then he would decide whether their allegations merited a full hearing.

When Monday came, Peter Baczynski and Terry Quigley weren't the only ones Gottlieb brought to court. He was accompanied by Ron Sussman, his law partner. The last time Sussman had appeared before Tisch, a year and a half before, it was to ask the judge whether he was running for district attorney and to recuse himself from the Tankleff case if he was. That hadn't ended well for anyone but James Catterson. Now Sussman was standing before Tisch again, saying, "We have an application to disqualify Judge Tisch from conducting further proceedings in the case of *People versus Martin Tankleff.*"

If anyone thought Gottlieb couldn't possibly have left anything out of the motion he had filed only four days earlier, Sussman was here to drop one more explosive legal device. Along with everything else they had been working on since the verdict, Bill Navarra had been trying to confirm whispers that Tisch had attended a Tankleff prosecution "victory lunch" a week after the verdict. Navarra had finally pinned it down to Gottlieb and Sussman's satisfaction. According to their sources, Tisch had been seen at the gathering with Collins, McCready, Rein, and others from the DA's office and the police homicide squad who had worked on the case. It was said to have been a raucous affair that lasted all afternoon and was held in the furthest thing from an out-of-the-way place. The alleged lunch was held at the Harbor Hills club in Belle Terre, and according to Gottlieb and Sussman's information, it wasn't the only socializing Tisch had done with members of the Tankleff prosecution team following the verdict.

Standing with Gottlieb, Sussman laid out what they had been told and asked Tisch if it was accurate: Was it true that he had attended a prosecution victory lunch at Harbor Hills? And was it true "that the Court went golfing at the very same club with Vincent Bove, Detective McCready, and Detective Rein following the verdict?" And that he had lunch with Collins and McCready on another occasion after the verdict? "Our client, Martin Tankleff, is entitled to judgment from a fair and impartial and detached magistrate," Sussman said, "and if the information brought to our attention is correct, then the Court must disqualify itself from further proceedings."

Sussman handed Tisch a written version of the information he'd just presented. "I don't know that it's necessary for me to even examine it," Tisch said. "I can categorically state at this time there is absolutely no truth to any of the three allegations you've made. I don't know how much you pay your investigator, but I suggest you pay him some more so maybe he can get some factual material. If that's the basis of your application, denied."

All Gottlieb and Sussman really had was an affidavit from a bartender at Harbor Hills who said he had been told about the lunch by another bartender and several other staff members. The attorneys considered their information solid enough to confront Tisch, but they had decided it would be unwise to pursue the issue if he denied it. "Your Honor, with that, we're ready to proceed with the hearing," said Gottlieb.

"Just let me finish amusing myself with this information," Tisch replied, reading the bartender's affidavit and looking decidedly unamused. He put the paper aside and spent the rest of the day listening to Baczynski and Quigley talk about Frank Spindel.

Both jurors recounted what Spindel told them about his signaling to Collins from the jury box during deliberations. Baczynski demonstrated what he saw, using his own finger, and Quigley said Spindel told her at another point that this was what he was doing. "We had gone back into the room, and he was standing there saying that he gave Collins encouragement. I remember I said to him, 'What do you mean "encouragement"?' And a couple of the other jurors were also asking. He said, 'Well, I gave him the'"—she made an "okay" sign with her fingers—"'meaning it was going his way."

Both Baczynski and Quigley testified about instances when it seemed that Spindel had inside information. In addition to the story of the cigarette butts, Quigley recalled Spindel at one point predicting that the defense would try to implicate Todd Steuerman in the Tankleff murders. What exactly did he say? Gottlieb asked. "Simply that Todd didn't have anything to do with it, and that he knew it, and that you would make accusations that he did." Did he say how he knew this? "He was 'informed.'"

After delivering their direct testimony, Baczynski and Quigley faced two rounds of cross-examination, one by Robert Caccese, the prosecutor now handling the case for the DA's office, and another by David Clayton, a sharp-tongued attorney who represented Spindel. The cross-examiners tried to attack the credibility of Baczynski's and Quigley's accusations by questioning their motives and suggesting they were pawns of the defense. It didn't appear to be a strong argument in Quigley's case: She said she had no reservations about the verdict and insisted that nothing Spindel said influenced her assessment of the case or her eventual vote for conviction. She presented herself as a disinterested party simply relating what she saw and heard. "Did you at the time it occurred regard it as misconduct in any fashion?" Clayton asked her. Replied Quigley, "I regarded it as B.S."

With Baczynski, the cross-examiners had more to work with. They made much of his change of heart about the verdict and what he'd said about it in the media. Soon after the verdict, he was quoted in newspapers saying things such as "the evidence just piled up" and "I think he definitely snapped and lost it." Two months later, on the tabloid TV show *A Current Affair*, he was heard telling a reporter for the program on the phone, "An innocent boy is sitting in jail." The day the story of his allegations broke, Baczynski began getting threatening calls—*We know where you live. Don't think you're gonna testify. You're not gonna live to Monday.* Several came while Gottlieb was at Baczynski's house that night. "I'm getting death threats up the kazoo," Baczynski told a reporter that day. "Somebody out there is very, very nervous about me coming forward."

Spindel's lawyer recited the quotes to portray Baczynski as a man un-hinged by regret. So on redirect Gottlieb allowed him to explain his change of heart and to talk about the havoc caused by his decision to come forward. "I've never been in jury duty before," Baczynski said. "I have never been under this kind of pressure before. And I said I just want to keep it to myself, not tell anybody, and I'll just live with it. When I went out and made all these interviews early on, I said if I can justify that Marty was guilty, then it's okay if there were things that weren't right. I kept try-ing to tell myself, 'He's guilty, he's guilty. It's okay.' Because even though you might have cheated and not played by the rules, he's still guilty. It's sort of like patting myself on the back—'Don't worry about it.' But as time went on, I couldn't live with myself. Saying whether he's guilty or not guilty wasn't the issue. The part that killed me was that I knew that these things happened, and it bothered me. . . ."

THAT THURSDAY, Tisch announced his ruling on the defense motion to set aside the verdict, and it was clear from his first words that he'd had quite enough of Gottlieb's postverdict maneuvers.

To Tisch's mind, Gottlieb had misled him in promising "new evi-dence" that warranted a postponement of the sentencing. "John Doe"— that's it? Tisch was so unimpressed that he didn't even take Gottlieb up on his offer to privately reveal the names of the principals and show him his source's affidavit. But the allegations of juror misconduct were not so eas-ily dismissed. Tisch said he would hold a full hearing to determine if Frank Spindel did anything improper and, if he did, whether it influenced the verdict. But in announcing his decision, a written ruling that he read in court, the judge left little doubt that he'd come to it begrudgingly, con-scious that the law required it and that he risked a reversal of the verdict on appeal if he refused. He made no effort to discourage the impression that he was about to preside over a three-week proceeding whose outcome he had already decided.

Tisch began by blasting Gottlieb's tactics, essentially accusing him of a bait-and-switch in promising new evidence that someone else killed the Tankleffs and then delivering a motion that focused on the conduct of the jury. "It could certainly be questioned whether fraud was perpetrated on this court," he said. Then he launched an appraisal of the case that flirted with the premise that Marty Tankleff's defense amounted to a spoiled rich kid stamping his feet, blaming everyone else, refusing to accept his punishment, writing checks all the way to prison. Tisch's words grew into a tirade—as much of one as the low-key judge could manage—of personal feelings that seemed to have been welling up for some time:

". . . The defense with its apparently unlimited resources available has chosen to attempt to portray the defendant as the victim of the great frame-up. The defendant, convicted by a panel of jurors he chose, confounded by a verdict he was apparently assured by counsel was unlikely, if not impossible, now seeks to attribute this conviction to every possible hypothesis but his guilt. We have had allegations and innuendos of misconduct about virtually everyone connected with this matter. Allegations have run the gamut from police collusion to jury tampering by the prosecutor. This week we were treated to character assassination of the presiding judge based on specious if not ludicrous grounds clearly attempting to intimidate the court and to dissuade it from carrying out its sworn duty. Although the defense has clearly degenerated from those lofty ideals so often espoused by counsel for the defense, this court refuses to engage in any unjudicial response to these deplorable tactics. This court is aware of its obligation to maintain a fair, objective, and impartial state of mind to provide both sides with justice to which they are entitled."

Tisch continued, "Apparently we have embarked upon a new and dangerous era, the era of jury bashing. It has the potential to develop into an insidious disease which will strike at the very heart of our criminal justice system." It should not be surprising, said Tisch, that emotions ran high after a long and emotional homicide trial and eight days of sequestered deliberations. "Certainly there will be lingering animosity, even after the verdict, between those who were most vociferous on behalf of the majority and those in the minority who ultimately yielded and joined in the unanimous verdict. The strong overcome the weak. It's human nature, and the weak resent it. Each juror was instructed that they were not to give up honestly held beliefs on the guilt or innocence of the accused unless convinced of the appropriateness of doing so. There was no report by the jury during deliberations of any deadlock. Disgruntled jurors are not permitted by law to impeach their own verdicts solely due to second thoughts, emotional stress, or postverdict coercion by others."

All that said, "the state of the law" determined that a hearing should be held. It would commence the following Tuesday.

Gottlieb stood. He said he had a few procedural matters to discuss, but that first he wished to make a comment. He told Tisch that it was "terribly unfortunate—and I think that is the way I will present it this morning—" that the judge felt it appropriate to suggest that his firm's vigorous representation of its client was a fraud, or improper in any way. "We have and will continue to do whatever is necessary in accordance with law, in accordance with the ethics of our profession, to represent Martin Tankleff. That is the appropriate way for the system to operate. That is the way, ultimately, for justice to be done. That's what this is about, Your Honor."

OVER THE COURSE of three weeks, nine of the twelve jurors who convicted Martin Tankleff were summoned to the very chair whose procession of occupants had once been the focus of their attentions. Now it was the jurors who would be questioned and cross-examined.

Assistant District Attorney Robert Caccese put five jurors on the stand and asked each of them what they knew of the various allegations of misconduct being made about one of their number by two others. All five said they saw nothing, heard nothing, knew nothing. Gottlieb was well aware by now of the alliances that had developed among the jurors. And he knew this: The day after Frank Spindel played golf with Collins and McCready, he called Peter Baczynski. Unaware of Baczynski's cooperation, Spindel told him not to talk to the defense investigator and said he was going to call all the others and tell them the same thing.

After testifying that she was aware of no misconduct by Spindel, a juror named Anna Tonis was asked by Gottlieb whether she had spoken to Spindel since the trial. She said she had not. Spindel himself took the stand the next day, and when Gottlieb asked which jurors he had spoken to, he said, among others, Anna Tonis. "She had left a message with somebody else to get in contact with me and I called her back." When? "Last week or the week before. It was right after Mr. Navarra came to visit her."

Another juror who testified that she was unaware of any improper conduct by Spindel was named Gertrude Bunk. She sat next to Spindel in the jury box, which meant she'd been at his side six hours a day, five days a week, for more than two months. She said he was a fidgety fellow who shifted in his chair and kept kicking her accidentally and apologizing, saying he had a lower back problem. She demonstrated exactly how he rested the right side of his face in the palm of his right hand, with his elbow planted on the arm of his chair. Then she shifted to the left, just the way he did. But as far as seeing him giving signals to the prosecutor, no, she never saw anything like that.

During Baczynski's testimony, Gottlieb had asked him whether he shared with others the news he heard from Spindel, on the first night of deliberations, that Shari Rother had been supporting the prosecution for a year and a half. Baczynski said he told Victor Muglia about it the next morning. Muglia now took the witness stand for the prosecution. He wore a T-shirt that said GO LIKE HELL on the back. He said he never heard anything about Shari Rother backing the prosecutors over her brother. As he recalled, his conversation with Baczynski that morning consisted of "Good morning" and "How's your knee?" By the way, Gottlieb asked on cross-examination, did there come a time when you threatened to hit Terry Quigley? Absolutely not, said Muglia, though they did have an argument when she accused him of miscounting the ballots.

At the end of the day, Carolyn Colwell, the *Newsday* reporter, noticed Quigley sitting in the hallway and asked why she was there. Quigley told her the district attorney's office had subpoenaed her to return to the stand for more cross-examination. She'd reported at 9:30 as ordered but was never called, and no one from the DA's office talked to her all day. "*That's* jury bashing," she complained. She'd heard Muglia's testimony on a TV monitor. Colwell asked her what she thought. "Victor Muglia lied," Quigley replied. "Everything he said he didn't know and he didn't hear, he most definitely did." She knew Muglia was aware of the news about Shari Rother because *everyone* knew about it. Spindel talked about it openly in the jury room, and Muglia "was in on the comments." As for the argument about the ballots, it wasn't about Muglia's counting, it was about his commentary. She wrote "not guilty." Muglia sarcastically announced it as "adamantly not guilty."

Frank Spindel wasn't an actual defendant, but he played one in this hearing. He took the stand in his own defense and denied everything: He didn't know John Collins before the trial, didn't signal him during the deliberations, and didn't tell any of his fellow jurors otherwise. His denials continued under Gottlieb's cross-examination: He didn't have inside information about Dot Depping's cigarette butts, didn't watch videotapes of the trial, didn't keep a diary. And he didn't talk about the case with his next-door neighbor, Kevin McNamara, a homicide detective.

The only thing Spindel admitted was the one thing he couldn't deny: that he made numerous phone calls from the motel in violation of the judge's sequestration orders. Those showed up on his home phone records, which Tisch had allowed Gottlieb to subpoena. (The judge denied

Gottlieb's request for Spindel's phone records going back to the beginning of the trial to search for possible sources of inside information.) Spindel claimed he received no information about the case in any of the calls he made from the motel; they were all personal or business. So, no, he didn't find out about Detective McCready's announcement that Shari Rother was on the prosecution's side. Since he didn't hear about it, he didn't tell any of the other jurors.

The prosecution's last witness was the prosecutor himself, John Collins. There was no suspense about what he would say, but the moment disappointed no one expecting theatrics from the cross-examination. Collins denied knowing Spindel before or during the trial and said he'd had no improper contact with him or any other juror. When Gottlieb brought up the day during the deliberations when he asked Collins to stop saying good morning to the jurors, they essentially began yelling at and over each other, their words "merging into a garbled roar," as Carolyn Colwell put it.

Collins's testimony did yield something intriguing. A major theme of the defense's allegations about Spindel was his apparent access to extracurricular information and his use of it to enhance his influence among his fellow jurors. Gottlieb had been thwarted in his efforts to find a possible source of information in Spindel's phone records. But maybe he didn't need a phone to hear things. Gottlieb asked Collins whether he had ever talked about Spindel with the juror's next-door neighbor, homicide detective Kevin McNamara. Collins acknowledged he had a conversation with McNamara during jury selection. He had initially challenged Spindel's seating on the jury but dropped his objection after speaking to McNamara. What did McNamara tell him? Only that he and Spindel had no more than a casual over-the-back-fence kind of relationship and that Collins would have to make up his own mind about whether to accept him as a juror. Left unclear was why Collins initially opposed Spindel's selection, and why the prosecutor dropped his objection after speaking to Spindel's neighbor if all the homicide detective said was that he didn't know him very well.

IN RIVERHEAD one evening, Collins and a few other assistant DAs and some police detectives rolled into the Rendezvous, a hangout popular with the legal crowd. They were a boisterous bunch, and when Bob Caccese joined the group a few minutes later he got a round of raucous greetings. It had been a good day in court for Caccese.

After learning that Bill Navarra had recorded his first interview with Baczynski, Caccese had demanded and received a copy of the tape. He found that Baczynski did not tell Navarra that day all the things he had since gone on to say in court. Caccese thought the tape was a smoking gun of inconsistencies and hauled Baczynski back into court, hammering him with his own words. Judging by the merriment at the bar, the prosecution team was feeling pretty good about how it went.

A lawyer named Reynold Mauro was having dinner at the Rendezvous that night and said hello to Caccese when the prosecutor came stumbling through the dining area after a trip to the men's room. Mauro asked Caccese how the case was going.

"*Great!*" Caccese roared. "We got the little Jew bastard now!"

Mauro was taken aback. "Tankleff?" he asked.

"No, Gottlieb! We got the little fucker good." Caccese added a few more expletives, then returned to the bar, which was getting louder by the minute with hoots and hollers, despite motions to suppress by the bartender and then the owner of the place. Mauro went into the bar to see what was going on and saw Caccese on the TV screen questioning Peter Baczynski in the courtroom. Then Gottlieb's face came on the screen, and the cheers turned to catcalls. "We'll finish him, that Jew shyster," Caccese said, to huzzahs from his colleagues. "He better have money in a Swiss account because he's finished practicing law in Suffolk County!" The group quieted to hear Gottlieb being interviewed after court. "They're dangerous," he said of the DA's office. Caccese yelled back at the screen, "You're fuckin-A we're dangerous!"

Late the next afternoon, Mauro was in his office on Veterans Highway when he decided to drop in on one of the other law firms in his building before going home: the offices of Sussman, Gottlieb & Needleman. Mauro had no desire to make enemies in the DA's office but after thinking about it for a day he decided the right thing to do was tell Gottlieb what he'd seen and heard at the Rendezvous. Gottlieb asked Mauro if he would give him an affidavit. Mauro wrote one on the spot.

The following Monday, Gottlieb attached Mauro's affidavit to a motion asking Judge Tisch to disqualify the Suffolk County district attorney's office from the proceedings and appoint a special prosecutor. He was supported by the New York State Association of Criminal Defense Lawyers, which accused Caccese of prosecutorial misconduct and said the incident, along with the response in general to the juror misconduct issue, "demonstrates that serving justice does not appear to be the main concern of the Suffolk County District Attorney's Office." What becomes of a defendant's rights, Gottlieb's fellow defense lawyers asked, when prosecutors are driven by a desire to inflict personal humiliation on his attorney?

In addition to Caccese's de rigueur denial, the chief of the DA's appeals bureau accused Gottlieb of completing a hat trick of judicial abuse—

"juror bashing, judge bashing, and now prosecution bashing"—and asked the judge to "put an end to this circus." Denying that his office was guilty of such blatant and vulgar anti-Semitism had to have been awkward for the bureau chief, Mark Cohen. He did, however, strike a chord with his "circus" comment: Others started using that word to describe the Tankleff case, some noting how far Marty Tankleff had faded into the background of his own case. Of course, everybody loves a circus. Even the district attorney himself couldn't resist shooting himself out of a cannon. "This man has an exaggerated idea of his own importance. I've always maintained he was the best weapon the district attorney's office ever had," James Catterson told *Newsday*, speaking of Gottlieb. "I can't hide my disdain of him. I didn't like him during the campaign, and I've never thought much of him as an attorney." In fact, said the district attorney, "I've had it with this turkey."

Tisch, too, said he'd had enough—with both sides, though he'd clearly had more than enough of one of them. He denied Gottlieb's request for a special prosecutor, suggested he take his complaints to the professional disciplinary authority, and told the state defense lawyers' association to stay out of it. A week later, on October 23, Tisch called everyone to his courtroom for what he made clear would be the last time. The defense motion to set aside the verdict was denied: No new evidence of any value had been brought forward and the allegations of juror misconduct were groundless.

According to Tisch, it wasn't Frank Spindel who was guilty of mischief, but Peter Baczynski: His testimony, Tisch said in a written opinion, "was for the most part so incredible as to approach the bizarre." Observing that "the burden of criminal service can be devastating to a frail psyche," the judge suggested that Baczynski was a man "tortured by pangs of regret" who was to be dismissed and pitied. "Whether Baczynski now actually believes that some of the incidents he described occurred is irrelevant. Whether he is hallucinating or prevaricating is also irrelevant. He is perhaps nurturing those seeds of remorse into a forest of fiction in the hopes that he can get off the hook for his guilty verdict. However, it will not work. He will simply have to live with his verdict the best way he can."

Tisch's ruling ran eight pages and never mentioned that most of Baczynski's testimony was independently corroborated by Teresa Quigley. The only time her name came up was when he wrote, in a list of "findings of fact," that "the Court finds that juror Frank Spindel did not refer to the content of a portion of a videotape of the trial while involved in a heated discussion with juror Teresa Quigley during the deliberations in the presence of the other ten jurors." Tisch found that Spindel's wife did videotape the trial but that "Spindel did not watch the videotapes." Among his other findings of fact were that Spindel had no knowledge of the source of the cigarette butts and did not tell any juror that he did, and that no juror was aware during deliberations that McCready announced that the defendant's half sister sided with the prosecution.

Tisch was merciless in his psychological analysis of Baczynski, but, curiously, he had nothing to say about why Quigley would lie. Since she firmly stood by her verdict, he couldn't accuse her of suffering hallucination-inducing pangs of remorse. So he did something that had a familiar ring in this case: He pretended she didn't exist. And while Tisch showed no reluctance to speculate about Baczynski's character, there was no evidence that he considered what was actually documented about Spindel's: ten uncontested legal judgments against him that he failed to disclose and numerous suspensions of his driver's license. In every instance, Tisch believed Spindel over Baczynski, who struck many people as nothing more than an earnest man with a strong conscience. It went without saying that Tisch swept away any suggestion that Spindel was a domineering figure in the jury room whose influence might have continued after the verdict. It was apparently more plausible to the judge that Baczynski and Quigley made up their stories than it was that the jurors who were called to testify for the prosecution had been badgered one last time by Juror Number 11.

It seemed the perfect ending to a railroading: a case that was off the tracks from the beginning.

ON THAT DAY, October 23, 1990, Marty Tankleff, age nineteen, approached the bench and declared, when asked by the judge if he had anything to say before sentence was pronounced, "I stand before you innocent of this charge. I loved my parents. I did not kill them."

Marty's Aunt Mickey requested to address the court. Tisch invited her to come forward. "I know Marty is innocent," she said, her voice quivering. "From the moment he was taken into custody, I believed he was innocent. Nothing that happened in this courtroom has changed my mind. . . . We will fight forever to free him from this injustice."

And then the judge handed down the sentence. Noting the brutality of the crimes of which the defendant had been convicted, Tisch imposed the maximum sentence: two consecutive sentences of twenty-five years to life in prison, a total of fifty years before Marty would be eligible for parole.

Marty was led away, leaving his aunts and uncles and cousins in tears once more. Reporters descended on the family as they left the courtroom. For only the second time, Marty's sister was among them, though she surely wasn't with them. Earlier, when the judge announced he was rejecting the motion to set aside the verdict and called a recess before the sentencing, Shari broke into a sob and left the courtroom on the arms of two men. On one side was her husband; on the other, Jim McCready. Later she talked to reporters. She would always ask herself how Marty could have done this, Shari said. "But tonight—two years, a month and two weeks after my father and my stepmother were murdered—I can go home and mourn."

The rest of the family—Marty's only real family now—vowed to go home and fight. "As far as we're concerned," said Ron Falbee, "this is just the end of the beginning."

PART THREE

The Best Years of His Life

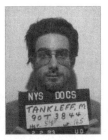

CHAPTER 27

9OT 3844

MARTY TANKLEFF, Department of Corrections number 90T 3844, reached Auburn Correctional Facility in January 1991, the month American troops were mounting Operation Desert Storm in the Persian Gulf War. Auburn was a decrepit prison, a place from another time. Thirty miles southwest of Syracuse, it was New York's first penitentiary, nearly as old as the state itself. The prison opened for business in 1816, and it was here, in 1890, that William Kemmler, convicted of murdering his girlfriend with a hatchet, became the first person in the world to be executed by electric chair. A century later, Auburn was the only maximum-security prison in New York that still didn't have electric gates. "It was an old, old lever-and-spring system, where you had to open each cell door and close it yourself," Marty remembered. "But no matter where you are, it's still that same sound of steel on steel, the closing and even the opening telling you where you are."

An older man took Marty under his wing and advised him to put on a good front and not to show his emotions. The helpful inmate—an "associate," Marty called him, using the proper terminology in a place where the word "friend" was not used loosely—had no idea that keeping his emotions wrapped would be the least of this kid's problems. Even in the relative privacy of his cell, Marty never cried. He thought about how he was going to get out—how his *family* was going to get him out. That remained his mind-set. From the beginning, they had handled everything, and so they would continue. In these early stages of his prison life, he maxed out his phone privileges and they visited when they could, all but his young twin cousins, Susanne and Carol, who couldn't bear to see Marty in prison.

But it was the lawyers Marty needed most, and there were more of them than before. Overturning a conviction was one of the hardest things to do in criminal law, not in the least because it was preceded by the over-turning of the burden of proof: The moment the jury foreman said the word *guilty*, it shifted to the defense. Appeals courts gave the benefit of doubt to the prosecution, and accorded "great deference" to the rulings of trial judges that were the basis of most appeals.

To develop Marty's appeal, Gottlieb recommended Mark Pomerantz, a New York attorney with a top-drawer résumé. Pomerantz had begun his legal career with a clerkship for U.S. Supreme Court justice Potter Stew-art, then spent several years as a federal prosecutor, eventually heading the appeals unit of the U.S. attorney's office in Manhattan. He was now a part-ner at Rogers & Wells, one of New York's most prestigious old-line law firms. He and a colleague, Warren Feldman, plunged into the Tankleff case and found themselves instantly consumed. "As a lawyer you're look-ing at the legal issues," Pomerantz reflected, "but as a human being, you want to know: Did he do it?" After excavating the case, reading the ten thousand pages that already made up the record and flying upstate to meet Marty at Auburn, Pomerantz and Feldman found the answer almost too obvious. "Patently, he didn't do it. I couldn't understand the jury's deci-sion. This was the walking definition of reasonable doubt, and the sheer magnitude of the injustice was staggering. Meeting Marty, I was struck by the ordinariness of him. He could have been any nineteen-year-old kid. As a lawyer, you rarely see such a stark and profoundly disturbing human drama."

Pomerantz and Feldman's job was to find winnable legal issues, and they spent more than two years doing it, finally producing an appeal that ran 180 pages. Their first point was an expanded version of the argument Gottlieb had been making since the beginning: that Judge Tisch should have suppressed Marty's alleged confession. The main prong was that the police didn't advise Marty of his rights until long after he was in legal cus-tody, as the laws of New York defined that status: Would a reasonable and innocent person believe he was free to leave had he been in the defendant's position? The appeal argued that Tisch's ruling before the trial was just too convenient: Marty wasn't in custody during the detectives' relentless drive for a confession, but the moment they managed to push him over the edge—*now* he was in custody. The timing of the Miranda warnings was closely tied to the other custody-related issue: that McCready's tactics in isolating Marty from his family, and particularly from the family friend who was an attorney, amounted to a denial of his right to counsel. Finally, Marty's statements should have been suppressed because the circumstances of the interrogation produced an unreliable confession—as demonstrated by its inconsistency with the physical evidence.

A second element of appeal was one that Gottlieb had promised when Tisch gave Collins free rein to ask in his summation why many of Marty's relatives had not testified in his defense. This improperly shifted the burden of proof to the defense. Finally, the appeal asserted that the jury's verdict that Marty was guilty of "depraved indifference" in the death of his mother was inconsistent with both the facts of the case and the jury's simultaneous finding of intentional murder in the case of his father.

Pomerantz and Feldman filed the appeal with the Second Department of the Appellate Division of the state Supreme Court in July 1992. Headquartered in Brooklyn, the Second Department was the busiest appellate court in the United States. Each year, its fifteen justices (five more would be added in 1994) decided some four thousand appeals and considered twelve thousand motions. The justices, who were appointed by the governor, were assisted in this mammoth caseload by a staff of fifty-nine attorneys and by whatever the court administration could come up with to make the wheels of justice move faster. The judges had traditionally sat in panels of five, but in 1978 they were reduced to four.

If it was true that the assignment of judges was by luck of the draw, it could not be said that Marty's fortunes were improving. The presiding justice for his appeal was Lawrence J. Bracken, one of the two justices on the appellate court from Suffolk County. Bracken had a solid history as part of the Suffolk County law enforcement establishment, but the potential for conflict was more specific than that.

During jury selection at Marty's trial, Gottlieb had wanted to excuse a prospective juror for what seemed to him an obvious bias. But for reasons he couldn't fathom, Judge Tisch refused his repeated requests. Gottlieb talked it over with his partner, Ron Sussman, and decided that keeping this person off the jury was critical enough to take the extremely risky step of going over the judge's head. Judges of the Appellate Division maintained chambers in their home counties. Gottlieb and Sussman went to Justice Bracken and presented him with a writ of mandamus, an order by a superior court to compel a lower court to correctly perform a mandatory function. As Sussman recalled: "We show up at Judge Bracken's chambers, we present it to him, he looks at it and he says, 'Eh, you don't need this. Go back—who knows, maybe he'll change his mind.' Bob and I drive back to Riverhead, talking the whole way about what just happened. I said, 'You think he's gonna make a phone call?' We get back to court, and Tisch has miraculously changed his mind. He lets the juror go."

What the lawyers didn't know at the time was that Tisch had been a protégé of Bracken's since the late 1960s, when the senior judge was in the top ranks of the district attorney's office and Tisch was starting out as a young prosecutor. Later it was Bracken's behind-the-scenes influence that helped get Tisch nominated for his first judgeship. And now Bracken was the head of a panel of judges that would be reviewing Tisch's rulings in one of the most high-profile and arguably the most intensely contested murder trials in the county's history. It was only natural to wonder how it might affect his consideration of the appeal, and even whether his assignment to the case was as random as advertised. At the same time, Justice Bracken was on a panel hearing an appeal in the Pius case, another notorious Suffolk County homicide involving confessions by teenagers.

Though Gottlieb and Sussman were bothered by Bracken's presence on the panel, Mark Pomerantz didn't agonize about it. "We speculated about it," he recalled, "but lawyers always speculate. The judges are who they are and you can't do anything about it. You assume judges are going to be straight and impartial." It was also true that Bracken was only one of the four judges who would decide the case. And if his perspective was worrisome, it might be balanced by that of one of his colleagues, Justice Geraldine Eiber. She was the rare appellate judge who had spent her entire prior career as a defense attorney. Moreover, she had participated in a famous case that bore some resemblance to Marty's. In 1965, Alice Crimmins was charged with the murders of her two children after her reactions to their deaths failed to meet expectations.

On September 27, 1993, Marty's lawyers and relatives converged on a courthouse that filled a block of Monroe Place in Brooklyn Heights. The three-story structure housed a single courtroom, a magisterial chamber with carved walnut paneling and stucco cornices, lit by a quartet of chandeliers. Appearing for the Suffolk County district attorney was Mark Cohen, the chief of the office's appeals bureau, who was accompanied by John Collins. The one person who wasn't in attendance, for the first time in the history of the case, was Marty Tankleff. His absence was symbolic of the new order of things. A defendant had the right to be present at his trial, but not at his appeal.

It was the job of an appeals attorney to argue matters of legal procedure, not to retry the case. But Pomerantz took an approach urged by Mike McClure. Still full of regret that he'd not taken a more active role with Gottlieb during the trial, McClure wasn't shy about offering his views to Pomerantz. One of the things he wished Gottlieb had done, he told Pomerantz, was to use a visual aid—a chart on an easel—to demonstrate to the jury how each element of the supposed confession was refuted by a corresponding piece of physical evidence. Pomerantz thought Gottlieb made the point piercingly clear, but he liked the idea of using a chart to underscore how obvious it was that the police produced a fictional confession. When Cohen contended during his oral argument that there was plenty of evidence corroborating the confession, Justice Eiber told him that was nonsense.

McClure smiled when he heard that. But something else concerned him. The day before, the family had met with Pomerantz and Feldman in their Manhattan office to talk about what to expect at the hearing. Mike noted the oddity that the panel had an even number of judges and asked what would happen in the event of a two-two split. Pomerantz told him that never happened. By custom, the judges gathered after each day's oral arguments, and nine out of ten cases they heard were cut-and-dried. The decisions were usually unanimous.

"It won't be in this case," Mike said.

The decision came two days after Christmas. The lawyers received it by fax and scanned it for the only words that mattered.

"ORDERED that the judgments are affirmed."

The appeal was rejected, but not in the usual way. The names of the judges were listed at the top of the page as always, but there were five, not four. It *was* a tie. And it was broken by a judge who sided with the presiding justice who wrote the majority opinion, Lawrence J. Bracken.

The judge selected to cast the deciding vote was Thomas R. Sullivan, a former district attorney of Staten Island and once the president of the New York State District Attorneys Association. Sullivan agreed with Bracken and Justice Vincent Pizzuto that Martin Tankleff was not in custody at any time prior to the moment he was advised of his rights and so his statements were properly admitted into evidence by the trial judge. They also rejected the argument that Detective McCready's ruse led to a false confession: "[O]n the contrary," Bracken wrote, "we find that the factual reliability of the defendant's confession was, if anything, enhanced by the nature of the particular ploy which was used to elicit it. Needless to say, we give no credence to the defendant's claim that he confessed because he was 'brainwashed.'" What of the confession's inconsistencies with the physical evidence? Bracken and his two concurring colleagues said nothing about it. And they rejected all the other grounds for appeal.

But it wasn't the majority's judgment that was most remarkable about the decision. It was the dissent by Justices Cornelius J. O'Brien and Geraldine Eiber. They didn't just want to reverse the verdict and order a new trial. They wanted to dismiss the case entirely.

The dissent was written by O'Brien, a highly respected judge whose prior career path had been the reverse of the standard model. He began as a private attorney and then joined the Queens district attorney's office, rising to the top ranks, including a term as chief of the appeals bureau, over the course of a decade. "At the time of the murders, the defendant was still a minor and special care should have been taken to ensure that his rights were protected," O'Brien wrote. "Instead, the police improperly isolated the defendant from his family for the purpose of interrogation, questioned him in an increasingly accusatory manner for hours without advising him of his *Miranda* rights, and employed a ruse to extract inculpatory statements. As the questioning progressed over the course of the morning, no reasonable person of 17 years of age, in the defendant's position, and innocent of any crime, would believe that he was free to leave the presence of the police." Even assuming Marty was not in legal custody at any time through most of the questioning, O'Brien and Eiber asserted, he certainly was the moment McCready told him his father identified him as his attacker. But the detectives didn't advise him of his rights even then.

O'Brien compared the case to one heard by another panel of this same court. After just an hour of questioning, a fifteen-year-old boy confessed to stabbing his sister to death. The detectives told him no lies and used no psychological manipulations; they simply pointed out inconsistencies in his story. The court overturned that conviction and suppressed the confession, saying that "as the session wore on it must have become apparent to the defendant that he had become a suspect and was not free to simply terminate the questioning and leave." In the Tankleff case, the conduct of the police "was more egregious," O'Brien wrote, yet the majority made the opposite ruling. He and Eiber came to a remarkable conclusion: "In view of the absence of any other evidence connecting the defendant to the murders, except for the confession which he disavowed at the trial, the indictments should be dismissed."

But O'Brien and Eiber weren't finished. They agreed with Marty's lawyers that Tisch willfully committed a reversible error in allowing Collins to ask why the defense hadn't called Shari and Ron Rother to the stand. So "even if I agreed with my colleagues that the confession should not be suppressed," O'Brien wrote, "I would dissent and vote to grant the defendant a new trial based on the court's error in permitting the prosecutor to comment during summation. . . ."

For Marty, his lawyers, and his family, the decision was painfully frustrating but not without a glimmer of hope. "We came so close," Gottlieb said that day, close enough to be optimistic that the state's Court of Appeals would hear the case. Acceptance was far from automatic, but O'Brien felt so strongly that he exercised his power to sign an order granting Marty's lawyers "leave to appeal" to the state's highest court.

Nine months later, on November 30, 1994, Pomerantz and Feldman brought the case to Albany. The Court of Appeals was established by the state constitution to decide issues of law, not fact, so Pomerantz needed to persuade at least four of its seven justices that Marty's convictions should be overturned as a matter of law. The decision came a month later, again the week of Christmas. And again it went against Marty. This time, it *was* unanimous.

IN THE USUAL course of a murder case, the family of the victim will be relieved at the news that a court has rejected the appeals of the person convicted of the crime. In the Tankleff case, the only relatives of the victims who were pleased by the appeals court rulings were Shari and Ron Rother. Shari discounted the strong dissenting opinion that forced the addition of a tie-breaking judge by the Appellate Division. "I don't believe the dissension came out of any belief that anybody thought that he might be innocent," she told a reporter, though it was plain that the opposite was true.

Shari had moved on with her life, and by the point of the decisions on Marty's appeals, it included a business venture that could only be considered peculiar. In the spring of 1993, Michael Slackman, a reporter for *Newsday,* heard that the Rothers were opening a bar in Riverhead. He also heard that the retired detective who put Shari's brother in prison was doing the construction. Slackman reached Ron Rother, who said it was true. He was always looking for business opportunities, he said, and it occurred to him during Marty's trial that Riverhead would be a good town to open a pub-style restaurant. He and Shari had gotten to know Jim McCready before the trial and they'd become friends. Since McCready had a construction business, why not? Rother told Slackman he had two partners but wouldn't say who they were. The name of the place would be Digger O'Dell's, after the friendly undertaker in *The Life of Riley.* "It's going to be a real classy place," Rother said. "Lots of mahogany."

McCready didn't see any problem with the arrangement. He was retired now, he told Slackman, and the Rothers could do with their money what they pleased. Did it matter that it was the money Shari inherited as a direct result of Marty's conviction? Not a bit, said McCready. What he didn't say was that he was benefiting from that conviction beyond merely being the Rothers' contractor. In fact, he was one of those unnamed partners. What made him unnamed was that he put his interest in his wife's name on the liquor license application. PUB STORY GETS MEATIER was the headline over the follow-up story.

For Bob Gottlieb, McCready's business venture with the Rothers triggered all the old feelings about the Tankleff case. He wrote to District Attorney Jim Catterson, asking for a grand jury investigation of the relationship between the detective who put Marty Tankleff away and the relatives who benefited from it. Were they discussing it during the trial? If they were, it should have been brought to the jury's attention. There's no conflict of interest here, Catterson responded. Nor was McCready's testimony at the trial suspect; it was corroborated by numerous witnesses. Catterson's defense of McCready was at once predictable and incongruous: He was at this very moment trying to put McCready in jail.

On the night of St. Patrick's Day in 1991, a few months after Marty Tankleff was tucked away in a cell at the Auburn Correctional Facility, Jim McCready was settled in at Harry's Bar with his fellow members of the Rocky Point St. Patrick's Day Parade Committee. Among the other patrons that night was Douglas Schuchman, a construction worker who departed with a dozen beers in his belly and a WE SUPPORT THE TROOPS banner in his hands. The sign was hanging outside and happened to be McCready's donation to the parade. When someone came in and announced the snatching, McCready and three others chased Schuchman down and walked him to a dark side street, where, it was alleged, they began to pummel him. This woke the neighbors, who would later testify that two police officers arrived separately during the assault, and each drove off without intervening. Schuchman himself would tell of his relief when a police car arrived and an officer lit up the scene with a searchlight—but then, after talking to McCready, got back in his patrol car and drove off. "I said, 'Please don't leave me. Help me.' And James McCready comes up to me and says, 'Nobody's going to help you,' and bang, bang, he punches me in the face." As a final act of humiliation, McCready's posse took Schuchman's clothes.

The incident became public when Schuchman and his lawyer announced their intention to sue the police department and the two officers who ignored his pleas for help. It put pressure on Catterson to demonstrate the kind of independence from the police for which his predecessors were never known. Catterson responded by bringing the case to a grand jury, which indicted the entire bunch—the four who beat Schuchman and the two cops who did nothing to stop it. McCready found himself facing charges of felony assault that carried the potential for serious time in state prison.

Leaving nothing to chance, McCready obtained the services of not one but two of the better-connected defense lawyers in Suffolk County, both former high-profile prosecutors. One was Tom Spota, the attorney for the Suffolk County Detectives Association who represented McCready before the State Investigation Commission. The other was William Keahon, who had also been ensnared in the SIC investigation. He was one of the two high-ranking assistant district attorneys accused by Judge Stuart Namm, and later by the investigations commission, of helping cover up a colossal lie by the lead detective in the James Diaz murder trial by twice giving "highly suspect" testimony themselves.

In the St. Patrick's Day assault case, Keahon started out representing one of McCready's co-defendants, a laundry manager named Albert DeLuca. This was an arrangement in which McCready had more than a casual interest: The most damning evidence against him, aside from the victim's testimony, was a signed confession by DeLuca in which he admitted his involvement but said that McCready led the assault and did most of the damage.

Much as he had good reason to be highly annoyed with DeLuca, McCready had even more reason to see to it that the man replace his no-name lawyer with Keahon. When the case was about to go to trial, Keahon made a motion to Judge Arthur Pitts to suppress his client's confession. The grounds: that DeLuca was in police custody the moment he left his house with two detectives after they asked him to come to the precinct; that the police didn't read him his rights as they claimed; and that they violated his right to counsel by telling his wife—who told his lawyer when he called the precinct—that they only wanted to speak to him as a witness, not a suspect. Judge Pitts held a Huntley hearing, and after watching one former fellow detective after another testify about their proper conduct in obtaining DeLuca's confession, McCready told reporters, "They're cheating. They're lying. And my life is at stake."

The hearing lasted three days. McCready didn't miss a moment of it, and when the judge announced from the bench that the police investigation of the case was so "troublesome" that he felt compelled to toss DeLuca's confession, McCready leaped to his feet and ran from the courtroom, shouting, "Yes! Yes!" Not that he wasn't still mad as hell. "The police officers lied," he said, "and the district attorney's office condoned it. They're persecuting me, they're not prosecuting me. The whole thing is a sham."

The priceless irony of McCready's indignation was not lost on the DA's office, and Catterson's spokesman called him on it. Said the flack, "McCready is raising the same charges against Suffolk County police officers that were leveled against him so many times when he was a detective, and against which this office successfully defended him. Is he now saying we were wrong?"

Without DeLuca's statement, the assistant district attorney conceded he had insufficient evidence to proceed against him. With no client to defend, Keahon jumped over to help Spota defend McCready. And with the favorable ruling, McCready took his legal team's advice to waive his right to be tried by a jury and go with a bench trial. He'd put his faith in the judge. "I think the issues in this case are too complicated for a jury to understand," McCready explained to a reporter, but to sophisticated observers the choice suggested the outcome. Spota made no opening statement and presented no witnesses, though he did tell reporters that the entire case was based on the testimony of "an admitted drunk and unmitigated liar" who didn't look so bad in the pictures the detectives took that night—just some black and blue marks and a little puffiness. Keahon added, "If he had fallen down because he was drunk, he could have gotten the same injuries."

Perhaps Keahon decided to test his own theory. The next morning, Spota arrived in court and asked for a day's adjournment, on account of his co-counsel's inability to appear, on account of the unfortunate accident he'd been involved in overnight. It seemed that Keahon was driving on Nesconset Highway at 2:15 A.M. when he crashed his Mercedes head-on into a car whose driver was, unlike Keahon, traveling in the right direction. The other driver was an emergency room doctor on his way home from the night shift. He wound up where he started and was fortunate to survive his injuries, while Keahon escaped with little more than a few black-and-blue marks, a little puffiness, and charges of driving both drunk and with a suspended license.

Spota finished the case himself. This involved cross-examining the prosecution's witnesses, saying the defense rested, and summing up by declaring that James McCready, who served this county with distinction for twenty years, could not be convicted and sent to prison on the word of a man who told "lie after lie" under oath. Judge Pitts retired to his chambers. He returned ninety minutes later and said he'd reviewed all the evidence, given the matter due deliberation, and found that the People had failed to prove its case. McCready burst into tears and threw his arms around Spota, and then his wife, as his supporters—brother detectives, including his two actual brothers—cheered and stomped their feet. Afterward, McCready said it was the happiest day of his life. The DA's office had been out to get him—for what reason, he didn't say—and he beat them.

But as things turned out, McCready and Ron Rother barely got one St. Paddy's Day out of Digger O'Dell's. By the second year, they were out of business and McCready was virtually penniless. He couldn't make the payments on his '94 Thunderbird, among other debts. In 1995 he declared bankruptcy and eventually moved to South Carolina.

JERRY STEUERMAN, on the other hand, was doing quite well for himself. The prosecutors always said Steuerman had no motive to kill the Tankleffs, because he would still owe their estate, but the settlement his lawyer negotiated allowed him to pay considerably less than the actual debt. It included signing over one of his bagel stores to Shari Rother, but that was okay: It was Jerry's good fortune to have a business-savvy son with a golden touch. Not Todd, who was only halfway through his seven years upstate, but Glenn, an aggressive entrepreneur who figured out how to modernize the bagel business by using new labor-saving ovens and selling franchises. By 1994, there were thirty Strathmore Bagel stores in New York and Florida.

Jerry was semiretired, living with his second wife in a gated community in Boca Raton. But he didn't head south without leaving a trail behind. A couple of years before his departure from Long Island—this time for good—Steuerman bought a car from an Infiniti saleswoman named Karlene Kovacs. To her, Steuerman wasn't just another customer.

In the spring of 1991, the man Karlene was dating, John Guarascio, invited her to his sister's house out in Suffolk County for Easter dinner. On the way there, Guarascio gave Karlene the rundown on the man his sister lived with, a guy named Joe who was, in John's opinion, a no-good wiseass. He was heavily into dope, and if he and Terry were married you'd call him a wife-beater. They had two kids together, a two-and-a-half-year-old boy and a baby girl born a few months ago. John wished his sister would find the nerve to get out. But it was the same old story: Joe would just come after her and make things even worse.

After they arrived, Karlene could see what John meant. Joe was cocky, she thought, like a low-level wiseguy. But he wasn't unfriendly, and not long after they got there, Joe asked them if they wanted to smoke a joint. Why not, they said, and followed Joe and a friend of his to the back of the apartment.

Karlene and Joe swapped small talk as they passed the joint around. It turned out they grew up in neighboring towns and knew some of the same people. And then the conversation drifted into strange territory. The entry point would later be a bit hazy, but somehow the name Steuerman came up. Maybe passing a joint around made it natural for Joe to mention that he was involved in dope dealing with Todd Steuerman before Todd got sent upstate. And maybe that led Karlene to mention that she'd sold an Infiniti to Todd's father. However it began, Karlene somehow found herself on the receiving end of a one-sided conversation. Suddenly Joe was talking about the Tankleff murders. He was talking about *being there* when it happened. He was saying he was with Steuerman, but he didn't say which one, father or son. He said something about crouching down behind some bushes and something about getting away quick and going to the Carolinas.

Karlene couldn't believe what she was hearing, so she pretended she didn't. She and Joe were having a kind of one-on-one, and John and the other guy weren't really involved. So she didn't bring it up in the car when they left, or any time in the couple of months they continued to see each other. And she told no one else.

Karlene moved from sales to the service department a couple of years later, and got to know her boss's father, who would drop by now and then. He was a retired cop, now a private investigator. His name was Bill Navarra. A jolt went through Karlene when he mentioned he worked on the Tankleff case for Bob Gottlieb, Marty Tankleff's lawyer. She had an impulse to tell him about that strange encounter on Easter Sunday but couldn't manage to do it. He won't believe me, she thought. We were smoking dope. He'll think I was hallucinating. Anyway, didn't the son do it? He confessed, right?

One day Navarra dropped by the dealership, and Karlene decided to just get it over with and tell him. He didn't think she was crazy. He asked her why she never told him about it before.

On August 10, 1994, Navarra brought Karlene Kovacs to Gottlieb's office, where she put her information in an affidavit. As new evidence went, it was on the thin side. She recounted driving to a house somewhere north of Exit 61 of the Long Island Expressway one day three years earlier, with a man she hadn't seen since soon after that; that they "went into a bedroom and smoked a joint" with a guy named "Joe" whose last name she did not know; that Joe "told me, in essence, that he was involved in the Tankleff murders in some way" and that she recalled him "saying something about hiding behind trees and bushes at the Tankleff house during the time of the murders and that he was with a Steuerman. He did not give the first name of the Steuerman he was with." She also remembered him saying that after the murders "he was afraid of being caught and therefore had to get out of town."

As sketchy as Karlene Kovacs's story was, it was the best thing anyone connected with Marty had heard in the four years since he went to prison. The first thing to do was talk to John Guarascio. Navarra found him at his job at a town garage. He was a slightly built man in his late thirties with blue eyes and a ponytail. He seemed wary when Navarra approached, but he agreed to talk. Yes, he said, he used to date Karlene Kovacs—her name was Burroughs then, she must have gotten married—and yes, he remembered taking her to his sister's house one Easter two, three years ago. And yes, his sister lived with a guy named Joe. But no, he didn't remember hearing Joe say anything about being involved in the Tankleff murders. Not that they spent a lot of time together. "I don't have much use for the guy, to be honest with you," Guarascio said.

What's this Joe's last name? Navarra asked.

"Creedon," Guarascio said.

GOTTLIEB WAS STUNNED by the news that it was *Joe Creedon* who had talked about being involved in the murders of the Tankleffs. It was Creedon who came to *him* during the trial with the story about Todd Steuerman shooting him and Todd's father threatening him. It allowed Gottlieb to promote his theory that Todd's drug dealing gave his father access to muscle for hire. It just hadn't occurred to him that the muscle might have been Creedon himself. Why would he go out of his way to inject himself into the case? Gottlieb decided it was because Creedon was playing him. "After the trial," Gottlieb recalled, "Creedon would come to my office and say he was bothered that Marty was convicted because he knew that Steuerman had to be involved." When the postverdict intrigue got the television show *A Current Affair* interested in the case, Gottlieb saw a chance for some publicity that might encourage people with information to come forward. He asked Creedon to go on camera. Creedon agreed and showed up at Gottlieb's office the night the TV crew came to tape the interviews. But he changed his mind at the last minute.

One day in August 1992, Creedon showed up at Gottlieb's office and asked him to handle an aggravated harassment charge, the kind of minor criminal trouble Creedon got himself into on a fairly regular basis. Gottlieb and Creedon signed a retainer agreement, though Gottlieb never did any work on his case or received any payments. "He would just show up in my office," Gottlieb said. "And when Karlene came forward, I said, 'Son of a bitch. Now it makes sense.' He knew I was continuing to pursue anything that would lead to Marty's exoneration. He was keeping close watch on me."

After Gottlieb took Karlene Kovacs's statement and Navarra talked to John Guarascio, Mark Pomerantz came out to Long Island to discuss what to do next. The lawyers found it disconcerting that Guarascio didn't corroborate her story, but Navarra told them they shouldn't assume he was telling the truth. He sensed that Guarascio was holding back out of concern for his sister, that he might just need some time to think about it. Gottlieb and Pomerantz decided to bring what they had to the district attorney. Gottlieb's relationship with Jim Catterson had warmed up considerably the last year or so. Once it became clear that Gottlieb had exhausted his political ambitions and was no threat to his job, Catterson became positively friendly. So Gottlieb called him. They exchanged pleasantries about their respective children, and then Gottlieb told Catterson he was in possession of significant new evidence in the Tankleff case. Catterson invited him in to talk about it.

The following week, Gottlieb, along with Pomerantz and Warren Feldman, went to the DA's office and spent an hour and a half with Catterson; John Collins; the appeals bureau chief, Mark Cohen; and the office's deputy chief investigator, Robert Plansker. They turned over Karlene Kovacs's affidavit and a report of Navarra's other investigative work identifying the "Joe" in her statement as Joseph Creedon. Gottlieb also recounted his unusual dealings with Creedon over the previous four years, pointing out that he was apparently smarter than he seemed. Catterson asked Gottlieb if he planned to go to the press. Absolutely not, Gottlieb told him—"We're here in good faith." All right, said Catterson. We'll look into it.

Gottlieb didn't hear anything for a month and a half. When he did, it didn't come from Catterson's office. It came from Joe Creedon. On the afternoon of October 17, he called Gottlieb's office in a lather. "I need to talk to Bob right away," he told Gottlieb's secretary. She told him he wasn't in the office. "Tell him the DA wants to question me," Creedon said. When Gottlieb got the message, he told his secretary to call Creedon back and tell him he was involved in a long trial and wouldn't be available for a while. Creedon wasn't pleased to hear this. "Bob told me whenever I had a problem to call him," he told the secretary, who wrote down everything he said in shorthand. "Now he's not keepin' his promise. The only reason I'm involved in this is because I was shot by Todd Steuerman, okay? And when *Current Affair* was callin', Bob was beggin' me to go on. When the DA wanted to question me during the trial he told me not to talk to them without an attorney. Now he wants me to wait until his trial is over to talk to him? I can't even go home and see my kids."

Gottlieb didn't call Creedon back. Instead, he called Monroe Freedman, the noted legal ethics expert at Hofstra. Gottlieb told him he was worried that he had inadvertently created a conflict of interest for himself by agreeing to represent a man who may have committed the murders for which his client had been wrongly convicted. The immediate question was this, he told Freedman: He had Creedon's private beeper number; could he give it to the DA's office? Freedman told Gottlieb not to worry: His obligation was to Marty Tankleff, and Creedon couldn't tie him up with a sham attorney-client privilege that he may well have sought for just that reason. Go ahead, Freedman said, give them the beeper number. And stay away from Creedon.

Gottlieb called one of the investigators at the DA's office and gave him Creedon's number. Then he waited. Months went by. Finally, in January, Gottlieb called Mark Cohen. In a "Memo to File" about his conversation that day with Cohen, Gottlieb wrote: "He told me that detectives spoke to Creedon when he was locked up in Nassau County on another charge.

[Creedon] adamantly denied making the statement. He indicated that he did hate Todd and if he had anything he would give it to them. The detectives apparently said that they would help him in the Nassau County charge to try to loosen him up. That did not help. I told him that if I thought of anything creative I would let him know."

Gottlieb didn't think of anything, and neither did Marty's appeals team. They turned their minds back to familiar terrain. If they were going to be creative, it would have to be in court.

The Clock Strikes 13

AFTER TWO YEARS at Auburn, Marty was moved to the Clinton Correctional Facility in Dannemora. Why? They didn't say. Pack your shit—that's what they said. Clinton was in the northeast corner of the state, about ten miles from Lake Champlain, and it was newer than Auburn. It opened in 1845.

At Clinton, Marty was housed in a section called APPU, for Assessment Program and Preparation Unit, prisonspeak for where they put inmates who needed to be separated from the general population—those who had high profiles or needed to keep low ones.

Marty was in the Lower H cell block. It had six tiers, three on each side. A cell measured eight by ten feet, narrow enough for some men to spread their arms and touch the walls on both sides. Most inmates tried to make themselves at home in their cells, sticking makeshift artwork on the concrete, filling their spaces with personal stuff as if it were a dorm room, but Marty resolved never to become so acclimated that he accepted that he *lived* here. "Some of these guys make up their cells so it's nice and designer and all," he explained one day years later. "They'll cover the walls with towels and posters. But why? Do you enjoy this life? Do you really want to look at it as your home? Not me. I don't ever want to get comfortable here. I may reside here. But I don't live here."

It was a game he played with himself, his way of keeping his focus on getting out. But the fact was that Marty *did* live here, and he found ways to make the best of it. At one point early on another inmate told him how to turn juice into wine. But then he got caught and was confined to his cell for thirty days. "My Aunt Marianne would say that was my 'little shit' period. The stupid Marty period. I was still a rebellious teenager."

Marty enrolled in the prison branch of Clinton Community College, taking classes that led to an associate's degree in liberal arts. That would be as far as he could go, once the state cut back on prison education programs. He ate his holiday meals on 2 Gallery, sliding bowls of food down to his friends, Chris and Erik and Danny and Kurt and Richie. But then August would come around, another birthday behind bars. People outside wondered what it was like in those moments, night after night after night, when he laid down to sleep knowing he was going to wake up in prison. But to Marty, "Nighttime is the *best* time. You're asleep and you don't know where you are. It's your only escape. Anytime you're awake you realize where you are. The worst time of the day is when you wake up in the morning."

Marty always assured his worried family that nothing bad had happened to him. "In the first few years I associated myself with some old-timers who kind of took a liking to me," he said. "They felt something was wrong that I was in prison. I had one guy, he said, 'Marty, I think you're innocent. If you're guilty, I don't mind you hanging out with me. But since I think you're innocent you get my respect, too.' That's just the mentality of prison. It's funny, prisoners have this class system. Like murder is perfectly acceptable as long as it's not a little baby. Because if you committed a murder, it's like, 'You're one of us.' Pedophiles, rapists, all that, they're the lowest of the low, and in prison word travels quickly. Usually when a new guy comes in, everybody's curious. Like, who's that guy? Especially a white guy. I tried to associate with the upper echelon kind of guys. You could decipher who they were. They carried themselves a little differently. They were the kind of guys who had a decent upbringing and something happened in their lives that put them in jail."

Chris Lue-Shing was doing eight to twenty-five after pleading to manslaughter for shooting someone who stole a gun from him. Chris was Marty's age, born two weeks before him, and grew up in an Asian American community of Queens. He'd gotten involved in a gang, but it wasn't who he really was. He was bright and articulate and soft-spoken. He and Marty, both residents of Lower H, met in the classroom.

Lower H had a collection of characters that Marty could never have imagined meeting, much less living among. There was Joey Fama, one of the gang of young white guys from the Bensonhurst neighborhood of Brooklyn convicted in a notorious racial killing, the murder of Yusuf Hawkins in 1989. There was a middle-aged man named Gary Cohen. He was a pedophile pediatrician from Suffolk County who was convicted of numerous counts of sodomy and sexual abuse but told everyone in prison he was framed. There was Jason Radtke. He was from Nebraska. Two weeks after he and his girlfriend moved to New York, he killed their baby son. He didn't mean to do it, but the baby was crying so much that he just lost it and threw him down on the floor. That's what he said when he finally confessed to a detective at the 104th Precinct in Queens. But on Lower H, his story was that he didn't do it. He certainly didn't talk about what he did with the baby's body. But judgment was a funny thing in prison. The moral class system that put child predators on the lowest rung competed with the social pressure not to judge the guy in the next cell by his crimes. Lue-Shing developed an anthropologist's eye for the ironies and absurdities of the environment. "Lower H was the biggest contradiction," he recalled a few years after he got out. "There was this feeling of moral superiority over the general population. But everybody did something. And everybody said they didn't do it."

Or at least that it wasn't *totally* their fault. There was every degree of disavowal—rationalizations, self-justifications, outright denial. If a guy asked Marty Tankleff about his case, he would tell him about it. But he didn't go around screaming that he was innocent.

IN PRISON YARDS across America, you can hear three languages: English, Spanish, and Latin. It is common knowledge, for instance, that a convict whose state appeals are exhausted has but one option, and that is to go federal, with a process called habeas corpus—literal translation, "you have the body." In the United States, the filing of a petition for a writ of habeas corpus is a demand to prison authorities to produce an inmate—to bring him to court so it can be determined whether, as he contends, his incarceration by the state is a violation of his federal rights.

To bring a federal writ, Marty needed a new lawyer. Bob Gottlieb had handed the appeal to Mark Pomerantz and Warren Feldman, and now they needed to hand it to someone else. Marty's family had spent hundreds of thousands of dollars on his trial defense and two rounds of appeal, and Pomerantz had worked many more hours than he billed, personally subsidizing some of the fees he was obliged to charge for his firm. If money had ever been no object, as Judge Tisch had once asserted, then those days were over. His sister had the money his parents left behind; Marty needed a free lawyer.

Ron and Carol Falbee came up to visit one weekend, and they talked about where to go from here. Marty thought the family should start writing to people for help—legal foundations, prison activists, politicians. He showed Ron a list of names he'd compiled.

Ron always had complex feelings about the injustice of Marty's arrest and conviction. His overriding emotion was rage against Suffolk County—

the cops, the prosecutors, the judge—but there were strands of other sorrows: anger at Seymour for bringing on the situation that led to the murders; at Mike Fox for his failure to protect Marty; regret about his own obliviousness to what the police were up to that day. And tucked away in a dark corner of his mind were some ambiguous feelings about Marty himself. Ron had given Marty a dose of tough love after he came to live with his family in Westbury. Now he gave him another one. Marty, he said, it's time for you to take responsibility for getting your life back. The family will never abandon you, but this fight is yours.

Ron knew it was a little harsh, but he needed to shake Marty up. He looked at the list of people Marty wanted him to write to and handed it right back to him. "How about *you* write the letters?" he asked. "You've got time."

Marty did have the time, and from that day forward he used it to do exactly what Ron demanded—and way beyond Ron's expectations. Later, they would both look back at this moment and see it as a turning point. Marty began to transform himself from the naïve and clueless teenager, the innocent victim who assumed everything would turn out okay as long as the grown-ups kept paying the lawyers and making the decisions. He became a voracious student of his case and a relentless advocate for his freedom. He obtained a manual typewriter and began writing letters. First to those ten people, then to ten more, then to ten after that. Now what he wanted most from his family was money to buy postage stamps and typewriter ribbons. They happily kept him in stock. The letters went out to lawyers and law firms and law schools and legal foundations—and to his own lawyers. He wanted Gottlieb and Pomerantz to send him the files of his case. He wanted everything—trial transcripts, appeal briefs, investigative reports.

Marty made the prison law library his second home, and eventually his place of employment. The pay was $1.55 a day and all the legal knowledge he could consume. He became the quintessential jailhouse lawyer, working on his own case as well as those of other inmates. He found it to be a winning survival tactic: "The guys that are good at law, they're the one group of guys that everyone wants to keep out of trouble. Because when they have a problem, who's the first one they go to?" He would pull friends and associates into the library to show them something he'd found in a law book, or in the latest issue of the *New York Law Journal*. He would help other inmates with their appeals, and years later one of them would gain his freedom even as Marty continued to struggle for his own.

In the spring of 1995, Marty was trying to get some help with his federal habeas petition when he got a letter from Laura Taichman—Earl L.

Vandermeulen High, Class of '86, and now a third-year law student at Northeastern University in Boston. Laura was three years older than Marty, so she barely knew him while growing up. But she did know Jerry Steuerman, having worked at Strathmore Bagels. In September 1988, she was on the ferry, heading up to Connecticut for her junior year at Wesleyan, when she picked up the paper and read about Marty's arrest. She had a gut reaction: *They have this all wrong.* Two years later, Laura shuddered when she heard Marty was convicted. She always thought Marty could have been anyone. Now, Laura was taking a third-year seminar in constitutional litigation and she had to pick a case and write a paper about it. She didn't have to think twice. *People v. Tankleff*—the case was chock full of self-incrimination issues. She wrote to Marty and began an exchange of letters. During a visit home, she interviewed his lawyers and read the trial record. She had always believed Marty was innocent, but it wasn't until she delved into the case with three years of law school behind her that she truly understood how horrendous the case was.

Approaching graduation, Laura went to Washington for a two-month internship at the law firm of Miller, Cassidy, Larroca & Lewin. Two young associates at the firm, Barry Pollack and Kirsten Levingston, took her out to lunch toward the end of her last week, and the subject of pro bono work came up. Levingston had a case she wanted to take on for the NAACP. Well, said Laura, if you're interested in a pro bono case, I've got a great one for you. She told them about Marty. The guy is innocent, she said.

Sure he is, said Pollack, already a little jaded at thirty-one. No, really, Laura insisted. It's an incredible case. Pollack asked to see her paper. He read it that night and couldn't put it down. "The more I read," he recalled, "the more I thought, 'This kid really did get railroaded.'"

The next morning, Pollack told Laura he was interested in taking the case. As an associate, of course, he had no authority. But his mentor, conveniently, was the partner in charge of the firm's pro bono work. Pollack didn't think he'd have a hard time getting his blessing. Steve will love this, he thought.

Stephen Braga was born and raised in Newport, Rhode Island, though not the Newport that the founder of Marty's hometown was trying to recreate on Long Island in the early 1900s. Braga's father was a television repairman who worked hard to provide for his wife and four children. Steve, the oldest, came of age post-Woodstock, but close enough to embrace the anti-authority values of the time. From his first year of law school, he knew his purpose in life was to defend the accused. "I have always been so philosophically aligned to the defense," he reflected thirty years later, "that I'm one of the few defense lawyers who has never worked a day as a prosecutor." But Braga was no firebrand. He had a quiet righteousness about him.

Braga went to work at Miller, Cassidy after Georgetown Law and a clerkship for a federal judge. The firm had an active pro bono practice, and he was quickly drawn to that work. One of the first cases he tried was a lawsuit against the District of Columbia on behalf of a man who had been brutally attacked while in the D.C. jail. Braga claimed the assault was a result of the jail's overcrowded conditions. "We won the trial and a six-figure verdict for the prisoner," he said, "and I was hooked."

On the last day of Laura Taichman's internship, Barry Pollack brought her to Steve Braga's office to talk about the case of Marty Tankleff. Laura explained the essentials—the background, the appeals, where the case stood now. Pollack told Braga he liked the case; a habeas petition wouldn't be all that complicated. Braga said it sounded good—let's go up, meet the guy, see what we think.

As Laura Taichman went back to Boston to finish law school and start her career, Steve Braga, Barry Pollack, and Kirsten Levingston traveled to the upper Adirondacks of New York to meet Marty Tankleff. They brought a gift in a brown paper bag. In a brief phone conversation with Marty, Braga had asked if there was anything they could bring him. A bagel, Marty said. A decent bagel, with cream cheese.

The journey to Clinton Correctional Facility involved a flight to Burlington, Vermont, a ferry trip across Lake Champlain, and a twenty-minute drive to Dannemora. "It was cold and rainy, an ugly day," Braga remembers, "and Clinton was a dark and desperate place no one should have to spend a day in." And here was Marty Tankleff, a twenty-four-year-old trapped in a life interrupted by the most desolate, Kafkaesque circumstances, but somehow maintaining an outlook that was as unshakable as it was incongruous. "We smuggled the bagel in Kirsten's bag, and in between bites we just fell in love with the guy," said Braga. "He was the world's most optimistic client." The other thing that struck them was Marty's command of his case. He knew off the top of his head what was in every motion, when it was filed, before what judge. "He just had this firm belief that the justice system got it wrong and somewhere, somehow, somebody's going to figure it out and fix it. He had utterly convinced himself that this was a temporary situation."

Leaving the prison that day, Braga told Pollack to get working on the habeas petition.

BARRY POLLACK began law school the week that Marty Tankleff became a murder defendant. Pollack grew up in Toledo and came to Washington in

1988, expecting to stay only as long as it took to earn his law degree from Georgetown. But when the time came, he had no desire to leave. "Inertia is a very powerful force," he explained. So was Plato Cacheris, a Washington defense lawyer with a client in every capital scandal since Watergate. Pollack was getting eight dollars an hour doing research for a law professor when he heard Cacheris was hiring law students—same pay, more interesting research. His celebrity client of the moment was Fawn Hall, Oliver North's secretary. Pollack had no notion of going into criminal law, and it would be hard to imagine him brashly protesting, as Cacheris once did, "My client is a fool, an ass, a boor! But he is not a cold-blooded strangler!" But he found himself drawn to the Sturm und Drang of Cacheris's work. "I loved his practice, I loved what he did."

Only four years after passing the bar, Pollack had his first murder case, if one that was well into its afterlife of appeals. His job was to study the record to date and identify issues on which to hang a claim that Marty Tankleff's imprisonment by the State of New York was a violation of his rights under the Constitution of the United States. Pollack thought the extraordinary dissent by two of the four original appellate judges was a good sign that Marty could win with the same custody and confession arguments in federal court. The habeas petition would also raise something new: that the trial judge made a reversible error when, during the jury selection process, he prevented Gottlieb from challenging the prosecution's exclusion of African American jurors. Braga and Pollack had solid footing for contending that Judge Alfred Tisch's action violated rulings by the U.S. Supreme Court.

In selecting a jury for a criminal trial, each side has a number of "peremptory" challenges—the right to dismiss a prospective juror without stating a reason. In the Tankleff case, Collins used peremptory challenges to exclude two of the only three African Americans who remained in the jury pool after the prescreening process. He wanted to strike the third one as well, but he eventually accepted him as the fourth of four alternate jurors rather than bring in more candidates for prescreening. Gottlieb contested each of these peremptory strikes with what is known as a "Batson challenge," an objection named for a landmark 1986 ruling by the Supreme Court that prosecutors could not use peremptory challenges to exclude jurors based solely on their race. If challenged by the defense, the prosecutor had to state race-neutral reasons for the exclusion and the judge would decide the issue.

In a case such as Marty Tankleff's, there was a practical reason why, all things being equal, the prosecution might have wanted a jury with no African Americans, and why the defense might have wanted one with as many as possible. As Pollack put it: "Generally, African Americans have had a different life experience with the police than Caucasians have, and they may have a different view of what goes on in a police investigation and of the credibility of police."

But when Gottlieb raised his objections, Tisch cut him off. "He obviously is not black," he said of Marty, so Collins wasn't obliged to explain why he was striking all the African Americans from the jury pool. The ruling may have been technically acceptable at the time, but a year after the trial the Supreme Court made a further ruling that closed that loophole: A prosecutor couldn't exclude a juror on a racial basis regardless of whether the defendant and the excluded juror were the same race. Though the high court's second ruling came after the Tankleff trial, it applied because the case was still under appeal. It gave Marty's federal habeas petition a new ground for reversal.

In the six years since Marty's conviction, his case had traveled from Riverhead to Brooklyn to Albany. Now the case was back on Long Island. The federal appeal was assigned to Judge Thomas C. Platt, one of the three judges of the U.S. District Court's Eastern New York District who presided from a small federal courthouse just off the campus of Seymour Tankleff's beneficiary, Hofstra University. Friendly as the setting might have seemed, however, that it would be Judge Platt who would hear the case was not auspicious news for Marty.

Platt had been on the federal bench for more than two decades, appointed during the last months of the Nixon administration in 1974. By the 1990s, he was widely known as a surly, biased judge whose decisions were frequently reversed by the court above him. A few years later, the low regard many attorneys held for Platt was given voice by the Robing Room, a website founded and operated "by lawyers for lawyers" and that stated its purpose with a catchphrase: "Judge the Judges." The website wasn't just a place to complain and disparage; many judges were given high ratings and enthusiastic praise. But the comments about Platt were uniformly unflattering and reflected disenchantment that went back decades: "Rude and dismissive . . . no party should have to rely on him dispensing 'fair justice.'" "This is the chamber of horrors for a defendant. . . ." "Spiteful . . . ignores the U.S. Court of Appeals." One lawyer wrote simply: "Ugh."

In January 1997, Steve Braga and Barry Pollack became the latest lawyers who wished their case had gone before a judge other than Thomas Platt. After "in-depth, careful and thoughtful consideration," Platt found the defense arguments to be of the sort that "might find acceptability in arenas removed from reality but not otherwise." He found nothing amiss in the way the case was approached by the police: "There was no leap to a premature conclusion, there was an opportunity given to a possible suspect, away from the highly charged, stressful scene, to offer whatever explanation he wished to give and there was a test made of his explanation which revealed to the son the futility of his position. Thereafter, the arrest was made, warnings were given, and a voluntary confession was given by the son which was corroborated by the scene of the crime itself."

The next stop for the appeal was a majestic federal courthouse on Pearl Street in lower Manhattan, home to the Second Circuit of the U.S. Court of Appeals. This court was composed of thirteen judges who reviewed, in panels of three, the decisions of all the federal district court judges in the states of New York, Connecticut, and Vermont. In early August, Braga and Pollack traveled to New York to argue the appeal to Circuit Judges Guido Calabresi, José Cabranes, and Fred Parker. Once again Mark Cohen argued the case for the Suffolk County district attorney's office. Once again Marty's relatives attended the proceedings. And once again they listened closely for hints of what the judges might be thinking. One of them, Calabresi, a former dean of the Yale Law School and a highly respected legal scholar, offered more than a hint. Nothing about this case makes sense, he told Cohen. It's like when the clock strikes thirteen— every stroke before becomes suspect. It seems as if this case went wrong from the outset. Braga and Pollack looked at each other. "I thought we had won the case," Braga said later.

But Marty's family left with higher hopes than expectations. There had been too many rejections over the years, too many disappointments. All told, the appeal had been considered by fourteen judges, and twelve of them had declined to reverse the verdict. Now it was up to these three. The only thing certain was that it wouldn't be a tie. But it turned out to be the most complicated and ambiguous of all the rulings so far—the closest a unanimous ruling could come to being a tie. It was written by Calabresi and radiated regret.

The judges thought that Marty should have been advised of his Miranda rights "much earlier than he was, and all of the inculpatory statements he made before receiving the warnings should have been suppressed." The problem for Marty was that after the police finally advised him of his rights, he waived them—and then "repeated and elaborated upon his confession." Under federal law, the subsequent statements could only be suppressed if the police tactics that led to the initial ones were "so coercive" that they made his waiver of rights involuntary. "The issue is a close one," the judges wrote. But in their view, the accusatory sequence of the interrogation, culminating in Detective McCready's decisive lie and the deft psychological pressure he and his partner exerted on Marty, "barely did not entail that degree of coercion that would irredeemably taint Tankleff's 'second,' *Mirandized* confession."

Still, there was an opening. The Second Circuit judges noted a kind of interjudicial catch-22 at work against Marty—a mismatch between the factual findings of the federal and state courts and the constitutional law each was obliged to follow. The federal court, adhering to federal law, found that Marty *was* in custody earlier than when he was given his Miranda warnings. But that was no help to him because of the way federal law allowed the use of statements made after Miranda even if the ones made before it were suppressed. New York law, meanwhile, made no distinction between before and after. It followed a principle, laid down by the state's Court of Appeals, that when it came to advising a suspect of his rights, "later is too late." The police had to issue Miranda warnings as soon as a suspect was the subject of a custodial interrogation, or the *entire* statement had to be suppressed. This interpretation would have led to a new trial for Marty and the suppression of his statements—if the state appeals courts had drawn the same conclusion about the facts as their federal counterparts.

"It might appear," Calabresi wrote, that the panel should rule the statements inadmissible because the case occurred in a state that used the "later is too late" principle. "But *we* can only grant habeas relief based on violations of *federal* rights. Thus, it is not for us to say whether Tankleff might or might not have any claim based on state constitutional law as a result of our holding that Tankleff was, under *Miranda* and its federal progeny, in custody at the time of his 'first' confession. We note that the validity of such a claim would seem to turn on whether the definition of 'custody' under the New York constitution tracks the definition of that term under the federal constitution."

Every lawyer who read the decision interpreted it the same way. As constitutional law professor Eric Freedman told *Newsday*, "It seems clear that the Second Circuit, which has serious doubts about the admissibility of this confession and possibly even the guilt of Mr. Tankleff, has attempted to design a ruling that would enable him to pursue the matter in state court."

That the Second Circuit judges had reservations about Marty's guilt seemed evident, ironically, from the language they used in rejecting another of the appeal's grounds. After Marty's trial, Jim McCready had told a television interviewer that in 1976 Jerry Steuerman hired a gang of Hells Angels to assault union picketers outside his bagel store. This information had never been disclosed to the defense. Was this prosecutorial misconduct, as the defense now claimed? The federal judges said it was a moot point because the information probably wouldn't have changed the verdict. But in explaining their thinking, Calabresi seemed to convey some puzzlement about the jury's: "The defense contends that this evidence could have been used for a devastating cross-examination of Steuerman, who when asked if he had anything to do with the murders testified that he would 'never do anything like that.' Arguably, hiring Hells Angels to settle a union dispute is akin to murdering your business partner." However, "Steuerman's credibility was already thoroughly undermined on cross-examination by evidence that he had threatened other people with whom he had business relationships. Moreover, Steuerman's bizarre behavior right after the murders also called his innocence into doubt." In other words, if the jury didn't get it by then, the Hells Angels story wouldn't have helped.

Marty read the decision and showed it to his friend Chris Lue-Shing. They worked in the law library together, and Lue-Shing had become as much a self-taught legal scholar as Marty. To other prisoners, they were a virtual law firm—Tankleff & Lue-Shing, inmates-at-law. Lue-Shing cursed Marty's latest decision, cursed the judges. He couldn't believe how close Marty had come—first at the Appellate Division, now the Second Circuit. It seemed there were judges out there who thought he was not only victimized by the police, but that he was actually innocent. And still, here he was.

Braga and Pollack took the Second Circuit's cue and went back to the Appellate Division in Brooklyn. But the state judges declined the guidance of their learned federal colleagues across the river. And so, more than a decade after the day Marty complied with James McCready's request to take a ride to headquarters, the legal issues surrounding what occurred that morning were finally put to rest. Barring a review by the U.S. Supreme Court, and the chances of that were mighty slim, Marty was out of appeals on the question of the admissibility or reliability of what he was alleged to have told the police that day.

But he was still not out of options. Deep within the Second Circuit's decision was a glimmer of light: the Batson challenge. It seemed that Judge Platt had disregarded the U.S. Supreme Court—twice in a single decision. First, he paid no heed to the high court's ruling that a defense attorney was entitled to question a prosecutor's exclusion of jurors for possible racial reasons, whether or not the defendant and the excluded jurors were of the same race. Second, Platt ruled that even if Tisch's decision was wrong, it was a "harmless error." According to the Second Circuit judges, *that* was an error by Platt, and not a harmless one. The circuit judges explained—in case Platt didn't know—that federal law divided errors into two categories. There were "trial errors," those that concerned evidentiary rulings. And there were "structural errors," mistakes in the conduct of the trial itself. Appeals courts could review trial errors to determine if they were "harmless," meaning they didn't affect the outcome of the case. But there was no such thing as a harmless structural error. By Supreme Court ruling, if one occurred, it *had* to be corrected.

It was hard to know whether the prosecution dismissed the prospective African American jurors based on race, said the judges, because Tisch cut off Gottlieb's attempts to raise Batson challenges. But the fact that the prosecutor tried to strike the only three blacks in the jury pool—all without explanation because the challenges were peremptory—"constitutes a sufficiently dramatic pattern of actions" to require the question to be examined even seven years later. If the prosecutors couldn't show that the three jurors were excluded for race-neutral reasons, the verdict would have to be set aside, the case retried. The U.S. Court of Appeals returned the case to Judge Platt and ordered him to either hold a hearing or send it back to the County Court from which it came. But if the passage of time and insufficient records made such a "reconstruction hearing" impossible, he "must then rule" that Marty Tankleff was entitled to a new trial.

YEARS AFTER he worked on Marty's first appeal, Warren Feldman met a lawyer who recognized his name. "You were on the Tankleff appeal, weren't you?" the lawyer asked him. He said he'd been a law secretary for Judge Platt at the time of the federal appeal. And he apologized. He'd tried to persuade Platt that he should rule in favor of Tankleff. "I argued with the judge for a solid year," he said, but he just couldn't budge him.

In January 1998, a year after his original decision, Platt found the case in front of him again. He was not pleased. Though not unaccustomed to being overruled by the Second Circuit, Platt griped about being ordered to fix the Batson problem. He had no interest in holding the hearing, so he sent the case back to Suffolk County. But not before issuing a document, which he labeled a "Decision," declaring what fools the judges up the line were, and taking his criticism all the way to the Supreme Court. It infuriated him especially that the Supreme Court's *Batson* decision didn't have only the defendant's rights in mind; it was also meant to protect the rights of the peremptorily challenged. And who loses? "The public must pay for the alleged wrongdoing by footing the cost of additional hearings and/or a new trial. Why innocent and unwitting citizens and taxpayers should suffer from the infliction of such penalties is unexplained."

The Batson hearing returned the Tankleff case to the Arthur Cromarty Courthouse eight years after Judge Alfred Tisch thought he had put an end to it by sentencing Marty to fifty years. Tisch knew there would be appeals, but he couldn't have imagined any of them bringing the case back to

Riverhead. In any event, Tankleff was no longer a concern to him. Tisch had decided not to run for reelection in 1995 and now he was selling real estate. The Batson hearing would be conducted by the county's supervising judge, Michael Mullen.

Most lawyers go their entire careers without finding themselves on the witness stand, let alone in one of their own cases. But John Collins was about to testify for the second time in the same case, both times on a juror-related issue. The first time was about juror misconduct; now it was about juror discrimination. Marty's lawyers were skeptical that there could be a legitimate reconstruction of the juror voir dire because the court record didn't include transcripts of the whole process. Collins professed to have no worries either about the feasibility of the hearing—he still had his notes, he said—or about the outcome. And who could blame him? Gottlieb, among others, had no illusions that a Suffolk County judge would seriously entertain throwing out Marty Tankleff's conviction because eight years ago the DA pulled a couple of black people out of the jury pool.

When the day of the hearing arrived, in September 1998, Collins testified that he knew exactly why he dismissed each of the African Americans: One said he had met Robert Gottlieb at a political event. The other was an emergency medical technician. "I was concerned," said Collins, "that he would view himself and be viewed by others as an expert in that particular area." Braga stood up to cross-examine Collins, but the judge stopped him. "Not in my courtroom," the judge told him. "He's an officer of the court."

After the hearing, Collins was moved to compliment Braga on his legal work but wanted him to know he was fighting for an unworthy cause. "You did a great job," Collins said, "but the kid's guilty." When Braga told him he disagreed, Collins brought up the day Marty took the stand at his trial. "I know he was lying," he said. "I know he did it." Braga knew it was pointless to debate the case with a man who was obviously beyond any ability to second-guess himself. "He just believed it, and nothing was going to change his mind," Braga said. "We could have Steuerman come in and confess, and he still wouldn't believe it."

A month later, Judge Mullen issued a ruling: The prosecutor's reasons for exercising the peremptory challenges were race-neutral. Petition for a new trial denied. Braga and Pollack tried to go back to federal court, arguing that Mullen's hearing was not what the Second Circuit ordered—the testimony and evidence didn't meet the standards for a reconstruction hearing, and it certainly didn't support the judge's decision. Pollack found similar New York cases in which new trials were ordered. But the court declined to hear the appeal. An application to bring the question to the full Second Circuit was also denied. And finally, the U.S. Supreme Court. On December 11, 2000, *People v. Tankleff* was on a list of cases the nation's highest court declined to hear.

Steve Braga thought back to the beginning, to that dreary day when he, Pollack, and Levingston traveled to Dannemora. They had left with such determination to get Marty out of prison, and such optimism. "We had this wonderful Miranda issue . . ." Braga remembered wistfully. But five years of futility had confirmed to him what he and every lawyer knew as well as they knew Miranda itself: A defendant's best chance is to win at trial. After that, the interest of the system is in finality. Braga was deflated, resigned to the reality that Marty was probably not going to get out of prison until a month after his sixty-ninth birthday.

But Marty just kept going: writing letters, reading law journals, looking for openings. One day he got a letter from Bob Gottlieb saying the producers of the TV show *America's Most Wanted* were doing a special on DNA, the latest thing in forensic evidence. They were looking for men imprisoned for murder who claimed they were innocent and thought they could prove it with DNA. The show would pay for the testing as long as the convict agreed to discuss the results on camera, whatever the outcome. The special, hosted by John Walsh, was called "Judgment Night: DNA— The Ultimate Test." Marty wanted to volunteer. He asked Braga what he thought. It was showbiz, said the lawyer, but with funds short it wasn't a bad idea, as long as the evidence was handled properly and tested by a reputable lab. Marty wrote to the producers and gave them a history of his case. They decided to include him in the program.

Braga and Pollack consulted with Barry Scheck and Peter Neufeld, a pair of New York lawyers who were pioneering the use of DNA to exonerate wrongly convicted prisoners. In 1992, they founded the Innocence Project at the Benjamin N. Cardozo School of Law and started a revolution in American criminal justice. Working with local attorneys, the organization had used DNA evidence to free dozens of wrongly convicted prisoners all over the country.

In October 2000, the Innocence Project attorneys joined Gottlieb in a motion asking Suffolk County to make available a large assortment of evidence, though ultimately they had to make a choice: *America's Most Wanted* would test only one item. After letters and phone calls among the five lawyers and their client, the decision was made to go with a group of rootless hairs found on Arlene Tankleff's body.

At Marty's trial, the forensic hair specialists for both the prosecution and defense found the hairs to be "similar to or consistent with" Arlene's known hair samples. The prosecution expert also testified that their broken, rootless condition would be consistent with the hairs having been pulled from Arlene's scalp during a struggle. But it was Marty's hope that DNA testing—which raised hair evidence to a level of certainty comparable to a fingerprint—would find that the hairs were not his mother's. The best-case scenario would be for the hairs to share the DNA properties of the hairs the crime lab staff took from Jerry Steuerman's hair weave three months after the murders.

The hairs were sent from the Suffolk County evidence vault to the forensic lab hired to conduct the tests for *America's Most Wanted*. Some weeks later, a producer and his crew went to Clinton. The camera came in tight on Marty as he was told the results: The hairs are your mother's. The results proved neither guilt nor innocence. From a remote studio, John Walsh told Marty, "This had to be a really big setback to you." Marty replied that it was no bigger than any of the others. "Unfortunately, we've had so many setbacks," he said.

"I've got to ask you," Walsh said, "aren't you reconciled to the fact that you're going to spend most of the rest of your life in prison?"

"No, not at all," Marty said matter-of-factly. "I'm confident that with the support of everyone out there working together as a team, we will prevail and I will get out of jail."

What Marty wanted to know was what he always wanted to know when he got bad news: What's next? Braga told him the options were not promising. The best shot now, probably the only one, was to come up with new evidence. He and Pollack had been brainstorming. How about suing Jerry Steuerman in a wrongful-death action, as Ron Goldman's family did against O. J. Simpson? Publicity and pretrial depositions might shake some trees. But it was something of a backward approach: The Goldmans had a ton of evidence to go after the right man. They weren't using a lawsuit to turn up evidence to free the wrong one.

Braga told Marty that the best use of his family's now-limited resources was to hire a private investigator to take a fresh look at the case. Marty, as usual, was upbeat, even wide-eyed. There have to be people out there who know the truth, he thought. All we have to do is find them. He got a list of private investigators and banged out a round of letters. Some didn't respond, and those that did weren't encouraging. One turned out to be a retired Suffolk County police detective. *Next.* The others wanted all kinds of money: $10,000 retainers, $1,000 a day.

One day, Marty's Aunt Marianne sent him an article clipped from *Newsday* that she had received from Seymour's old friend and golfing partner Paul Lerner. The story was about a man named Fred Chichester, who was serving twenty-five years for murder. The homicide was in January 1989, four months after the deaths of Marty's parents. It occurred in Suffolk County, where it was prosecuted by John Collins. And there was evidence that Chichester was innocent. The story described how a private investigator had found several people who said that another man had told them he committed the murder. The investigator was a retired New York City police detective named Jay Salpeter. Marty read the article and thought he might have heard that name before. *Wasn't that Austin Offen's investigator?*

Late one night in 1996, a brawl erupted outside a club in the Hamptons, and when it was over a young black man named Shane Daniels lay bloody and unconscious on the pavement. When the police sorted it out, three white men were under arrest, including an off-duty New York City detective. The one in the worst trouble was Austin Offen, who was identified in news accounts as "a 25-year-old weightlifter from Queens." He was accused of hurling racial epithets as he repeatedly struck Daniels over the head with a metal device used to lock a car steering wheel—the Club, as it was called, ironically enough. Daniels lay in a coma for a month as the incident took on a life of its own in the New York media.

Marty met Offen in the Suffolk County Jail in the fall of 1998, when he was brought down for the hearing on the Batson challenge. In prison, Marty had learned to fit in with men of every stripe, having decided long ago that the only judgments worth making about people were the ones that had something to do with your own welfare. He and Offen got to talking about their cases, and Marty explained where his was at the moment. He'd been trying to get his conviction overturned for eight years and now it came down to claiming he didn't get a fair trial because the DA wouldn't let any blacks on his jury. Offen said his problem was the opposite: He would have walked if he'd had an all-white jury.

What happened, said Offen, was that his mom got a private investigator out of the Yellow Pages, and this guy was awesome. *He comes up with all kinds of shit on the DA's witnesses, and my lawyer kicks their asses.* The jury was all white, except for the foreman. And they couldn't come to a verdict, even after the judge made them go back and keep trying. All the whites thought there was too much contradictory evidence to say beyond a reasonable doubt that Offen was the one who hit Daniels. But the black juror refused to vote for acquittal. So finally the judge declared them a hung jury.

Two years later, toward the end of 2000, Marty ran into Offen again—in an exercise room at Clinton. The second trial hadn't turned out so well for Offen. Actually, it never went to trial. The prosecutors came up with DNA evidence proving he struck the blows that nearly killed Shane Daniels. His lawyer negotiated a deal that got him ten years for assault rather than the thirty-six for attempted murder he faced if he went to trial and was convicted.

Offen asked Marty how he was doing in his case. Marty said he was out of appeals and needed to come up with new evidence. He was trying to get an investigator. Someone who wouldn't charge a lot. He wondered if private investigators did pro bono work like lawyers. Offen said he should try the investigator he had on his case. Jay Salpeter. He didn't know what he charged, but the guy did an awesome job.

The Reinvestigator

JAY SALPETER was a man who always seemed to need a vacation. There were his cases—CRIMINAL, MATRIMONIAL, BACKGROUND, SURVEILLANCE, said his ad in the Yellow Pages. There was the check-cashing business in Queens he took over from his father. And there was everything else. Salpeter was by nature the sort of person who seemed perpetually preoccupied by the needs of other people. Always on the phone, always a thousand things on his mind. So when he did take a vacation, all he asked was a pool, a chaise longue, and a good bar waiter.

Salpeter spent Christmas week of 2000 in Cabo San Lucas, Mexico—he and his wife, Cheryl, and the four girls, two each from their first marriages. They stayed at the Fiesta Americana, a beachfront resort with five pools. Salpeter would have liked to stay a few more days but the girls wanted to get back for New Year's Eve. So they flew home on the thirty-first, and he and Cheryl went out to dinner at their favorite place, and then it was back to the office at 7 A.M. on New Year's Day.

Salpeter had been a private investigator for eight years after two decades in the New York Police Department, and you could get a sense of how he was doing by where his desk was. When he first started out, he worked out of his basement and used the Dunkin' Donuts in Roslyn, next to Joanne's Gourmet Pizza, when he had to meet someone. He called it his annex. Now he rented space from his lawyers, Alex Fine and Barry Bassik, in a reconfigured house in Great Neck, though not in the prime location of the otherwise well-to-do town. Salpeter's office had a veranda but it overlooked a string of car repair shops. Soon, though, he would be moving to an upscale building nearby, taking an office in a suite with two receptionists.

There wouldn't be much to move. For a guy who made his living collecting information, Salpeter wasn't big on paperwork. Mostly he had his framed news clippings—the front-page story from the *Post* about the homicide case that sent him into retirement; articles about his cases in *GQ* and *Vanity Fair*—and his array of New York Jets memorabilia. Season tickets was the other thing he inherited when his parents moved down to Delray Beach.

At forty-nine, Salpeter had a head of wavy brown hair and a thick, graying mustache. He was a beefy man who tried to keep his weight down with the assistance of a personal trainer at the North Shore Gym. On days when he planned to stay in and work the phones, Salpeter wore warm-ups or jeans and a sweater. There was little mystery about this investigator; he seemed made for his life. He'd grown up a few miles over the Queens line, in Bayside. As a teenager, he had no particular career aspirations, least of all thoughts of becoming a cop. It wasn't the most common path for a Jewish kid. "When I was thirteen, I couldn't play football because I had to go to bar mitzvah lessons," he remembered. "My mother didn't want me to get hit in the face because of the pictures." Five years later, his father had an idea. "He was a blue-collar Queens Jew, my father—drove a cab, had the check-cashing business, little this, little that. Everyone called him Salty. He was friends with a lot of cops, and he thought that would be good for me. I had no direction, I wasn't college material, I gave my parents what we say in Jewish—*tsuris*—and he figured joining the police department would keep me out of trouble. You get a salary, he says, you get benefits. So I went in."

Salpeter took to the work with a vengeance. As a patrol cop in Brooklyn early in his career, he acquired a reputation as an arrest-obsessed cowboy who sometimes pressed the boundaries. Working in a tough precinct, he wouldn't hesitate to be rough with a suspect—tune him up, as they said—and might be less than courteous with an uncooperative witness. Some of Salpeter's aggression came naturally and some of it came from insecurity. He was surrounded by Irish guys from cop families and wanted to show that he was one of them. More than a few incidents accumulated in his personnel file, but none serious enough to bring formal discipline, and he managed to tone down his act before doing any serious damage to his career.

In those days, the early 1970s, Salpeter had long, bushy hair that violated department regulations, so he secured it with a net and a bunch of bobby pins and wore a wig of short, straight blond hair. It was good training for the Street Crimes Unit, an undercover assignment that involved playing dress-up to catch a thief. The disguise depended on the venue. When there was a rash of assaults and robberies outside the Ramrod, a famous gay club in Manhattan's West Village, Salpeter went out as a transvestite. On another night in another neighborhood, he suited up as a Hasidic Jewish woman. And then there was the time he played a generic frail old lady, holding a kerchief over his face to hide his mustache. A mugger went for the bait, and Salpeter dropped the scarf in the struggle. *"Shit— this bitch got a muthafuckin' mustache!"* the skel exclaimed. That shining moment for New York's finest was captured by a crew shooting a documentary for HBO.

Salpeter made detective in 1983 and went to work in the 69th Precinct, a classic Brooklyn neighborhood of Italians and Jews. His very first case was the theft of a torah from a yeshiva in Canarsie, one of a rash of crimes that fed a thriving Russian black market for the ancient scrolls. Salpeter worked the neighborhood and tracked the thief, who ditched the torah in a trash can in the stairwell of his building when he heard Salpeter was coming. The dean of the yeshiva, Rabbi Jacob Jungreis, was astonished when Salpeter showed up with the stolen torah. "It's unheard of!" he exclaimed. Salpeter was hailed as a hero cop—a hero *Jewish* cop. Rabbi Jungreis invited him to carry the torah into a party to celebrate its safe return. He wrote a letter to the city's police commissioner: "From the start, Officer Salpeter assured me, 'Rabbi, I will not rest until I get your Torah back.' I sincerely believe that this officer did not rest and, miraculously, within 48 hours the Torah was returned and a suspect apprehended! I believe this is a significant investigative breakthrough, which we in the Jewish community hope will lead to a cessation of the devastating Torah-theft epidemic."

Salpeter went from stolen torahs to dead bodies. He worked dozens of homicides through the 1980s, and developed a method of investigation that combined equal measures of persistence, personality, and dumb luck. By his own appraisal, he flew by the seat of his pants, a method that didn't change with experience: "Half the time I don't know what I'm doing—I'm like a fuckin' Clouseau. Somehow I get it done, I really don't know how. I schmooze, I treat people nice, I bullshit, whatever I have to do to get the information I need for my case." But when it came to suspects, sometimes he didn't treat people so nice.

In 1990, Salpeter was working at the 104th in Queens. He was always the first one in on the day tour, so sometimes he started working cases on his own. A call came into the precinct one hot summer morning from a young father who said he and his girlfriend had woken up and discovered their six-day-old baby gone. "The dog may have ate the baby," the desk sergeant told Salpeter nonchalantly.

"What the *fuck*?" Salpeter said and headed out.

Jason Radtke and Linda Boyce were a pair of nineteen-year-olds with

Midwestern twangs who had been in New York just two weeks. Radtke wanted to raise and train guard dogs, so he and his girlfriend had driven from Nebraska to Maine to buy a German shepherd, then down to New York so he could learn obedience training at a school in Queens. They rented the upstairs of a house, Radtke started classes with his prized shepherd, and a week later Linda gave birth to a baby boy.

When Salpeter got to the apartment, he found a baby's nightie soaked in blood and fragments that looked like shavings from a sharpened pencil. He had the dog picked up and x-rayed by the ASPCA, and when the results came in later that day he was revolted but resolute. He shut down part of his brain, as he always did when he had a job to do, and brought Radtke into a room at the precinct. He started gently: "Jason, I know something went very wrong and I need to know what it was." When Radtke said he didn't know, Salpeter told him what *he* knew, and when Radtke clung to his denial, Salpeter went to his repertoire—cajoling, accusing, threatening, taunting. He sang to his young suspect: *You're a murderer, I know you're a murderer.* At one point he left Radtke alone in the steaming room, then came back in and told him, "You know, I fucked your wife." Radtke stood up and hurled his fist into the wall. Salpeter kept at him for hours, and finally Radtke began to crumble: It was in the middle of the night and the baby was crying. He got up to change him, got the diaper off, and the baby peed on him. He got mad and threw the baby on the floor, smashing his skull. And then Radtke told Salpeter what he did with the baby's body.

The grisly story was on the front pages of all the New York tabloids. "The crime was a hundred times worse than anything we have in New York," Jimmy Breslin wrote the next day in his column in *Newsday*. "It is out of a Russian novel, with babies being torn to bits by wild dogs."

Salpeter didn't sleep that night, and in the morning an assistant district attorney brought him before a grand jury and asked him to read the confession. Salpeter could barely get the first sentence out before he broke down and cried, a shock to his own self-perception. He had worked on seventy-five homicide investigations through the years, thought he'd seen it all, and never had trouble putting his emotions in a box. Salpeter realized he was at a crossroads. He had been growing weary the last couple of years. The job had taken a heavy toll on his marriage, an occupational hazard that afflicted a lot of cops. It was why he asked for the transfer out of Brooklyn. Queens was almost the suburbs by comparison. And now this. *Fucking Jason Radtke from Nebraska.*

Salpeter left the grand jury room, left the courthouse, and decided right then and there to leave his job. The state had just announced a change in pension rules that would allow a police officer's time as a trainee to count toward his years of service. It gave Salpeter his twenty-and-out. A week after he arrested Jason Radtke, Salpeter put in his papers. And a week after his last day on the job, he and his wife split up.

Salpeter spent a year or so running the check-cashing business. It was lucrative but unexciting, and eventually he felt ready to get back to doing what he knew best. He passed the test for a private investigator's license and went in with his old partner from the 104th Squad, Dan Daly, who got a perfect score. They called themselves Eagle Trace Private Investigation, hijacking the name from a condo community in Florida that sounded more like a detective agency than a place you go when you retire. The name was all they had. The ex-cops worked out of their respective homes and collaborated on cases, which weren't exactly top-notch: "Looking at a woman in a bathroom whose husband thought she was doing drugs," as Salpeter described a representative case. "That's what we were getting."

Salpeter considered Daly one of the smartest detectives he knew and one of the handful of people he could truly count on. But they didn't mesh as business partners and split up after little more than a year. Salpeter went on his own as Jay S. Salpeter & Associates, the associates being various retired detectives he could call on when he needed someone to do a surveillance or an interview or go out to a courthouse to pull records. Salpeter called them his guys: There was Andy Cilenti and Everett Grant and Vinny Pepitone, whose brother Joe used to play first base for the Yankees. There was Bob Gundel, the best surveillance and tail man around—he lost *nobody*—and James Worthy, a large African-American man who made Salpeter feel safe when he might not be. He had specialists, too—Joel Reicherter on polygraph, Charlie Haase with crime scenes, Denise Pantori on persuasion. She was the only one of Salpeter's guys who wasn't a guy, or an ex-cop. She was a bartender—"a knockout brunette with the balls of a man," in Salpeter's estimation.

Salpeter built his criminal business by getting cases from some of the defense attorneys whose clients he once put in jail. It felt strange to him at first, but he considered himself no different from a prosecutor who became a private defense attorney. If you stripped it down, criminal justice was an industry—everyone was in it to make a living, whichever side they were on at a given moment—and Salpeter went about his work the same way whether he was carrying a shield or a PI's license. There were things he couldn't do once he relinquished his police powers. Get search warrants, for one. Intimidate witnesses, for another. But there were other ways to do the job. Salpeter had an uncanny ability to make people feel comfortable giving him what he needed, even when that was not their inclination and sometimes when it wasn't in their best interests. It was a natural skill that he honed as a member of the NYPD's hostage negotiating team. So when Austin Offen's mother picked Salpeter out of the Yellow Pages because it said he was a "former NYPD Detective 2nd Grade," he did what he'd always done. He went out and did background checks and interviews with more than two dozen people who witnessed that brawl in the Hamptons that left Shane Daniels in a coma and Austin Offen facing attempted murder charges. Then he delivered the results to the lawyer trying the case. The only difference was that it was a defense attorney instead of an ADA.

In this case the lawyer was Bruce Barket, a former Nassau County prosecutor who was earning a name for himself as one of the county's best young defense attorneys. Lawyers and investigators usually found one another through referrals, but Salpeter and Barket were brought together by their mutual client. They both had strong, idiosyncratic personalities and were used to doing things their way, so they regarded each other warily at first. But when Barket saw Salpeter's work on the Offen case, he decided they made a pretty good team. Salpeter turned up major contradictions among the various eyewitnesses to the incident, and he found that some of the people testifying for the prosecution had what could charitably be called credibility problems. The key ones had connections to the Gambino crime family (for which, incidentally, Salpeter had also once done some work, a case being a case). Barket turned Salpeter's work into a hung jury, though Offen ultimately took a plea bargain and went away for ten years. And that was fine with Salpeter. "Austin Offen was guilty as sin, as it turned out," he said. "So I did my job and they did theirs, and justice was done. It was a win-win."

Then something unusual began to happen: Salpeter found himself working on behalf of people who were *not* guilty as sin. It changed the nature of his work—and of how he perceived justice. After twenty-five years as a detective, it even changed his view of who he was.

It all started with a call he got one day in 1997 from Hank Chichester. He was a bank executive from Suffolk County who'd gotten Salpeter's name from an attorney in Manhattan. They arranged to meet, and Chichester told Salpeter that his son, Fred, had been in prison for murder for seven years, with another eighteen to go. According to Chichester, his son was innocent. Okay, said Salpeter. Tell me why you think that, other than because he's your kid.

In January 1989, twenty-four-year-old Fred Chichester was arrested for the murder of a woman named Maryann Meola. She lived in a bungalow behind the house he was renting. The primary evidence was a bloody impression found beside the body. It matched the bottom of one of Fred's Avia sneakers. The other problem was that the apparent murder weapon was found in a drawer in his kitchen. The Suffolk County homicide detectives questioned Fred for more than fifteen hours but couldn't get him to confess. Teams of detectives took turns interrogating him, but he kept saying he didn't do it. He said he'd had a bunch of people over the evening before, and they'd partied through the night. One of them was an on-and-off friend of his named Jeff Ciraolo. Jeff borrowed Fred's sneakers because his own shoes were wet from horsing around in the snow. Fred, meanwhile, had an alibi for nearly the entire time frame of the murder. But they arrested him anyway.

Fred Chichester was prosecuted by John Collins, who apparently considered the case something less than open-and-shut because he offered Fred a deal: plead guilty to manslaughter and go away for eight years, a third of the time he would get if he were to be convicted of murder. An excellent deal for a guilty man, but Chichester insisted he was innocent. He rolled the dice and he lost.

All along, Chichester and his parents believed the murderer was Jeff Ciraolo. He was unstable and violent, and earlier that day he had gotten high on crack and threw Fred into a wall. Ciraolo was the one who reported the homicide, telling the police that he found Meola's body when he went to her bungalow to invite her to the party—at 6:30 in the morning. Soon after Fred's conviction, his parents hired a private investigator who went to the town in the Catskills where Ciraolo lived for a time after the murder. He found two people who said Ciraolo had made statements to them hinting at his possible involvement in the murder. But the information was too vague to bring to court. Now it was years later and Hank Chichester wanted Salpeter to pick up the case. The problem was money. After eight years of fighting for their son, he and his wife were tapped out.

Salpeter liked Chichester. He told him he'd do some preliminary work for $500. He read the case file and thought the Chichesters were right to believe that the killer was Jeff Ciraolo and not their son. He took the case, worked it for two years, and never asked for any more money. By the spring of 1999, Salpeter had affidavits from three key people. One of them, whom Salpeter found in Florida, admitted he had not told the earlier investigator everything he knew. According to this man—who passed a polygraph test arranged by Salpeter—Ciraolo told them that he killed Maryann Meola when she spurned his advances: "He was screaming and yelling about why this girl didn't want to do anything with him. He pushed the door in and knocked her to the ground. He went in and that's when he said, 'I had to get that cunt. I wanted her and she didn't want me.'"

Salpeter also got a statement from a man who had roomed with Ciraolo and recalled him pulling out a stack of newspaper articles about the murder and saying he knew for a fact that Chichester didn't do it. Eventually he admitted to the murder, as well as to setting Chichester up: He said he was wearing Chichester's sneakers when he killed Meola and that he put the knife in his drawer. "How does it feel to have a killer in the house?" the former roommate quoted Ciraolo as saying.

Salpeter thought he had more than enough to get the case reopened. The Chichesters brought the statements to Fred's original lawyer, Paul Gianelli, who decided the best approach was to go right to John Collins and ask him to take a new look at the case. No court motions, no formal letters. Just a request, lawyer to lawyer, Paul to John. But Collins wasn't the least bit interested. Neither was his boss, Jim Catterson. The case, they said, was closed.

Not yet, Salpeter hoped. The DA's office had its own squad of investigators, and two of them were retired NYPD detectives. The head of the DA's squad, Bob Plansker, had been one of the bosses in Queens Homicide. And Salpeter had worked undercover with Bill Krebs in the Street Crimes Unit when they were both early in their careers. "I went to these fellas, I said I have unbelievable statements here," Salpeter recalled. "They loved it. They thought there was enough there and they're all set to go to Florida and interview one of my witnesses. Then I get a call from Billy Krebs. 'We're not going.' 'You're not going? Whadya mean you're not going?' 'I can't get into it.'"

The only choice now was to go to court with a motion requesting a hearing to reopen the case on the basis of newly discovered evidence. Salpeter called Bruce Barket, who filed the motion as a favor. Two months later, in December 1999, Judge Gary Weber issued his decision: The statements were insufficient to warrant even a hearing, let alone a new trial. Salpeter had grown close to Hank and Mary Chichester. Breaking the news to them was one of the hardest things he'd ever had to do. Hank was a tough man with the handshake of a Marine sergeant, but when Salpeter told him they'd lost in court, he cried like a baby.

Soon afterward, Salpeter got a note in the mail from Bill Krebs: "Sorry I couldn't have been more helpful. . . . It was not from a lack of effort on my and Bob Plansker's part. Best regards, Bill."

To Salpeter, the Chichester case was infuriating—and mystifying. He couldn't understand how the prosecutors and even the judge could so casually dismiss such strong indications that the wrong man was in prison. At least talk to the people, bring them to court, cross-examine them all day long if you want. Don't just sweep it aside like an inconvenience. The irony was that Salpeter had spent two decades on a job in which becoming jaded was as guaranteed as a twenty-and-out pension. But one case out in Suffolk County was enough to leave him disillusioned.

Of course, bad cases could happen anywhere, and that certainly included the borough of New York where Salpeter spent the bulk of his police career. On December 30, 1997, a masked gunman walked into a bodega in the Brownsville section of Brooklyn and shot the owner dead with a .38-caliber revolver. Then he chased a teenage employee down an aisle, stood over him, and killed him, too. A week later, the police arrested Antowine Butts, a twenty-seven-year-old songwriter and rapper. They said he had been picked out of a lineup by an eyewitness. The Brooklyn district attorney, Charles Hynes, announced he might seek the death penalty. Bruce Barket took the case as an assigned counsel.

Barket was a devout Catholic who opposed the death penalty. In 1991, after five years as an assistant district attorney in Nassau County, he quit his job and entered a Jesuit seminary in Syracuse. "I didn't like prosecuting people much," he later explained. "The sin of being self-righteous and judgmental was too tempting for me. And my nature is to be a little more of a rule-breaker than a rule-enforcer." He wasn't sure he wanted to be a priest, but he was sure he wanted to find out. It took about a year. First of all, "there was the whole celibacy thing." Secondly, he wound up doing some emergency pro bono legal work while at the seminary. "It occurred to me that I didn't know how good a priest I would be, but I was probably a pretty good lawyer."

Barket returned to Long Island and started a private practice. When New York State brought back the death penalty in 1995, he volunteered for duty with the state's Capital Defender Office, an agency established by the state legislature to ensure representation for indigent defendants in death penalty cases.

From the day he met Antowine Butts, Barket was convinced he had the worst-case scenario for a lawyer: the responsibility of defending a man who could be executed for a crime he didn't commit. Butts had no criminal record and a solid alibi, while the evidence against him was reed-thin. The only witness against him, the supposed eyewitness who picked him out of a lineup, was a crackhead named Martin Mitchell, who was stoned out of his mind on the day of the murders.

If any case was in need of a defense investigation, this was it. Barket brought in Salpeter, who was appalled at the work of the detectives in his former command. Barket had one assignment for him: Find Martin Mitchell and try to bring him in. Salpeter used his NYPD contacts to get Mitchell's priors, which led him to his girlfriend's apartment. He took one of his guys, Everett Grant, into the Brooklyn night.

Salpeter knocked on the door, identified himself, said he was looking for Martin. The girlfriend didn't answer. Then a booming voice came through the door. *I'm not talkin' to you mothafuckas, get the fuck outta here!* Mitchell, evidently. He was pounding on the door, making the hallway shake like an earthquake. Salpeter and Grant stood to the side in case Mitchell had a gun. But it was just more screaming like a crazy man, more pounding on the door. Salpeter almost hoped he wouldn't open it. He called Barket, who could hear the commotion over the cellphone. "Just get him in here," Barket said wearily. Salpeter could hear that he had a terrible cold. Probably didn't want to be waiting all night. Salpeter tapped his inner hostage negotiator. "C'mon, Martin," he said, not quite soothingly. "I'm a nice guy. I'm not here to make trouble for you but I got an innocent guy. I just wanna talk to you. C'mon, open up."

Mitchell finally stopped screaming and came out. "I really need your help," Salpeter told him. "Antowine needs your help. I'd like to take you out to the Island to talk to the lawyer. Whadya say? Will you do that for me?"

Everett sat in the back with Mitchell as Salpeter drove through Brooklyn. It was like the old days, bringing a guy to the station house. Salpeter hit the LIE and Mitchell looked out the window. "Where the fuck you takin' me?" he asked. "This don't look like Staten Island."

"Not Staten Island," Salpeter said. "*Long* Island."

Salpeter brought Mitchell up to Barket's office on the sixth floor of a mirrored-glass building at the edge of Roosevelt Field. Barket turned on a tape recorder, told Mitchell he knew he was lying about Antowine Butts, and asked him what really happened. And Mitchell told him. He said the Brooklyn detectives told him they would lock him up if he didn't cooperate. And so he picked Butts out of the lineup, even though he knew he was fingering the wrong man.

"If I showed you a picture of my client, could you tell me if he's the guy who shot those two people?" Barket asked.

"Yeah, sure," Mitchell said.

Barket put a photo of Antowine Butts in front of him. "Do you recognize him?" he asked.

"Oh, yeah, that's him."

"Excuse me?"

"That's the kid from the lineup."

"Okay. Is that also the kid from the murder?"

"No, that was somebody else."

When Antowine Butts went on trial for murder a month later, Martin Mitchell was the cornerstone of the prosecution's case. Under Barket's cross-examination, Mitchell admitted he was out of his mind on crack, marijuana, and alcohol throughout that day. Asked at one point what time the shootings occurred, he said, "I can't remember *people*. How am I going to remember time?"

Butts was acquitted in March 2000, though not before spending two years in jail for a murder he didn't commit. One of the jurors later said they made up their minds in half an hour, but stayed in the jury room awhile for appearances. The *New York Times* op-ed columnist Bob Herbert wrote two columns on the case. The prosecution of Antowine Butts, he said, showed "the frightening reality of a criminal justice system gone haywire—a system that simply closed its eyes to the most elementary aspects of truth and falsity, guilt and innocence."

Salpeter's eyes were opening a little wider to the idea that bad and even corrupt police work was perhaps not so rare. Then came yet another case. In January 2000—one month after Fred Chichester's motion for a hearing was turned down in Suffolk County and two months before Antowine Butts was acquitted—Salpeter read about a murder case on the Caribbean island of Tortola. Four American men were being charged. Whether they were guilty or innocent, Salpeter figured they could use an investigator and imagined there were worse places to work a case in January. Salpeter called the father of one of the suspects and offered his services. It took a while but Salpeter eventually got the job. He called Barket and asked him if he wanted to take a trip to the Virgin Islands.

Lois McMillen was an artist from an affluent Connecticut family. A few days after her body was found on a rocky shoreline, the local police charged a man from Virginia whose family owned the villa where McMillen was staying; they also charged his three American houseguests. Roaming the island in sandals and shorts, Salpeter and Barket found that the police had failed to do the most routine investigation. Salpeter spent another two weeks there after Barket went home, long enough to hand his client's lawyers the ammunition they needed to dismantle the prosecution's case. The trial judge dismissed the charges against three of the four defendants, and the fourth was later exonerated on appeal.

The chief defense attorney in Tortola was Michael Griffith, a New Yorker famous for defending Americans charged with crimes overseas. For sheer drama (real and cinematic), he probably never topped the case of Billy Hayes, a young man from Long Island who wound up in the hell of a Turkish prison in the 1970s after he tried to leave the country with several bricks of hashish taped to his body. It was made into the 1978 film *Midnight Express*. A few years after the Tortola case, Griffith told a writer for *New York* magazine: "Jay is the best investigator I've ever used, and I've been practicing for thirty years with clients in over a dozen countries."

The headline on the article was THE REINVESTIGATOR. But it wasn't about the Tortola case. That was just background.

SALPETER DROVE to Great Neck, flying along Northern Boulevard early on New Year's Day. The roads were deserted, as was the law office of Fine & Bassik. Salpeter unlocked the front door and climbed the stairs, entering his office to find the pile of mail that had accumulated while he was lying by the pool in Cabo. He sat behind his desk and started flipping through it. Couple of bills. Some checks on bread-and-butter cases, matrimonial surveillances that he jobbed out to his guys. Then, something different. A letter from someone in prison. The return address had a name and a DIN—Department of Corrections Identification Number.

> Martin Tankleff 90T 3844
> Clinton Correctional Facility
> 1074 Cook Street
> Dannemora, New York 12929-2001

> December 21, 2000

Dear Mr. Salpeter:

Several years ago I read about your involvement in the Henry Chichester case. Recently, I was speaking with my work-out partner Austin Offen and he spoke of you highly. He felt that you could obtain justice in my case. . . .

As you may know from media reports in Newsday and Channel 12 news, in 1990 I was wrongfully convicted of murdering my beloved parents. I can state to you, as the facts support, that I am 100% innocent. I don't want to convince you of this, I would rather you draw your own conclusions. . . .

Over the past 10 years, investigators and lawyers have obtained a great deal of exculpatory information. However, when trying to follow up some of the information, we ran into many brick walls. We just learned that the Suffolk County D.A.'s office lied to us regarding some exculpatory information they said they were going to investigate. I know this doesn't surprise you. What will surprise you is how little of an investigation they did in my case.

My family and I need someone such as yourself but I wonder if you would be willing to work on my case on a <u>pro bono</u> basis or a primarily <u>pro bono</u> basis. Please know that your services are greatly desired. I have all the investigator files for your review. . . . We are confident that the truth is out there to be found.

Thanking you in advance for your time and cooperation in this matter. I anxiously await your reply. In addition, I want to wish you and yours a happy and healthy holiday season.

Very truly yours,
Martin Tankleff

Another innocent man in prison? How many could there be? Salpeter was still a cop at heart, still assumed that people in prison belonged there, and that included men who wrote him claiming they didn't. That this was a Suffolk County case didn't raise any red flags, either. Just because they got the Chichester case wrong didn't mean they made a habit of convicting innocent people of murder. Salpeter had only a vague recollection of the Tankleff case. In 1988, he was a detective on the 69th Squad in Brooklyn and had his own cases to worry about. He knew about Tankleff from the papers and TV, but didn't follow it closely enough to remember the details. He'd assumed the kid was guilty and forgot about it.

Still, a case was a case. If his family could come up with a little money, Salpeter was happy to take a look. He figured he'd do some work, make himself a few bucks, then tell him sorry, looks like you're guilty, I can't help you. Then again, he lived by the simple assumption that an investigator never knew where he was going on a case until he got there. "Martin, I wish I was financially secure enough to work for you on a pro bono basis," Salpeter wrote back. "I am not as liquid as a Washington based law firm. Your case would take me many hours to review and of course then the investigation. If you are able, I would take your case on a flat fee of $5,000 for the duration of the investigation."

Salpeter got a quick response from Marty and a phone call from Ron Falbee. Marty's cousin and onetime guardian came to Salpeter's office and gave him a ten-minute version of the twelve-year history. What Marty needed now, he explained, was something along the lines of a gift from heaven.

I'm no miracle worker, Salpeter said.

A few days later, he took Marty's collect call from Dannemora. Marty told him all the things he and his family had been doing—collecting information through freedom of information requests, working with the Innocence Project on getting DNA testing. Salpeter was impressed, but he wanted to get one thing straight right up front. "If you're innocent," he told Marty, "the only way I'm getting you out of prison is to solve the case. And I'm not gonna lie to you, that's a hard thing to do. I'm not a New York police detective anymore. I'm on my own. I have nothing to offer anyone for coming forward. I can't subpoena. I have to do it the hard way. So I don't want to run around and then find out you're *not* innocent. If you're guilty, don't hire me."

"I *am* innocent," Marty said.

"I mean, don't waste my time. If you killed your parents I can't help you."

"I didn't kill my parents. I am a hundred percent innocent. You'll see that once you start digging into the case."

Salpeter got off the phone thinking: This kid is different. Intelligent, articulate. In fact, he sounded less like a prison inmate than a prison inmate's lawyer. "He was very aggressive on his innocence—that was the biggest thing," Salpeter recalled. "The innocence was coming out of his pores. Even over the phone, I felt it. The vibrations from this kid were, 'Let's go. This is going to be good.'"

Salpeter filled out an agency agreement that didn't reflect high expectations on his part. He crossed out "retainer fee" and replaced it with "flat fee" of $5,000. At the bottom of the second page he handwrote a provision: "At client's request this investigation can be terminated and money refunded on unused investigative hours." Salpeter came across the agreement in his files years later and it made him chuckle.

A check arrived from the law firm of Baker Botts in Washington. A year earlier, the only firm Steve Braga ever worked for—Miller, Cassidy, Larroca & Lewin—had merged with Baker Botts, a storied international firm of eight hundred lawyers in eleven cities whose roots went back to 1840s Texas. The original Baker of Baker Botts was Judge James Baker, and he was by followed by five more of the same name. James Baker III was President George H. W. Bush's secretary of state (and, just a few weeks before this point, the field general of Bush's son's Florida recount battle). So Marty Tankleff was now represented by one of the most influential law firms in the United States, as well as another. Barry Pollack had departed Miller, Cassidy a few years earlier and was now with Nixon Peabody, another megafirm with hundreds of lawyers in many countries. (He would later move again, to a partnership at Kelley Drye & Warren, one of Washington's oldest firms.) And there was Jennifer O'Connor, who came to Miller, Cassidy after several years as a lawyer in the Clinton White House. She joined Marty's case when Pollack left the firm, though he, like Braga and O'Connor, would bring his pro bono commitment to Marty wherever he went in his career travels. If nothing else, Marty was lawyered up—a supreme irony considering how it all started.

But no matter how many high-powered Washington law firms he had behind him, there was virtually nothing any of them could do for Marty without dramatic new evidence. And that was now in the hands of a lone private detective whose office overlooked an auto body shop.

Salpeter called the offices of Baker Botts in Washington to see about getting started on the case files. The first person he spoke to was Steve Braga's assistant. He expected an executive secretary type. What he got was a force to be reckoned with named Meg Griffin. She was an intense woman in her late thirties who seemed to be the authority on all things Marty. She could cite chapter and verse on the trial and all the appeals, and kept every significant fact of the case on file in her head. Marty wasn't just another client to her.

Meg had become captivated by his case almost from the day she went to work for Braga after the merger. Her first assignment was to go through the box of videotapes from the trial and label them. The first one she happened to pop into the VCR had Steuerman on the stand. "And I laughed out loud," she recalled. "His drama queen–ness was just hilarious. *I'm not the one on trial here!* Just like when he was crying in the airport when McCready brought him back from California when he was pretending he was dead, which was on another tape." She watched tape after tape, and they didn't make her laugh. They made her angry. When Salpeter joined the case, Meg sent him a package of files with a note saying there was a lot more at Bob Gottlieb's office on Long Island. If he was going back to the beginning, that was the place to start.

Salpeter drove out to Gottlieb's office on Veterans Highway with his crime scene guy, Charlie Haase. Salpeter wasn't all that interested in talking to Gottlieb. He preferred learning about a case on his own, from documents and live witnesses, and found that lawyers tended to put a spin on things.

Gottlieb put Salpeter and Haase in a conference room with several boxes of files, and within twenty minutes Haase made Salpeter glad he brought him. He was going through the crime scene material, looking at photos and lab reports, when he came upon a diagram of the interior floor plan of 33 Seaside Drive. Next to Seymour Tankleff's office was a notation that stopped Haase cold. "Jay, what is this?" he asked. "Does that say 'mud stains'?"

Salpeter peered down. That's what it looked like to him. *Mud stains 31˝ from E wall.* It seemed to be referring to a spot inside the office, near the east wall. That would put it right in front of the sliding glass doors and a few feet from Seymour's body. Salpeter was no expert on the case, not yet, but he knew enough to realize that a mud stain in that spot would not be inconsistent with the defense theory of the crimes. This couldn't have been overlooked, could it? In any event, the goal was new evidence. Anything in these files was old. "Nice but nothing," was how Salpeter termed the notation of a mud stain.

Salpeter and Haase watched the crime scene video. They weren't impressed. There were a lot of panning shots of rooms and not many close-ups; the police videographer seemed to put more time into shooting the exterior. "It's like a real estate video," Salpeter remarked. "Nice property, though. Gorgeous views."

Salpeter read Marty's written "confession," the one McCready wrote but never finished and which Marty never signed. And the typed report titled ORAL STATEMENTS — MARTIN TANKLEFF. Salpeter had been told that the statement didn't match up with the forensics, but he was struck as much by how it didn't match up with common sense. The kid goes to bed pissed off at his parents over bullshit, plans to get up early and kill them? He flips out, but he waits to get a good night's sleep before pounding them with his barbell and slicing them up with a watermelon knife? And he does this naked? It didn't sound right.

IN ONE OF their first phone conversations, Salpeter had asked Marty if he would take a polygraph test. Marty didn't hesitate. He had pleaded with McCready and Rein to give him one that morning at police headquarters, right after McCready told him his father woke up and said he did it.

One thing Salpeter shared with McCready—perhaps the only thing— was that he worked on instinct. The difference was that he recognized their limits. That's why he was a big fan of the polygraph. "It tells me if I'm going in the right direction or I'm wasting my time. I love a polygraph. When I was in the police department I used it all the time. I don't care if it's not admissible in court. It's a tool. You don't have a crystal ball when someone's sitting in front of you. I can't get into your mind. I can't get into your heart. We're all gullible. We all sometimes hear what we want to hear. Why did McCready and Rein refuse to do it? If I were the detective on this case and Marty said, 'I'm innocent, I'll take a lie detector,' I'd hook him up on the spot. Because I want to know. They had the opportunity. They should have done it."

Salpeter's polygraph examiner, Joel Reicherter, was one of the leaders in the field. His c.v. ran twelve pages and included everything from teaching at the Department of Defense Polygraph Institute at Fort Jackson, South Carolina, to offering his expert commentary for CNN's Greta Van Susteren when JonBenét Ramsey's parents were polygraphed in 2000. Reicherter wasn't cheap. He charged $750 a day plus expenses, and the long distance from his home on Long Island to the prison in Dannemora would make his examination of Marty Tankleff a two-day job. Marty wrote to Salpeter, saying he was eager to take the polygraph—"But we have very little money saved up right now and the polygraph isn't going to get me home. I wonder if there is any way he could make the trip in a single day. Maybe fly JetBlue to Burlington and take the ferry across?" Salpeter was impressed with Marty's involvement in the details, but knew his powers were limited. He called Steve Braga, who told him to have Reicherter go to Dannemora however he liked. Baker Botts would take care of it.

Reicherter drove upstate, stayed the night in Plattsburgh, and arrived at Clinton at 8:50 on the morning of September 11, 2001. Crossing the prison yard, he heard a couple of guards talking about something on the news about a plane flying into the World Trade Center. Reicherter paid it little mind, figuring it was a Piper Cub or something. He was brought to a small room, where he unzipped his computer case and flipped open his Compaq Presario. In the modern world, a basic laptop could be a lie detector, so long as it was loaded with the right software. Reicherter used the Axciton polygraph program with computerized algorithms developed at the Johns Hopkins University Applied Physics Laboratory.

To prepare for the exam, Reicherter had read a summary of the case and talked with Marty's lawyers by phone. The last and most important part of the preparation was an interview with his subject. After Marty was brought to the room, Reicherter began a process that was a kind of benign version of the interrogation by the police thirteen years earlier. He asked him first to recount in as much detail as possible the hours surrounding his parents' murders, everything he did from the afternoon before until the moment he made his 911 call. Then he asked him to sketch a floor plan of the house and use it to describe his movements from the time he awoke until he discovered his mother's body. Finally, Reicherter asked Marty to describe in more detail the condition of his parents when he found them. From all this, Reicherter devised the questions Marty was to be asked.

Then he hooked him up. He attached transducers to Marty's abdomen and chest and electrodes to the inside surface of the second and third fingers of his left hand. He asked him some random questions to acquaint him with the process. And then he conducted the test. There were ten questions in all, but only three relevant ones. The rest were unrelated, used either for comparison or as tension breakers. Reicherter started all his exams the same way. "Is today Tuesday?" he asked.

Then he asked the first of the three relevant questions: "Did you put gloves on your hands in the early morning hours on the day your parents were attacked?"

"No," Marty said.

Two unrelated questions, and then the first direct question about the actual commission of the murders. To avoid a compound question—a basic rule—Reicherter referred to only one of Marty's parents and assumed his guilt or innocence applied to both. "Are you the person who hit your mother on the head the night she was beaten and stabbed?" he asked.

"No," Marty said.

The last relevant question: "When you found your mother on the bedroom floor, was that the first time you saw her since you went to bed that night?"

"Yes."

The results, as Reicherter put them in his report: "The polygraph examination numerical scores indicate Mr. Tankleff answered all relevant questions stated above truthfully. The Johns Hopkins Applied Physics Laboratory computer algorithms indicated: **No Deception**, with a statistical chance of error of two percent against a database of known outcomes. The Axciton computer software evaluated Mr. Tankleff as: **No Deception**. . . . In my opinion, Mr. Tankleff did not stab or bludgeon his mother on 7 September 1988."

Reicherter's report put Salpeter's investigation on a swift upward trajectory. "It gave me a huge emotional lift," he said later. "It told me the one thing I needed to know. It made me want to work on this."

An Imperfect Savior

IF JAY SALPETER could have dreamed up one prime lead, one dangling thread that might unravel the whole thing, he would have been hard-pressed to come up with something better than the single page he found in a thin manila folder in Bob Gottlieb's files.

Karlene Kovacs, being duly sworn, deposes and says . . .

The affidavit was just four paragraphs long. It was dated August 10, 1994—seven years ago. Salpeter asked Gottlieb what the story was. Somebody named Karlene Kovacs saying a guy she smoked a joint with told her he was involved in the Tankleff murders. What happened—turned out to be bullshit? Gottlieb frowned at the mention. It wasn't bullshit at all, he said. It was great information. We gave it to the DA's office. They said they looked into it, but they didn't. They went through the motions. We took it as far as we could.

Along with the affidavit was a four-page report to Gottlieb from Gary Trobe, whose private investigation agency employed Bill Navarra. Kovacs said she went to "Joe's" house with John Guarascio, whose sister was Joe's girlfriend. So Navarra had talked to Guarascio. Trobe wrote:

> John stated that the "Joe" we are interested in is Joe Creedom [*sic*], who is no good, and who he would like to see separated from his sister. He stated that Joe Creedom [*sic*] was, and is, into drugs, and in with bad people. . . .
> John denied knowing about the Tankleff case, other than what he read in the paper. . . . It is our investigator's belief that John Guarascio knows more than what he is saying, and perhaps needs

some time to mull over what was presented to him during the course of the interview.

When Guarascio was next interviewed, according to the file, it was by investigators Thomas McDermott and Frank Shields, who were identified as members of the district attorney's Public Integrity Unit. A report by McDermott said he and Shields were assigned to follow up the information after a meeting between the Tankleff legal team and DA James Catterson and two of his top deputies, including the trial attorney, John Collins. But such a high-level meeting apparently didn't lead McDermott and Shields to pursue the information with much urgency. The report of their investigation ran just a page and a half. It contained no reference to an interview with Kovacs herself and indicated the investigators worked on it when they had nothing else to do. It recounted three interviews over four months. John Guarascio told the detectives that if he'd known anything he would have reported it to the authorities. Three weeks later, the DA's investigators went to see Guarascio's sister, Terry. She said Creedon never said anything to her about the Tankleff murders. Three months later, McDermott and Shields went to see Joe Creedon himself.

> On January 4, 1995, the undersigned spoke with Joseph Creedon, who was residing in a Nassau County detention facility. Joseph Creedon stated that he did not know the Tankleffs; never was on their property, and did not know any Steuerman except Todd, who shot him. Joseph Creedon did claim that Todd Steuerman had once asked him if he knew anybody that would cut Marty Tankleff's tongue out of his mouth, because his father would pay a lot of money. Creedon stated he never followed up on that remark because he does not like Todd Steuerman and the main reason is because Todd shot him.
>
> The undersigned did ask Joseph Creedon what he was being incarcerated for. He stated that he had an attempted grand larceny in Nassau County and aggravated harassment in Suffolk County. The undersigned told Joseph Creedon that the District Attorney could help him in his legal woes if he could supply any information regarding the Tankleff homicides. Joseph Creedon appeared to understand the severity of his plight and stated that he wished he had information so he could help himself but had none. He stated he knew nothing of the Tankleff murders.

Salpeter found McDermott's report laughable. In fact, he laughed out loud when he read it. *Tell me you committed these murders and I'll help you out with that aggravated harassment case. What the fuck kind of work is that?* Salpeter thought of the Chichester case—a guy sits in prison for murder, people come forward to say someone else confessed. And then, nothing. He understood why the DA's investigators did nothing more than a cover-your-ass investigation, but what about the defense investigators? Salpeter called Gary Trobe. "It looks like you guys were going in the right direction," he said. "Why'd you stop?"

"The money stopped," Trobe told him. After six years of legal battles, the family was strapped. Marty had just lost at the New York Court of Appeals, and there wasn't even any money to bring the case to federal court. Then Marty got his pro bono lawyers in Washington. The Kovacs lead seemed to fall by the wayside as everyone focused on the federal appeals, which took five years to play out.

"WHERE HAVE YOU BEEN?" Karlene Kovacs asked Salpeter when he called her.

It had been ten years now since that Easter Sunday in 1991 when Kovacs found herself smoking a joint with a professed murderer, and it had been seven years since she gave her sworn statement about the encounter to Bob Gottlieb.

"I only met him that one time," she told Salpeter when he asked about Joe Creedon. In fact, she never knew his last name. Could she describe him? Yes, she said. "He was short but muscular, very Italian-looking, and he was definitely what John had said, a wiseguy. He was arrogant. Very cocky."

Tell me what happened that day, Salpeter said.

"They were preparing dinner and Joe invited me and John to go into one of the rooms to smoke a joint of pot with him," Kovacs said. "And so we went in. And I don't know how the conversation started in regards to the Tankleff murders but he said something about Steuerman. What I recall is that Steuerman's son bought dope from Joe. Then he said regarding the Tankleff murder that he and a Steuerman hid behind bushes. He was saying something about running and they had to hide behind bushes, that things were bloody and he was afraid. Then they ran and he was nervous and his adrenaline was flowing and they had to get rid of their clothes."

"And he mentioned there was blood?"

"Yeah, there was a lot of blood."

"Now when Joe was telling you this story, did you feel he was being sincere?"

"Well, like I said, he was very cocky, and I don't know if he was showing off but, yes, he came across as being truthful, and maybe he didn't realize what he was saying or who he was talking to."

Kovacs's account was more detailed than the one-page affidavit she gave Gottlieb. Most conspicuous was her recollection that Creedon said there was "blood all over." Her 1994 statement didn't mention blood at all. But Salpeter didn't regard it as an inconsistency per se. Like most experienced detectives, he had a pretty good sense about people and their motivations. Karlene Kovacs seemed credible, and he couldn't think of a thing she had to gain. Still, he wanted to know for sure. Not that I doubt you, Salpeter told Kovacs, but would you take a polygraph?

Joel Reicherter read Kovacs's 1994 affidavit and a transcript of Salpeter's taped interview with her. Then he went to her house, interviewed her, and came up with three relevant questions: "Did Joe Creedon tell you he and a Steuerman were hiding in the bushes on the Tankleff property the night of the murders?" "Did Joe Creedon tell you they were full of blood and had to get rid of their clothes the night of the murders?" "Did Joe Creedon tell you he was scared and his adrenaline was flowing and had to get out of there?"

Karlene answered yes to all three questions. Reicherter's computer indicated "No Deception" on each one, with a chance of error of one percent against the database of known outcomes. According to Reicherter, there was virtually no doubt that she was telling the truth.

WHEN HE WAS approached in 1994—first by investigators working for Marty Tankleff's lawyer, then by the pair from the Suffolk County district attorney's office—John Guarascio had denied knowing anything about Joe Creedon and the Tankleff murders. In both interviews, he said he had nothing but disdain for Creedon, and would gladly tell them if he knew something.

It wasn't exactly the truth. As Bill Navarra had suspected, Guarascio was holding back out of concern for his sister; he needed some time to think about it. Maybe not seven years, but that's how much time had passed by the time Jay Salpeter found his way to him. Guarascio told Salpeter that he did hear Creedon saying something about the Tankleff murders that Easter Sunday. He just didn't know it at the time. He was on the outskirts of the conversation, he recalled, and wasn't paying much attention. Karlene and Joe were talking about people they knew in common. At some point Joe said something about hiding in bushes, being "pumped up," watching a card game. That was about all Guarascio could remember. He didn't put the pieces together until the investigators came calling three years later. "I didn't know he was talking about the Tankleff murders," he said. "I thought it was one of his drug deals, one of his little burglaries."

He didn't tell the truth back then because his sister already had enough trouble with Creedon.

Salpeter asked Guarascio if he would put him in touch with his sister. Guarascio said he couldn't do it. "She's out of state now," he said. "Creedon doesn't even know where she is. He's been out of her life for years and she wants to keep it that way. She doesn't need any trouble from Joey Guns Creedon. Did you know that's his nickname? Joey Guns."

Salpeter called Guarascio a few days later, and again a week after that, and the week after that. Have you talked to Terry? Will she speak to me? Can you ask her again? He called Guarascio every week, sometimes more than once.

And at Salpeter's suggestion, Marty made his own plea directly to Terry. "I'm sure you know that I have been incarcerated in a New York State prison for almost 12 years for a crime I had nothing to do with," he wrote. ". . . I now understand that you may have the key to open the door to my freedom. Each day in here I fear that the truth will never come out. I fear that the people who killed my parents may find a way to keep the truth from ever being known. You can set that fear free and help me and my family out by providing any and all information you have to Jay. . . . Please help me, I beg of you to help. . . ."

Salpeter asked John Guarascio to get Marty's letter to his sister. John sent the letter to Terry. She read it more than once. She told her brother to tell Salpeter that she sympathized, but she really didn't know anything.

SO WHO WAS Joe Creedon? Among the documents Meg Griffin had sent Salpeter from Washington were arrest records on Creedon that Marty had obtained at one point through freedom of information requests to Suffolk County. Between those documents and Kovacs's story, Creedon didn't seem to be anyone's idea of a professional hitman. He'd had his share of arrests, but most were for garden-variety garbage. Joey Guns loved his nickname but his documented history included two shootings and in both cases he was the victim. One was the Todd Steuerman incident in 1989. The other was in May 1995, five months after DA's investigator McDermott visited Creedon at the Nassau County Jail. There was a photocopy of a brief news story in Gottlieb's files. It said that Creedon had been shot in the arm and cheek, that he told the police it happened while he was standing at a phone booth. "We're not sure if the story is straight," a police detective was quoted saying. This was apparently because Creedon claimed he was shot on the day he was supposed to be in court on an aggravated harassment charge (the same charge the DA's investigators had offered to help him with).

Creedon had done two stretches of state time. The first was for statutory rape in 1982—Creedon was twenty-three, the girl fourteen—for which he spent a little over three years upstate. A conviction for attempted grand larceny sent him back for another two years in 1996. But most intriguing to Salpeter was a collection of documents relating to a burglary that occurred just a few months after the Tankleff murders. Attached to the arrest report were confessions by Creedon and a young accomplice.

On December 29, 1988, twenty-year-old Glenn Harris was charged with burglarizing the post office in the South Shore town of Moriches. He was taken to the nearest precinct, the Fifth, and there he told the detectives who were processing him that besides confessing to this particular burglary he'd like to add a few others. Seven, all told. A clearance confession, they called it. One of the burglaries on his list was the break-in of a Fayva shoe store a couple of nights before. According to Harris's statement to Detective Floyd Jones, he and Joe Creedon were together the night after Christmas. They stole a van, then used it to smash the shoe store's plate-glass window. They stole the store's safe, which contained about $400.

Creedon's statement, like Harris's, was handwritten by Detective Jones. But it was dated some four months later, and blamed everything on Creedon's junior partner. According to Creedon, it all started when he was at his father's house, minding his own business, "and Glenn Harris came over with a Strathmore bagel truck."

Now this is interesting, Salpeter thought. This wasn't some random vehicle these two knuckleheads happened to use to break into a shoe store and grab a few hundred bucks. It was a truck that belonged to the Steuermans. Not that it was out of the blue. Salpeter already knew that Creedon had a connection to Todd Steuerman. But still.

The file also contained copies of three typed letters Creedon wrote to Suffolk County police officials—one to the commissioner, two to Internal Affairs—complaining that he had been coerced into signing his statement. He said it happened when he went to the Sixth Precinct to see about getting his girlfriend's car back after the police impounded it as evidence in his shooting by Todd Steuerman a week before. While he was at the precinct, Creedon explained, the detective who had the Fayva case saw him and asked him to come into a room. "Det. Jones closed the door and told me sign the fucken paper or I'll break your fucken arm at which time he began to tug at my arm. At this time my right arm was in a sling cast from a bullet to my right elbow. . . . I know a Glenn Harris But know nothing of this incedent. I would ask with all do respect ask that this matter be throughly Investagated. Respectfully, Joseph S. Creedon."

Salpeter rolled all this around in his mind. If Joe Creedon was so casual with his secrets that he talked about the Tankleff murders to a complete stranger while getting high on Easter Sunday, what were the chances he might have mentioned something about it to a guy he ran with? And what if one of the guys he ran with happened to be a criminal with such a guilty conscience that he was moved to confessing to seven burglaries when all the cops were asking him about was one?

ON JANUARY 3, 2002, Salpeter punched a number into his cellphone, hoping he might find Glenn Harris on the other end.

"Hello." It was a woman's voice.

"Hi. Is Glenn there?"

"Who's calling?"

"My name is Jay Salpeter. I'm a private investigator. Can I speak to Glenn?"

"Well, he's not here. This is his mother. Can I help you?"

Glenn Harris's mother sounded like a pleasant woman, and it wasn't Salpeter's style to play games with nice people. "Well, as I said I'm a private investigator," he said. "I'm a retired New York detective. I'm working on a case, the Tankleff case. I don't know if you remember it. Two people who were murdered in Belle Terre and their son was convicted for it."

"I remember it. They had it on TV. Wasn't that years ago?"

"Yes it was. But I've been hired by Martin Tankleff to take another look into it."

"What does it have to do with Glenn?"

"I think he might be able to help me. What's your name, by the way, if I can ask?"

"Virginia."

"Virginia, I'll be honest with you. I'm looking for some information on Joe Creedon. I understand that Glenn knew him. So I'd like to talk to him and see if he has some information that can help me. Sometimes things change over the years, you know what I'm saying? So if you could ask him to call me. I'll give you my cellphone number."

A week later, Salpeter got a call back from Virginia Harris. She said she had talked to Glenn.

"And will he talk to me?" Salpeter asked.

"Well, he's in prison," Virginia said. "He's up at Clinton. And I told him what you said."

"And what did he say?"

"He said to tell you that you might be on the right track."

Tantalizing as this was, Salpeter couldn't pounce on it. He couldn't call Harris; even if he could, the phone didn't feel like the right approach. And it wasn't his style to drive nearly to Canada without a clue. That left the U.S. mail. Salpeter wrote to Harris, explained who he was and what he was after. He said he'd like to come up and talk to him, but only if Harris had something to tell him.

Prison mail was notoriously slow, but it was less than a week before an envelope arrived at Salpeter's office with the return address Glenn Harris 93A5047 at Clinton Correctional Facility. The envelope was fat. Salpeter opened it and found ten pages from a yellow legal pad filled with large, back-slanted cursive.

> Dear Sir,
>
> What took you so long and who put you on to me? At this point that is not important. What *is* important is that Mr. Tankleff be released as soon as *we* can prove it. He has suffered enough. When I found out you were lookin' for me I reflected back and did the math. I have some info. I believe my "theory" to be correct. And its not just a theory. (I know it, you know it, Martin knows it, and piece O shit McCready knows it. Can't forget Jerry either. (Even *I* can play detective!)
>
> Sir, I feel I was wronged too. I feel I don't belong here either yet I'm guilty. I'm a drug addict and by societies standards a "scumbag"! To know Martin has been subjected to this shit pains me. All I gotta do is look around. Yet time after time I've subjected myself to this bullshit. Obviously there is something wrong with me and once and for all I am trying to nip this in the bud and put an end to this madness. I've been serving life on the installment plan. I was released now & again to hang out with scumbags & basically slowly kill myself. I'm not gettin' the help I need here! I can cry out, scream out, beg, and no one heres my cries. And they expect me to become a better person. As you can see I'm extremely bitter. I am lookin for redemption and I don't know if I will find it through Martin but it cant fuck me up more than I already am.
>
> So fly your ass up here in ya jet. . . .
>
> I am an arrogant, cocky bastard! My credibility is shot! I wont be trusted and/or believed. I guess you can help me. I can use my

intelligence when I need to. Deceitful, yes and no. Put it this way. I can be articulate. I want someone to pay. Yes, I'm angry! Nothin is gonna give 13 yrs back to Martin. It was a big political conspiracy. THEY KNEW! Yet an innocent man was sent to jail! They didn't play fair Mr. Salpeter. By the way, nice fake name! (Only kidding). I am gonna need a lawyer. I don't wanna get implicated in this F-U-C-K-I-N-G TRAVESTY OF JUSTICE.

I don't want to get personal but what are you in this for? Who do you work for? Department of Justice? I'm curious as hell as to who put you on to me. At this point it doesn't really matter. Call it fate or whatever. I am going to have to implicate myself in a crime to corroborate my "theory." I would need immunity. Just get up here! Sorry this letter is so long and drawn out but I've been waiting. I've been holdin' it in and I couldn't any longer, Magnum P.I. (Joke laugh ha-ha) You better have a sense of humor Sir! Its the only thing that's been keeping me going for the last 12½ of 15 years.

I believe I can feel compassion for another now. It has opened my eyes, a blessing in disguise. As far as I know your close and you may not even need me. But I believe I can prove my theory. The thing is will I be believed. As I said, either way, I can sleep at night. There is no blood on my hands nor demons (of that sort) tormenting my soul. . . .

> Goodnight.
> Glenn

Salpeter had no idea what to make of Harris's letter, other than that it was equal parts enticing and bizarre. Clearly Harris knew something, but clearly he was also some kind of head case. *Fly your ass up here in ya jet.* Not yet. Salpeter decided to take it slowly, feel him out while establishing a rapport that might pay off later. Harris seemed to be a troubled man who wanted someone to talk to. So Salpeter talked to him. No, I'm not from the FBI, he wrote back. Just a private investigator trying to find the truth so an innocent man can get out of prison. He sent him a copy of the newspaper article about the Fred Chichester case.

Harris wrote back, and then he wrote again without waiting for a reply. Salpeter found himself with a pen pal. Harris's letters rambled between goofy jokes and vivid introspection and serious unburdening: His father was a Marine who sexually abused Harris. His sister committed suicide. His life was an endless cycle of drugs and crime and prison and parole. In one of his letters he mentioned his "meds." He had bipolar disorder. Not surprising, since he wrote Salpeter just about every day for two months, and most of the letters went on and on for pages. One day a letter came with the return address "Jose Rodriguez 98A5599." Harris had maxed out on his mailing privileges and used other inmates' names.

In every one of Harris's letters, "Martin" came up sooner or later, usually in the context of his own beleaguered existence. "This is not about just me but in a way it is. It's about me, it's about Martin. Two totally different individuals with so many similarities and coincidences. At the moment its still beyond my comprehension. And its about you, a caring compassionate man who believes in what he does, who believes in right and wrong, good and bad. Who believes in justice. Justice will prevail. I never had a chance Jay! Or did I have too many? My head is sooo far up my ass (and has been for some time now) that I am having a hard time excavating it Jay. But I am beginning to pull it out. I can breathe and I can see light. . . ."

So what did Harris know? Another coy confession by Joe Creedon? By March, after two months of letters, it was time to find out. Since his client was in the same prison—and he had yet to meet him in person—Salpeter made plans to see Marty, too. He wrote one more letter to Harris. "It's a long trip," he said. "Don't bring me up there for nothing." Harris responded in his usual way.

Jay,

I've decided you are my savior in disguise Youre my white knight. It's Monday the 11th. I am patiently anticipating your visit. I hope all goes well. I have been going through a range of emotions as I have previously stated in my letters. I (we) may have some damage control to do. . . . I shared what is going on with me with a few people I felt I could trust. How could I be expected to keep it to myself?! As I said, I want the world to know Martin didn't do it, Martins a good person. I'm a good person, you're a good person for believing in it and investigating it. I've been having my own self "think tanks" and self analysis sessions with myself. Overall, I am not too displeased. I am getting the help I need here for the most part. I need to get out of jail and progress forward. Can you get me into a half way house Jay? What are my chances of getting parole? Be honest, am I shooting too high?

Glenn

Salpeter called Virginia Harris and asked if she'd like to visit her son. She was thrilled by the invitation. Salpeter booked two rooms at a motel in Plattsburgh, then headed off for a nine-hour drive with a woman he'd only spoken to on the phone. First, though, he stopped at Oggi Domani, the salon in Queens that he visited two or three times a week. Salpeter didn't spend much time worrying about how he dressed, as some detectives did, but he cared a great deal about how his hair looked. "So we stop to get our hair done. We're sitting next to each other in the chairs and waving to each other. She loves it. And then we get on the road. Virginia does most of the talking. If you know Glenn, you know his mother. Just not so crazy. She was a nice lady. She worked for years for the IRS. Eventually we got there. We go out to dinner that night in Plattsburgh. The next morning, we're going to the prison. It's only twenty minutes away and she says she knows the way, but she gets us lost. Takes us an hour out of the way. She can't find the fuckin' prison. I'm getting a little annoyed. *Virginia, where's the prison?*"

They finally found it. Virginia waited in the reception area while Salpeter went in to meet Glenn alone. He went through several sets of metal gates, each one opening and closing with a reverberating clang, then entered the visitors' room and handed his yellow pass to a guard at the desk, who told him where to sit and wait. Harris would be out shortly. Salpeter had asked Virginia for a picture of her son, and now he watched the area where the inmates entered the visiting room, looking out for a man in his mid-thirties, compactly built with a square jaw and a goatee.

That's him. Harris checked in at the desk and the guard pointed out Salpeter. Harris walked down the aisle to the chair opposite where Salpeter was waiting for him. They shook hands over the low partition that separated them. There was some small talk about the trip up. Your mother couldn't find the prison, Salpeter said. Harris was nervous, jumpy, all over the place, just like his letters. Then Salpeter got down to business. Talk to me about Joe Creedon, he said.

Harris began with the Fayva shoe store burglary. There was a little more to it than what was in the arrest report. His statement to the police started after he and Creedon had stolen the Strathmore bagel truck. How they got it was another story. According to Harris, they had started the evening by breaking into the bagel store itself. Creedon knew where the safe was.

How did he know? Salpeter asked.

He knew, Harris said.

Anyway, they couldn't get the safe out. It was too big. So they decided to steal the truck. Once they had the truck, they decided to use it to crash into the Fayva shoe store.

"So what do you know about the Tankleff case?" Salpeter asked.

Harris was finally silent. He sighed heavily.

"If you know something, Glenn, now's the time," Salpeter said. "That's why I'm here."

"This has been botherin' me for a long time," Harris said. "But what's gonna happen to me if I tell the truth?"

"Nothing's gonna happen," Salpeter said. "What's there to be afraid of?"

"I'm gonna need a lawyer."

"What're you gonna need a lawyer for? For telling the truth? You're not gonna need a lawyer."

Harris sighed again. Then he said, "I drove them there."

Salpeter's heart skipped a beat. *Do I have the driver of the fucking car?* He tried to seem unfazed. "You drove them there," he said. "Are you lying to me now?"

"No, it's the truth," Harris said.

"This is the truth. You drove them there."

"Yes."

"Who did you drive there?"

"Creedon."

"And who else? You said 'they.'"

"Peter Kent."

"Who's Peter Kent?"

"One of the scumbags I used to run with."

"So you drove Joe Creedon and Peter Kent. Where did you drive them?"

"To Belle Terre."

"All right," said Salpeter, his heart thumping. "Let's start at the beginning."

It was in the summer. A few months before me and Creedon did the Fayva burglary. We were gettin' high and Creedon says he knows where there's a safe. He and Kent are gonna do it and he asks me if I wanna go along 'cause they need a driver. It's a house in a rich neighborhood. So I say yeah. I had a '71 Grand Prix I just bought off a guy. We went up to Belle Terre. We go through Port Jeff and get to the arches, the pillars, whatever, up there in Belle Terre. Creedon told me where to go. It was somewheres off to the right of the main road. We come up to a house by the bluffs up there and he tells me where to park and tells me to wait. They get out and start walking toward the house. I lost sight of them in the dark. I waited in the car for maybe fifteen, twenty minutes, then I seen them running up to the car. They get in, and they're all nervous and Creedon says to get the fuck out of there. He tells me to take him to his mother's house in Selden, he has to take care of something. When we got there Kent got out too. He lived about three houses away.

What did you do then? Salpeter asked.

I just stayed there. I got into the backseat to go to sleep. But I couldn't sleep and I sat up and saw Peter around the side of a house. He was doin' somethin', it looked kinda suspicious so I got out of the car and went up to him. He was burn-

ing his clothes. I asked him what's goin' on, what's he doin'? And he says, "Never mind, just mind your own fuckin' business." I walked away but I thought somethin' bad went down. I went back to my car and wanted to get some sleep. When I woke up I turned on the radio and heard that somethin' happened to a couple in Belle Terre. I thought, Holy fuck. I put two and two together. I was scared. I swear I didn't know what they were up to. I'm a drug addict. I'm a thief. They said they were doin' a safe.

What clothes was Kent burning? Salpeter asked.

Jeans and a sweatshirt. With a hood.

Did you see a murder weapon?

No, but Creedon had gloves on when he was getting in the car.

What kind of gloves?

Rubber. He took them off and put them in his jacket pocket.

Was there blood on them?

I couldn't see.

Did they have a weapon?

Harris didn't answer. His face said, *Enough for now.*

Salpeter was flabbergasted. He had come up thinking Harris was going to tell him he'd heard things—maybe, if he was lucky, that Creedon told him he was involved. Not in his wildest dreams did Salpeter think he had someone who may have been involved in the actual murders. This is a home run, Salpeter thought—but is this guy telling me the truth? Is this bullshit? Marty's in this prison—is this something they could have cooked up together? But how in the world do two guys come up with something and then pray that Jay Salpeter drops from the sky and writes to Glenn Harris?

This is sensational stuff you're telling me, Salpeter said. But I need to be sure it is the truth. Will you take a polygraph?

Yeah, said Harris. Why not.

After he finished with Harris, Salpeter visited his client. Marty greeted him with a wide smile and bright eyes, excited to finally meet the man he prayed would unlock his cell door. But when Salpeter told him what Harris said, Marty's reaction struck him as oddly low-key. Maybe it was that he'd had so many close calls and disappointments over the years that he lacked the ability to register joy at anything short of freedom itself. And maybe that was simply Marty—boundless optimism, restrained emotion.

Salpeter asked Marty if he knew Harris, or ever came in contact with him. "I'm in the honor block," Marty said. "I don't have contact with the regular population. I wouldn't know him if he was sitting right next to me."

While Salpeter was seeing Marty, Harris was visiting with his mother. He told her what he'd told Salpeter, said he'd wanted to get it off his chest for a long time. He couldn't wait to write his next letter to Salpeter, so he jotted a note on the back of his mother's yellow Inmate Visitor Receipt and asked her to give it to him. "Jay, This wasn't random. It was a planned act no? Did they use me as a pawn? I remember Kent said he was goin' to take a shower and he had like a sense of urgency to do so. Jay, am I gonna get in trouble for this?"

Since Salpeter had come as a regular visitor—it wasn't a "legal visit"— he couldn't take any notes when he was with Harris. He wrote down everything he could remember as soon as he could get his hands on a pen and paper. He called Steve Braga's office in Washington and spoke to Meg Griffin. "Oh my God," Meg said, and got Braga on the phone. Salpeter filled him in. That's wonderful, Braga said—do you believe him? Salpeter said he thought so. He wanted to polygraph Harris, but he couldn't imagine why in the world anyone would involve himself in a double murder if it wasn't true. Everything Harris said fit with what Creedon told Karlene Kovacs. And there was this: Harris said that Creedon had rubber gloves— a *huge* detail. It would be consistent with the forensic evidence and answer one of the enduring mysteries of the case. Braga asked Salpeter to put everything in writing and send it to him.

A few days later, Salpeter got a letter from Harris.

Jay,

I just got back from our meeting. I don't know how and what to feel Jay. I feel uneasy. I feel good & bad at the same time. I feel sorta dirty, guilty, used but I feel elated. I feel cleansed in a way too. I've trusted ya on blind faith. You're a good guy, good first impression. Straight Shooter.

You told me not to worry but I am Jay. I'm scared. I'm scared as hell. You helped me bring up some things, memories, that I've been suppressing. Bring on the lie detector test. That's all I gotta say. You said you'd look out for my best interests. I believe you. I trust you. I have faith in you. You didn't make me any promises Jay and you asked for the truth, just the truth but when your mind is so fucken twisted and you suppress the truth. . . . I didn't believe it, didn't wanna believe it and/or I stuffed it. If I'm correct I remember seeing Creedon in and or around the bushes, shrubbery. I was trying not to look cause I didn't want him to know I was scared of him and I was afraid of what I was possibly involved in, how I was used.

What was the link between Joey and Jerry? You probably told me but there's a lot of things you didn't tell me and for your own reasons. I respect that. I'll say it again, I trust you Jay. I trust you like I've never trusted another in my life! I don't know where this comes from Jay but I remember twilight. Maybe it was lights on the house, outside lights and I recall facing the water, facing where the house would be on my right facing towards the water. I guess the direction would be N. And it wasn't too far into Belle Terre. It mightve even been on Belle Terre Road right inside the gates. . . . Was it a ranch Jay? One story ranch. Enough! Poor Marty.

Harris's memory that the Tankleff house might have been on the main road and "right inside the gates" didn't match its actual location. But his letter included a carefully drawn diagram showing houses on a side street just east of the main road, with a notation that the house he went to that night was "in here somewhere . . . to the right." It was almost exactly where the Tankleff house was in relation to Cliff Road.

In another letter, Harris speculated about who besides Creedon and Kent might have been involved in the murders: "Jerry, Joey, possibly more? . . . Do you think McCready knew and when he got caught up in it it was too late?"

MARTY'S LAWYERS were excited and hopeful about Glenn Harris's story, but his letters made them anxious. Someone involved in a murder did not figure to be a choirboy, but Harris apparently had the added baggage of mental instability. At the same time, if Harris was telling the truth, the question might become whether he was telling *all* of it. His first letter to Salpeter after their meeting contained a sentence with possible implications: He saw Creedon "in and around the bushes" but was "trying not to look" because "I was afraid of what I was possibly involved in, how I was used." Was Harris saying he was aware that he might be involved in something more than a burglary? Did he do more than sit in his car and wait, unaware of what was going on inside?

A few weeks after his first trip to Dannemora, Salpeter went back up again. This time he was accompanied by Barry Pollack. They flew separately to Burlington, Vermont, and met for the first time in the lobby of a hotel near the airport. They rented a car and got better acquainted on the Lake Champlain ferry. Pollack had made this trip before, when he and Braga first took on the case, seven years earlier.

The meeting with Harris was arranged as a legal visit, so Salpeter and Pollack were able to talk to Harris in private. As Harris repeated his story for Pollack, Salpeter listened closely for inconsistencies. But the story was the same. Salpeter had also established to the lawyers' satisfaction that they could refute any suggestion that Marty had something to do with

Harris's story. He'd obtained prison records that confirmed they were housed in separate units that never mixed.

Pollack was confident that Harris was telling the truth. "He was not somebody who was leaping at the opportunity to do this," he recalled. "He seemed very reluctant to be doing it, in fact. He was very scared. I couldn't figure out a reason why he would be telling this story if it wasn't true. He had details. He was also quite candid about the things he couldn't remember. He didn't try to embellish or make it up. He wasn't looking for an opportunity to add things to the story. At one point I asked him something, and he looked at me and kind of laughed. 'It's *fifteen* years ago.' That being said, clearly he had some mental health issues, he had some drug issues, he's not the ideal witness in a lot of ways. It doesn't mean he's not telling the truth. But I hoped we would be able to get other witnesses to corroborate what he was saying, because if he's all we've got, that's a tough sell."

The question of truth was confronted on June 19, 2002, when Salpeter made his third trip to Dannemora, accompanied this time by Joel Reicherter. Reicherter had administered some 1,200 polygraph exams in his career, but he wasn't sure he had ever tested someone quite like Glenn Harris. Jumpy during the pretest interview, Harris said at one point that he wanted to stop. Reicherter watched in amazement as Harris suddenly stood up, went over to a wall, and did a handstand, saying he wanted to get blood to his brain. Reicherter looked at Salpeter and had to restrain himself from laughing.

It must have done the trick. Harris finished the test, though it took nearly the entire day. Salpeter wanted Harris tested more extensively than Marty or Karlene Kovacs, so Reicherter had to devise a second set of questions.

The first three relevant questions were about what Harris did and what he saw in the early morning hours of September 7, 1988.

"Did you drive Kent and Creedon to the Tankleff residence the night they were killed?"

"Yes," Harris said.

"Did you see Kent burn jeans and a black hooded sweatshirt at his house after the Tankleff stabbings?"

"Yes."

"Did you see gloves in Creedon's left pocket when he got out of your car at the Tankleff property that night?"

"Yes."

Reicherter found that Harris answered the first two questions truthfully. His answer to the third question, however, indicated he was "either deceptive or at least not certain of the truthfulness of his answer." A possible explanation could be found in Harris's inconsistent memory about the gloves. While he answered yes when Reicherter asked if Creedon had gloves in his left pocket when he got *out* of the car when they arrived at the Tankleff property, he had told Salpeter that Creedon had the gloves in his pocket when he got *in* the car when they were leaving. It didn't necessarily mean he didn't see him with gloves, just that he wasn't sure *when* he saw them. Considering all the factors—a traumatic event, a brain with chemical imbalances both involuntary and self-induced, the passage of fourteen years—Reicherter wasn't surprised.

The next set of questions gave further support to the overall veracity of Harris's story. Each one was based on the premise that he was with Creedon and Kent at the Tankleff house that night.

"Did you know before you arrived at the Tankleffs' house that Steuerman wanted the Tankleffs killed?"

"No."

"When you were driving Kent and Creedon to the Tankleffs' house, did you know they were going to kill the Tankleffs?"

"No."

"When you, Kent, and Creedon left the Tankleffs' house that night, did you know, then, that the Tankleffs had been stabbed?"

"No."

According to Reicherter, the polygraph revealed that Harris answered all three of these questions truthfully.

GLENN HARRIS'S polygraph test gave Marty his first solid hope in years, maybe his best chance in all the years since his imprisonment. Salpeter thought it was enough to bring into court. In Washington, Steve Braga and Barry Pollack agreed it was enough to start working on a motion arguing that Marty's conviction should be vacated and a new trial held. Not because the police didn't read him his rights early enough, not because John Collins said some things he shouldn't have in his summation, not because there were no black people on the jury. Because Marty was innocent. After a decade of failed appeals, it was a ground for reversal that had never been tried.

The mechanism was called a 440 motion, after the section of New York's Criminal Procedure Law that provided a way for a person convicted of a crime to try to overturn the verdict and win a new trial based on the discovery of new evidence. "Discovery" was the key word. The law considered only evidence "which could not have been produced by the defendant at the trial." And to warrant a new trial the evidence had to be "of such character as to create a probability" that it would have changed the verdict had it been presented to the jury. Marty wrote a draft of the 440 motion himself.

The Washington lawyers agreed they needed a lawyer on Long Island running point, and Salpeter, naturally, suggested Bruce Barket. Would he do it pro bono? Salpeter knew Barket well enough to assume it wouldn't be a problem. "It didn't sound like much work," Barket recalled. "They needed a local attorney, someone to sign a few documents, appear in court, kind of negotiate their way around."

Barket read the motion brief and saw that Glenn Harris was the key to it. He had one question: "Where's his statement?"

"We don't have one," Salpeter told him.

Harris had been transferred from Clinton down to Sing Sing, the maximum security facility closest to New York City and the state's most famous prison. On August 29, 2003—Marty's thirty-second birthday, as it happened—Salpeter made his fourth trip to see Harris, bringing Bruce Barket with him. They sat in a legal conference room, and Barket asked Harris to tell him his story. Take it slow, he said, give us every detail you can remember, and Jay will write it down. Salpeter didn't expect anything new, not after all those letters and the trips upstate. But this was Glenn Harris. There *was* something new, stunningly new, in the first words out of his mouth: "I ran into Peter Kent and Joseph Creedon at Billy Ram's house. While there we were using crack . . . Creedon says that he knows where there is a safe. Myself, Creedon and Kent went to a house in Belle Terre. . . ."

Salpeter stopped writing. "Billy Ram?" he said. "Glenn, who the fuck is Billy Ram?"

"Another guy I used to do shit with," Harris said.

Why didn't he mention him before? Why had he said he and Creedon and Kent left from Creedon's house? Harris had his reasons. Or he had no reason. Or his brain was misfiring again. Maybe he was confusing it with some other night that started with "We were hangin' out, doin' crack, and decided to go out and . . ." With Glenn you never knew. For now, Salpeter was pleased to hear no more surprises. The rest of Harris's statement was consistent with the story he had told from the beginning, down to the color of the hooded sweatshirt he saw Kent burning. Salpeter wrote it on a yellow legal pad, and Harris signed it in front of a notary.

The emergence of Billy Ram, though disconcertingly late in the game, gave Salpeter another key witness to pursue, the kind he and the legal team could have only wished for: someone who might corroborate Harris's story—enough of it, at least, to establish the reliability of the rest—without worrying about implicating himself.

"Jay," said Barket, "find fucking Billy Ram."

Back in Great Neck, Salpeter ran a data search and hit the phones. He reached a lot of people named Ram, none of them the right one. He got wrong numbers and wrong relatives, left messages on answering machines that weren't returned. The only thing that seemed certain was that Billy Ram was no longer living on Long Island.

CHAPTER 31

Buckle Up, My Friend

MARTY TANKLEFF'S last chance for freedom would hinge on a legal brief arguing for a reversal based on newly discovered evidence. The brief ran fifty-six pages. Only two of them contained what might be strictly considered new evidence. There were the statements of Glenn Harris and Karlene Kovacs. The rest was a history of the case that put them in context—a narrative organized under a series of nineteen subheadings that were as much a commentary as anything turned up lately: "The Police Fail to Investigate the Prime Suspect," "The 'Confession' Is Not Supported by the Physical Evidence," "The Government Misleads Jurors About the 'Confession.'"

Since the moment of his convictions, Martin has been relentless in pursuing any and all means of proving his actual innocence of these horrible crimes. He is now able to do so. The truth of the statements by Glenn Harris and Karlene Kovacs had been substantiated by one of the country's leading polygraph examiners, the motion declared. Though given years apart by two people who didn't know each other, they "verify and corroborate each other by virtue of their interlocking factual detail." Creedon told Kovacs, for instance, that he and his accomplices were full of blood and had to get rid of their clothes after the murders. And Harris reported seeing Peter Kent burning his clothes. Both statements, moreover, were consistent with a previously overlooked notation on a crime scene diagram that indicated a "mud stain" inside an unlocked sliding glass door in Seymour Tankleff's office.

Wrongful convictions are becoming less and less aberrational as many cases of falsely accused individuals come to light. In Martin's case, his erroneous convic-

tions regrettably flowed from two separate and substantial violations of his Constitutional rights. The first was the familiar one—the Miranda violation found by two state and three federal appeals judges, to no avail. The other one was an assertion Marty's attorneys made reluctantly: that Marty's trial counsel was "ineffective." The lawyers saw some missteps in Bob Gottlieb's defense, and their duty to their client left them no choice but to make them part of his appeal. Appraising the job Gottlieb did was not a simple thing. As Barry Pollack put it, "Of course he could have done some things differently. But you know what? You try that exact case, exactly the same way, and nine out of ten juries would acquit. He got the one that didn't. That's one of the scariest things about this. This isn't one of those horror stories where a guy has a schlock court-appointed lawyer who was sleeping at the trial. He had a good attorney who did a good job. The jury got it wrong, and the system is not built to correct that."

But Marty's family had never forgiven what they considered the fatal flaw in Gottlieb's defense: his failure to counter the prosecution's bogus picture of Marty as a psychopath. Now, thirteen years after the trial, a dozen of his relatives gave affidavits saying why they had never wavered in their belief in Marty's innocence and what they would have testified had they been given the chance. The motion asserted that Gottlieb's disregard of the crucial contribution they could have made to the defense represented "an extremely significant departure from acceptable representational standards." (Gottlieb assumed a whatever-it-takes public posture when the motion was later filed, though he was obviously wounded by the "ineffective counsel" argument. "Marty better walk out of jail while I'm still alive if they're going to throw that in," he said one day with a faint smile, before emphasizing for the record that "they should file whatever they deem appropriate in order for justice to be done.")

The motion argued that it all added up to Marty's *actual innocence*, a legal precept meaning there was "clear and convincing evidence that no reasonable juror could convict the defendant of the crimes for which he was found guilty." If a judge were to find this to be the case, he would not only have to vacate the verdict but dismiss the indictment and set Marty free. That's what made the argument perhaps overly optimistic. For Marty, a more realistic hope was a new trial. He would sign for that on the spot.

"Our procedure has always been haunted by the ghost of an innocent man convicted," the motion concluded, a quote from Judge Learned Hand that had become the watchwords of the wrongful-conviction movement. "This case presents an opportunity for the Court to rid the system of just such a ghost. . . . This Court has a very clear opportunity to correct an obvious

and tragic injustice, to vacate this innocent young man's conviction, and to permit, for the first time, an honest, impartial, and professional investigation of the real facts pertaining to the murders of his beloved parents. . . ."

The brief made the rounds among the lawyers and Salpeter until there was a consensus that it was ready to go. Then Bruce Barket had an idea. In 2001, after twelve years of Jim Catterson, a district attorney with a well-earned reputation as a bully who used his office to settle political scores, the voters of Suffolk County were ready for a change. Tom Spota was interested in trying to unseat him, but he was a Republican like Catterson. Rather than buck the powers of his own party, Spota defected to the Democrats and ran as a reform candidate. TOM SPOTA FOR DISTRICT ATTORNEY— A PRINCIPLED PROSECUTOR, said the bumper stickers. He defeated Catterson easily.

Barket thought Spota was a straight shooter who had no built-in bias because he had nothing to do with Marty's original prosecution or the appeals that followed. Spota's roots were in the DA's office, but that was a long time ago. Barket wanted to bring the 440 motion to him before it was filed. Give him the chance to do the right thing, Barket told his colleagues, and he might do just that. He can investigate quietly, before Creedon and Kent lawyer up, and if he's as fair as I think he is, he'll see what we have and consent to a hearing. He'll be a hero.

Bullshit, said Salpeter. Spota will do nothing like that. He will sit on it.

Salpeter's point of view came partly from his hard-nosed inclinations, partly from his occupational impatience with lawyers. But it was mostly because he took a dim view of the Suffolk County district attorney's office. He did not hold Tom Spota in such high regard.

It was about the Henry Chichester case. Salpeter hadn't forgotten about it in the two years he had been working on Marty's case. If anything, Marty's case *kept* him from forgetting about Fred's. They had too much in common. Salpeter still bristled that the courts and prosecutors in Suffolk County refused to take a new look at the case despite strong evidence that the wrong man was in prison. So in the spring of 2003, four months before Marty's 440 motion was set to go, Salpeter had decided to try to get an answer to a question that had bothered him for years. It was a question that had become only more relevant as he worked on Marty's case.

Four years earlier, Salpeter had brought his work on Chichester to Bill Krebs and Bob Plansker, the fellow NYPD retirees who had gone to work for the Suffolk DA's office and were charged up to interview the strongest of the new witnesses, but then bailed at the last moment. In his desk, Salpeter still had the note Bill Krebs sent him, saying he was sorry he and Plansker couldn't have helped more, that it was not for a lack of trying. Krebs wouldn't talk about it back then, but now he and Plansker were both retired. Salpeter found Krebs in the Carolinas and called him. "You guys were ready to jump on it," he said. "What happened?"

"Jay," Krebs said, "I don't want to get involved in anything here, but we were all ready to go when John Collins found out about it. And he came into the office and reamed Plansker and me brand-new assholes. He shut us down. He just shut us down."

Collins had won two convictions of Chichester: first in 1991—his next trial after Marty's—and again three years later, after the first conviction was overturned on a legal issue. He had since risen to chief of the homicide bureau, and was now one of Tom Spota's top deputies. Salpeter was hardly shocked to hear that Krebs and Plansker had been stopped by someone above them; the hand of a boss was obvious to any veteran of the NYPD. But hearing that it was Collins, the same ADA who had put Marty Tankleff in prison, set Salpeter off. He fired off two letters—one to Collins, the other to Spota. He demanded to know why Collins "would not allow investigators to interview persons that might have the ability to exonerate an innocent man." He made the letter to Collins both personal and accusatory: "Our job within the criminal justice system, Mr. Collins, is not to obstruct justice, but to seek out the truth. . . . I implore you to reconsider your decision to terminate the additional interviews, as I feel confident they will prove Mr. Chichester's innocence."

Salpeter was in Manhattan, about to go on Court TV to give his expert commentary on the murder trial of the moment, when he got a call from Tom Spota. Salpeter was startled to hear from the DA himself. He expected a written reply, if anything. "I received your letter about the Chichester case," Spota said. "I'd like to know the names of the detectives you're alleging were interfered with by John Collins."

"Why don't you ask Mr. Collins?" Salpeter replied. The conversation went downhill from there. The next day Spota wrote to Barket, inviting him to come in and talk about "the serious allegations of misconduct alleged by Mr. Salpeter against Mr. Collins . . . and whatever information you believe tends to exculpate Mr. Chichester in the commission of this homicide." He specified that Salpeter was not invited to the meeting. Barket met with Spota the following week but nothing came of it. Barket told Salpeter he gave it a shot. But it was Spota's call.

The Tankleff case would be Spota's call, too, and Barket thought the DA might see this one differently. There was so much reasonable doubt in the original trial that the jury stayed out eight days, and the appeals came so close. A fair-minded prosecutor should see the new evidence in that light. But Barket wasn't taking something vital into account. Having grown up and gone to law school in Connecticut, and practiced in Nassau County, he presumed that things in Suffolk County worked the same as anywhere else. He didn't grasp that Spota, whatever his recent reputation, was a product of Suffolk County's entrenched criminal justice system. He had allegiances that went back twenty-five years, to a time when he was making his name prosecuting cases such as the murder of thirteen-year-old Johnny Pius, hardly an untainted prosecution itself. Spota had an unbreakable bond with the police and their associations. He was the lawyer for the detectives' union, and they had helped get him elected. And he had John Collins across the hall. For Spota to ignore all that on the word of Glenn Harris would be an act of courage and independence that Salpeter found impossible to imagine. "Let's file the fuckin' motion," he told Barket and the Washington lawyers on a conference call. But Braga and Pollack deferred to the lawyer on the scene. They had little to lose, they agreed, and a lot to gain.

The day after taking Harris's sworn statement at Sing Sing, Barket brought a draft of the 440 motion to Spota and promised it would not be filed so long as his office was actively investigating its claims. Spota told him he would look into the information promptly and give it fair consideration. In the interest of full disclosure, he acknowledged that he had represented Jim McCready in a criminal case. It was ten years ago, when he got McCready acquitted of assault in the Rocky Point beating. He had also represented him back in the 1980s, when McCready had a problem with the State Investigation Commission and Spota was the lawyer for the detectives' union. But it would have no bearing on the Tankleff information, Spota assured Barket.

Barket left the office encouraged. "I thought he would work with us," he said later. "I thought he would consent to a hearing." He talked with the lawyers in Washington about Spota's prior representation of McCready. It was something to be aware of, they agreed, but not a clear conflict of interest. Since McCready's conduct wasn't directly related to the new evidence, and Spota deserved the benefit of the doubt, and Barket felt Spota was receptive, they decided to leave it alone.

Salpeter kept in close touch with his witnesses, waiting to hear if they had been contacted by the DA's office. A week went by, then two. Neither Glenn Harris nor Karlene Kovacs heard from anyone. Three weeks. Four. On September 30, nearly five weeks after Barket gave the draft motion to Spota, he went back to the DA's office. Spota acknowledged he had done nothing with the information. He promised again that he would investigate it thoroughly.

Barket called Salpeter and told him he was right. "He's sitting on it," he said. "We need to file it." Barket was genuinely surprised and disappointed, but he now realized that it was going to take a fight to get this case reopened.

Not just a fight, Salpeter thought: a war. And it would have to be fought on two fronts. To get the case to court, he believed, they would have to bring it to the court of public opinion. Salpeter had an old high school friend who ran a boutique public relations agency. This will be perfect for Lonnie, he thought.

Lonnie Soury had done PR and "crisis management" work for major corporations like General Motors and Calvin Klein, but he identified more with the work he did in the arenas of politics and public policy. He had a master's in social work and was a public affairs staffer for various city government agencies before going out on his own. He was a PR man with a strong social conscience, along with an appreciation for the allure of true crime as popular culture. His wife, Marlene Dann, was the executive vice president of Court TV. Soury and a colleague, Eric Friedman, became the newest of Marty Tankleff's pro bono advocates.

Soury and Friedman planned a big splash for the filing of the 440 motion. Their plan was to have the story in the morning papers on the day the motion was filed, followed by a news conference by the family at the Garden City Hotel, the most elegant on Long Island. It would give the story two days of coverage.

Soury brought the story first to Bruce Lambert of *The New York Times*, a reporter he knew and trusted from the days when he worked for the city and Lambert was in the *Times*'s City Hall bureau. He gave Lambert the motion brief several weeks in advance, on the condition that his story not run until the day it was to be filed. Barket, meanwhile, gave the brief to *Newsday*'s legal affairs reporter, Robin Topping. And Salpeter sent a note up to Marty:

> Do you remember a couple of years ago when I took the case I said that if you're innocent I'll be taking you for a ride? Buckle up my friend, we're about to take off . . .
>
> Jay

The motion was filed at the Suffolk County Courthouse on October 2, 2003. The reporters filed their stories the night before, after calling the DA's office for a comment. "This office will conduct a fair and comprehensive investigation of the claims made by Mr. Tankleff's attorneys," Tom Spota promised.

NEW EVIDENCE IN 1988 SLAYINGS, *Newsday* announced. DA TO EXPLORE INMATE'S STATEMENT ON BELLE TERRE KILLINGS.

At the news conference, one after another of Marty's relatives declared that they had never doubted his innocence or lost faith that the truth would eventually come out. They were confident the new evidence would finally free him. "He's a jewel of a boy," said his Aunt Mickey, who still had Marty's high school senior portrait on a credenza in her dining room. "We always believed in Marty's innocence," said Uncle Norman. Asked whether Marty would seek damages from Suffolk County—a premature question, to be sure—Ron Falbee said, "We want to get Marty out; that's number one. But ultimately we want people responsible to pay for putting this family through hell."

In the back of the room, a tall, lanky man in a suit sat casually, his arm draped over the back of his chair. His name was Leonard Lato. He was an assistant Suffolk County district attorney, assigned to handle the case by Tom Spota, who made a point of saying that he chose Lato because he was a recent hire with no ties to the case. Not that Lato was unfamiliar with the territory. He lived in Suffolk County and joined Spota's staff after a decade as a federal prosecutor assigned to the U.S. attorney's Long Island office.

Barket was not displeased to hear that Lenny Lato would be handling the Tankleff case. He'd known Lato for years, even played golf with him on occasion, and didn't think he was coming in with an agenda. On the other hand, he could imagine Lato adopting his *boss's* agenda and going full throttle. Among people who knew him, Lenny was considered susceptible to zealotry and self-righteousness, and Barket knew from personal experience how dangerous that could be in a prosecutor. For some reason, an image from the golf course popped into Barket's head—Lenny prone on the green, flat on his stomach, to line up a putt. And if random quirks contributed pieces to the puzzle of a person's nature, some people found themselves mystified when Lato told them he collected stray dogs, following in his car when he spotted one. He had more than a dozen at home.

When the reporters asked Lato about Marty Tankleff's 440 motion, he could have replied in any number of safe ways to assure everyone involved that he was an objective seeker of truth with no inclination toward prejudgment. What he said instead was this: A murder conviction couldn't be thrown out on the basis of a statement by a convicted burglar. And the DA's office wasn't going to decide whether to consent to a hearing "based on a press conference."

The ultimate decision, if the DA's office opposed the motion, would belong to Suffolk County Court judge Stephen Braslow. After the motion was filed, Braslow called the parties to court for a conference. Lato asked for two months to investigate the defense's new claims and decide whether to consent to a hearing or oppose one. For Marty, that was the threshold to be reached. A hearing would give his lawyers the power to subpoena. Braslow set December 12 as the due date for the DA's reply.

*   *   *

WITHIN MARTY'S CAMP was one family with unique views of Tom Spota and whether the DA would examine the case objectively. As a Suffolk County police sergeant, Kurt Paschke was perhaps an unlikely supporter of Marty's. Even more unlikely was how he and his family came to be part of Marty's fight. Paschke's son, Kurt Jr., was a good friend of Marty's in prison.

The younger Kurt was an honor student and a talented artist, but in 1992, when he was seventeen, he found himself in the wrong circle of friends. He thought they were just a bunch of kids who were into punk rock like him. The trouble started when he realized they were actually neo-Nazis and he tried to break free. Late one June night, they cornered Kurt behind a pizzeria and pummeled him into momentary unconsciousness. He managed to escape, but the incident continued after he fled, escalating into a brawl involving other teenagers who happened to be passing by. In the middle of it, a member of the skinhead group—the one who had led the initial confrontation—was fatally stabbed. But he was still conscious when he arrived at the hospital, and before he died he told a nurse that Kurt Paschke was the one who stabbed him. Despite flimsy evidence, Kurt was charged with murder. His father followed the recommendation of a friend and hired Tom Spota to defend him.

The case was mired in so much ambiguity that it took three years to reach trial, and by then the charge was reduced to criminally negligent homicide. Earlier in the case, the judge had made sure the Paschkes were aware of a potential conflict of interest for Spota. Some fifteen detectives were involved in the case, all members of the union represented by Spota, and any number of them could be called as witnesses. It was for that reason that Spota rarely tried felony cases anymore. But the Paschkes decided to stick with Spota. They liked Spota and were satisfied his relationship with the detectives' union wouldn't be a problem. They felt confident he would keep Kurt out of prison, even when a new judge took over the case and barred Spota from introducing key evidence—that the victim in the case was a member of a group that called itself the Revolutionary Aryan Workers Front, that he had a knife, and that the police later found batons and billy clubs in the car he and his friends rode in. Spota told the Paschkes not to worry—it would be good for the appeal if they lost.

And then the original judge's concerns came to pass. Early in the prosecution's case, Spota cross-examined one of the detectives. The questioning was routine, but the next day Spota told Kurt Sr. that he had gotten a call from a detectives' association official. Apparently the detective had taken offense, and the official threatened to fire Spota as the union's counsel if he gave any more of its members a hard time on the stand. "After that, Spota's whole approach changed," recalled the senior Paschke. "He hardly gave a summation." Said Kurt Jr.: "That's when I knew he sold me out. When he sat down I was just glaring at him so he knew that I knew he had fucked me."

Kurt was convicted and spent nearly three years in prison. The Paschkes always believed he was a pawn in a political game—that he had been prosecuted only because higher-ups in the police department were worried about the bad PR of dropping charges against the son of one of their own, something that had happened before and led to inclusion in the 1989 State Investigation Commission report. Their views were at least partly vindicated after the verdict, when the prosecutor went into the jury room and bragged to the jurors about all the evidence he had been able to keep them from hearing. Outraged, several jurors wrote letters to the judge saying they wouldn't have convicted Kurt had they known the whole story and urging him to be lenient in his sentencing. The judge declined, sentencing him to the maximum. In prison, Kurt received letters of apology from four jurors and even visits by two of them.

A decade later, the Paschkes were wary of Spota's election as district attorney, but at the same time hopeful that it would be a good thing for Marty. The reason was that Spota had discussed the Tankleff case with the family several times during Kurt Jr.'s case and told them he never believed Marty was guilty. The Paschkes remembered one conversation in particular. They were talking with Spota at their kitchen table. "He said he had seen the crime scene photos," the senior Paschke recalled. "He said there was no physical way one person committed those murders and no way a kid Marty's size could have done it. He said he hoped someone would come forward someday and the truth would come out."

GOING PUBLIC made Glenn Harris even edgier than usual. In late summer—before he put his name on an affidavit—he had begun going to a discussion group conducted on Saturday mornings by Sing Sing's Catholic chaplain, Father Ronald Lemmert—Father Ron, as everyone called him. Harris immediately made his presence felt, talking nonstop about his problems, complaining that he'd been in and out of prison for more than a decade and never gotten any help from anyone in the system. He dominated the class to such an extent that Lemmert finally made a suggestion. "If you've got all these problems, why don't you come and talk to me? I'll counsel you one-on-one."

Harris took him up on the offer. He talked to Father Ron about his long history of drug abuse, petty crime, emotional instability, his endless cycle of prison and halfway houses. Lemmert listened, offered his particular brand of spiritual guidance for the criminally wayward. A white-bearded man in his mid-fifties who had been at Sing Sing for nearly a decade, Father Ron did the work of a prison chaplain with the patience of a saint. With equal parts compassion and tough love, he insisted that inmates who sought his counsel or attended his classes make their best efforts at redemption. He told Harris it was good that he seemed to acknowledge that his life was a series of bad judgments or no judgment at all. Now he needed to commit to changing.

For all his outpouring of tribulation, there was one thing weighing on Harris's mind that he didn't talk about with Father Ron. He wasn't sure he could trust him. So he talked to another inmate about it, and asked *him* to talk to Father Ron. The other inmate approached Lemmert after Mass one morning and said he had a friend with a problem: He knew of a crime for which an innocent man was serving a life sentence. If he told what he knew, the guy could get out. But he was scared. The inmate told Lemmert that his friend wanted to talk to him but he wasn't sure he could trust the priest. It had to be confidential. Well, *of course* it would be confidential, Lemmert said. I'm a priest. The rules are the same, even in here.

Lemmert had no way of knowing that the anxious inmate was Glenn Harris, until he went home that night and put on the ten o'clock news. *Tonight, lawyers for a Long Island man convicted of brutally murdering his parents fifteen years ago say they have new evidence that could prove his innocence. Martin Tankleff is serving a fifty-year sentence for the 1988 killings in the exclusive waterfront community of Belle Terre. But now an inmate at Sing Sing Prison has given a sworn statement saying that he drove the real killers to and from the murder scene. Glenn Harris says . . .*

The next morning, Father Ron went to see Harris, who was already in protective custody. Salpeter had given Harris a heads-up that the story was about to break, and his brother arranged the transfer. Father Ron assured him that the publicity had no bearing on their relationship, that anything he told him would be held in the strictest confidence. Harris stared at the floor. He told Father Ron that he had been wanting to talk to him for a while, that he had written him several letters but ripped them up each time. "I can't sleep, I'm having nightmares," he said. "I don't know what to do. I know what I *should* do, but I don't know if I can."

Why don't you start by telling me what happened, Lemmert said. Harris recounted the events of that night in 1988 and said it had bothered him ever since. But it wasn't until a private investigator came calling that he told anyone about it, and now he wasn't sure he should have done that. He didn't know how far he could take it. He was worried about implicating himself, and he was scared for his life. "Creedon has friends up here," Harris told the priest. That's why he was in protective custody.

Harris and Father Ron were to discuss his predicament many more times. "Every time I saw him we talked a little bit more about it," the priest said later, after Harris had released him from his obligation of confidentiality. "He wanted to do the right thing but he was scared. I mean, he was really scared. I told him he had a moral responsibility to tell the truth. Yes, there were consequences; yes, it was frightening. But it's the right thing to do. I said, 'You've told me you've made a mess of your whole life. This is finally your opportunity to make something right.'"

Four days after the 440 motion was filed, Harris finally got the visit Salpeter had been telling him to expect for more than a month. He was brought to a conference room, where he found two men waiting for him. "Mr. Harris, my name is Detective Warkenthien," said one, "and this is Detective Flood. We're from the Suffolk County district attorney's office. We want to talk to you about the statement you've given to this investigator, Salpeter." He started pulling a copy of the affidavit out of a folder, but Harris said he didn't need to look at it. He knew what he said. All right, said Warkenthien, why don't you tell us?

Harris went through his story, starting at Billy Ram's house and ending when he dropped off Creedon and Kent in Selden. But he added a few incidental details that weren't in the affidavit. He agreed to go with Creedon because he was a "burglary/safe man." When they drove into Belle Terre, they passed a "guard shack" with no one in it. They went up a long road that he remembered from childhood, when his mother would take him up to the bluffs to look at the sailboats out on the sound. He parked, then "Creedon and Kent got out of the car and vanished in the dark," as Warkenthien would later relate it. He "slouched down in the seat so no one could see him. He was worried about the constable being on patrol." Creedon and Kent "came back to the car all out of breath."

Warkenthien would later say that Harris seemed distracted as he was telling his story. "The only time he actually looked at me is when he told me about his mother taking him to Belle Terre when he was a little kid. The rest of the time he was all around the table, never looking at me . . . just talking and going on. . . ."

He told Harris he found his account hard to believe. "It's inconsistent with what you told Salpeter," he said. "For instance, you didn't tell us you saw Kent burning his clothes. Isn't that what you said in your statement?"

"I think maybe now I need to have an attorney," Harris said, according to Warkenthien.

"Fine," Warkenthien told him. "How about I give you a couple of weeks to get one?" He gave Harris his business card and told him to have his attorney contact him. "And if you have a problem finding a lawyer, how about I bring you down to Riverhead and maybe your family can help you out with that?"

Harris liked that idea. He looked at the business card—"Walter Warkenthien, Office of the District Attorney"—and said, "Thanks, Wally." Warkenthien got up to leave. Then he turned back to Harris.

"Listen," he told him, "you know, when someone gets killed during the commission of a felony, everyone involved is guilty. That goes for everyone, even a nonparticipant in the homicide. So if the statement that you gave Mr. Salpeter is true, you may very well be trading places with Marty Tankleff."

Harris's reaction, according to Warkenthien: "He sat back in the chair, his mouth wide open, he was red as an apple as he was during most of that entire interview. And we left."

Back in his cell, Harris asked to see Father Ron. When the priest came to talk to him, he found that the balance of Glenn's fears had toppled over. He was no longer worried for his safety. "He was afraid he would end up doing the rest of his life in prison," Lemmert said. "After Warkenthien came to see him, he was afraid he could get screwed."

Harris's visit from the DA's investigators confirmed Salpeter's expectations. To him, Warkenthien's remark—*You may be trading places with Marty Tankleff*—was no offhand comment. It was a purposeful, veiled threat that raised serious doubts about Spota's promise of a fair investigation. The lawyers agreed and decided to make a move. Barket wrote to Spota. He and his colleagues had the utmost respect for him, he told the DA, but they now believed his past representation of the detective "whom we maintain improperly extracted a confession from an innocent man" posed a significant conflict of interest. He asked Spota to recuse himself from the case and allow a special prosecutor to take over.

Spota declined. What he *would* do, he said, was give Leonard Lato complete independence to investigate the new information and make recommendations as he saw fit. As Lato later put it, "Mr. Spota erected within his office an attorney's version of a 'Chinese Wall' so that neither he nor anyone else from the office would attempt to influence me during my investigation."

But could such a wall really exist between a boss and a subordinate? To investigate the case, Lato would be using the office's resources and talking to other prosecutors—including, as it would turn out, John Collins. Moreover, it would be a stretch to regard his principal investigator, Walter Warkenthien, as independent. He had known Spota for thirty years, since Spota's earliest days as a prosecutor. He had been personally

hired by Spota after his election, and unlike the office's other investigators, he reported directly to the district attorney. Warkenthien had one
more connection that inspired little confidence in his independence. He
worked with Jim McCready and Norman Rein on the homicide squad in
the 1980s.

TWO WEEKS AFTER Warkenthien's visit to Sing Sing, the Suffolk County
sheriff's office brought Harris to Riverhead. Lato would later say he
arranged the transfer so it would be easier to interview him. But perhaps
there was another reason. By happenstance, according to Lato, soon after
Harris's arrival at the county jail, the DA's office was contacted by two inmates offering information about Harris. In the prosecution business,
these incarcerated informants are known informally as jailhouse snitches.
According to Lato, the first snitch reported that Harris came up to him in
the jail's law library and asked if he'd heard what was going on with the
Tankleff case. "Harris started to laugh and then stated, 'The funny thing
is, I made the whole thing up.'" The snitch contacted the DA's office,
spoke to Walter Warkenthien, and agreed to wear a wire. Then he sought
Harris out and struck up a conversation. He asked him how he'd gotten
wrapped up in all this and what he'd told Tankleff's investigator when he
came around.

"I told him the truth," Harris said. "I told him the fuckin' truth."

"So it's all bullshit, right?" the informant asked, none too subtly.

"Nah."

"So that shit can blow up in your face, can't it?"

"I hope not. I don't talk unless I shoot a fuckin' deal, you know what I
mean? I'd rather wish this thing to just go away. . . ."

"But there's no way they can figure out that it's all bullshit, even after
you give your testimony to get him out."

"It's not bullshit, it's the truth."

At another point, the snitch apparently asked Harris whether Marty
Tankleff had anything to do with him coming forward. "I never met him
before in my life," Harris told him.

"By him getting out, then who goes in, in his place?"

"Two other individuals. Not me, that's for sure. Two scumbags that
told me to give them a ride." Harris paused. "This is how it went down,
between me and you."

"Yeah?"

"I was hangin' out [in] a fuckin' house in Selden where a bunch of
dudes were getting high. We ran into Joey Creedon. Joey Guns. He asks
me, can you gimme a ride? I'm like, sure, where to? He tells me up in Belle

Terre. I'm like fuck, I'll give ya a ride. . . . So we go up into Belle Terre, he tells me to stay out in the car, I'm thinking fuckin' either a burglary's goin' down or a drug deal, know what I mean? The two guys go in the house, they come out, go, 'Get outta here, go, go, go.' I'm like, what the fuck?"

"All of a sudden you come out and tell this shit now," the informant said, "ya know what I'm sayin'? I was reading the paper, like I can't figure this guy out."

"They came to me, ya know what I mean?" Harris said. "They came to me."

At that, the informant gave up. "I thought they was fucked, rounding up Martin Tankleff in the first place," he told Harris. "Reading about it, I was only a kid then."

"The kid caught a raw deal, bro," said Harris.

According to Lato, the second snitch contacted the DA's office and told Walter Warkenthien almost exactly the same thing as the first one: that he was in the law library when Glenn Harris came up to him and asked if he'd heard what was going on with the Tankleff case. When he said he had, Harris told him he'd fabricated the whole thing. Warkenthien wired the informant and sent him off to talk to Harris.

In this case, according to the transcribed excerpts, Harris said at one point, "Nah," when the snitch asked if his statement was the truth. But then he spent the next twenty minutes giving an expanded account of that night in Belle Terre, including the aftermath back in Selden: "Creedon tells me stop here, jumps outta the car, runs over towards his mother's house. Peter says, 'Yo, let me out at my mother's.' I let him out. I parked my car on the little fuckin' side road near Newfield High School. I'm sittin' there and I'm like, what the fuck happened here, ya know? I'm sittin' in the car, the sun's coming up, I see fuckin' smoke coming from the back of the house, ya know? So I'm like, damn, what the fuck? And I run over there and I see a pile of clothes on fire, ya know? I'm like, 'Damn, man, what the fuck happened?' He said, 'Just forget about it, just get outta here,' ya know?"

A few months later, "Me and Creedon went on a little run. I was like, 'Do you know where we can get some money?' He was like, 'I know where a safe is.' I was, like, 'Where?' He was like, 'Strathmore Bagels.' I was like, 'How do you know there's a safe there,' ya know? He was like, 'Because I've been in the office before.' So I get there, me and him. I get in through the roof. Strathmore Bagels, right? I get into the office, there's a safe about fuckin' four feet by six feet—"

"Does this have anything to do with this fuckin' statement you wrote?" the snitch asked impatiently.

"Yes it does," said Harris.

"Go ahead, go ahead."

"Because the owner of the bagel store—"

"Strathmore Bagels."

"Right. Jerry Steuerman. He was there that night."

"In the house where the shit went down?"

"Right. When the killings took place."

"How'd you know that?"

"I didn't."

"You come to find out?"

"Right. Later on. Now I'm putting two and two together."

"All right, so go ahead."

"... So, from what he alluded to in the bagel store, knowing that I was up there that night, I knew, I didn't think it was coincidental, you know what I mean?"

"It was planned?"

"Yeah, you know what I mean?"

"How the fuck did the kid get involved?"

"It was his parents."

"... Let me ask you a question. If you already signed a statement, what part of the statement is false?"

"Nothin'. None of it. You know where my dilemma comes in? ... I'm scared of the district attorney trying to say, 'You know what? We think you were down with the fuckin' crime.' You know why I'm hedging? I'm hedging because I'm trying to fuckin' implicate myself the least possible way. ... If I don't get immunity, I'm not swearing to nothing. They gotta guarantee me immunity, you know what I mean?"

IN JANUARY 2002, Thomas J. Spota was sworn in as district attorney of Suffolk County by Patrick Henry, a predecessor and mentor who was now a judge. Spota had been chief of the homicide bureau under Henry in the early 1980s, though he had left for private practice by the time the office began the prosecution of Marty Tankleff. That Henry swore Spota into office demonstrated that their bond was stronger than politics. Henry was a rock-ribbed Republican, while Spota had bolted the party for the chance to unseat Henry's successor. Among the speakers at Spota's inauguration were two of his now-fellow Democrats, U.S. senator Charles Schumer and New York's attorney general, Eliot Spitzer. They hailed Spota as a man who would bring integrity and impartiality to the office.

Then Spota himself spoke. He pledged to strive "in every thing we do and in every way we act" to be fair and unbiased; to "enforce the law with temperance and without malice, to seek truth and not victims, to serve the law and not fractional purposes, and to approach these tasks with humility and respect." His speech became a permanent page of the office's website. Appearing under the heading "Message from the District Attorney," it began with a quote from the American Bar Association's Standards of Criminal Justice: "The duty of a prosecutor is to seek justice, not merely to convict."

No case was to test Spota's obedience to this most fundamental principle more than Marty Tankleff's motion to vacate his verdict on the basis of new evidence. It was a nearly poetic juxtaposition of events: Spota's first day of business as district attorney, January 2, 2002, was the very day that Jay Salpeter called Virginia Harris, looking for her son Glenn.

In November 2003, a month and a half after the Tankleff defense team filed its motion for a new trial, Ron Falbee wrote to the district attorney to request a meeting to discuss the progress of his investigation. He pointed out that in the long history of this case, the family had never been interviewed by the police or prosecutors, never had the opportunity to present its side of the story. Spota wrote back: "I deem it unwise to jeopardize Mr. Lato's independence by meeting with you." If you want to meet with Lato, Spota told Ron, feel free to write to him.

Ron thought it was a bit silly that Spota was so intent on keeping up the pretense of the "Chinese Wall" that he didn't simply pass his letter on to Lato. But he followed his suggestion, and in early December he and a retinue of Marty's relatives met with Lato in his office. They told him about Marty's close relationship with his mother and father, assured him that the idea that Marty felt smothered, a pawn in his parents' marital troubles, was completely false. Marcella Falbee told Lato that she had practically lived with Arlene and Seymour and Marty that last summer, and knew about the tensions with Jerry Steuerman firsthand. One day, she said, Arlene told her that Steuerman pulled Seymour across a counter at the bagel store and threatened him.

Lato listened politely, but asked few questions and revealed nothing—until the end of the meeting, when he took them by surprise with a comment that raised their hopes. He told them that a close colleague of his in another office, his mentor, was always convinced that Marty didn't do it. With that parting comment, Lato thanked Marty's relatives for coming in and escorted them out. "His attitude was, 'I have no skin in this game, I'm just here to investigate the facts,'" Ron recalled. "We left the meeting thinking maybe they're finally going to look at this. He had us totally snookered."

One week later, Spota announced the results of Lato's investigation of the new evidence: It was not credible and most of it wasn't even new. The Tankleff defense had Karlene Kovacs's affidavit since 1994, yet didn't turn up Glenn Harris until 2002. And another year went by before a motion was put forward. All too late, said the DA, to meet the "due diligence" standard required of newly discovered evidence in a motion to vacate a verdict. So there should be no hearing of the defense's new claims, never mind a new trial.

The DA's formal reply came in the form of a *Report of the People's Investigation of the Defendant's Claim*, a sixty-eight-page document that often seemed at odds with its opening declaration that "prosecutors should endeavor not to win but to seek justice and the truth." The report was written by Lato in a format that combined the styles of standard legal brief, first-person narrative, and interoffice memo. But it was signed both by Lato and his boss, whose appearance at a news conference tore down any illusion of a Chinese Wall. "No rational finder of fact would believe a word Mr. Harris says," Spota announced.

Harris's veracity was apparently beyond the imagination of prosecutors who regularly made deals for information with criminals. Give up someone bigger, get your charge knocked down and your jail time cut in half—*that's* how it worked. This guy was giving up two people—for a double murder he himself was involved in—because it was the right thing to do? He *had* to be lying.

Lato and Spota said they found too many inconsistencies in Harris's story. For instance: "Harris told Reicherter that he drove Creedon and Kent to the Tankleff residence . . . yet told Warkenthien and Flood that he parked by 'the bluffs,' which was six-tenths of a mile from the Tankleff residence. . . ."

Was this really an "inconsistency"? As Warkenthien would later testify, the spot that he clocked at six-tenths of a mile from the Tankleff house was a scenic overlook at the end of Cliff Road, a cul-de-sac that locals knew as "the turnaround." This was Harris's point of reference when he said his mother took him "up to the bluffs" when he was a kid. But he never said it was where he parked the night he drove Creedon and Kent to Belle Terre. Lato was scrambling Harris's words to *create* an inconsistency. "Harris's statements, although incredible, may not be the product of a conscious intent to deceive," Lato mused. "[H]e may be suffering from a mental disease or defect that renders him incapable of differentiating between reality and fantasy."

As further evidence of Harris's unreliability, Lato presented excerpts of the transcribed conversations with the two jailhouse snitches, whom he designated "CS-3" and "CS-4" (for confidential source). According to Warkenthien, CS-4 claimed that Harris told him "he fabricated the whole thing. Harris also told CS-4 that he knew that Marty killed his mother and father but that he wanted to help Marty Tankleff because he felt that

Marty Tankleff had served enough time." Of course, the transcripts of the recorded conversations between Harris and the informants told a completely different story.

Lato found inconsistencies in Karlene Kovacs's statements as well. In both her 1994 and 2002 affidavits, she said Creedon made his admissions to her while they were smoking marijuana in a rear bedroom. But according to Lato, when he and Warkenthien interviewed Kovacs she said they were outside, behind the house. And while she said in all her recent statements that Creedon told her he was covered with blood after leaving the Tankleff house, there was no mention of blood in her 1994 affidavit. "I do not credit the bulk of Kovacs's version of events," Lato wrote. But he *did* credit her statement that Creedon professed his involvement in the Tankleff murders. "I find that Creedon made inculpatory statements to Kovacs, to John Guarascio"—and to two other people the Tankleff team didn't even know about. These were confidential sources—one brought to Lato by a police detective, the other by a lawyer—who said that Creedon had told them years earlier that he was involved. The detective vouched for his source's reliability and said he wasn't surprised by his information. "In the mid-1990s a lot of drug dealers who got arrested in Suffolk County were saying that there was a rumor that Creedon had killed the Tankleffs," Lato quoted the detective saying.

But Lato thought it was Creedon himself who started the rumor—an attempt by Joey Guns, he concluded, "to enhance his violent reputation." He ventured no guess as to why Creedon, if he were going to claim responsibility for murders for the purpose of street cred, would pick *these* murders: a middle-aged couple whose son had apparently confessed to the crimes. But Lato had his reasons for believing Creedon didn't do it. First of all, he was Joey *Guns.* "Although a career criminal," Lato reasoned, Creedon "used firearms, not knives or blunt instruments, to facilitate his crimes." For another thing, "Other than his boasts and Glenn Harris's unquestionably false statements, there is no evidence whatsoever to connect Creedon to the murders or to the Tankleffs."

Not that Lato didn't ask Creedon if he did it. Creedon came in voluntarily with his lawyer, then signed a sworn statement putting it on the record: "I have no idea what Kovacs and Harris are talking about. I did not kill the Tankleffs, nor have I ever been to Belle Terre. I have never spoken with or met Jerry Steuerman."

Then there was Creedon's seemingly silent partner. While Joey Guns went around boasting about the Tankleff murders, Peter Kent apparently stayed mum. Kent was thirty-five and had a string of arrests and convictions that began when he was eighteen. He had done two stretches in state prison, and was once accused of threatening to kill police officers who were going to testify against him at a parole violation hearing. Most recently, he was awaiting trial on a trifecta of charges—stealing a car, driving it drunk, resisting arrest. "Fuck you," he replied when the arresting officer asked Kent if he wanted a lawyer.

After beating up another inmate, Kent was confined to his cell in the county jail the week Marty Tankleff's 440 motion was filed. They called it being "in the box." No newspapers, no TV, no visitors. So when a pair of sheriff's officers brought him to the district attorney's office, Kent didn't know what it was about. Unlike Creedon, he walked in with a swagger instead of a lawyer.

Lenny Lato told Kent that Glenn Harris was putting him in the middle of the Tankleff murders.

And Peter Kent began to cry.

This was the kind of moment Bruce Barket had envisioned when he brought the new information to Spota a month before making it public: Get them by surprise, no lawyers.

Lato and Warkenthien told Kent not to worry.

"Fighting tears," Lato wrote, "Kent stated that he did not kill anyone and that he has never been to Belle Terre. He stated that he and Harris have a drug problem and they had committed a lot of burglaries together over the years, but that they had never hurt anyone or even encountered anyone during any of the burglaries. . . . Kent stated that he has no idea why Harris was involving himself and others in the Tankleff murders. . . . Kent stated that although Creedon was capable of committing a murder, Kent was not, nor was Harris."

When the members of the Tankleff legal team read this paragraph, they were incredulous. But nobody was more furious than Salpeter: "This could have been the whole case *right there*. Why is Peter Kent crying? He's crying because he's about to go for a double murder. His buddy has given him up. He knows they have him. And they just let him go. You can put down that date—October 7, 2003. That's the date this should have ended. If I'm a detective in that room, I see those tears and I say, *Okay, Pete, here's your Queen for a Day. Give it up now or you're going for the murders all by yourself. We've got a one-day-only deal right here. Tell us what happened. This was all Creedon, right? You were just along for the ride. This wasn't supposed to happen.* He would have given it up in a second. Like taking candy from a baby. But they put this guy in a comfort zone. *Don't worry, Pete. Can we get you a tissue?* How can they do that? *Why* do they do that? This was the point when I knew these people are in another stratosphere. They are not here to seek justice or the truth. They are going to keep Marty Tankleff locked up in prison. Even if it means protecting murderers."

If his report suggested an almost incomprehensible lack of skepticism for a pair of characters like Creedon and Kent, Lato couldn't help but look askance at Jerry Steuerman. He called him at his condo in Boca Raton. "I told Steuerman that even though he had testified at the Tankleff trial, I had some questions for him," Lato wrote. "I asked him why, about 10 days after the attack on Arlene and Seymour Tankleff, he fled to California, explaining to him that his behavior was consistent with a consciousness of guilt." Steuerman gave Lato the same explanations as he had at the trial, and assured him that he did not profit from the Tankleffs' deaths.

Lato's report made no mention of whether he raised the name Joe Creedon during his conversation with Steuerman. But he did ask Steuerman's son about Creedon. Todd was now thirty-eight and living near Albany. "[Todd] Steuerman denied that he and Creedon had ever done anything illegal together," Lato reported. He also said he had never discussed the Tankleff case with his father. "When I advised him that that was hard to believe given that Marty had accused his father of the murder, Todd replied that no one in his house had spoken about anything important since he was five years old."

After dismissing the new evidence on various evidentiary grounds, Lato addressed Marty's "actual innocence" claim: "Creedon's and Harris's statements, *even if true* (and they are not true), do not establish Tankleff's actual innocence. At best, the statements demonstrate only that others *in addition* to Tankleff may have committed the murders. They do not demonstrate that Tankleff *did not* commit the murders." The district attorney's chief witness in support of this preposterous premise: Glenn Harris. Lato actually quoted from one of Harris's recorded conversations with a jailhouse snitch: "They're askin' me to help prove this kid's innocence. I can't do that. . . . I don't know if he was responsible in any way, shape or form, I don't know if he knew Joey."

Meanwhile, Lato, perhaps trying to fulfill Spota's promise of a "comprehensive" investigation, came up with two prison snitches trolling for deals in exchange for information about Marty Tankleff. One was a convicted murderer named Brian France, who wrote to Spota saying that in 1996 Marty confessed to him in the law library at Clinton. France quoted Marty saying, "When the cop told me my old man regained consciousness and told them I did it, I knew I was fucked, so I told them everything."

Lato had France brought down to Suffolk County. France told him he wrote to the DA's office after reading about the Tankleff case in *The New York Times*. He also mentioned that he'd be up for parole in a couple of years—might the DA's office put in a word for him? Lato said he told France he wouldn't make any recommendations, but that he would "inform the parole board of his cooperation."

Marty knew Brian France as an inmate who came to the prison law library a few times when the officer in charge assigned him to help France with his case. Kurt Paschke, Jr., knew France better. He told Salpeter that France tried to befriend him at Clinton because he thought they shared a worldview, misinterpreting the neo-Nazi element of Kurt's case. "He was a white power supremacist skinhead," Kurt said, later putting his recollections in an affidavit. "He talked against blacks, against Jews, against Jewish conspiracy theories. He was a conman, a liar. A portrait of probably what everyone thinks of a bad-guy inmate. A real low-life, backstabbing, manipulating, extorting person. He would extort people for food with threats." Not your typical *New York Times* reader. Oh, and one more thing, said Paschke. "It was known that I was an artist in prison, and one Christmas Brian asked me to draw a picture of a Satan raping Jesus Christ. Because Brian was also a self-professed Satanist."

It defied plausibility that Lato found it reasonable to believe that Marty Tankleff would spend years fighting for his exoneration—pounding out all those letters, poring over all those law books, doing something to prove his innocence virtually every day of his incarceration—and then casually confess to someone like Brian France. Stupid, Lato was not, so it appeared that he was without shame. His use of France was a textbook case of a practice long condemned as unreliable and typically corrupt. As the *Pittsburgh Post-Gazette* found after a two-year investigation in the late 1990s, "[I]nmates in federal prisons routinely buy, sell, steal and concoct testimony, then share their perjury with federal authorities in exchange for a reduction in their sentences. Often, these inmates testify against people they've never met. They corroborate crimes they've never witnessed. Prosecutors win cases. Convicts win early freedom. The accused loses."

The practice was no different in state prisons. Lato found Glenn Harris "wholly incredible." He scrutinized every word Karlene Kovacs, a law-abiding suburban mother, had to say on the subject. But he had Brian France sign an affidavit, which he submitted in his brief of the "People's Investigation." With a tin ear for irony, Lato concluded by borrowing from Thomas Platt, the federal district court judge who rejected Marty's habeas petition in 1997. "Tankleff's attorneys have magnified the significance and importance of the evidence that they have presented," Lato wrote, "but only in 'arenas removed from reality' could such evidence establish that Tankleff is 'actually innocent.'"

CHAPTER 32

Better Than a Polygraph

"MIND-BOGGLING" was Bruce Barket's appraisal of the district attorney's response to the new evidence, and it summed up the reaction of everyone on the defense team.

It was easy to attribute Tom Spota's posture to the usual impulse of a prosecutor to protect his institution from the blemish of a reversed conviction. But was it more than that? And that question led to another: What did it mean that the case was assigned to Judge Stephen Braslow?

The courthouse in Riverhead operated like a political clubhouse, and Braslow had a patron better than most: his father. Jack Braslow was an old-line lawyer and power broker in the county's Democratic Party. His base was Babylon, a township of two hundred thousand in Suffolk's southwest corner across the bay from Fire Island. Jack Braslow put his political weight behind his son's career, from an appointment as the Babylon town attorney to his nomination for a District Court judgeship, and then, in 1997, for a coveted seat on the County Court bench. Most relevant to anyone concerned about the influence of personal and political relationships was Jack Braslow's connection to the district attorney. Braslow shared an office with the county's Democratic leader, and together they had engineered Spota's conversion and his ensuing ouster of the party's nemesis, Jim Catterson. Now Braslow's son was presiding over a case in which the DA seemed to have an agenda. At the risk of prejudging the judge, the Tankleff camp had reason to wonder if Braslow's assignment was entirely random, and whether it signaled that this new phase of Marty's case was but a continuation of the old one.

The potential role of political factors made it all the more important for the Tankleff team to reply to the DA's opposition not only with legal arguments but with more new evidence. Glenn Harris and Karlene Kovacs might not be enough. Barket pressed Salpeter to keep digging, to pursue every lead.

Salpeter started with something already in hand—another sworn statement that, like Karlene Kovacs's, was years old but had never seen the light of day. At Clinton in the mid-1990s, Marty had met an inmate named Bruce Demps. He was in his late twenties, doing time since he was nineteen for robbery, rape, and assorted other crimes. Demps sought Marty out because they knew someone in common. *You're the guy Todd Steuerman was always talking about,* Demps told a startled Marty. *You're the guy in for murders you didn't do.*

Demps told Marty that he had gotten to know Todd Steuerman at Clinton in 1990, soon after Todd began serving his seven years for felony drug possession. According to Demps, the subject of the murders first came up when Todd told him about a kid named Marty Tankleff he was worried about. Tankleff was just convicted of murdering his parents, Todd told Demps, and if he's sent up here and we run into each other there's gonna be problems. What kind of problems? Demps asked. According to an affidavit he gave Marty's lawyers in 1997:

> Todd Steuerman explicitly told me that he knew for a fact that Martin Tankleff had not committed these crimes and that a Hells Angels friend of his father's had indeed committed these crimes. He informed me that he believed that if Martin Tankleff ever met up with him there would be serious problems and that Martin Tankleff would force him to tell the truth. . . . [H]e felt that he would need protection from Martin Tankleff. . . .
>
> At some point, Todd Steuerman informed me that there was some kind of transaction that his father conducted which involved a sum of $60,000. . . . As I can recall, this discussion was in regards to the Hells Angels friend that Todd's father used to commit violent acts against others.

The affidavit went on to say that when they met up again at a different prison a few years later, Demps and Todd Steuerman "entered into [a] business agreement and we needed someone on the outside that would be respected and feared to appear as representatives for me and Todd. And considering what Todd was in jail for, I knew he had connections. At that time, Todd once again called on his father's friend who was a Hells Angel biker residing in Long Island. . . ." Demps said Todd told him that his father's connections came in handy one other time: when Todd found out that his wife was having an affair with a corrections officer. "And he once again had his father call in the Hells Angel biker friend. From what he explained to me, they (a group of about 4 men) beat up [the corrections officer] pretty bad. . . ." As a result, Todd was transferred to another prison.

Marty's lawyers had decided to play down the Demps affidavit in the 440 filing. For one thing, it was six years old. For another, they were reluctant to feature yet another prison inmate. They attached Demps's affidavit to the motion but discussed it only briefly and in small type: as a one-sentence footnote to the section on Karlene Kovacs's statement connecting Joe Creedon to "a Steuerman."

Salpeter had been aware since early in the case that Jerry Steuerman was known to use Hells Angels as muscle. So he had looked for a link between Creedon and the biker group. Creedon had the trappings—he rode a Harley and had tattoos—and over time Salpeter picked up information that while he wasn't an actual member he was *associated* with them. "He was in tight with them, without a doubt, and I heard this from many sources," Salpeter said. "He did a lot of work for them." Was Creedon the Hells Angel in Bruce Demps's story? It wasn't hard to imagine Todd Steuerman referring to Creedon that way, or Demps drawing that inference.

Though the 440 motion technically didn't cite the Demps affidavit as part of the new evidence, Leonard Lato addressed it in his response. He said he asked both Steuermans about the suggestion that Jerry hired a member of the Hells Angels to commit the murders of the Tankleffs. "Steuerman denied the accusation," Lato wrote of Jerry, while Todd "stated he did not know what Demps was talking about and that Marty had killed his parents."

While Lato's report said his investigators couldn't locate Demps, Salpeter tracked him down with a couple of clicks on his computer: Demps was still in the New York State prison system. Salpeter wrote to him at his current residence and asked if he would be willing to testify for Marty Tankleff should a hearing be granted. Demps wrote back: "I am in receipt of your letter and it came as a shock to me cause I had forgotten all about Marty since I had never heard from him. . . . I have not talked to any detectives about this but I do think you and I need to talk about this whole situation as I am about to possibly create a lot of trouble for myself if my name becomes involved with this case."

Salpeter talked to Demps by phone and got confirmation of everything in his affidavit. He also got the feeling that Demps was angling for some help in return for testifying. Nothing explicit, Salpeter told Barket, just a feeling. Barket told him to nip that right in the bud. Prosecutors could dole out favors for testimony—a letter to the parole board, say—but defense attorneys and their investigators could offer nothing. Write to

Demps, Barket told him, and make it clear that whether he testified or not was his decision, but under no circumstances would he be getting anything in return.

Barket, meanwhile, obtained the name of the informant, brought to Lato by a police detective, who said that Creedon had implicated himself in the Tankleff murders. Salpeter brought the man to Barket's office. His name was Gaetano Foti. He said he first encountered Creedon around 1991, at a bar called Mr. Lucky's. "He shot a friend of mine in the behind." He didn't remember what it was about, but drugs and money was a good bet. Foti was working at another bar a couple of years later when Creedon came in and tried to shake down the owners for a percentage of their drug business, claiming he was representing the interests of a drug dealer named Frank Flammia. But when Flammia made his regular call to the bar, collect from prison, he said he didn't know anything about it. Creedon dropped his extortion demands, but he still came by the bar and one day he and Foti got to talking about the Tankleff murders. "I said it was a shame because I thought the kid was innocent and he's in jail. And Creedon said, 'I know he's innocent because I did it.'"

Foti said he didn't pursue it. "I knew who I was talking to." But he brought it up a couple of months later, when Creedon was in the bar talking about straightening out a guy who owed some money. He said he'd shoot him if he had to. A friend of Foti's was at the bar and expressed some skepticism that Creedon would shoot someone over a few bucks. Foti told him that Creedon was involved in the Tankleff murders, and Creedon nodded.

IN THE WAKE of Glenn Harris's stunning admissions and the press conference to announce the motion for a new trial, most of the major network television magazine shows wanted the Marty Tankleff story. Soury and Friedman set up meetings with the producers, but to Marty and his family the choice was obvious. None told the tales of American true crime better than CBS's *48 Hours Mystery*, and with its format of one in-depth story per episode, it was the only one that guaranteed a full hour. The story would be reported by Erin Moriarty, a veteran correspondent who was trained as a lawyer, and a seasoned producer, Gail Zimmerman.

Getting the story out to a national network audience would be a major turning point. It could build local pressure for a hearing and encourage people with information to come forward. And in a very basic way, the show could start to turn around the vast misperception of the case. For fifteen years, the name Martin Tankleff triggered the image created by the prosecution and burnished by the media from the earliest moments of the case. Back when Marty was arrested and prosecuted, he and his family perceived—not unreasonably, in many cases—that reporters were the enemy. But it was also true that the family put up a wall, too overwhelmed and unsophisticated to cultivate the press for Marty's advantage, as the prosecutors did for theirs. They had no inclination to disobey their lawyer's edict that they would fight the case in court, not in the press.

Two decades later, everything was reversed—because the legal burdens were. The only way out for Marty was to go on the offensive. Fortunately for him, his personality and his circumstances had a way of capturing the hearts and minds of people who could help him do that. So he had a PR team. He had lawyers who spoke out often and aggressively, and who placed no restraints on the family to do the same. They allowed Marty to give interviews, though these were carefully controlled. The media were gradually becoming as much an instrument of his drive for freedom as they were of the prosecution's to convict him, if only after years when they were hardly aware of him. They were finally giving him his voice.

The initial publicity surrounding the filing of the 440 started bringing in new leads. Salpeter jumped on one of them. It came from a retired NYPD detective named Eli Thomasevich. He didn't know Salpeter but read about the Tankleff case in a newspaper in South Florida, where he was now working as a private investigator. Thomasevich called Salpeter and told him that a friend of his, another former NYPD cop named Tony Picarelli, was working in the Strathmore bagel restaurant near Boca Raton. It was run by Jerry Steuerman's son Glenn, but Jerry spent a lot of time there. When the story hit the local paper, a waitress asked Jerry what it was all about. According to Picarelli, Steuerman said, "So what—I slit their throats. What're they gonna do, give me fifty years at my age?"

Salpeter flew to Florida, but it turned out that Picarelli hadn't heard Steuerman's remark from Steuerman. He'd been told about it by a waitress named Nancy Barton. Salpeter talked to Barton. She said she'd heard it from two cooks named Sean and Scott. Salpeter waited for Sean and Scott to finish work and approached them in the parking lot. One said he didn't know what Salpeter was talking about and walked away. The other said nothing and got in his car. But Picarelli and Barton said Steuerman's chilling comment was the talk of the place, and the place wasn't so big that an untrue rumor would still be circulating months later.

So was this anything? It would never fly at a trial, but there was agreement among the lawyers that they should go with anything that could possibly help get a hearing. It's a brick, Barket liked to say. Just keep laying bricks and eventually we'll have something solid. Though second- and third-hand, Steuerman's purported remark became a prominent piece of the Tankleff team's reply to the district attorney's opposition to the hear-

ing. SON JAILED IN KILLINGS SAYS ANOTHER MAN ADMITS TO CRIME, declared
The New York Times.

Aside from rebutting the DA's responses to the 440 motion, the defense's reply brief featured the conclusion by two experts in police interrogation techniques that Marty's statements on the day of his parents'
murders were a classic false confession. Richard Ofshe was a professor of
sociology at the University of California at Berkeley who had spent years
studying false confessions. He found Marty's confession to be "inherently
unreliable"—coerced by psychological manipulation and proven false by
its inconsistency with the physical evidence. The other expert, Richard
Leo, a criminology professor at the University of California at Irvine,
called the confession "almost certainly false." Because the field was in its
infancy at the time of Marty's trial, the defense asserted, the research and
testimony of Ofshe and Leo qualified as new evidence.

With the decision on a hearing now in Judge Braslow's hands, the wild
card remained Glenn Harris. Lato made his position clear: Harris wanted
full immunity before he testified and the DA's office had no intention of
granting it. Therefore, there was no point in the judge granting a hearing.
But Harris's lawyer, Richard Barbuto, was telling reporters that his client
wasn't necessarily holding out for full "transactional" immunity, meaning
he couldn't be prosecuted in the murders under any circumstances. He
might testify with the more limited "use" immunity, which would bar the
DA only from using Harris's testimony against him. He could still be
prosecuted with other evidence. And there was no immunity from prosecution for perjury.

Harris, meanwhile, was telling Salpeter that he *would* testify, with or
without immunity—at least that's what he said most days. Salpeter would
talk it through with him: How can they prosecute you for murder, he
asked Harris, if they're on record saying they don't believe a word you're
saying?

Harris had been paroled in January, and for the first time in the two
years since Salpeter had made contact with him, his star witness was out of
prison. Salpeter felt responsible for him, and not just because of the case.
He genuinely cared about Harris. "With all the people I met in this case,"
he later reflected, at a point when he had met dozens, "Glenn was the one
I felt I had a real bond with. He had a tough past. But he never hurt anyone. If I was a social worker I'd say here's a guy who was misdirected."
One night, he took Glenn out to dinner with Cheryl at La Bussola, their
favorite place in Glen Cove. She wasn't happy. It wasn't unusual for Jay to
mix business with social, but clients were one thing; lawyers, other PI's,
fine. Glenn Harris? Cheryl wasn't happy, but she understood.

The probation department placed Harris in a "sober house." Salpeter gave him a stack of his old clothes—the featured garment a Jets jacket from his collection—and bought him some underwear and socks, a pair of boots, and a basketball. He gave Harris a prepaid cellphone to keep tabs on him, and an old watch so he wasn't late for his appointments with his parole officer. Harris went back to working part-time with his brother in the land surveying business, but sometimes he'd be a little short on cash. So Salpeter would throw him an occasional twenty, thirty bucks to tide him over. No drugs, that was the deal, and Salpeter kept on top of Harris to make sure he wasn't using, looking in his eyes every time he saw him. Just because he was in a "sober house" didn't mean he was staying clean.

So far, so good. And then came a positive sign about Harris's intentions of testifying: He agreed to be interviewed by *48 Hours*. The TV crew turned a room at the Garden City Hotel into a studio, and Harris showed up with Barbuto, took a seat opposite Erin Moriarty, and told his story on camera. When Moriarty asked who he was with that night, Harris's first response was the same as when he revealed it to Salpeter in a prison visiting room two years earlier. He took a deep breath. Then he said, "Joseph Creedon and Peter Kent."

During his trip to Florida, Salpeter had been trailed around by Gail Zimmerman, the *48 Hours* producer, who brought a crew down to get some "B-roll," footage of the PI working his case. They filmed Salpeter at the wheel of his rental car, dressed in shorts and sandals, and got a long-lens shot of him in the parking lot outside the Strathmore restaurant, approaching the two men who were said to have heard Steuerman's chilling remark. Zimmerman had tried to get an interview with Steuerman, but like other reporters she couldn't even get him on the phone. His wife answered the phone at their condo in Boca West and said he wasn't talking. So the crew staked out the restaurant and got a shot of Steuerman driving up in a new convertible. He looked relaxed, happily chatting with people outside the restaurant. Now sixty-four, his hair weave was neatly trimmed and mostly gray. He wore a black shirt with a pattern that looked from a distance like large floating circles and on closer inspection turned out to be bagels. The crew also filmed Salpeter outside the entrance of Boca West. "They're both in gated communities, my client and Jerry Steuerman," Salpeter quipped, standing in front of the entrance's lovely gardens. "But only one of them is allowed to leave."

When the story aired in April, Salpeter appeared in the introduction, the camera in tight, accentuating the emotion in his eyes. "This *kid* is *not* guilty," he said. "It just hits you in the face." From there the story unfolded: a baby picture of Marty, another of him with his parents at his bar mitzvah, and finally Marty in prison at age thirty-two, saying, "There's no way I could have hurt my parents. I loved them." He talked about his happy and privileged childhood and tried to answer the question he'd been asked so many times over the years. "They had me believing I did it," he told Moriarty.

"But how?" Moriarty asked him.

"I don't know," Marty said.

There was Richard Ofshe, the interrogation expert. "You know that everyone listening to this is saying, 'You couldn't make me confess to a crime I didn't commit,'" Moriarty told him.

"Wanna bet?" Ofshe replied. "Happens all the time." He explained how—the psychological manipulations of a naïve teenager at his most vulnerable, the suggestion of a "blackout" that allowed him to reconcile the conflict between knowing he didn't do it and being told that he did by police officers who had the proof and wouldn't lie. And the paradox created by the physical evidence: "His confession is actually evidence of his *innocence*."

There were Marty's relatives, a dozen of them sitting in two rows—the way the show often set up interviews with juries after a trial—telling Moriarty why they never believed Marty was guilty, not for a second. All except Shari, who was interviewed separately and said, "I feel like I'm the black sheep of the family." What did she see that no one else in the family did? "I saw a very manipulative young man who was able to manipulate two adults, Arlene and Seymour, into believing that he was the quintessential child." But did she ever see any hint of violence toward them? "Oh, no. Never."

There was Glenn Harris, telling his story, explaining why he came forward: "I did something right for once. I told the truth. . . . Making good, that's all I'm trying to do at this point in my life."

And there was Lenny Lato saying he didn't believe Harris for a second. Nor did he believe Creedon's admissions to all those people. "A lot of people have bragged to killing President Kennedy," Lato told Moriarty. "Doesn't mean that they did it."

"Why do you believe Joe Creedon couldn't possibly have had any involvement here?" Moriarty asked.

"Because Joe Creedon, based upon his criminal history—"

Moriarty began listing Creedon's convictions, counting them with her fingers. Lato cut her off. "Murder? No," he said after each one.

"Even Peter Kent, another career criminal who knows him, says he's capable of murder," Moriarty said.

"So what?" Lato replied. "A person is capable of murder. That doesn't mean the person committed this murder."

"Are you saying that those jurors still would have convicted Marty had they known about a career criminal who was *bragging* that he had done it?"

"In my view, they probably would have," Lato said. ". . . Look, two people are brutally murdered. One person slept through the whole thing. That's bad for Marty Tankleff from the beginning."

Putting his money on sixteen-year-old snap judgments, Lato made a matched set with Jim McCready, whom Moriarty interviewed at his home near Myrtle Beach, South Carolina. McCready was saying yes to all TV and newspaper interviews. He seemed unfazed by the recent developments in the most famous case of his career. Actually, he seemed mostly clueless as Moriarty virtually interrogated him. She asked him, for instance, to describe the scene he found on Seaside Drive that morning. McCready said he went into the master bedroom, where Arlene Tankleff lay dead on the floor beside her bed. "It was an eerie feeling—it was always an eerie feeling. And it was dark."

This was not what McCready said at the trial. In fact, he testified—repeatedly, insistently, and to significant effect—that it was *not* dark in the bedroom, even before he got there, so Marty *had* to be lying when he said he didn't see his mother's body the first time he looked in the room.

"She was nearly decapitated," McCready continued, "and it appeared to me that she had struggled with whoever assaulted her."

So why were there no marks on Marty? Moriarty asked.

"It doesn't necessarily mean he's going to have injuries."

Was there any physical evidence tying Marty to either of his parents' bodies?

"I don't recall."

There wasn't, said Moriarty.

"Why would there be?" McCready asked.

More important to him, he said, was Marty's demeanor. "He was sitting as calm as could be. . . . As the conversation developed, I could see that he was just—he was lying."

"And how did you know that?" Moriarty asked.

"It's not so much the way—what is said, it's the way in which it's said."

Moriarty pointed out that after his own big lie in the interrogation room later in the morning, McCready and his partner refused Marty's pleas to be polygraphed. "So you're better at telling whether someone's lying—"

"I think I'm better than a polygraph machine."

Salpeter had never spoken to McCready, but the *48 Hours* story gave voice to the intense professional contempt he had developed for him. "This is a *bad* detective," he said flatly on the broadcast. "It's just mind-boggling what this man did to this kid." Of the confession, he said, "You give me a kid like that, I'll have him tap-dancing that he killed his parents. Is it right?" The confession wasn't Marty's story, Salpeter told Moriarty, it was McCready's.

"Once you have that confession, aren't you kind of caught?" Moriarty asked McCready.

"Well, I'm not taking a confession from an innocent man," he replied. "I would never do that."

"If Marty wanted to kill his dad, why would he call 911 when he was still alive?"

"I don't think he knew his father was still alive," McCready said.

"But he could hear him gasping," Moriarty pointed out.

"He was brain dead," McCready said.

"But he was gasping," Moriarty repeated. "Why would Marty call 911?"

"You'd have to ask Marty that."

Moriarty asked McCready to explain how the forensic evidence disproved the details in the confession. "Every confession does not have a hundred percent of the truth in it," said McCready.

"What happened to the gloves?" she asked.

"I don't know," said McCready.

"And that doesn't concern you?"

"No."

"Why would Marty kill his parents? Why?"

"One of the simplest old things in the world," McCready said. "Greed." But under the terms of his parents' wills Marty wouldn't have inherited their estate for another eight years. "Were you aware of that?"

"No, I was not," McCready said. "No, I was not."

That was because neither he nor anyone else on the homicide squad ever talked to any of Marty's relatives. When Moriarty asked him about that, McCready said, "No, that's not true."

"Are you saying they're lying?" she asked.

"Yes," said McCready, a position he held for about three seconds.

"Did you ask to speak with them and they said no?"

"No, I never directly asked to speak to them. I didn't have to. What were they going to add to my case?"

Moriarty was incredulous again. "Jim, isn't it important to talk to everybody before you settle on someone, when you know their entire life could be ruined by this?"

"No," said McCready. "Under the circumstances, in this case, everything we needed to know we pretty much knew in the first day."

"Are you proud of what you did in this case?"

"Absolutely."

"Would you do anything differently?"

McCready looked down. "Given the same set of circumstances," he said softly, "I don't, I don't see anything I would have done differently."

THE *48 HOURS* broadcast had a major impact on public perceptions. Even Shari apparently now had doubts about Marty's guilt. "I'm back on that fence again," she said on the broadcast. ". . . I'm questioning a lot of the things that have happened and the things that are going on. And I would like some answers, too."

The story aired just as Marty's lawyers were about to submit their reply to the DA's opposition to a hearing. They had momentum. But did they have their star witness? Glenn Harris had told his story to millions of people on national television. The question was whether he would tell it to the judge, the only person who mattered, and under oath.

Harris was still wrestling with the possible consequences, and one day he told Salpeter that while he was in Sing Sing he had talked about his moral dilemma with two Catholic chaplains, Father Ron Lemmert and Sister Angeline Matero. What'd they tell you? Salpeter asked. They both said to do the right thing, Harris said. Sister Angeline practically demanded it.

Salpeter decided to call them both. He thought it would be good to make contact with two people who could keep Glenn on track about testifying, but he also had something else in mind. Harris said he told them the whole story. That meant they were potential witnesses.

When Salpeter called Father Ron and started talking about Glenn, the priest cut him off: You're aware, he said, that I can't say a word about this. I'm a priest. I can't break that confidence, not without Glenn's permission. In writing. And notarized.

Forgive me, Father, Salpeter said.

Harris signed the waivers, and Father Ron and Sister Angeline told Salpeter what Glenn told them. Lemmert portrayed Harris as a deeply flawed but still redeemable man. He's tormented, struggling to find it within himself to do what he knew he should. Father Ron said he would testify if called upon. Barket, the lawyer who nearly became a priest, savored the prospect. *Now, Father, would you please tell the court . . .*

In early May, Harris's lawyer informed Lato that he would testify without immunity. Lato and his boss now had a decision to make. They had staked their opposition to a hearing on the immunity issue. They could

maintain their resistance on the basis of their other stated reasons—
chiefly, their disbelief of Harris. Or they could consent to the hearing,
have Lato cross-examine Harris into oblivion, and be done with it.

Spota wrote to Judge Braslow. Based on the assurances of Harris's attorney that he would testify without immunity, the DA's office was now
dropping its opposition to a hearing. A week later, Braslow granted the
hearing. It would begin two months later, in mid-July.

FROM THE DAY Glenn Harris first told him about that night in Belle
Terre, Salpeter knew Harris was holding back one thing. He would inti-
mate that he knew something about a murder weapon, but whenever Salpeter brought it up, Harris would just nod or smile or change the subject.
Salpeter took a patient approach, expecting he would get it out of him
eventually. And then one day, Harris finally opened the door. It was unexpected, even unintended, and it wasn't Salpeter he told.

Before Harris's release from jail, Bruce Barket went to talk to him
alone. He wanted to see what kind of witness Harris would make. Would
he crumble under the pressure of cross-examination, show himself to be as
mentally unsteady and untrustworthy as Lato claimed? And he wanted to
press Harris for the whole story. Barket had always been skeptical that
Harris waited in his car outside the Tankleff house that night if he thought
all Creedon and Kent were doing inside was a burglary. And he had a running debate about it with Salpeter, who was adamant that Harris would
not have participated in the murders. "In all his arrests, there's not one violent crime," Salpeter would say. "He's a drug addict, he's a thief. He
doesn't hurt people."

Salpeter had no trouble believing Harris was lying about *something* to
minimize his exposure to prosecution. Maybe he knew why they were
going to Belle Terre. Maybe he went into the house at some point and saw
more than he was saying. But he was sure Harris didn't participate in the
actual murders, if for no other reason than common sense: He wouldn't
have come forward if he did.

Barket sat across from Harris in a legal conference room at the jail and
conducted a mock cross-examination. "I'm telling him that the statement
is bullshit," Barket recalled, "that it is not possible he knows this and nothing else. We're going back and forth, I'm yelling at him, he's yelling at me,
and then he blurts out, 'What if I told you about the pipe?' I said, 'What
pipe?' It just slipped out. He didn't want to talk about it. He said, 'If I tell
you they piped the people, then I'll be in trouble for the murder because I
knew there was a weapon.'" As Salpeter had always told Barket, Harris
might be a head case, but he's not stupid.

Harris wouldn't say anything more about the pipe. But as Barket and the rest of Marty's legal team later learned, he already had—to one of the county jail inmates who secretly recorded him on behalf of the DA's office. "When Peter got out of the backseat of the car," Harris told the informant, "he fuckin' bent down and grabbed like an eighteen-inch-long pipe out of the backseat."

Soon after Harris was paroled, he and Salpeter were sitting in the food court of the Smith Haven Mall. They had done a little shopping and were about to go on a long-planned trip up to Belle Terre. Harris was going to retrace his route on the night of the murders and point out where he parked, where Creedon and Kent went after they got out of the car, where they came from when they returned.

"Jay, I got a present for you," Harris said.

"Oh yeah?" Salpeter said.

"You wanna see what happened to the pipe?"

They drove up in Salpeter's blue Mercedes SUV. At the entrance to Belle Terre, Harris pointed out the constable booth that was unoccupied each time he drove past it that night. Salpeter drove up Cliff Road, but Harris couldn't direct him to Seaside Drive. All he remembered was that it was somewhere near the main road and off to the right. Salpeter knew where it was, so took the road a mile up, turned right on Crooked Oak, then the quick left on Seaside. Harris said that this looked like the road. He remembered that Seaside was like a narrow country lane with a sharp bend right where the Tankleff house was.

"That's it," he said. "That's the house. We were looking for a place to park. Creedon said to keep going." They went past the house, all the way to the turnaround at the end of the road. They backtracked and approached the former Tankleff house. "I parked right over here," Harris said. Salpeter pulled over. They were just to the east of the Tankleffs' house, between their property and their neighbors at 29 Seaside, the Hovas. It was almost exactly the same spot where Jim McCready parked his car only four hours later. Where Marty sat on the hood as the detectives interviewed him. Where he was when Mike Fox made his brief appearance.

"They got out over here, went toward the back of the house," Harris said, pointing out a path that would have brought Creedon and Kent to the back near Seymour's office.

"What about the pipe?" Salpeter asked.

"Creedon got rid of it before we left," Harris said.

"Where?"

Harris told him to continue back toward the main road, make the right off Seaside onto Crooked Oak. Right over here, Harris said, pointing to a wooded area that seemed to be part of an adjacent property. They got out and walked to the edge of the woods. Creedon went about ten yards in, Harris said, and just hurled the pipe. Harris was wearing his green Jets jacket. He cocked his arm and simulated a throw like Joe Namath going long. Salpeter looked out at the small forest that unfolded in front of him. It was heavily wooded, covered with more than a few seasons of dead leaves and a light blanket of snow.

The next day, Salpeter went back to Belle Terre with Barket and knocked on the door at 61 Crooked Oak Road. An older gentleman answered. His name was John Trager. He and his wife, Ruth, had lived in the house for thirty-two years, since 1972, a year after the Tankleffs moved into their new house around the corner. Never one to mince words, Barket told Trager there might be a murder weapon from the Tankleff homicides out there somewhere, and asked if it would be all right if they conducted a search.

Salpeter later returned with Charlie Haase, his crime scene man, and a high-powered metal detector. Haase began the electronic search in one section while Salpeter, dressed in shorts, a blue West Point T-shirt, and hiking boots, explored another area with a stick. After three fruitless hours in the woods, Salpeter decided to take a break and pick up some lunch for Haase and himself. First, though, he did something else a guy might do in the woods. He wandered off to a discreet location, stood there relieving himself, and looked around. Something caught his eye. Something rusty peeking out from under a pile of brush. Salpeter zippered up and got down on the ground. *Holy Shit! Charlie! I found it! Holy shit!*

It was a pipe, all right. It was weathered, rusty, badly pitted. "Definitely been there quite a while," Haase said. Salpeter went to the house and brought the Tragers back to look at it. They said they'd never seen the pipe and had no idea where it came from. Had they ever done any work back here? None at all, Trager said. It had been untouched since they bought the property more than thirty years ago.

Salpeter called Barket but couldn't raise him. He reached Pollack, who told him to leave the pipe where it was and cover it. He'd call Lenny Lato in the morning about having the county crime lab people take possession. Salpeter returned to the property in the morning. Barket spoke to Lato, told him what Salpeter had found, and asked him to get the crime lab people out. Lato told Barket he'd have to look into it, that he wasn't sure what they were going to do. Salpeter spent the day sitting in his car, waiting for word that never came. The next day, it seemed clear the DA was not interested in the pipe.

Chances were slim that the pipe, if it was the murder weapon, had any DNA material on it after all these years. But there was always a chance.

Pollack called Barry Scheck, the cofounder of the Innocence Project, who suggested he send the pipe to a lab in California called Forensic Science Associates. Pollack talked to a forensic biologist there named Ed Blake, who told him to wrap the pipe in butcher paper and bubble wrap, then FedEx it out. They'd give it a shot.

The results came back negative, as expected. Still, the Tankleff legal team considered the pipe a helpful piece of its case. The absence of DNA could be regarded as consistent with the pipe having been exposed to the elements for sixteen years. And certainly consistent with Harris's story.

"WE'VE GOTTA keep him on the reservation," Barket told Salpeter. With the hearing approaching, Salpeter knew better than anyone how important it was to keep Harris straight, and how hard it might be. The crime that appeared most frequently on his rap sheet was parole violation.

Salpeter saw Harris regularly and talked to him on a daily basis. Then one day in late May he couldn't reach him. He tried again. No answer. He was starting to worry. Finally Harris called. Salpeter listened for a few seconds, then said, "Jesus, Glenn, are you fucking kidding me? Let me get this straight . . ." It seemed Harris had gone on a cocaine binge. With the manager of the sober house. Who was now under arrest. For stealing the van that belonged to the sober house and possessing drug paraphernalia. "Are you with the guy?" Salpeter asked. "You're not locked up? Where are you now?"

Salpeter grabbed his gun and drove out to Selden. He found Harris in a seedy motel room, packets of drugs scattered around. "Get your fuckin' clothes on and let's get outta here," Salpeter told him. He drove Harris to Queens and had him admitted to Hillside Hospital, a psychiatric facility where Harris detoxed and got back on his bipolar medicine. Salpeter picked him up two weeks later. "I'm taking you to Peekskill," he told Harris. "I called Father Ron. You're going up to stay with him." Glenn asked for how long. "As long as he can put up with you. Fuckin' knucklehead. I'm trying to keep you alive. At least until the hearing."

Harris and Father Ron were glad to see each other, but Salpeter may have been the happiest of the three. It was now June, just a month till the hearing. I'll take care of him, Father Ron assured him. Harris settled into the priest's house, and they picked up where he left off when he departed Sing Sing eight months earlier. "He was terrified about testifying," Lemmert said later. "He literally broke out in hives when he talked about it." Which was nearly all the time. When he wasn't talking to Father Ron about it, Harris was talking to Sister Angeline.

Harris was in Peekskill for barely a week when he got a call from a parole officer in Riverhead, asking him to come down to the office. Are you violating me? Harris asked. No, said the parole officer, I just need to talk to you. Harris showed up and was promptly arrested. So let me get this straight, Harris said. You put me in a sober house that's run by an addict who takes me out on a binge. Now you're violating me because I missed my meetings—because I was in rehab? Pretty much, said the parole officer. Back to the Suffolk County Jail went the star witness.

Martin Tankleff 90T3844
Clinton Correctional Facility
1074 Cook Street
P.O. Box 2001
Dannemora, New York 12929-2001

December 21, 2000

Jay Salpeter
JAY SALPETER & ASSOCIATES
1010 Northern Boulevard
Suite 208
Great Neck, New York 11021

Dear Mr. Salpeter:

Several years ago I read about your involvement in the Henry Chichester case. Recently, I was speaking with my work-out partner Austin Offen and he spoke of you highly. He felt that you could obtain justice in my case and break down the brick walls. So I wrote to Bruce Barket who provided me with your address.

As you may know from recent media reports in Newsday and on Channel 12 news, in 1990 I was wrongfully convicted of murdering my beloved parents. I can state to you, as the facts support that I am 100% innocent. I don't want to convince you of this, I would rather you draw your own conclusions. To gain more information on my case, I would encourage you to log onto www.angelfire.com/wy/tankleff/. This is a web site about my case. In addition, I would encourage you to ask me any questions.

Presently, I am represented by Robert C. Gottlieb and Barry Scheck (and others) on a DNA motion. The motion has been granted and we are now in the process of transferring the evidence to the experts. A Christmas gift (tentative as of this date) from FOX news was given to us they are paying for all of the DNA testing. In return, they want to interview me, my family, attorneys, and videotape some of the testing process. The tentative airing date is February 2001.

In addition, I am represented by Steven Braga and Jennifer O'Connor of MILLER, CASSIDY, LARROCA & LEWIN, LLP (in Washington, D.C.). These attorneys have represented me for the last 5+ years on a pro bono basis and continue to represent me. They will take my case wherever it takes them. Everyone knows and believes that with the right private investigator on the case. I believe you are the right private investigator because of your extensive investigation in the Chichester case.

Over the past 10 years, investigators and lawyers have obtained a great deal of exculpatory information. However, when trying to follow-up some of the information, we ran into many

His appeals finally exhausted ten years after his conviction, Marty began writing to private investigators. Another inmate recommended Jay Salpeter.

Karlene Kovacs (left) first came forward in 1994. Her affidavit led Salpeter to Glenn Harris (below left), who eventually told him that he drove Joe Creedon and Peter Kent to and from the Tankleff house on the night of the murders. Below is a section of Harris's handwritten affidavit.

It was a gated community — Creedon diedted me to the house — I parked my car on the street where Creedon told me to stop. Creedon and Kent got out of the car and walked towards the house on the grass. At this time I lost sight of them towards the rear of the house — Anywhere from 10 mins — to half of an hour they came running to the car — Creedon opened the

96A6092
CREEDON, JOSEPH
5'5" 160lbs
DATE 7/27/98

NY9 DOCS

Salpeter found this rusted pipe (left) in the woods near the Tankleffs' old house, just where Harris told him to look. The photo of the rear of the house, taken by a police photographer on the day of the murders, illustrated several points supporting the scenario laid out by the new witnesses: Harris said he lost sight of Creedon and Kent as they approached the rear of the house, and Kovacs said Creedon talked about watching a card game and hiding behind bushes. The sliding glass doors at the left are in the office where the poker game was played and Seymour Tankleff was attacked.

Complicated justice: Acquitted of a serious assault in 1993, Jim McCready broke into tears and hugged his lawyer—Tom Spota (right). As district attorney a decade later, Spota assigned Leonard Lato (below left) to fight Marty Tankleff's bid for a new trial. The evidence was considered by Judge Stephen Braslow (below right), whose father was one of the political power brokers behind Spota's election to DA.

Marty's family fought for him from the beginning, never so poignantly as when they spoke to Erin Moriarty of CBS's *48 Hours*. The 2004 broadcast was a turning point in Marty's long fight for freedom.

On the first day of the hearing of new evidence in July 2004, Barry Pollack and Bruce Barket arrive at court with boxes of files.

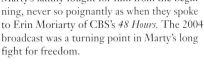

MARTY
DIDN'T DO IT.
www.MartyTankleff.org

The martytankleff.org website drew supporters from around the world.

Joe Creedon (right) and Peter Kent (below) came to court, took the stand, and said they had nothing to do with the Tankleff murders.

Billy Ram testified that Creedon, Kent, and Harris left his house to go "straighten out a Jew in the bagel business."

Joe Graydon came forward to testify that he accompanied Creedon on a failed attempt to kill Seymour Tankleff at the bagel store earlier that summer.

Brian Scott Glass (right) leaves court with his lawyer, William Wexler, after testifying that he was only kidding when he told Marty's lawyers that he was the link between Steuerman and Creedon. A few months later, the DA's office dropped an armed robbery charge against Glass.

Creedon reunited with his son, Joe Guarascio, in the spring of 2004 (left). A year and a half later, young Joe came up from Florida, accompanied by his mother, Terry Covais, and testified that his father had told him that he and Kent killed the Tankleffs.

The only principal figure who managed to avoid the hearing was Jerry Steuerman. A *48 Hours* cameraman got a shot of him in Florida, looking carefree in his bagel shirt.

JAMES CARBONE/*NEWSDAY*

A few days after his convictions were reversed in December 2007, Marty arrived in Riverhead in the back of a Suffolk County sheriff's car—an image that was a bookend to the memorable photo of him in the back of a police car the night of his arrest nineteen years earlier.

JAMES CARBONE/*NEWSDAY*

Finally released but still under indictment: many microphones, just a few words.

Hugs and kisses from cousins Autumn Asness (left) and Lynne Kadan.

Tom Spota (above left) announces that he will not retry Marty—but only because of legal technicalities. Shari Mistretta (right) said that letting Marty go was an outrage. But Jim McCready (above) said he didn't care. Still carrying his shield twenty years later, he said Marty Tankleff would have to answer to God.

All smiles after Spota's surprise announcement: With Marty are (left to right) Lonnie Soury, Eric Friedman, Ron Falbee, Jay Salpeter, Marianne McClure and her daughter Jennifer and son-in-law Dan, and Carol Falbee.

Team Tankleff celebrated at the Falbees' house after the New York attorney general's office announced it was dismissing the indictments against Marty. Left to right: Dawn Murphy-Johnson, Jay Salpeter, Bruce Barket, Jennifer O'Connor, Marty Tankleff, Barry Pollack, and Stephen Braga.

A seven-year battle: Marty and the man behind his freedom.

A free man.

CHAPTER 33

Riverhead Redux

ON JULY 19, 2004, fourteen years after his conviction, Marty Tankleff returned to a seat at the defense table in a Suffolk County courtroom. He sat with different lawyers, opposite a different prosecutor, in front of a different judge. The jury box was occupied not by jurors but by reporters, an accommodation by the judge that gave them a rare vantage point and made more seats available for spectators.

Marty's relatives were back, full of hope that things would be different this time, and Judge Braslow gave them a lift when he announced he would be liberal about allowing in evidence. This was not a trial but a hearing, and since "actual innocence" was one of the claims he would be considering, he would relax the rules, permitting hearsay testimony so long as it was relevant and probative. He wanted to hear everything the defense had to offer.

The first witness for the defense was Jay Salpeter.

With Barket leading the way, Salpeter laid out his investigation to date. It was his first public account of the trail that had begun three years earlier with Karlene Kovacs's 1994 affidavit and led to the day he drove to Belle Terre with Glenn Harris. "Glenn told me to stop the car," Salpeter said, "and he showed me the place where Joe Creedon exited the car and disposed of the murder weapon."

There was a stir in the courtroom—this was big news.

"Which murder weapon was that?" Barket asked.

"The pipe," Salpeter said, causing another stir.

Braslow's open-gate policy allowed Salpeter to put into the public record information that would never be permitted under the conventional rules of evidence. He recounted his trip to Florida, when the Strathmore restaurant employees told him that Jerry Steuerman had professed no worries when the case broke back into the news: "So what—I slit their throats. What're they gonna do, give me fifty years at my age?"

Salpeter was permitted to testify as well about another piece of information that was tantalizing, but indirect and unverified. It came from a man whose cousin worked for the Steuermans around the time of Marty's trial. On the day before Bari Steuerman was to testify, he told Salpeter, "She told one of the employees that she was very upset because she was going to have to go to court and lie for her father." The next day, Bari testified that her father woke her up to let him into their house at 3:15 A.M. because he forgot his keys, a story that Bob Gottlieb mocked in his closing as "lame," all but accusing her of perjury. Salpeter contacted the person to whom Bari was said to have confided, but the man reacted irately, demanding to know where Salpeter got his information. The call ended more calmly, and a few days later Salpeter sent the man a copy of the *48 Hours* story. He called again but the man still wouldn't confirm the story.

Lenny Lato began his cross-examination of Salpeter by asking him whether he preferred to be addressed as Detective or Investigator.

"How about Jay?" Salpeter suggested.

"Now, Jay . . . when you got this case you decided basically that an injustice had been done."

"I didn't think a proper investigation was done," Salpeter responded. But yes, he had since come to believe that Marty Tankleff was unjustly prosecuted and imprisoned.

Lato wondered how much Salpeter had been paid and by whom, the standard hired-gun tactic. Five thousand dollars from the law firm of Baker Botts when he began three years ago, Salpeter said, and then recently Marty's family gave him another five thousand, though they weren't obligated. Lato suggested that wasn't a lot of money for all the work Salpeter had put into the case—so why was he doing it? For the publicity, perhaps? "In fact, there was an article in *The New York Times* just yesterday, correct, with your picture in it?"

"How did I look?" Salpeter replied.

"Good," said Lato. ". . . And *48 Hours*, correct?"

"So were you," Salpeter said.

"I'm not going to ask you how I looked," Lato said.

"I'll stipulate that Mr. Lato looked good," Barket volunteered.

Lato concluded the trivialities and moved on to the core of his cross-examination. The subject of his interest was Salpeter's star witness and occasional social work project, Glenn Harris.

As part of discovery, Barket had presented the prosecution with copies of Harris's endless letters to Salpeter, and to Lato they were a treasure trove. They provided him with an abundance of material with which to portray Harris, with his own words, as unstable and unreliable. In one letter, Harris described himself as "a criminal, a drug addict, a deadbeat dad and by society's standards basically a good ol' piece of shit." He began an early communiqué, before he met Salpeter, "Yes, it is me again, the psychopath. I am crazy, insane, a psycho-babbler," punctuating the greeting with the first of many smiley faces. "I'm not crazy, society's crazy," he observed in another letter. ". . . I feel like I'm caught up in a Greek tragedy. . . . I will probably make a terrible witness. I would need help with my credibility."

"Fair to say Harris looked to you as a father figure?" Lato asked Salpeter.

"Yes," Salpeter replied.

". . . You're cultivating a relationship with Glenn Harris to the end of helping Marty regain his freedom, correct?"

"To get the truth."

"Well, you're not retained to get the truth, are you?"

"Yes I am."

"Well, Jay, you're not a detective now, correct?"

"But, Lenny, I'm an investigator and my job as an investigator is to get the truth, whether it benefits my client or it doesn't."

Lato wanted to know why there were no tapes of Salpeter's conversations with Harris. "Because you don't want the judge to know how you spoke to him to get him to say the things he said?" Lato asked, oblivious to the irony that was plain to anyone who knew the history of the case. In fact, Lato asserted that Salpeter manipulated an emotionally needy and mentally unstable man into making, essentially, a false confession.

"Now, you have a dislike of the DA's office in Suffolk County?" Lato asked.

"Yes, I do," Salpeter answered candidly. "I dislike district attorneys that don't allow the truth to come out."

BARKET AND POLLACK had decided to put Glenn Harris on the stand after laying the foundation for his testimony with Salpeter and their other witnesses. Building to the big witness was a standard strategy, but in this case it was also a matter of hedging bets. Harris's testimony was still not a sure thing. Apart from his anxiety about being prosecuted, Harris told Salpeter that another inmate had brought him a message from Peter Kent: "He says to tell you he knows where your kids are."

If Harris backed out, it would take the air out of the case, so Barket and Pollack wanted to make sure they got the others on first—starting with one of their prime targets. Joe Creedon found himself called as a witness by the side that was accusing him of murder. He would be questioned by a defense attorney playing the role of a prosecutor, then "cross-examined" by a prosecutor who took the position that he had nothing to do with the crimes. In this topsy-turvy proceeding, Creedon was accompanied by his attorney, Anthony La Pinta, who took a seat in the jury box, ready for consultation with his client should things get even more strange.

Creedon's menacing reputation was little in evidence as he took the witness stand. He wore a well-tailored dark suit with a white shirt and a burgundy tie and his hair and goatee were fastidiously groomed. He seemed anxious, even as Barry Pollack began by asking how old he was. Creedon said he was forty-five. Pollack asked him how old that would have made him sixteen years ago.

Creedon hesitated. "Thirty-two," he said.

"Does twenty-nine sound about right?" Pollack asked.

"Yes."

"I know that wasn't fair. I didn't tell you there was going to be math."

Pollack got down to business. "During those years, did you make some of your income through criminal activities?"

"Yes I did," Creedon said.

"What sorts of criminal activities?"

"I would say I collected money."

"As far as I know it is not illegal to collect money," Pollack said. "What made it a criminal activity?"

"Well I believe some of it might have been drug money," Creedon replied.

"Might have been?"

"I'm sure it was. How about that?"

Pollack asked Creedon to talk about the work. How would he go about collecting a bill from someone? Well, said Creedon, first he would knock on the person's door and ask him "to fulfill his obligation." But it wasn't always so simple. "Somebody that owes that money probably doesn't have it all at once. At that point, you would ask that person if he could fulfill his obligation weekly."

"Put him on a payment plan?" Pollack asked.

"Basically," said Creedon.

"But I'm assuming, Mr. Creedon," Pollack said, "there are some people that you ran into in your line of work that either weren't able to be put on the payment plan, weren't willing to be put on a payment plan, or maybe were on a payment plan and missed payments. As a drug money collector, what did you do in that situation?"

"Judge, can I get a drink of water?" Creedon asked.

Sure, said Braslow, then reminded Creedon that he could consult with his attorney any time he wanted. "We spoke in chambers about that, okay?" said the judge. "Don't be reluctant to do that. He's right over there."

"Thank you," said Creedon. Then he explained what he would do when collecting money from someone who might be having some cash flow problems: "I would probably convince him that it was in his best interests to pay the money."

"I'm sure you were a very persuasive guy," Pollack said. "How would you go about convincing him?"

"I would speak to him."

"Did you ever do anything more than speak with him?"

"Yes."

"Like what?"

"Maybe punch him in the face."

"Anything else?"

"Maybe pull a gun."

"Did those two techniques tend to work?"

"They sure do. They used to. I haven't done that in a long time."

Pollack brought up Todd Steuerman. Creedon readily admitted he collected drug debts for him, but he was not willing to put the time frame before the Tankleff murders. He acknowledged knowing Todd since 1986—even remembered they met in the Port Jefferson bowling alley—but when Pollack asked him when he started collecting for him, Creedon said, "I'd say it was in 1989."

Let's talk about Todd's father, Pollack said. Did you ever meet Jerry Steuerman? Creedon said he never did. Ever speak to him on the phone? Nope. What about the affidavit he signed in 1990 for Robert Gottlieb, in which he said Jerry Steuerman told him he was "fucking with the wrong people" when he turned down Jerry's $10,000 offer to drop the shooting charges against Todd.

"There is a mix-up on who I spoke to," Creedon said. "I never spoke to Jerry, I spoke to Todd."

"You simply made a mistake in signing the affidavit that said Jerry Steuerman." He handed Creedon the document. "It says Jerry not once but twice. You missed it both times?"

"I believe that I was misled at that time by Mr. Gottlieb."

"Mr. Gottlieb misled you?"

"I believe so because I never heard or talked to Jerry Steuerman or met with him, so that there was supposed to be Todd. That's what I thought I was signing. I never met Jerry Steuerman."

Pollack asked Creedon about all the people who were saying he talked about his involvement in the Tankleff murders: Karlene Kovacs and John Guarascio, along with the two sources cited in the DA's report. Creedon said they were all mistaken.

"Do you recall in 1993 telling a gentleman at the Gallery Pub by the name of Gaetano Foti that it was too bad about Marty Tankleff because he didn't do it?"

"I've always held that position," Creedon said.

"Didn't you go a little further with Mr. Foti and in fact, say that you knew that Marty Tankleff didn't do it because you were at that murder?"

"Absolutely not."

Lenny Lato conducted a brief "cross-examination." He clarified a few things from Creedon's direct testimony, then asked him what a defense attorney might ask his client: "Have you ever killed anyone?"

"Absolutely not," said Joey Guns.

TERRY GUARASCIO—now Terry Covais—flew up from Florida under subpoena. She had initially agreed to testify voluntarily, but changed her mind. "I was afraid of Joe finding out," she explained when Barket asked her about it on the stand. And why did that make her afraid? "Because Joe is not a very nice person."

Terry had no smoking gun to offer about Joey Guns. Creedon talked about the Tankleff murders to a variety of people, but not to the woman he lived with, more or less, for eight years. So she testified about Creedon the man. "He was very cruel to me. He used to beat me. I've seen him beat up many people." She recalled him coming home one night and telling her that he had taken a drug debtor into a friend's basement and lit the guy's face and hands on fire with gasoline. He threatened to do the same thing to her if she told anyone about it.

Karlene Kovacs finally told her story in a courtroom. Lato challenged her about the inconsistencies in some of the details she was giving thirteen years after the fact, but none of them changed the thrust of it. When Pollack asked her if she was getting anything for her testimony, Kovacs replied, "Agita."

John Guarascio followed her, testifying that he heard Creedon mention something about hiding in some bushes, watching a card game. "I just tuned it out," he said. "With Creedon, the less you knew, the better."

Gaetano Foti testified about the day in the Gallery Pub in 1993 when Creedon told him he knew Marty Tankleff was innocent because he himself was guilty. Lato challenged Foti about the words Creedon used. "Didn't you tell me something different last year?"—that Creedon said, "The kid didn't do it, I was there." Foti replied, "It sounds like the same thing to me." Lato asked him which version he recalled more. "He did it, that is my recollection," Foti said. "I wouldn't have come forward and told you that if that wasn't the case."

Bruce Demps came from prison to testify about the things Todd Steuerman told him in 1992, when they were both inmates at Clinton. "He said he would probably have to move because Tankleff would be coming to Clinton," Demps said, "and then he told me why. His father had a beef with the Tankleff family, and his father hired some guys to take care of the business for them." Barket asked him to clarify. "He said they had put a hit on them," Demps said.

"Did Todd tell you what the problem was between his father and the Tankleffs?"

"Todd's father owed them money. He said he had borrowed some money. He was supposed to do one thing with it but then he went to open a business with Todd and it didn't work out well."

Todd told Demps that he was so worried about running into Marty Tankleff when Marty was transferred from Auburn to Clinton that he put him on his list of inmates he couldn't be housed with. Todd was like that, a nervous guy in prison. "He couldn't hold his own. He couldn't fight." At the same time, Demps was impressed with how Todd got his father to call on his Hells Angels friends when there was a problem on the outside— when Todd's wife was having an affair with a guard, or when Demps had a similar problem back in Brooklyn. "There was a guy messing with a girlfriend of mine and me and Todd talked about it," Demps said. "He called his father, wherever he was at, and they sent somebody over there."

Interrogation expert Richard Ofshe spent several hours on the stand. "False confession is a regular occurring phenomenon in modern America," he said, and the case of Marty Tankleff was such a classic that he had included it in one of his published studies. Pollack wanted the judge to know that Ofshe was not some self-proclaimed expert who saw evidence of his theory everywhere he looked. In more than half the cases he examined for defense attorneys, Ofshe said, "I would do a brief review and report back to the attorney that I saw no reason for me to be involved in the case." But he was testifying here, without being paid, because the case was so egregious. His conclusions had been included in the first federal appeal, but eight years later Marty was still in prison. "Failing to be here would be an unacceptable act in my own view," Ofshe said.

THREE TIMES THAT WEEK, Barket went to the jail after court to prepare Harris for his testimony—the cross-examination in particular. Salpeter went with Barket on one of the visits, just to keep Harris on track. He used everything, including Harris's children. They were fifteen and eleven, and Harris's mother-in-law, who was virtually raising them, had told Salpeter that they were proud of what their father was doing. Harris always talked about what a failure he was as a dad. This is your chance, Salpeter told him. Make them proud.

Harris would get that chance on Friday, and when the day came the courtroom was packed, anticipation in the air. But then something else was in the air. There was a delay in the proceedings and indications of unusual activity behind the door that led to the judge's chambers. Kurt Paschke was sitting in the spectator section, waiting with everyone else, when the side door opened for a moment and he caught a glimpse of Tom Spota. And then, after two hours of suspense, Braslow adjourned the hearing until Monday without explanation.

Harris wasn't ready. He was scared. Barket and Pollack made another pitch for immunity, but Lato waved it off with a sneer. He said he'd known all along that Harris would never testify—the guy knows the cross-examination will show him to be the liar that he is. Barket asked Braslow for the weekend; maybe Harris would be ready on Monday.

When Monday came, Harris entered the courtroom through a side door and approached the witness box. His lawyer, Richard Barbuto, was nearby, sitting in a corner of the jury box with the reporters. Harris looked downcast as he stood to take the oath. From his seat in the gallery, Salpeter knew something was wrong.

"Mr. Harris, your attorney is here," Braslow said. "You can confer with him at any time."

Barket faced Harris from the lectern. "Good afternoon," he said.

"What's up, Bruce?" Harris muttered cheerlessly.

Barket asked Harris how old he was. Barbuto cut in. "May I confer with my client?" he asked the judge. Barbuto whispered in Harris's ear and Harris nodded.

"I refuse to answer any questions on the grounds I might incriminate myself," Harris said.

Gasps could be heard from the gallery, reactions from Marty's family reminiscent of moments long ago. Salpeter sat stunned, glaring. Harris met his gaze, then averted his eyes.

"Judge," Barket said, "I think he can only take the Fifth to questions that would tend to incriminate him. His age would not be one of those."

Braslow agreed. Harris said he was thirty-five. Barket continued with a series of questions that would not tend to incriminate him—how old his children were, whether he had any brothers or sisters, where he was born. He answered those. Then Barket asked, "Mr. Harris, do you know an individual by the name of Joseph Creedon?"

"Yes, I do," he said, raising hopes in the gallery for an instant.

"Objection," Barbuto said. "I would like him to assert the Fifth Amendment."

Braslow asked Harris if that's what he wished to do. "Yes," said Harris.

"Do you know an individual by the name of Peter Kent?"

"I refuse to answer the question."

"In early September of 1988, you took Peter Kent and Joseph Creedon to Belle Terre?"

Harris hesitated slightly. "He will not answer the question," Barbuto said.

"Is it correct that Mr. Kent and Mr. Creedon went into a house for about a half hour at three o'clock in the morning, or at least in the early morning hours—"

"I refuse to answer the question."

"I haven't finished. The two of them came out, that they brought with them a three-foot-long pipe and they had blood on their clothes?"

"Once again, I refuse to answer the question."

"Is it correct that you took them out of Belle Terre and on the way out, you were ordered to stop by Mr. Creedon and Mr. Creedon took that very pipe and threw it into some woods?"

"Once again, I refuse to answer the question."

From the front row of the gallery, Salpeter looked on, disgusted. *I wanted him to look at me. But he just sat there, hunched over, almost in a fetal position, staring down at the floor, taking the Fifth.*

Finally, Barket told the judge he wouldn't prolong the exercise. He had just one more question for Harris: Would he testify if he were given immunity? Barbuto said he wouldn't answer that question, either. Barket turned to Braslow and asked him to direct the district attorney's office to grant immunity to Harris. This was normally a prosecutor's decision, he acknowledged, but the judge could find that the DA's office in this case was exercising an "abuse of discretion" and direct it to grant immunity.

"By their very conduct, Judge," he said, "they have caused what we have here today." First Warkenthien tried to scare Harris with the threat of a life sentence for murder. Then he and Lato had two jailhouse snitches try to get Harris to recant his story. When that failed, the inmates told Harris he'd be going to jail if what he was saying was true, that Creedon would be out to kill him, that he didn't really want to be known as a rat in jail, did he?

But the ultimate hypocrisy, Barket told Braslow, was Lato's refusal to grant immunity from charges he had no intention of ever making. "There is not one chance in the world that Mr. Lato is going to prosecute Mr. Harris, Mr. Creedon, and Mr. Kent for those murders. If there is, then let

Marty go, because he can't have it both ways. He can't continue to insist that Martin Tankleff did these murders and at the same time stop us from putting on exculpatory evidence in the form of Mr. Harris by threatening him with the very same prosecution. It certainly is an obstruction of the truth-finding function that this Court is supposed to be engaged in."

Barket turned to Lato. "You can still prosecute him for perjury if you think he is lying. But let the Court hear what the man has to say." He turned back to the judge. "Mr. Lato does not want the Court to hear what Mr. Harris has to say because what the Court will find out is that Mr. Harris said repeatedly for two years that he was involved in those murders with Creedon and Kent." The only exception was a few sentences in one of Harris's letters when he claimed he made the whole thing up. But that was the exception that proved the rule, Barket asserted: a moment of fear put into Harris's mind by the DA's office. Every other page of every other letter, scores of them, supported his story. To say nothing of the polygraph.

Judge Braslow listened to Barket's pitch, then told him that granting immunity to witnesses wasn't in his job description. "I'm not inclined to step in the shoes of the district attorney."

Marty's relatives were devastated by the day's turn of events. "When he took the Fifth," said his Aunt Ruthie, "it was like somebody put a knife in my heart." She and the others went down the hall to the DA's office and asked to speak with Lato. Warkenthien came out to the reception area and said Lato would see two people for ten minutes. Mike McClure would have been one of them, but he had expected Harris to testify on Friday and had to get back to California. So Marianne went in and gave her layperson's version of Barket's argument for immunity. Lato told her he couldn't do it. It was the office's policy to grant immunity only in exchange for information that could be used to prosecute others. Harris didn't qualify because what he was saying wasn't true. Marianne asked Lato why he was so convinced Harris was lying when his story dovetailed with what Karlene Kovacs was saying, and *her* story supported what the family believed happened in the first place, that Jerry Steuerman hired someone to kill Seymour and Arlene. With all that, plus all the evidence of innocence at the trial, how could Lato still be so sure Marty did it?

"How can you be so sure Marty *didn't* do it?" Lato replied.

SALPETER WASN'T SHOCKED by Harris's collapse of conscience, but he took it hard and very personally. He sent Harris a greeting card cutout of the Cowardly Lion of Oz. "Do you know this guy?" he wrote. "He did find the courage." Inside he asked: "Do you remember these words, 'I want to give an innocent man back his freedom'?"

With Dick Barbuto's permission, a condition set by the judge for members of the defense legal team, Salpeter went to see Harris at the jail. He found him as he expected: contrite, full of excuses, unable to think about much but his own self-preservation—still the same old Glenn. "Jay, I just couldn't do it," he said. Though his lawyer told him it was very unlikely he would be prosecuted for the murders, he found the threat too terrifying. He rationalized that Marty's lawyers still had his affidavit and would get him out with or without his testimony—so why take the chance? But Harris's feeble excuses made Salpeter only angrier. He followed the visit by taking a page from Glenn's book. He wrote him a long letter on yellow legal paper, a tirade of guilt and betrayal that went on for three pages. *You are gutless, a man with no balls. . . . I thought I saw a good guy with a troubled past. Glenn, you fooled me. . . . You should have seen what you looked like on the stand. I was embarrassed for you. . . . If you become a man in the next couple of days and decide to do what you have told everyone you would, call your attorney. This hearing ends next week. . . .*

Harris's refusal to testify was a crushing blow to Marty's case, but Barket and Pollack saw an upside: no worries about the cross-examination. With Harris's affidavit in the record, its truth supported by a polygraph, his story would remain intact. Father Ron would be on the stand the next day, and to the lawyers it would be almost as if he were speaking for Harris, testifying without the baggage.

At the same time, the Harris episode had a subtle effect on the case. It was an effect on perceptions, starting with the reporters covering the hearing. Some began to have the sense that something was not quite right. Why *wouldn't* the DA grant Harris some form of immunity? Lawyers could come up with lawyerly reasons not to do it, but Barket's arguments about the DA's pretzel logic seemed to make more sense than Lato's declarations, which bordered on the sanctimonious, that he was *positive* that Harris was lying. Put everything together—the polygraph, the things he wrote to Salpeter and said to Lato's jailhouse informants, the unlikelihood that someone like Harris would put himself through such torment to help someone he didn't know—and it seemed to add up to a flawed witness telling a truthful story.

That a sense of injustice was in the air could be gauged by the increasingly open reception Marty's PR team was receiving. Armed with the work of Salpeter and the lawyers, Lonnie Soury and Eric Friedman were turning support for Marty into something of a movement. Soury was a relentless pitchman for media coverage of the case. In the three years since the

440 filing, he had become as consumed as anyone in the brigade of pro bono advocates that Marty dubbed Team Tankleff. Marty called him several days a week (and Friedman on the others) to talk about what was going on. There was plenty. Soury was constantly on the phone with reporters and producers, columnists and editorial writers, explaining the history of the case, pushing whatever outrage was most on his mind at the moment, his manner somehow simultaneously patient and frenetic. Sometimes he didn't react well to the results. Reporters who got an important fact wrong or, much worse, took the DA's slant on an issue, were apt to find a rant from Soury the next time they checked their emails. His fury could be measured by the number of misspellings and typos. Sometimes Salpeter worried about his old friend.

Friedman was Soury's complement—the inside man with the discreet personality. He had a sly wit and an encyclopedic knowledge of the case, which he applied to the influential website he created and oversaw. Martytankleff.org was a bountiful source of information, the first stop on the Internet for people who heard about the case from the media coverage and wanted to know more. Friedman posted updates, legal briefs, links to news coverage, and thumbnails on all the players. Rana Strazza, a friend of Marty's from high school, created a "Tankleff Case Character Map" that highlighted the connections between some of the major ones. Supporters could get MARTY DIDN'T DO IT T-shirts and view PDFs of artifacts of the case: the certified demand letter Marty's father sent to Jerry Steuerman, the confession that McCready stopped writing mid-sentence. Followers of the case could feel the family's pain and share its anger by clicking on "Marty's Aunt's Letter to DA" and see outtakes of Erin Moriarty's jaw-dropping interview of McCready on *48 Hours*.

Friedman also wrote a blog and under the moniker Doctor News he presided over a discussion board that drew passionate supporters, from across the country and occasionally from around the world, usually after one of the American crime documentary programs turned up on overseas television. By the middle of 2008, the number of posts on the forum would exceed four thousand, most by a core group who could cite chapter and verse on the case and went online regularly to denounce their favorite villains. The two most active posters were former police detectives: Bob Olson, once a New York State Police investigator, and Pete Fiorillo, a retired NYPD detective who had worked on the personal staffs of the current and prior Manhattan district attorneys. His screen name on the forum was In Support of Marty.

An occasional visitor to the website was someone who was occasionally mentioned on it: Stuart Namm, the whistle-blowing judge of the 1980s, who was now living in North Carolina and spending his retirement making documentary films. His first one, in 1998, was also the first to revisit the conviction of Marty Tankleff. Namm had always been captivated by the case—still a judge when Marty was prosecuted, he had sat in on the trial whenever he had a break from his own cases—and in 1998 he began working with a British filmmaker on *A Question of Guilt: The Martin Tankleff Story.* Hokey reenactments by actors and Namm's wooden voiceovers made it a somewhat unpolished production whose first public distribution would be in DVD sales through the Marty Tankleff website a decade later. But the film was not without its compelling moments. It was to Namm that Shari Rother acknowledged the depth of her resentment about Marty's inheritance, saying, "He wasn't a part of this family. He was brought *into* this family." Namm also persuaded Jim McCready, his one-time antagonist, to sit for an interview—in the witness box of an empty courtroom near Namm's home. "He said he would do it if I put him up in a nice hotel," Namm recalled. "And he said something about he and his brother wanting to be in the movies."

Though the website forum was the province of Marty supporters, there were occasional postings by visitors who assured everyone that Marty was guilty as sin, sometimes in a manner that suggested an undercover operator. Friedman was all for open discussion and rarely edited the board, but he would sometimes issue "troll alerts" to warn newcomers who might not be up to speed on the case. And there was little question that the prosecution side was monitoring the website. At one point prior to the hearing, Karlene Kovacs posted a signed message saying she looked forward to the day Marty would be freed and she could give him a hug. The post wound up in a prosecution brief as evidence that Kovacs had an agenda.

The one person who could not surf martytankleff.org was Marty Tankleff. Prison inmates lived in a pre-Internet world, and Marty more than most. He may very well have been the U.S. Postal Service's best individual customer. He once calculated that he'd written fifty thousand letters, and anyone who corresponded with him or sent him stamps had no trouble believing it. Marty's address was prominently displayed on the website's home page, and as the case generated more and more publicity he began receiving letters from two new categories of people: complete strangers and high school classmates.

One day Marty heard from Marc Howard—Earl L. Vandermeulen High, Class of '89. They had known each other since their earliest years, and when Marty was arrested Marc came to his defense as the editor of the school paper, *The Purple Parrot.* While Marty was sent to prison, Marc went to Yale. He studied economics and ethics, went on to earn a doctorate in political science at Berkeley, became fluent in Russian, German, and

French, and was now an associate professor of government at George-town. But when he heard about the new developments in Marty's case in 2004, he was drawn back in time. With Marty back on Long Island for his hearing, Marc decided to come up and visit him. It initiated a friendship they never had as kids and stirred an admiration that Marc couldn't have predicted. He was amazed at how Marty was able to convince people to join his fight, and then he became one of them.

Marc visited Marty half a dozen times, exchanged letters with him, and found himself doing research for Marty's case online, sending packages of printouts to prison. "As if caught in a spell, I became heavily invested in Marty's life," he later wrote in a piece published in the Sunday opinion pages of *Newsday*. "How could someone so utterly powerless—who had spent his entire adult life locked up in a tiny cell—manage to persuade others to sacrifice their time and resources to help him?" Marc decided it was Marty's disarming genuineness as much as anything—a simple au-thenticity that was not necessarily his reputation as a teenager. "When we would meet, he never seemed self-conscious about his prison clothes, and he always welcomed me with a huge smile and cheery attitude—a stark contrast to the somber people sitting around us in the visiting room." Like anyone else who visited Marty in prison, Marc couldn't help but notice that pretty much everything about Marty was a stark contrast with the sur-roundings. "Strangely enough, I never had the sense that Marty was suf-fering in prison." He was, of course, but not in the way Marc or anyone else could have expected. He still made friends, educated himself, and somehow managed to stay positive. He signed his letters to Marc, as he did to everyone else, "Write when you can."

AFTER GLENN HARRIS'S day of reckoning, Father Ron was the defense's only remaining witness. But the media coverage, especially of the Harris situation, was helping make the hearing a self-sustaining process.

After court on the day Harris was on the stand, Barket and Pollack were back at Barket's office in Garden City, taking stock of the case and preparing for the next day. Salpeter arrived with Father Ron, who was ac-companied by Sister Angeline for moral support. Salpeter was in a grumpy mood over Harris, but you take your lumps, he liked to say, and keep going. He took the priest and the nun to the Hilton Garden Inn for the night.

Barket went through the day's phone messages. There was one from a Mrs. Fischer who said her husband had information about the Tankleff case. Barket returned the call, and when he got off the phone he told Pol-lack that Father Ron wouldn't be their last witness after all.

In 1988, Neil Fischer was starting up a kitchen-cabinet-making business. Trying to drum up some customers, he posted signs on telephone poles. One of the first calls he got was from Jerry Steuerman, who hired him to install cabinets and countertops in one of his bagel stores. And then in another, and another after that. Steuerman turned out to be his best customer, if you didn't count having to chase him for payment.

One day in the spring of 1989, Fischer was installing shelves under the counters of a bagel store Steuerman was opening in the South Shore town of Oakdale. Steuerman was there with the man who had sold him the oven. It wasn't working right, and Steuerman was letting the guy have it. "He was screaming at him," Fischer told Barket, "something to the effect that he had already killed two people and that it wouldn't matter if he killed *him*, too."

Barket asked Fischer the obvious question: Why didn't he come forward with this at the time? Marty Tankleff's trial was still a year away, and it was hard to imagine that it wouldn't have helped. As Fischer told it, he wasn't sure Steuerman really meant what he was saying. The guy was incredibly high-strung. And Fischer admitted he was reluctant to risk losing his best customer over something that might not be what it sounded like. So he let it go. Fischer probably wouldn't have come forward even now if not for his wife. She pushed him to tell what he knew. Barket told Fischer he needed him to tell his story in court the next morning.

No sooner had Barket lined up one last witness when Salpeter called him from the lobby of the Hilton Garden and said they might have yet one more. "Scott Glass just called me," Salpeter said. "He may talk to us."

"See if he'll come in," Barket said.

A few weeks earlier, Salpeter had gotten a call from a woman in California who had known Marty in high school. She'd heard what was going on and wanted to help. She gave Salpeter the name of someone she knew back then who ran in the same circles as the Selden drug crowd. Salpeter found the man, who said he'd talk to him, just keep his name out of it. He knew all the players—Creedon, Kent, even Billy Ram, whom Salpeter had been trying to find for nearly a year. Did he know where Ram might be? No, he hadn't seen him in years. Was there anyone else who ran with Creedon and might know something? The guy thought for a second. Scotty Glass, he said. Creedon did a lot of shit with him back then. Have you talked to him?

Brian Scott Glass had been involved with drug dealers for twenty years—collecting for some, robbing others, all part of the same job description. Glass had two felony convictions—one for drug dealing, the other for weapons possession—and Salpeter's source had heard he was wanted on his latest charge, an armed robbery. He'd pulled a knife in a drug deal with a guy who came out $500 short and had the temerity to report it. But Glass was slippery, and the cops hadn't found him yet.

The data search listed Glass with his mother. Salpeter called her, told her who he was and why he was calling. It had worked before. And after two weeks of messages, it worked again. Salpeter was at the check-in desk of the Hilton Garden with Father Ron and Sister Angeline when his cellphone rang.

This is Scott Glass. Whadya want? Salpeter went through his standard spiel—I'm trying to get an innocent guy out of prison, maybe you can help me. Glass said maybe I can, but what's in it for me? Salpeter considered the do-the-right-thing pitch, but something about this guy told him not to bother. Why don't we just get together and talk? Glass said he'd call him back.

It was after dark and Salpeter was home when Glass called him back. Pick me up in Ronkonkoma, Glass said. At the Amoco station on Portion Road. There's a Carvel there.

Cheryl wasn't happy. Her husband had been making a habit of going out by himself to meet shady characters he didn't know. Salpeter told her what he always told her: Don't worry, I'll be careful.

Brian Scott Glass was the kind of edgy smart-mouth who could be found in any self-respecting street gang, still playing that character at the age of forty-four. But he was punctual. Salpeter picked him up and drove him to Barket's office.

Glass had information, but he also had an agenda. He needed a lawyer to handle his inevitable arrest on the armed robbery. It was a bullshit case, he said, but it would be his third felony, which meant he was looking at some serious time. Barket told Glass he could give him a long list of lawyers to call, as many as he wanted. Other than that, he couldn't help him. Glass said he didn't have any money to pay a lawyer. That's why he was looking for a free one. Sorry, Barket told him, you won't find one here.

This was what it was like trying to get people like Scott Glass to cooperate. They wanted something out of it, and the defense team had nothing to offer. All Barket could do was try to find the right button and push it: "If they hate the government, it's 'I hate the government more than you do. Here's your chance to stick your thumb in the eye of the man.' If they're religious, I'm religious, too. Or give them my 'Do the right thing' speech." But none of that was going to work with Scott Glass. Ultimately he talked because he just felt like it. "He had a 'fuck 'em' kind of attitude," said Barket. "'Fuck Creedon, fuck the DA.'" For now, anyway.

This was what Glass had to say: He used to run around with Joey

Creedon—doing drugs, some collecting, a few burglaries. Mostly "we pushed up on people." Pushed up on people? Pollack asked. Yeah, said Glass, rob 'em. He knew Todd Steuerman—they met through a guy named Vinny at a Super Bowl party at a topless joint—and through Todd he knew Jerry. And Jerry tried to hire him that summer of 1988 to do "a piece of work" involving his business partner, Seymour Tankleff.

"What do you mean, 'a piece of work'?" Barket asked.

"Do a number on him," Glass said. "Send him a message. Because he owed Steuerman money."

Barket told him that wasn't right—Steuerman owed *Tankleff*. No, said Glass, you got it backwards. Steuerman told him it was Tankleff who owed *him*. Then why don't I just collect the money? Glass said he asked Steuerman. The whole thing made no sense, so he turned down the job. And then he passed it on to Creedon.

Glass was off on the key element of the story, but it wasn't impossible that Steuerman claimed Tankleff was in debt to him. With Jerry, nothing was impossible. The main thing was that Glass was saying Steuerman tried to hire him to hurt Seymour Tankleff. So would he testify? Maybe, Glass said. But he was afraid he'd walk into the courthouse and get locked up for the robbery. Barket told him not to worry. "You'll go, we'll get you in and out. You'll be gone before anybody who knows anything about the robbery will ever hear about it."

Glass said all right, but Salpeter wasn't so sure. Only hours earlier, he'd watched Glenn Harris lose his nerve—and he was a guy who really did want to do the right thing, for nothing in return. Glass was not that kind of guy. Salpeter knew that the second he met him. He also knew there was only one way Glass was getting on the stand in the morning, and that was by keeping him in sight overnight. "C'mon, we'll put you up," Salpeter said lightly. "We'll share a room." Glass said no thanks. He said he wanted to spend the night with his girlfriend and take care of a few things in case Barket didn't get him in and out so fast and he wound up in handcuffs. Salpeter drove Glass back to the Amoco station and watched him walk away. That's the last we'll see of him, he thought.

The next morning, Father Ron testified about all the things Glenn Harris told him—about driving Creedon and Kent to Belle Terre and about how tormented he had been about testifying. Emerging from the courtroom afterward, a smiling Pollack told the reporters, "We just heard from Glenn Harris. I don't think anyone thinks he lied to the priest."

And then it was Neil Fischer, the cabinet guy who heard Steuerman screaming to the oven guy about killing two people. That night the media were reporting that a "surprise witness" had come forward to give the first direct evidence against Jerry Steuerman. Barket and Pollack had hoped to have *two* surprise witnesses give direct evidence against Jerry Steuerman. But Brian Scott Glass never showed up. No surprise there.

AMONG THE DEFENSE TEAM, it was an article of faith that there were more people out there who knew things. Maybe just one thing. Maybe just a tip that someone else might know something. And maybe something would push them to make a phone call, like Neil Fischer.

Joe Graydon was following the coverage of the Tankleff hearing with more interest than the average Joe. He was part of the Selden crowd in the mid-1980s, and ran with Joe Creedon. He'd met Creedon in typical fashion: "I looked at his girlfriend Terry and he flipped out. I guess he was a little jealous." On this occasion, Creedon found words sufficiently persuasive, and he and Graydon went on to become friends, along with partners of a sort. "We sold drugs, we robbed drug dealers," Graydon reminisced. "Mostly the Dominicans in Port Jeff. We would just go and kick down their door and steal their stuff. What're they gonna do, call the police?"

Graydon shared a house with Creedon and Terry for a while. They had the first floor; he was in the apartment upstairs. But that was years ago. They'd gone their separate ways and Graydon had straightened out. By his telling he owed his turnaround to a judge who gave him such a break on a sentence that he figured it had to be a case of divine intervention. "God told me, 'That's it, enough is enough.'" Lately, he'd been living up in Seneca Falls, working as a cook, planning to buy a little restaurant that was in foreclosure. The pastor of the Finger Lakes Christian Fellowship had turned him into a churchgoer and a Bible student.

One day in July, Graydon was on a bus going back upstate, reading a copy of *Newsday* he'd grabbed for the trip. Usually he'd just read the sports section—he was still an inveterate gambler, Bible study notwithstanding—but this week he'd been checking out the front of the paper for developments in the Tankleff case. The headline this day stopped him: KEY TO DEFENSE CASE PLEADS FIFTH; DA REFUSES TO GRANT IMMUNITY. Graydon looked at a picture next to the story. Marty's Aunt Ruthie was crying, a friend trying to comfort her. Graydon understood Glenn Harris's decision, but it forced him to think about his own choice.

When he got to Seneca Falls, Graydon called his pastor, Jerry Graziano. "I go, 'Pastor, I got something to tell you. You're not gonna like it.' He says what is it? I tell him there's this kid in jail for killing his mother and father. He didn't do it. He says, 'How do you know?' And I explained the story to him. And I said what should I do? He says, 'You should do the right thing, and I know you know what the right thing is.'"

The next day, Graydon was on the phone with Bruce Barket, telling him something astonishing. Barket was nearly as stunned by the timing as he was by the information itself. Only two days after Brian Scott Glass told about the "piece of work" he passed on to Joe Creedon, here was another of Creedon's old cohorts surfacing with information that dovetailed perfectly with Glass's.

"Have you spoken to Scott Glass?" Barket asked skeptically.

"Scotty Glass?" Graydon replied. "I haven't seen him in years."

"When can we get you down here?"

The following week, Graydon was on the witness stand, talking about the old days with Joey Creedon. "We sold drugs, we did drugs, we robbed drug dealers, we got into a lot of fights in places together. And then there was a time that somebody wanted a partner eliminated and it happened to be at Strathmore Bagels. Summer 1988. It was a Sunday. . . ."

The courtroom was rapt, hanging on the words of this raspy-voiced, world-weary man. "Creedon said he was offered some money. Some partner owed another partner money. As far as the names, I don't know. All's I know is Strathmore Bagels. The guy was going to be there alone on a Sunday. He didn't work there, he picked money up. Friday, Saturday, Sunday was when the most money was going to be there."

"Mr. Creedon told you that one partner had hired him to kill the other partner?" Barket asked.

"Yes, and to make it look like a robbery because of the amount of money that was going to be there on a Sunday."

According to Graydon, Creedon said he was being paid $25,000 for the murder, plus whatever money he got from the store's weekend receipts. He told Graydon they would split everything fifty-fifty, which sounded good to him. He wasn't looking to be involved in a murder, but he needed the money. "I had made a few bets, football bets that I owed money for almost a year. They started coming around and they wanted the money. I had gotten back together with my wife. She was getting nervous."

On that Sunday evening—it was in July or August, he couldn't get it closer than that—he took his wife's Honda and picked up Creedon and drove to the Strathmore bagel store in East Setauket. Creedon had a gun with him, as usual. But when they got there, the place was locked and dark. "We went around back. Nobody was there, no car there. We drove back around front, drove around the parking lot. Then we went to the parking at the end. We made a right, continued along the shopping center. Joey said stop. He threw a garbage can through a window. I'm going to say a stationery store because that's what I remember. And he came out with a little box that they had, I guess, money in it."

"As you were driving there, what feelings did you have?" Barket asked.

"I really didn't want to do it," Graydon said, and when the plan didn't work out, "I was kind of happy." When Creedon wanted him to come for another try a few weeks later, "I didn't want no part of it."

Barket asked Graydon if the murders of the Tankleffs a few weeks later set off any bells in his head. "Yes and no," said Graydon. The Strathmore bagel connection was all over the news after Steuerman's disappearance, but "I was led to believe, you know, I thought the kid did it." Marty Tankleff's confession was the main thing, but it was also that Creedon's job "wasn't supposed to happen in the guy's house, it was supposed to happen in the store," and he never mentioned "a wife or a lady . . . it was supposed to be a man. So when I saw a husband and wife . . ."

When Glenn Harris's statement went public in the fall of 2003, Graydon read about it in the paper. "I was in shock," he said. It was the first time he'd heard Creedon's name connected with the Tankleff murders. "I put two and two together." As Harris had done fifteen years earlier. Why didn't he come forward at that point? "Because I thought Creedon was getting blamed for it and I thought the kid was getting out. I didn't think there was no need to say anything, to be honest with you."

Then last week, nine months later, he read about Harris taking the Fifth. "And I saw this poor little old lady." It was the picture of Marty's Aunt Ruthie, crying in the hallway. "I don't know who's who. I don't know the Tankleffs. But it's time that something was said to help. It's time to help the guy out."

"You're referring to Marty?" Barket asked, motioning in his direction.

"Yes, I'm sure that's him because he came in with cuffs."

"It is a dead giveaway, isn't it?"

"I didn't make the phone call at first. I talked to my pastor, Pastor Graziano. He said, 'God is touching you, finally.' He goes, 'You know what to do.' I picked up the phone. I called the DA first. I asked for the number of the lawyer, and they wouldn't give it to me."

"Wait a second," Barket said. "You called the district attorney's office?" He had been so focused on the hard news of Graydon's story, and so anxious to get him on the stand before he changed his mind, that he was hearing this for the first time like everyone else.

"I told them I had information," Graydon said. "I used to live with Joey Creedon and I know about him. I asked for the lawyer's name. He wouldn't give it to me."

"Who did you speak to?"

"Walter something. All he wanted to know was my Social Security number."

"Walter Warkenthien?"

"Yes. He calls me back and wants to know my Social Security number. Nothing else. Hung up."

"How did you find my number?" Barket asked.

"I had to go back in my dumpster, jump in the garbage, and get the *Newsday* out because your name was in there. Barket, Garden City. That's how I got your number. I called information, 411."

Graydon brought out the best and worst in Lenny Lato's skills as a cross-examiner. "Stop yelling at me," Graydon told him at one point. Argumentative to a fault, Lato sometimes seemed to be trying to win a debate, and may have asked one question too many about Graydon's attempts to report his information to the DA's office. Did you get into any substantive conversation with Warkenthien? Lato asked.

"I said I used to live with Joey Creedon," Graydon said. "He said, 'Did you see him do it?' I said no, I did not see him do it. Then he said that is speculation. I said, no, it is not. Two plus two is four. The kid didn't do it. And then he started getting wise and angry, like you are."

Graydon wanted to make sure everyone was clear that he was just acting as Creedon's driver. "I wasn't going to do the actual killing," he said. And after Lato asked him if he was "the type of guy to go out and kill somebody," Graydon shot back, "I wasn't doing the killing. Stop saying that, *please*. I was driving."

Lato asked Graydon why he'd been reluctant to give his home address when he took the stand. Was he scared of Joe Creedon?

"I'm more scared of you people than I am of Joey Creedon," Graydon replied. "He can't hurt me."

CHAPTER 34

Tricknology

THE CALLS KEPT COMING. But not all who came forward were as determined as the dumpster-diving Joe Graydon, or as fearless as he was of the men involved in the murder conspiracy the defense was exposing piece by piece.

On the very same day that Graydon surfaced, a woman called Barket's office and said she had information—but she was scared. Barket wasn't in, so his assistant called Salpeter, who called the woman back. Danielle Nichols—the name we will use here—had worked at Strathmore Bagels as a teenager in the early 1980s. She was friends with Todd Steuerman in those days, though she didn't approve of his side business, which he ran from the back of the store without much concern about getting caught. Eventually Todd told her why it was so easy. "He said the police were paid off," she said. "I wasn't sure I believed him. I saw him selling drugs but I never saw him paying the police."

One day a man came into the store and went behind the counter with Todd's father. "Jerry put his arm around him and called him his card partner," she recalled. "Then they went into the little office in the back of the store, where Jerry had his safe. One of the people working in the store told me that this guy, Jerry's 'card partner,' was a police detective. At first I was nervous for Todd with a detective being back there. I was young and naïve then. Then I got a chill because I realized that maybe Todd was telling me the truth about the police being paid off. I didn't see it, but it all kind of added up in my mind."

The Tankleffs were murdered a year or so later, and then Jerry went missing. "Todd said he knew where his father was and he was fine. He said that the day before he disappeared he took all the cash he kept in the safe.

When they found Jerry in California and brought him back, he was in the papers and TV with the police. And I immediately recognized the detective. James McCready. He was the one I saw in the bagel store that day with Jerry. I even said something to Todd and he laughed. He said, 'Yeah, they sent my father's friend out to get him.'"

Danielle asked Salpeter if what she was telling was important. Very important, he told her. He asked her why she had waited so long to come forward. At the time, she said, she thought that what she knew was common knowledge. And now she realized it wasn't, and it bothered her. It *always* bothered her. But she was also scared. So that's why she didn't say anything before.

Danielle agreed to come to Barket's office that night, and after she went through her story again Barket asked if she would put it into an affidavit. She was nervous about it, but said she would do it. She started again from the top as Barket sat at his computer, typing her recollections. He printed it out, and Danielle read it over. She made a couple of changes. Then it was time to sign the statement and notarize it. But first she had a question: Would she have to testify? Barket told her that's what they needed. Danielle froze. She had started out thinking she would help with a tip over the phone. The next thing she knew she was in a lawyer's office. And then she was agreeing to sign a statement. And then she was being told she would have to testify in court. If she did that, her name would be in the newspapers. There could be consequences. She was a single mother. "These people are murderers," she said. "Who will protect me?"

She got no answer back.

"I'm not doing it," she said.

Salpeter cringed. It was Barket's way to be completely straight with witnesses. Salpeter wished he had a little finesse sometimes. When Danielle asked if she would have to testify, Salpeter would have deflected the question. First, get her statement. If she doesn't testify, she doesn't testify. But at least you've got her statement.

Barket and Pollack didn't get that, but they would get a chance to use her information to back up someone else's. Amazingly, only a few days later, a second person came forward linking Steuerman and McCready. Lenny Lubrano was watching Court TV one night and saw a documentary on the Tankleff case that had initially aired two years earlier. The program was the first of a series called *The Wrong Man?* and featuring a private investigator named Jerry Palace, like Salpeter a retired New York City police detective. Toward the end, Palace was seen showing up at McCready's door in South Carolina, at night and unannounced. Palace was miked but the cameraman stayed back, shooting the scene from the street. When McCready opened the door, Palace said he was from Court

TV, doing a show on the Tankleff case. "You fuckin' kidding me?" McCready said. He didn't seem annoyed, just surprised, and he invited Palace in. After interviewing McCready at his kitchen table, Palace was shown driving off into the night as he said in voiceover, "I was shocked to hear McCready say he never considered Jerry Steuerman as a suspect. It seemed strange to me and I wondered if there was more to their relationship. But I was never able to find a connection."

Lenny Lubrano watched the show and realized that he—like Danielle Nichols—knew something that was apparently not common knowledge. He told his wife he thought he should get in touch with someone. She was against it. Don't get involved, she said. Lubrano told her no, he had to.

Lubrano had owned a pizza restaurant for twenty years, and one of his regular customers in the early days had been Jim McCready. McCready was putting up houses in the area at the time, his side business, and he would come in to pick up lunch for his crew. As he got to know McCready, it occurred to Lubrano that he knew him from somewhere. He couldn't place it at first, but then it hit him: Strathmore Bagels. Before he opened the pizza place, Lubrano sold wholesale baked goods to restaurants and institutions, and Jerry Steuerman was his bagel supplier. He would pick up bags of them at Strathmore Bagels seven days a week. He'd seen McCready there numerous times, talking to Steuerman. How could he be sure? It was McCready's wristwatch. As he explained, "I like watches. I notice them. And the thing that stuck out in my mind was that McCready had a Rolex that I admired when I saw him talking to Jerry. And when he came into my restaurant he was wearing the same one. That's what stuck out, and also that he was a very polished dresser." Did he remember anything else? One other thing: McCready once mentioned doing some construction work for Steuerman.

As they had with the other over-the-transom witnesses, Barket and Pollack brought Lubrano to court the day after he called them. And they brought something else: pages 3625 and 3626 of the transcript of Marty's trial. Lubrano came directly from work, apologizing to the judge for his pizza maker's attire as he stepped up to the witness chair. His direct testimony was brief, and when Pollack was finished, he told the judge that he had an application to make. "Your Honor," he said, "at the trial in this case, Detective McCready testified unequivocally that he did not know Jerry Steuerman prior to the Tankleff murders."

Pollack recited Bob Gottlieb's cross-examination of McCready: "Did you know Jerry Steuerman?" "No, sir, I did not." And then: "Did you ever meet Jerry Steuerman?" "Did you know anything about Jerry Steuerman?" "Did you know anything about his background?" "Did you know anything about Jerry Steuerman's children or his family?" McCready's answers were emphatic, ranging from "Absolutely not" to "I didn't know one thing about Jerry Steuerman." At the Huntley hearing, he had said: "Oh, God, no. I never heard of him."

Pollack looked up at the judge. "The conduct of Detective McCready is now directly at issue in this proceeding," he said. And since Tom Spota had twice represented McCready, the district attorney now had a clear conflict of interest. The defense, Pollack told Braslow, intended to move for the disqualification of the DA's office and the appointment of a special prosecutor.

Braslow declared the hearing on hold, and within the week the Tankleff lawyers presented him with a thirty-four-page motion. They supported Lenny Lubrano's testimony with the information from Danielle Nichols, whose fears about going on the record, they contended, were not unrelated to Spota's conflict of interest. Barket wrote that he and Salpeter talked to their unnamed source for hours, and it was apparent to them that she knew even more than she was telling—not only about the relationship between McCready and Steuerman but about the murders themselves. "The source asked, 'What if a person knew the motivation for murder? How could you protect that person?' I had to answer honestly that I could not." An independent prosecutor had to investigate the source's claims, Barket wrote, and clearly Tom Spota, the lawyer who defended McCready whenever he got in trouble, could not be that prosecutor.

Lenny Lubrano was not to be the only person to come forward, on the record, with information putting McCready and Steuerman together. Though he was not to surface until later, William Sullivan provided persuasive evidence of the connection—first to Marty himself. "This letter is long overdue," William Sullivan wrote. "Please pass this to your lawyer."

In the late 1980s, Sullivan had been the manager of Carrington's, a restaurant and catering establishment in Stony Brook. As he later said in an affidavit, the restaurant had Wednesday singles nights, which Steuerman attended regularly. In another room, also on Wednesday nights, the Suffolk County Detectives Association held its monthly meetings. Sullivan said he saw Steuerman and McCready in conversation outside their respective events at least twice. He offered a detailed account of how he knew the two men and why he was sure of where and when he saw them together: He was introduced to McCready by the restaurant owner's brother, a former Suffolk County PBA president. "Jim McCready was a regular customer of Carrington's," Sullivan said in his affidavit, "and I can say with certainty that I saw, greeted, and chatted with him at least once a month." He was introduced to Steuerman, meanwhile, by another customer. And he was hard to forget: "He dressed in the real disco fashion, with a polyester shirt open at the collar that was ten years behind the fashion at that time."

Sullivan said he saw McCready and Steuerman talking twice, each time on the landing near the entrance to the nightclub. The second time, he stopped to chat with them at the top of the stairs; he remembered talking about how packed the place was, and something about McCready's construction business. Seeing Steuerman and McCready together reminded Sullivan of Starsky and Hutch, though Steuerman was not smooth in the least. "Jerry seemed kind of nervous and ancy [sic] and I thought that maybe he was a married man about to stray into the affair zone. That is why I also found noticeable and strange [that] Steuerman didn't really mingle in the crowd. I never saw him dance or hang around or even have a drink at the bar. It seemed to me he was just a freeloader who came in, talked to McCready, and would then leave without spending any money."

Crucially, Sullivan was able to narrow the period to before the Tankleff murders—between the fall of 1987 and early 1988, based on the Wednesday night events and the décor he saw in his mind's eye. In January 1988, Carrington's had a major interior renovation that completely changed the look and atmosphere of the restaurant's upstairs club level, and "it was not how the club was decorated at the time I saw these men together."

"Why did McCready lie about this?" asked the defense motion for a special prosecutor. "Why didn't McCready tell his superiors that he had a relationship with Steuerman? Did he disclose this relationship to anyone else connected to this prosecution? Did he come to learn any of the facts that have been developed during the course of this hearing? The implications of McCready's perjury are potentially far-reaching. It is possible McCready may very well be implicated in a conspiracy to cover up the identity of the actual killers. . . . It would be outrageous to suggest that the head of the office responsible for such an investigation should be McCready's former personal attorney, Thomas Spota."

The Tankleff team's argument went beyond the immediate issue, pulling no punches in tying Spota not only to McCready but to Suffolk County's checkered criminal justice system. They called attention to an allegation by the State Investigation Commission in 1989. In the early 1980s, according to the SIC, Spota and his law partner at the time, Gerry Sullivan, were implicated in an arrangement to kick back a percentage of their fees to an assistant district attorney and police officers who referred drunken-driving cases to them. Two police officers gave sworn statements saying that the assistant DA gave them his business card and asked them to refer people they arrested. "He would then refer them to Spota and we would all make some money," one of the officers said. But the accusations were quietly buried within the DA's office, according to the SIC, which found "conflicts and interrelationships . . . which allowed Spota and Sullivan to be exonerated by a mere telephone call in which they denied any improprieties." That call was to James O'Rourke, the chief of the special investigations bureau, who found "no prosecutable crime" and put the matter to rest. When it became public as part of the SIC investigation five years later, O'Rourke was a partner in Spota and Sullivan's firm.

Marty's legal team argued that Spota's handling of the new evidence in the Tankleff case was prima facie evidence itself of his conflict of interest. It started with his failure to do any investigation in the month before the 440 motion was filed—an opportunity an "unconflicted office" would have used to talk to reluctant witnesses out of the public spotlight and interview the alternate suspects before they got lawyers. Instead, Spota and his office did nothing. And doing nothing turned into active obstruction. Rather than investigating Glenn Harris's claims, the DA's office tried to discredit and intimidate him—first with Walter Warkenthien's "trading places with Marty Tankleff" threat, then with the jailhouse inmates the office used as its agents, even after Harris was represented by a lawyer— a clear violation of his rights. "In any other context this would be considered witness tampering," the motion asserted, adding: "It would have been interesting to hear what Creedon and Kent had to say if the district attorney had chosen surreptitiously to record them instead of Glenn Harris."

This "disturbing pattern" continued with the office's refusal to grant immunity to Harris and its failure to so much as interview Joseph Graydon. "Mr. Lato's unwillingness to believe any witness who has testimony inconsistent with Mr. Tankleff's guilt is itself compelling evidence of the lack of objectivity of the District Attorney's office in this case." To say nothing of his unwillingness to *disbelieve* anyone with testimony supporting guilt—even Brian France, the skinhead who claimed Marty confessed to him one day in the law library.

On August 17, Lato filed his response to the Tankleff team's motion for a special prosecutor. He didn't rebut Lubrano's testimony that McCready knew Steuerman (with an affidavit from McCready, for instance). Nor did Spota himself reply to the defense's direct question of whether he and McCready discussed the Tankleff case in the course of their attorney-client relationship. (Did Spota's silence on this question virtually confirm that privilege, and thus his conflict of interest?) The reply simply argued that Spota's prior representation of McCready posed no conflict; that, regardless, the Tankleff lawyers knew about it even before they filed the 440 motion and had their chance then to move to disqualify him; and that the whole thing was a desperate attempt by the Tankleff lawyers to rescue a "foundering" case by asking the court to replace Lato with a less formidable prosecutor.

But it wasn't the legal arguments, or Lato's self-regard, that was most notable about the DA's reply. It was the affidavit, dated that day and signed by Spota himself, that was hastily attached. The district attorney revealed that his former law partner, Gerard Sullivan, had represented both Jerry and Todd Steuerman. The timing of this disclosure was interesting. On the previous days and that very morning, one of Salpeter's guys, Steve Naklicki, had been in the court clerk's office searching records for the names of lawyers who had represented the Steuermans.

Though perhaps an attempt to avoid an unpleasant headline by divulging himself what Salpeter's investigator was about to discover, Spota's affidavit nonetheless fell short of full disclosure. The statement said that Sullivan represented the Steuermans after he and Spota dissolved their partnership. That was technically true for Todd Steuerman's *second* drug arrest in 1989. Spota and Sullivan were no longer official partners by then. But they still shared an office and support staff, and Spota later admitted that when he asked his current staff to look through his files for cases involving the Steuermans, they found that 1989 case. In any event, as Lato acknowledged in court that day, Spota and Sullivan were formal partners when Jerry Steuerman hired Sullivan to represent his then seventeen-year-old son in his first narcotics case in 1983. By law, that meant that the Steuermans were Spota's clients, too. So Tom Spota had prior legal relationships with Jim McCready, Jerry Steuerman, and Todd Steuerman.

The Tankleff lawyers used the new information in its reply, noting that it wasn't until they moved for Spota's disqualification—nearly a year after the proceedings began—that he revealed his firm's ties to the Steuermans. The defense submitted an affidavit by Roy Simon, the director of the Institute for the Study of Legal Ethics at Hofstra Law School. According to Professor Simon, the conflicts at play here were intricate, severe, and irreconcilable—not even a close call: "The entire Suffolk County district attorney's office is disqualified."

Aside from legal experts, the Tankleff defense got support from *Newsday*. The paper's editorial page had been an enthusiastic supporter of Spota since his campaign for DA but thought he was wrong to insist on staying on the Tankleff case: "Spota's reputation for fairness is an asset to the people of Suffolk," said the editorial, "and we hope Braslow will help him preserve it by taking him off the case."

Braslow declined the advice. Spota's past representation of McCready "may appear to be the appearance of impropriety to the layman," the judge wrote, but it had "nothing to do with this case." That it would affect his conduct of the hearing "is remote and speculative." The Steuermans posed no conflicts, either.

But Braslow had some thoughts about the defense lawyers: He wanted them to stop complaining so much. The burden of finding new evidence to vacate the verdict fell squarely on the defense, he said; the DA's office was under no obligation to reinvestigate the case. So all this criticism the defense was heaping on Spota for sitting on information, or for refusing to grant immunity to Glenn Harris, or for asking Joe Graydon for his Social Security number when he called to offer new evidence—irrelevant, all of it. Braslow, it appeared, had a somewhat narrow interpretation of the prosecutor's obligation "to seek justice, not merely to convict."

The case's ups and downs were taking their toll on Marty and his camp. The tactics of the DA's office had become increasingly infuriating to them, and now here came the judge with a decision that seemed to go through contortions to favor Spota. "It's distressing," Barket told a reporter, "not just for Marty, but for the system of justice they purport to have in Suffolk County."

Braslow's decision fed suspicions that the ultimate decision about a new trial was preordained. To Barket, it confirmed what he was being told by a well-connected person he knew in the Suffolk courthouse: "You're going to lose. They let you have the hearing so they can bleed you dry. Then Braslow will shoot you down and they'll be rid of this kid forever. That's the plan."

Lonnie Soury heard the same thing. He and his wife lived in Manhattan but had a weekend house on Suffolk County's North Fork. One of their neighbors was a retired judge who told Soury something he found astonishing and outrageous. "Everyone knows he's innocent," said the former judge. "And you're going to lose."

THE DEFENSE LOST its bid for a special prosecutor, but the battle had an unexpected benefit: It bought time. The hearing paused for nearly three months, at a point when Barket and Pollack were out of witnesses. When it resumed in late October, they had a new one—someone Salpeter had been pursuing for nearly a year. In fact, he had all but given up when he got a call one day in late September, a few days after Braslow's decision on Spota.

"This is Bill Ram. You've been calling my mother looking for me."

Salpeter was always calling someone's mother. He had to think for a second who Bill Ram was. Then it hit him. *Billy* Ram. The guy whose name Glenn Harris wrote in the very first sentence of his affidavit. The guy who could corroborate Harris's story—or blow it up. Salpeter told

Ram what he wanted. The Tankleff murders. Glenn Harris, Joe Creedon, Peter Kent.

Ram chuckled.

"I just want to know if they left from your house that night," Salpeter said.

"I know what you want," Ram said. "I'm not talking on the phone. If you want to come down here . . ."

"Where are you?"

"Tampa."

The next day, Salpeter took an early flight and checked into the Marriott at the Tampa airport. He'd arranged to meet Ram for dinner, so he spent the afternoon lying in the sun. A few minutes before five, he went to the lobby to wait for Ram, worried, as usual, that he wouldn't show up. He panned the lobby, looking for someone along the lines of a Glenn Harris. Then he saw a heavyset man approaching. He was well dressed in slacks and a button-down shirt. He wore glasses. Salpeter thought he looked like an accountant. At six-two, three hundred pounds, a very large accountant.

"Hello, Jay. Bill Ram."

Ram drove Salpeter to a restaurant and told him about his new life. In his younger days, he was like the rest in his crowd whose lives revolved around drugs—using them, dealing them, stealing to get them. He grew up with Harris and Kent. Creedon was a few years older but he knew him from the neighborhood, and after high school he was pretty good friends with him. They lived together at one point. Ram had been convicted of various degrees of possession and sale of drugs, and, "you know, things that go along with that." Sometimes when Ram was having a hard time getting his money out of a customer, he would bring Creedon along. Ram was very big and Creedon was small, but it wasn't about size. "If you showed up at somebody's house with Joey," Ram said, "people knew it was time to go get their money."

Ram had also done the usual burglaries, some with Harris, some with Kent, some with both. He'd spent a total of six years in prison, most recently in Florida. He got out two years ago and was still on probation. But he had his act together now, he said. Since he got out of jail, he'd been selling vacation timeshares, and doing quite well with it. His girlfriend was in sales, too—insurance. They'd been together five years and bought a house together. "In sales, you constantly have to build for the future," Ram said. It was all about getting leads and pursuing them.

"Just like my business," Salpeter said.

"So what do you want to know?" Ram asked.

"I want to know if you can confirm what Glenn is telling me. He says he and Creedon and Kent were at your house before they went to Belle Terre. Is that true?"

"I'm not testifying," Ram said. "I'm telling you that up front."

"I'm not asking you to testify," Salpeter said. "Just talk to me. You can do that, right?"

Ram looked Salpeter over. "Not here," he said. Then he changed the subject. They talked sports.

They left the restaurant and got in Ram's car, heading back to Salpeter's hotel. Ram put the radio on, turned the volume way up, and started talking. Salpeter could see Ram's lips moving but couldn't hear a thing above the blasting music—country music, which he hated. Salpeter laughed. *"I can't hear a fuckin' word you're saying!"* he yelled. Ram turned down the volume, but not much. Salpeter could just about make out the words *Jew* and *bagel store.*

Can you cut this shit out? I promise I'm not taping you. Just talk to me, what's the big deal?

Ram pulled into the parking lot at the hotel. He turned the radio off, then turned to Salpeter. "All those guys were over my house that night," he said. "Harris, Creedon, Kent. Creedon wanted to use my mother's car because he was going up to an exclusive neighborhood to straighten somebody out. My mother's car was like brand-new at the time. She had a Honda Accord or a Prelude. I'm not sure. I'm not good with cars. I guess he thought it wouldn't stick out in that neighborhood."

"Did Creedon say what neighborhood he was going to?"

"Sure, it was Belle Terre. He wanted me to drive him or let him borrow the car. He said there's some money in it for me. I told him no."

"Did he say who he was going to threaten, or what it was about?"

"He said he was going up there to straighten out a Jew in the bagel business. Joey was working for a guy who was in the bagel business, and it was a partner or someone he was in business with. And it could have been some money in it for me if I helped him. Maybe because of my size he felt I could help interrogate this guy or hold him while Joey threatened him or scared him or did whatever he was gonna do. I told him I wasn't getting involved in that, and it turned out to be the Tankleffs."

"Were you doing drugs at your house?"

"Crack."

"Okay, so then what happened?"

"They went in Glenn's car, which was an old beat-up car, like from the late sixties or early seventies. That's why I guess he figured he had a better chance with my mother's car in Belle Terre."

"How did you find out it was the Tankleffs?"

"The next day I saw Glenn. He came to my house and he wanted to borrow some money. He was really shook up. He said when they left he drove them there, wherever Joey had to go in Belle Terre and Joey came out with blood on his clothes. Peter looked like he saw a ghost and they went and burned their clothes. I told him I didn't want to hear any more about it. I didn't want to be involved. I told him to leave, and keep his mouth shut."

Salpeter knew he had a home run. Ram perfectly corroborated the core of Harris's story. In the process, he may have also answered the only real point of doubt about it: Harris's claim that he drove to what he thought was a burglary and sat outside in the car. Ram's account was the missing link. Harris presumably knew Creedon and Kent were going to Belle Terre to do some dirty work—not necessarily to commit a murder but to "straighten somebody out." That might explain why Harris stayed outside, and why he would lie about thinking it was supposed to be a burglary. Admitting he knew what was planned—even if he couldn't have known it would get out of control—might get him in deeper than he was willing to go.

Salpeter loved how Ram presented himself. Whatever he'd done in the past, he seemed to have found a way to clean himself up. He was articulate and credible. He would come across much better than Harris would have. But the first thing Ram had said was that he wouldn't testify. With the hearing ongoing, Salpeter had no time to go through the usual routine of cultivating and coaxing a reluctant witness.

"Billy," he said, "I need you to testify."

"Okay," Ram said.

Salpeter was stunned. He had a much longer speech planned. "You will?" he said. "Wonderful. Great. You're doing the right thing."

Ram said he knew. That's why he was doing it.

BARKET AND POLLACK flew Ram to New York the following week. They interviewed him, got his affidavit, and sent him home. Then they brought him back up three weeks later with his girlfriend, Heather Paruta. Ram had talked to her about his knowledge of the Tankleff murders years earlier—around 1999, she thought—and again after the case returned to the news. And she had been instrumental in his decision to testify. When Salpeter left the messages at Ram's mother's house, it was Heather who got him to call back. And it was she who told him he had to come forward and testify. "He didn't want to do it," she said. "I talked him into it." That's why Ram agreed so quickly when Salpeter came to Florida. He had already made the decision. And now, as the hearing resumed after its three-month hiatus, she would follow him to the stand.

Ram and Paruta were scheduled to testify on Monday, but they were brought up on Friday to give Barket time to prep them. Heather had relatives on the Jersey shore, and Salpeter saw no harm in renting them a car to make a family visit over the weekend. He met them at Kennedy Airport, got the car, then checked them into the Marriott adjacent to Nassau Coliseum, a few minutes from Barket's office. They got the full Salpeter treatment: dinner with Cheryl to keep them on board and a prepaid cellphone to keep them close.

Ram and Paruta drove down to New Jersey on Saturday, and when Salpeter went to the hotel on Sunday to bring them to Barket's office, Ram had in his possession a filthy, smelly stray dog that he'd found along the Long Island Expressway and sneaked up to his hotel room. He was on the phone with the airline, trying to find out how much airfare would be for a little dog. It turned out to be a fortune, so then he started looking up animal rescue shelters. "This big guy takes a liking to this little dog," Salpeter said. "He gets it a bullshit leash and he's walking it around Bruce's office. This was when I started feeling anxious."

But it wasn't just Ram's testimony Salpeter was worried about. He had one more thing in mind, and he needed him to be of sound mind. He wanted him to try to hook up with Peter Kent. While wearing a wire. There was a risk of some bells going off in Kent's head—Billy Ram showing up out of the blue with all that was going on—but Salpeter wasn't worried. Neither was Ram. He said he'd do it.

Salpeter had one of his guys, an old pro on matrimonial stakeouts, confirm where Kent was living, and Ram went there and rang the bell. Kent's girlfriend answered and said he wasn't around. But she got him on the phone, and Ram made plans to see Kent later. Salpeter had Ram wired with a tape and sent him off, expecting him back in a couple of hours. But Ram went off the reservation. He stayed out all night, incommunicado. Salpeter stayed up, waiting to hear from him, trying to reach him. He dozed off on his couch a little before daybreak. Ram finally checked in around seven. He said he and Kent wound up driving into Manhattan. Did he say anything? Nothing direct, Ram said, but he complained about Harris "running his mouth" and Creedon "talking about every crime he ever committed." And he told Ram to keep his own mouth shut. If anyone asked him about that night in 1988, "You should just say we weren't there." But when Salpeter played the tape later that day, there was nothing intelligible on it.

Ram's testimony was moved to Tuesday. That meant another night to worry about for Salpeter, and Ram didn't disappoint. When Salpeter called the hotel room early in the morning, Heather said Billy went out, she didn't know where. Shit, Salpeter said. Fuck. Then Barket called. How's Ram? Salpeter said he hadn't talked to him yet, not exactly lying. He hung up, alternately cursing and praying. One of them worked. His phone rang.

"What time you picking us up?" Ram asked, his voice like gravel.

"Right now," Salpeter said.

He was at the hotel in ten minutes. He didn't ask Ram where he'd been. Judging by the way he looked, it wasn't tucked in bed.

"IT WAS A JEW in the bagel business," Ram said, when Barket asked him how Creedon described the person he wanted Ram's assistance in "straightening out" that night in Belle Terre.

Salpeter watched from the second row of the gallery, relieved—and impressed. Ram didn't look so good starting out that morning, but somehow he got it together. He was alert, articulate, forthright.

"Did you agree to do that?" Barket asked.

"No," said Ram.

"Why not?"

"Several reasons. The first being I wasn't in the habit of actually hurting people . . . I never really liked that. Number two . . . I didn't believe in bothering innocent people." And one more thing: "In a neighborhood like that, you're going to stick out. It's going to be investigated. Chances are you're not going to get away with it."

When Ram told Creedon no, "I think the only car available to him was Glenn's car." And Glenn said yes. The next day, Harris showed up back at Ram's house in an awful panic. "He said he thinks he's going to be in trouble. He thinks they did something bad. I think he went in with the mind that they were doing a burglary or something, not going to do what they did. And he said, 'They came running out of the house. They had blood on them. Peter was white as a ghost. Something bad happened.' And after that they went and burned their clothes. And I heard enough at that point. He was concerned about what he should do. I told him, you know, the best thing he could do is just keep his mouth shut and stay away from those guys."

What did he think when he heard later that day that a couple named the Tankleffs had been murdered in Belle Terre? "That there was a Jew in the bagel business," Ram said. And from that day forward he knew who killed the Tankleffs, and who didn't. It was an unspoken secret among their circle, though it came up from time to time, in veiled and offhanded ways. There was a rumor going around at one point that Harris and Kent were snitching on each other about a burglary. Ram talked about it with Creedon. "I told him, 'You know, if they're snitching, you'd be in jail for murder. So obviously they're not snitching.'"

"I want to bring you right up to today," Barket said. "Why didn't you come forward before now to talk about what you knew about the murders of Arlene and Seymour Tankleff?"

"Because back then I was in a real criminal lifestyle," Ram said. "I didn't want to be viewed as a snitch. I didn't want to be the one to break this whole thing open, you know?" After any of his many arrests and incarcerations, did he ever think of trading what he knew to help himself out? "Not really. I've always been against snitches and snitching. I believe if you're involved in something and you get caught, you take the time and you do it. It's a risk you're taking, you know? I mean, I had plenty of opportunities to snitch on people for other things. I was looking at a lot of time. It just wasn't in me to do it."

"What led you to do it now?"

"A few things. First of all, after spending six years in prison, I know what it's like. I know the hell that it is to be there for something you did do. And to know that this guy is in there for something that he *didn't* do, for much longer time, well, it just kind of weighed on my conscience. Then when I heard other people came forward, I wasn't going to be the only one, you know? I don't really view this as snitching, what I'm doing now. I'm not really trying to put somebody in jail. I don't care if those guys, frankly, whether they go to jail or not. That's not my business. I feel as though I've waited too long, and I need to help him get out if I can, you know?"

"Him being Marty?"

"Marty, yes."

"Are you getting anything for this?"

"Not at all."

"How is this going to help or hurt your parole?"

"It's probably going to hurt it. Because I don't think they're going to be, you know, favorable to me helping somebody out. It's kind of like going against them. That's why initially I didn't get back in touch with Jay. I just didn't want to be involved at all. I kind of look at parole, and the police and the district attorney—it's all one team, you know? I mean, I'm going against the team. I don't want to, but it's something I feel as though I have to do."

SALPETER BREATHED a huge sigh of relief when it was over. He thought Ram was "brilliant," and putting Heather on after him was a good move.

She was a solid citizen who wasn't from his world. She confirmed that Ram told her about the Tankleff case years earlier, and maybe she served as a kind of character reference for him.

Salpeter drove Ram and Paruta back to the hotel. When he arrived home, he noticed the prepaid cellphone he'd given Ram. He brought it inside, and early that evening a call came in on it. Salpeter answered it.

"Billy, what the fuck!"

Salpeter knew right away who it was. He decided to play along. "Whadya mean, what the fuck?"

"You tell me you're in fuckin' Chinatown coppin' drugs when you're on the stand testifyin' against me?"

"We got a problem now?" Salpeter said, trying his best to sound like Ram, trying to provoke Kent. "You don't like what I did?"

"Who the fuck is this?" Kent said. Then he hung up.

Salpeter called him back. "Peter, this is Jay Salpeter," he said.

"What the fuck do you want?" Kent asked.

"I want to talk to you."

"Fuck you."

"You don't want to talk to me? You really should talk to me."

"Why would I talk to you? I got no words for you, jerk-off. I got an airtight alibi."

"You got an airtight alibi?"

"Go fuck yourself," Kent said, and hung up again.

Salpeter had a thought. He flashed to that day a year earlier when Lato and Warkenthien could have had Kent but let him go. Salpeter decided to take a shot—play like the cop he used to be, try to persuade Kent that it was all over, Ram's testimony sealed the deal, better get out front, blame it all on Creedon. It was a real long shot, but Salpeter figured what the hell. He hit redial. The call went to voicemail. He left his pitch.

Hi, Peter, it's Jay. Apparently you don't want to speak to me, so maybe you can listen to my message. I'm sure you know what happened today in court. Bill testified, and of course we have knowledge of what happened that evening, that you were at Billy's house and you left with Joe. . . . The truth is coming out, there's no doubt about it, and believe me, Peter, there is more to come. So we'd love to have you aboard and I think Billy broke the ice with you regarding that the other day, that you're probably better off with being on the winning side, so please give me a call. . . .

Kent did give Salpeter a call. "I don't want your money," he said.

"What are you talking about?" Salpeter asked.

"I'm not takin' your money. Billy told me all about the fifty grand."

"Fifty grand? What the hell are you talking about?"

"You're talking about a winning team. Why would I want to come on your team? For what? Come on, man. And I'm forwarding this tape right now on to Lenny Lato."

A 440 HEARING is the mirror image of a trial, everything in reverse. The defense rests, and then the prosecution presents its own witnesses. When Lato began with Peter Kent, the hearing took on a bizarre quality, as if it were a crossover episode of *Law & Order* and *The Twilight Zone.*

Kent was straight out of central casting, a tall, thin man with a shaved head and a perpetual smirk. He emerged from a side door in an ill-fitting jacket and a tie that ended several inches above his waist. He was a thuggish man who didn't walk so much as strut. He fell into malapropisms whenever he veered from the street slang that seemed to be his native tongue. Where Creedon had been a little tense on the stand, Kent seemed to be enjoying himself. "Copy that," he would say, and give long, rambling answers that the judge would finally have to cut off: "Mr. Kent, he asks the questions and you give the answers, okay?" Copy that, Judge.

Lato had Kent run down his criminal history. This was so he could lay a foundation for his alibi, which was that he couldn't have been in Belle Terre committing murder because he was engaged elsewhere that night, robbing people and doing drugs. "I was actually indicted and arrested and served time for an armed robbery charge I did that day," he said cheerfully.

And he had the records to prove it. Lato handed Kent a parole document to refresh his recollection of his younger days. It showed an arrest for a string of robberies between August 31 and September 9, 1988, most of them committed with a man named Daniel Raymond. When Braslow expressed impatience with Kent testifying by simply reading from his arrest record, Lato told the judge, "I need to go through this because I'm establishing where he was at the time of the murder." He sounded like Kent's defense lawyer, though if an actual defense lawyer tried to claim Kent's testimony "established" an alibi, an actual prosecutor would have been hard-pressed not to laugh out loud.

The arrest record did indeed show two robberies on September 7, the date of the murders. Unfortunately for Kent, there are twenty-four hours in a day. The robberies were at 9 P.M. and 10:30 P.M. That was eighteen hours after Seymour Tankleff's poker game broke up.

"So where were you then, say, between three, four, five o'clock A.M. on September seventh?" Lato asked.

"I was in the city," Kent said.

"Doing what?"

"Cocaine and heroin."

And that was Kent's airtight alibi.

Then there was the business about Glenn Harris saying he saw Kent burning his clothes after he dropped him off at his mother's house in Selden. "Are you aware of that?" Lato asked.

"Yeah, I'm aware, I'm aware," Kent said. "I find that impossible, though, because my mother's house wasn't there. It was in Center Moriches."

"Did your mother ever live in Selden?"

"Yes, she did. But at that time on that date when this kid's family was murdered, my mother was not living in Selden."

"How do you know?"

"How do I know? Because I was in prison. When I came home, it was the year 1988 and I was arrested that year and that also happens to fall on my mother and sister's birthday, the date that this kid's parents were killed. . . . My mother's birthday is the third but they celebrate it together being their birthdays are so close. And they always done that year after year since I've been born, you know?"

Translation: In the middle of the robbery spree, he went to his mother's house for the birthday celebration. That was in Center Moriches. He remembered that because that's where she was living when he got out of prison. The problem was that Kent didn't even *enter* prison for the first time until nine months later. That was for the robberies for which he wasn't even arrested until five days after the murders.

"And another thing," Kent said, unprompted. "I read in the statement where he says that he's sitting in the car? Glenn was never one to be sitting in the car anywhere hanging out being a getaway driver for a burglary. That's ludicrous. Glenn was always the first one always to go into the house."

When he heard about Harris's statement about the Tankleff murders, he couldn't imagine why Glenn would make up such a story. And then he got the chance to ask Harris himself. It was a few weeks later, when they were both in the Suffolk County Jail. They ran into each other in the outside yard, though they were in different units so were separated by a fence. "I says, 'Glenn, what the fuck?' I said, 'Why the fuck would you do this to me? I never ever did nothing wrong onto you.' He says to me, 'Pete, you fucked with my old lady. You were doing my wife.'"

"By the way," Lato interjected, "were you?"

"Yeah," said Kent.

Later, on cross-examination, Barket asked Kent how Harris found out. "Lisa told him she hated his guts, she wanted nothing more to do with him," Kent said, "and he just, he's overcompulsively obsessed with her. I used to always tell him, 'Listen, bro, there's mad girls out there. Why you always obsessed with her?' She was my childhood sweetheart but I moved on, you know? I got numerous amounts of girlfriends over the years, you know what I'm saying? Just like I'm sure yourself, you would have too before you got married. I just haven't settled down yet."

"Okay, you're doing it once again," Braslow told Kent, then asked the spectators to stop laughing.

"My bad," said Kent. "I'm sorry. I'm just being real, man."

So how did Harris go from being mad at Kent for messing around with his wife to saying he drove him to a house where he and Creedon murdered two people fifteen years ago? "He says to me, 'I was propositioned while I was upstate in Clinton in the year 2000'—I think it was when he was doing a violation up in Clinton—'through a third party to find another party to tie up with Creedon that had involvements, already gave statements, onto this Tankleff case.' And he couldn't think of another better than me to fulfill his bendetta—his vendetta—onto me because, you know, he was hurting over the fact that I was doing his old lady. . . . He was also hurt to the fact that his kids were, you know, saying good things about me, that I was taking care of them. And you know, I just bought them basically simple stuff. You know, a couple pairs of shoes, some clothes for them. And you know basically I was just doing that to please the mother, know what I mean? Stay in good graces with her."

Translation: Four years ago, some "party" in prison told Harris he was arranging for Creedon to be blamed for the Tankleff murders and wanted to know if Harris could come up with someone else who could be blamed with Creedon. And Harris came up with Kent. Because he was mad at him for doing his wife and buying shoes for his kids.

Apparently this all sounded reasonable to Lato. "Now, did the subject of money come up in the conversation between you and Mr. Harris?" he asked.

"Yes, in fact it did," said Kent. "He told me that he was propositioned that if he could find somebody to hold down his statement with him he would be well taken care of and his kids would be taken care of, and he wouldn't have to worry about them. Like, he doesn't worry about them already as it is, but at least he would know that they would be well provided for."

"While you were talking with him, did you go over with him past crimes that the two of you committed?"

"Yeah, we happened to engage in a conversation like that. We did. I says to him, 'You know, you're crazy for even wanting to think that you could possibly have done this with me and Joey and you because it never went down. You know you're telling a lie.' He said, 'I know I'm telling a lie,' but he says, 'I want to try to help somebody out and do the right thing for once in my life.' . . . I said, 'You didn't do this, I wasn't there, you weren't there, this is all a lie. Why are you going there with this?' Then, in addition, we started talking about history about us together hanging out and some goofy times that we did."

Kent's cellphone rang. "My bad," he said.

"Nice beat," said Judge Braslow.

SO YOU HEARD that Glenn Harris had given you up in a double murder, Barket said to Kent in his cross-examination. And a few weeks later you ran into him inside the jail. "And you chatted about old times?"

"That's right," said Kent. Unlike an encounter he had with an inmate named Reyes. He went into the man's cell and beat him up. That's what got him sent to the special confinement area called the box.

"What did Mr. Reyes do to incur your wrath?" Barket asked.

"He disturbed my sleep when I asked him politely and nicely to not make any noise near my cell," Kent said. "And everybody else in the tier respected me, so there's no reason for him not to be an exception to the game."

"I'm sorry?"

"An exception to my rules and ethics to how I practice living."

"So you told him to let you sleep, he didn't, and the answer is he got beat up?"

"Bottom line, yeah."

"But Glenn, who accused you of murder, got a chat about the glory days of your teenage years?"

"Sure," said Kent. Then he added, "Man, if I could have got my hands on him, I would have beat flames out of him."

"Did you tell Glenn if you could get your hands on him, you'd kill him?"

"I didn't tell him I would kill him. I told him I would beat him up, because I'm not a killer."

Barket backtracked a month, to October 7, 2003, the day Kent was brought to the district attorney's office. It was five days after the 440 motion was filed and Harris's statement became public. "Had you heard at that point in time from newspaper accounts that Glenn Harris had implicated you and Mr. Creedon in the murder of Marty's parents?"

"Actually, I was in the box when the incident took place. And we're not allowed no newspapers up in there."

"And you were told that fact by either Mr. Lato or Mr. Warkenthien, is that correct?"

"Correct."

"And at that point in time, you began to cry?"

"I was upset over the fact, yeah."

"The reports I have here indicate that there were tears in your eyes, that you began to cry."

"Is that what it says?" Kent asked.

"I'm asking you if that's what happened, sir."

"I was emotionally disturbed of the fact, yeah. Yeah. Sometimes when I get emotional, I cry, sure, no question about it. I cried."

"You've been arrested twenty times?"

"I've never been arrested for murder."

"You've done six years in a state prison, you did other time in local prisons, yes?"

"Yes."

"When Mr. Lato and Mr. Warkenthien said Harris implicated you in the murder of the Tankleffs, your reaction was to shed tears."

"Yeah."

"You knew Glenn had just given you up, didn't you."

"No."

". . . Now, in your quest to get money for drugs, you've testified, you were willing to do armed robberies . . . to break into people's houses . . . to point a gun in somebody's face and steal money from them, correct?"

Yep, said Kent, all those things.

"So if Joseph Creedon and Glenn Harris had said to you, 'Hey, we got a burglary to do to get some money up in Belle Terre,' that would have been just par for the course, right?"

"Never took place, though. Never happened. We were never to-gether."

"You were never together?"

"Not that night."

Barket kept at him, until Kent finally shot back, in a moment reminiscent of Marty's trial, "I was not there. I'm not a defendant, man. This is crazy."

Barket read again from Lato's report: *Kent stated that although Creedon was capable of committing a murder, Kent was not, nor was Harris.* "What made you think that Joey was capable of murder?" he asked Kent.

"Because he has the name Joey Guns," Kent replied.

"Because you watched him beat Marty's mother and father to death, didn't you!"

"No, you're wrong. You're wrong."

"You didn't think there was going to be a murder that night, you thought it was just a robbery or a burglary to get money for drugs—isn't that true, sir?"

"Untrue. I was never there."

"And we know that, of course, because you were busy committing other robberies and buying drugs for yourself, right?"

"That's right."

TO LENNY LATO, Kent's night out with Billy Ram in October was a gift. And it became the gift that kept on giving.

Kent's elaborate account began with Ram's appearance at his door out of the blue. "He said we need to talk, hang out and get high for old times' sake," Kent said. "I says, 'Sure. Right now I'm a little broke on cash and I'll be more than happy to get high, help you spend some of your money, no problem.'"

So Ram picked him up and they drove into the city. On the way, "We spoke about how he was supposed to be the go-between man between me and the Tankleff guy. Jay Salpeter had set up an account for some money for me to take . . . because he was getting paid for his statements."

"Did he tell you how much money he was getting?" Lato asked.

"Yeah. He said he was getting ten grand and he said he had an account number for Western Union numbers set up for me to receive fifty thousand dollars. That's what he said."

Then they got to the city. "We copped some heroin and crack. We went to a bodega, picked up a crack pipe, some screens . . . We proceeded to drive around the city, getting high, and we stopped at a few spots here and there 'cause, you know, he kept rambling on about how I should take this money, it's a window opportunity, just take it and join the winning team, get ahold of that cash cow while you can get it. And I said to him, 'I'm not taking nothing. You ain't going to talk me into taking nothing.' I said, 'I don't even want to talk about this.'" Later on, "He continued to tell me about the cash cow. He [wanted to find out] where a Western Union machine is so we can get this money. He just kept saying, 'Come on, let's get this money.'"

Salpeter sat in the gallery, trying to make sense of what Kent was saying. He would have dismissed it altogether if not for one thing: the reference to Western Union. That *was* how he had wired money to Ram to cover his travel expenses. Did Ram try to get Kent to talk by telling him there was money in it for him? Was this something cooked up between Kent and the DA's office? The only thing clear was that Ram's escapade began a game of inane intrigue. Kent didn't know Ram had a concealed tape recorder with him that night. Salpeter didn't know whether Ram deliberately botched the recording. And the defense team didn't know, until now, that *Kent* later tried to get *Ram* on tape for the district attorney's office. Twelve days before he took the stand, he'd sat with Warkenthien at the DA's office and tried to call Ram in Florida. "We were attempting to catch Bill stating that he was getting paid for his testimony," he said. But they couldn't reach him and didn't try again.

Kent was in high spirits when he came out of the courtroom. He was trailed by reporters and stopped to answer a few questions. Such as, why he cried when Lato told him about Harris's statement. "When they brang me in," Kent said, "they told me that, 'We don't believe that you did this.' I mean, I thought maybe like they were trying to play tricknology games with me, you know? Saying, 'Yeah, Peter, we don't think you really did it, but just come on, come forward,' you know?"

Apparently even Kent himself couldn't believe that Lato and Warkenthien didn't go for the kill when he started to cry. He sure was relieved when he realized they weren't playing any tricknology games; they just wanted to help him with his airtight alibi.

SENDING BILLY RAM out to get Kent incriminating himself on tape turned out to be one of those decisions Salpeter wished he could take back. Not only didn't it work, but it caused a lot of unnecessary trouble. Though Ram's supposed promise of a $50,000 payment from a "Western Union machine" was absurd, Lato seized the opportunity to suggest that the Tankleff team was going around bribing witnesses. That word even made it into a headline in the *New York Daily News:* TANKLEFF CASE BRIBE HINT.

Lato subpoenaed Salpeter to the stand. But since he had no actual evidence, the prosecutor didn't bring up anything about cash cows and Western Union accounts, leaving that for the TV cameras in the hallway. Instead, he questioned Salpeter about the $4,000 paid to Ram to cover his lost pay for the two trips to New York. Ram himself had testified about the reimbursements, and Barket had since provided Lato and the judge with Ram's pay stubs and a letter from his employer, verification they had told Ram they would require. The defense also cited state bar ethics rules, showing that the payments were permissible and routine.

Barket and Pollack were seething about Lato's attack on their integrity, but there was an upside to Lato putting Salpeter on the stand. "Crossexamining" his own investigator gave Barket a forum for setting the record straight. "After you heard Peter Kent's testimony about a fifty-thousanddollar account," he asked Salpeter, "did you go to Western Union to determine whether or not that was even possible?"

"I learned that they do not offer an account where you could put money like a bank account or an ATM account," Salpeter said. "That's not one of their services."

"In fact, the only use you made of Western Union was to reimburse [Ram] for the two days he was up here to be interviewed by us," Barket said, virtually testifying himself by simply having Salpeter confirm his statements. "And from a defense cost standpoint, that was actually cheaper for us than having myself, Mr. Pollack, and you fly to Florida, lose time for, forgive me, from our hourly billing."

Barket tried to handle the issue straightforwardly, but his anger wasn't far beneath the surface, and it erupted during an argument that escalated until Lato finally asked, "Will you stop yelling?"

"You want me to yell?" Barket shot back. "You want me to yell? Don't accuse us of bribery! That's what this is about, Judge. Let's not put any mask on it. It's nonsense!"

To the Tankleff team's chagrin, Billy Ram continued to plague the case long after he left the witness stand. In the very week that Kent was on the stand testifying about his night on the town with Ram in October, Ram was back in Tampa creating even more problems for the Tankleff defense, and certainly for himself. He went on a spree of armed robberies that led to a shootout with the police, putting him first in the hospital and then back in prison for a long, long time. Salpeter wasn't shocked that Ram fell into his old ways, but he felt partly responsible. It was likely Ram's drug binge with Kent that set his downward spiral in motion. Ram had told Salpeter he lost his job after he returned to Florida, and the rest wasn't hard to imagine. The only thing that surprised Salpeter was how spectacularly Ram flamed out.

Salpeter found himself trying to keep up with Ram's brushfires. He was on the stand to explain the money Ram was paid, but now he had another job: persuading the judge that Ram's recent relapse, extreme as it was, didn't mean his testimony wasn't credible. To do that, Barket had Salpeter testify about a source he'd developed in the old Selden crowd who had corroborated Ram's testimony even before Salpeter found Ram. Don Oakes had told Salpeter that Glenn Harris was telling the truth about that night, at least the part about being at Billy Ram's house with Creedon and Kent and leaving from there to do a job in Belle Terre. Oakes knew this because way back in 1990—during Marty's trial—Ram told him the same thing. But Oakes refused to testify out of fear of Creedon. "If you subpoena me, I'll disappear," he told Barket and Salpeter. But because of the developments with Ram, Barket decided to out him—over Salpeter's strenuous objections.

All this took a toll on Salpeter. Lato had made him a target since the very first day of the hearing, when the prosecutor suggested he was in this for the publicity and grilled him about his relationship with Harris. When he returned to the stand five months later to answer questions about how much Ram was paid, Salpeter started feeling chest pains. He knew he had done nothing wrong. But as tough as he could be in some ways, he was a man who took things very personally and just couldn't let them roll off his back. The chest pains came and went the rest of the day, and when he finally said something to Cheryl over dinner, she insisted he go to the hospital. At least let me finish my salmon, he told her. After a night on monitors, the news was good. Diagnosis: stress.

Lato wasn't finished trying to show that Ram had been bought. Warkenthien called Ram's lawyer in Tampa, Hubbell Losson, and proposed a trade. "We know Ram was bribed," Warkenthien said, and if he were to "come clean" and admit his perjury and implicate members of the Tankleff legal team, the Suffolk County DA's office would talk to the Florida authorities about reducing his sentence. Ram's response when his lawyer told him about Warkenthien's offer: He wasn't bribed, he didn't lie, and "they have an innocent kid in jail up there."

Salpeter heard about this first from Ram himself. Then Barket called Losson, who confirmed the account and put it in a sworn statement that Barket submitted to Braslow as evidence of witness tampering and slander. But the most significant thing about Warkenthien's maneuver was its failure. In that way, he did the defense a favor. "Ram's refusal to even consider recanting his testimony before this Court—even for a reduction in a lengthy prison sentence—adds to his credibility," Barket wrote. "If Ram were the sort who would commit perjury in exchange for money, as the prosecution has suggested, one would expect him to jump at the chance to reduce his prison sentence, especially if all that he needs to do is to 'come clean.'" Lato's reply claimed that Warkenthien simply told Losson "that there were allegations that some of the Tankleff witnesses may have been paid," and that he asked the lawyer to ask Ram if he "knew anything about it."

FIFTEEN MINUTES OF FAME. Jealousy. Love. Hate. Revenge. Money. These were the motives Lenny Lato attributed to the defense witnesses. But the truth was that it was the prosecution that had the power to influence testimony with either inducement or intimidation, and no one illustrated the point better than the case's most elusive witness. Four months after he told the defense team that he passed the Tankleff "work" on to Creedon after Jerry Steuerman offered it to him first, Brian Scott Glass finally came to court.

There had been some developments since that night when Glass came to Barket's office looking for a free lawyer. Two weeks later, Glass surrendered on his outstanding armed robbery charge, appearing at his arraignment with a lawyer at his side. Not a lawyer, however, that an unemployed street criminal such as Scott Glass might be expected to retain. William Wexler was one of the more prominent criminal defense attorneys in Suffolk County. The son of a federal judge, he was a specialist in white-collar crime whose previous cases included a ninety-count indictment of the county sheriff and undersheriff for using their office as a political shakedown operation. Two other interesting facts about Scotty Glass's new lawyer: He shared an office with Jack Braslow, father of the judge, and Richard Schaffer, the Suffolk County Democratic chairman, both key political patrons of Tom Spota. And Wexler also happened to be a good friend of Lenny Lato's.

Though Glass had served two stretches in prison and was now charged with a violent felony, the district attorney's office consented to his release without bail—ROR, as it was known, for "released on his own recognizance." Two months later, Glass was in trouble again. He was accused of calling an adversary on the phone and saying, "I'm going to kill you and put you in a box." An arrest warrant was issued, but the police didn't find Glass until late one night two weeks later, at which time he claimed to be someone else. While searching Glass's pockets, the police found a crack pipe with some cocaine residue. All told that night, he was charged with criminal possession of a controlled substance, criminal impersonation, and the initial aggravated harassment.

At his arraignment the next morning, which Wexler did not attend, an assistant district attorney told the judge that in addition to the three new misdemeanor charges, Glass had an open felony charge (the armed robbery for which he had been ROR'd), two other open warrants, six prior failures to appear in court, and one probation revocation.

"I can't afford bail," Glass told the judge.

The judge looked at his rap sheet. "Based on the fact that you have twenty-five total arrests, six failures to appear—"

"And my lawyer is Bill Wexler . . ."

"ROR," said the judge.

When Barket caught wind that Glass had surfaced with Wexler as his lawyer, that he'd been released without bail on the armed robbery charge and again only weeks later, he suspected something was up. He called Wexler, who told him that Glass was no longer willing to testify in the Tankleff hearing. He says he made up the story he told you, Wexler told Barket. Now Barket was sure something was up. He had no objection to putting the story out.

Barket laid out the sequence of events for *Newsday*'s Zachary Dowdy: A witness gives us exculpatory information and agrees to testify. He needs a lawyer for an armed robbery charge. We tell him we can't help him with that. He says he'll testify anyway. He bails on us. Two weeks later he surfaces with a well-connected attorney and turns himself in. It's a violent felony, the guy has a record as long as your arm, but the DA consents to spring him with no bail. And the guy withdraws his exculpatory information. "You tell me who influenced that witness," Barket said.

Dowdy called Lato, who told him Barket's allegation was ludicrous. Then Dowdy asked him why Brian Scott Glass, a repeat felon, had been given an ROR on a violent crime that could send him away for twenty-five years. Lato said he didn't know the particulars of Glass's case, but that it was common practice for the DA's office to consent to low bail or none at all in exchange for help in making other cases. Was that the case here? Lato couldn't say, since he didn't know the particulars. But one thing he did know: The defense lawyers were creating a conspiracy in their minds. "There isn't a shred of evidence that anybody intimidated this guy."

Not yet. Barket called Wexler and told him he was going to subpoena Glass to testify. He was going to get to the bottom of this. No need for a subpoena, Wexler told him. He'll testify voluntarily.

In early December, Glass strutted to the witness stand in a turtleneck and sport jacket.

"Good afternoon, Mr. Glass," said Barket. "We've met before, is that correct?"

Sure, said Glass.

In July, did you tell my colleagues and me that Jerry Steuerman came to you about hurting his business partner? "Yep." And that Steuerman told you the partner owed him money? "Right." And that you turned it down because you didn't see why the job was to hurt the partner rather than to just collect the money he owed? "Yeah."

"And you—do you have a phone ringing or something?"

"It's not a phone. It's a pack of cigarettes."

"I saw you reaching for something, so if you're distracted I'll wait a second."

"It was a gun," said Lato, such a kidder.

"And you indicated," Barket continued, "that you had passed that work, if you will, on to a person by the name of Joseph Creedon, correct?"

"No, I said he might have learned in passing as I was speaking about it," Glass said.

"Now, the information you gave us . . . did those events actually occur?"

"No."

"You made that up?"

"Yeah."

"And what led you to do that?"

"Umm, I don't know," said Glass. "I was bored."

"So you made up an account of Mr. Steuerman offering you work to harm his business partner . . . because you were bored?"

"No, because you offered to get me a lawyer."

By Glass's telling, he went to Barket's office with no intention of asking for anything. But right up front—starting in the car, when Salpeter picked him up—the Tankleff defense team came out and offered to get him a lawyer for his armed robbery case. So he figured, hey, great, and made up a story.

"So, but for the fact that I somehow represented that I'd find a lawyer to help you with your third felony, you wouldn't have lied to us?"

"Listen," said Glass, "you were bullshitting me and I was bullshitting you. Let's face it. So was Jay. Come on."

"And somehow you ended up with a lawyer within a couple of weeks."

"Yeah, I borrowed five thousand dollars off my mother."

"And the lawyer that you ended up with is the gentleman sitting over here," Barket said. "And how did you find your way to Mr. Wexler?"

"I went down to Sunrise Highway to Bay Shore toward Deer Park Avenue."

"He's giving you directions," Lato observed.

"Yes, I gather that," Barket said. "How did you learn of Mr. Wexler's name?" he asked Glass.

"I'm going to object, Judge," Wexler interjected.

Barket told Braslow the whole thing smelled, and he had the right to get to the bottom of it. "Mr. Glass's account of this is incredible on its face. He's telling the Court that he was willing to posit some story about Mr. Steuerman in exchange for me getting him, quote-unquote, a 'free lawyer.' Three weeks later, he ends up in court with the son of a federal judge, the good friend of Mr. Lato, and an ROR after making a deal with the DA's office. But those circumstances have nothing to do with the fact that he is no longer willing to testify to the fact that Steuerman offered him money to hurt Marty's father, just before Joseph Graydon went out to hurt Marty's father on behalf of Creedon."

If he couldn't ask Glass about it, Barket wanted to put Wexler himself on the stand. Denied, said Braslow. He demanded to know what evidence Barket had that there was a deal to keep Glass from testifying truthfully.

"This is circular," Barket said: How could he show that without questioning the people involved?

"Ain't that client-lawyer privilege?" Glass chimed in at one point.

Barket cited federal case law to support his position, but when he tried again, asking Glass if he had made a deal with the DA's office, Braslow shut him down. "Mr. Barket, you're done," said the judge.

Glass left the courtroom with Wexler, and when a photographer stepped up to take a picture as they made their way to the elevator, Glass smiled and put his arm around his lawyer, who seemed to be making an effort not to look as uncomfortable as he appeared.

WITNESS CHANGES HIS STORY was the headline in the next day's *Newsday*. At the Nassau County Jail, Mark Callahan read the article, did some soul-searching, and decided to write a letter to Marty Tankleff. The next thing he knew he was getting a visit from Bruce Barket. Do you know Marty? Barket wanted to know. No, said Callahan, I don't even know what he looks like. You never bumped into each other in jail? No, never. Why are you coming forward? I don't know, Callahan said. I really don't. I just am.

Mark Callahan had known Scott Glass since he was a kid. Glass and his crowd were a decade older, and Callahan looked up to them. "They were the guys that people feared in our neighborhood," he said. "They had beautiful girls, they had endless amounts of parties, drugs. I wanted to be like them." When Callahan was eighteen, Glass talked to him about loyalty. He used the murder of two people that he was somehow connected with as a reference. "It was like a threat, 'You could end up like that if you ever turned on me.'" The reference wasn't so vague the next time. Glass told Callahan that he was offered the Tankleff murders. "He told me he passed that down. He could have had the chance to do it himself but he passed it down to Joey Guns."

Barket had always been puzzled by Glass's stated reason for turning down "the work" from Steuerman: that he "didn't like the way he put it." In fact, Barket told Glass that night in his office, "This makes no sense. Why would you turn it down? It's what you *do*." Callahan had the answer: It was common knowledge among their crowd that Glass didn't have the stomach for serious violence. Dead bodies spooked him. He discovered this when he was involved in a shooting back in the 1980s, and it traumatized him, gave him nightmares. He got teased about it.

Callahan ran into Glass over the summer. "He told me what was going on, that you guys have contacted him and he was thinking about helping you guys." And then he saw Glass again a couple of months later. This time they were in a holding cell at one of the Suffolk County district courts. They were both waiting to be arraigned—Glass on his various new charges, Callahan for violating an order of protection. Callahan asked him what was going on with the Tankleff case. Glass told him he'd changed his mind about testifying. As Callahan later put it when he took the witness stand, "He said he's not going to go through with what he originally was going to go through, and that was helping you guys. And in more words than one, he pretty much put it that the district attorney is putting pressure on him to change his statement and he's looking at a lot of time because he was charged with an armed robbery. . . . He didn't exactly say who, but he said somebody told him that if he goes through with it, they're going to make it tough for him. And he's a two-time violent felony offender as it is, so he's looking at twenty-five to life."

But Glass didn't spend a day in prison. Eight months later, the armed robbery charge disappeared, as did the assorted lesser offenses.

CHAPTER 35

Son of Guns

IN FEBRUARY 2005, the hearing came to a close after thirty-six witnesses had testified over twenty days spread intermittently across six months. The defense and prosecution were to submit their posthearing briefs and final arguments by the end of the spring. And then Judge Braslow would decide whether Marty Tankleff's convictions should be vacated and a new trial held.

One morning a few days after the hearing ended, Salpeter was getting coffee in the cafeteria of his building when his cellphone rang. Terry Covais was calling from Florida. She sounded anxious. "Joseph wants to talk to you about something," she said. "Something important."

"What's going on?" Salpeter asked.

"It's about his father. But it has to be between us. He's scared, Jay."

Salpeter knew that Terry's sixteen-year-old son had had a reunion with his father a year earlier. He told her he'd call her back in a few minutes. He went upstairs, engaged his tape recorder, and punched in Terry's phone number. Her son answered. "Hi, how ya doin', man?" he said.

"How you doing?" Salpeter said. "So, right, it's between us."

"Yeah, uh, I had a talk with Mom, y'know. What I'm saying, he told me some stuff when I was up there."

"What did he tell you?"

"I don't even want to say right now."

"But you did call me to tell me something."

"Yeah. I called you to tell you that if there's any way I can get in touch with him I could probably crack your whole case."

"In touch with who, your father?"

"Yes. . . . My mom's on the phone right now."

"Terry, you on?" Salpeter asked.

"Yeah, I'm here," Terry said.

"I think you've learned to trust me, Terry."

"Yeah," said Terry, "but let me tell you, what I heard last night is pretty damn scary. So scary that I couldn't sleep last night and I couldn't go to work today."

"What did you hear?"

"I can't say."

"Should I come down there and talk?"

"I don't know. He's scared, Jay, and so am I."

JOSEPH CREEDON, JR., was five years old when his father put an Uzi in his hands. "I'm holding on to the gun, my finger's under his finger," he remembered, "and we're shooting out the window of the dining room."

Such was life as the son of Joey Guns.

And such was life that his early memories were sprinkled with images he wished he could forget. "I remember walking into the house and seeing him having my mom by the throat up against the wall. One time when we were at my Aunt Maryann's house, I looked out the window. My mom was sitting on the swing set and he just punched her in the mouth. She started crying. She had a tooth in her hand."

In January 1995, when he was six and his sister, Crystal, was four, their mother had had enough. Terry had an option. Over the holidays, she had reconnected with her high school boyfriend, Lenny Covais. Conveniently, Lenny lived three thousand miles away. He went home and sent her three plane tickets to Seattle. Creedon had made it clear he wouldn't stand for her taking his kids away from him—"He told me he would chop me into little pieces and nobody would ever find me," Terry said—so there could be no goodbyes. "I packed our bags and got the hell out of there."

Terry changed the children's names to Guarascio, her maiden name. Eventually she married Lenny and became Terry Covais. But she never stopped feeling as if they were on the run from Creedon. In her house, he was a forbidden subject. But Joseph didn't quite understand why he didn't see his father anymore. One day he found a picture of him in an old photo album. He took it out and hid it from his mother inside his pillowcase. "I looked at it every time I went to bed," he said. "Then my mom caught me looking at it one night and she took it away. I found it in the garbage ripped up. I kind of got angry—'That's messed up. He's my dad.' She would say he's a bad man and she put up with his abuse for nine years. And I started thinking, Yeah, that did happen and I didn't want that to happen. But then I kept telling my mom maybe he changed."

When Joe was ten, he came home from school one day and found his mother crying. "Your father found us," she told him. "He called the apartment." She changed their phone number and gave a picture of Creedon to the principal at Joseph and Crystal's school. A few months later, Lenny was laid off from his job at Boeing. They moved back across the country, to Sarasota, Florida, where Terry's sister and brother lived. Years went by without any contact from Creedon, but Terry never completely let her guard down. It was why she wouldn't talk to Salpeter for nearly a year, and why it was months more before she agreed to see him. Then everything changed.

One day in the fall of 2003, when he was fifteen, Joe was getting his hair cut, as usual, by Carol Fields at a salon in Sarasota called Today's Cut. Fields was a transplant from Long Island, and so was one of the other haircutters in the shop. Port Jefferson came up and Joe remarked that his father was from around there. "Did you ever hear of the Tankleffs?" he asked Carol.

"Yeah, I heard of the Tankleffs," she said. "Why?"

"They think my dad murdered them," Joe said, almost matter-of-factly.

Carol stopped cutting and stepped in front of the chair. "Who's your dad?" she asked.

"Joe Creedon."

"You're *Joe Guns's* son?"

"You know my dad?"

"Yes, I know him. I cut his hair for years."

Joe told her he hadn't seen his father in more than eight years. Carol said she knew that. She cut his hair for years, remember? Before he left, Joe asked her if she could get in touch with him. Carol told him she probably could—did he want her to? Joe said he wanted to think about it. And talk to his mom. He said he'd let her know and left. A few minutes later, Terry came roaring into the shop. "She was shaking, crying, begging," Carol remembered. "'Do not tell him where I am. He will kill me and my children. Do you know what he's done? He will kill us.' I told her, 'I won't, I won't, calm down.' She needed a Xanax."

But Carol had a problem: The next time young Joe came in, he told her he'd been thinking about it and he really did want to talk to his father. "Joey begged me to get in touch with his dad," she recalled. "I was adopted, so I knew what he was feeling." And there was one other thing: What if Creedon found out she knew where his kids were and didn't tell him? Joe Guns was not the kind of guy you wanted mad at you. Carol called her friend Patricia on Long Island. They worked together at the hair salon in Selden, and Patricia had introduced Carol to Creedon. "I told Patricia, 'I found Guns's kids. What should I do?'" Carol said. "I was a nervous wreck. We went back and forth, and finally Patricia said she would tell him if I didn't. I said, all right, go ahead. She gave him my number. He called and says"—she mimicked Creedon's wiseguy voice—"'You found my fuckin' kids?'"

When Joe came in for his next haircut, Carol asked if he wanted to speak to his father. Now Joe hesitated. He wanted to connect with his father, but he was worried about his mother. "Yeah," he said finally. Carol handed him her cellphone.

Joe talked to his father for the first time in eight years, more than half his life. And they both cried. "Don't you tell no one," Creedon said. "Nobody's ever seen me cry."

Joe may have been hesitant about talking to his father, but now that he had him, he wasn't shy. He asked him why he broke up the family by beating his mother. Creedon told his son that he was a changed man—he had gone to anger management, he was doing a lot better, and he would never hurt her again. Would it be okay if I came down? No, Joe told him, thinking of his mother, not just yet.

In March 2004, Creedon's sister and father flew to Sarasota and spent a day with Joe. They took him to get a cellphone, and the first call he got was from his father. "I told Grandpa to get you some new clothes," Creedon told Joe, "anything you want." When Joe came home with a cellphone and a stack of new clothes and a pair of shoes, Terry asked him what was going on.

Joe fessed up. "Momma," he said, "I've been talking to Dad. He's been sending me money, and he sent Aunt Maryann and Pop Pop down."

Terry was scared, but she felt that Joe was old enough to have a say in all this. She asked him if he wanted to see his father. Joe said he thought so. But something besides his mother's fears was still holding him back. As he put it, "Should I meet up with this guy that's supposedly a murderer?" He didn't want to believe it and told himself maybe it wasn't true. Yeah, he told his mother, he wanted to see his father.

That night, Terry called Creedon. She was shaking, her heart pounding, but she managed to punch in the number. To her surprise, to say nothing of her relief, he didn't sound angry—he sounded almost contrite. "I'm not the way I used to be," he told her. "I don't do drugs no more, I don't collect. I got a body shop. I'm doin' really good." They talked for a couple of hours, but the one subject Terry did not bring up was the Tankleff murders. She didn't want to know. And when Creedon asked if it would be all right if he came down, she said okay. Because he asked. But she still didn't want him to know where they lived. They would meet at the Sarasota Square Mall.

Creedon flew down the next day. "He took a taxi from Tampa. It cost him a hundred ninety-two dollars," Joe recalled. "When he first saw me, he said, 'My boopee-doopee boy!' I said, 'What the hell are you talking about?' He said, 'You used to call me boopee-doopee dad.' He threw his necklace around my neck. Big necklace with a nice cross. I was nervous, and was afraid for my mom. She didn't want to come, but she did it for me. You should have seen her face when he got out of that taxi. All she could do was hold on to me and cry, for a good fifteen minutes. I'm trying to talk to him and he's like, 'What's she crying for?'"

Terry said, "I always said God made Joseph big to be my bodyguard against Joe Creedon."

Creedon's sister and father joined them for dinner, but his thirteen-year-old daughter didn't. Crystal didn't remember her father, and based on what she'd heard she had no interest in meeting him now.

Her brother, though, was clearly happy to be reconnecting with his father. He cut school the next day to hang out with him at his hotel—unbeknownst to his mother. They played shuffleboard at the hotel. In the middle of the game they had a push-up contest. Joe did ten, but his father couldn't match him. Creedon used to be able to pump out fifty, no sweat, until he got shot in the arm by Todd Steuerman.

At one point Joe broached the subject of the Tankleff murders. "I ain't worried about it," his father told him. "My lawyer told me I got nothing to worry about. If I did, I wouldn't be in this country." Joe didn't pursue the implication. When his father left for the airport later that day, they hugged each other goodbye, promising another visit soon. Maybe next time in New York. Until then, they'd stay in touch by cellphone.

The next visit came sooner than expected—only a couple of weeks later. Terry's brother, John Guarascio, called to say that his wife, Marilyn, had died of the cancer she'd been diagnosed with only a few months earlier. Terry, Joe, and Crystal came up for the funeral, their first time back on Long Island since they left without a forwarding address.

After the wake, Joe called his father, and they spent some time together that night. Creedon took Joe around in his black Mercedes, introducing him to all the people he knew. He showed him his Harley and Joe was impressed. The next morning, they went out to a bagel store. The line was out the door, but Joe followed his father straight to the front. But when he asked about the body shop his father said he owned, it turned out it was his friend's shop. When Joe asked his father what he was doing for work, Creedon admitted that he was still collecting.

As they cruised around town, Joe had something on his mind. In the two weeks since his father's visit to Florida, *48 Hours* had aired its segment on the Tankleff case. Salpeter had called Terry to let her know it would be on, and she and Joe watched it together. "I made him watch," Terry said.

Joe saw a mug shot of his father and heard Erin Moriarty's ominous voiceover: *Joseph Creedon, known on the street as Joey Guns, has a long criminal record. Apparently, Creedon has bragged to several people over the years that he was involved in the killings.* Glenn Harris was seen telling his story, then being asked if he was afraid of Creedon. "Of course I am," Harris said.

Joe was unsettled by what he saw. "Do you think he's involved in these things?" he asked his mother.

"It kind of looks like it to me, Joe," she said. "I have no trouble believing it."

While they were driving to the bagel store, Joe decided to put it to his father. "I saw that TV show," he said. "They had that investigator saying he knows you did it."

Creedon laughed. "He don't know his ass from his elbow," he said.

"Well, did you do it?" Joe asked. Creedon was taken aback by his persistence, but waved off the question and pulled up to the bagel store. He came out with a baker's dozen and a newspaper. "I wonder if my face is in the paper today," he said.

Later that day, Creedon brought Joe to his mother's house in Selden. It was the house where Harris said he dropped Creedon that night in 1988. Joe spent a few minutes with his grandmother, then went upstairs with his father. Creedon brought him into his old room, which had a bed, a dresser, and a safe.

Creedon went into the closet and brought out a folder of papers. There was information about Terry and her husband—their address in Seattle, where Lenny worked, Social Security numbers. "He said the only thing that stopped him from killing my mom and my stepdad was that it would traumatize me," Joe later said.

Creedon bent down to the safe and dialed the combination. "He opened it up and there was a whole bunch of stolen jewelry that was still in a display case," Joe said. "Rings and necklaces and chains. The rings still had the little tags on them. It was like a jewelry store. There was money on the bottom, stacks and stacks. He told me if I moved up with him and left my mother this would all be mine. You know, 'If you come live with me you'd get anything you want.'"

Seeing that his father was apparently not leading the straight life he had professed, Joe was moved to bring up the Tankleff murders yet again. He asked him if he was worried about the man he saw on television, the one who was saying he drove him and the other guy to that rich neighborhood. Harris? Creedon asked. Nah, he wasn't worried about him. He reached under the bed and pulled out a black bag, opened it, and showed his son a gun, a pair of handcuffs, and ankle shackles. "This is for Harris if he testifies," he said. He reached under the mattress and pulled out three more guns.

Joe was unnerved by his father's show-and-tell session, but it made him more curious. He kept probing. "I just had to know," he said later. "When we were on the way back from my grandma's house, I asked him again, I said, 'Dad, did you do this?' At first he just sort of changed the subject. I said, 'Seriously, did you do this?' And he got very serious and he said, 'Yeah, I did it.' And he began telling me how he did it. He said it was him, Peter Kent, and Glenn Harris, but Harris didn't go in with them. He said his buddy Todd, his dad was waiting and gave them a signal and he and Peter Kent went into the house. He said he brought a brake cable from a bicycle that had the cover stripped off and he used it to choke the man. They hit him with a snub-nose .38 special. He said Kent stabbed the lady in the bed."

Joe was stunned. "Just think about a fifteen-year-old boy hearing all this stuff from a dad he hasn't seen in ten years. I'm thinking to myself, 'I'm in the car with a murderer. He's supposed to be my dad.' I felt sort of unsafe but I didn't want to show it. I didn't want to say anything, I didn't want him mad. I didn't want him to think, 'Oh, I messed up big time telling this kid.'" His father continued revealing details, almost randomly, as if running the events through his mind for the first time since that night. "He said he went up some steps and looked into Marty's room and saw he was asleep. When they left, they had to go back because they left the pipe. As they were driving away, Harris tossed the pipe. And then he went to a house where a guy named 'Ronnie Reefer' lived and burned his clothes in his basement. He said that was the basement where he used to torture people."

And he said something else: that Jim McCready was paid $100,000 to protect the actual murderers. "He said they were friends and still talked now and then," Joe later said, "and he was still in touch with Jerry Steuerman."

That night, Joe's aunt, Creedon's sister Maryann, told him, out of the blue, "If you ever testified against your dad, they're going to put him away for life." Joe looked at her blankly, taken aback. He was so troubled by everything he heard and saw that day that he told no one, not even his mother. *Especially* not his mother. "If my dad thought I told my mom," he explained later, "she might be in danger from him."

The Tankleff hearing began three months later, and when Terry told Joe she was being subpoenaed to testify, he begged her not to go. But he wouldn't tell her why. She told him she had to testify, and it was the right thing to do. Joe was hugely relieved when she returned home safely. And then he went back to trying to lock away what he knew. Tried to pretend that day with his father never happened. But it was impossible. He couldn't stop thinking about it.

Months went by, and hardly a day passed without his father's admissions invading his thoughts. And then, finally, one night in February 2005, ten months after the trip to New York, he couldn't hold it in any longer. Lying in bed, he suddenly burst into tears. He went into his mother's room and told her he had something to tell her. "I knew it had something to do with Joe," Terry recalled. "I thought maybe he wanted to see his father again or something. And then he started to tell me. And I couldn't believe what I was hearing."

They talked through the night. Joe told her everything. Finally, Terry asked, "Do you want to talk to Jay?"

"Do you think I should?" Joe asked.

Terry thought he should. "What if someone killed me," she said, "and you got blamed for it? Wouldn't you want someone who knew the truth to come forward?"

Joe turned the question around. "What if I killed somebody and I told you—would you tell?"

Terry thought for a second. "Joseph, I would have to," she said. "Because that's what you have to do. You can't kill somebody and not take the consequences for it."

In the morning, Joe told his mother, "I'll talk to Jay."

"HE'S SCARED, JAY," Terry was telling Salpeter a few minutes later. She and Joe were both on the phone.

"I understand that," Salpeter said.

"No, you really don't understand," Terry said.

"You don't," said Joe.

"Well, can you tell me, and then let's see where we can go with it?" Salpeter asked.

"What it basically is," Joe said, "he told me some stuff."

"Can you tell me what he told you?"

"I really don't feel comfortable, Jay."

"You know," Salpeter said, trying to nudge him forward, "maybe I'm mistaken but you guys called me."

"Well, there is one thing I can tell you," Terry said. "His aunt told him if he was to testify against his father, his father would go away for the rest of his life. It's serious stuff he has to tell you, Jay, but we are very scared."

"Terry, I don't think I've ever violated your trust," Salpeter said. "I mean, we've almost cried together with what you went through, and you gotta understand where I'm coming from, too, and you do, because you know we have an innocent kid there in jail and he's not a kid anymore, he's a man."

"I know," Terry said, "and that's what I've been talking to Joseph about since last night."

"Do you have a tape recorder on this phone right now?" Joe asked.

"No," Salpeter said.

"You give me your word?"

"Joe, I give you my word, I'm not going to do anything with this but at least let me know what you have. And you know I'm good, I could work with it or we can see what we can do with it. But to call me and to, like, put a prime rib in front of my face and say you have information and then you say you can't talk but then you call me . . . You know, Joe, you're growing up now, you're a man . . . I know it's your father and it's very difficult . . ."

"See, I'm in a hard place right here, you know what I'm saying?" Joe said.

"Well, I tell you, Marty's in a harder place."

"I know that," Joe said.

It went on in that vein for another minute or two. And then Joe abruptly began to talk, as if diving into a freezing ocean. "Your buddy, Glenn Harris, he knew what was going on."

"What did your father tell you?" Salpeter asked.

"He knew why he was driving there."

"So he knew they were going to go there to kill the Tankleffs?"

Joe stopped talking. "Uh, Jay," he said, "I think it would be better if you came down here."

Salpeter said he'd make the arrangements and call her back. "He's scared, Jay," Terry told him once more before hanging up. "What you're going to hear will make your head spin."

Salpeter called Barket. "I think we may have Creedon's kid," he said.

SALPETER FLEW to Florida and heard it all. And Terry was right. It made his head spin. He called Barket, who was in Atlanta on another case and about to head home. Barket booked a flight to Sarasota instead. Barry Pollack met him there. Terry, meanwhile, called her brother John in New York. He got on the first flight to Tampa. They all sat in a meeting room at the Marriott, and Barket and Pollack and Guarascio heard Joe's story for themselves.

Always the skeptic, Barket questioned Joe closely. This was too big, too important to skirt the boy's possible motives, or the details of his story. When Joe said his father told him about going up a few steps to look in Marty's room, Barket said hold on. The house was a ranch, all one level.

"All I'm telling you is what he told me," Joe said. But when Marty heard about it, this was the detail that excited him most. His house had a sunken living room separating the two wings. Creedon didn't say he went up a stairway, just "a few steps." It was the kind of obscure fact—even Marty's own lawyer was unaware of it—that bolstered the credibility of Joe's information. And Creedon's disclosure about checking Marty's room confirmed what Marty and his family knew since the day the county crime lab reported that the bloody impressions around his light switch were made with a glove that was never found.

But there was one big problem with all this: Joe wasn't ready to go on the record. It was to be five months, until late July, a few weeks after his seventeenth birthday, before he decided that he would give a sworn statement and testify in court. The lawyers flew him to New York, went over his story again, and prepared a three-page affidavit. They decided to omit one area of Creedon's admissions: his statements that Jim McCready was paid $100,000, and that he still kept in touch with both him and Steuerman. Marty's lawyers wanted to keep that under wraps until Joe testified.

Getting him on the stand, though, was no sure thing. The affidavit was in hand just as the lawyers were preparing to submit their final posthearing brief to the judge. Now they put Joe Guarascio's statement into a motion asking Braslow to reopen the hearing. "Joseph Creedon has already been implicated in these murders by no less than six other people," said their brief. "To that list, the Court can now add Creedon's own flesh and blood. The admission is startling because it provides the first window into what took place inside the Tankleff home the night of Seymour and Arlene's murders. It is consistent with much of the testimony heard by the Court . . . and proffered by a witness with no personal interest in the outcome of Martin Tankleff's case."

The news was dramatic both for the message and the messenger. This was a story of fathers and sons. The forces that drove Seymour Tankleff's life led to the ruin of his son's. It was through Todd Steuerman's drug trade that his father found a man to do his dirty work. And now, a generation later, came Joe Creedon's son to try to help bring a belated justice. Joe Guarascio was born on July 8, 1988, two months before the Tankleff murders. He was now seventeen, about to begin his senior year of high school, just as Marty was then.

That recognition triggered a memory for Terry. One day when Joseph was a baby, just a few months old, Creedon showed up with his hand in bandages. He said he'd had an accident with his motorcycle. Terry remembered thinking at the time that he was lying. The motorcycle didn't have a scratch.

*   *   *

LENNY LATO'S RESPONSE was familiar: The affidavit from Joe Creedon's son was too late, his testimony would be inadmissible at a trial, and, anyway, he was lying, just like the rest of the defense witnesses. According to Lato, Joe Jr.'s affidavit was an attempt to counter the "disaster" of his mother's testimony at the beginning of the hearing, a year earlier. It was an odd take. Lato had scored a couple of points in his cross-examination of Terry Covais, but they were innocuous in the scheme of things. In any event, she was hardly one of the defense's principal witnesses, especially in light of those, such as Billy Ram, who emerged as the hearing unfolded. Casting her testimony as a disaster, so damaging that the defense was scrambling to repair it a year later, was a major spin even for Lato. But even more peculiar was how he backed up his position that Joe Guarascio's affidavit was a collection of fabrications:

> . . . Guarascio's claim that at first he was impressed by his father's "Harley" is Tankleff's attempt to show that Creedon was "the biker" that Bruce Demps assumed to be the member of the Hells Angels who had killed the Tankleffs. Guarascio's paragraph 9 claim that his father showed him guns, handcuffs and leg shackles is an attempt to support Covais's claim that Creedon had guns and had tortured people. . . . Guarascio's paragraph 11 claim that, when he asked if his father had killed the Tankleffs his father answered, "Yeah, I did it" is a quote from Detective Rein's trial testimony. According to Rein, in response to Detective McCready's question whether Tankleff had killed his parents, Tankleff answered, "Yeah, I did it." . . . Guarascio's claim that, according to his father, "he and Peter Kent waited outside of the house until Jerry Steuerman gave them a signal," is a response to a portion of page 238 of the People's post-hearing brief, which reads that, at the Tankleff house, the windows and doors were undamaged, and there was no sign of a break-in. . . . Guarascio's claim that Kent stabbed Arlene "by or in the bed" is Tankleff's attempt to have Guarascio's affidavit match the trial testimony that Arlene was attacked in her bed and that her body was found near the bed. . . .

"The DA tops himself in a tour de force of the breathtakingly absurd," Eric Friedman blogged in response to Lato's tortured logic. Lato's words—in court, in briefs, and especially in the media—made him a reviled figure in Marty World. When giving interviews, he favored the snide metaphor. Glenn Harris wasn't granted immunity because "you don't give immunity like you're giving away candy." Marty didn't deserve a new trial because "this isn't a game of stickball where you get do-overs." At one point, Lato responded to a defense filing by emailing reporters: "They can call as many incredible witnesses as they like. Marty Tankleff killed his parents and the misfits that Tankleff's attorneys have dredged up cannot change that." A few days later, Soury and Friedman assembled Father Lemmert, Karlene Kovacs, and others who testified for the defense to decry Lato's slur. It wasn't easy, they said, but they did the right thing and told the truth. For that they were ridiculed, and by a man whose sworn duty was to serve and protect the public. Asked for a response, Lato said he didn't mean *all* the defense witnesses were misfits, adding, "What they've said about my witnesses is far worse than what I've said about their witnesses." He had a point, considering that his main witness was Peter Kent.

For every question, Lato had an answer. When the question was why he seemed to be fighting the case with such fervency, he denied the premise, claiming he had no investment in the outcome and presenting himself as a humble civil servant doing an honest job for the people. "I looked at it openly. I basically think there's nothing there," he told an interviewer for the A&E network's *American Justice*. But his words inevitably betrayed him. "Marty's lawyers are saying that Jerry Steuerman murdered Marty's parents," he said in the same interview, his voice rising by the word. "That to me is an *outrage*. Before they go and blame an innocent man they better have some good evidence. They have *none*. They had none at the time of the trial and they have none now."

JUDGE BRASLOW found no legitimate reason to bar the testimony of Joseph Guarascio. He scheduled it for Monday, November 14, 2005— eleven months after the last defense witness took the stand.

Joe wanted to bring his mother, his sister, and his girlfriend—a group of moral supporters that was too big for the lawyers' comfort. They were worried about Lato waving around the expense receipts along with another round of insinuations. Joe Creedon's son was the most dramatic witness Salpeter had come up with in the entire case, but getting him on the witness stand proved to be one more battle—the culmination of all of Salpeter's skirmishes and struggles with the lawyers, all his anxieties about getting his witnesses to the stand and about how they would do once they got up there. This was where Salpeter's head was now:

I can't talk at home anymore about the case. I can't talk to the attorneys. Sometimes they look at me like I got three heads. I get information, sometimes it sounds wild, but I'm not pulling it out of thin air. Ninety-nine percent of the time I'm doing this alone. I'm trying to keep our witnesses with us. I'm fighting with the attorneys. All this bullshit about who comes up with Junior. Who cares what it looks like? Let it go, just get him up here. The other day it got so bad that Marty heard about it. He dictates a letter to Meg over the phone and she emails it around. He's asking us to all please get along. Shit, sometimes I even get pissed off at him. *He has things he wants me to do. Meanwhile, Bruce has ten things he wants me to do. So I talk to myself. How many times I've been driving and people are honking and I'm so absorbed in the case I hardly hear it. And in my mind I've spoken to Arlene and Seymour. I promise them I will bring Marty home. It sounds crazy, but I believe that people that are gone, they're watching. And I've told them, "I'm going to bring your son home so you guys can rest in peace." Because how can they be resting in peace seeing their son in prison like this all these years?*

The negotiations over who would accompany Joe Guarascio to New York went on for days before Salpeter finally exploded. He stood in his kitchen screaming at Barket over the phone. Barket conferred with Pollack and Braga, and on Saturday, Joe arrived in New York with his mother, his sister, and his girlfriend.

The weekend was to be spent preparing Joe for his testimony, and Salpeter knew the first order of business was his. From the airport he took the family to the Bayside Diner for a bite to eat before going on to Barket's office. He took Terry aside before they went in. "Listen," he said, "remember when you first called me about Joe having something to tell me, and he kept asking if I was taping the call?"

"Yeah," said Terry.

"And I kept saying no?"

"Yeah?"

"I was taping it. And I have to tell Joe. Because we had to give the tape over to the DA, and Lato will probably ask him about it. How do you think he'll take it?"

Salpeter was genuinely worried. Lying to your witness was never a good thing, and if anyone had a right to be tense, it was a seventeen-year-old kid who was about to testify that his father told him he murdered two people. Terry said she didn't know how Joe would take it. "But I guess you'll find out."

They ordered lunch, then Salpeter invited Joe outside for a smoke. Standing in the parking lot, Salpeter confessed. Joe dragged on his cigarette. "Jay, I know it's your job," he said. "Don't worry about it."

Barket and Pollack spent a couple of hours with Joe that afternoon, going over his direct testimony. On Sunday they did a mock cross. And then Monday came. He and his entourage were back in Barket's office.

They weren't due in court until the afternoon. Barket and Pollack thought they should go over things one more time.

Joe sighed. "I don't need to do this," he said. "I'm okay."

"Everybody out," Barket said.

Salpeter took the family to a diner for lunch. As soon as the food came, Terry's cellphone rang. It was Joe. "I've had enough!" he screamed. "I'm outta here!"

"We'll take it to go," Salpeter told the waitress.

They went back to Barket's building and found Joe in the parking lot, pacing and smoking. Terry calmed him down, gave him a cheeseburger. And off to Riverhead they went.

The group came down the corridor at the courthouse and found a big crowd of media and more than the usual number of Marty's family, friends, and supporters waiting. Marianne and Mike McClure came in from California. Meg Griffin was there from Washington. Father Lemmert and Sister Angeline from Peekskill. The entire Paschke family. And Peter Reilly, a teenager when he was convicted of his mother's murder based on a false confession and later exonerated. He was fifty now and working at a motorcycle dealership. For a long time, he felt as if he had gone through something as rare as one of those diseases nobody ever heard of. But the wave of DNA exonerations had brought wrongful convictions into prominence, and Reilly felt connected to every one of the 174 "exonerees" listed on the website of the Innocence Project (forty-four more would be added over the next three years). He felt a special kinship with those who endured the emotional burden of being victims of their own false confessions.

It was an excited crowd, people buzzing about the drama of this final piece of the overwhelming case for Marty's innocence. Salpeter brought Joe and his family into one of the legal conference rooms next to the courtroom and had Vinnie Pepitone guard the door. Salpeter emerged after a few minutes, looking as stressed as anyone had seen him. It didn't help that the proceedings were late in starting. Half an hour after the appointed time, the courtroom was still empty. That's when word started going around that Lenny Lato had been taken to the hospital. He passed out just as he was about to come downstairs, someone said. There was a rumor he might have had a stroke.

The testimony was postponed, and Barket told the media his concern now was for his friend Lenny. Salpeter bristled. Lato had bred so much contempt that there were jokes among Marty's supporters that it couldn't have been a heart attack; that perhaps it was a ploy by Lato, like icing the field goal kicker in the last minute of a football game.

Lato's emergency passed, and he was back in court for Joe Guarascio's rescheduled testimony a month later. Joe flew up again—with just his mother this time—and finally took the stand. With Pollack leading the way, he recounted his reunion with his father and how it led to their conversations about the Tankleff murders: the initial exchange, when he broached the subject as they were going out for bagels; then the moments in his grandmother's house, when his father showed him his safe full of stolen jewelry and stacks of cash, and the gun and ankle shackles and handcuffs he said were for Glenn Harris if he testified. "I was kind of shocked, stunned," Joe testified, "starting to think that maybe the stuff on TV is true." And then, driving around with his father, asking him again if he did it, because "I had to know." And his father telling him yes, he did it, he and Peter Kent, and here's how, from waiting for Jerry Steuerman's signal to burning his clothes in his friend's basement.

"Did you understand your father to be serious when he was telling you this?" Pollack asked.

"Yes," Joe said, "very much so."

It wasn't until the closing moments of the direct questioning that Pollack detonated the bombshells—the only things that had been kept out of Joe's affidavit.

"In the conversations you had with your father, did he say anything about his relationship with Jerry Steuerman?"

"That he was one of his best friends' dad and that they still keep in touch."

"Did he tell you anything about his relationship with a Detective McCready?"

"He told me that him and McCready were friends and that he had paid him a hundred thousand dollars to keep his name out of it."

Murmurs filled the courtroom.

"Did he say whether he continues to be in touch with Detective McCready?"

"Yes. He told me that they still talk every now and then."

"NOW, MR. GUARASCIO, are you trying to get your father?" Lato asked to open his cross-examination.

"No," said Joe.

"Now, Mr. Guarascio, are you aware that your mother, right about the time you filed your affidavit, is trying to get your child support from Joseph Creedon?"

"No."

Joe wasn't aware of it because it wasn't true. If it were, Lato surely would have introduced evidence of it. The question was whether he was making it up, or Creedon was feeding him false information. Lato asked a number of questions that made clear that he called on Creedon to help him cross-examine his son—once again seeming more like a defense lawyer than a prosecutor.

He asked Joe how many times he had talked to his father on the phone, producing Creedon's cellphone records to assist him. He scorned the idea that his mother was afraid of Creedon, showing Joe a group photo taken by Creedon's sister during the trip to Florida. "Does it look like everyone's smiling to you?" Lato asked.

"Not my mom," Joe said. ". . . She had a smirk on her face but it ain't no smile."

"That's your interpretation," Lato replied.

Lato eventually got to the substance of Joe's testimony: "You said you were shocked when your father showed you the guns and the leg shackles . . . but you weren't so shocked or stunned to prevent you from asking him these questions about the Tankleff case."

"What would that have anything to do with how shocked and stunned I am?" Joe replied. "I just wanted to know the truth."

"Isn't it a fair statement that when you were in New York you were smoking some marijuana or weed?"

"The only time I did," Joey replied, "was when my dad asked me to take a hit, sir."

"Now, you said your father admitted to you that he and Jerry Steuerman are friends . . . and that your father said that he gave McCready a hundred grand."

"That's what he said."

"You're sure it wasn't two hundred grand?"

"I only told you what he told me, sir."

". . . Basically, sir, didn't you find out, oh, right around February or so of this year that Marty Tankleff was buying and you decided to sell?"

"Was what?" Joe responded. "I'm confused."

"You know something, Judge—" said Barket.

"Hold on," said Braslow, visibly irritated. "Hold on. Hold on. I'm going to strike that from the record. Mr. Lato, that was inappropriate."

JOE GUARASCIO was a hero to many that day. There were thanks and hugs from Marty's family and supporters. "Good for you!" Sister Angeline told him. "You're marvelous." He stopped to talk to the clot of media. "I'm just doing the right thing," he said. "Marty was the same age I am." Terry said, "The only thing I can say is I'm very proud of my son." A few days later, Catherine Crier had Joe on her Court TV show. "I know how hard this must have been for you," the former judge and prosecutor told him, "but you are to be congratulated. You are a very brave young man. This is very important, what you've done."

The defense and prosecution each offered its take on Joe Guarascio's testimony in the form of a letter to Braslow, its last words before he delivered his decision on the case. Lato had the young man in the middle of a dazzlingly inane conspiracy. According to the prosecutor, it all started four years earlier, in 2001, when Marty wrote to Joe's mother, pleading with her to speak to Salpeter. "It would be months before Harris would implicate Creedon and give Salpeter a reason to contact Covais," Lato wrote—ignoring the most obvious fact that Salpeter knew from the very beginning that Karlene Kovacs implicated Creedon all the way back in 1994. "So it appears," Lato continued, "that, contrary to Salpeter's claim that he found Harris using 'old-fashioned detective work,' Tankleff, Salpeter, and Harris had reached an accord before Tankleff wrote to Covais."

Lato didn't say how Salpeter found Harris, if not by detective work, implying that Marty met him in prison, though it had been well established that he hadn't. In any event, here's what happened next, according to Lato: "Salpeter furnished Harris with details of the murders, but Tankleff's plan to frame Creedon and Peter Kent suffered a setback when Harris recanted and declined to testify and when a recorded statement of Covais, and the testimony of Maryann Testa [Creedon's sister] exposed Covais as a liar. But Tankleff and Salpeter are resilient, and, in Guarascio, created what was arguably the biggest liar at the hearings. Annoyed with Harris, who denied being a knowing part of the murder plot, Tankleff had Guarascio retaliate with, 'Jay, your buddy Glenn Harris, he knew what was going on,' and with making Harris, not Creedon, the 'pipe thrower.' As for the loyal Covais, Tankleff had Guarascio *and* Covais accuse Testa of covering up Creedon's involvement in the murders. And to rebut the People's accusation that Salpeter had furnished Harris with details of the crime, Tankleff had Guarascio call 'a surprised' Salpeter with an offer to 'crack the whole case.'"

It all added up, said Lato, to "an outrageous story of conspiracy and cover-up."

CHAPTER 36

Nefarious Scoundrels

ON ST. PATRICK'S DAY of 2006, nearly everyone involved in the legal campaign to free Marty Tankleff—everyone but Marty himself—was glued to the website of the Suffolk County court administration, hitting the refresh button every fifteen or twenty seconds. Judge Stephen Braslow's decision was to be released and posted online at high noon. It was like waiting for a virtual verdict.

"I can't get on," Jay Salpeter said, staring at the computer screen in his office. There was a MARTY DIDN'T DO IT bumper sticker across the top of his monitor. "Must be too many people trying at once."

It had been more than five years since Marty first wrote to Salpeter. Sixteen since he went to prison. And now it was a minute past noon. Salpeter still couldn't get on the website. He called Meg Griffin at Baker Botts in Washington.

She was crying.

"We lost?" Salpeter said. "Meg, listen, we're not giving up. This wasn't unexpected. We knew we weren't going to win in Suffolk County. Now we get it out of there. What'd the decision say? Denied everything? That's just amazing. We're not finished, believe me. He's gonna come home."

He called Cheryl. "We lost," he said. "I know, it's unbelievable. But we knew this was coming. . . . No, I don't know if he knows yet."

Salpeter drove to Bruce Barket's office building. He stepped off the elevator into a clot of television crews, each waiting for a one-on-one with Barket, who was in his office, talking on the phone with Bruce Lambert of the *Times*. ". . . And as far as reasoning, what, they're *all* lying? How do Glass and Graydon come to us three days apart, having not seen each other in years, telling two parts of the same story?"

The first of the TV crews came in and set up. "Bruce," the reporter asked, "your reaction?"

"My reaction is it's a ridiculous legal opinion," Barket said. "It's sickening. But not unexpected. And I think this is going to say much more about Braslow and Spota and Lato and the whole gang out there than it says about Marty."

"Does Marty know yet?"

"Not yet."

The judge had ordered Marty sent back upstate two months earlier, which nobody had taken as a good sign. He was now at another ancient state prison, this one near Lake George and tauntingly named Great Meadow. Barket was fuming that Braslow hadn't kept Marty on Long Island until the decision. "I don't want him hearing about this from some jail guard," he said. He had called Meg in Washington. If he calls you first, he told her, just tell him we need to talk to him and patch him through.

"Yeah, we lost," Salpeter was saying into his cellphone, saying it over and over, chewing on a toothpick. Selim Algar of the *New York Post* came into the office and Salpeter told him, "It's horrible. It's one of the great miscarriages of justice. But, you know, we're gonna keep going and we're gonna bring him home." Algar got some quotes from Barket and from Ron Falbee, then called his desk in New York and began dictating his story for the paper's website and the next morning's paper: "Despite evidence pointing to his innocence, a Long Island man convicted of slaughtering his parents in 1988 had his bid for a new trial denied yesterday. . . ."

Braslow's ruling so closely resembled the arguments and attitude of the district attorney's office, and even its contemptuous language, that the dark joke among Marty's camp was that the decision was only *signed* by Braslow. Most memorably, he dismissed the credibility of the defense witnesses with a broad stroke of disdain: "The defendant has introduced what he has characterized as newly discovered evidence, which consisted mainly of the testimony from a cavalcade of nefarious scoundrels paraded before this court."

Salpeter took this more personally than anyone. After all, these were his witnesses. "How dare he?" he said. "These are people who came forward, and for what—to be called names? They came forward to help free an innocent man. Do they have a past? Do they have records? Yes. So what? Who else is going to know the things they know? Choir boys? Prosecutors use people like this all the time." Eric Friedman blogged about the "nefarious scoundrels" line: "It was a turn of phrase at once reminiscent of ADA Lato's famous 'misfits' epithet and dialogue from *Deadwood*. Any judge saying this would sound more like a man with a horse in this race than an impartial finder of fact."

Those who said Joe Creedon made admissions to them, according to Braslow, "were shown to be unreliable, incredible, contradictory, and possibly motivated to harm Creedon by having him convicted of these murders." Most dubious of all, it seemed to Braslow, was Creedon's son. The judge presumed that Joe Guarascio's mother was out for revenge against Creedon for his abuse when they were together and his failure since then to pay child support. "Accordingly, the court finds the testimony of Joseph John Guarascio to be incredible and unreliable and due to the motivations of his mother."

Braslow's assumptions about young Joe were astonishing to the Tankleff camp, as well as to those among the media corps who found Creedon's son perhaps the most credible of all the witnesses. Braslow's presumptions seemed curiously aligned with Lato's. They were unsupported by any testimony; if anything, the evidence was that putting her son up to a phony murder allegation would be the last thing Terry would be motivated to do. She had testified only under subpoena, and Braslow himself noted that Creedon's abuse when they were together "caused her to run and hide from him with their son." Nor was there any testimony that Terry had ever made an issue of child support. Braslow obviously picked this up from Lato, who asked Joe, based on nothing, if he'd ever heard anything about it. As Braslow presumably instructed jurors in his trials, questions by attorneys are not evidence, nor is their own speculation.

"The testimony of Karlene Kovacs also lacks credibility and reliability," Braslow wrote. Like Lato, he put great emphasis on inconsequential differences between her 1994 affidavit and her recollections a decade later, but said nothing about what motivation she would have had for making up a story about a stranger, or about the polygraph that confirmed she was telling the truth, or how it was that her account supported, and was supported by, other witnesses with whom she had no connection.

As for Glenn Harris: "There was substantial evidence that Harris is mentally unstable and equivocal, often recanting his statements. Additionally, there was evidence that Harris sought details of the crime from Salpeter, the defendant's investigator, which would indicate that he probably had nothing to do with committing the crimes. Moreover, evidence was provided at the hearing which indicated that he wanted to incriminate Peter Kent because Peter Kent had an affair with his wife."

On Billy Ram: "He is clearly an individual who has always put his personal interests above society's . . . and this court does not believe that he would do anything like testifying in favor of this defendant out of some underlying need to see justice done." On why Ram didn't grab the chance to recant in exchange for some help in his Florida case, which sent him to prison for fifteen years soon after, Braslow ventured no speculation.

On Neil Fischer's testimony that he overheard Jerry Steuerman telling someone during an argument only a few months after the murders that he had already killed two people: "This statement was overheard by Fischer while he had his head in a cabinet and he was probably not paying close attention to what was being said. The statement was taken out of context, may have been made facetiously since the defendant had been accusing Steuerman of the murders ever since they were committed."

On the pipe: Though it was found where Glenn Harris told Salpeter to look, Braslow was unimpressed with the defense argument that the absence of forensic material was consistent with the pipe being exposed to the elements for sixteen years. Braslow's view was not unreasonable, but the way in which he supported it was. "The People's investigator found other pipes of the same type of varying lengths on the lot," he noted— once again parroting an inaccurate assertion by the prosecution. Those pipes were actually not the same type as the one found by Salpeter, and they were not loose. They were buried in the ground.

On Richard Ofshe's expert testimony that Marty's statements to the police amounted to a classic case of a coerced, false confession: "There was no conduct by the detectives that would have rendered the defendant's confession false." But Braslow said nothing about the point Ofshe stressed most: that the complete inconsistency with the physical evidence was the strongest evidence of a false confession. Instead he trotted out the enduring myth of Marty's "lack of emotion" on the morning of the murders as evidence of a true confession.

On pizzeria owner Leonard Lubrano's testimony that Steuerman and McCready knew each other and that McCready told him he was doing construction work for Steuerman: Braslow wasn't interested in the merits of the defense claim that this was evidence of perjury by the lead detective on a key question that might have changed the verdict. The reason he wasn't interested, said the judge, was that this issue had already been addressed—sixteen years earlier, by Judge Alfred Tisch. Among the grounds of Bob Gottlieb's postverdict motions was a sworn statement from a high school student who said McCready told her class that he'd known Steuerman for years and that he was beyond suspicion. Tisch ruled then that this evidence could not have been introduced at the trial to impeach McCready's credibility because it would have been "collateral to the issues." Salpeter had pursued the statement from the high school student, tracking down her former teacher at a golf course in Florida. But the teacher couldn't corroborate the story. Braslow, meanwhile, found Lubrano to be "a very honest individual and a very credible witness." But he ruled it irrelevant, claiming he was obliged to apply Tisch's 1990 ruling on a similar issue. In fact, he was not so obliged. Nor did he distinguish between Lubrano's credible, firsthand testimony and the high school student's uncorroborated hearsay.

Apart from finding problems with every defense witness, Braslow adopted the DA's fundamental argument that it was all too late. Among the requirements of Section 440, he pointed out, was that a defendant trying to vacate a verdict based on newly discovered evidence had to bring a motion "with due diligence" after the discovery of the new evidence. "The defendant has not adequately explained why he sat with the Kovacs statement for nearly nine years," Braslow wrote. "In fact, Jay Salpeter, the defendant's investigator, did concede at the hearing that an investigator could have developed that lead at that time and located Glenn Harris." Of course, Salpeter also said it couldn't be assumed Harris would have responded in 1994 the way he did in 2002 or that an investigator would have been able to turn up the witnesses who surfaced after the 440 motion was filed.

Braslow based the bulk of the ruling on his finding that most of the new evidence would be barred by hearsay rules if there were to be a new trial. Apart from that debatable conclusion, the law took that factor out of the equation in an "actual innocence" claim, the theory being that innocence ultimately trumps procedure. So Braslow was required to consider all the evidence presented, including hearsay, in determining whether there was "clear and convincing evidence" of innocence. But there was no suspense by the time Braslow reached this part of his decision. To him, it seemed, there wasn't even a little evidence of innocence. In making this judgment, he relied heavily on a single observation: Nothing was taken from the Tankleffs' house. "This court," said Braslow, "finds it hard to believe that characters such as Creedon and Kent would not have looked for something to steal."

The judge concluded, "After thoroughly reviewing this matter, this court reaches the same conclusion that the jury reached seventeen years ago and every state appellate court and federal court that has reviewed the case, and that is that Martin Tankleff is guilty of murdering his parents."

It was an astonishing misstatement, not only of the history of the case but of the essential function of appellate courts. None had ever addressed Marty's guilt or innocence; they had only found that his *legal grounds* for reversal fell short. In fact, judges at both the state and federal levels had made it clear that they had serious doubts about Marty's guilt—and that was without any of the new evidence presented to Braslow.

"HI, MARTY," Meg Griffin said, trying to sound nonchalant. "Bruce and Barry want to talk to you."

"As soon as I heard her voice," Marty said later, "I knew. But Bruce had me prepared, so it was in my head that Braslow was going to shoot us down and then we would get it out of Suffolk County and go to the Appellate Division. So I wasn't shocked. But it still hurt to hear it. And then there were so many people on the call—Bruce, Ron and Carol, Meg—and they had all read the decision and they're saying, 'It's so bad that it's good.' I didn't understand what they were talking about until I read it for myself. Steve Braga once said to me, 'You know, they can walk away looking good if somebody would just have the integrity to say, "We made a mistake."' They wouldn't be alone. There are wrongful convictions everywhere. For the DA not to do that is one thing. But this is a *judge*. And when I read the decision, I thought, The integrity of the judiciary just went out the door. This is a day that Suffolk County will regret because it's finally going to expose just how dirty the county is."

The question was: Why? What was it about this case that made it so important to keep Marty Tankleff in prison? The question was so obvious, the answer so elusive, that reporters couldn't help but raise it, even if they had to report their stories straight.

"Bruce, off the record," asked a radio reporter who had covered the hearing, "what do you think is going on here?"

"What I think, and I'll say this *on* the record," Barket replied, "is that Suffolk County justice is a fucking train wreck."

THE OUTRAGE SPREAD that day and for weeks, even months to come. Among the dozens of posts on the Marty website was this one: "So sorry to hear today's result, but I'm sad to say that it was predictable. Unfortunately, the faces may have changed in Suffolk County, but nothing else seems to have changed." It was signed by retired judge Stuart Namm. "P.S. Justice will triumph in the end!" Another message came from Saul Kassin, a false confession expert at Williams College in Massachusetts: "How tragic; what a scandalous breach of common sense. I am so sorry for Marty, his supporters, and the millions of us who are so deeply offended by injustice."

And, of course, there were dozens from regulars on the Marty discussion board: "This is truly heart-wrenching and frustrating for justice-seekers everywhere," a poster wrote from San Diego. "What can we say about Braslow? His behavior was akin to any other party hack. His decision was morally repugnant."

Someone posted McCready's reaction to Braslow's decision, quoted on the Court TV website: "I'm ecstatic. I never had a doubt he was going to deny it. I just couldn't believe he would listen to so many lies and innuendos. Tankleff had his day in court, so the hell with him." The comment brought a string of responses about "McCreepy," as he was commonly known on the board. "What a vile piece of crap this guy is," said one.

While it seemed there was no limit to McCready's eagerness to defend his case—or to his proclivity for inciting his legion of hecklers with each new utterance—conspicuously silent were the two other men who played the key roles in Marty's conviction. In the two and a half years since the motion for a new trial had been filed, John Collins had said not one public word about it. Norman Rein, meanwhile, was all but forgotten. McCready's last partner had retired from the police department, worked a few years as a private investigator, and had recently sold his house in Patchogue and moved to the Orlando area. Reached there one day, Rein was pleasant, though unwilling to meet for a discussion of the Tankleff case. He seemed not to be bothered in the least by recent developments. He felt "righteous" about his work in the Tankleff case, he said, and assured his caller that if he felt he had put the wrong man in prison he would be "the first one" to fight for his freedom.

McCready, meanwhile, never stopped talking. But his most stunning and provocative remark of all never became public.

Later in 2006, the *Dr. Phil* program featured Marty's case in a show on false and coerced confessions. The producers brought Salpeter to Los Angeles, where he was joined by Marty's Aunt Marianne and her daughter Jennifer, along with Steven Drizin, the legal director of the Center on Wrongful Convictions at the Northwestern University law school. They also invited one of Salpeter's star witnesses—Joe Guarascio—and sat him in the first row. The one guest they wanted but couldn't get was McCready. That is, they couldn't get him to fly to California for the privilege of being surrounded by some of Marty Tankleff's closest relatives and fiercest advocates. But at the last minute, McCready agreed to call in during the taping. It gave Salpeter the chance to do something he'd fantasized about for years.

When McCready came on, Dr. Phil asked him the basic questions and got the usual defiance. "The evidence clearly shows that Marty did this," McCready said, his raspy voice blaring over a speakerphone. The new evidence was all a "bogus lie that's made up." The people who testified were "looking for their fifteen minutes of fame."

Then the host turned to Salpeter. "I got a couple of questions, if you don't mind," Salpeter said. "You're a terrific detective, you've told everyone on television. Can you name one thing in Marty's confession that fits the crime scene?"

"Can I name one thing that fits the crime scene?" McCready replied. "Everything in that confession fits the crime scene."

"Okay, let me ask you a question: The dumbbell that you wrote in the confession—was that a murder weapon, yes or no?"

"As far as I know it was."

"Oh, please, you *know* it's not, it's been proven it wasn't, James. Let's go to the knife that you put in your confession—was that the knife that was used to kill Arlene and Seymour?"

"I believe it was."

"It *wasn't*—how could you say that on television? You're lying to this audience!"

"No I'm not."

"James, you know for a fact that those are not the weapons."

"I believe that was the murder weapon. I'm not going to argue with you."

"You're not arguing, you're *lying*."

Dr. Phil cut in. "Wasn't the knife found with watermelon juice on it?" he asked.

"No, I don't believe that's true at all," McCready said. "Both those weapons were totally clean. He took a shower and tried to clean himself too. He didn't do a good job."

"But wasn't the shower drain also tested for blood?" Dr. Phil asked.

"Did we take the traps and all that to see if we could grab something out of it? Yeah, but you're not always going to find something in there. That's just an investigative procedure."

"Do you have a history of perjury in Suffolk County?" Salpeter asked.

"No," said McCready.

"You weren't cited by the New York State Investigation Commission for committing perjury?"

"No."

"Are you telling the truth?"

"I'm telling the truth."

Now Dr. Phil turned to Joe Guarascio, introducing him as "the son of Joe Guns, the alleged hit man." Joe recounted his father's detailed admissions but McCready was unfazed. "I give that kid no credibility," he said. "My understanding is there's no love lost between the father and son over child support payments and things like that."

"He also told me he paid Detective McCready a hundred thousand dollars to keep his name out of it," Joe added.

"He probably wants his money back," Dr. Phil remarked, to chuckles from the audience. Then he asked McCready, "Is that true?"

"No, that's not true," McCready said. "And if it *were* true, that means he lost money, I mean, he only got paid fifty thousand to do the murder."

It was a stunning moment—Salpeter and Drizin looked at each other, as if to ask, *Did he just say what I think he said?*—but it came and went as McCready kept talking and Dr. Phil followed with a question about the perjury allegation, and thanked him for coming on. "You're welcome, have a nice day," McCready said, and he was gone before anyone could point out that he had apparently just confirmed that Creedon committed the murders or ask him how he knew how much Creedon was paid.

The guests huddled as soon as the cameras went off, comparing their memories of McCready's precise words. They all thought he said the same thing, but it seemed so unbelievable. Salpeter called Barket, starting what became months of negotiation by Marty's lawyers to get a copy of the tape from CBS, the show's owner. The network had a policy against releasing any material before a show was broadcast. Then, when the show aired a few months later the key remark was missing—edited out by order of the CBS legal department for the most ironic of reasons: The company lawyers didn't want their network held responsible for what amounted to McCready's allegation that Joe Creedon committed the murders. It left this odd moment in the version that was broadcast: Dr. Phil asking his next question as Marianne and Jennifer looked at each other, visibly stunned by the preceding ten seconds that the TV audience never saw.

After the show aired, the CBS lawyers told the Tankleff defense they would turn over a copy of the unedited tape—but only with a subpoena. At this point Marty's lawyers had no subpoena power because they had no open 440 motions. Lonnie Soury got an off-the-record confirmation of McCready's statement from a producer, but the attorneys were not to get the actual tape until after the appeal was filed. At that point, they decided to keep it for possible use at a retrial.

JAMES MOORE was watching the news on the night of Braslow's decision and realized, like so many other people over the previous two and a half years, that he had a decision to make. For several years, he'd known something that could help prove Marty Tankleff's innocence, but kept it to himself for one of the usual reasons: It was obvious Marty would get a new trial anyway—so why get involved? But on that Friday night, Moore heard the news that Marty was *not* getting a new trial, and saw Barket and Salpeter and the Falbees raging at the relentless injustice of Suffolk County. Salpeter wasn't around, so Barket went to talk to Moore himself. He was at Moore's doorstep by noon.

For four years, until 2003, Moore worked for Truly Blue Pools, a company that built and serviced swimming pools. He would work with three or four other guys, and in 2002 one of those guys was Peter Kent. "When you're working on a crew with somebody," Moore told Barket, "you're stuck in a hole with them all day and sometimes you're tired and you just get sick of each other. Kent was a guy who talked on and on. One day we were working in Wading River. We were grading the hopper—that's the slope from the shallow end to the deep end—and he just wouldn't stop talking bullshit. I got really bothered and finally I said, 'Can't you just shut up?' He started threatening me, saying he was going to kill me. I thought he was full of it. We went back and forth and then I said, 'Dude, how you gonna kill me? You never killed nobody.' He said, 'Wanna bet?' I said, 'Oh, yeah, who?' And he told me he killed the Tankleffs out in Belle Terre with a pipe. I said, 'Oh, really, and who's that?' I didn't know anything about it. I was like eight when it happened. Kent says, 'It was a long time ago. It was in the papers.' At that point, the foreman told us to get back to work."

Moore worked with Kent just that one season. But a year later, in the fall of 2003, he read about Kent's central role in Marty Tankleff's attempts to get a new trial. "It really kicked me in the head because he had told me he did those murders," Moore said. A few months later, Moore was on line with his wife and their baby son at the McDonald's inside the Wal-Mart store on Nesconset Highway. "Kent saw me and walked up to us," Moore said, "and the first thing out of his mouth was, 'I just got out of jail and the cops were questioning me about the Tankleff murders.' I asked him if he was in trouble. He said, 'They ain't gonna catch me.'" Right there on the McDonald's line, Kent told Moore about the murders. "He said that he and his friend—I forget the name of his friend—were 'paid to do the deed.' He said this was so the dead guy's partner could get control of some business. He said he wasn't worried about it now because they would have kept him in jail if they had anything on him."

Barket took a statement from Moore and called Salpeter from his car on the way back. "So Kent never opened his mouth?" he said.

Over the next few days, Salpeter tried to verify Moore's information. Truly Blue Pools was out of business, but Salpeter tracked down the owner, Frank Messina, by way of his father in Florida. Messina verified that both Peter Kent and James Moore worked for him, though only Moore was a regular full-time employee. "Peter was the type of worker who would just show up to work and if I had work I would use him," Messina said. "But it was just about a year or so. I fired him when he went to sleep in the woods on a job in Wading River."

But Messina did more than confirm that Moore and Kent worked together. He told Salpeter something truly astonishing. Sometime in the off season between 2001 and 2002, he sent Moore and Kent on a service call to fix a pool leak for one of his new accounts, the Serabians in Belle Terre. When they came back, Moore told the boss that they weren't able to fix the leak. He also mentioned that Kent said he'd been to the house before. Kent had worked for other pool companies, so Messina assumed he'd serviced the pool for one of them. He called Kent into his office and remembered the conversation this way:

"Peter, Jimmy says you worked on the Serabian pool before. How come you couldn't fix it?"

"Do you know whose house that was?" Kent replied.

"No," said Messina.

"It's the Tankleff house," said Kent.

"Okay," Messina said, missing the reference. "So have you been there before?"

"Yeah, I've been there," Kent said.

"So you know the pool?"

"I didn't work on the pool," Kent said. "I had business there."

Messina was puzzled. All he wanted to know was whether Kent knew what the problem might be with the pool. "What did you do there if you didn't work on the pool?" he asked.

"I had my business there," Kent said.

Messina told Salpeter, "I wasn't getting an answer so I just walked away at that point. I didn't connect it with the Tankleff murders at the time. I didn't connect it until I saw his name in the paper."

A few days later, Messina sent Salpeter an account card showing six service calls to 33 Seaside Drive in the time period Kent worked for him. "Still leaking," it noted on the last one.

Barket prepared a new 440 motion, asking Braslow for another hearing. Kent's statements to James Moore and Frank Messina, the motion declared, meant that "the defense has now presented admissions by all four people involved in the murders of Arlene and Seymour Tankleff. An objective and honest prosecutor would have, long ago, agreed to release Marty Tankleff and would have sought an indictment against these men. . . . We can only hope each time that, in the face of all other evidence, this will be the day Martin Tankleff is set free." The responses were pro forma: Lato opposed the new motion and Braslow rejected it on hearsay grounds.

But there was still more to come. After Braslow's St. Patrick's Day ruling, Salpeter set up a tip line, which was advertised on the martytankleff.org website. Calls went to a cellphone Salpeter set up for the purpose, which he carried with him along with his personal phone. One day in the summer of 2006, Salpeter picked up a voice mail on the tip line from a woman named Heidi Kulp. When he called her back, she told him that her information concerned an old friend of her husband's named Danny Raymond.

Salpeter recognized the name instantly. Danny Raymond was Peter Kent's supposed alibi. After Kent testified that he was committing robberies and doing drugs with Raymond throughout the week of the Tankleff murders, Salpeter had tried to find Raymond. He did his usual—data checks, phone calls and messages to various relatives—but got no response and moved on to other leads. Now it was a year and a half later. Heidi Kulp told Salpeter that Raymond had visited her husband at their house a few weeks earlier. And he had a lot to say about Peter Kent.

In 1989, Jason Kulp was arrested for burglary and spent six months in the Suffolk County Jail with Raymond and Kent after their arrests for the string of robberies they committed the first week of September 1988. All three of them were twenty years old then and about to be shipped off to state prison for the first time. They were together for a while at their first stop, Elmira. Kulp developed a friendship with Raymond, but not so much with Kent. He told Salpeter that Raymond talked "on numerous occasions" back then about Kent being involved in the Tankleff murders.

Kulp got out of prison in 1991 and didn't see Raymond for fifteen years. And then, just a few weeks ago, he ran into him at a McDonald's. They got reacquainted, and a couple of weeks later Raymond and his girlfriend spent an afternoon at the Kulps' house. Sitting around the kitchen table, the subject turned to Peter Kent—and the Tankleff murders. Raymond told the Kulps that Kent had been leaning on him to be his alibi for the Tankleff murders. "Dan said Tankleff was innocent but he didn't want to rat out Kent," Jason Kulp told Salpeter. "And he didn't want to get involved because this goes high up to the DA's office and the judge."

The tip from the Kulps got Salpeter back on the trail of Danny Raymond. Armed with Raymond's cellphone number, he began leaving messages—long, incessant, baiting messages. *You hold the key, Danny. Your silence is not only keeping an innocent man in prison but it's allowing dangerous killers to roam free. Can you look yourself in the mirror, Danny?* Another, after he heard that Raymond had found religion. *Hello, Danny. It's Sunday morning. Maybe you'll call me after church.* He called Raymond at least once a day. And one day Raymond called him back.

DANNY RAYMOND was indeed a key to the case. It wasn't so much that he put the lie to Kent's alibi—Kent pretty much did that himself when he testified—but that he shed a bright light on how the DA's office established a symbiotic relationship with a murderer.

That relationship began on October 7, 2003, when Lenny Lato and Walter Warkenthien told Kent about Glenn Harris's admissions and responded to his tears by helping him with his alibi. As Lato himself disclosed in the form of a question during Kent's testimony, "You basically said you're going to look at your record and you wanted us to look at your record to see if we could figure out where you were, to reconstruct it?"

Danny Raymond became the foundation of that reconstruction. The records showed that he and Kent committed several burglaries in the days surrounding the murders. Kent learned—from whom, it could be presumed—that Raymond's current residence was the Mohawk Correctional Facility, a medium-security prison near Syracuse where he was serving time for grand larceny. Fourteen years after he'd last seen Raymond, Kent went to see him, unannounced. It was mid-July 2004, a week before the Tankleff 440 hearing was to begin. Raymond didn't even recognize Kent at first glance. "What's up?" he said when he did. "I guess this isn't a social call."

Kent told Raymond he was in trouble and needed his help. "They're looking at me heavy for the Tankleff murders," he said. His face was red, and he was sweating, breathing heavily. "I need you to be my alibi." Raymond told Salpeter and Barket, "He was ranting, 'I can't do fifty to life, I can't do fifty years.' He started talking about the robberies we did the week of the Tankleff murders." Kent had their arrest records with him. They showed that one of the robberies was on the date of the murders— but at least fifteen hours later. "He told me I was supposed to say I was with him at the time of the murders. He kept talking about the murders. He said it was Creedon who actually killed them, not him. He talked about how dangerous Creedon was. He said Harris is a dead man. 'He's gonna disappear and there won't be a body this time.'" Then Kent got back to the alibi. "He kept going over it, and then he said he's glad I'm gonna do this because there are serious people involved with this. He named Creedon and Jerry Steuerman and he said, 'They're watching your family. They know you have three kids that live with your wife in Hicksville.'"

Kent's information was accurate, and it got Raymond's attention. "I didn't want to get involved," he said, "but I was afraid for my family." After Kent left, Raymond put everything Kent told him in an affidavit: That on the night of September 6, 1988, he picked up Kent from his sister's house and they went on an eighteen-hour binge of cocaine and heroin. "Peter Kent and I did use said illicit substances together all throughout the evening of September 06, 1988, through the entire morning of September 07, 1988, and into the early afternoon . . . at which time I dropped Peter Kent back off at his sister's place of residence in Ronkonkoma, New York, so he could attend her birthday party. . . . At no time during that period of time . . . did I witness Peter Kent ever having any contact or communications of any kind with any person or persons named Glenn Harris."

Raymond signed the affidavit in front of a prison notary and sent it to Kent. Two months later, he was released on parole. Soon after he returned to Long Island, he got a phone call from Walter Warkenthien. The assistant district attorney on the Tankleff case wants to meet with you, the investigator told him. Raymond suggested a diner in Lindenhurst near where he was working. On November 12, a month before Kent was to take the stand as the People's first witness in opposition to Marty Tankleff's bid for a new trial, Raymond sat in a booth with Lato, Warkenthien, and another investigator.

Lato wanted Raymond to testify to the alibi he provided in his affidavit. But Raymond knew he was essentially an *anti*-alibi: Not only couldn't he account for Kent's whereabouts in the critical hours, but Kent himself had told him many times that he *was* involved in the murders. Raymond had decided to draw the line at the affidavit—he wouldn't lie for Kent on the witness stand. But like anyone who lived the life he did, Raymond was wary of antagonizing the DA's office. So he did a bit of a tap dance. He told Lato he really couldn't be sure whether he was with Kent in those hours—it was such a long time ago and he was, after all, doing a lot of drugs at the time. That's not what you said in your affidavit, Lato replied, not gently. It says right here you were with him. Raymond responded that he wrote the statement after Kent visited him upstate, implying he did it because Kent asked him to but stopping short of saying it was under duress. As Raymond would later say in another affidavit, this one for the defense, "I did not trust them enough to tell them about Kent's comments about my family. I just kept telling them that I could not help them."

In response, Lato raised something that Raymond took as a threat of another kind: He asked about his parole status. According to Raymond, "I knew they could violate me if I didn't cooperate. But I wasn't going to lie for Peter Kent." So he kept prevaricating, until Lato apparently realized it would be dangerous to put him on the stand. "Lato then asked if I was going to testify for the defense. I told them that I would not." Of course, the defense didn't even know of Raymond's existence at that point. It would be another year and a half before he decided to respond to Salpeter's phone calls. By then he was off parole.

Barket filed Raymond's new affidavit, recanting everything he said in the one he wrote for Kent, with yet another 440 motion. "Piece by piece the case against Martin Tankleff continues to crumble," Barket wrote, opening the motion with his favorite metaphor. ". . . Brick by brick the case against the actual murderers—Creedon, Kent, Harris and Steuerman—continues to be built."

But the new motion raised the stakes in another way: It accused the DA's office not only of shielding the true murderers in its defense of a conviction but of actually colluding with one of them to "construct what we now know is a false alibi." It asked, "If Raymond really is an alibi witness for Kent, why was the first interview of this critical witness performed not by Mr. Lato, a police officer, Warkenthien, a lawyer for Kent, or even a private investigator—but by Kent himself?" Maybe because "only Kent could bring the message he delivered—'I am glad you are going to help because there are serious people—Creedon and Jerry Steuerman—who know where your family lives.'"

Lato responded by clinging to the alibi with a ludicrous claim: "Court and district attorney records confirm that Raymond and Kent were together from 11:40 P.M. on August 31, 1988, through 10:40 P.M. on September 7, 1988." The records obviously didn't confirm that the two men were together twenty-four hours a day for eight straight days. To the contrary: There was a gap of *five days* between a robbery on September 2 and the last two late on the night of September 7, nearly twenty-four hours after Seymour Tankleff's poker game broke up.

Lato also denied Raymond's account of their meeting at the diner. Though he himself led the interview, Lato attributed his version to Warkenthien. "Raymond stated that he is willing to help us," Warkenthien wrote, "but after Lato explained that if Raymond testified his testimony and criminal record would definitely be printed in Newsday, he stated that he would rather not testify because he has gotten his life together." Lato had spent nearly three years famously disparaging the defense witnesses as liars and criminals and misfits, but it seemed he was so respectful of Danny Raymond's delicate feelings that he would rather give up a key witness than force him to suffer the embarrassment of testifying and, even worse, *having his name in the newspaper.*

It was a commentary on the state of affairs that a man who had spent half his life in prison seemed more credible than a prosecutor and an investigator who were two of the district attorney's most trusted people. The Tankleff team called Lato on it with one more affidavit from Raymond in which he stated, flatly and finally, "I know that Peter Kent's claimed alibi for the night the murder of Marty Tankleff's parents occurred is false because it was concocted by myself and Peter Kent in the visiting room of the Mohawk Correctional Facility." Not to be outlasted, Lato submitted a reply declaring that the latest defense filing was part of "Tankleff's ever-changing theory." To which the defense responded with a point that was beyond dispute: If only one thing had *not* changed since the moment he discovered his parents, it was Marty Tankleff's theory of the crimes. Like all theories that bear out, the full picture evolved with each new discovery. "The prosecution," on the other hand, "has redefined blind stubbornness. In its latest defense of the flat-earth theory, the prosecution now adds Daniel Raymond to its list of diverse witnesses who are willing, for unknown reasons, to lie for Marty Tankleff."

The legal thrust and parry was uncommonly barbed but ultimately moot. Marty's lawyers knew Braslow would reject the latest motion as he had all the others, and that it would be just more fodder for the appeal. He did, and it was.

"LEAVE TO APPEAL," the formal request to the Appellate Division to accept an appeal, was granted only a month after it was filed, an unusually quick response that Barket did not discourage people from reading as a positive sign.

Shifting gears after three years of 440 motions, Marty's legal team was reorganized, with Steve Braga and Jennifer O'Connor assuming primary responsibility for the appeal and Barket and Pollack stepping back from the front line and into consulting roles. Continuing the perpetual motion of the lawyers' careers, O'Connor had moved from Baker Botts to another major firm, Wilmer, Cutler & Pickering, where she recruited yet one more team of young lawyers to Marty's cause. Chief among them was a rising star named Roberto Gonzalez, who had only recently finished a prestigious clerkship for Supreme Court justice John Paul Stevens. It was Gonzalez's second federal clerkship. The first was with Guido Calabresi— the judge of the Second Circuit Court of Appeals in New York who wrote the 1998 decision that conveyed serious doubt about Marty's conviction but couldn't quite find a way to overturn it.

The lawyers reexamined the entire history of the case, analyzing it from every possible angle of New York and federal law. After seven months of intense research, discussion, writing, and rewriting by lawyers in separate offices who knew their work could well be Marty's last chance, the brief was submitted to the Appellate Division on January 5, 2007. Though O'Connor emerged as the principal author, the appeal bore the names of no fewer than eleven attorneys from six different firms. Among them were Mark Pomerantz and Warren Feldman, who had brought the first appeal in 1992. As the lawyers liked to say, nobody ever leaves Marty's case.

Approaching its twentieth year, *People v. Tankleff* may well have been the nation's longest-running criminal litigation. So not surprisingly the brief was hardly brief. It ran 158 pages (plus twenty more citing precedents and authorities), and included information from the six people who had given sworn statements since the end of the hearing. "Because Marty is innocent," the brief noted, "it is unsurprising that this investigation continues to yield results."

The appeal took great umbrage at Braslow's decision, but in language that was relatively restrained—highlighting legal errors and poor reasoning rather than the judicial corruption that the facts suggested. Among Braslow's errors, according to the Tankleff defense team:

- He considered the witnesses in isolation, ignoring how they corroborated one another. Astonishingly, he claimed not to believe a single one of the six people who reported that Creedon made statements to them implicating himself. Even Lato said in his initial 2003 report that "too many persons unconnected with one another have reported that he did"—and several more emerged during the hearing. Braslow offered no explanation of why they would all come forward only to commit perjury.

- He adopted a virtual rule dismissing the credibility of anyone with a criminal record—the very kind of person prosecutors everywhere were so eager to use that they routinely offered inducements for testimony. In the case of those such as Glenn Harris and Joe Graydon, who had links to the crimes themselves, the brief quoted John G. Douglass, once a top federal prosecutor and currently dean of the law school at the University of Richmond: "Accomplices make the best witnesses. . . . Sometimes, they provide the only direct, eyewitness account. Without information from cooperating accomplices, many crimes would never be prosecuted at all."

- Instead of considering the evidence from the perspective of a reasonable juror at a retrial, as he was required to do, the judge adopted the perspective of the prosecution. Assessing the defense witnesses, Braslow, like Lato, seized on trivial inconsistencies that were easily explained by the passage of time—while dismissing or altogether ignoring the corroboration of their most critical testimony by other witnesses. And in one critical instance—his declaration that Joe Guarascio was "motivated by his mother" to lie about his father—the judge had no basis at all. "The court manufactured this motivation out of whole cloth," the defense said flatly: It was an act of blatant speculation that was revealing of the *judge's* motivation.

- Braslow's evaluation of Glenn Harris was especially unsound and biased. Harris's statements were corroborated by other witnesses, verified by a polygraph exam, and repeated to many people, including his mother, his wife, a priest, and a nun, over a period of years. Another witness was found after the close of the hearing—a prison inmate who said Harris told him, in the mid-1990s, that he was racked with guilt about his knowledge of a man serving life for murders he didn't commit. This was years before Harris was approached by Salpeter. "Harris has no plausible motive to fabricate his account—in fact, he has every reason to *deny* his involvement in a double homicide."

- Braslow had no legal basis for refusing to consider McCready's false denials of his relationship with Jerry Steuerman. "Indeed, if McCready were so committed to protecting Steuerman and implicating Marty that he would go so far as to *perjure* himself repeatedly in open court— an act that shows his consciousness of bias and wrongdoing—a reasonable jury would likely find that McCready was wholly unworthy of belief. Such impeachment would have ripple effects throughout the prosecution's case. Once McCready's bias and lack of credibility were established in this way, a reasonable juror would be far more likely to accept Marty's account of what happened in the interrogation room. . . ."

- Braslow wholly embraced the original prosecution's view of the case— that Marty's reactions to the murders were "inappropriate" and that he gave the police "conflicting and confusing accounts"—as if he hadn't heard the new evidence. "Although the testimony at trial showed that the defendant was upset and agitated that morning," Braslow wrote, " . . . overwhelming grief, fear, panic, bewilderment, did not appear to be present. Instead, he immediately set about trying to steer the detectives to Jerry Steuerman as being responsible for the attacks." The appeal noted that the descriptions of Marty's "inappropriate" behavior came from the police, who were hardly unbiased observers, especially in light of McCready's concealed relationship with Steuerman. Moreover, the new evidence established that Marty was right to "steer" the detectives toward Steuerman, something others tried to do as well.

ATTACHED TO THE defense's main appeal were six amicus curiae ("friend of the court") briefs, a collection of documents reflecting how prominent—how notorious—the Marty Tankleff case had become in the national movement that had grown around wrongful convictions. It was also an indication of Marty's indefatigable campaign on his own behalf. Steve Braga joked about the time he mentioned Marty to his opposing counsel in another case. "Martin Tankleff?" the other lawyer said. "I got a letter from him."

One of the amicus briefs was filed by the Center on Wrongful Convictions at the Northwestern University law school. The center was founded in 1999 and had already been involved in eleven exonerations of Death Row inmates in Illinois alone. Its brief was submitted on behalf of the Innocence Network, an umbrella for thirty-three organizations representing the wrongfully convicted in the United States, Canada, and Australia. A separate amicus brief was filed by Barry Scheck and the Innocence Project. Still another brief was submitted by several "exonerated false confessors." One of them was Connecticut's Peter Reilly, whose false confession to his mother's murder in 1971 was eerily similar to Marty's case. Three decades after he was exonerated, Reilly maintained a public profile in support of later generations of false confessors.

A major focus of the amicus briefs from the wrongful-conviction organizations was Judge Braslow's assertion that nothing McCready and Rein did would have led Marty to confess to something he didn't do and that McCready's ultimate trick was the kind of tactic that "has been deemed . . . the least likely to result in a false confession." To support this claim, Braslow cited a single sentence in a ruling by a federal judge in Wisconsin: "A lie that relates to a suspect's connection to the crime is the least likely to render a confession involuntary." But in an elaboration that Braslow conveniently omitted, the Wisconsin judge wrote that lies about *evidence* could lead to unreliable confessions, especially when police make "repeated false statements designed to induce a suspect to believe that the evidence against him is overwhelming." The consequence of police trickery, he added, "is further compounded if the suspect is young and impressionable."

Said one of the briefs, from the Center on Wrongful Convictions, citing several books and hundreds of peer-reviewed articles: "Contrary to Judge Braslow's findings that false evidence ploys are among the 'least likely' to result in a false confession, study after study and case after case have shown exactly the opposite. . . ." (The brief noted a fact particularly relevant to Marty's case: According to the police interrogator's bible, *Criminal Interrogation and Confessions*, suspects who volunteer to take a lie detector test are usually innocent.)

The amicus organizations asserted that Braslow's blatant intellectual dishonesty—cherry-picking one sentence from one case, taking it out of context—was matched by his disregard of the expert testimony of Richard Ofshe. "Inexplicably," Scheck and the Innocence Project wrote, "even though the People did not present contrary expert testimony and the County Court did not contest Dr. Ofshe's qualifications or methods, the County Court rejected the substance of Dr. Ofshe's testimony and held that it would not change the verdict." The Innocence Project recounted, among others, New York's infamous Central Park jogger case, in which five teenagers falsely confessed to a rape. Three years later, a convicted rapist confessed to the crime, and his confession was corroborated by DNA evidence.

Along with the amicus briefs by the innocence organizations, one was submitted by thirty former New York area prosecutors—assistant DAs in both Long Island counties and four of the five boroughs of New York City, as well as former assistant U.S. attorneys and New York attorneys general. (The Suffolk DA's office later pointed out that all were now defense attorneys.) Yet another brief was submitted jointly by three national and state criminal defense lawyers' associations and two retired judges. One, John S. Martin, Jr., was the U.S. attorney for New York's Southern District before he became a federal judge. The other, Herbert A. Posner, spent twenty years as a state Supreme Court justice, presiding over more than two hundred criminal trials. He read the hundreds of pages of transcripts from the Tankleff hearing and told Bruce Lambert of the *Times:* "I never saw a similar case where a defendant was so obviously innocent."

And finally, there was an amicus brief authored by Marc Howard, who organized a high school reunion of an unusual sort. Fifty-three members of the Earl L. Vandermeulen Class of 1989 signed on to a friend-of-the-court brief with a poignant friends-of-the-defendant argument. "It has often occurred to many of us that what happened to Marty could have happened to any one of us," Howard wrote on behalf of his classmates, blasting Braslow's "speculation, conjecture, and a pseudo-psychological understanding of what 'should' have been Marty's 'level of emotion.'" We knew Marty, the classmates said. "He was not someone who was prone to expressive outbursts, of either sadness or joy. More important, perhaps, is the fact that Marty was very impressionable and was always seeking to receive approval from authority figures. In a nutshell, he was a naïve kid who had a relatively weak sense of himself and who wanted to please and impress others. . . . [H]e would have been particularly vulnerable to the kinds of interrogation techniques that are known to produce false confessions—especially one that begins with 'Could I have blacked out and done this?'"

LIKE THE DEFENSE, the prosecution reargued the case from the beginning. Unlike the defense, it had nothing new to say. Its 195-page brief featured subheadings such as "Tankleff's Mood Swings and Outburst at Seymour," "Fear That Seymour Might Awaken Leaves Tankleff Speechless," "Resenting His Parents and Feeling Smothered," "Detailing How

He Murdered His Parents," and even "Physical Evidence Is Consistent with the Confession"—a presumably key section that ran all of four sentences. It recounted crime scene detective Charles Kosciuk's interpretation of the blood patterns on Seymour's desk and reported that he "found a knife in a position different from the one in which Bove, the card game's last user, had left it." (Even at the trial, the prosecution made no showing that Bove was in fact the last to use the knife, to say nothing of its failure to counter the overwhelming forensic evidence that the knife had nothing to do with the murders.)

When it came to the new evidence, Lato's brief read like an expanded version of Braslow's ruling. Under the headings "Tankleff Calls Biased Witnesses" and "The Witnesses Get Worse," he quoted bits and pieces of testimony to show how his cross-examinations exposed them all as "bad" witnesses—a cavalcade of nefarious scoundrels.

While preparing what would likely be its last defense of the conviction of Marty Tankleff—whatever the decision—the district attorney's office had become aware of a line of investigation by the Tankleff team and countered it aggressively. Toni Marie Angeli, a lawyer in Barket's office, had set about revisiting the case with the jurors who had convicted Marty a decade and a half earlier. She knocked on doors, hoping personal visits would lead the former jurors to go on record saying they wouldn't have found Marty guilty had they known then what they knew now. What she found didn't surprise her. "As a group," she said later, "they were tormented."

Angeli called on the jurors in order of their likelihood of being swayed by the new evidence—Peter Baczynski and the two last holdouts at the top of her list and Frank Spindel at the bottom. Baczynski now lived in Florida, and when Angeli reached him by phone she heard the voice of a haunted man. His anguish seemed so fresh and consuming that Angeli wondered if he'd had a day of peace in sixteen years. But Baczynski was no longer alone in thinking a terrible mistake had been made. Difficult as it was to come to terms with, most of the other nine jurors Angeli visited told her they found the new evidence credible. Though they still thought they had made their best judgment based on the evidence presented at the time, several agreed to provide statements saying they wouldn't have convicted Marty had the new evidence been available. But it wasn't unanimous. Angeli found a couple of the jurors determined to justify the verdict against any evidence to the contrary. "Even if there was a video of someone else, I wouldn't believe he wasn't involved," said one. "Not without DNA."

Angeli asked the jurors about the allegations of misconduct by Spindel that surfaced after the verdict. Several told her that despite Judge Tisch's findings, the mischief was as serious as Baczynski and Terry Quigley claimed, and Quigley herself intimated it was even worse. She said she wanted to think about it before saying anything more, but asked Angeli to come back, telling the attorney she would be astonished by the full extent of what went on.

But Angeli never heard the rest of the story. One of the last jurors she visited alerted the district attorney's office, and when Angeli called him back he told her he'd been instructed not to discuss the case. Though the DA had no legal authority over the former jurors, Angeli found them all suddenly uncooperative. "I don't know what they were told," she said, "but they went from being willing to talk and feeling very badly for 'the boy'—they all called Marty 'the boy'—to a totally different attitude. I kept hearing the same sound bite—'There's no DNA, and without DNA there's no proof he wasn't involved.'" That's what she heard from those who would talk to her at all. The rest cut her off completely. Angeli's pursuit of the jurors didn't make the appeal, but to the Tankleff team it was one more indication of the DA's abuse of the judicial process.

As it happened, that kind of grievance now had the attention of an agency of state government that had a history with the criminal justice system of Suffolk County.

Sometime earlier, Marty had written to members of the State Commission of Investigation. Joseph Kunzeman, a retired justice of the Appellate Division who was now a part-time special counsel to the SIC, got one of the letters. Kunzeman began looking into the case and proposed an official investigation to the commission's chairman, Alfred Lerner. The idea resonated. It had been twenty years since the SIC's investigation of the conduct of the Suffolk County police and prosecutors, particularly in homicide cases. The Tankleff case was clearly a product of the way things were done in those days—the overreliance on confessions, inadequate investigation, poor supervision. But what Kunzeman wanted to focus on was *now*. The way the case had been handled by Tom Spota's office, and the ruling by Braslow, indicated, as Stuart Namm said, that nothing had really changed. Lerner gave the green light to begin a new investigation, and the first person Kunzeman called was Marty Tankleff's private investigator.

Salpeter spent several hours with the commission's staff of lawyers and investigators, leading them through the case, furnishing documents. Over the next year, he kept them abreast of developments. But the investigation remained low-key and under wraps because the commission didn't want to interfere with the judicial process. Once the appeal was decided, it would go into high gear. So for a year and a half, the SIC's investigation was known only to its staff and to the inner circle of Marty's legal team. But it was a one-way street. "They give me nothing," Salpeter said one day when a colleague asked if he had a sense of where the SIC was going. It wasn't a complaint. Salpeter knew it had to be that way. Eventually, it would all come out.

LONELY HEARTS, a 2006 film based on the true story of a Long Island couple who swindled and murdered lonely war widows in the late 1940s, was written and directed by Todd Robinson, the grandson of the lead detective on the case. Robinson got John Travolta to play his grandfather and James Gandolfini to play his partner. And he hired Jay Salpeter as his technical consultant to make sure the details were right. In one scene, Travolta's character shows up at a house where the body of a woman has been found in a bathtub. "You don't have him securing the crime scene," Salpeter told Robinson. "You got cops putting their fingerprints all over the place." In the eventual movie, Travolta said, "All right, I want names and badges."

Salpeter became friendly with Gandolfini during the movie's production, and they kept up after it wrapped. Gandolfini even put Salpeter in a scene in *The Sopranos*. "It's after he gets shot, he's in Atlantic City, and he's dreaming he's some other guy," Salpeter told his friends. "He goes over to a table with some guys he's met and he's got me with a blond at another table. No lines, though. It's a union thing."

Anybody who knew Salpeter heard about Marty Tankleff before long. Gandolfini found the story no less fascinating than anyone else, and in August 2007 Salpeter asked him for a big favor. Marty's birthday is coming up, he said. He'll be thirty-six. Any chance you want to take a drive upstate? Gandolfini had a tight week, getting ready for the premiere of an HBO special on Iraq War veterans. "How important is this to you?" he asked Salpeter.

"James," Salpeter said, "you do this for me, I'm your investigator for life, no charge. Anything you need."

On Marty's birthday, Salpeter drove up to Great Meadow with Steve Braga and Lonnie Soury. It was a four-hour trip from the city, and Gandolfini came up separately with his driver. He had a friend opening a bakery in the Catskills and was planning go there afterward. Salpeter got to the prison with Braga and Soury, and they waited in the parking lot. When Gandolfini showed up, he was behind the wheel—his driver was sitting next to him. "He got tired," Gandolfini explained with a shrug.

Marty was shocked when he came into a private visiting room and saw his lawyer, his investigator, his public advocate, and Tony Soprano. They spent a couple of hours together and genuinely hit it off. Gandolfini told Marty, "I'm here for you. If there's anything I can do, you let me know.

But you better do it fast." He smiled. *The Sopranos* had recently and famously faded to black. "Couple months from now, nobody will know who I am. I'll be just another fat man."

A month later, Gandolfini offered a public show of support for Marty, joining Salpeter at the long-awaited oral arguments before the four judges considering the appeal in Brooklyn. He demurred when Soury asked if he'd like to make a quick comment to the media, and the horde kept an unusually respectful distance as Gandolfini and Salpeter made their way into the courthouse. Braga greeted Gandolfini and thanked him for coming. Salpeter told Braga, "I've had the case for six years and I'm giving it to you for one day. Don't fuck it up." The three men broke into a hearty laugh.

The hearing was in the grand courtroom of the Appellate Division's Second Department. It was here, fourteen years earlier to the week, that Mark Pomerantz delivered the argument on Marty's direct appeal, the one that came so close to freeing him. The courtroom had 120 seats for spectators, and not one was unoccupied. Barry Scheck was there, and so was Jeffrey Deskovic, a false confessor whom the Innocence Project had recently helped exonerate with DNA evidence. Also in attendance was Bennett Gershman, a law professor who became involved in Marty's case—and began lecturing about it in his classes—after receiving one of Marty's thousands of letters. No surprise: Gershman was one of the country's leading authorities on prosecutorial misconduct and judicial ethics.

Up front sat the four justices, evenly spaced across a bench that ran the width of the ornate courtroom. Unlike the last time, when the presiding justice was from Suffolk County and a mentor to the trial judge, the makeup of this panel raised no red flags for Marty's chances. In fact, on paper, it seemed as favorable a group as he could hope for. The presiding justice, Reinaldo E. Rivera, was from Brooklyn; he was the first Hispanic appointed to the Second Department in its 106-year history, and had never been a prosecutor. Justice Gabriel Krausman, also from Brooklyn, had been on panels that overturned three murder convictions. Mark C. Dillon was from Westchester, where he worked briefly as an assistant district attorney before spending the bulk of his career in private practice and then as a judge. Anita Florio was from the Bronx and had once been a counsel to Mario Cuomo, who later appointed her to the bench. She was also on the panel that reversed Jeffrey Deskovic's conviction.

By now the justices had studied the four hundred pages of appeal briefs, the amicus briefs, and the 1,800 pages of hearing transcripts, which themselves made frequent references back to the thousands of pages that made up the record of the trial and the subsequent state and federal appeals. There were great stacks of those papers in front of them, each

tabbed with countless yellow Post-its. It was said that judges in these proceedings already knew how they were going to rule by the time they
reached the oral arguments, though observers were advised against assuming that their questions or manner telegraphed what it would be.

Braga took the podium first, and after a brief presentation of his main
points the justices peppered him with questions, challenging him to respond to some of the prosecution's points of view, and to some of their
own. Braga responded smoothly for forty-five minutes, mixing legal dis-
course with occasional moments of righteousness, and his performance
seemed to satisfy the judges.

When Lenny Lato stood to address the panel, the tone changed
slightly. The judges seemed skeptical, for instance, when Lato argued
against the credibility of the defense witnesses with criminal records. "You
yourself use them all the time," Justice Krausman told him.

"*I* don't," Lato replied defensively.

Lato was unfazed, however, when he was challenged about the cumulative nature of the numerous witnesses whose testimony contributed to
the defense theory of the crimes.

"Quantity is no substitute for quality," he said. "Twenty times zero
equals zero."

Of the four judges, Krausman seemed squarely in the defense's corner.
Braga at one point had explained how the physical evidence contradicted
the confession the detectives attributed to Marty. He noted that the forensic lab took apart the knife presumed to be one of the murder weapons and
couldn't find a trace of blood.

"In fact, the knife had watermelon on it," Krausman pointed out.

And when the judges indicated that they were not inclined to revisit
the Miranda issue because it had been decided by a prior panel of the same
court, Krausman added a revealing aside. He said he would have been with
the minority—the two justices who thought the confession should have
been thrown out and, in the absence of any other evidence, the indictment
dismissed.

There seemed to be some hints also in comments by Rivera, the presiding justice. He asked at one point if the consideration of new evidence
should take into account when a case "didn't go quite right," an apparent
acknowledgment that there were problems even with the original case.

The hearing lasted two hours, much longer than the usual oral argument. "All we've ever been fighting for," Braga told the media outside the
courthouse, "is for somebody to take a good, long, hard look at the facts
and render a fair and impartial judgment."

Now, it was time to wait again.

*   *   *

A CALL CAME into the Tankleff tip line that night from a woman named Tina Malloy. It had nothing to do with the hearing in Brooklyn; she didn't even know about it. But she and her boyfriend knew Joe Creedon and became the latest people to say he incriminated himself in the Tankleff murders. Salpeter and Barket went to see them the next day and heard a story that was by now not surprising, though a piece of it was revealing in a new way.

Malloy said she'd dated Creedon for a few months earlier in the year, a romance that included accompanying him on several robberies. "He would joke and say I was his 'partner in crime,'" she said in an affidavit she signed that day. At a friend's house one day, Creedon went online and Googled up a picture of his son. He called Malloy over. He told her he couldn't believe his son testified against him but didn't deny anything he said. "He was hurt, upset that his son told people what he said," Malloy said. But not too upset. He said he wanted to write a book about the Tankleff case, or make a movie and play himself.

"But did you actually kill those people?" Malloy said she asked, and Creedon replied, "Yeah, I did, but they can't prove it. I'm untouchable." He seemed to act as if he were. Knowing Malloy's mother wasn't happy she was involved with him, he snickered, "How does she feel about her daughter dating a murderer?"

Malloy had split up with Creedon, and now she was with Dennis Piacente. That may have been a factor in the trouble Piacente was having with Creedon earlier in the summer. Piacente told Barket and Salpeter that he'd known Creedon since he was a kid and didn't take his threats lightly. So he had decided to call a contact in the Suffolk police department he'd made through his work shooting freelance news video. When Piacente told Malloy he was going to the police about Creedon, she told him to tell them about the things Creedon had told her about his involvement in the Tankleff murders. Piacente's contact, a detective sergeant in the Major Crimes Bureau, told him to call 911 if Creedon bothered him. As for Tankleff, the sergeant asked Piacente if it would be all right if he passed the information on to the DA's office. Piacente said sure. The sergeant was Bob Doyle. Apparently, he didn't tell Piacente that he had been in charge of the Tankleff homicide investigation all those years ago.

Three days later, Piacente got a call from Walter Warkenthien, and two weeks after that Warkenthien, Lato, and another investigator came to Piacente and Malloy's apartment. Lato did most of the talking.

Malloy said in her affidavit: "I told Mr. Lato and the other two about Joe's admissions. Mr. Lato made jokes. He seemed not to care at all. Mr. Lato also made fun of me by saying things like, 'Who's to say anyone is going to believe you?' He laughed about my boyfriend's speakers. (He has a big stereo system in my apartment.) He also said that 'just because he robs drugs dealers does not mean he is a murderer.' I said 'I know what he told me. I am telling you what he admitted to me.'"

Neither did the prosecutor and his investigators seem interested when Piacente told them what he saw when he helped Creedon move some things from his mother's house during the summer. Creedon took him into the garage, dialed the combination to a large safe, and showed him the "work items" he kept inside. There was a .22-caliber automatic weapon, leg irons, handcuffs, a security guard's badge on a neck chain, and a black stocking. Piacente said the only thing that got much of a reaction from Lato was a bullet that Creedon gave him. Piacente gave it to Lato, who laughed.

"Lato sat in my house defending Creedon and making jokes," Piacente said in his own affidavit. "Every time I told them about something Joe had done or said he did, they would try to explain it away or make it seem like it was not a big deal."

When Lato and his men left that day, they told Malloy and Piacente he would be in touch. That was now two months ago. Hearing nothing since, Piacente and Malloy decided to pick up the phone themselves. They called the Tankleff tip line. By sheer coincidence, they did it the day of the arguments on Marty's appeal.

Marty's lawyers put the latest statements in yet another 440 motion they filed in Suffolk County Court. Braga wrote the key words: "A killer is walking the streets of Suffolk County with a feeling of impunity. One can hardly imagine a more dangerous situation, and this one is—quite literally—the DA's own creation." The motion accused the district attorney's office of prosecutorial misconduct for suppressing exculpatory evidence, pointing out that Lato made his oral arguments to the Appellate Division within weeks of obtaining it. "We can only wonder, of course, how many other witnesses have come forward to the DA's office with further instances of Creedon's or Kent's admissions of participation in the Tankleff murders. Such witnesses have and will continue to come forward because Marty Tankleff is innocent, and they know it."

Why did Creedon continue to tell people he killed the Tankleffs, even after his own son gave him up? "I'm untouchable," he seemed to think, and with good reason judging by the response from the Suffolk County district attorney's office. And that—more than yet another of Creedon's admissions—was the real meaning of the information Malloy and Piacente brought forward.

Not that this was news to Salpeter. A year earlier, he had received information from a source he had developed who was close to Creedon. The source was direct and reliable, and in the summer of 2006 he told Salpeter that Creedon was threatening to kill him as well as Barket once the case was over. He said that Creedon had paid off a probation officer for private information on them from a law enforcement databank.

Barket told Lato about this. And Lato laughed.

6,338 Days

FOR MARTY and everyone involved in his case, the entire fall of 2007 was like those eight days in June 1990. Like waiting for another verdict—not for days but months. The oral arguments were heard on October 4, and rumor had it that the decision would be out by Thanksgiving. But Thanksgiving came and went. In early December, up at Great Meadow, Marty went to the prison infirmary. The doctor took his blood pressure. "It's very high," he said. "Have you been under any stress lately?"

One day in mid-December, Salpeter got a phone call from a source whose boss, a judge, had connections. The decision's coming next week, she said. But by the following Thursday, there was still nothing. Monday would be Christmas Eve. "Do you realize that if the decision comes down tomorrow, that'll be December twenty-first?" Salpeter said that day. "That's the exact date of Marty's first letter to me: December twenty-first, 2000. Seven years to the day."

The next morning, Salpeter called Lonnie Soury's office. Lonnie wasn't in yet. Are you hearing anything? Salpeter asked his secretary, Roz, who was also his mother-in-law. Nothing, she said. Seconds later, Salpeter's phone buzzed. It was Gail Zimmerman from *48 Hours*. "Jay, I'm online," she said, hesitatingly. "I think they reversed the conviction. I'm reading it. I think that's what it says."

Salpeter called Barket, just as Barket was calling Salpeter.

"We won!" Barket shouted into the phone. "I just got a call from the *Law Journal*. They vacated—we won!"

"Are you fuckin' kidding?" Salpeter said. "We *won*?"

"Get your ass up here!"

Salpeter called Cheryl in tears. "We won!" he said, and kept saying it.

He made another call and then another. "We won! Conviction vacated, new trial! We overturned a jury verdict *without DNA*! We fuckin' won!"

Barket called the superintendent's office at Great Meadow and said he needed his client to call him immediately. Marty called half an hour later.

"Pack your shit," Barket told him. "You're going home."

Marty took a deep breath, then offered up his unique brand of understatement. "Finally," he said. "Finally, justice starts to tilt our way."

The next step, as he already knew, was to get him released on bail. The court's ruling turned the clock back to the second before the guilty verdict was announced on the morning of June 28, 1990. Marty was out on bail then, so there should be no reason why he shouldn't get out on bail now. Barket gave him a rundown of the decision and said he'd fax it up.

"There is a God," Ron Falbee said when Barket called him with the news. Ron called Mike and Marianne in California. Mike answered, Ron broke the news, Mike shouted it to Marianne. "For the first time since I've known her," Mike told Ron, "Marianne is speechless." It was Ron's call that morning in 1988 in reverse, as if the rewind button had finally been pushed.

In Washington, Jennifer O'Connor called Steve Braga, who was on a train to New York with his family, and Braga called Barry Pollack, who told him, "You won the appeal!" No, said Braga. "*We* won." Braga's next call was to his dedicated assistant and Marty's passionate supporter, Meg Griffin. It was a bittersweet call: Meg was recovering from a stroke. "Praise the Lord," she said, and they both cried. But it wasn't until he got to his hotel in New York that Braga was able to talk to his long-imprisoned client. Marty could hardly hear Braga—his lawyer's whole family was screaming congratulations in the background.

Salpeter flew to Barket's office, and when he got there they did something they had never thought of doing through all the years and all their cases together: They hugged. Later, they joked about it. "I'm not a hugger," Barket said. "I'm not either," said Salpeter. Copies of the Appellate Division ruling spewed out of a printer, the magic words leaping from the seventh line of the first page: "vacate the judgments and the sentences imposed thereon . . . remit the matter for a new trial."

The Falbees arrived and there were more hugs. "It's been a long time," Ron told the first of the reporters and TV crews. "A long, long time."

Even the reporters were excited. It was a great story, sure, but it was a happy one, too. It had long been obvious that the journalists covering the case most closely were pulling for him. They had an affection for his family that was not unlike the empathy reporters could be expected to develop for the loved ones of hostages, or of coal miners trapped a mile underground as rescuers worked to save them. It was the prosecution—indeed,

Suffolk County's criminal justice system as a whole, once Judge Braslow's decision was announced—whom reporters tended to look upon with disapproval. They found themselves incredulous at some of the things they had heard from the mouth of Lenny Lato over the course of three years, and when Braslow's decision came down they couldn't help but join the Tankleff camp in ridiculing his idea of justice.

"Justice" and "injustice"—the words hovered in the air as Marty's legal team and family exhaled. "The way the DA's office has handled this," Ron told one of the New York television reporters, "to me, it's criminal."

THE UNANIMOUS RULING by the four justices of the Appellate Division was an extraordinary rebuke of Judge Stephen Braslow—and by implication, a recognition that something was terribly wrong in Suffolk County.

"It is abhorrent to our sense of justice and fair play," wrote the presiding justice, Reinaldo E. Rivera, "to countenance the possibility that someone innocent of a crime may be incarcerated or otherwise punished for a crime which he or she did not commit."

The court was dismissive of the district attorney's argument, and Braslow's agreement, that the defense brought forward its new evidence too late to meet the "due diligence" requirement of the 440 statute. Indeed, it seemed to the judges that the defense showed remarkable diligence in presenting "a body of new evidence which required time to accumulate." Then the court laid into Braslow's appraisal of the evidence: "The County Court's determination amounted to a misapplication of its gatekeeper function. . . ." Braslow was "obligated to conduct a critical analysis of the evidence. [He] cannot merely engage in the mechanical exclusion of such evidence."

The Appellate Division justices castigated Braslow for failing to judge the evidence not only reasonably but cumulatively. Had he done so, he would have had to conclude that had the jury heard this evidence, it probably would have acquitted Marty. "The County Court completely disregarded a crucial fact which is pivotal to our determination," Rivera wrote. "Namely, many of the witnesses who testified at the CPL article 440 hearing were *unrelated* to each other, and their genesis as witnesses was separated by both space and time." But Braslow "erroneously applied both a narrow approach and methodology in evaluating the evidence. The County Court, in effect, applied a blanket disqualification of all of the defendant's proffered evidence. It viewed almost all of the defendant's witnesses as questionable, untrustworthy, or unreliable. It dismissed, outright, the possibility that witnesses with criminal records, drug addictions, and/or psychiatric issues may nevertheless be capable of testifying truthfully. As noted by my learned colleague, the Honorable Gabriel Krausman, at the oral argument before this Court, the People 'use [such witnesses] all the time.'"

The court also rejected as "sheer conjecture and speculation" the assertions of the district attorney and embraced by Braslow that some witnesses had ulterior motives for testifying. For instance, "We cannot conclude that multiple witnesses who admittedly expressed fear of or contempt for Creedon perjured themselves in order to implicate Creedon in the murders." Nor could it be said that the testimony would be inadmissible at a new trial. "In fact, significant competent evidence in admissible form was elicited at the CPL article 440 hearing from disparate and wholly unrelated sources. This evidence warrants a new trial."

As they had signaled during the oral argument, the judges declined to revisit the Miranda question after two decades of litigation. But they did revisit, in effect, the question of who told the truth about the interrogation—the detectives or the defendant. Had the jury been presented with the new evidence, it probably would have found Marty's version of how his confession was obtained more plausible than McCready and Rein's.

THE REVERSAL OF the verdict triggered an explosion of media coverage that surprised even Marty's tireless publicity men, Lonnie Soury and Eric Friedman. On their front pages, *Newsday* and the *New York Post* ran photos of Marty as a teenage defendant next to recent ones of him as an inmate with a receding hairline. "FINALLY, JUSTICE!" announced the *Post*. "WRONG MAN" WINS LI RETRIAL. The *Daily News* cover was a time warp—a photo only of young Marty next to the headline COURT TOSSES TEEN'S CONVICTION IN HIS PARENTS' BRUTAL MURDER.

While reporters filled their notebooks with reactions from the Tankleff camp, they had to wait a day to hear from District Attorney Tom Spota, beyond a terse written statement saying his office disagreed with the decision. "Let me say this," Spota said at a news conference on Saturday. "It's very clear that this court has said that they are not exonerating Mr. Tankleff's claim of actual innocence. They directed that a new trial be held."

"Do you still believe that Martin Tankleff killed his parents?"

"I never said that Martin Tankleff killed his parents," Spota replied. "I never said that he did or did not. What I have consistently said is that I do not believe that the people that the Tankleff team has said killed these people did indeed kill these people."

Actually, Spota did say Martin Tankleff killed his parents. Asked about the case while running for reelection in 2005, he told *Newsday* that he was convinced of it because "it was a crime of rage and passion," not the work of a professional killer. This was the opposite of what he told the Paschke family a decade earlier: He had seen the crime scene photos and there was no way scrawny little Marty Tankleff did it. And it was consistent with the evidence presented by the defense that the murders were committed by two coked-up street thugs—hardly professional hit men. Why was Spota now so adamant that the Tankleffs were not killed by Creedon and Kent on behalf of Steuerman? No one asked. They did ask whether he would retry Marty and Spota said it was too soon to say. But for now, it was only right that he be released from prison with a "reasonable bail." That turned out to be a million-dollar surety bond.

From the moment he heard about the reversal, Marty was to have six more days in custody. It would have been one or two but the weekend and then Christmas got in the way. Time always went slowly in prison, but these were six of the longest days of all. He barely slept. Suffolk County would transport him down to Riverhead on Wednesday afternoon. The bail hearing would be Thursday morning. Ron and Carol Falbee would sign the bond guaranteeing his appearances at all future court proceedings. And then Marty would be free.

Marty stayed up all night Tuesday, waiting. He sat on his bed. He looked out the window. And he wrote letters. Steve Braga liked to joke that Marty wrote him every day for ten years, and if he missed a day he would write two the next day. "This will be my last letter to you from a prison cell," Marty wrote to Braga on his dependable Brother 500 electric. "As I type this, my bags are packed and I'm ready to go. I've been looking out my window at the snow capped mountains and look forward to when I can roam those mountains as a free man. . . ."

And he wrote one more last letter:

Dear Jay,

By the time you get this letter, I should have been able to hug you and thank you properly in person. But I really wanted you to know how thankful I am for you coming into my life. . . . I still remember when you wrote me the letter about getting ready for the roller coaster ride. Never could I imagine it would have so many twists, turns, loops, upside down twists and more. But the ride is nearing an end and it's all because of you and your dedication and hard work. Lonnie has joked often that he wants me out of jail so he can get rid of me. Well, I'm letting you know you'll never get rid of me for life, since you've given me my life back!! I don't want to cut this short, but I have to finish getting ready for my last few hours in a prison and get ready to spend some very, very, very long overdue quality time with family (that means you) and friends.

Love,

Marty

Late the next afternoon, Marty heard goodbyes and good wishes from prisoners and guards alike. He bequeathed his typewriter to another inmate and walked, handcuffed, out of Great Meadow and into a Suffolk County Sheriff's Department car. He had made trips back to Long Island before, for the federal Batson hearing in 1998 and the 440 motion six years later. But this time he was less than a day from freedom. When the sheriff's car arrived at the county jail in Riverhead that night, a cluster of photographers and TV crews emerged from the darkness and shined their lights into the backseat. "Marty! Hey, Marty!" they yelled, the way the paparazzi do to get their quarry to look their way and smile. Marty stared out, squinting, looking utterly baffled. It was carried live on Long Island's Channel 12 and led the eleven o'clock news on all the New York City stations.

The next morning, an excited crowd gathered outside the courthouse doors. The McClures were in from California once more, this time with their daughter Jennifer. She had testified at the trial as an eighteen-year-old, and would never forget driving Marty's car home with her mother after he was convicted. Now they were back here, all these years later. Marianne was wearing one of the yellow MARTY IS INNOCENT buttons they all wore to the sentencing before Judge Tisch made them take them off. Two of Marty's cousins, Autumn Asness and Lynne Kadan, hugged when they saw each other, then suddenly broke out in the giddiest of songs: *If you're happy and you know it, clap your hands!*

Bob Gottlieb was here. "I've always said I would be there the day Marty walked out of prison," he said, smiling wistfully. Buried somewhere in his mind was the sting of the "ineffectiveness of trial counsel" grounds in Marty's final appeal. It was quietly put to rest in the last sentence of the ruling: "In light of our determination, we need not consider the defendant's remaining contentions." Hardly anyone noticed.

The bail hearing could have been conducted by any one of the eleven County Court judges. But this was the week between Christmas and New Year's, so whatever judge was around would take it. The daily printout of cases posted in the courthouse lobby said it would be Judge Doyle. But there was a change. The crowd was directed to the familiar courtroom of

Judge Braslow on the third floor. The room was packed when Braslow entered and took his seat at the bench. He looked as though he would rather be anywhere else.

"Your client will be coming out forthwith," he said softly to Barket and Pollack.

Marty was brought in a few minutes later. He smiled toward the crowd of family and friends and supporters, who restrained the impulse to break into applause, or cheers, or something. Braslow got through the formalities of the bail—Ron and Carol came to the lawyers' lectern to affirm under oath that they were guaranteeing the bond—and said this would end his involvement in the case. "This will now be Judge Doyle's case."

In the judgment of Marty's relatives, Braslow seemed embarrassed, almost contrite. It would only be natural, given the way the Appellate Division dismembered his decision, like a law professor telling a first-year student that maybe this wasn't the career for him.

"Keep in touch with Mr. Barket," Braslow said to Marty, as if he were a garden-variety defendant represented by a public defender he'd just met for the first time. "Good luck to you, sir."

Now came the applause, the way it does at the end of a wedding ceremony. Marty turned to Barket. "I'm not a convicted felon anymore," he said. "I can vote."

He was taken through a side door, then to another part of the building, where he reconnected with Barket and Pollack, along with Jennifer O' Connor. The handcuffs came off.

After 6,338 days in prison, Marty was free.

The foursome went out a back door and circled back toward the main part of the courthouse, trailed by a clot of cameramen and a news helicopter above. "This is a live shot from Chopper 12," an anchorman for Long Island's cable news station was saying from the studio. "Marty Tankleff is going back inside to meet his family and speak to the media." A court officer cleared a path as random people in the parking lot smiled and applauded. "Marty, how's it feel to be out?"

A few minutes later, Marty emerged through a door and into the third-floor lobby, where he was enveloped by his family, a tearful scene of almost unbearable bittersweetness. Then Marty made his way to the lectern, microphones arrayed in front of him, cameras trained from every angle. He read from a written statement, a moment reminiscent of the last time he was released on bail, the day before his father's funeral. If everything else had changed, his voice hadn't. He still spoke with the rushed cadence of a teenager.

It's great to see all of you here today. If my arrest and conviction was a night-

mare, this is a dream come true. I want to thank everyone who made this possible. Jay Salpeter, for reading a letter I sent him one day, and then taking it upon himself to go out and solve this case. My entire, incredible legal team. The people who have been getting the truth about my case out through the media and the website. The witnesses who have come forward just because it was the right thing to do. The appellate judges whose ruling demonstrates they did a thorough review of the case record and acted accordingly. All my friends and supporters, in Suffolk County and across the nation and literally around the world, for your interest and for making my fight your fight. Most of all, my family, who have stood by me from day one right up to this moment. Remember that while I am innocent, I am still accused by the Suffolk County district attorney of the murder of my parents, and I am awaiting a possible retrial. I do hope that I can continue to count on everyone's support as I defend myself once again. I always had faith this day would come. I look forward to welcoming in the new year with my family. Happy New Year.

Salpeter looked for Bruce Lambert in the crowd. The *New York Times* reporter wrote the first story about the new evidence in 2003 and had covered the case closely and cogently ever since. Salpeter had had a phone conversation earlier that morning and gotten a green light to leak a piece of information he'd been keeping confidential for a year and a half. He'd jotted a note, folded it, and put it in the inside pocket of his suit jacket. Now he spotted Lambert outside the courtroom and sidled up to him, a little mysteriously. He handed him the note and walked away. "For the past year and a half the State Investigation Commission has been investigating Suffolk County's conduct in this case."

AFTER STOPPING at a gas station for his first cup of coffee brewed outside prison walls, Marty returned with the Falbees to their home—his home, too, until the morning of June 28, 1990, and now again. His twin cousins, Susanne and Carolyn, were eleven then. Now they were near thirty and on their own, but today they were here to welcome Marty home.

Relatives, friends, members of Team Tankleff, and a few select journalists gathered for a celebration like no other. TV trucks were parked on the street, and newspaper photographers milled about. They would be there in shifts for days. Marty Tankleff's homecoming was getting the full Big Media treatment. Inside, Marty sat on the sofa in the family room with a laptop. He went on the Internet for the first time and headed straight for martytankleff.org. Someone gave him a cellphone and he looked it over with a kind of bemused awe. "It's mine?" he said. He ate a plate of food and declared himself ready for another. Laughter filled the house into the night. "It's Marty Gras," said the senior Kurt Paschke. People gazed at Marty doing the most ordinary things and found the scene positively surreal.

"It's like the whole family got out of prison today," said Marty's cousin Lynne.

On Saturday, the family escaped to Ron and Carol's weekend home in Pennsylvania. With the media still camped out, it was a major decoy operation. Ron and Carol and the twins left from the driveway as the cameras recorded their departure. Marty went out the back, through a neighbor's yard. Ron picked him up, and they made it to the Poconos without being tailed. The following week, Marianne emailed photos of Marty skiing to the rest of the family and friends.

The day they left, Bruce Lambert broke the story of the State Investigation Commission in the *Times*. "The commission is looking at how Suffolk County handled this case," he quoted an official to whom he'd been directed by Salpeter. The SIC viewed its inquiry as a follow-up to its report eighteen years earlier, said the source. The question to be answered: "Are there still systemic problems and should anyone be held accountable for the arrest and prosecution of Mr. Tankleff?"

Newsday picked up the story the next day, with the commission's chairman, Alfred Lerner, going on the record. "We're going to look at the whole thing," he said. He told the newspaper that the SIC began looking into the case after getting a "complaint." He didn't reveal that the person who made the complaint was Marty Tankleff himself.

Over the next few days, there were calls on the opinion pages of newspapers for Spota to finally step aside and let a special prosecutor take over. The revelation of the SIC investigation was a major boost: How could Spota pursue a retrial while his own actions in the case were under scrutiny? But Spota did something more, and it caught everyone by surprise. On January 2, he announced that he would not retry Marty Tankleff. But it wasn't because he thought Marty was innocent. "I firmly believe that the various theories advanced as to others who may be responsible for the murders are just not supported by the credible evidence," Spota said, reading a prepared statement at a news conference. "The manner in which Arlene Tankleff and Seymour Tankleff were killed is totally inconsistent with a hit or a burglary, as has been suggested. Nevertheless, for legal and factual reasons the prosecution against this defendant is over."

It was hard to prosecute any twenty-year-old murder case, said Spota—witnesses die, memories fade—but the primary reason behind his decision was a change in the law that would hamstring any effort to reconvict the defendant. Marty Tankleff was acquitted of intentional murder in his mother's death but convicted of the "depraved indifference" count. In

2004, the New York Court of Appeals ruled that prosecutors could no longer charge murder defendants under two incompatible theories and give juries a choice. Marty was acquitted of intentional murder in one death, so the rule of double jeopardy barred him from being tried again on that charge. "The evidence shows that both victims were intentionally murdered," Spota said. ". . . I believe that attempting to try half of the case against Tankleff is futile and I will not do it." He carefully avoided any acknowledgment that the futility of retrying Marty had anything to do with the mountain of evidence brought by the Tankleff team, or the specter of a cross-examination of McCready that would feature, among other things, a few questions about why he perjured himself about his relationship with Jerry Steuerman.

Finally, Spota offered his personal view of the case. He laid out, rather defensively, all the ways in which he had performed his duties honorably. "After nearly twenty years of successful appellate litigation, *I* consented to the defense request for a hearing to vacate the conviction of Martin Tankleff," he said, skipping the nine months when he opposed it. "When the Appellate Division vacated the defendant's conviction *I* agreed to a bail the defendant was able to post and assured that Tankleff was produced in court as expeditiously as possible." And finally, a dramatic announcement: Once the indictment was formally dismissed, "I intend to request that the governor consider the appointment of a special prosecutor to resolve any residual doubts with respect to the potential prosecution of other individuals the defense claims participated in these murders."

Marty rejoiced at the news that he would not be retried, ignoring Spota's obstinacy about the matter of his guilt as if it were an annoyance only to be expected. It seemed, at least, that the district attorney was finally doing a proper thing by allowing a special prosecutor to decide whether to pursue "other individuals."

Soury and Friedman went into high gear, alerting the media to a news conference the next day at Baker Botts's Manhattan office. The firm's large meeting room was packed—a huge gathering of media equaled by Marty's army of lawyers, family, and friends, many wearing FREE MARTY buttons. One after another, the principal players spoke and took questions, and then Marty took the stage to speak for himself, fielding questions about his feelings and his future. A reporter asked if he could foresee a reconciliation with his long-estranged half sister, Shari.

"Shari who?" Marty replied.

The next night, Shari came out of her house and stood before a smaller number of cameras in the cold night air of Long Island. In 2004, Shari had said on *48 Hours* that the new evidence brought by Glenn Harris and Karlene Kovacs had her "back on that fence" about whether Marty did it or

not. She was so *confused* now, she said. That was before the hearing—
before Billy Ram and Joe Graydon and Joe Guarascio and a dozen others.
What did she think now, after all their testimony and the unequivocal ruling overturning the verdict? "Mr. Spota's decision not to try to appeal this
case is senseless and illogical," she said, her face contorted with rage, her
ex-husband, Ron Rother, standing behind her. "These latest developments have left me, my family and friends appalled, ashamed, discouraged,
and disillusioned in our judicial structure." Among her estranged family, it
was assumed that Shari's wrath had something to do with another question
about her that Marty had been asked but had not answered: Would he sue
his half-sister to recover some of his inheritance?

The Rothers' former business partner, on the other hand, said he
couldn't care less—all this meant nothing to him. "I did my job," Jim
McCready told a reporter over the phone from South Carolina. "The kid
is still guilty. I don't care if they let him out of jail."

But Shari cared, and she was presumably pleased by what came next.
Spota had announced he would ask Governor Eliot Spitzer to "consider"
appointing a special prosecutor after the charges against Marty were formally dropped on January 18. But in a curious move ostensibly of his own
volition, Spitzer stepped in six days before that court date, announcing the
immediate appointment of the state attorney general, Andrew Cuomo, to
take over the case. Cuomo, in turn, announced that his office would investigate the Tankleff case from the beginning, follow the evidence wherever it led, and then decide what to do. Until then, the indictment of
Martin Tankleff would remain in place.

The turn of events had the scent of political arrangement: Why did
Spitzer (whose patronage of prostitutes would force him to resign two
months later) jump the gun, negating what could be argued was the first
sound decision Tom Spota had made in the entire case? Under similar circumstances, a district attorney might be expected to vigorously protest
such big-footedness by the governor. But there was no protest from Tom
Spota. He gladly washed his hands of the entire mess—saved by the governor, at the eleventh hour, from the awkwardness of being known among
the lawmen of Suffolk County as the guy who let Marty Tankleff walk.
Meanwhile, the selection of Attorney General Cuomo—as opposed to the
more typical appointment of a former prosecutor or judge—left the polit-
ically savvy among Marty's camp feeling wary of the outcome. In New
York power circles, Cuomo was widely viewed as a ruthless operator who
made no move without assessing its impact on his career. He certainly had
not achieved the exalted moral reputation of his father, in whose footsteps
he had long hoped to follow as governor.

* * *

A FEW DAYS AFTER Cuomo took over the case and put Marty back in limbo, Salpeter received a package in the mail from Marianne McClure. Inside, framed and under glass, was the note he had written to Marty six years earlier: "Buckle up my friend. . . ." Marianne sent it before Cuomo's announcement postponing Marty's ticket to permanent freedom. But it was still relevant, not a memento quite yet.

With still one more decision to wait out, Marty spent the next few months alternately preparing for the possibility of a second trial and laying the groundwork for his long-delayed adult life. He made himself at home again with the Falbees, and Ron resumed his role as surrogate father, even as his own daughters, eight years Marty's junior, were out on their own. The day after Marty's release, Ron suggested he call Hofstra University. The trust his father left the university was still there, ready to be tapped for tuition. Spring semester was starting in a couple of weeks. Marty said he'd call in a few days. "I think you should call today," Ron said. Yeah, Marty said, later in the week. "Marty," Ron said, "I really think you ought to call *today*."

Marty spent the semester studying philosophy and sociology at Hofstra and the changes in New York's law on depraved indifference murder charges at Bruce Barket's law office. He failed his first attempt to reacquire his driver's license so he had to get rides to school and sometimes rode a bicycle to Barket's office, where he had a desk and a place for the boxes of files shipped down from prison.

For six months, meanwhile, a team of lawyers and investigators from the attorney general's office reviewed and reinvestigated the murders of his parents. The AG's people, led by Benjamin Rosenberg, the office's chief trial counsel, interviewed dozens of people—from all-but-forgotten trial witnesses such as fitness trainer Dan Hayes to Braslow's cavalcade of nefarious scoundrels—and some of them testified before a grand jury. Rosenberg wanted to interview Marty, as well as Jerry Steuerman. True to form, Marty was willing and eager. Ever vigilant, his lawyers huddled, but after a round of negotiations between Pollack and Rosenberg, Marty sat down with the attorney general's team and answered all their questions. But the investigators never got the chance to interview Steuerman. He refused to talk to them.

On June 30, 2008, six months after the verdict was set aside, Rosenberg came to Judge Robert Doyle's court with his staff to announce whether he intended to proceed with a second trial or dismiss the indictment for good. The courtroom was packed with all the familiar faces:

Marty's aunts and uncles and cousins, supporters from the website, the full complement of media. Behind them all, against the rear wall of the courtroom, stood a line of stone-faced men in jackets and ties. They were the latter-day brothers of Jim McCready and Norman Rein, members of the Suffolk County homicide squad. Marty was well represented himself: Five of his lawyers were in attendance.

The attorneys from both sides were summoned to the judge's chambers, leaving Marty alone in the well of the courtroom. He looked oddly calm, even for him. It was the people in the spectator section who fidgeted anxiously as the minutes went by, pondering and speculating what the lawyers could be doing back there that was taking so long. Either they were going to try him or they weren't—what was there to discuss? Unless it was pretrial motions. Finally the legal teams emerged from the inner sanctum. Eyes fixed on Barket and Pollack and Braga and O'Connor, but all anyone saw was one poker face after another. Until, finally, Barket took his seat next to Marty at the defense table, said something in his ear, turned back to Salpeter, and smiled.

Rosenberg stood and faced the judge. "After extensive review," he said, "the attorney general has determined that although there is some evidence that the defendant, Martin Tankleff, committed the crimes charged"— dubious looks washed over the spectators—"after twenty years the evidence is insufficient to conclude or to prove beyond a reasonable doubt that he did so."

In the interests of justice, he said, the indictments should be dismissed.

The front of the gallery seemed to exhale collectively. But Marty barely reacted—it turned out he knew the decision even before he entered the courtroom. Barket had gotten a call on his cellphone while he and Pollack were on their way to Riverhead. Marty would not be retried. And no one else would be prosecuted, either.

The reasons for both decisions were spelled out in a summary of the investigation that Rosenberg filed with his motion to dismiss the indictments. It was an odd and often confounding document. This, for instance, was what he meant by "some evidence" that Marty Tankleff did commit the murders: "There was no sign of a break-in or of a robbery, and the defendant, who was the only other person in the house, was unharmed." Also, the defendant "made direct confessions to some fellow inmates in prison." Rosenberg didn't name them but he was apparently referring to the two discredited prison snitches Lenny Lato dredged up in 2003, one of them being the neo-Nazi skinhead satanist who claimed Marty took a break from his legal research one day to confess to him in the law library. Such a blind and misleading reference seemed an arbitrary thing to feature in a document presented as a summary of the most salient evidence.

But of course it wasn't arbitrary. Rather, it appeared part of an effort to portray this as a case too ambiguous to ever be resolved. This was an approach that allowed the attorney general to cite evidence in Marty's favor, suggesting an unbiased investigation, while making sure it ended here.

For instance, Rosenberg acknowledged there was "controversy" surrounding Marty's alleged confession, and he became the first prosecutor in the history of the case to concede that the key details were contradicted by the forensic evidence. But he qualified it by saying there was no physical evidence "strongly" linking Marty to the crimes. Meanwhile, he noted that there was "testimonial evidence from a number of sources, some of which are clearly independent of any of the others, that other persons may have committed the murders." But in his judgment, "on balance, the defense theory does not appear to be supported by clear evidence." For one thing, just as there was no forensic evidence firmly linking Marty Tankleff to the crimes, there was also none connecting Creedon, Kent, Steuerman, or Harris. Another problem, according to Rosenberg, was that a number of witnesses who testified at the 440 hearing "recanted their testimony or changed their stories when we interviewed them."

This was where the attorney general's investigation became truly confounding. Though Rosenberg named no names, the defense team was aware of one recanter, and it was no surprise. A few weeks earlier, Glenn Harris had called Salpeter and told him he made up his entire story and had signed an affidavit to that effect for the attorney general's office. Barket talked to Harris's lawyer, who told him that the attorney general's people believed Harris when he said he fabricated his story in an attempt to help Marty Tankleff because he thought he was innocent.

Salpeter got a copy of the affidavit, and to him all signs pointed to a more sophisticated and successful version of Lato and Warkenthien's attempts to frighten Harris five years earlier. Harris told Salpeter he'd gotten a visit from four people from the AG's office—Rosenberg, his deputy counsel, and two investigators—a day before his latest parole from Sing Sing. Why then and why there? Salpeter wondered. What message would that send such a weak-willed and easily intimidated man as Harris? The result was a statement in which he recounted all the things he had sworn to four years earlier and had since repeated to everyone from his wife to a national television audience—and then recanted everything. He did not drive Creedon and Kent to Belle Terre. He did not wait in the car as they went inside the Tankleffs' house. He did not see them come out with bloody clothes and a pipe, which he did not see Creedon throw into the woods before he did not drive them back to Selden, where he did not see Kent burning his clothes. Harris also claimed he told Salpeter and Barket that his story was a lie, but they just wouldn't listen. And then came Paragraph 10: "I understand that if the facts set forth in Paragraph 2 were correct—which they are not—it could be argued that I was criminally responsible for the murders of the Tankleffs. I was not criminally responsible, however, because the facts set forth in Paragraph 2 are not true."

Salpeter subsequently learned that Harris, back in Port Jefferson after his release, went to the emergency room of Mather Hospital two weeks later, asking to be admitted to the psychiatric unit. A security guard on duty that night said that Harris sat with him for half an hour, talking about how he was the driver in the Tankleff murders. Nothing had changed, Salpeter thought. Harris was the same head case he always was, the same frightened little man who wanted to tell the truth but kept hearing the voice of Walter Warkenthien in his ear. Marty Tankleff was out of prison now—maybe Harris was feeling the prophecy of trading places with him drawing closer. Salpeter knew by now that this was how Harris's mind worked. But it wasn't his story that was the issue anymore. The real question was why the AG's people would look at his original account—its veracity supported by a polygraph, corroborated in different ways by Billy Ram and Karlene Kovacs and Joe Graydon and Joe Guarascio—and believe his retraction was true and pure, worthy of a sworn statement setting the record straight. If Rosenberg found Harris to be an unreliable witness—certainly a prudent judgment—why not simply ignore him? What was his motivation in memorializing a patently false recantation?

Still, the attorney general's investigation could not be called a whitewash. It found what appeared to be a piece of previously overlooked forensics that added to the body of evidence that the wrong man was prosecuted: a bloody imprint made by a knife on the bedsheet in the room where Marty's mother was killed. It didn't match any of the knives in the house. Like the rubber gloves that were also never found, the newly discovered knife impression pointed to a killer from the outside. But not to anyone in particular, which was why Rosenberg saw it as a reason to dismiss the indictment against Marty, but not a reason to prosecute the other suspects.

But to the Tankleff team, the finding of new forensic evidence after all these years was stunning: The knife print was the closest thing to a smoking gun. "It is the most damning piece of evidence to date that Marty's confession was completely false, fabricated and fed to him by McCready," Braga said. "Up to now, the argument for the false confession was that it failed to match any of the physical evidence. But this knife print gives us evidence affirmatively proving that something entirely different happened in that house that night. Just as important is the question it raises: Did the original crime scene investigators completely miss the knife print—or did they see it and bury it? That's an even more sinister scenario of corruption than we imagined."

The state investigators came up with one more new piece of information. They spoke to witnesses from the original police investigation who said that James McCready showed them crime scene photos. There was no legitimate reason for him to do this, Rosenberg wrote, and it constituted misconduct that would be "problematic" at a retrial. "[H]is wrongdoing, which was unknown prior to our investigation, would make the case harder for the People to try." But what of McCready's far more serious misconduct—his evident perjury about never having met Steuerman, to say nothing of his contributions to the "controversy" surrounding Marty's alleged confession, which would certainly be scrutinized more closely at a second trial than they were at the first? Rosenberg, unaccountably, said nothing about either.

The revelation that McCready had shown crime scene photos to witnesses came as no surprise to Salpeter—because he had spoken to one of them only a week before. He had gotten a call from Dan Hayes, whom he had interviewed several years earlier. Hayes wanted Salpeter to know that the attorney general's investigators seemed headed in the wrong direction with old and discredited information.

In the summer of 1988, Marty had ordered a large quantity of nutritional supplements through an ad in a bodybuilding magazine. He charged them to the gym and planned to use some and sell the rest, but Hayes intercepted the delivery and informed Seymour. The product was legal and harmless, Hayes assured him, but he couldn't have Marty making unauthorized purchases through the gym. Seymour confiscated the supplements and Marty apologized to Hayes. But the story put out by the prosecutors was that Marty was using *steroids*, suggesting "'roid rage" was a factor in the murders of his parents, though Marty's unimpressive physique belied the theory. Apparently, however, it was another myth that wouldn't die. Hayes had firsthand knowledge of several important aspects of the case—Seymour's fears about Steuerman, for instance—but when the attorney general's investigators came to interview him twenty years later they focused on the one that was meaningless. "Their big concern was the so-called steroids, asking whether it was 'roid rage that gave Marty the strength to kill his parents," Hayes told Salpeter when he met him early one Sunday morning. "I told them no way—he couldn't even get away with selling protein powder. But they were trying really hard to make it work. They just couldn't let it go." (The state investigators' theory was nothing if not ironic all these years later. Outperformed on the weight machines by his mother when he was a teenager, Marty was now putting his investigator to shame. Salpeter took him to his gym and watched in amazement as Marty pressed 350 pounds.)

Salpeter asked Hayes what else he told the state investigators. Hayes said he recounted the day he was called to testify for the prosecution at Marty's trial. "I was waiting in a room," he recalled, "and McCready comes in and says, 'I need you to come with me.' He takes me into an evidence room. There's two other guys there. They tell me they've got the murder weapons on a shelf over there. One of them says they found the dumbbell in the backyard and he couldn't believe how the kid was trying to get away with it. Then McCready showed me a book of pictures from the crime scene. I saw Arlene with her neck slashed, and I didn't want to see any more."

The subject of McCready led to something that stunned Salpeter, even at this late juncture. Hayes told him he had personal knowledge that off-duty Suffolk County police detectives provided security for Todd Steuerman's drug business. He said he knew this because he slept at the gym to save money on rent, and on weekends he worked security with other off-duty cops at the roller rink next door. Both businesses were in a shopping plaza that shared a parking lot with the one next door that included Strathmore Bagels. Hayes said he would see men standing guard outside the back of the bagel store at two or three in the morning, and the cops he worked with at the roller rink told him they were fellow members of the force protecting the drug operation. One of the men he saw, Hayes said, was McCready.

Salpeter asked Hayes the obvious question: Why didn't he tell him all this when they first talked several years earlier? The answer he got was one Salpeter had heard before: "I thought it was common knowledge." In some respects, it was. The attorney general's office filed its report a week later and Salpeter was unsurprised to find nothing like this in it. It would have been naïve to hope that Rosenberg's team would conclude its investigation by opening such a Pandora's box, much less that it would focus specifically on the possibility of a cover-up relating to Todd Steuerman's drug business—the element that Salpeter himself had come to see as the single most important component in Marty's continuing incarceration. Nevertheless, the motion to dismiss struck Salpeter as being chock-full of disingenuous findings, selective omissions, and roundabout language that seemed designed to do the one thing that clearly had to be done—cut Marty Tankleff loose—while carrying on Tom Spota's determination not to embarrass Suffolk County's law enforcement establishment. In short, it was a political document.

*   *   *

MARTY'S LAST DAY in court was followed by one last appearance before the media. It was established custom by now for Bruce Barket to open the proceedings, with Barry Pollack chiming in when he felt the urge. The attorneys applauded the more vital half of the attorney general's decision but lamented the other, suggesting it was premature to call this case closed. But that was a fight for another day.

Marty stepped to the lectern. He expressed his infinite relief to be finally, unconditionally free, and his gratitude to all who made it possible, but for the record, "It's twenty years overdue." He took questions, none of them unfamiliar. He'd answered them any number of times in the months since his release, whether for television cameras or strangers on the street. He was a celebrity of an unusual sort—the recipient of random acts of kindness and odd mixtures of condolence and congratulation. Someone recognized him having dinner with Salpeter one night and insisted on picking up their check. "Welcome home," people said, no other conversation necessary, and some were moved to gestures of solidarity. They treated him like a freed hostage, told him they always thought he was innocent, shared their outrage at the people who put him in prison and kept him there—*They should go to jail themselves.* After so many years of condemnation and deprivation, Marty basked in the overwhelming public approval. He liked the attention, but what he cherished was the validation.

Still, Marty's reentry wasn't perfect. A few days after he started classes at Hofstra, *Newsday* dispatched a rookie reporter to get campus reaction. Judging by the story in the next day's paper, most of the handful of students the reporter spoke to had never heard of Marty Tankleff and still didn't know much about him after he filled them in. They wanted to know why the university didn't use its post–Virginia Tech security procedures to notify the campus of his presence. "I think it's pretty unsafe if he's just here under no watch," said a business major, while another suggested, "Have professors keep tabs on him." Marty was hurt by the story, but only momentarily. He chalked it up to ignorance, something he knew was out there and he would have to deal with.

Are you bitter? a reporter asked, a standard question that was often accompanied by an observation: You don't even seem angry. Marty always said bitterness served him no purpose in prison. But now that he was out he allowed that those emotions might surface over time. Some who knew him best thought they might not. That's just Marty, as they always said. In the early years, his closest relatives worried that prison would harden him, change who he was—it seemed almost inevitable, a cliché for good reason. But there came a point when they realized that there was much more character inside Marty than they ever imagined when he seemed no more complicated than any other overindulged teenager. Somehow, he became stronger than his circumstances, adapting to them without surrendering to them. He never subscribed to the idea that prison was a slow death—not for him, anyway—or that you couldn't find things to laugh about behind those endless walls. Ron and Carol saw all this most viscerally when they went upstate for a "family day" visit in his early years at Clinton. He introduced them to his friends—one fierce-looking inmate after another with a story behind his name: Sonny and Pirate and Molly and Prince. He was unself-conscious and good-humored. There was no question he grew up in prison, but maybe deep down this was who he was all along.

Are you planning to sue the county? Marty was asked. That was yet to be determined, Barket cut in to say, though certainly Marty deserved some kind of compensation for all those lost years. What about the people he believed to be his parents' actual murderers? Would he press the attorney general to prosecute? Or file a civil suit like the Goldman family did against O.J.? The questions were too big for today. But he answered them broadly. "This isn't over for us," he said. For now, though, "I'm just looking forward to getting on with my life."

What are your plans? he was asked, another question he got on a daily basis. He would finish his degree at Hofstra—though his last day in court made him miss his first day of summer classes. With his associate's degree from prison—and "life experience" credit from the university—he was close to earning a degree in sociology. Then he would go on to law school. And finally, sometime around his forty-first birthday, he would begin a career. He would not be a "businessman" like his father. He would be a criminal defense attorney, with a specialty: Freeing the wrongfully convicted would be his life's work. As it had been.

Marty's words came with the slightly bemused half smile that tended to play across his face when he talked about his case, his life, his emotions. It had been this way since the first television crew came to prison years ago, hooked by one of his letters and disarmed by his resolve. It was an expression that said: *This is really unbelievable, isn't it? But it is what it is, and I'm just going to keep going, and in the end I'm going to win.* From the distance of a TV screen, some perceived a little cockiness. But perhaps it was a case of expectations coming full circle, an echo of when people thought Marty lacked emotion and held it against him to tragic effect. Two decades later, it could be jarring to see a man in prison for something he didn't do displaying such buoyancy.

Jay Salpeter stood to the side as Marty spoke. Jay was in familiar pose—head up, eyes alert, arms to the side. It was the stance of a cop, whether there was a shield in his wallet or a PI's license. His expression was like the way his father, Salty, made a living: little this, little that. Happiness for Marty, of course, maybe a hint of sentimentality. For himself, less joy than pride. Satisfaction. Weariness. It was almost inconceivable to Salpeter that a job he took based on a letter from prison, a case he expected to work a month or two for a quick five grand, had consumed his life for seven and a half years. It was as hard to believe that Marty was actually free; that his murder convictions were erased, as if they'd never happened, by the kind of old-fashioned gumshoe work that seemed almost quaint in the age of DNA. That's what made him proud: He did the job the police never bothered to do.

Salpeter waited for the moment, which almost always came, when the reporters were out of questions for Marty and his lawyers and his cousin Ron, who was more than ready to retire from his job as the family spokesman. Usually, Salpeter winged it when the TV people wanted a sound bite. He was good that way—articulate on his feet with a flair for spontaneous poignance. But this time he had something prepared. Lately he'd been thinking about what he might say when the case was finally over. He wanted to do justice to the moment, and to all the years that preceded it.

"Jay, what are your thoughts today?" asked a radio reporter.

Marty stepped aside for the man he called his savior. Salpeter leaned in to the microphones. "My only thought is something I would like to say to Marty's parents," he said with the slightest quiver. "Arlene and Seymour, it's time now that you can finally rest in peace. Your son is home, and he's home to stay."

ACKNOWLEDGMENTS

RICHARD FIRSTMAN

I owe a great debt of gratitude to many people for their help and support over the course of my work on this book. I first thank my partner, Jay Salpeter, for trusting me with the case of his career, and for his countless contributions to the success of our collaboration. Being alongside a great investigator as he followed the trail that freed an innocent man has been one of the highlights of my own career.

I thank Marty Tankleff for the many ways in which he made my job easier, starting with the six hours he spent patiently answering my questions the first time I interviewed him at Great Meadow Correctional Facility in 2006. I've lost count of the number of times I've written or spoken to him since then, and I thank him for always being attentive and accommodating. I'm grateful also to his family, particularly Marianne and Mike McClure and Ron and Carol Falbee, for their candor in recounting the events of twenty years ago and for their many kindnesses.

I thank the members of Team Tankleff, then and now, for helping me piece together the long history of this case, from Bob Gottlieb and Ron Sussman to Steve Braga, Barry Pollack, Bruce Barket, Jennifer O'Connor, Rick Friedman, Lonnie Soury, and Meg Griffin. Special thanks to Steve Braga for the many hours he spent helping assure the book's accuracy, and for his support along the way. He is my idea of a great lawyer in every regard.

Others who have my appreciation include my former *Newsday* colleagues Carolyn Colwell, Bruce Lambert, Bob Keeler, Joe Demma, and Tom Maier; my friends Paul Vitello and Paul Levitt, whose insights and encouragement were a blessing; and Dorothy Bonardi and Sue Rubin for their able assistance. Gathering the many photographs we used in the book was a major task, and it couldn't have been done without Cathy Mahon and Erica Varela at *Newsday* and Sara Ely Hulse and Gail Zimmerman of *48 Hours*. Thanks also to Frank Norberto for his loan of the videotapes of Marty's trial that he kept in a box all these years.

It would be hard to imagine a better publishing experience than the one I've had with Mark Tavani, as graceful an editor as he is a person. I am enormously grateful to Mark for his unflagging support, patience, and wisdom. Thanks, also, to associate copy chief Beth Pearson for her skill and dedication; Laura Goldin for her wise and careful counsel; Liz Cosgrove for her smart design; and Tom Pitoniak for his conscientious copyediting.

My agent, David Black, saw me through this long project with unfailing encouragement. An author is fortunate to have David in his corner.

Finally, I am grateful most of all to my family: my amazing wife, Jamie, and our children, Ali, Mandy, and Jordan (an eighth grader when I began this project, a high school senior when I finished). I thank them with all my heart for their enduring patience, support, and love. And I thank my parents, Elaine and Bob Firstman, and my sister, Meryl Schlossberg, for their endless love and encouragement.

JAY SALPETER

First, to my wife, Cheryl: Seven years we lived this case together, and you put your faith in me and supported me all the way to the end. Without your love and understanding, I don't know that I would have been able to do my part to bring Marty home. Having you next to me on the day of Marty's release made it all worthwhile. I love you.

To my daughters, Jaime and Jodi, and stepdaughters, Stacie and Jaimie: Thank you for all your support and for always understanding the effort it took to bring Marty home. To Mom and Dad: I guess you were right about having a career in the NYPD. Yes, the benefits and the pension were great, but giving the gift of freedom and life back to Marty outshines it all.

To Vinnie Pepitone, James Worthy, Andrew Cilenti, Charlie Haase, Stephen J. Nackliki, and Joel Reicherter: Thank you for being part of my investigative team. Yes, we won.

To Stephen Braga, Bruce Barket, Barry Pollack, Jennifer O'Connor, Lonnie Soury, Eric Friedman, Roz Dann, and the rest of Marty's defense team: Without your brilliant work, this book would not be possible. I thank you for the opportunity to work with all of you. Many times we were knocked down, but we all had the courage and endurance to get back up and keep going.

And a special thanks to Meg Griffin. You gave your heart and soul for Marty and the rest of his team. We all pray for your continued recovery.

Author and Investigator: Notes on a Partnership

BY RICHARD FIRSTMAN

I was a reporter for *Newsday* at the time of Marty Tankleff's arrest in 1988, though not on the local staff that covered the story. So I followed it like any other reader who saw headlines such as DEADLY TEMPER TANTRUM? and presumed that the story the police and prosecutors were putting out was true. Like many, I had my doubts when Jerry Steuerman disappeared. But then he came back, somehow convincing enough in the role of the erratic but harmless business partner. Because, we were told, the kid confessed. The trial was covered live by the local cable news channel, but few outside the jury heard all the evidence. And they found him guilty. For the next decade and a half, the mention of the name Martin Tankleff brought to mind the image of the spoiled rich kid who slaughtered his parents because he didn't like his crummy old Lincoln.

In the fall of 2003, eight years after I left *Newsday*, I was astonished to read that a private investigator had unearthed evidence suggesting that Marty may have been innocent all along. I became fascinated by the idea that truth could be so far from perception—and haunted by the possibility that a young man had been wrongly imprisoned for the worst crime imaginable. I found myself wondering whether Marty Tankleff, after losing his parents to murder, had been robbed of the best years of his life—perhaps the *rest* of his life—by a criminal justice system that was not just imperfect but reckless, maybe even corrupt. The idea of writing a book about the case began percolating in my mind. One Sunday in December 2004, a day before the hearing of new evidence was to resume after a six-week pause, *The New York Times* and *Newsday* featured stories on the case based on a joint interview with Marty, his first ever with the newspapers. The articles by Bruce Lambert and Zachary Dowdy were sympathetic to Marty, but it was the photographs of him in that bright orange prison jumpsuit that seized my attention. No longer the teenager of our memories, Marty Tankleff was a pensive man looking out from the news pages through large round glasses, his hairline receding as he approached his mid-thirties. The next morning, I drove out to the county courthouse in Riverhead to have a look.

I met Jay Salpeter that day, and over the next few months we discussed his idea of collaborating in some fashion. It wasn't my initial intention to write the book with someone involved in the case, but there were good reasons to consider it. Jay had spent three years on the case to this point, working virtually pro bono. He had accumulated a great deal of information and sources, obviously, and he was actively pursuing new leads. The advent of DNA evidence had led to the exonerations of some two hundred wrongfully convicted people in the United States, but Jay and the Tankleff legal team were on a much more difficult path: trying to free an innocent man *without* DNA. I began to see a partnership with the investigator who had opened the courthouse door as a rare opportunity: the chance to tell an extraordinary story, and an important one, from the inside. First, though, I had to be satisfied that it was the right story—that the new evidence proved beyond my own reasonable doubt that Marty really was innocent.

I read all the legal filings by both the defense and the prosecution, transcripts of the hearing thus far, and other background material provided by Jay. I spoke to Marty's lawyers and relatives, and spent an hour with Marty himself at the Nassau County Jail. Ultimately I found myself persuaded, though not just by the new evidence, compelling as it was. What I found equally striking was how much I had never known about the original case. How the forensics, for example, made Marty's supposed confession the best evidence of his *innocence*, as the false confessions expert Richard Ofshe put it so incisively. Getting up to speed all these years later, I wondered how Marty had been convicted in the first place. That question was to become a major focus of my work, and part of the answer, I came to realize, lay in how effectively the prosecution skewed perceptions by selling a fiction. One of the most common views of the case was that Marty had hurt himself by taking the stand; that the jury and a lot of other people had found his demeanor, and thus his words, unconvincing. But when I watched a videotape of his testimony, I thought he did fine. And then I remembered something: Fifteen years earlier, I had watched Marty's testimony with some *Newsday* colleagues on one of the overhead televisions in our newsroom. And I hadn't found him convincing either. That was the power of preconceived notions.

I learned much more as the case continued to unfold, both from Jay's investigation and my own research, and our collaboration produced a book that is something of a hybrid. The story is necessarily told from the point of view of one side of a highly contested case, and I have made no attempt to disguise my own perspective and sympathies. But at the same time, I maintained a journalistic approach to the story. From the beginning, we agreed that everything would be documented and verified with the same kinds of sources as in any other work of nonfiction: interviews with the principal figures, court transcripts, case reports, archival material. And we agreed that a book about a search for the truth could be nothing but honest itself. This meant writing frankly about Marty's shortcomings as a teenager and how his parents' actions contributed to their murders. It meant being candid about Jay's own missteps, such as the fiasco that took some of the luster off Billy Ram's powerful testimony. And it meant dealing objectively with some strongly held beliefs about the case that were not necessarily consistent with the available facts. There was a balancing act for Jay in all this, and to his credit he never flinched.

In the course of his investigation, Jay interviewed some seventy-five people, many of the key ones on tape, and obtained or had access to hundreds of pages of documents. This work, over seven years, not only provided the basis of the final third of the book but informed the first two. Additionally, because investigating a murder case is not the same as writing about one, I conducted my own research, studying records of the case and interviewing the main players. The most important, of course, was Marty Tankleff. After our initial meeting in January 2005, I had a six-hour recorded interview with Marty at Great Meadow Correctional Facility in Comstock, New York, on April 11, 2006. I met him there again on August 30, 2007. We also corresponded often and had many conversations after his release from prison in December 2007.

Marty's lawyers, relatives, and friends were also interviewed extensively. I spent many hours with Robert Gottlieb in his offices on Long Island and in New York City, and interviewed his former partner, Ronald Sussman, and appeals attorneys Mark Pomerantz and Warren Feldman as well. Stephen Braga and Barry Pollack were interviewed at their firms in Washington, D.C., and Bruce Barket in Garden City. All were consulted by phone and email at other points along the way. I also had interviews and conversations with many others who helped flesh out the background of the Tankleff family, the murders of Arlene and Seymour, and the prosecution of their son. The most substantial family interviews were with Ron Falbee, Marianne and Mike McClure, and Norman and Ruth Tankleff. Mike Fox was interviewed for several hours at his home in

Palm Beach Gardens, Florida, the only interview he has ever given to a journalist.

Several key figures in the investigation that ultimately freed Marty were also interviewed: Glenn Harris; Joe Guarascio and his mother, Terry Covais; and Joe Graydon. Stuart Namm was interviewed at his home in Hampstead, North Carolina, where he showed me the unreleased documentary he made in 1998. The film contained interviews with James McCready and Shari Rother that provided material for the book that is attributed in the narrative. Other interviews and personal conversations: Dr. Vernard Adams, Autumn Asness, Estelle Block, Lawrence Bracken, Benjamin Brafman, Michael Cahill, Fred Chichester, Carolyn Colwell, Joe Demma, Janette Drexler, Steven Drizin, Lee Ekstrom, Carol Fields, Eric Friedman, Meg Griffin, Carolyn Gusoff, Marc Howard, Jesse Kornbluth, Karlene Kovacs, Bruce Lambert, Father Ronald Lemmert, Myra Lerner, Paul Lerner, Kirsten Levingston, Christopher Lue-Shing, Thomas Maier, Sister Angeline Matero, Jim Mulvaney, Frank Norberto, Frank Oliveto, Kurt Paschke Jr., Kurt Paschke Sr., Joel Reicherter, Steve Saperstein, Barry Scheck, Lonnie Soury, William Sullivan, Laura Taichman, Marie Vieira.

It should be noted that certain key people are conspicuously absent from the list of those interviewed—the people who put Marty Tankleff in prison and fought to keep him there. The two district attorneys in office during the prosecution and subsequent appeals, Patrick Henry and James Catterson, did agree to speak with me. But the major figures in the case did not. Over a period of months, I made four written requests to the office of District Attorney Thomas Spota for interviews with him, Leonard Lato, and John Collins. All the requests were ignored. I also attempted to interview retired detectives James McCready and Norman Rein. Though he has given interviews to virtually every print and broadcast reporter who has asked, McCready told me he would speak with me only if I paid him. I declined. During a trip to Florida, I called Rein, who had recently moved to the Orlando area, but he declined to meet with me, suggesting that his trial testimony would be the most complete and reliable source of his recollections. Two other major figures also declined to be interviewed: Shari (Rother) Mistretta and Jerry Steuerman.

Apart from Jay Salpeter's personal account and the interviews detailed above, the book is based on thousands of pages of documents. These include complete transcripts of all the legal proceedings in the twenty-year history of the case: the Huntley hearing in March 1989, the trial in 1990, the posttrial proceedings involving allegations of juror misconduct, and finally the hearing of new evidence conducted intermittently over a seventeen-month period beginning in July 2004.

The trial record runs 5,143 pages and includes the testimony of all fifty-two witnesses, opening statements and summations, and all the evidentiary discussions between the attorneys and the judge that were conducted in chambers or at sidebar, out of the presence of the jury and the public. (In addition, videotapes of the live trial coverage by Long Island's News 12 were viewed.).

Another vital source of material was the case reports written by members of the Suffolk County police homicide squad between the day of the murders in 1988 and the trial in 1990. This includes Detectives James McCready's and Norman Rein's handwritten notes and typed reports of their interviews and interrogation of Marty on September 7, 1988, and interviews they conducted with others, including Jerry Steuerman. Many of these are cited in the text. Other documents include the autopsies of the Tankleffs, hospital records for Seymour, notes and reports by the forensic scientists at the Suffolk County criminalistics lab, and crime scene photographs taken by the police.

We also drew from the files of the Tankleff defense: reports written by John M. Murtagh of the O'Connor Investigation Agency, detailing his investigation in behalf of Marty's defense between September 1988 and April 1990; documents he and Gottlieb gathered regarding the financial arrangements between the Tankleffs and Steuerman; and the work of investigator Bill Navarra for the postverdict motions to set aside the convictions on the basis of new evidence and juror misconduct. A key document was a transcript of Navarra's recorded interview with juror Peter Baczynski on August 20, 1990.

The chapters covering Marty's state and federal appeals were based on the briefs and decisions in those appeals as well as the recollections of the attorneys involved. The proceedings that began in October 2003 and led to the reversal of Marty's convictions four years later included more than 1,200 pages of testimony and several hundred pages more of legal briefs, affidavits, and other documents. Many of these are cited specifically in the text.

A more complete and detailed list of documents and sources may be found at www.ACriminalInjustice.com.

Notes to the Narrative

CHAPTER 2

Marty recounts waking up on the morning of September 7, 1988: The italicized paragraphs of Marty's recollections of discovering his parents are his own words. They are drawn from the interview with him recorded on April 11, 2006, and his trial testimony on June 7 and 8, 1990.

CHAPTERS 2 AND 3

McCready as the first detective at the scene: Among those who have closely followed Marty Tankleff's case, there has been a widespread belief that McCready was scheduled for a day off on September 7, and thus that it is peculiar that he was the first detective on the scene, showing up in a jacket and tie less than twenty minutes after being alerted. The suspicions have been fueled since 2003 by the discovery that McCready and Steuerman had a hidden relationship prior to that day, and by the testimony by Joseph Guarascio that his father, Joe Creedon, told him that McCready was paid off. However, we have found no evidence that McCready was scheduled to be off on September 7 and base our account on the available record: the testimony of McCready and his sergeant, Robert Doyle, at the Huntley hearing and trial, and the recollection of Doyle during a conversation with Richard Firstman (hereafter RF) in 2005. According to Doyle, his team of detectives was off-duty but on call at the time the case was reported, shortly after 6:00 A.M. At the Huntley hearing in 1989, McCready testified that he was at his construction shop, less than a twenty-minute drive from Belle Terre, when he was reached by Doyle at about 7:15 A.M. It is possible that this testimony has been misinterpreted over the years to mean that he alone was off-duty and scheduled to be so for the entire day.

CHAPTER 4

McCready and Rein's interrogation of Marty at police headquarters: In the absence of an electronic recording of what transpired in the interview room between 9:40 A.M. and 1:22 P.M., the interview is reconstructed as accurately as possible based on all the available sources. At the trial, there was little substantive dispute about the interview prior to 11:54 A.M., when, the detectives claimed, Marty began to confess. The questions and answers up to that point are recounted without quotation marks, indicating they are reliable in essence but not verbatim. In his testimony, Marty confirmed that he asked, "Could I have blacked out?" From that point on, however, the interview defies precise reconstruction. Partly for that reason, the narrative stops there and the key moments of the interrogation are recounted through the words of the three participants in later chapters. In Chapter 6 (pages 60–62), on the night of September 7, Marty tells Robert Gottlieb and Mike Fox what he remembers of the interrogation that morning. This passage is based primarily on interviews with Gottlieb and Fox. An additional source is the transcript of an interview of William Strockbine by Joe Demma of *Newsday* on October 28, 1988. Strockbine, whose son was a longtime childhood friend of Marty's, was the first person to visit Marty at the Suffolk County Jail the morning after his arrest. Marty gave Strockbine a detailed account of his interrogation, which Strockbine related to Demma. That interview is arguably the best documentation of what Marty said about his alleged confession in the hours immediately afterward. Marty's version, along with McCready and Rein's, is recounted in detail through their testimony in the chapters covering the trial.

Newsday's coverage of the Tankleff case in the months after the murders: These passages are based on the files of the newspaper's reporters. These include transcripts and notes of interviews, memos between editors and reporters, and public records gathered on Seymour Tankleff, Jerry Steuerman, and others. Joe Demma's interview with Jerry Steuerman on November 16, 1988, was recorded and transcribed. But for a few brief quotes, it remained largely unpublished. The excerpts in this chapter are published with Demma's permission. The appraisal of *Newsday*'s December 13, 1988, article is based in part on a comparison between material in the files and the published article.

CHAPTER 27
McCready assault case and partnership in Digger O'Dell's bar with Ron and Shari Rother: Shari (Rother) Mistretta has long downplayed her role in the bar partnership and sometimes denied it altogether, claiming that only her husband was involved with McCready. But in 1998, during a filmed interview with Stuart Namm for his documentary *A Question of Guilt*, she acknowledged that the bar was financed with her money, thereby confirming that McCready went into business with money gained from Marty's conviction.

Selected Media Sources

"America's Most Wanted Presents Judgment Night: DNA the Ultimate Test," May 17, 2001.

Amon, Rhoda, "His Heart Belonged to Belle Terre," *Newsday*, November 14, 2000.

Barthel, Joan, *A Death in Canaan*. New York: E. P. Dutton and Co., 1976.

"Belle Terre Murder: Victim in Extremely Serious Condition," *Port Jefferson Record*, September 9, 1988.

Bridson, Susanna, "Patrick Schoendorf: What Really Happened?" *Three Village Herald*, 1995.

Bugden, Walter F., Jr., and Tara L. Isaacson, "Crimes, Truth and Videotape: Mandatory Recording of Interrogations at the Police Station," *Utah Bar Journal*, October 30, 2006.

Cerra, Frances, "Police in Suffolk Defend Methods of Interrogation," *The New York Times*, June 25, 1979.

Chisholm '72: Unbought & Unbossed, Public Broadcasting System P.O.V. documentary, REALside Productions, 2005.

Colen, B. D., and Joshua Quittner, "Nurse Indicted on Murder Charge in Hospital Death," *Newsday*, January 14, 1988.

Colwell, Carolyn, "Bail Denied to Murder Suspect, 17, Despite Support Letters of 30 Relatives, Friends," *Newsday*, September 16, 1988.

———, "Family Posts $1 Million Bond to Free Tankleff," *Newsday*, October 12, 1988.

———, "New Questions in Tankleff Case; Defense Says Reports Clear Accused Son; DA Says Link Is Stronger," *Newsday*, October 14, 1988.

———, "Reward Offer in Tankleff Case; Family Maintains Son Innocent of Killings, Puts Up $25,000," *Newsday*, October 15, 1988.

———, "Tankleff's Daughter Contests Will," *Newsday*, January 26, 1989.

———, "A New Twist in Tankleff Trial," *Newsday*, April 28, 1990.

———, "Alternate Juror's 'Verdict': After Release, Says She Would Have Voted to Convict Tankleff," *Newsday*, June 25, 1990.

———, "Juror: Confession Was Disregarded," *Newsday*, June 30, 1990.

———, "Tankleff Family: Jury Goofed," *Newsday*, July 3, 1990.

———, "Tankleff Comforted Behind Bars," *Newsday*, July 12, 1990.

———, "Maximum for Tankleff," *Newsday*, October 24, 1990.

Colwell, Carolyn, and Jenny Abdo, "School Bars Tankleff; Knife Threat Alleged," *Newsday*, October 13, 1988.

Colwell, Carolyn, and Michael Slackman, "Ridge Man: Ex-Cop Beat Me; Says Officers Ignored His Pleas," *Newsday*, April 2, 1991.

Colwell, Carolyn, and Kinsey Wilson, "Cops: 'Bagel King' Fled Trauma; An Aimless Journey After Friend's Slaying," *Newsday*, September 30, 1988.

"A Confession in Question," *American Justice*, A&E Network, 2005.

Corry, John, "Arthur Miller Turns Detective in Murder," *The New York Times*, December 15–16, 1975.

A Current Affair, October 9, 1990.

de Cuba, Natalia, and Kinsey Wilson, "At Funeral, Family Supports Accused Teen," *Newsday*, September 11, 1988.

Demma, Joseph, "Tankleff Stands to Inherit Millions," *Newsday*, November 2, 1988.

———, "Murder Victim's Estate Sues Partner of Tankleff; Took Assets and Owes $900,000, Lawsuit Says," *Newsday*, November 30, 1988.

Dowdy, Zachary, "Courtroom Surprise: Man Key to Defense Case Pleads the Fifth, Frustrating Tankleff Kin as DA Refuses to Grant Him Immunity to Testify," *Newsday*, July 27, 2004.

———, "Spota Reveals Client Connection," *Newsday*, August 18, 2004.

———, "Their Missing Witness," *Newsday*, October 30, 2004.

———, "Misfit Talk Riles Tankleff Witnesses," *Newsday*, March 30, 2005.

Drizin, Steven A., and Richard A. Leo, "The Problem of False Confessions in the Post-DNA World," *North Carolina Law Review*, March 2004.

Drizin, Steven A., and Marissa J. Reich, "The Need for Mandatory Recording of Police Interrogations to Accurately Assess the Reliability and Voluntariness of Confessions," Wrongful Convictions Symposium, *Drake Law Review*, Summer 2004.

Esalen website, www.esalen.org.

Finn, Robin, "The System Worked? A Defender Begs to Differ," *The New York Times*, January 4, 2008.

Geller, William A., "Videotaping Interrogations and Confessions," National Institute of Justice, March 1993.

Gusoff, Carolyn, "Tankleff on Trial: 'Sweet' or 'Cowardly'?" *The New York Times*, June 3, 1990.

Harris, Amanda, "Police Kill Holdup Man After Ex-Cop Is Wounded," *Newsday*, June 10, 1976.

Herbert, Bob, "The Wrong Man," *The New York Times*, March 2, 2000.

———, "Why This Man?" *The New York Times*, March 6, 2000.

Howard, Marc, "Tankleff Case: An Overview" and "Irresponsible Journalism," *The Purple Parrot*, Earl L. Vandermeulen High School, October 14, 1988.

Innocence Project website, www.innocenceproject.org.

Kassin, Saul M., and Gisli H. Gudjonsson, "True Crimes, False Confessions: Why Do Innocent People Confess to Crimes They Did Not Commit?" *Scientific American Mind*, May 24, 2005.

Keeler, Bob, "Tankleff Evidence Cries Out for a New Trial," *Newsday*, October 5, 2005.

Kirschner, David, "Adoption Forensics and the Tankleff Case," *Crime Magazine*, March 3, 2008, www.crimemagazine.com/08/marty_tankleff,0303-8.htm.

Kleiman, Dena, *A Deadly Silence*. New York: The Atlantic Monthly Press, 1988.

Kleinfield, N. R., "Unraveling Puzzle of L.I. Car Dealer Reveals Layers of Personal Mystery," *The New York Times*, April 19, 1992.

Korbluth, Jesse, "Trouble Boys," *New York*, August 30 and September 6, 1982.

Lambert, Bruce, "15 Years Later, Pushing to Clear His Name in Murder of Parents," *The New York Times*, October 2, 2003.

———, "Questions About a Son's Guilt, and a Cop's Methods," *The New York Times*, April 4, 2004.

———, "Key Witness Fails to Testify in L.I. Man's Murder Appeal," *The New York Times*, July 24, 2004.

———, "L.I. Killer Loses Motion on Prosecutor in Retrial Bid," *The New York Times*, September 24, 2004.

———, "State Panel Investigates Prosecution of L.I. Man," *The New York Times*, December 29, 2007.

Lewis, Anthony, "High Court Gives Views of Police; Throws New Light on Use of Coercion to Obtain Criminal Confessions," *The New York Times*, March 27, 1961.

Maier, Thomas J., "2 Testify, 4 Called in Police Probe," *Newsday*, December 30, 1986.

———, "One Judge's Evolution: The Old Namm Highly Praised Suffolk's Law Enforcement, the New Namm Is Sharply Critical," *Newsday*, January 26, 1988.

Maier, Thomas J., and Rex Smith, "The Confession Takers," *Newsday* series, December 7–19, 1986.

Martin, Alex, "Juror: Defendant Convicted Himself," *Newsday*, June 29, 1990.

MartyTankleff.org (website of the Tankleff defense team).

McNamee, Thomas, "Island Dreams," *Natural History*, May 1998.

Moreno, Sylvia, "Bullish on Demands," *Newsday*, August 29, 1978;.

Moushey, Bill, "Win at All Costs," *Pittsburgh Post-Gazette*, November 22, 1998.

Muha, Laura, "For Suspect's School, a New Tragedy," *Newsday*, September 9, 1988.

Nash, Pati, "It's Tougher Than It Looks," *Newsday*, January 20, 1986.

News 12 Long Island, coverage of Tankleff trial, 1990.

Orth, Nancy, "The History of Belle Terre," www.belleterre.us/History/tabid/58/Default.aspx.

Perlman, Shirley E., "Cops: Son Killed Parents in Fear They Would Cut Off Tuition," *Newsday*, June 3, 1987.

———, "Deadly Temper Tantrum? Prosecutors: Anger Led to Son's Attack," *Newsday*, September 9, 1988.

———, "2 Asst. DAs Barred in Tankleff Trial," *Newsday*, October 29, 1988.

Perlman, Shirley E., and Patrick Brasley, "Tankleff Associate Is Found; Bagel Shop Owner Jerry Steuerman Located in California Motel," *Newsday*, September 29, 1988.

Perlman, Shirley E. and Joseph Demma, "A Child of Suburban Wealth, Martin Tankleff's House Was a Place of Luxury—and Tension," *Newsday*, December 13, 1988.

Perlman, Shirley E., and Phil Mintz, "Twist in Tankleff Case? Father's Partner Disappears After Receiving Threats," *Newsday*, September 20, 1988.

"Prime Suspect," CBS News *48 Hours Mystery*, April 7, 2004, and subsequent segments.

Pulitzer, Lisa, *Murder in Paradise*. New York: St. Martin's Press, 2003.

Puzzanghera, Jim, "Victim's Partner Glad It's Over," *Newsday*, June 29, 1990.

———, "Evidence Made Sister Doubt Belief in Tankleff," *Newsday*, June 30, 1990.

Puzzanghera, Jim, and Carolyn Colwell, "Sister Feels Tankleff Guilty, Ex-Cop Says," *Newsday*, June 22, 1990.

A Question of Guilt: The Martin Tankleff Story. DVD, Legal Eagle Productions, 1998.

Quittner, Joshua, "In Tankleff Case, a Preview of DA Race," *Newsday*, March 14, 1989.

———, "How Many in Court Running for DA? Tankleff Lawyer Asks Judge If He's in Race," *Newsday*, April 11, 1989.

———, "Judge's GOP Meeting Questioned," *Newsday*, April 27, 1989.

———, "Second Thoughts on Judge's DA Bid," *Newsday*, April 29, 1989.

———, "PBA Backs Catterson," *Newsday*, September 27, 1989.

———, "Suffolk DA Race: Insider vs. Whiz Kid," *Newsday*, October 15, 1989.

———, "Tankleff Juror Misconduct Alleged," *Newsday*, September 26, 1990.

Quittner, Joshua, and Adam Z. Horvath, "In Defense of a Defender: Experts Question Ads on Gottlieb's Practice," *Newsday*, October 25, 1989.

Quittner, Joshua, Thomas J. Maier, and Rex Smith, "NY Investigator: Suffolk DA Ignored Perjury by Police," *Newsday*, January 29, 1987.

———, "Tense 2nd Day Caps Hearings on Suffolk Police Procedures," *Newsday*, January 30, 1987.

The Robing Room, ratings of federal district court judges, www.therobingroom.com.

Rosenbaum, Ron, "The Devil in Long Island," *The New York Times Magazine*, August 22, 1993.

Sargent, Greg, "The Reinvestigator," *New York*, March 7, 2005.

Slackman, Michael, "GOP Leaders Back Judge for DA," *Newsday*, April 9, 1989.

———, "Ex-Detective Indicted: Assault, Robbery Charges Expected in Alleged Beating," *Newsday*, April 20, 1991.

———, "Pub with a Twist: Cop in Slaying Case Building for Tankleff Kin," *Newsday*, May 11, 1993.

———, "Pub Story Gets Meatier," *Newsday*, May 19, 1993.

Smith, Andrew, "DA Against New Trial; Says Evidence Doesn't Clear Tankleff In Parents' Deaths," *Newsday*, December 13, 2003.

Smith, Don, "Lawyer Indicted on DWI Charges," *Newsday*, October 9, 1993.

Smith, Don, and Thomas J. Maier, "Confessions to Be Taped in Suffolk," *Newsday*, November 14, 1985.

Strickler, Andrew, "No Regrets for Ex-Cop," *Newsday*, January 5, 2008.

Tayler, Letta, and Michele Salcedo, "Shock over Teen's Arrest; Suspect in Fatal Stabbing Called Popular Student," *Newsday*, June 30, 1992.

Topping, Robin, "Jury Selection Process Becomes Issue in Appeal," *Newsday*, September 30, 1998.

———, "Detective in Tankleff Killings: Dogged by Scrutiny of Old Murder Case," *Newsday*, August 15, 2004.

Topping, Robin, and Andrew Smith, "New Evidence in 1988 Slayings," *Newsday*, October 2, 2003.

Vitello, Paul, "One Side Isn't the Truth," *Newsday*, September 21, 1988.

———, "Probing Interrogation's Bond," *Newsday*, March 15, 1989.

———, "Father-Figure's Murder: A Battle Between 'Sons,' " *Newsday*, May 3, 1990.

Wasserman, Elizabeth, "In Court, It's Cop vs. Cop: Ex-Detective Wants Statement Suppressed," *Newsday*, May 5, 1993.

———, "Statement Barred in Assault Case," *Newsday*, May 6, 1993.

———, "Victim Recounts Beating; Ex-Cop the Leader, Ridge Man Testifies," *Newsday*, May 13, 1993.

———, "Cop Trial Stalled After Attorney Injured in Crash," *Newsday*, May 15, 1993.

Whittle, Patrick, "Unease over Tankleff Studies," *Newsday*, January 29, 2008.

Wick, Steve, "Tankleffs' Wills Scrutinized," *Newsday*, December 23, 1988.

———, "How His Sister's Trust Was Shaken," *Newsday*, October 24, 1990.

———, "Fellow Officers Shocked by Accusations," *Newsday*, April 24, 1991.

———, "Dad Fights to Clear Son of Murder," *Newsday*, May 1, 1994.

———, "Pressing Ahead," *Newsday*, January 2, 2000.

Wilson, Kinsey, "Husband Held in Wife's Slaying," *Newsday*, June 26, 1988.

Witherspoon, Gary, and Michael Slackman, "MD Hurt, Lawyer Charged with DWI," *Newsday*, May 14, 1993.

The Wrong Man? Court TV, 2002.

Zion, Sidney, "Man Who Fought Confession Loses; Huntley, for Whom Hearings Are Named, Denied Retrial," *The New York Times*, April 10, 1965.

About the Authors

RICHARD FIRSTMAN is an award-winning author and journalist whose books include *The Death of Innocents*, a *New York Times* Notable Book of the Year and Edgar Award winner co-authored with his wife, Jamie Talan. He has written for numerous publications, and his work as a producer has appeared on *60 Minutes*. He was previously a reporter at large and an editor at *Newsday*.

JAY SALPETER, a highly decorated former New York City police detective and hostage negotiator, is one of the country's top private investigators. His work has led to frequent appearances on *Dateline*, *48 Hours*, MSNBC, Fox News, and Court TV (now truTV). In 2008, he co-founded the Fortress Innocence Group, the nation's first private investigations firm devoted to overturning wrongful convictions.